# THE MACRO POLITY

*The Macro Polity* provides the first comprehensive model of American politics at the system level. Focusing on the interactions between citizen evaluations and preferences, government activity and policy, and how the combined acts of citizens and governments influence one another over time, it integrates understandings of matters such as economic outcomes, presidential approval, partisanship, elections, and government policy making into a single model. Borrowing from the perspective of macroeconomics, it treats electorates, politicians, and governments as unitary actors, making decisions in response to the behavior of other actors. The macro and longitudinal focus makes it possible to directly connect the behaviors of electorate and government. The surprise of macro-level analysis, emerging anew in every chapter, is that order and rationality dominate explanations. This book argues that the electorates and governments that emerge from these analyses respond to one another in orderly and predictable ways.

Robert S. Erikson is Professor of Political Science at Columbia University. He has coauthored six editions of *American Public Opinion: Its Origins, Content, and Impact* (with Kent Tedin) and has won the Heinz Eulau Award of the American Political Science Association and the Pi Sigma Alpha Award of the Midwest Political Science Association.

Michael B. MacKuen is Burton Craige Distinguished Professor of Political Science at the University of North Carolina at Chapel Hill. His previous publications have received recognition in the form of the Heinz Eulau Award of the American Political Science Association and the Pi Sigma Alpha Award of the Midwest Political Science Association.

James A. Stimson is Raymond Dawson Distinguished Professor of Political Science at the University of North Carolina at Chapel Hill. He has won the Heinz Eulau and Gladys Kammermer Awards of the American Political Science Association, the Chastain Award of the Southern Political Science Association, and the Pi Sigma Alpha Award of the Midwest Political Science Association.

Cambridge Studies in Political Psychology and
Public Opinion

General Editors

James H. Kuklinski, *University of Illinois, Urbana-Champaign*
Dennis Chong, *Northwestern University*

Editorial Board

Stanley Feldman, *State University of New York,
Stony Brook*
Roger D. Masters, *Dartmouth College*
William J. McGuire, *Yale University*
Norbert Schwarz, *Zentrum für Umfragen, Methoden
und Analysen ZUMA, Mannheim, Germany*
David O. Sears, *University of California,
Los Angeles*
Paul M. Sniderman, *Stanford University* and *Survey
Research Center, University of California, Berkeley*
James A. Stimson, *University of North Carolina*

This series has been established in recognition of the growing sophistication in
the resurgence of interest in political psychology and the study of public opinion.
Its focus ranges from the kinds of mental processes that people employ when
they think about democratic processes and make political choices to the nature
and consequences of macro-level public opinion.

Some of the works draw on developments in cognitive and social psychology
and relevant areas of philosophy. Appropriate subjects include the use of heuris-
tics, the roles of core values and moral principles in political reasoning, the effects
of expertise and sophistication, the roles of affect and emotion, and the nature
of cognition and information processing. The emphasis is on systematic and rigorous empirical analysis, and a wide range of methodologies are appropriate:
traditional surveys, experimental surveys, laboratory experiments, focus groups,
and in-depth interviews, as well as others. These empirically oriented studies also
consider normative implications for democratic politics generally.

Politics, not psychology, is the primary focus, and it is expected that most
works will deal with mass publics and democratic politics, although work on
nondemocratic publics is not excluded. Other works will examine traditional
topics in public opinion research, as well as contribute to the growing literature
on aggregate opinion and its role in democratic societies.

Other books in the series

Asher Arian, *Security Threatened: Surveying Israeli Opinion on Peace and
War*
James DeNardo, *The Amateur Strategist: Intuitive Deterrence Theories and the
Politics of the Nuclear Arms Race*

*Series list continues on page following the Index*

# THE MACRO POLITY

**ROBERT S. ERIKSON**
*Columbia University*

**MICHAEL B. MACKUEN**
*University of North Carolina*

**JAMES A. STIMSON**
*University of North Carolina*

CAMBRIDGE
UNIVERSITY PRESS

CAMBRIDGE UNIVERSITY PRESS
Cambridge, New York, Melbourne, Madrid, Cape Town, Singapore, São Paulo

Cambridge University Press
The Edinburgh Building, Cambridge CB2 2RU, UK

Published in the United States of America by Cambridge University Press, New York

www.cambridge.org
Information on this title: www.cambridge.org/9780521563895

First published 2002

*A catalogue record for this publication is available from the British Library*

*Library of Congress Cataloguing in Publication data*
Erikson, Robert S.
The macro polity / Robert S. Erikson, Michael B. MacKuen, James A. Stimson.
  p.   cm. – (Cambridge studies in political psychology and public opinion)
Includes bibliographical references and index.
ISBN 0-521-56389-5 – ISBN 0-521-56485-9 (pb.)
1. Political participation – United States.   2. Public opinion – United States.   3. United
States – Politics and government.   I. MacKuen, Michael B.   II. Stimson, James A.
III. Title.   IV. Series.
JK1764 .E75 2001
323′.042′0973 – dc21

00-066711

ISBN-13  978-0-521-56389-5 hardback
ISBN-10  0-521-56389-5 hardback

ISBN-13  978-0-521-56485-4 paperback
ISBN-10  0-521-56485-9 paperback

Transferred to digital printing 2006

To: Angus Campbell, Phillip E. Converse, Warren E. Miller, and Donald E. Stokes

# Contents

# Figures and Tables

## Figures and Tables

# Figures and Tables

## Figures and Tables

### TABLES

# Figures and Tables

## Figures and Tables

# Preface

Filing into the voting booths in November 1994, most American voters knew almost nothing about the Republican Party's "Contract with America." Most could not say who would lead that party if its contract succeeded. Many were even unsure which party was in control going into the election, although American voters make better guesses at party control in those increasingly rare instances, like 1994, of one-party control of both White House and congress. Most Americans did not vote at all, and as usual that familiar majority of nonvoters knew even less than those who did.

This story of unmotivated, ill-informed, and inattentive voters is as old as the first examinations of individual voters, and it is confirmed anew by every subsequent voting study. Looked upon as individuals, most Americans care little about politics and possess a level of knowledge of the details of political life that is consistent with not caring. Whereas large numbers could cite NFL football standings, list the details of the private lives of celebrities from the entertainment industry, and recall almost verbatim the scripts of television commercials, relatively few know much about government beyond the identity of the president. The minority who vote with any regularity do so, it appears, from a sense of obligation more than anything else. Good citizens, they believe, watch their diets, floss their teeth daily, and vote from time to time.

All this is true for voters as *individuals*. All of it is well documented and well known. But it is also wrong for voters when considered as a collective electorate. All these facts, insofar as they lead us to believe that the electorate acts without purpose, lead us astray. For when we look to whole electorates, we see a different picture entirely.

We now know that the American electorate of 1994 was in a relatively conservative mood after the liberalism of Bill Clinton's first two years. We have no doubt whatsoever that the ideologically active electorate knew which party would propose and enact more conservative policies.

We believe that it acted, in the aggregate, with purpose, and got some of what it wanted from Newt Gingrich and the G.O.P. 104th Congress.[1]

What we see here is a radical discontinuity between the impressions and conclusions reached from the study of individuals and aggregates. That discontinuity does not require us to deny one or the other set of facts. Although they have strikingly different implications for the democratic polity, both sets of facts are simultaneously true. Both even are known – but the individual-level facts are much better known, and their implications more often believed.

Analysts of the early voting studies were impressed with the degree to which experiences long in the past shaped party preferences and loyalties. Respondents in the 1950s and 1960s repeatedly referred to Herbert Hoover and Franklin Roosevelt when asked to account for their current party views. From this, the natural inference is of great sluggishness in response to the events of current politics. Thus we have the view of an electorate slow to acquire new information and slow to adapt to it when it does, a view of backward-looking and inertial behavior. These are the individual-level facts.

The aggregate of such an inertial electorate should show a very slow and very partial adaptation to the stream of events in politics. And that is wrong. The real aggregate is quite nimble, changing its partisan balance in response, for example, to real economic indicators of the last quarter or two, reacting to the president more swiftly. That reaction, far from being a slow adaptation to a new stream of facts, adjusts itself to expected "facts" about the future before they occur.

If we ask again which of these views is correct, historically rooted and slow-adapting individuals or the nimble aggregate, the answer again is that both are. The implications that flow and the inferences one draws cannot both be correct, but the simple facts are. Our task will be to draw the right inferences for the right level of analysis, which is a matter of perspective.

The lore of the cloakroom holds that overwhelming proportions of voters cannot recall how their member or senator voted on a single issue during a session of congress. And that lore is undoubtedly rooted in fact. We know that large numbers of voters cannot recall the name of the member, let alone his or her behavior in office. Details about congress sink into that large gray zone of inattention to politics. More visible than important acts of the Federal Reserve governors or the FTC, congress

1 This is not to suggest that it wanted all of what it got. The data are consistent with a story of an electorate demanding a moderate correction to the right, but not a "Republican Revolution."

still is no competitor to sports, romance, and work life, the things that most often command attention.

That lore would be consistent with a casual decision style for members; voting "right" can't matter when voters have no memories of what members do. That again is starkly inconsistent with what we observe. Members behave as if their every action were monitored in exquisite detail, a committee of constituents viewing from the gallery. How can members simultaneously believe that constituents are largely uninformed about their behavior and still fear for their political lives from a bad vote? They fear because they have seen others, friends and opponents, lose elections when they could not defend their public positions. But why should this inattentive public opinion monster rear up on them? For that we need to return to the familiar contradiction of individual and aggregate, micro and macro. There we see that most individuals need not remember a vote in order for the member to get into electoral trouble. Elections are won and lost in the aggregate. And the aggregate moves at the margin; a few percent doing this or that systematically produce big, sometimes shocking, aggregate effects.

Professionals in politics – journalists and politicians – see issues as bundles of similar debates over similar concerns. Ordinary Americans draw only loose connections. The data seem to suggest that they come to each issue policy controversy anew, without concern for how what they believe about other controversies might impinge upon what they ought to believe about the current one. They are largely, in Converse's (1964) term, "unconstrained." Where professionals see issues as instances for the application of higher abstractions, ordinary citizens seem often to lack this abstract structuring mechanism. When asked to describe their preferences, their words are rich in reactions to the persons and events of politics, relatively impoverished in ideological classification. Abstractions that do arise are typically quite limited in connotation, unlike similar language used by those who make their living from public life.

This lack of connection suggests an electorate in which every issue is *sui generis*, a function only of the facts and context of the times. In such an electorate, thinking about change over time would be pointless. Lacking a stable set of relationships between issues, there are only particulars, nothing general worth observing. This is not the case. When we look to the associations of issues with one another over time, they are quite predictable and quite high. High associations within bundles of issues suggest that something stable lies beneath them. This something, public-policy mood, turns out to be orderly and predictable, moving through time in response to the events of politics. It is as if the aggregate order were impossible to square with the individual-level disorder we so commonly observe.

Which of these views is correct, individual disorder or aggregate order? In one, conventional views – and no less, democratic theory – square with observed behavior. In the other, politics is characterized by large elements of randomness and only small elements of order. It is a politics of chance, where nothing is orderly or particularly meaningful. Both views we will see to be correct. We will build a portrait of orderly aggregate behavior in this book without challenging the consensus that individual behavior involves large elements of caprice and disorder. Choosing between the views becomes a matter of what questions are to be answered. Questions about citizens are answered with individual data and individual conclusions. Questions about how electorates interact with parties, candidates, and events over time are answered with the aggregate, orderly view.

What individual voters know about economics is much less documented than what they know about politics. We presume that this is true in part because voters know so little about macroeconomic policy debates that it is pointless to ask for preferences on surveys.[2] We think it safe to assert nonetheless that most individuals lack any working knowledge of fiscal or monetary policy, do not know the function of the Federal Reserve or the identity of its leadership. Faced with a serious debate on alternative courses of national economic policy, most voters would not understand the key terms of the discussion.

We can get some gauge of the matter by looking at the language politicians use to address their audience. There serious debates about the possible role of the federal deficit as a lever on real interest rates become homilies about government operating just like the typical family, balancing what comes in with what goes out. Expansive monetary policy is "government printing money" – and we would not be surprised to find the Bureau of the Mint chosen by many citizens as a key economic policy maker. Virtually every act of taxing and spending is described by proponents as "producing jobs" and by opponents as "costing jobs," all with little apparent concern that both claims cannot be simultaneously true.

---

2 We do have some modest experience with the related issue of taxation. There, attempts to gauge sentiment toward progressivity, the central issue of taxation controversies, run afoul of voter misunderstanding. The evidence is that large numbers of lowest income and least educated respondents gravitate to response options that would substantially increase their own tax burdens relative to the wealthy. The political popularity of "flat tax" ideas – at least so long as they are not implemented – is related evidence of the same propensity. An intriguing question is whether evident enthusiasm for a flat tax seen in surveys erodes when the issue becomes the focus of a salient political campaign.

## Preface

Americans are quite well aware that many of the goods they consume are made in other countries, and they worry about the impact on American jobs. They are quite unaware that huge numbers of American jobs, and maybe even their own, are dependent upon exports to many of those same countries. Debates about foreign trade consequently must take place on two levels, where decision makers deal with real balances between gains and losses, and most of the public knows only rhetoric, for example, "the giant sucking sound." Political leaders regularly ignore expressed public preferences on these matters, knowing that the preferences arise from a weak grasp of the central facts.

But all this changes when we look to macro politics. There we learn that public expectations of the future course of the national economy closely mirror those of economic forecasters. We learn that presidential approval rises and falls with revised expectations about the future. We learn that incumbent success at reelection is predictably dependent upon the state of the economy and expectations for its future. Again it is tempting to regard these two accounts as contrasts, one true and one false. But they are both true. It is true that individual Americans have a weak grasp on the essentials of economics and economic policy, and it is also true that Americans, in the aggregate, are highly sensitive to real economic performance. After worrying about the terrible effects of the combination of cynical politicians with myopic electorates, we now know that electorates are not myopic; they cannot be manipulated by the here and now because they attend to the future.

This book is a sustained examination of American politics from the aggregate perspective. We will see routinely that implications from the best sustained generalizations from the study of individual attitudes and behavior do not hold at the macro level. At one level, this is just a tired restatement of the maxim that we ought to restrict generalizations to the level of data that support them. And this would be a sermon to our readers about the dangers of cross-level inference. But our interest is the substance of American politics, not methodological sermons. We care about what is believed to be true about how American politics works. Our goal is to contribute to that body of knowledge by a systematic analysis of the whole. We will not achieve that goal. But at least we will be as systematic as we know how to be, and we will cover as much of the whole as we can grasp and squeeze between two covers.

As we move from topic to topic, we will keep returning to one set of questions. We will ask: Which is the real American politics? Is it ignorant or informed? Is it sensitive to real political context or the aggregate of a kind of meaningless babble? Is it the expression of, and governing response to, real preferences, or is it manufactured symbols that move voters and politicians in a surreal dance? The answers will usually be "both." And then the important question becomes which of the contrasting perspectives is more appropriate for the particular question at hand.

Our starting point, and a major theme of this book, is the point of our several examples: *The operation of the macro-political system produces a more sophisticated and intelligent response than we would expect from what we know about the individual actors who compose it.*

# Acknowledgments

---

The research program on which we report began in 1986. In this long period, the three of us have accordingly accumulated debts quite beyond the usual numbers. Universities that have supported this project through various means include The University of Houston (Erikson and Stimson), The University of Missouri, St. Louis (MacKuen), The University of Iowa (Stimson), The University of Minnesota (Stimson), Columbia University (Erikson), and The University of North Carolina, Chapel Hill (MacKuen and Stimson). We have also benefited from the hospitality of other institutions away from home. These include Cal Tech (Erikson), The Center for Advanced Study in the Behavioral Sciences (Stimson), and The Center for Political Studies of the Institute for Social Research, University of Michigan (Stimson). While few have seen early drafts of the complete manuscript, many of our colleagues have offered valuable commentary on its parts along the way. These include Chris Achen, Andrew Austin, Larry Bartels, Nathaniel Beck, Janet Box-Steffensmeier, Henry Brady, Charles Cameron, Mark Crescenzi, Darren Davis, Susanna DeBoef, Ray Duch, Lee Epstein, Stanley Feldman, Morris Fiorina, Charles Franklin, John Freeman, Jim Granato, Michele Hoyman, Larry Jacobs, John Jackson, Jane Junn, Paul Kellstedt, Rod Kiewiet, Gary King, Kathleen Knight, George Krause, Michael Lewis-Beck, David Lowery, John Matsusaka, Greg McAvoy, Michael McDonald, Kevin McGuire, Timothy McKeown, Walter Mebane, Warren Miller, Rebecca Morton, Calvin Mouw, Thomas Oatley, Rich Pacelle, Benjamin Page, Martin Paldam, David Papell, Douglas Rivers, Robert Shapiro, Renée Smith, Steven Smith, James Snyder, Richard Sobel, Marco Steenbergen, Terry Sullivan, Michael Ting, Herb Weisberg, John Williams, Chris Wlezien, and Gerald Wright. Graduate and undergraduate research assistants include Robert Durr, Paul Kellstedt, Tami Buhr, Larry Grossback, Greg Pettis, Nate Kelly, Chris Reinard, Pat Taylor, Callie Rennison, Joe Bafumi, and Jordan Hirsch.

# Acknowledgments

Our earlier journal articles have drawn a good deal of published criticism, of which we are the beneficiaries. Some of the chapters in this book show changes in position and emphasis that reflect what we have learned from our critics. These include Warren Miller, Paul Abramson, Charles Ostrom, George Bishop, Renée Smith, Janet Box-Steffensmeier, Helmut Norpoth, Harold Clarke, Marianne Stewart, Donald Green, Bradley Palmquist, and Eric Schickler.

Formal support for this research program came from the National Science Foundation (SES 9011807 Politics Eras and Representation) directly and also, indirectly, from its ongoing support of the Political Methodology Society, which has been the audience of choice for most of our work during its development. We owe a debt of gratitude to all of those Political Methodology participants who have argued with us, informed us, and in general pushed our work to a higher standard.

Our data came mainly from archival sources, among them, The Roper Center, The Inter-University Consortium for Political and Social Research, The United States Department of Commerce, and The Conference Board. We are particularly grateful to Jeff Segal, Jeff Cohen, Kathleen Frankovic, Ian Budge, Richard Hofferbert, Michael McDonald, Donald Green, Bradley Palmquist, and Eric Schickler for the contribution of specialized data to our research. We owe a special debt to Philip Converse, whose initial help pushed us toward the study of macro politics.

We should like to thank James Kuklinski and Dennis Chong, the series editors, for the opportunity to publish our work. And we want to express our appreciation for the patience and perseverance of both Alex Holzman and Lewis Bateman, our Cambridge University Press editors, who nurtured this long-lasting project and helped bring it to fruition.

Finally, we would like to nod our heads to Kathleen Knight, Michele Hoyman, and Dianne Stimson, who encouraged, sustained, and sometimes good-naturedly tolerated our commitment to this years-long project.

# 1

## A Model of the Macro Polity

This book is about politics in the United States. We examine the attitudes and behavior of American citizens. We study their evaluations of the president. We study their perceptions of the economy and the political responses that result. We study their party identifications. We study their policy views and ideological leanings. We study not only attitudes but also one important form of political action, the voting choices people make at the ballot box. And we don't study just ordinary citizens. We also study politicians and their responses to the voters – and the voters' responses to the politicians' actions.

These several topics will be familiar to readers who know the empirical literature on American politics of the post–World War II era. But our book diverges from the norm in one crucial respect. Our focus is on the macro rather than micro level of analysis.

For most studies of political behavior, the unit of analysis is the individual – the mass survey respondent or the member of some political elite. That is the study of "micro politics." This book is about "macro politics," not the politics of the individual but the politics of the aggregate – the "macro polity." Here when we study citizens, the subject under investigation is the electorate rather than the voter. When we study elites, our subject is the institution rather than its members, or even the composite acts of the national government rather than its specific institutions.

We study the macro polity over time. Thus, our statistical analysis consists largely of a series of dynamic time-series equations. We ask questions such as how one aggregate changes when we change another. Ours of course is not the first time-series analysis of macro-level politics. By far the most heavily researched topic in political time series is *Presidential Approval*. Starting with Mueller's (1970, 1973) pioneering work, numerous books and articles have been written about the president's approval rating and, for other nations, the popularity of governments in general. A second familiar type of political time series is the study of

1

election results over time. With Kramer (1971) as the pioneer, macro-level studies of elections have become routine, although often with forecasting as the major goal at the expense of explanation.

Typically, whether the focus of explanation is *Presidential Approval* or whether it is elections, the dominant predictor variables are from the realm of economics. Numerous economic variables have been collected; they vary over time; and there is strong reason to believe that they are politically relevant. Thus, the macro-level study of political variables has largely been the study of why economics is important to politics. The economy is politically important, as subsequent chapters will attest. But it is not the sole source of changes in the public's evaluation of its leaders.

The kinds of political explanations that are important in micro-level political behavior research were largely ignored, until recently, in macro-level research. Micro-level analysis focuses on variables like party identification, policy positions, and ideology. Why did these explanations escape macro-level attention? There are two reasons.

Most importantly, these political aggregates were thought to be constants rather than variables, and therefore hardly worthy of dynamic analysis. Starting with *The American Voter* (Campbell et al. 1960), it became widely recognized that people rarely changed their party attachments. Indeed, aggregate stability was evident in the Democrats' dominant lead over Republicans in reported polls on party identification. Policy positions, if meaningful at all, were thought to be constant, too. While responses to policy questions were fragile and susceptible to change (or even minor variations in question wording), changes in response to a specific question were attributed mainly to "doorstep opinion" rather than thoughtful reappraisal (Converse 1964). Moreover, opinion polls rarely showed much movement on policy issues in the aggregate.

A second reason that aggregate-level measures of these political variables went ignored was that the databases of party identification, liberalism-conservatism, and views on any issue did not exist with sufficiently regular measurement to form a meaningful time series. Advances in archiving the historical record show the existence of variability where none was thought possible. The first systematic measurement of aggregate party identification was not published until MacKuen, Erikson, and Stimson's (1989) assembly of quarterly readings of Gallup's party identification. The change observed in what we labeled *Macropartisanship* has been the subject of considerable research and controversy. The next important breakthrough was the demonstration that macro-level positions on policy issues changed in meaningful ways. Page and Shapiro (1992) showed that macro-level positions on policy issues changed and changed in ways that could be described as a rational response to

2

the political environment. About the same time, Stimson (1991, 1998) reported the measurement of the public's *Policy Mood* as a composite indicator of policy views as they fall on the liberal-conservative continuum. And Wlezien (1995, 1996) showed that mass opinion actually reacts to policy decisions. Public opinion, it turns out, moves after all and in meaningful ways.

This book is made possible by the collection of a rich set of macro-level political explanations and their indicators. From the economic realm, we have both objective indicators of prosperity and the public's subjective perceptions of prosperity (*Consumer Sentiment* and its components). As political evaluation, we have the omnipresent *Presidential Approval* and partisanship, our *Macropartisanship* series. For the public's issue preferences, we have *Policy Mood*. Of course, we have national election results, every two (congressional) or four (presidential) years.

A crucial set of our measures is for political elites rather than the electorate. We have measures of the ideological direction of the major parties as written in their party platforms (Budge and Hofferbert 1990; McDonald, Budge, and Hofferbert 1999). We have dozens of measures of congressional, presidential, and judicial behavior that go into our measure of the government's *Policy Activity*. And we develop a measure of the ideological direction of major legislation drawn from Mayhew's (1991) list of major laws. For each congress, the measure is laws; over time, *Laws* accumulate to form the measure of national *Policy*.

### The "Voter" and the "Electorate": Macro vs. Micro

The crucial actor in the democratic political process is the individual known as "the voter." Viewed at the macro-level perspective, the voter transforms into "the electorate." Although the electorate is simply the sum of voters, our knowledge of the individual voter turns out not to be a reliable guide for generalizing to the electorate and its role in democratic politics.

### The Voter at the Micro Level

At the dawn of the era of survey research in social science (circa World War II), it was widely assumed that voters and electorates acted as democratic theories required; that they had preferences over policy alternatives, knowledge about choices, and interest in outcomes; and that all of these were encapsulated in the vote. These attributes, "electoral intelligence" for short, ensured a two-way communication. They produced electoral response to the things government actually did on the one hand, and they sent a message about preferences back to government on the other.

This happy picture was dashed by the early voter studies (Berelson, Lazarsfeld, and McPhee 1954) and then dashed again by the most influential *American Voter* (Campbell et al. 1960) and the follow-up work of the Michigan voting behavior school. The citizens who emerged from this work had few policy preferences (and little cognitive structure to hold those few together), abysmal levels of knowledge of political facts, and little interest in their citizen role. Nowhere is the impression of voters who don't measure up more vivid than where they speak for themselves in the *American Voter*'s "Levels of Conceptualization" analysis. They sounded just like people we knew, but somehow seemed to be aberrations. To see what was typical of American voters was to see a picture that did not resemble any conception of electorate as partner in a dialogue over political choices.

It is not too much of an exaggeration to say that the American voter portrayed by early survey research studies was a political fool, hardly equipped to handle the responsibilities of democratic citizenship. More recent scholarship resurrects the voter's reputation somewhat, by ascribing to the voter what Popkin (1991) calls limited information rationality. The voter *is* capable of complex, rational judgments, so the argument goes, given the limited information available. (See also Lupia and McCubbins 1998.) Still, the problem of low information remains. Either because of a low supply of information available or the voter's perhaps rational choice not to use it, our voter – while more sophisticated than once thought – remains ignorant.

Indeed, the best analysis of voters' attention and awareness shows no appreciable gain in voter knowledge over the years (Delli Carpini and Keeter 1996). Let us imagine that we have a good scale of general political knowledge and can rank people accordingly. The typical voter, at the 50th percentile of general political knowledge, would be challenged to name such commonplace political objects as both home-state senators, the House speaker, and the chief justice of the Supreme Court. This typical voter could name the president, the governor, and probably one home-state senator, but would have only about a 50-50 chance of possessing even a rudimentary knowledge of the terminology of political ideology (e.g., "liberal," and "conservative") or of the latest hotspot in the world where the United States is involved (e.g., Nicaragua, Kosovo).

How does this typical voter make political judgments and vote in elections? Our typical voter's political beliefs have no particular ideological structure. If responding in a survey, our voter at the median level of information would offer a mix of liberal and conservative viewpoints on

4

different issues – and if given the opportunity, might express agreement with both the liberal and conservative sides of the same issue (Zaller 1992). It is often observed that the typical voter makes judgments not by evaluating facts but by an emotional response to political stimuli. Perhaps fortunately, our typical voter may have the anchor of a party identification, which provides a baseline for voting decisions. But our typical voter has not arrived at this party choice from thoughtful deliberation as much as from family inheritance and habit, much in the same way people who attend religious services decide which one to attend based more on family tradition than a personal theological appraisal.

Our negative portrayal of the typical American voter is one that is ingrained in students of American political behavior with their exposure to the available survey-based literature. Our depiction of the limitations of the typical voter at the 50$^{th}$ percentile of political awareness may exaggerate some (we hope it does), but for the sake of argument, let us accept it as true. What then are the implications for the value of public opinion and ultimately, for the quality of democratic governance?

One obvious answer would be extreme skepticism about any signs of intelligent life, along the lines of the following. When pollsters conduct their polls on presidential approval, party identification, policy issues, and economic performance, we should be wary of subjecting them to elaborate interpretation, as if changes in the mass response had any meaning. And we should not attribute any particular intelligence to the voters' collective decisions at election time.

Election results would be explained as voter responses to vestigial party identifications, or to candidate promises of bread and circuses, or to orchestrated emotional appeals.

While there is sometimes a grain of truth to this obvious answer, it is largely wrong. To understand the political behavior of the American electorate is not to understand the political behavior of the typical voter. Let us see why.

## The Electorate at the Macro Level

One can agree that the average citizen is not particularly informed, not particularly thoughtful, and not particularly attentive, but still find these characteristics emerge in the aggregate. There are many aspects to this argument, but its simplest summary is that citizens at many different levels of information, thought, and attention determine the electorate's collective behavior. Those at the low end of the scale have little input on aggregate movement; those at the high end have major input. The net result is that the more informed, thoughtful, and attentive citizens contribute disproportionately to aggregate movement.

## The Macro Polity

The key to the macro-micro discrepancy, of course, is that aggregation accentuates the orderly. One can have an electorate in which large numbers of citizens act as if at random and other large numbers have unchanging loyalties that commit them to the same side for a lifetime – and yet still observe in the aggregate response an orderly response to real political events. When we aggregate over time, those who act as if at random cancel out. Those who act always the same produce no variance. The aggregate "signal" arises almost wholly from those who are orderly in their behavior. The important misconception is that the normal or typical individual attributes dominate the aggregate. They do not. When individuals are disorderly or constant over time, then their attributes contribute trivially to the movement of the whole.

The point is that the macro perspective is – and should be – very different from the micro. To understand (micro) voters, one must focus upon normal and typical behavior. To understand (macro) electorates, the focus must be on their orderly movement over time. And we shall see again and again that such movement *is* orderly, *is* responsive to real political events, and *does* send a message that politicians ignore at their peril. *The irony of this shift of perspective is that it is a shift back to the conventional wisdom of political observers before the scientific study of politics.*

To elaborate, consider the simplified illustration of an electorate composed of two types of individuals. Group A is composed of ideal informed citizens who pay political attention and respond in meaningful ways to political cues. Group B is composed of people who pay virtually no attention to the political (and economic) environment. Suppose we survey group B at regular intervals. Group B respondents might give random responses to survey questions or reach back to some stable predispositions to provide answers, but in the aggregate there will be no variance. For instance, when the economy changes, they do not see it, and the record of *Consumer Sentiment* will be a flat line.[1] When the president succeeds or fails, they do not see it, and their degree of *Presidential Approval* will be a flat line. When the candidates propose new policy solutions, they do not see it, and the election result is unaffected. Meanwhile, in all these circumstances, group A responds to the political stimuli as expected, given its attention and interest in politics.

By definition, our hypothetical two-group electorate consists of the addition of groups A and B. The electorate, that is, is the sum of meaningful variation and a flat line. It is easy to see that the responses of group A are solely what drive the macro-politics indicators. When *Consumer*

---

1 Alternatively, they perceive their personal economic experiences but not the economic experience of the aggregate.

*Sentiment* changes, it is people who are informed about the economy who move. When *Presidential Approval* changes, it is people who are aware of the president's activity who move. When candidates change their policy positions, it is the interested, informed voters who shift their votes, although in different directions depending on their policy views. Most importantly, in each case the change is not unpredictable or random movement; it is orderly and predictable. Neither informed voters nor uninformed voters are going to collectively move without a collective reason – a net response to available signals.

The electorate of course does not divide simply into groups A and B, but at any one time, some people are attentive and others not. Imagine again our scale of political information, from which we drew the typical voter as the voter at the median. We know that the more informed the voter is, the more responsive the voter will be to the political environment. In this way, the informed electorate drives the macro polity system to a degree that may not be immediately apparent.

At the same time, we should not write as if aggregation from the individual to the aggregate solves all the problems of democracy. And we should see the limits of the argument. At least two important limitations deserve attention. One is that even as they dominate the change in the political indicators, informed voters might be too low in number to have any political impact. If only 10 percent were in the ideal group A category, their influence would be less than if, say, 50 percent were in category A, even though group A's dominance over the aggregate indicators would be the same in either instance.

A second limitation is that circumstances could exist where the "errors" of uninformed voters do not cancel out but instead represent the systematic response to some erroneous signal. Suppose that ignorant voters are just alert enough to respond to some false signal of economic well-being. Or suppose that they evaluate the president not on objective indicators of which they remain ignorant, but rather on superficial indicators like the president's general demeanor when appearing on television news bytes. Similarly, whereas the informed voters respond to candidate issue positions, suppose their votes are swamped by less informed voters who are just attentive enough to follow the siren call of the demagogue.

In theory, macro-level analysis *could* show the voice of the attentive voter drowned out in these ways. But we do not find that. We are struck by the facts leading in the other direction, to the extraordinary sophistication of the collective electorate. Here is a preview of some examples: When the citizenry forms expectations of the economy, it responds as if to the best information available, *and* it uses this information rationally to evaluate the president. Similarly, according to our estimates, the electorate's collective policy proximity to the two parties matters at election time to a degree most observers would find surprising. And we find evidence that when national policy responds to assuage public opinion, public opinion responds accordingly, lowering its demands for further action. In each instance, these responses of the collective electorate are far more than we expect the typical voter of survey research lore to be able to perform.[2]

## Political Dynamics

This book is about the American political system. To examine American politics, we do not describe its state at any given moment but instead observe how it changes, how it evolves, over the course of time. We are interested in dynamics, in how each of the various pieces impinges upon each of the others, in how change flows from electorate to government and back again.

The *Macro* in our title connotes our level of analysis throughout. Our interest is in system-level equations. When we explore how government economic performance affects the electorate's political support and future elections, or the interrelationships between government policy and citizen preferences for policy, each shaping the other, we focus on the systemic relationships between citizens and governments. We model the system as a system, and explore the interactions of things influencing other things and feeding back through multiple layers of causal relationships.

All of these questions are about the whole, not the parts, of American politics. Consequently, we explore them nearly always with aggregated macro data. This is not, however, an exercise in ecological inference – the inference of individual behavior from aggregate information (Erbing 1990; Achen and Shively 1995; King 1997). For the questions that drive us are macro-level questions; making inferences to micro behavior is another line of research altogether. Often we will start with micro-level models to deduce macro characteristics, but we do not cross levels to go back again to the micro.

Although we deal with research questions – for example, the causes of presidential approval or the influence of government economic performance on political evaluation – that are familiar in the political

2 The value of studying politics at the macro level is not limited to time-series analyses. It extends as well to cross-sectional analysis (cross-national, cross-states in the United States) of politics. For a discussion of many of the issues raised here as they apply to aggregate-level cross-sectional data, see Erikson, Wright, and McIver 1994.

science literature, it is uncommon to design research that focuses unrelentingly on the macro side of the ledger. That is what we shall do. Never delving far into the minds of citizens or politicians, our explanatory goals are at the system level. We care about questions such as whether shifts in mass preferences drive government policy. Such questions involve individual citizens and individual politicians. But it is not the individual behaviors that are our primary focus.

As political scientists, our model is the sister discipline of economics, in which the distinction about levels of analysis is formalized into the micro and macro domains. We are quite self-conscious in our emulation of macroeconomics, in its starting idea that movements of aggregates influence one another at a level of analysis removed from the understanding of individual choices. Markets are macro phenomena, interactions of individuals producing properties, which are not themselves the properties of the individuals who engage in market behavior. Along with the economists, we have learned that good macro theory springs from micro foundations, from explicit linking of the models of individual behavior to macro and aggregate consequences.

In this regard, we are better off than the early students of macroeconomics. Thinking about macro and micro questions in economics ran roughly in parallel. Culminating ultimately in the intellectual crisis preceding the rational expectations revolution, it became clear that the absence of micro foundations in macroeconomics allowed confused and contradictory perspectives. We begin perched on the shoulders of five decades of micro-behavior theory and research into the behaviors of citizens, voters, politicians, parties, and the myriad of institutions that structure and constrain their interactions. Not wholly separate enterprises, as was the case early in the history of micro and macro studies of economics, we have good micro theory to build on. And we shall exploit everything we know.

Because our approach is unusual for political science, we have an unusual need to explain ourselves, to lay out what we believe and how we shall proceed in the analyses to come. Sketching out some of our prior beliefs and commenting on our macro approach to politics are the main business of this chapter.

## COMPONENTS OF THE MODEL: MICRO AND MACRO

Citizens choose. They vote. They take up or abandon an identification with a political party. They decide to approve or disapprove of the president's performance in office. Politicians also choose. They decide to support or oppose particular policies. If they are legislators, they decide to support or oppose the administration. They choose sometimes to highlight their acts by seeking publicity for them. At other times, they obscure them by acting quietly, perhaps by taking positions that are contradictory or confusing.

These are acts of the sort that are the main focus of political scientists who study American politics. They are individual behaviors, understood by studying individuals one at a time. Often these acts, micro behaviors, aggregate over the populations of citizens or politicians to a total that is exactly the sum of its parts. In these cases, our understanding of micro behaviors, the micro polity, becomes also an understanding of the whole, the macro polity. When this is the case, the study of micro behavior is exactly the right way to go about a science of politics. This is the dominant style of American political science, and we believe that on balance it is a good one.

Often, too, macro behaviors have a character, which is not well understood by summing the pieces. If we wished to understand, for example, how presidential approval responds to the vicissitudes of events experienced in the presidential term, we would not get far by the study of individual citizens. If we wished to account for their behavior, we would be impressed by explanations that discriminate between them; factors such as partisanship and ideology would dominate our explanations. Things that affect all citizens equally (or nearly so) – factors such as international crises, honeymoons, and the zigs and zags of the macro economy – would not emerge as important understandings. These matters, which vary over time, but not among citizens, do not help to discriminate among citizens at any one moment of time. The reverse is also true; the factors that best discriminate among citizens at a given time vary little over time and do not therefore emerge as dominant understandings of dynamics.

Macro-level understandings differ from micro-level understandings for two classes of reasons. One is that some political behavior is *social*; groups of people interacting with one another do things, which are different from what would have occurred from the summation of atomized individuals. A good knowledge of the preferences citizens bring to a precinct caucus, for example, does not give impressive leverage in predicting its outcome, because things change when citizens begin to talk to one another. They can change quite dramatically when strategic considerations enter the fray.

But more humble differences between the micro and macro level are also important. Understandings of micro and macro differ also from the design of research appropriate for the two. Macro-approval research, for example, holds nearly constant those factors that discriminate among citizens and emphasizes variation in those that move all together. That makes it possible to observe subtle causes of behavior without the disruption of powerful – but not very interesting – individual factors, such as whether or not the citizen shares the president's party affiliation. Even where social interaction does not modify behavior at the macro level, the different levels of analysis permit different questions to be addressed and lead to different understandings.[3]

It is pointless, we believe, to argue whether micro or macro theories are superior or which is the appropriate strategy for understanding politics. In those cases where micro theory produces macro understanding, then micro theory *is* better. An understanding of the whole that proceeds from understanding the parts is better than an understanding of only one or the other. We pursue macro designs not from any belief in inherent superiority, but because we believe they offer the best opportunity *given the knowledge of this moment* to enhance our ability to explain politics. That knowledge of the moment is heavily based upon micro-research programs.

Our starting assumption is that we know quite a lot about politics and that we know it mainly from micro theories, micro models, and micro-research designs. A substantial limitation of micro knowledge – perhaps the largest – is that it is not easily integrated. Impressive bodies of knowledge, for example, about citizen attitudes and behaviors and congressional attitudes and behaviors leave the connections between the two largely in the domain of speculation. A query as simple as, "If citizens change their preferences on some policy question, will Congress respond with changed policy?" cannot be answered from the sum of micro understandings of citizens and politicians. The strength of the macro approach of this book is that such questions are readily addressed, and we shall address them.

We wish ultimately to say how politics works in America. That is a tall order, and we shall quickly have to retreat to less comprehensive understandings. But goals matter, and that comprehensive knowledge is the object to which we aspire. We are at the task of building bridges between bodies of knowledge, and we look to the macro level to learn the rules of bridge construction.

## POLITICS IN THE UNITED STATES: MICRO MODELS, MACRO BEHAVIOR, MACRO DATA

We seek to know macro behavior. We seek to understand it, when we can do so, from theories of individual behavior. That leads to a self-conscious modeling strategy in many of our efforts. We first lay out a

---

3 The classic statement of the levels of analysis conundrum for political economy remains Kramer (1983).

micro theory and model, usually static and usually pretty simple. Then we ask what happens under aggregation over time and derive a macro model, usually dynamic, from the static micro understanding. The macro model produces predictions about macro behavior, and it is these predictions that confirm and disconfirm the theories and models from which they are derived.

This is not the only legitimate and useful way to proceed, nor is it the most common. More normally micro models produce micro predictions, the accuracy of which reflects simply on the models that produced them. One can then generalize *theories* to the system level. The hazard in doing so lies not in the logic of inference, but in the fact that micro theory rarely crosses the boundary between citizens and government. It is about one or the other, but rarely about the junction between them. But our title, *The Macro Polity*, is our interest. So our question is not the usual one, "Is the theory good?" but rather "Does the theory aggregate up to produce useful macro understanding?"

The payoff for this constant focus on the macro level is that it becomes possible to unify our understanding of how politics works. Insofar as we can derive predictions from simple coherent theories, we can use our macro understanding to tie together what is known about the interactions of citizens and officials that we call politics. Our promise is less to produce new macro findings – although we do quite a lot of that – than it is to integrate what is known about the macro into a coherent package.

## OUR PRIORS

In the spirit of Bayesian inference,[4] it is clear that conclusions that emerge from analyses come partly from confrontation with data and partly from the prior beliefs, which structure the analysis. Here we lay out some of the priors for this book. We have two sets, one about citizens and one about politicians. We begin with citizens.

### Citizens

In the abstract models to come, citizens act in four capacities. They *evaluate* governments, sometimes approving, sometimes disapproving what they see. They *identify* – or choose not to identify – with political parties and ideological groups. They *hold preferences* about what government ought to do and how it ought to do it. And last, they *choose* between candidates and parties in elections. We begin with evaluation.

4 See Bartels (1997) for an explication of Bayesian logic.

*Evaluation.* Citizens sometimes approve of governments – presidents, congresses, courts, and maybe parties in office – and sometimes disapprove. To understand why is a major task of this volume. We begin that task with the question, "What is it that citizens want from government?" with the hope that its answer will lead us closer to understanding. We postulate that citizens want three basic attributes, competence in the administration of public affairs, control of the direction of government, and agreement with the citizens' policy preferences. We explore each in the following paragraphs.

*Competence*: Citizens want government to succeed, that is, to achieve the goals it sets. This is the centerpiece of most analyses of presidential approval, that governments govern well by achieving consensual goals such as peace and prosperity. We presume that success arises from competent direction, that prosperity, for example, is the result of steady hands on government economic levers, not the luck of the times or the result of decisions beyond government's reach. This notion that government policy is a major influence on the quality of economic outcomes is controversial among economic theorists – but not apparently with citizens, who are willing to give credit or blame to those in control, usually of the White House.

Economic outcomes dominate analyses of citizen evaluation of government competence. And they will loom large in ours. We wish to emphasize, however, that the central standing of economic management probably is due chiefly to its readily quantifiable outcomes. This is true not only for the *study* of citizen evaluation, but for the thing itself. In no other arena can we index performance and compare it to historical norms. We believe that competence of diverse sorts matters for citizen evaluation, that citizens form appraisals of how well presidents or congresses do all the things they do and that these appraisals matter.

*Control*: Successful implementation of policy requires something more than competence of a limited sort; it requires also that policy actors such as presidents be in control of events. A competent president who is a bystander, either to events no one controls – Jimmy Carter and the Iran hostage crisis comes to mind – or to other political actors, will not win high marks.[5] Control may be seen as psychic reassurance; citizens want the ship of state actively directed, not drifting to and fro. It is also the

---

5 Seen in this light the perennial unpopularity of legislative bodies makes some sense. The public debate over outcomes that is their essential character – "bickering" to the public – is continuing evidence that no one is in control.

logical connection that projects competence and policy agreement into the future. To agree with a political leader or to think he or she is competent still doesn't reassure citizens about the future where there is doubt about control.

*Policy Agreement*: One of the more basic beliefs of nearly all observers of politics is that citizens want government not only to succeed, in an objective sense, but also to do so along a path that honors the citizen's beliefs and values. That is, citizens want policy agreement. If they are moderate or liberal or conservative, they want government to pursue policies that are moderate or liberal or conservative. *Ceteris paribus*, liberals ought to be more likely to approve governments that pursue liberal policies, and conservatives ought to be more approving of conservative governments. Much of our understanding of politics is predicated upon just such a thesis.

It is remarkable, therefore, to note that our research literature on citizen evaluation – chiefly that on presidential approval – ignores this aspect of evaluation. There, the focus is almost wholly on *what* governments achieve, not on *how* they go about it. This oversight arises more from research design than theoretical rejection. While policy direction is in principle observable (to citizens and researchers) over time, it comes contaminated with the personality and party of the president. And then, our focus on explaining how the central tendency of approval moves over time usually leads us to ignore *who* is doing the approving and disapproving. We take up some of these issues in Chapter 2.

Competence and control are universal goods. Let us call the combination "performance" for short. Policy divides citizens; interesting policy disputes arise when different citizens desire different ends. Citizen evaluation of government should depend upon both. Within limits, good performance will win approval even from some policy opponents. Similarly, those who agree with government policy may approve even in the face of performance problems. Both play a role.

Citizens may "play" the political game as neutral spectators or become associated with the teams as fans. Which they do influences the dynamics of the play. Competence and control as goals are unifying and are consistent with wholly individual and neutral behaviors. Policy divides; it tends to organize government into competing teams and tends to lead citizens to think of themselves as belonging to one side or the other. That self-identification is our next analytic task.

*Identification*. Citizens may be cool observers of the political world, scoring points for one side or the other in the manner of the polite upper crust of British society at a cricket match. Or they may get into the fray, take sides, and think of themselves as contestants in the party or ideological tug-of-war.[6] The micro behavior literature fails to resolve this issue of the nature of citizen attachment to party, in particular, whether it is fundamentally based upon rational appraisal of outcomes or on "identification" in its strongest sense, a self-image of commitment to one side. We shall not take sides on this issue because we believe that each of these models is appropriate for some citizens some of the time, and not for others or at other times.

Whatever models analysts find plausible as accounts of how partisanship works for individuals, we can be certain that the aggregate will be not one of them, but rather a mixture. Thus whatever the deducible dynamics of the micro models, if they differ, we can be confident that the macro result will be in between. In this case, we will not have a micro model yielding a macro model, but rather competing micro models, the mixture of which yields a macro model.

If identification is no more than a cumulated version of evaluation, its aggregate should share properties with evaluation. It should move in time with some of the same properties and in response to the same forces. This suggests a variable *Macropartisanship*. In contrast, if identification is the formation of a self-image in the manner of *The American Voter* (Campbell et al. 1960), then we expect it to be formed earlier in life and to be highly resistant to later change. This suggests a highly cumulated *Macropartisanship* that moves, if at all, with glacial smoothness. If partisanship is a mixture of the two types, then *Macropartisanship* should have much of the "stickiness" of the identification conception and some of the movement expected of a rational evaluation of outcomes.

Thus we think *some* citizens will be responsive to the factors that influence incumbent evaluations. We will model *Macropartisanship* as a response to domestic economic performance, which is the best conceptualized, best measured of these influences. Because others (i.e., the "identifiers") will not be responsive, we expect the aggregate response to show a more limited translation of economic events into political outcomes than is the case with evaluations.

Evaluations, for *some* citizens, will carry over to identifications. Those who approve of the president's actions in office are more likely to come to "think of themselves" as members of the president's party. And disapprovers are likely to identify with the opposition. But evaluation is more transient than identification. Evaluation can be, and often is, little

6 Most of our treatment of identification will be of identification with *party*, one of the central facts of American politics. But thinking of oneself as a liberal or conservative is also identification and should entail similar processes and similar understandings.

more than a momentary response to a recent presidential action. Thinking of oneself as member of a party is a more basic, and hence more lasting, attitude. Thus we expect some portion of approval and disapproval (but not all of it) to register on identification. And we expect the process to be quite cumulative over time.

Citizens, to be sure, want government to achieve its goals. But if that were all they wanted, we wouldn't need politics. For one of the things essential to politics is that goals themselves are open to controversy. When government takes from some and gives to others, for example, merely being efficient at the transfer isn't likely to please all citizens. Citizens have differing preferences. To come to terms with how citizens function in a democratic polity, we must come to terms with those differing preferences.

*Policy Preference.* Students of micro-level political behavior study citizen policy preferences and causes and effects on other activities, especially vote choices. Policy preferences are often treated as public opinion itself. Opinion is what citizens want government to do. In this book, we focus on an important subset of issues, those that involve how large and how active the (federal) government ought to be.

*Citizens as Consumers of Government:* Citizens are consumers of government. They want the collective benefits government is organized to provide. They want national security, paved and maintained highways, airport security, and social welfare. Sometimes they want these things for themselves, sometimes for others more in need. Narrowly conceived, some of these benefits can be thought of as self-interest. But we should not lose sight of the fact that government does many things (e.g., sponsoring exploration of the Moon) that convey no such direct benefits, but nonetheless draw wide public support.

Are citizens *rational* in their political choices? If forced to use a term too laden with complexity to provide much meaning, we would answer in the affirmative. By standard conceptions, most of the time as individuals and even more frequently as the collective electorate, citizens are indeed rational. By this, we mean nothing more than that citizens have their reasons for their actions, an assertion that is almost tautologically true. This is a conception that helps the analyst: To understand the actions, look for the reasons.

The assertion of rationality can breed surprising controversy and misunderstanding. In our sister discipline of economics, the conception of rationality tends to narrowly focus on narrow goals of individual self-interest, as if rational citizens support only government activities where they see actual or potential personal benefit. This does not rule out collective goods – an economic conception itself – but it pretty nearly does rule out classes of collective goods that reasonable citizens think will not benefit them personally or benefit family members or others they might care about. In fact, citizens often support spending programs for those less fortunate than themselves for reasons that do not include the probability of personal gain, present or future. Is this "rational"? The answer is, "of course." Pursuing individual self-interest at the expense of others is far from the only reasonable criterion of rational behavior. But it has a long and honored history in economic theory, where its limitations are not so obvious as they become in politics. We have no quarrel with a rationality postulate – indeed, we could not do without it. It is the narrow criterion of personal self-interest that is problematic.

We observe that many citizens express preferences for government activities that benefit mainly others. Are we to regard this as irrational? Are such citizens an amalgam of fools, who fail to make good self-interest calculations, and saints, who make them and then ignore the result? Clearly, the standard debate between those who want government to do more and those who wish it to do less cannot be well understood if one position – "do less" – is characterized as rational and the other – "do more" – cannot be understood at all with such concepts.

The rationality postulate permits citizens to gain utility from social goods. We have no difficulty understanding that citizens might wish to be surrounded by physical beauty – lakes, streams, and trees – and be willing to pay to enhance it. We postulate also social goods such as equality of opportunity, decent treatment of victims of misfortune, and the like as pleasing aspects of a society that rational individuals could value and be willing to pay for. With this conception in hand, we can explain citizen preference for a variety of government activities with the same logic of choice as the preference to limit government activities. The debate over more or less government becomes then a debate between (equally) rational citizens who bring different preferences to bear, not of the rational versus the foolish-and-saintly.[7]

*Micro Consumers, Macro Electorate*: Assume that much of what we call policy preference is captured by this simple idea of wanting or not wanting more of the product and cost of government. If that is how individuals see choices, we explore here what we would expect (1) of the macro electorate and (2) over time. We can think of the electorate as composed of two groups, those who want (and are willing to pay for) more government, and those who want less. The dichotomous choice for individuals becomes a matter of proportions for the aggregate electorate.

7 We borrow here from Durr (1993).

It consists of a proportion that wants more government – we shall call them liberals – and a proportion that wants less – we shall call them conservatives.[8]

This is a useful simplification, but we should keep in mind that many individuals are both liberal and conservative. In the sense of Zaller (1992), the same individual, depending upon the considerations of the moment, is capable of sincerely advocating more government at some times and places and less at others. This idea violates common understandings of politics, but it should not. Just as consumers are sometimes driven to buy by desire for the product and other times are restrained by its cost, we should not expect political consumers to make a lifetime decision that either "more" or "less" is always superior.

Circumstances change with time and experience, and thus we should expect the proportions that want more or less government also to change. Thus our policy preference concept is longitudinal. While its base is the individual citizen choosing between more and less, the focus of our analyses will be the proportions of both sides as they change over time.

Having said what our conception is, it is worthwhile also to point out what it is not. It is not laden with symbols, emotion, or moral judgments about the right and wrong of politics. All these things are decisively important ingredients of politics; they just aren't useful for operational definition. We do not assume, also, that citizens choosing either left or right will be conscious of how that choice impinges upon their self-conception. Whether those who are liberal by this definition think of themselves as "liberals" is open to investigation, an empirical matter. It will turn out that there is considerable slippage between preferences and self-descriptions and, in particular, that many who cheerfully advocate more activist government in case after case equally cheerfully refer to themselves as "conservatives."

Last, this conception is at odds with the long tradition of voting-behavior scholarship – a tradition in which each of the authors is rooted – in which the central questions are whether or not citizens can have meaningful preferences about public life, and whether, if they do, they

---

8 Political scientists are capable of creating an awful tangle arguing what these words "liberal" and "conservative" mean, or ought to mean. And that tangle grows worse when common usage fails to follow *any* of the philosophical suggestions. We use these terms henceforth to mean exactly what they are defined to mean, for example, a liberal is someone who advocates government action to solve problems. This has three virtues: (1) we know exactly what the words mean, (2) that meaning is closely matched by the operational indicators we will bring to bear to measure the concept, and (3) it is close to usage on the street.

18

can express them at the polls. This preoccupation arises from a conception of public policy controversies as too technical and specific for a part-time electorate with limited knowledge and interest. If public policy becomes the simple question, "more or less?" over and over – with the specifics less central than the fundamental issue of government itself – then a part-time electorate with limited knowledge and interest is still quite capable of having meaningful preferences and of expressing them.

*People, Issues, and Time*: Preferences can vary among people. This is the subject of much work in micro behavior. But it has little macro consequence, and we shall not pursue it. Preferences differ across issue domains. This can be understood as the application of a cost-benefit calculus to varied aspects of public life. In some areas, for example, education and environment, the goals are especially dear to many citizens, who are then willing to pay the price. For other endeavors, for example, public assistance for nonworking mothers, there is less support for the goals and less willingness to pay. Or, where the goal is highly valued, for example, reducing violent crime, citizen beliefs about the inefficacy of government action might still undercut support for a greater government role.

We will choose to deemphasize preference variation across issue domains, treating the varied issues – and the survey items that are their operational indicators – as specific instances of the general phenomenon we wish to track, which is variation across time in the cluster of attitudes that tie together all issue domains. We will pursue the public's *Policy Mood* as citizen demand for more or less government. We believe that it influences both election outcomes and policy making and that it is in turn influenced by citizen response to previous episodes of policy making.

*Choice.* Citizen choice, the micro phenomenon studied in voting behavior, becomes election outcomes when aggregated to the macro level. We pursue outcomes as a function of all of the other citizen opinion attributes. We postulate that outcomes turn on evaluation – of the national economy on the one hand and of the incumbent's performance in other matters on the other. We postulate that the movement of outcomes over time follows movements in identification, or *Macropartisanship*. And we believe that longitudinal movements of global preferences matter as well, that elections signal the evolution of public preferences.

Elections are very well studied in American politics, but much of the research is partial. Questions such as "Does the economy matter?" and "Why does the presidential party lose seats in midterm House elections?"

dominate much of the scholarly output of political scientists and economists on the issue of outcomes. We wish to build on this work in the direction of more comprehensive understandings. We seek greater inclusion in two directions. First, we try to come to terms with all sorts of (national) elections, not merely the presidency or one or the other kind of House elections. Second, we seek a more comprehensive understanding of the causal factors that move elections of all kinds. Toward that end we entertain models in which alternate explanations, for example, economic performance and changes in the public's *Policy Mood*, compete for a full explanation.

Figure 1.1 outlines our basic elections model. It projects electoral choice of all kinds as a function of evaluation (approved presidents and members of congress are more likely to be reelected), of identification (movement toward either party aids that party at election time), and of preference (movements toward liberalism produce Democratic votes; movements toward conservatism produce Republican votes). Each of these, in turn, is influenced by performance, for which our best indicator will be the state of the national economy.

### Politicians

Public officials in a democracy exist always in a dual state: They govern by making and enforcing policy, and they seek election and reelection. We wish to understand why they behave as they do, and then what consequence that carries for the macro polity. Our starting assumption is that both aspects of the job move behavior. Politicians are not merely policy makers, but are required always to have an eye on the next election. Nor are they merely election seekers. That one-sided view of the political life has some appeal, but it will serve us badly when we try to account for what politicians do in their official capacities.

Popular commentary about politicians is hindered by a moralistic screen that prevents objective appraisal of who they are and what they do. It is common to regard election seeking as a mean and disreputable behavior. Then the politician who has policy goals and also wants to protect his or her electoral career is seen through a haze of cynicism, "They all want to be reelected." We hold no such view. Democratic institutions require politicians to have some ambition as a means of enforcing responsiveness to the public. After paying a high entry cost to begin a political career, in most circumstances it would be less than rational not to seek to sustain it through reelection. For us, the reelection motive is normal and expected behavior. It may even be dominant. But it matters for our theory that it not be exclusive, and we posit that it is not. We think most politicians care about the (nonelectoral) stakes of the policy

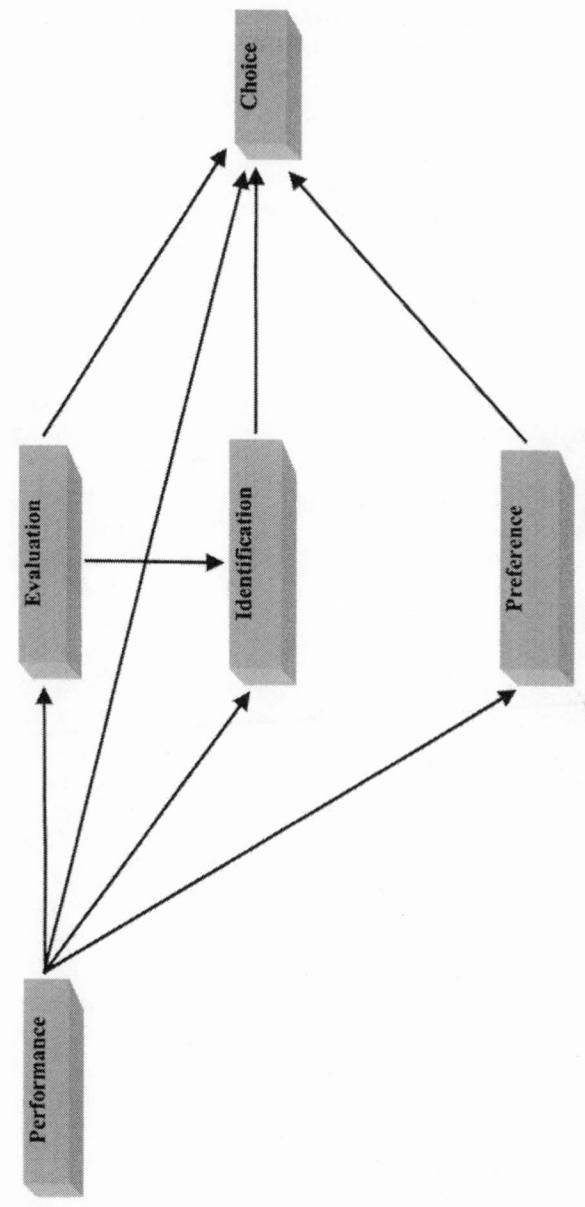

Figure 1.1. A Micro Model of Election Choice

debate, that they seek a public career in part because moving the direction of public affairs seems a worthwhile goal.[9]

*Policy Choice.* We postulate democratic politicians who are partly ideologues committed to a set of policy preferences and partly reelection seekers attuned to signals from the electorate. Because politics is their profession, we expect them to have thought through public controversies and to have arrived at a coherent world view. Coherent views are not necessarily pure or ideologically extreme, but people who think about public controversies for a living are more likely to arrive at relatively extreme positions than is the amateur electorate, which is moderate of necessity by aggregation.

Individual politicians will often then hold views that are different from – often more extreme than – their constituencies. On each policy choice they are likely to have not a single position that is simultaneously their policy ideal and optimal for reelection, but rather some trade-off between the two. In current American politics, often Democrats will hold a policy ideal that is more liberal than what is electorally most advantageous, and Republicans will face a choice in the opposite direction.

Reelection is a future event. And how the various causes add up to create the electoral outcome is never known with full certainty, not even on the eve of the election. Although the risk will vary, to the politician all elections are gambles. Thus politicians cannot *know* what policy position is optimal for reelection, but must instead infer from available information. Then politicians must balance these uncertain estimates of what is electorally optimal against their own policy preferences. The more they value promoting their own beliefs, the greater electoral risks they take; however, they must be wary that the greatest risk against influencing policy in future election cycles is to risk electoral defeat in the present.

Now we ask, what do politicians do when public preferences change? Politicians, who are professionals in the business of reelection, should be adept at sensing that change and then at adjusting their estimates of optimal positions. Because careers can meet an

---

9 By the same token we find discomfort from the moral implications of the term "shirking," which economists use to describe the politician who departs from constituency views. Like political scientists, economists study elections but from their unique perspective. Not directing their attention to available knowledge about actual voters, they rely on the median voter theorem (Downs 1957) to conclude that the median voter's position decides elections. The political scientist asks: what is the evidence that politicians are driven by electoral anticipation? The economist assumes the answer as given. Their puzzle is to understand why politicians "shirk."

inglorious end from failure to make such calculations well, we posit that successful career politicians survive in part because they are very good at it.

*Politicians as Teams.* Politician behavior is not so unstructured as we have written in our little model just described. For politicians' behavior in national government is only partly independent. They also choose to be members of teams, which we call political parties. Free to go it alone when they choose, the fact that they organize into teams does nonetheless bring more structure to their behavior than would otherwise be the case.

Assume that citizens are imperfectly informed about the policy behaviors of individual politicians and also about the typical behaviors of party groups. In the absence of specific information about individuals, reasonable citizens will then make inferences about individuals from the information they possess about parties. This will give a directional bias to the citizen construction of politician positions. Individual Democrats will, on average, be perceived to be more like the Democratic norm than they in fact are, and individual Republicans will be perceived to be more like the Republican norm than they are. This gives individual politicians an important stake in the policy image of their party and provides a motivation to cooperate within party for the collective good.[10] Along with personal ideology, this should form a continuing basis for politician preferences that diverge from those most approved by voters.

### THE DESIGN OF THE BOOK

Our understanding of the political dynamics of American politics begins from two vantage points: (1) how government *performance* affects citizen evaluations and subsequent identifications, and (2) how *policy* preferences affect government policy making. These two aspects, performance and policy, structure the chapters to come. In Part I, we take up matters of performance and its political consequences. In Part II we turn to policy, examining how electorates and politicians shape and respond to one another.

The nature of this task requires the selection of a specific time period for analysis. Our choice of time frame is 1952–1996. Thus, politics

---

10 This expected bias of perceptions also helps to explain the election-time disassociation of some candidates with the symbols of their party, for example, its presidential candidate. If the party norm is unpopular at the moment, or in a particular place, this almost hostile "I am not one of them" behavior is a necessary means to limit the extent of perceptual bias.

before the election of Dwight Eisenhower as president escapes our analysis. So, too, does all that has transpired since Bill Clinton's reelection. The discipline imposed by these limits is necessary for the telling of our story. Still, our subject matter is large – American politics over nearly half a century.

## Performance

Chapter 2 begins our empirical analysis with a discussion of *Presidential Approval*. As an exception to the general rule, macro-level *Approval* has been the subject of considerable analysis by political scientists. Standard explanations for the fluctuations in *Presidential Approval* include presidential honeymoons, public reactions to presidential handling of unexpected events, and the economy. Our analysis shows that these explanations do indeed tell much of the approval story. We also include an extended discussion of the policy basis of presidential evaluation, its difficulty of measurement, and the possible implications.

Chapter 3 extends our analysis of *Presidential Approval* to elaborate an argument that we have made earlier (MacKuen et al. 1992): When citizens evaluate the president based on economic performance, they respond as "bankers" rather than "peasants" – that is, citizens evaluate the president based on expectations of the future rather than simple extrapolations from the past. Actually, the central variable of this chapter is the component of *Consumer Sentiment* we call *Business Expectations*. Chapter 3 argues that citizens form expectations and evaluate the president as if using rational expectations, efficiently weighing past performance and available information about the economic future.

Chapter 4 presents a discussion of *Macropartisanship*, a concept we introduced earlier (MacKuen et al. 1989; Erikson, MacKuen, and Stimson 1998). *Macropartisanship* is the macro-level reading of party identification. Here we consider over 50 years of *Macropartisanship* from 1945 through 1996, using all available Gallup poll readings. We show that *Macropartisanship* responds to presidential approval and (both directly and indirectly) to public evaluations of the economy. We show also that certain political and economic inputs on *Macropartisanship* are permanent, so that *Macropartisanship* represents the cumulative permanent memory of partisan evaluation.

Chapter 5 continues our exploration of *Macropartisanship*, this time with central focus not on the Gallup measure but the CBS News/*New York Times* measure. Our focus here is on how we are to understand the longitudinal movements of partisanship, and in particular the role of race, region, and gender. We give a special focus to age and generational differences, and from age differences in partisanship among older respondents, trace the early movement of *Macropartisanship* going back to the pre-poll era.

## Policy

Chapter 6 introduces a discussion of macro-level policy preferences. Much of this discussion involves *Policy Mood*, a concept introduced earlier by Stimson (1991, 1998). *Mood* is an indicator of public liberalism, based on the statistical analysis of available opinion data on diverse domestic policy preferences, from 1952 to 1996. Chapter 6 also discusses a parallel time-series measure of political ideology based on self-reports of ideology from the early 1970s to 1994.

The analysis of national elections of Chapter 7 draws on both performance and policy indicators. It examines U.S. national elections as a time series of the 12 presidential elections and 23 congressional elections from 1952 to 1996. Its design draws from three competing traditions for explaining election outcomes: the political economy, the response to candidates and campaign, and the influence of party positions and voter preferences. *Macropartisanship* and *Policy Mood* emerge as more important at the macro level than commonly supposed and statistically dominate over economics and candidate appeal for the explanation of the vote – both for president and congress.

Chapter 8 extends our earlier analysis of "dynamic representation" (Stimson, MacKuen, and Erikson 1995). It examines the effects of both mass policy preferences (*Mood*) and the party division determined by election outcomes on government *Policy Activity*. This chapter highlights the annual *Policy Activity* of governance in Washington, what congress, the president, and the Supreme Court do – measured by indicators based on roll-call votes and Supreme Court decisions – in response to changing public demands. We find strong responsiveness to public preferences, which differs by institutional design.

Chapter 9 shifts our attention to *Policy* as measured by the cumulation of major legislation. Exploiting Mayhew's (1991) analysis of "important" laws, this chapter measures the liberalism of each Congress's major legislation (*Laws*), which cumulates to form our measure of *Policy*. The public's policy demand (*Mood*) and party control of president and congress determine the liberalism of the biennium's legislation (*Laws*). In turn, *Policy* liberalism influences the liberalism of the public *Mood*. *Policy* liberalism lowers the public's demand for more liberalism (*Mood*). The resulting interplay between politicians and the public governs the public policy system.

# The Macro Polity

## American Politics as a System

Chapter 10 is our portrait of the big picture of American politics. We use this penultimate chapter as an opportunity to think seriously about politics as a system in which each of the components impinges upon each of the others, often through multiple layers of causal structure. We develop a set of equations that exemplify our analytic findings from earlier chapters and tie together everything we know. We ask what properties this system has and how it differs from the understandings we reach by treating the components as separable and isolated.

Finally, Chapter 11 summarizes our results and offers a more flattering portrayal of the American public's role in the democratic process than scholars generally concede. Whatever the defects of individual voters might be, we find that *in the aggregate* (which is what counts), the electorate responds to its environment as if alert to new information about the economy, political events, and public policy. Moreover, at the ballot box the public relies on its seemingly rational performance evaluations and policy demands. The political elite's anticipation of this behavior adds further to enhance government's responsiveness to the public's demands for both performance and policy satisfaction.

In this continuous world, where our story will feature interactions between citizens and politicians, each influencing future states of the other, there is no proper place to begin. We are breaking into an ongoing set of interactions, none of which is really the beginning and each of which could be. But we must be arbitrary and start the story somewhere. We choose to begin with performance, and, in particular, citizen evaluation of government, the topic of Chapter 2.

# PART I

*Performance*

# 2

## *Presidential Approval*

When he took office in 1993, Bill Clinton was an easy mark. Elected in a three-candidate contest with far from majority support, he quickly took on the aura of a politically troubled president. Fierce attacks from talk radio and his Republican opposition questioned his ideas, his policies, his appointments to office, and, most of all, his character. Lacking the customary bubble of public support we call the honeymoon, Clinton started his presidency in trouble with the public and stayed there for his first two years. Democrats were depressed over his (and their) prospects. Potential Republican challengers for 1996 emerged early and in number, planning to fight the "real" presidential election in Republican primaries – a prelude to an easy contest with Clinton. Then it got worse. When he fought the "Republican Revolution" in the 1994 congressional elections and lost, the election was universally interpreted as a repudiation of the Clinton Presidency. After it was over, Speaker of the House Newt Gingrich pronounced the president "irrelevant."

But then something happened. As a beleaguered Clinton began to oppose a congress controlled by his political enemies, his standing with the public began to rise. Ever so slightly, month by month, more Americans began to say that they approved of the way he was handling his job as president. As he contested with the Republican congress over the budget – and ultimately over the scope of the federal government in American life – he began to become tenacious in defense of moderate positions. He gave ground in compromise after compromise, but surprised his opponents (and, it appears, pleased the public) by standing firm after each compromise. With the help of immoderate opponents and a new reputation for fighting for his beliefs, his public standing continued to rise. Never particularly notable, the rise was slow and regular. But by the spring presidential primary season of 1996, he was no longer an easy mark. By summer, he was beginning to look formidable. By fall, experienced observers knew that he had won reelection long before Americans went to the polls.

What happened to Bill Clinton is that American citizens engaged in evaluation. Unfavorable early in his term, then increasingly favorable, these evaluations were the political stock with which he won the 1996 elections. This process we call *Presidential Approval* is the business of this chapter. We wish to understand why citizens sometimes approve and sometimes disapprove of their most visible leader. Some of that process is the chemistry of personality and public that we can appreciate when we see it, but find hard to explain. But much of it is the ordinary stuff of social science, behaviors that are uniform and explainable from simple postulates. Out task here is to put together such postulates, deduce their implications for macro behavior, and observe how well those implications map onto presidential approval.

We begin this task with a good deal of knowledge. There is a strong empirical literature on this topic.[1] We shall adapt it to our micro/macro structure, we will extend it in time, and we will build on it. But much of the structure that emerges will be extant knowledge of why citizens approve or disapprove of presidents and when they change.

In this chapter, we will lay out a micro foundation for citizen evaluation of politics in general and *Presidential Approval* in particular, and then focus on macro dynamics. We take on the always contentious issue of the nature of macro approval, whether it follows a deterministic time path and whether it tends to equilibrium after it is disrupted. Then we model the substance of approval, bringing in indicators of presidential competence and control. We take on the issue of how – or whether – citizen agreement with presidential policy leads to enhanced approval. And, last, we conclude by noting that this well-known indicator carries much more general information about citizen response to government than merely, as its words seem to imply, an evaluation of how well the incumbent is performing his or her job. We begin with micro theory.

*Micro Theory and Model*: Our micro model for this mainly macro topic was presented in Chapter 1. There we argue that citizens want two things from government generally (and from presidents in particular). First, they want competence in achieving commonly shared policy goals

---

1 This literature begins with Richard Neustadt's (1964) speculations about approval and presidential power and John Mueller's (1970, 1973) systematic explorations of macro approval. Important extensions are found in Kernell (1978, 1993), Edwards (1983), MacKuen (1983), Ostrom and Simon (1985), Chappell and Keech (1985), Brody (1991), Brace and Hinckley (1992), and Ostrom and Smith (1993).

(peace, domestic tranquility, prosperity, and so forth). This is the dominant, and more often exclusive, conception of micro processes in the *Presidential Approval* literature. For the president, competence involves more than the achievement of results; citizens also seek reassurance of control. For confidence in the future, they want the president to be in charge and to seem to be in charge. This is particularly crucial when dramatic events impinge upon government. Drama gives presidents an opportunity to assert mastery and control, and doing so, in turn, reassures citizens that someone is in charge.

Second, citizens condition their approval of a president upon the degree of policy agreement. We see this at the micro level when we find survey respondents more frequently approving the president when they support his policies than when they oppose them. While goals such as peace and prosperity draw nearly universal assent from citizens, the policy choices of who gets what from government and who pays the cost are inherently conflictual. Citizens can observe who wins and who loses in such conflicts and support or oppose presidents accordingly.

*Macro Implications*: Most of what we know about macro-level *Presidential Approval* is driven by the competence postulate. When the president scores success or failure in foreign policy or the economic realm, citizens observe a common phenomenon and usually respond the same way. People prefer success to failure and often agree on the evidence of success or failure in achieving common goals. For these reasons, the competency response is easily observed at the macro level. The policy response is different in that the goals are divisive. When the president pushes policy to the left or to the right, some citizens will applaud while others will react negatively. Thus, unlike the competence response, the policy response is more difficult to observe at the macro than the micro level. Still we know that presidents take varied positions on the left-right dimension of American politics, and (as we will see in Chapter 6) the public moves also in this same policy space over time. Distance between president and public should be inversely related to approval. Presidents who hit the moving target of public opinion should be approved; those who veer away from it not.

We turn now to the business of approval as a macro concept and variable. We begin the chapter by describing the statistical properties of the *Presidential Approval* time series. This is a necessary prerequisite for substantive modeling to follow. After that, we introduce the familiar macro components of the *Approval* story, prosperity, international events, honeymoons, and so forth, adding one at a time to move toward a comprehensive account. We show that a president's popularity can usually be accounted for by these factors. We briefly take up the special issue of control. We turn to policy agreement at the end; although we cannot easily predict a president's approval from the president's policy behavior, we are reminded that policies are assessed differently by different people. The degree to which the president's approval numbers move is greatly constrained by the fact that Democrats and Republicans (and liberals and conservatives) view the policy world differently.

## THE APPROVAL TIME SERIES, 1953–1996

The Gallup poll first asked its presidential approval question in 1938, only a few years after the beginning of scientific polling. Gallup monitored Franklin Roosevelt's approval only sporadically. But once Harry Truman ascended to the presidency upon Roosevelt's death, Gallup began to monitor approval with a near monthly frequency. Our analysis of presidential approval begins with the Eisenhower administration in 1953 and extends through 1996, Clinton's first term.

Gallup's approval question is the model of simplicity:

*Do you approve or disapprove of the way that [president's name] is handling his job as president?*

Although some respondents say they have "no opinion," attention always centers on the proportion of all respondents (approvers, disapprovers, and nonopinion holders) who say they "approve" the presidential performance. Following this convention, we define *Presidential Approval* as the proportion of all respondents in the survey who say they "approve."

We measure *Approval* on a monthly basis, 1953–1996. For each month, we pool the approval numbers for all Gallup polls and (starting in 1976) all CBS News/*New York Times* polls (using the same question wording). With over 3,000 respondents per month (on average), the monthly readings of *Approval* are subject to only minuscule sampling error.[2] Moreover, most months are covered. We have missing data (no survey) for only 26 of the 528 months, or less than 5 percent. For the *Approval* series itself, see Figure 2.1.

Our first task is to classify *Approval* by type of time series. For instance, is it stationary, unit root, or some more complex order of

---

2 For each month, we estimate the error variance due to sampling as $p(1 - p)/N$, where $p$ is the proportion approving and $N$ is the sample size. The observed variance in aggregate approval (as a proportion, not percent) is the total variance. The difference between the total and error variances represents the true variance. The proportion of the total variance that is true rather than error is the statistical reliability of the measure. For monthly *Approval*, this ratio is .99.

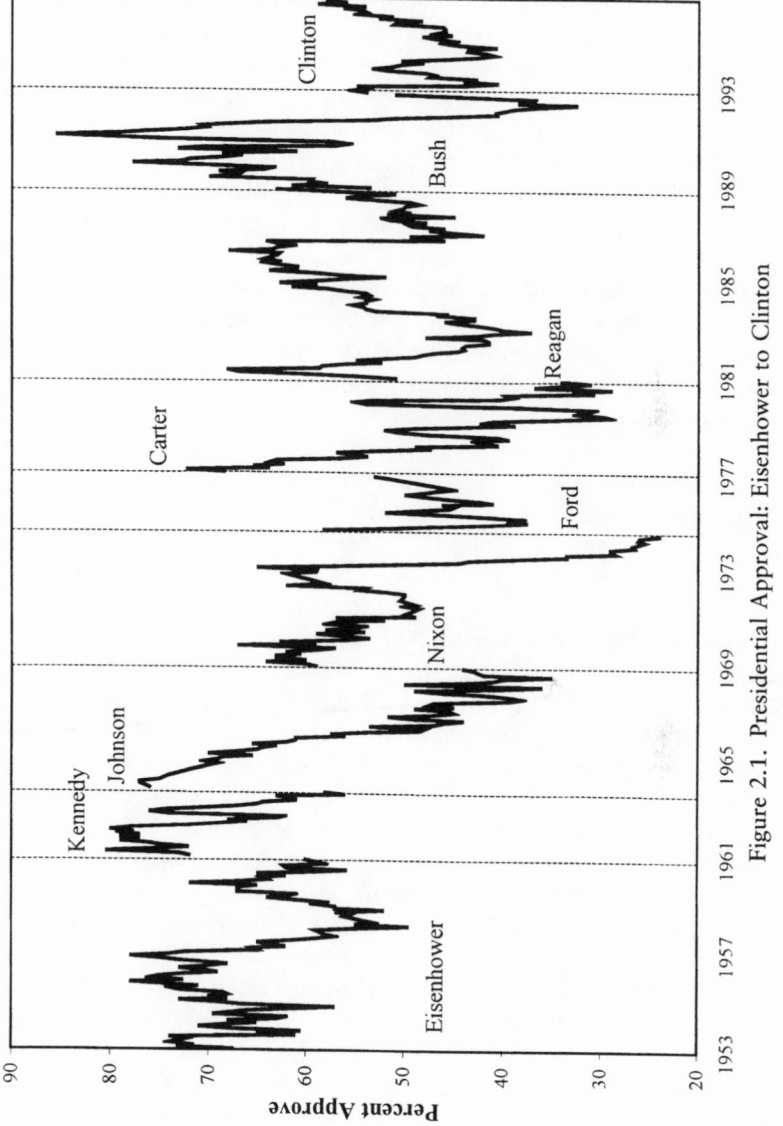

Figure 2.1. Presidential Approval: Eisenhower to Clinton

integration? And is its behavior first-order autoregressive (AR(1)) or something more complicated? While the answers bear on how the variable should be analyzed as a dependent variable, more important for us are the possible substantive implications. Fortunately, the diagnosis is unambiguous: The evidence clearly shows that *Approval* moves as a stationary series. Moreover, it is autoregressive. This simplifies our task. An autoregressive stationary series is a well-behaved series.[3]

When a series is first-order autoregressive, denoted AR(1), if one predicts the current level from past values, only the most recent values matter. This means that as an autoregressive process, current *Approval* can be modeled solely as a function of *Approval* from the previous month $(t - 1)$. Adding *Approval* readings from earlier months $(t - 2, t - 3$, etc.) makes no further statistical contribution. The autoregressive model may be written:

$$y_t = \phi y_{t-1} + \varepsilon_t$$

where $\phi$ is less (in absolute value) than 1.0. (For $\phi = 1.0$, the series would become "unit root" integrated at order 1.) Using the available values of *Approval*,[4] we estimate a $\phi$ of .94.

As a stationary series, *Approval* can be moved by the events and conditions of a presidency, but tends to return to a stable mean value as the impact of those factors recedes in time. The micro-level interpretation is either that people forget much of the past when they evaluate the president, or that they choose to discount it when evaluating the performance of the moment. The macro-level interpretation is that the president is evaluated based upon the flow of recent events, with earlier history mattering little. If, counterfactually, the series were integrated, there would be no forgetting or discounting, and current *Approval* would be a function of the president's cumulative record and not just recent history.

We can say more. An AR(1) series has an interesting signature in the pattern of the variable's autocorrelations (correlations with its past values at various lags): The autocorrelation at lag $t - m$ will be $\phi^{-m}$, a pattern that (allowing for sampling error) is approximated by the actual autocorrelations, shown in Table 2.1. As the lag length increases, *Approval* autocorrelations converge toward zero. Judging from the .56 autocorrelation over 12 months, one can forecast a president's rating one

---

3 We discuss the diagnostic tests next.
4 This equation is based only on cases where neither current or lagged values are missing. The first two months of an administration are omitted, so that the first observation of each presidency is for month 3 *Approval* predicted from month 2 *Approval*. First-month readings are irregular and generally too soon after inauguration to hold much content.

Table 2.1. *Correlations Between (Monthly) Approval and Lagged Approval from Lags of 1 to 24 Months*

| Lag | Correlation | Lag | Correlation |
|-----|-------------|-----|-------------|
| 1 | .94 | 13 | .52 |
| 2 | .89 | 14 | .49 |
| 3 | .85 | 15 | .44 |
| 4 | .81 | 16 | .41 |
| 5 | .78 | 17 | .39 |
| 6 | .74 | 18 | .37 |
| 7 | .70 | 19 | .34 |
| 8 | .67 | 20 | .30 |
| 9 | .63 | 21 | .29 |
| 10 | .60 | 22 | .27 |
| 11 | .57 | 23 | .25 |
| 12 | .55 | 24 | .20 |

*Note:* N's range from 276 to 475 monthly readings, 1953–1996. Correlations are based only on lagged readings with the current president in office.

year in the future only vaguely from the same president's rating today. With a 24-month autocorrelation of only .20, a president's rating in two years (a temporal distance that can seem like a short horizon) is virtually unpredictable from today's ratings. Over 36 months (not shown in the table), the correlation vanishes to near zero. One lesson is that one cannot predict at all how a president will be judged after a full four-year term from knowing what the *Approval* rating is after one year in office.

This carries an important substantive lesson. The obvious stability of *Approval* when observed over one or two months presents the illusion of persistence and permanence. When the president's popularity is measured over one or two years instead of months, the stability vanishes. This follows from the nature of the time series. *Approval* has a "what have you done for me lately" quality that is not fully evident from the short-term record. Reversals of fortune affect presidents both negatively and positively. The most dramatic reversal occurred when George Bush's *Approval* ratings hit the high 80s at the end of the Gulf War in early 1991, only to dip into the 30s the following year when the economy turned sour. Bill Clinton's changing standing with the electorate provides the opposite scenario, as we wrote in this chapter's introduction.

## TIME AND APPROVAL

New presidents start with a higher than average level of political support, with approval ratings of 70 percent or more not being unusual. Then, as the presidency unfolds, the approval level undergoes a gradual decline. This decline sometimes stabilizes or even reverses, but often continues to the end of the presidency. The initial high support for a president is often called the presidential "honeymoon." It is not surprising that presidents start out with an aura of goodwill, with even supporters of the defeated opponent offering their tentative approval. The interesting question is why the honeymoon fades.

Some say the reason why presidents lose support over time is that they cannot please all segments of society all the time. This theory is often called the "coalition-of-minorities" argument. The idea is that presidents begin with a large, fragile, winning coalition that eventually dissolves. Eventually, this theory goes, the president must upset the expectations of some supporters, and this disillusionment creates a spiral of declining approval (Mueller 1973). Indeed, one might imagine a general rule that with political support continuously decaying, leaders inevitably become less popular the longer they govern. The implication is that no matter what presidents do to solve national problems, their political support will continue to erode.

A "disillusioned voter" theory, once offered by Stimson (1976), makes the same prediction, but by a different route. Suppose that voters at the start of a presidency tend to be naive optimists, with unrealistically high expectations for what a president can accomplish. As the president's agenda gets stalled by politics, or as promises seem to go unfulfilled, the once naive optimists turn against the president. The result is that presidents decline in popularity due to inevitable popular disillusionment.

An "elite leadership" theory, articulated by Brody (1991), emphasizes that a president's honeymoon popularity represents an artificially high starting point at the outset, rather than a natural base of support. The reason for the high initial popularity is that newly elected (or ascending) presidents start out free of criticism, either from other politicians or from the media. Politicians and journalists respond to a new presidency with words of support. Ordinary citizens take their cues from these expressions of goodwill. They too express approval.

As argued by Brody, it is the nature of elite political discussion that allows, and then ends, the honeymoon. When the new president takes office, the opposing politicians hold their fire for a number of reasons. They wish to obey rules of political rectitude following the electorate's hallowed verdict. Their silence persists because it takes a while for the president to make mistakes. It also takes time for the opposition to devise strategies to initiate criticism.

Citizens, then, are faced with unrelenting good news about the new president. For entrenched supporters and opponents, mostly strong partisans, this matters little. But for the vast middle, the disapproval it might otherwise express is suppressed by the absence of public criticism. They are, accordingly, likely to echo elite approval in what must be a fairly shallow sense of goodwill.

As a president's term evolves, the president must take actions that are open to second-guessing and criticism from the media and political opponents. As a result, the news people receive about the president no longer has the positive bias found at honeymoon time. The news does not have to be mainly bad. It could be good and bad in equal amounts. Even as neutral news replaces the positive messages at the start of a presidency, the result is a decline in presidential popularity, as it descends to its more natural level.

As the reader surely has noted, these three theories of the decline of approval are not totally different from one another, and a serious attempt to sort out the truth among them would be a daunting task. The more recent theory by Brody has perhaps the greatest appeal today. Voters early in a presidential term are positive not because they are naive or easily fooled. Instead, they are positive because that is the plausible response given the positive information they are told. Later, when the news they are told is the more usual mix of negatives and positives, their support for the president stabilizes at its normal level.

Suppose we depict the typical flow of approval for the first four years of a presidency. Figure 2.2 does this, by presenting a composite of the first four years, for the seven recent presidents who actually served 48 months or more in office (Eisenhower, Johnson, Nixon, Carter, Reagan, Bush, and Clinton). Its data points are actual averages over the seven presidencies, the smooth line a function that describes the data. It starts with month 2 (readings are too sparse in month 1 to include) and ends with month 48.

The figure shows a steady pattern of approval decline, consistent with the various stories of honeymoons and temporal decay of support. We can ask: What is the nature of this decline? Does approval decline linearly, as in a straight-line drop? Averaged over seven presidents, the picture suggests a steady, but possibly curvilinear, pattern of decline. The first few months maintain the honeymoon boost, and then the decline begins. Once four years take their toll, the average approval is no more than about 50 percent.

*Approval,* on average, declines from one month to the next – 56 percent of the changes are negative – but there is considerable dispersion. Suppose we perform a simple $t$-test to see if the mean monthly change in *Approval* is significantly different from zero. The mean is a decline of 0.29 percentage point per month. Summed over 48 months of a full presidential term, that amounts to some 15 points per presidential term. Yet by the simple $t$-statistic $-1.52$, the mean monthly decline is not

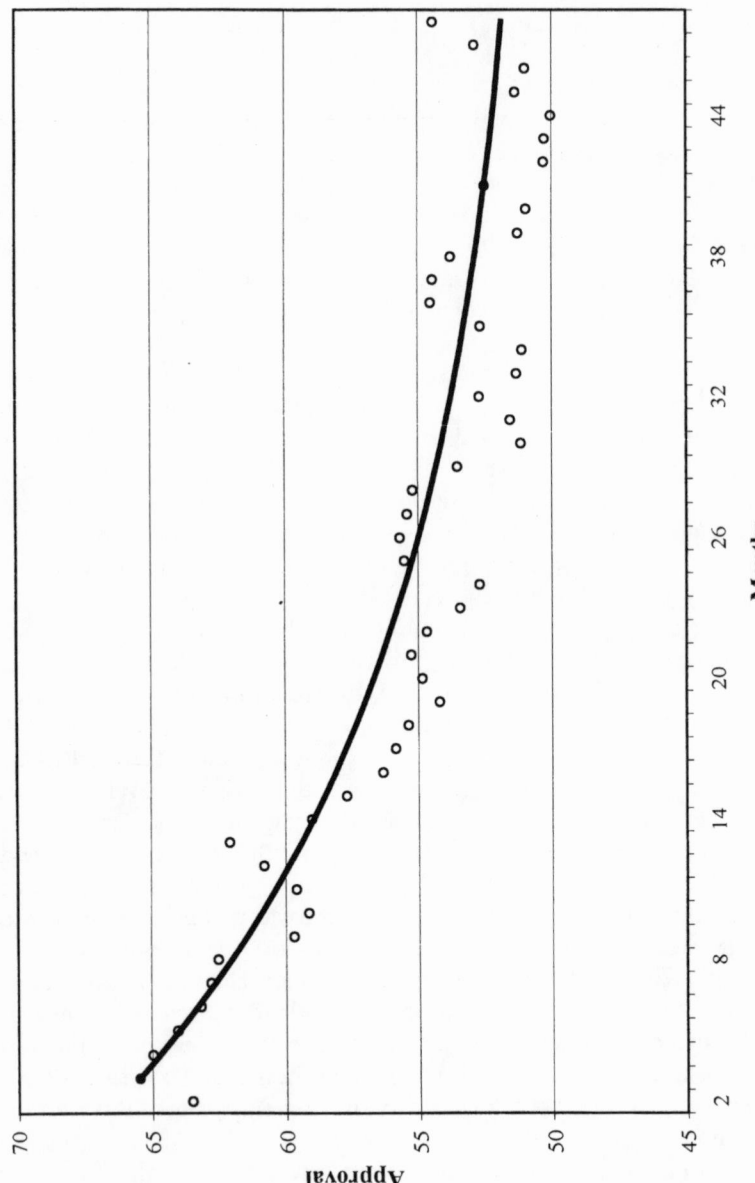

Figure 2.2. Average Approval over the First Four Years for Seven Presidents

Table 2.2. *Monthly Change in Approval by Lagged Approval and Time*

| | Dependent Variable: Approval$_t$ – Approval$_{t-1}$ | | |
|---|---|---|---|
| | (1) | (2) | (3) |
| Intercept | 2.48[a] | 2.87[a] | 2.58[a] |
| | (3.03) | (2.93) | (3.14) |
| Approval$_{t-1}$ | −0.05[a] | −0.05[a] | −0.05[a] |
| | (−3.53) | (−3.43) | (−3.67) |
| Months in Office | | −0.01 | |
| | | (−0.72) | |
| Honeymoon | | | 1.32 |
| | | | (1.29) |
| Adjusted $R^2$ | .02 | .02 | .02 |
| Standard Error of | | | |
| Estimate | 4.21 | 4.22 | 4.21 |

*Note*: Based on 487 monthly approval readings, 1953–1996. Honeymoon = 1 if Months in Office <5; otherwise 0. $t$ values in parentheses.
[a] $p < 0.5$.

sufficiently different from zero to be statistically significant.[5] We could accept this verdict as an invitation to conclude that approval does not move systematically with respect to time after all. However, that is too conservative a conclusion. We persist in asking: Why does *Approval* decline with time?

Table 2.2 presents the results of some regressions that help us diagnose the *Approval* time series. We model, in each case, Δ*Approval*, the month-to-month *change* in *Approval*. Column 1 models Δ*Approval* as a function of lagged *Approval* alone. The test whether $\beta$ is significantly different from zero in this equation is the basic test for whether the series is stationary or integrated. We must decide whether to reject (at the usual .05 level) the null hypothesis that the coefficient for lagged *Approval* is zero. Using the Dickey-Fuller test (Dickey and Fuller 1979; Hamilton 1994), the appropriate critical value is a $t$-value of −2.88. Given the observed $t$-value of −3.51,[6] we can reject the null hypothesis of an integrated (or unit root) series.[7]

5 The critical value for a one-tailed test for $\alpha$ = .05 is −1.65!
6 The same conclusion results when our estimate is based on data that are quarterly instead of monthly ($\beta$ = −0.10, $t$ = −3.08, $N$ = 182).
7 The Dickey-Fuller test is a conservative one, tending to err on the side of false positives regarding the null hypothesis of unit roots. Although in our view, the clearly

## Performance

Column 2 adds time as a variable in the equation, measured as the president's number of months in office. Note that time has no independent effect here. Thus, we account for the decline in *Approval* solely in terms of lagged *Approval* and not the passage of time itself. *Approval* declines as a move toward equilibrium following the artificially high starting values during the presidential honeymoon.

It can readily be shown that *Approval* trends toward an equilibrium at the value $-\alpha/\beta$, where $\alpha$ is the intercept and $\beta$ the slope predicting *Approval* change from lagged *Approval*.[8]

$$Approval^* = -\alpha/\beta$$

Above this equilibrium value, *Approval* trends downward. Below, it trends upward. From the coefficients in Table 2.2, column 1, we can solve for the equilibrium value for presidential approval. This turns out to be 49.8 percent, which we can round to virtually 50 percent. Below this approval level, a president generally gains. Above it, the president's approval generally falls. If presidencies could be allowed to continue for the truly long run, their approval would converge to 50 percent. The observed mean value is actually higher (55.5 percent) because every president gets a head start from the honeymoon and less popular presidents do not survive to reelection.

With no independent effect for time, the general decline in *Approval* is solely a function of artificially high starting values. As presidents begin with a honeymoon *Approval* in the 60–80 percent range, their approval can only fall toward equilibrium. As their approval level falls toward equilibrium, the expectation is that it will not decline further. Meanwhile, presidents below the equilibrium level generally improve.

A possible elaboration of the honeymoon argument is that presidents not only start with high approval levels, but also that their high approval numbers continue at an inflated level throughout a brief honeymoon

---

significant *t*-values and other diagnostic evidence rules out the unit root alternative, this conclusion is more controversial than one might think. Some authors (Ostrom and Smith 1993; Clarke and Stewart 1994; Freeman et al. 1998) claim that the unit root test hypothesis cannot be rejected for *Approval*. Some of these reports may be due to smaller Ns. Small Ns limit the rejection of the null hypothesis. Others may be flawed by the mingling of different presidents in a common time series rather than the appropriate decision to treat each presidency as a separate regime. If presidents are mingled in the quarterly data, the Dickey-Fuller test yields a nonsignificant *t*-value.

8 At equilibrium, the expectation is that *Approval* equals lagged *Approval*. In general, substituting generic Y for *Approval*, assume $Y_t - Y_{t-1} = 0 = \alpha + \beta Y_{t-1}$. Then, $-\alpha = \beta Y_{t-1}$, so $Y_{t-1} = Y_t = -\alpha/\beta$.

period. We can think of this as a honeymoon "bubble," with high approval sustained for a short burst until the process of decline begins. We show this with a honeymoon variable, coded 1 for months 3 and 4 of the new term, in the third column of Table 2.2.[9] Presidents gain about a point more than they deserve based on past *Approval* in their early months. Note, however, that the honeymoon variable is not statistically significant.

We now have an understanding why *Approval* declines. At the onset of a presidency, the president benefits from an inflated approval rating, as the news people receive about a new president is almost uniformly positive. We want to account for what happens next.

As a stationary series, approval decays toward its equilibrium with time, although at a slow rate. In terms of citizen psychology, we can infer that the initial good news about the president gets forgotten with time. As people begin to receive the more typical mix of good and bad news about the president, the approval numbers gradually approach an equilibrium value. We are not required to believe that news gets repeatedly worse for the president, only that after the honeymoon, news reverts to a more normal range of good and bad.[10]

This story of time and approval is told devoid of substance. As a president's approval evolves, the sources of change are lagged approval plus other things that we have modeled simply as random shocks. The shocks provide the substance that moves approval beyond the trajectory toward the middle of the scale. In the next section, we begin the search for this substance.

### THE SUBSTANCE OF APPROVAL: PRESIDENTIAL COMPETENCE

We have asserted a micro model in which perceptions of competence and policy satisfaction drive the citizen to approve of the president or not. In this section, we show that at the macro level we can generally account for a president's *Approval* level in terms of variables that reflect on

---

9 Recall that each president's *Approval* series begins with the third month. Readings in the first month are rare and usually too soon after inaugural to have any meaning. The second month's reading is the lagged value to predict the third month's reading.

10 We emphasize that the *Approval* time series we analyze is actually nine different time series for nine different regimes (presidencies) pooled together. In our analysis, we never assume one president's approval is a function of his predecessors. The nine autoregressive series are similar enough to be summarized as one. For instance, if we add dummy variables for different presidencies, they are not collectively statistically significant.

presidential competence. These include economic events and the president's positive or negative handling of important events.

## Economic Performance

One major cause of a president's *Approval* rating is the state of the national economy. People expect a president to produce prosperity, and they blame presidents who do not. There is a bit of irony here. Presidents do not manage the economy in any precise way, and all close observers of economics know this. At best, presidents set general policies and hope that the specific applications prove helpful. Mostly, they must rely on private economic decisions and exogenous circumstances to provide economic good times. Much like baseball managers, presidents, in reality, must avoid making dramatic mistakes and otherwise hope that fortune smiles kindly. Yet, for more than a century, politicians have promised prosperity in exchange for voter support and have expected retribution for failure. Even today, presidents win and lose elections on the nation's economic standing. So we should expect that booms and busts in the national economy will produce rises and falls in the public's estimation of the sitting president, whether or not its attribution of credit and blame exceeds the president's actual marginal impact.

This system of credit and blame makes more sense than is evident at first glance. Consider again the analogy of a baseball manager. A team's fans will judge the manager based on how he manages crises and on matters of policy, but certainly also the team's record of success, current or projected, compared to some baseline of initial expectations. For some fans, the net team performance may be the only criterion on which people hold the information to judge. And all can agree on whether this performance is good or bad. Some fans will be at a higher information level and judge based on policy and strategy decisions, but they will disagree among themselves, yielding little aggregate consensus. In the court of public opinion, a manager's fate will be tied to team performance, because that is the only criterion upon which all agree.

Just as it would be wrong to claim baseball fans are irrational when they take team performance into account when evaluating the manager, it is wrong to accuse the citizenry of collective irrationality when they evaluate the president based on economic performance. Even if the economy is only marginally influenced by presidential behavior, the economy is one of the few measures of performance upon which most can judge and most can agree. Even when citizens disagree over other measures of performance and over matters of policy, economic movement brings aggregate change in the president's *Approval*. And we should consider the consequences if people did not hold the president responsible for the economy. If nothing else, the citizens' responsiveness to the economy serves to concentrate the mind of the president to do what can be done to maximize economic performance.

Most of our story about the economy and the president will be told in the following chapter. Here, we present our first verification that the economy matters, by modeling monthly *Approval* as a function of the state of the economy. To measure the status of the economy, we want to pick up the aspects of the economy that register with the public. We start with the public's assessment as measured by the University of Michigan's *Index of Consumer Sentiment* (a combination of survey items). *Consumer Sentiment*, the subject of the next chapter, has been measured on a monthly basis since 1978. Prior to 1978, however, the measurement was quarterly, with surveys in February, May, August, and November. To obtain monthly readings of *Economic Performance* going back to the 1950s, we regress available monthly *Consumer Sentiment* readings on a host of contemporaneous economic indicators. The product of this endeavor is a predicted value for each month representing a composite of the objective economic conditions that best predicts the public's overall subjective evaluation. In the end, we have a monthly series that represents fluctuations in the real economy that manifest themselves in the general public.

Our index of *Economic Performance* is, in effect, a weighted sum of several economic indicators, with the weights determined by the coefficients of the regression predicting *Consumer Sentiment* from the objective economic indicators. The regression weights are shown in Table 2.3. Since the goal of this particular exercise is merely prediction, the derived weights merely document our *Economic Performance* indicator.[11]

We now want to see whether this measure of *Economic Performance* predicts approval. It does. In Figure 2.3 we see first our measure of *Economic Performance*. It shows the cyclicality that characterizes the U.S. economy, with the recessions of 1958, 1974, and 1982 most apparent. The effect on *Approval* is suggested by Figure 2.4, where monthly measures of *Approval* (on the vertical axis) are plotted against *Economic Performance* (on the horizontal axis) for the years 1953–1996. The solid line represents a regression that translates economics into approval. Observe two things: First, note that good economic times (toward the right) are truly associated with higher *Presidential Approval*. The worst economic times produce no popular presidents, and the best times produce no unpopular presidents. And second, note that the relationship

11 An explanatory model, on the other hand, would want to be much more parsimonious and would require considerable care to avoid multicollinearity problems in interpretation. These are not concerns in a prediction exercise.

## Performance

Table 2.3. *Creation of the Index of Economic Performance*

| Indicator | Parameter | Standard Error |
|---|---|---|
| Index of Leading Indicators, Growth over Previous Month | 1.77 | 1.21 |
| Index of Leading Indicators, Growth over Three Months | 0.20 | 0.21 |
| Index of Coincident Indicators, Growth over Previous Month | −0.69 | 1.43 |
| Index of Coincident Indicators, Growth over Three Months | 0.63 | 0.23 |
| Index of Lagging Indicators, Growth over Previous Month | 0.14 | 1.50 |
| Index of Lagging Indicators, Growth over Three Months | 0.78 | 0.19 |
| Civilian Unemployment Rate | −1.82 | 0.32 |
| Civilian Unemployment Rate, Change from Previous Month | 2.27 | 2.62 |
| Civilian Unemployment Rate, Change over Three Months | −4.33 | 1.91 |
| Consumer Price Index, Growth over Previous Month | −0.11 | 0.19 |
| Consumer Price Index, Growth over Three Months | −1.49 | 0.24 |
| Intercept | 100.64 | 2.16 |
| Adjusted $R^2$ = .64, N = 304 monthly readings, 1953–1996 | | |

*Note*: The Index is derived from this regression, predicting the Index of Consumer Sentiment. The Index is then created by multiplying each of the monthly variables by its respective coefficient. It is available for all months, 1953–1996.

between economics and politics is sloppy rather than precise. Much of the variation in *Presidential Approval*, especially when the economy is only middling-good, remains to be explained. And, as we will see, it is too simplistic to model *Approval* as a function of the economy only for the current month. In actuality, *Approval* is a function of the economy as it has performed over several months.

We begin our exploration in Table 2.4, which presents some regression equations where *Approval* is a function of *Economic Performance*.[12] The first equation shows that current *Economic Performance* by itself can statistically account for about 20 percent of the variance in current *Approval* (note the adjusted $R^2$ of .20). This is the equation generating the regression line in Figure 2.4.

The equation of column 1, however, is not the correct specification. The reason is that current *Approval* is a function of both the current economy and, somewhat discounted, the economy of previous months as well. A more appropriate specification is to regress *Approval* on

12 The equations in Table 2.4 are based on *Approval* in months past the inaugural, interpolating for missing data on *Approval*. This is necessary because our scheme for the statistical accounting of *Approval* (see ahead) does not allow missing data.

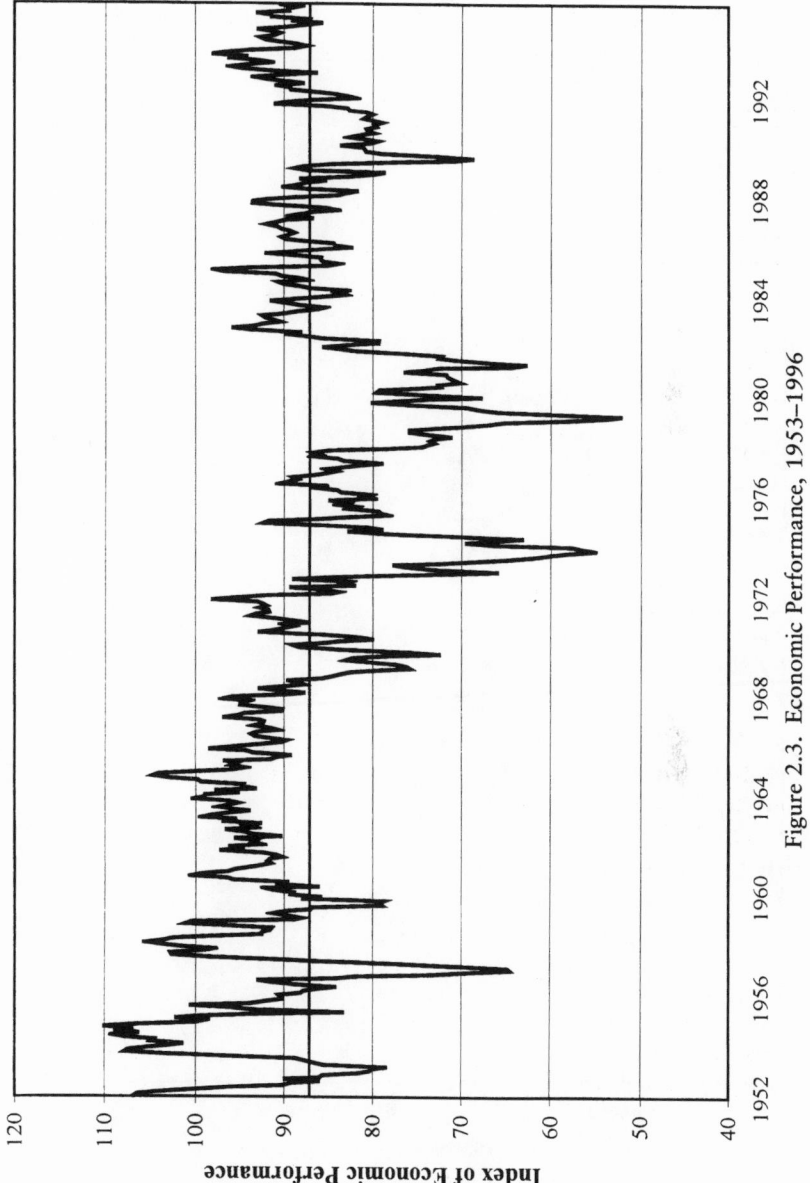

Figure 2.3. Economic Performance, 1953–1996

45

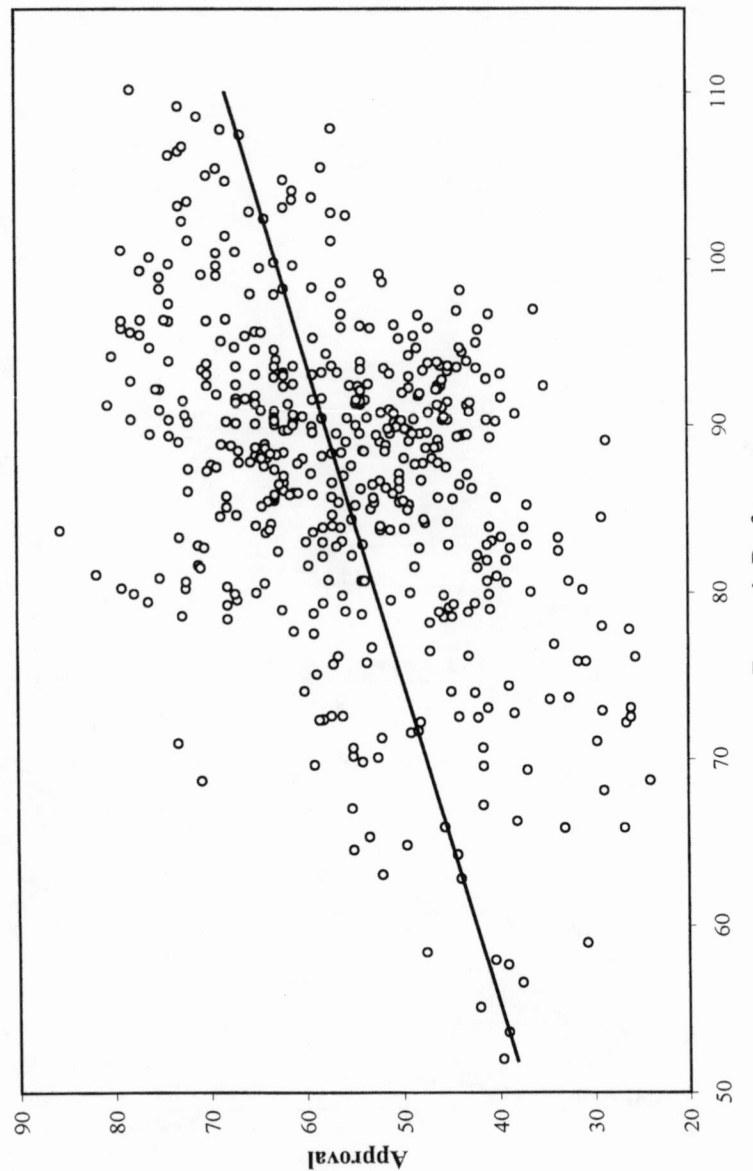

Figure 2.4. Presidential Approval as a Function of Economic Performance

Table 2.4. *Economic Performance and*
*Presidential Approval*

|  | (1) | (2) | (3) |
|---|---|---|---|
| Approval$_{t-1}$ |  | 0.91$^a$ | 0.89$^a$ |
|  |  | (55.83) | (43.85) |
| Economic Performance | 0.54$^a$ | 0.09$^a$ | 0.11$^a$ |
|  | (11.00) | (4.45) | (4.33) |
| Vietnam Deaths |  | −1.91$^a$ |  |
| (thousands) |  | (−2.35) |  |
| Kennedy |  |  | 0.54 |
|  |  |  | (0.63) |
| Johnson |  |  | −1.62$^a$ |
|  |  |  | (−2.19) |
| Nixon |  |  | −1.07 |
|  |  |  | (−1.40) |
| Ford |  |  | −0.17 |
|  |  |  | (−0.15) |
| Carter |  |  | −0.74 |
|  |  |  | (−0.83) |
| Reagan |  |  | −0.05 |
|  |  |  | (−0.07) |
| Bush |  |  | 0.86 |
|  |  |  | (1.10) |
| Clinton |  |  | −1.96 |
|  |  |  | (−1.94) |
| Adjusted $R^2$ | .20 | .90 | .90 |
| Standard Error of |  |  |  |
| Estimate | 10.96 | 3.87 | 4.03 |

*Note*: *t*-values are in parentheses. $N = 512$. Based on monthly
approval readings, 1953–1996.
$^a$ $p < 0.05$.

current *Economic Performance* plus lagged *Approval*. We also add a variable representing American casualties in the Vietnam War under Johnson to capture Johnson's exceptional decline.[13] This specification is shown in column 2. Here, we see a statistically significant effect of current *Economic Performance* with lagged *Approval* controlled. We also observe that the coefficient for lagged *Approval* has declined from its value of 0.94 in the simple autoregressive equation to 0.91 when *Economic Performance* is in the equation.

13 Monthly deaths are interpolated from quarterly casualty data. Vietnam deaths are coded as zero for non-Johnson years.

## Performance

We add presidential dummies in column 3. Although they are not collectively significant, it is useful to consider the coefficient for *Economic Performance* with this control. If anything, the effects of *Economic Performance* are even stronger with specific presidents controlled. This is reassuring about the presence of a true effect. The economic "effect" is not due to popular presidents presiding over prosperous economies. (If anything, presidents who show signs of being relatively popular in their own right tend to preside over subpar economies.) The crucial matter is that the economy affects *Approval* within specific administrations. That is, controlling for lagged *Approval*, each president's greatest popularity tends to be at times of greatest prosperity.[14] The evidence is clear; *Economic Performance* matters.

## Events

Virtually every day, new and unexpected events require presidential attention. How presidents respond to these surprises, or when a presidential initiative is itself the source for the surprise, the decision is subject to evaluation by Washingtonians. We can almost surely expect political journalists to comment on presidential action and frequently we can expect both the president's supporters and opponents to voice their judgments. Inside the Beltway, judging the president is standard cocktail party fare. Presidential actions affect the evaluations by the general public, too, both directly and indirectly. Commentary by the editorial writers, television celebrities, and Washington politicians register in the attentive public.

One category of presidential events is what John Mueller (1970, 1973) called "rally points," when presidents are called upon to react to dramatic events in the foreign policy sphere or take initiatives themselves. In the past, most rally points were related to the Cold War. Early examples include the Soviet shooting down of a U.S. spy plane (the Francis Gary Powers U-2 incident) in 1960; the Cuban Missile Crisis in 1962; and seizures of U.S. ships by Communist foreign governments in 1968 (the U.S.S. *Pueblo* by North Korea) and in 1975 (the *Mayaguez* by Cambodia). Other rally events involve favorable presidential initiatives rather than reactions to anxiety-provoking events. Examples include major treaties (e.g., Nixon's Moscow treaty of 1972), major "summits" (starting with Eisenhower's Geneva summit conference with Soviet leaders in 1955), and peace efforts such as Johnson's bombing halt (1968) or Carter's Camp David Accords (1978) establishing the foundation for peaceful relations between Egypt and Israel.

14 The presidential dummies can be thought of as providing different thresholds of economic expectations for different presidents.

## Presidential Approval

What these events have in common is a focus on presidents dealing with foreign policy. Generally, major foreign policy events are followed by a surge in support for the president – what is called the "rally around the flag" effect. These are special moments when eyes turn to the president, and the media and national politicians are seen to unite behind the president.

Going to war is a special case. In the short term, wars traditionally result in the showering of approval on the president. An early example from the early days of polling is World War II. While Franklin Roosevelt's *Approval* in the late 1930s averaged respectably in the high 50s, entry into World War II saw his numbers surge into the 80s. More recent wars show similar patterns. Harry Truman gained 9 points following the start of the Korean War in 1950. Lyndon Johnson gained 8 points following the major escalation of the Vietnam War in 1966. Lesser conflicts, such as Johnson's 1965 invasion of the Dominican Republic and Ronald Reagan's invasion of Grenada, also were followed by surges of presidential popularity. The biggest gain from war was George Bush's popularity surge to 87 percent *Approval* in March 1991 following the brief Gulf War against Iraq.

But the political rewards from wars and invasions can be short-lived. The Johnson administration, for example, certainly suffered from the U.S. public's lack of taste for a prolonged war in Vietnam. In just a few years, Johnson's *Approval* fell from the 70s to the low 30s. Truman's popularity declined further, into the 20s, as did Jimmy Carter's during the Iran hostage crisis. Bush's unique popularity in the afterglow of the Gulf War shows what a short successful war can do for a president's popularity. But Bush's popularity declined from the 80s to the 30s in little over a year. These slides in approval had direct electoral effects. Seeing their *Approval* at levels that threatened defeat, both Truman and Johnson declined to seek reelection. Carter and Bush fought on, only to be decisively defeated at the polls.

To summarize, in most foreign-policy crises the public rallies behind the president at least in the short term. In the long term (e.g., with a prolonged unresolved crisis or war), the result can be more hazardous for the president. What accounts for the public's short-term rally behavior? A common view is that the public is simply supporting the president in a patriotic "my president right or wrong" fashion. Indeed, even presidential blunders such as John Kennedy's Bay of Pigs invasion (1961) will often create public support for the president. But more than the most mindless form of patriotism may be involved. Consider again how the public responds to elite commentary.

Recall Richard Brody's (1991) argument that much of the standard political fluctuation in the president's fortunes is due to strategic calculations by Washington politicians. We have already discussed the honeymoon as the most obvious example – the president enjoys a "free ride" in the opinion polls when the disorganized opposition waits to mobilize its forces. In a foreign policy crisis, too, the president dominates the political agenda, a natural advantage. The president also stands unopposed in the field of public opinion. Even the president's partisan opposition will be cautious about criticizing the commander in chief, especially when they see the public's natural inclination to support him.

A classic example is provided by Reagan's invasion of the island nation of Grenada in October 1984. At the time of the invasion, Reagan's approval was under 50 percent and his administration was reeling politically from the bombing of a Marine base in Lebanon and the subsequent withdrawal of troops from that nation. Many of Reagan's Democratic opponents in Washington, as well as many commentators in the media, thought the invasion to be wrong and foolhardy. Yet it became clear that public opinion was largely behind the president, happy to see what appeared to be a successful exercise of bold U.S. leadership. With this reading of public opinion, the potential opponents dropped their public complaints and acquiesced (Brody 1991; Kernell 1993).

Support for a president is not automatic, however, and the exceptions can prove the rule. During Bill Clinton's September 1994 American invasion of Haiti, for example, politicians read the opinion polls and expert commentary, and most of them decided that the operation was dangerous and uncertain of success. President Clinton's Republican opponents jumped into the fray to voice loud and persistent disapproval. His nominal supporters in the congressional Democratic Party, on the other hand, stood mute. When it appears that people will see the president as taking decisive and successful action, then he can expect supporters to nod their heads and opponents to defer comment. When he takes chances or faces the expectation of failure, then he will stand alone in the face of a pack of circling opponents, each hungry for the kill. Actually, at least in the short run, Clinton's actions proved successful and perhaps worth the political risks.

As the Grenada and Haiti examples make clear, the politicians' dance brings information to the public. In the Haiti case, the outside observer could see the eager Republican pawing and the Democrats shunning the president as a signal that the "inside" view expected failure rather than success. But most Americans pay only casual attention to Washington politics. Instead of a subtle partisan game, they see a one-sided voice criticizing the president. Of course, when the president takes action that seems likely to succeed, the opposite reaction arises. And the public sees uniform praise for the president.

## Presidential Approval

Even in the polls following the Haiti invasion, President Clinton's *Approval* rose a few points, but not by an amount to signal a clear boost in support. Some presidential events, on the other hand, are clearly negative in their political consequences. An example is Gerald Ford's pardon of Richard Nixon in 1974. Ford's observable decline in popularity was thought by him to be worth the risk at the time. Nixon's Watergate revelations certainly were not pluses for *Presidential Approval*. Clearly negative events can appear in the foreign policy sphere as well, as Reagan's plummeting popularity following the Iran-Contra revelations (November 1986) will attest.

We now have two stories, both plausible, for why the public response to crisis is normally positive. In one, the president is the relevant actor, responding to crisis with presidential leadership and thereby projecting an "in command" image. In the other, just told, it is actions of others who directly influence the public. It is tempting to bring statistical tools to the task of sorting which is right or which works better. But we think that both are right and they are so inextricably bound up that it is foolhardy to try to separate them. Later we will take up a measure of presidential control to see if we can sort out its impact to some degree.

*Identifying Events*: Getting empirical purchase on the effects of events on presidential approval is problematic. We have no unequivocal measurement of what the president does in terms of "events" at any given time. At best we have the content of the contemporary press. But even this measure reflects only the momentary evaluations of the media. In any case, given the nature of the beast, the "news" always has something about the incumbent president and always encourages some sort of evaluative comment. Thus, we are left in the position of knowing that "something happens every day" and that we cannot know independently the intrinsic value of any particular series of presidential actions.

Here we take a second-best approach. We want to see what happens to presidential approval when we can identify both a political event and a public response. We look at 21 "events" that have been commonly identified as generating a shift of *Presidential Approval* and that indeed caused a shift of 4 or more percentage points over two months. This is a parsimonious list. We exclude some possible event candidates such as the Glassboro Summit (Johnson) or the U-2 incident (Eisenhower) because they did not generate the necessary 4 percent shift in approval. We exclude many shocks of more than 4 points because they are not accompanied by identifiable events. In some, one or more events can be identified, but these are not very plausible causes of major *Approval* shifts. Examples of such excluded events include "Neutron

Table 2.5. *Political Events and Their Impact on Approval*

| Year | Month | Approval Change | Event |
|------|-------|-----------------|-------|
| 1955 | 7 | 6 | Big Four summit (1955.7.18) |
| 1961 | 4 | 5 | Bay of Pigs invasion (1961.4.24) |
| 1962 | 11 | 12 | Cuban missile crisis (1962.10.22) |
| 1968 | 2 | −8 | Tet Offensive (1968.1.30–2.08) |
| 1971 | 2 | −8 | US invades Laos (1971.2.03) |
| 1972 | 2 | 5 | Nixon goes to China (1972.2.17) |
| 1972 | 5 | 8 | Nixon summits with Russia and mines Haiphong (1972.5.08–5.20) |
| 1973 | 2 | 16 | Vietnam War over (1973.1.23) |
| 1973 | 3 | −8 | McCord sends letter to Sirica (1973.3.29) |
| 1973 | 7 | −5 | Butterfield reveals White House tapes. Nixon refuses to turn over tapes. Erlichman and Mitchell testify (1973.7.16–7.30) |
| 1974 | 9 | −16 | Ford pardons Nixon (1974.9.08) |
| 1975 | 5 | 11 | *Mayaguez*: Ford sends troops (1975.5.15–5.20) |
| 1977 | 9 | −12 | Bert Lance hearings/resignation (1977.8.05–9.15) |
| 1978 | 9 | 11 | Camp David Peace Agreement (1978.9.06–9.17) |
| 1979 | 11 | 20 | Iran seizes embassy (1979.11.04) |
| 1981 | 4 | 7 | Reagan wounded (1981.3.30) |
| 1983 | 11 | 8 | Grenada invasion (1983.10.25–11.25) |
| 1986 | 11 | −16 | Iran-Contra revealed (1986.11.06–11.14) |
| 1989 | 12 | 8 | Bush-Gorbachev first summit (1989.12.01–12.04) |
| 1990 | 8 | 15 | Iraq invades Kuwait; Bush leads reaction (1990.8.02) |
| 1990 | 10 | −15 | Budget summit and congressional fight (1990.9.30–10.25) |
| 1991 | 1 | 18 | Gulf War (1991.1.12–1.15) |

*Note:* The dates in the month column are the months to which each event is assigned. The dates in parentheses along with the description give the calendar dates when the events began and some sense of the duration. The assignment dates reflect the next Gallup survey in which the event's impact was felt.

bomb deferred" (Carter) and "Labor Secretary Durkin resigns" (Eisenhower).

The result of this culling is the list of 21 major events shown in Table 2.5. These are events heavily chronicled as major shocks, with accompanying evidence that *Approval* moved in response. By no means does Table 2.5 supply a complete list of presidentially relevant events. We are not attempting to measure the impact of day-to-day politics on *Approval*. Instead, we want to examine those instances when we can confidently identify the effects of specific events to see if we can characterize those effects.

Our concern here is the duration and permanence of the popular reaction. Are the immediate reactions recorded in Table 2.5 quick bounces followed by fast equilibration? Or do the effects last so long as to endure throughout the presidency? If the impact of a presidential event persists for months beyond the initial action, it should be evident in the monthly readings beyond the initial event. In actuality, we already have the basis for predicting the lagged effects of presidential responses to our selected events. This is from our statistical analysis of lagged approval on current approval. Before taking into account the economy, expected approval converges toward its equilibrium value at about 0.94 times the gap per month. Taking into account *Economic Performance*, the movement is 0.91 per month toward an equilibrium conditional upon current *Economic Performance*. Over $m$ months, the expected persistence in the approval response is 0.94 or 0.91 (depending on the model) to the $m$ power.

For our purposes here, we need not get very technical. We observe that shocks to *Approval* persist for a long time, but do eventually decay. We can observe the shocks from our events series and monitor their decay. We consider the 13 major events that occurred at least a year before the end of a presidency and at least 12 months before the next event of our series. Then, we observe the mean change in approval from the month prior to the event (the baseline) to the period one year after the event. To smooth out the idiosyncrasies from event to event, we take an average. We divide events between those that are positive events, identified as those where the initial shock was favorable to the president, and negative events, where the initial shock was a negative movement in *Approval*.

As a baseline for the 12-month projection, we can use zero, or no change. The idea is that the best guess of what *Approval* would be 1 to 12 months into the future if the event did not occur is the *Approval* level one month before the event shock. But we know that is not quite right. Most events are positive, and more often than not, if nothing special happens, approval declines (toward equilibrium) rather than rises. Accordingly, we compute a 12-month baseline expectation where *Approval* moves toward its equilibrium. The expectations at times $t$ to $t + 12$ are computed using the parameter estimates of Table 2.4, column 2. For each event, we estimate *Expected Approval* for times $t$ (the month of the event) to $t + 12$. For $t$, expected *Approval* is the prediction from the regression of *Approval* on lagged *Approval* and *Economic Performance* at $t$. For every subsequent month, $t + m$, expected

# Performance

*Approval* is estimated from *Approval* at $t - 1$ and *Economic Performance* at $t + m$.[15]

Figure 2.5 shows an example, the change in President Kennedy's approval following the resolution of the Cuban Missile Crisis in 1962. The graph shows Kennedy's *Approval* from September $(t - 1)$ through October 1963 $(t + 12)$, along with expected *Approval*. Gallup's October monitoring of *Approval* overlapped slightly with the crisis itself, making it an ambiguous benchmark. Clearly, however, Kennedy's *Approval* spiked in November and then decayed. Kennedy's *Expected Approval* also declined, as his September 1962 reading was above its equilibrium value. The difference between expected and observed approval represents the estimated residual effect from the October 1962 crisis. After one year, Kennedy's *Approval* actually declined to a point slightly below where one would have forecast based on the expectation of September 1962 information. On balance, Kennedy's *Approval* boost for dealing with the missile gap was typical of our estimated spike-and-decay patterns, although the estimated residual effect evaporated a bit faster than the theorized 0.91 per month pattern.

Figure 2.6 presents our mean estimates of event effects, from the month of the event to 12 months after. For months $t$ to $t + 12$, we measure the effect as the deviation of *Approval* from expected *Approval*. When the event is negative, we flip the direction so that all *Approval* shocks are "positive" in direction, and all expectations are in the direction of the initial shock. Our means are based on a sparse set of 13 events where the aftershocks went uninterrupted for 12 months by either a new presidency or the shock of another event from our series.

In Figure 2.6 we see *Approval* change gradually but progressively from the initial shock. *Approval* in the month of the shock is less than the month after, for the simple reason that many *Approval* readings during the month of the shock occur before the event occurred. The better reading is the estimated effect one month after the shock, when the temporal sequence is unambiguous. On average, the estimated effect in month $t + 1$ is a major 11.5 percentage points. From 2 to 12 months after the event, the residual response to the initial shock progressively declines. The mean decline is reasonably close to the expectation of 0.91 per month. After 12 months, the shock of the average event has partially dissipated, at about 45 percent of its original value.

---

15 The prediction at time $t + m$ is $\alpha + \beta^m Approval_{t-1} + \gamma Economic\ Performance_{t+m}$ $+ \phi Vietnam\ Deaths_{t+m}$. where $\beta$, $\gamma$, and $\phi$ are the estimates of the causal parameters and $\alpha$ = the intercept. For month $t$, expected *Approval* is simply the prediction from the base equation, Table 2.4, column 2.

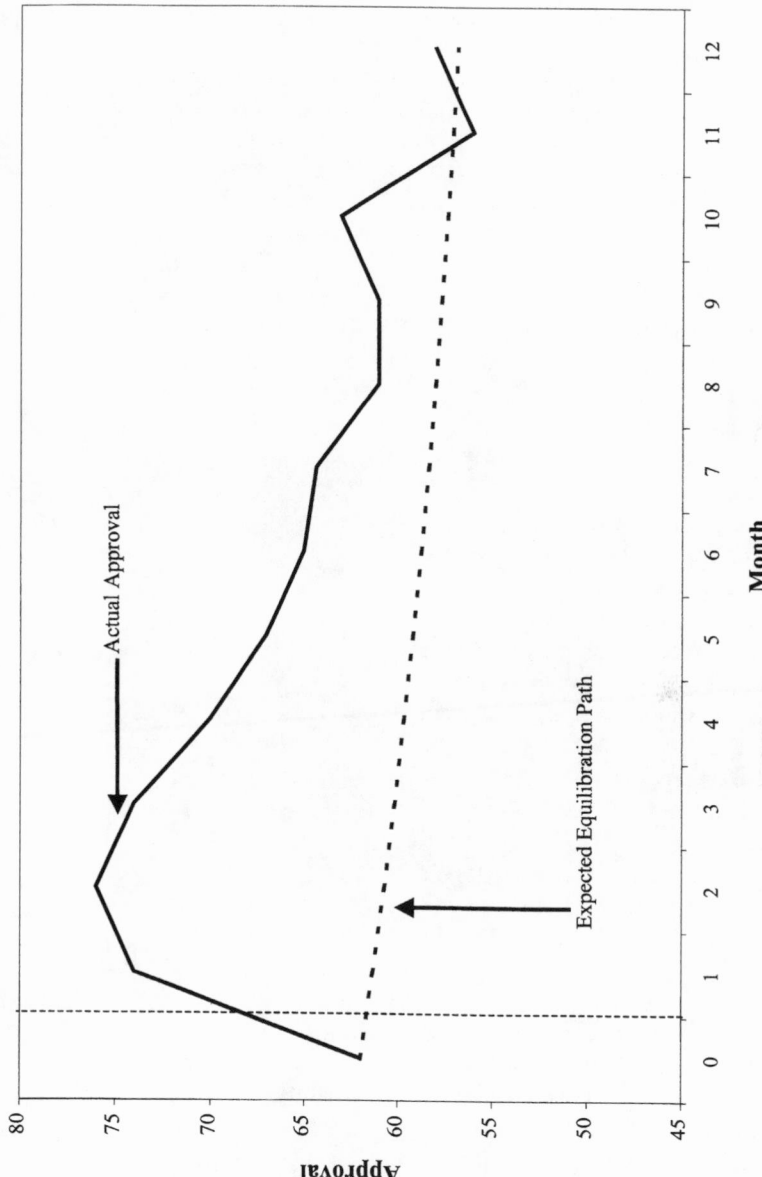

Figure 2.5. The Cuban Missile Crisis: Actual and Projected Kennedy Approval

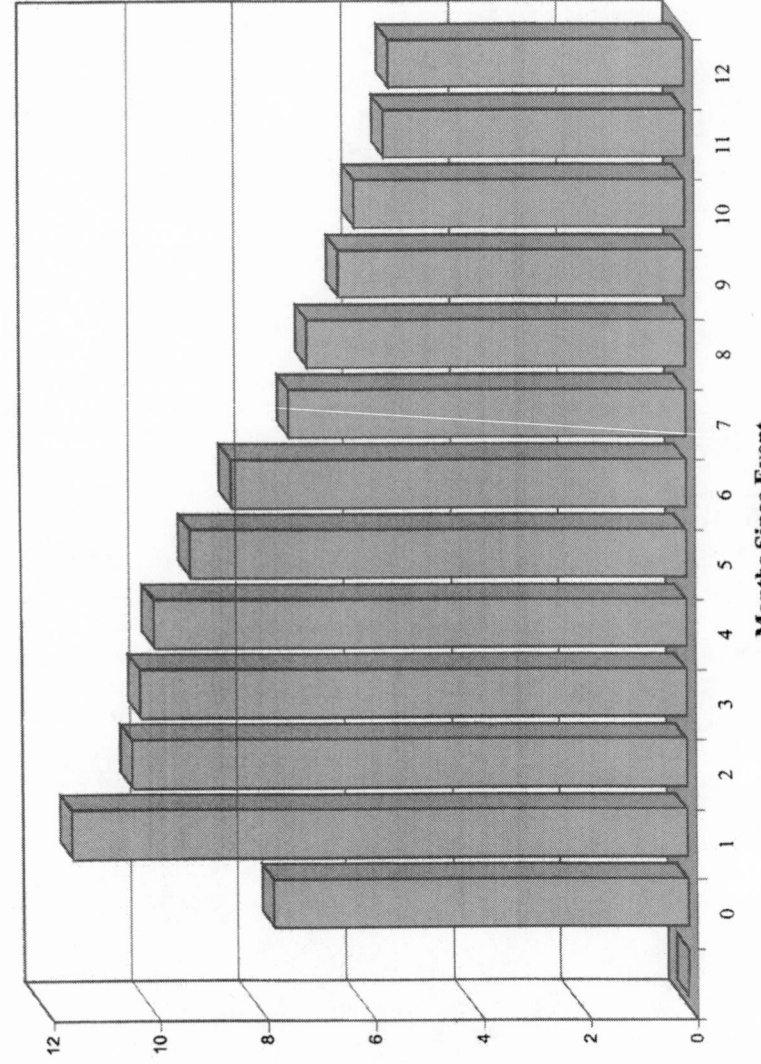

Figure 2.6. Estimated Event Impact from Onset to Month 12: All Events for All Presidents

## Presidential Approval

We have illustrated that effects of events on *Presidential Approval* are somewhat long lasting but far from permanent, with a half-life of less than a year. A few months after a major presidential event, the response will still register in presidential approval. After a year, the response has faded to less than half its original value. When people judge the president, they discount rally points and other major events from the past at about the same rate as they discount ordinary shocks from the past.

### Explaining Presidential Approval: A Summary

To this point we have posed explanations of the president's public standing and tested them one at a time. The tests tell us what matters, and we have exploited them for that purpose. They do not tell us particularly well *how much* any of the components matter. Is it all economics? Is perhaps the long-term equilibration process the dominant flow, with other factors mere wrinkles around the edge? What keeps us from sensing the magnitude of the contribution of the pieces to full explanation is the model structure in which the previous months' *Approval* is a dominating force in the analysis.

We understand that this "previous month" actually incorporates prior inputs of the factors that we care about. But we can't actually see it. We wish to do so, to get a sense of how much each component matters, a more descriptive issue. To get an answer we turn to an unconventional approach to simulating the joint contributions of our several factors, building a summary *Approval* from the ground up using the components. We will take the parameters we have estimated and use them, one component at a time, to build a predicted contribution of that component, so many points for each month to economics, so many to events, so many to reequilibration, and so forth. Then we add them up to re-create *Approval*.

We wish to divide the sources of *Approval* into the cumulative impact of five components: the honeymoon, the economy, major events, Vietnam (Johnson only), and the residual impact from unmeasured sources. We ask, to what extent is *Approval* explainable from observable sources past and present, and to what extent is it a function of things we do not know – originating in the residual shocks past and present?

*Equilibration Through the Term*: We start by projecting post-honeymoon *Approval* levels, given the president's initial popularity and the normal trajectory from honeymoon to equilibrium. We start with the president's initial reading (month 2) and project to month $t$.

$$Honeymoon_t = \beta^{t-2}Approval_2$$

57

where $t$ is the number of months since the start of the presidential term and *Approval* is calibrated as the deviation from its equilibrium level – its long-term mean. Thus, the *Honeymoon* represents the *Approval* level expected given the president's initial (inflated) popularity level and the time evolved since then.

*Economic Performance*: The economic performance component represents the combined effects of the current economy – and past economy readings, with decay – on current *Approval*. To estimate this cumulative effect for month $t$, we sum across the months from the start of the administration to time $t$, discounting each monthly input by its time lag, $\beta^{t-j+1}$.

$$Cumulative\ Economic\ Performance_t = \gamma \sum_{j=3}^{t} \beta^{t-j+1} Economic\ Performance_j$$

*Events*: We have 20 months in which major events occur.[16] For the 20 months when presidential events occur and the month following, we measure the event effect as the observed residuals. For generic month $t$, we are interested in the vestigial effect of the most recent presidential event, occurring at $t - m$. We measure this effect as:

$$Effect\ of\ Earlier\ Event_t = \beta^{t-m-1} e_{t-m+1}$$

We continue until either the next event or the next presidency.[17]

*Cumulative Vietnam Deaths*: For the Johnson presidency only, $\theta Vietnam\ Deaths_t$ is cumulated; adding the current tally to the cumulative past, discounted by $\beta$.

*Cumulative Residuals*: This is the unexplained component. For each month, cumulative residuals are simulated as the weighted summation of current and past residuals, each weighted by $\beta$ times the lag in months:

$$Cumulative\ Residuals_t = \sum_{j=3}^{t} \beta^{t-j} e_j$$

16 One event (Ford's pardon of Nixon) coincided with the first reading of the presidency. Without a pre-event reading of Ford's *Approval*, we lack the benchmark to score the effect of the pardon. Thus, the original 21 events are reduced to 20 here.

17 In this way, the estimate of the net effect at $t + 1$ is not affected by whether the initial shock is fully absorbed in surveys at month $t$ or month $t + 1$.

Table 2.6. *A Summary of Contributions to*
*Explaining Approval*

| Component | Variance Accounted for | Percentage of Total |
|---|---|---|
| Economic Performance | 45.0 | 30.1 |
| Events | 32.5 | 21.7 |
| Honeymoon | 12.1 | 8.0 |
| Vietnam Deaths | 12.6 | 8.4 |
| Residual | 60.0 | 40.0 |
| Total | 149.7 | 108.2 |

*Note*: Because they are modestly correlated with one another, the variances of the five components do not add exactly to the variance of observed Approval.

From this quantity, we then subtracted out the simulated impact at time $t$ of the most recent *Cumulative Event* (from time $t - m$).

By definition, *Approval* for month $t$ is an exact linear function of these five components, plus equilibrium *Approval* given the mean *Economic Performance (Approval\*)*. In theory, the five components should be statistically independent of each other, allowing the straightforward calculation of the proportion of the variance in *Approval* that can be accounted for by each component. In practice, the five components are mildly correlated with each other, so that the summation exercise is an approximation.[18]

The results, given in Table 2.6, suggest the portions of *Approval* that we could reproduce from reasonable postulates and the knowledge at hand, one piece at a time. *Economic Performance* and *Events* emerge as the most important to our understanding, while Vietnam deaths and honeymoon come in third and fourth.[19] Together these four components account for about two-thirds of the variance in the *Approval* series. We have not exhausted all sources of a president's *Approval* rating. We can increase the variance explained further by adding extended dummy variables for Watergate, Iran, and the Bush presidency post–Gulf War. We could pack our list of events with

18 Most notable is a slight tendency for positive events to erupt when the economy is bad.
19 *Cumulative Economic Performance* generally increases as a predictor of *Approval* as the presidential term progresses. The peak correlation is .88 after 44 months of a presidency.

added entries, as every event not included goes in the residual. And we could improve our measure of the economy, as the *Economic Performance* measure is but a surrogate monthly measure of *Consumer Sentiment*.

Figure 2.7 illustrates our statistical accomplishment and its limitations. It shows observed *Approval* for nine presidents as an additive function of the four substantive components (honeymoon plus cumulative economy, events, and Vietnam deaths). In general, the model performs quite well, although gaps can be identified. For instance, John Kennedy was more popular than predicted for most of his presidency, and Ronald Reagan had an unaccounted-for bubble of extra support mid-presidency. Jimmy Carter was less popular than expected, and Richard Nixon's Watergate-related loss of popularity is not fully accounted for by our model. The worst prediction is for Bill Clinton, who underperformed most of his first term, catching up toward the end.[20] If we add presidential dummy variables to the mix, we can further boost the explained variance from .62 to .72.[21]

The key point is that most of the time, the path of *Presidential Approval* follows a predictable trajectory as a function of a small set of variables. We start with knowing the first *Approval* reading of a presidency, which is of course almost entirely the function of the political history that preceded the presidency. We know the history of *Economic Performance* from the start of the presidency to the current month. We take into account the effect of *Vietnam Deaths*, which remind us of the political effects of protracted wars. We identify a slim set of 21 major events where presidential support either spikes upward or downward in response. This factual information is combined with our understanding of how the public discounts past sources of *Approval* as it updates from new information. The statistical result is that we can explain most of the variance in *Presidential Approval*.

20 Although Clinton's first term contained no major events as we define the term, there are several noticeable inflection points in the Clinton trajectory. For instance, Clinton's approval started to decline around the time of the 1993 gays in military "don't ask, don't tell" executive order and the 1994 collapse of the health-care plan. It started to climb in 1993 around the time of Clinton's health-care speech and again in late 1995 during Clinton's skirmish with congress. These turning points may have been due more to shifting perceptions of competence than to the policy substance of the issues involved, but of course we cannot be sure.

21 Earlier we noted that presidential dummies are not significant. Here presidents obviously make a difference in the cumulative effects of variables. The lesson is that when presidents have good or bad "luck" the effect carries over somewhat into the future.

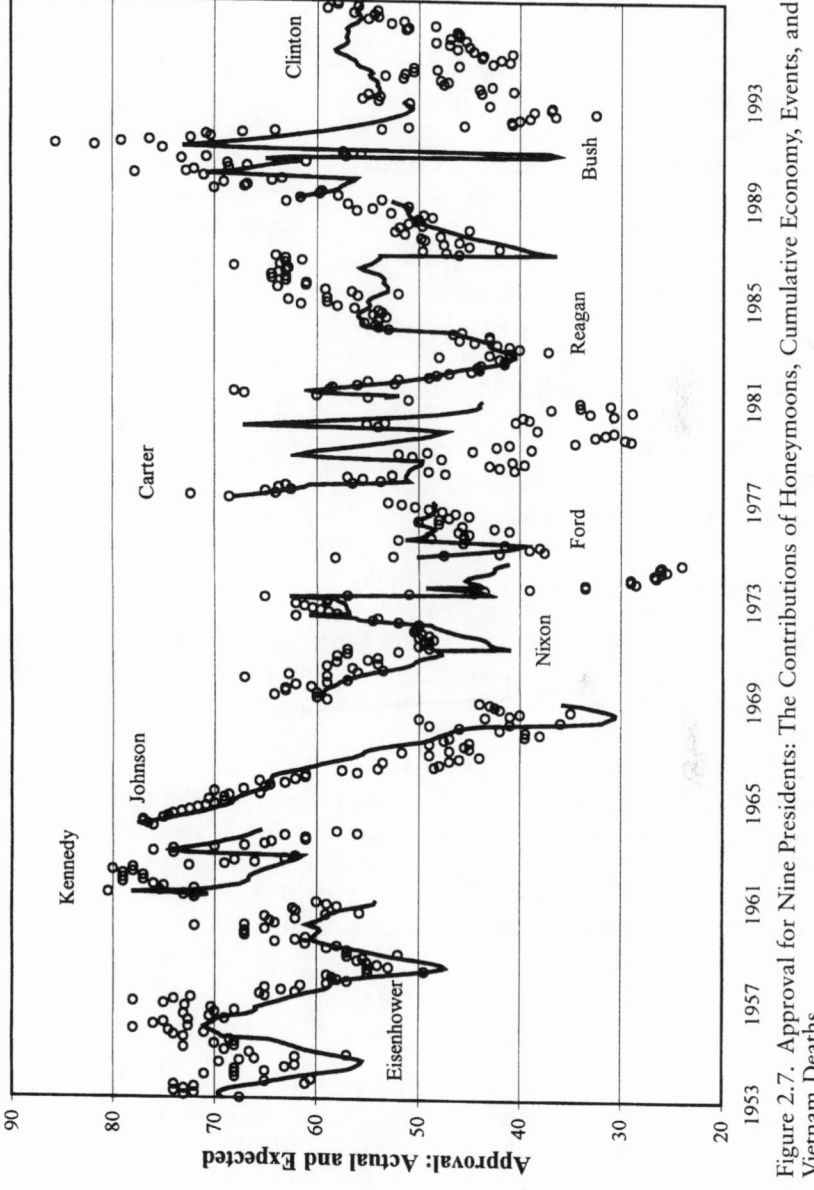

Figure 2.7. Approval for Nine Presidents: The Contributions of Honeymoons, Cumulative Economy, Events, and Vietnam Deaths

# Performance

## PRESIDENTIAL CONTROL

When the public takes into account the seeming evidence of presidential competence, it does not do so in a vacuum, but in the context of media commentary and evaluation. At its simplest level, the process is that the media provide images that the president is or is not in control of events. We ask whether we can observe statistical evidence of this process.

*Presidential Control*, the degree to which citizens see the president as in charge and mastering events, lacks conceptual development, a literature, and an established measure. It is not therefore quite comparable to the more standard materials we have just examined. But we think that it matters – that it is part of the full story of citizen response to presidents.

Here we will develop an indirect measure of control and conduct a brief examination of its effects. We have no measure of citizen perceptions of control. Therefore we turn to an indirect and imperfect alternative. We ask instead what citizens would have seen about the president as conveyed through media treatments of the presidency over time. Our instrument is a computerized content analysis of stories about presidents. We sample stories from the "National Affairs" section of *Newsweek*, where the president's actions are regular material for reporting (and no small amount of editorializing). The weekly news magazines closely reflect stories that have appeared in both print and electronic media accounts during the week and are a good summary of what is being said at the time.[22]

Our particular interest, and the keywords for our search, are presidential stories that describe mastery. Such stories describe the president with words like "calm," "assertive," "authoritative," "confident," "masterful," "strong," "confronting," "demanding," "ordering," "forceful," and the like. Often these words go with the title "commander in chief." The negation of these words, or others such as "burdened," "anxious," "crippled," "hostage," "captured," "in a corner," "begging," "floundering," "torn," "vacillating," "waffling," and "zigzagging," captures the opposite image of a president who is a prisoner of events, not in charge.[23]

---

22 Of course we do not assume *Newsweek* readership is universal or even particularly widespread. The idea is that *Newsweek* commentary should mirror, perhaps only roughly, the general media content at the time.

23 Our method employs the Fan (1988) interactive algorithm for coding the content of electronic text. The period of our analysis (1975–1994) is dictated by the availability of such text. For illustration of the portraits these words create imagine George Bush asserting, "This shall not stand" in response to the Iraqi invasion of Kuwait or the same George Bush a few months later begging the Japanese government for trade concessions to boost U.S. employment.

Two measures emerge: One is a count of the number of president-in-control stories, and the other a similar count for president-not-in-control stories. Each produces an average of about eight stories per month (for this 20-year span) with in-control stories slightly more numerous than not-in-control ones.

We return to presidential events to illustrate the interplay with media coverage. We postulated that events were unusual opportunities for presidents to take center stage and assert control. If that is the case, we should see "in-control" images rise during and after these episodes. Figure 2.8 illustrates that this is indeed the case. The base condition, before event onset, is near zero, a balance of control and not-in-control references. In the onset month, *Control* references begin to dominate. That grows substantially in the weeks after the event (which in some cases represent the first post-event publication opportunity of a weekly outlet) and

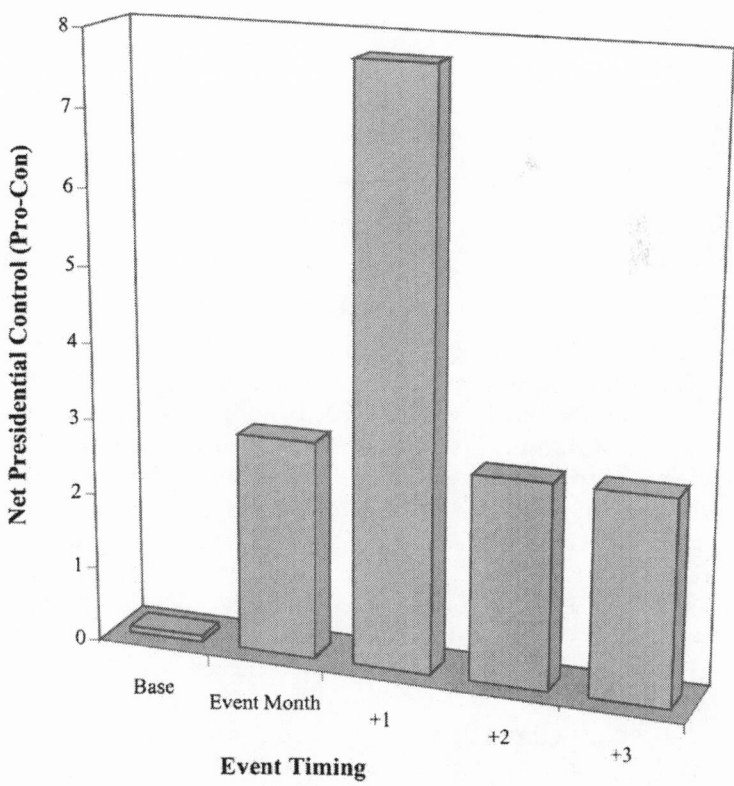

Figure 2.8. Media Portrayal of Net Presidential "Control," Before, During, and After Rally Events

Table 2.7. *Estimating the Effect of Presidential Control: Monthly Approval by Lagged Approval, Control, and Presidential Dummies*

| | | Dependent Variable: Approval$_t$ | |
|---|---|---|---|
| | (1)<br>Base Model | (2)<br>Base Model<br>with "Control"<br>Variables | (3)<br>Base Model with "Control"<br>Variables and Presidential<br>Dummies |
| Intercept | 4.07[a] | 4.07[a] | 5.08[a] |
| | (2.90) | (2.45) | (2.75) |
| Approval$_{t-1}$ | 0.92[a] | 0.92[a] | 0.89[a] |
| | (34.75) | (34.01) | (29.57) |
| "President in<br>Control" Stories | | 0.14[a]<br>(1.99) | 0.18[a]<br>(2.36) |
| "President Not in<br>Control"Stories | | −0.15<br>(−1.84) | −0.13<br>(−1.66) |
| Carter | | | −1.26<br>(−0.99) |
| Reagan | | | 0.52<br>(0.44) |
| Bush | | | 1.25<br>(0.93) |
| Clinton | | | −0.49<br>(−0.34) |
| Adjusted $R^2$ | .85 | .85 | .85 |

*Note*: Based on 233 cases, 1975–1994. *t* values in parentheses.
[a] $p < 0.05$.

then decays as the event ages. With only eight positive events and 20 years of media data, we cannot make particularly strong confirmation claims here. But the pattern is what we expected it to be, and it is quite similar to the flow of *Approval* following events. The control story is plausible.

We hypothesize that in-control references build an in-control perception in the public and lead to enhanced approval. And, equally, the reverse: Floundering presidents should be less approved. To test the thesis more systematically, we reestimate our base model for the restricted time period of this analysis (Table 2.7, column 1), producing essentially the same result as for the full period. Then (column 2) we introduce our control measures. There we see modest effects in both directions, as hypothesized. *Approval* goes up with media images of presidential control and goes down with images of helplessness and indecision. This is not, however, a large effect. It predicts movement of a point or two following events, as we have illustrated, and larger movements at extreme values of the measures.

Is presidential control a real influence on approval, or might we mistake it for popular presidents always perceived in control and unpopular ones the reverse? To test that possibility, we again include presidential dummy variables (excluding Gerald Ford as reference category). (See Column 3.) The result provides some support for the control thesis. The two control measures do not weaken and even gain a little strength in the presence of administration controls. Their explanatory power, though weak, works within administrations, not between them.

Competence, we know, matters. And the more suggestive evidence we have just seen suggests that control contributes something as well. We now turn to the third of our trio of citizen preferences about government – policy agreement – to see if it, too, extends the approval story.

## PRESIDENTIAL POLICY CHOICES AND APPROVAL

Confirming that people evaluate presidents in terms of competence holds little surprise. After all, the popular press treats the public's *Approval* rating as a measure of the president's character or strength. But to discuss a president's job performance solely in terms of competence ignores another input into the approval numbers, the matter of public policy. When Americans pick one presidential candidate over another during an election campaign, they are voting on more than simply the general qualifications for the particular individual who will hold office. Much of the debate and the actual deciding is based on questions of policy direction, much of it with a liberal-conservative content. And in office, presidents are very different in the sorts of policies they pursue; and they are very different in fairly well-understood ways. For instance, Ronald Reagan was clearly a very conservative president, while John Kennedy, Lyndon Johnson, and Bill Clinton pursued liberal policy directions.

The question is whether presidential policies affect the public's approval. People who approve of a president's policy choices should, other things equal, increase their estimation of the president. After all, the president is the most visible of all politicians – the press and the public will quickly see his role in policy proposals, legislation, and executive acts. Those who detest the policy should similarly disapprove of the president, blaming his actions for political outcomes.

That policy choices affect presidential evaluations is very clear from micro-level evidence. How might we detect a policy influence on macro-level *Approval*? One approach is to derive inferences based on the assumption that presidents typically take policy stances that are distinctive from the median voter. Democratic and Republican presidents advocate policies that are typically either more liberal (Democrats) or more conservative (Republicans) than the median voter.[24] When we look at the president's support for legislation, that support is almost always consistent with the main ideological direction of the president's party. When we look at policies actually passed by congress, a crucial ingredient for the ideological pace of this legislation is the president's party.[25]

This leads us to believe that policy moderation rather than ideological extremism should help a president's *Approval* rating. The expectation is that presidents who pursue policies most desired by the public will gain the most support. Presidents must choose between pursuing their and their party's ideological preferences on the one hand and appeasing a largely moderate public on the other. For testing, we must measure presidential ideology, which we can do by drawing on measures of presidential *Policy Liberalism* (Chapter 8) or the liberalism of major *Laws* (Chapter 9) passed by congress, usually with the president's initiative, each measured annually or biennially.

Whichever policy measure we use or whichever presidential party we examine, with or without multivariate controls, we find no relationship between presidential moderation and *Approval*. The reader is spared the details. Does this prediction failure mean that presidential policy does in fact not affect *Approval*? For a variety of reasons, we think not.

Consider first that while presidential policy can affect *Approval*, the reverse is also true. When presidents are popular, they have two extra incentives to push their ideological agenda. First, popularity is political capital that the president can spend on policy. Popular presidents can afford to spend some popularity to achieve their policy goals. Unpopular presidents cannot. A second incentive for spending on policy when popular is that presidents will be more successful with the congress and the public. A popular president could actually succeed in enacting a favored program, whereas an unpopular president pressing the same agenda could not.

Such complications are standard fare in discussions of presidential policy making (Edwards 1983, 1989; Rivers and Rose 1985; Bond and Fleisher 1990; Brace and Hinckley 1992; Mouw and MacKuen 1992). Statistically, the complication is that we cannot sort out the crosscutting causal processes. Popularity causes policy extremism, but extremism

---

24 This assertion is certainly true in the public's mind. It can readily be verified using the National Election Study 7-point scale assessments both of respondent positions and of presidential candidates on liberal-conservative scales. Consider the relative ratings of those NES respondents willing to make ideological evaluations. In every election since 1972 when ideological ratings began, most saw the Republican nominee to their right and the Democratic nominee to their left.

25 These regularities are discussed in Chapters 8 and 9 ahead.

causes unpopularity, a combination that leads to the very absence of a statistical relationship between *Approval* and policy, which we observe.

A second consideration is that we probably err when we assume presidential initiatives are unpopular. Most major legislation that passes with the blessing of congress and the president is in fact popular with the voters. Can one imagine congress and the president pushing major legislation through to passage that polls show to be distinctly unpopular with the voters? President Clinton's health-care plan provides an illustration. It appeared to be popular when introduced in 1993, and congressional actors behaved as if passage in some form was inevitable. When opinion turned against the plan in 1994, its backers knew the plan was doomed.

Even dramatic policy shifts like Lyndon Johnson's Great Society and the Reagan Revolution had the approval of the median voter at the time and were therefore unlikely to generate downturns in *Approval*. We may ask, though, how policies could be both ideological and popular, i.e., favored by the median voter? As we will see in later chapters, the policy demands of the public are not constant. Sometimes the public demands more liberalism or more conservatism. These shifts can affect the next election and, by anticipation, the behavior of political leaders.

This leads to the third and final consideration. Even when presidential policy affects individual voters greatly, it is unlikely to affect aggregate *Approval*. As we have repeatedly noted, while presidential competence is valued almost uniformly, policies are perceived divisively. Even policy changes that pass for mandates from the public are opposed by significant minorities.

In summary, even when opinions about the president are influenced by policy considerations, there are several reasons why the policy response is disguised when we observe the macro-level relationship between presidential policy and *Approval*. First, with simultaneous causation, popular presidents are most likely to undertake policy initiatives that might be unpopular. Second, we should not assume presidential policy initiatives are unpopular just because they arise from some ideological direction. Third, because of the public's division of opinion, specific policy initiatives or changes rarely generate visible ripples in macro-level *Approval*.

## *Party, Ideology, and Presidential Approval*

Even though the impact of policy on *Approval* is not directly observable at the macro level, we find circumstantial evidence when we subdivide the national sample by party identification or by ideological identification. Democrats and Republicans see the political world differently.

## Performance

People divide into Democrats and Republicans for many reasons, including parental inheritance, perceptions of party competence, and the different policy tendencies of the two parties. Not all voters are motivated by policy issues, but those who are most attentive to policy often choose their partisan allegiance based on their ideological (liberal vs. conservative) orientation.

Figure 2.9 displays *Approval* over time separately for Democratic and Republican identifiers. Democrats and Republicans view the sitting president differently, each naturally more favorable to presidents who are one of their own. On average, according to 44 years of the Gallup poll, 78 percent of identifiers with the president's party approve of the president's performance. In contrast, on average, only 37 percent of the out-party supporters approve. The party polarization on presidential evaluation is stronger for some presidents (e.g., Reagan, Clinton) than for others (e.g., Eisenhower, Carter) and generally grows over the course of the presidential term. Whichever president is in office, to predict whether a citizen approves or not, it is far more important to learn his or her individual party preference than to know the president's general *Approval* level within the general population.

Democrats like Democratic presidents better because they promote liberal policies, and Republicans like Republican presidents better because they promote conservative policies. That is at least part of the equation. We observe the role of ideology more directly by comparing the *Approval* trends for liberals and conservatives. For 20 years (1977–1996), the CBS News/*New York Times* poll data has provided the information for such a comparison, shown in Figure 2.10. Because of the relative sparseness of the data (compared to Gallup's polling frequency), only annual means are shown.[26]

Predictably, liberal identifiers like Democratic presidents the best, and conservative identifiers like Republican presidents the best. The gaps between the two types of ideological identifiers for any point in time are less distinct than the gaps between the *Approval* levels of Democrats and Republicans. But the two ideological groups comprise a surer division in terms of policy preference. Interestingly, the gap is less for the two one-term presidents (10 points for Carter, 16 points for Bush) than for the two-term presidents (20 points for Reagan, 32 points for Clinton). Presidents draw support from their ideological supporters and opposition from their ideological opponents. These two processes tend to cancel out, obscuring a clear view of the policy-*Approval* connection.

---

26 Gallup now also reports *Approval* by ideological identification, but only since 1990.

68

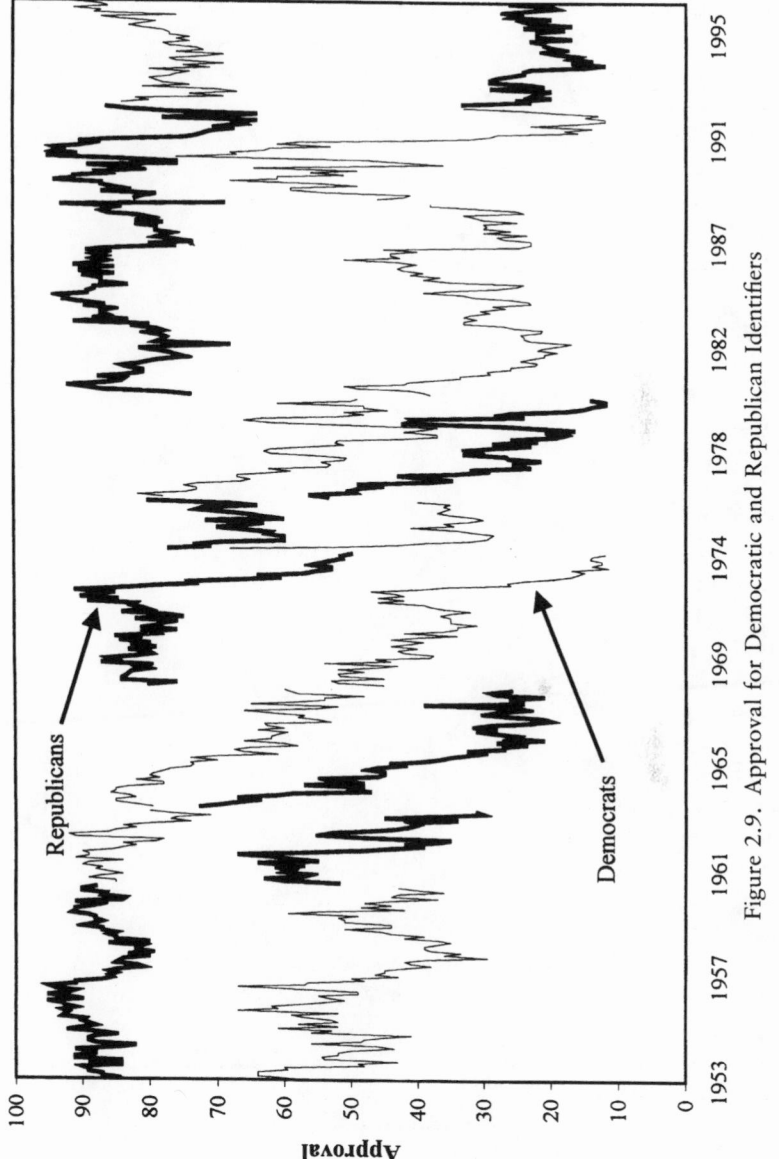

Figure 2.9. Approval for Democratic and Republican Identifiers

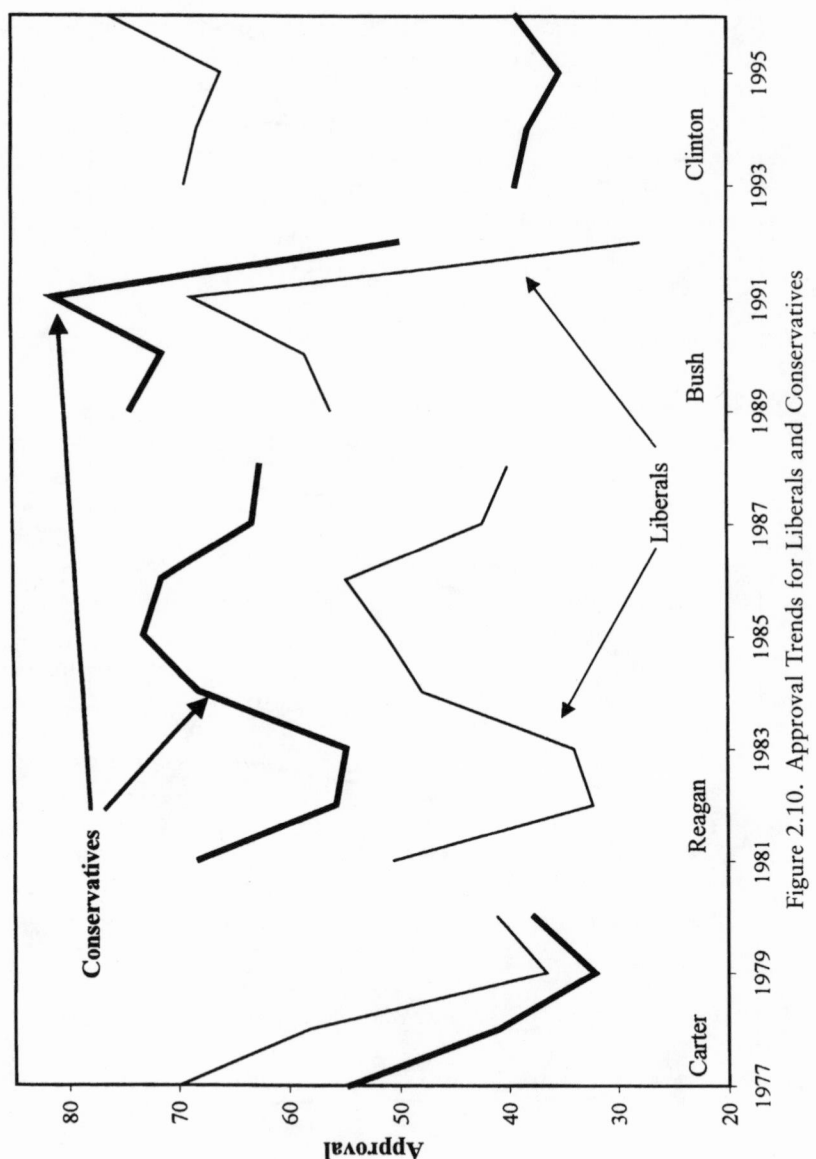

Figure 2.10. Approval Trends for Liberals and Conservatives

## Presidential Approval

For another indirect view of the policy connection, we return to the separate *Approval* series for Democrats and Republicans. As a starting point of our discussion, we note that the two partisan groups respond identically to the variables that contribute to evaluations of presidential competence. When *Approval* rises or falls due to an apparent change in public confidence, Democrats and Republicans move in tandem to create the change. For instance, for the starting months of our event series, the before-after changes (month before to month after) in *Approval* for Democrats and Republicans correlate at a whopping .95. Whether rallied by a Gulf War or shocked by an Iran-Contra, Democrats and Republicans move in the same direction by about the same amount. Where they differ is in their initial levels of *Approval*.

But what about routine movement of *Approval* of the sort that does not get captured by our *Approval* equation? Much of the day-to-day politics that dominates the newspapers carries an implicit partisan tone: The president's actions today will move his program forward (or not), or will help (or hurt) his party's chances in the upcoming elections, and so forth. If presidential action is seen by the public as having policy implications, as following a political philosophy or targeting social groups, then Democrats and Republicans should react differently.

When *policy* issues affect *Approval*, Democrats and Republicans should be pushed in different directions. Thus, we ask how similar are Democratic and Republican movements when the variables that predict presidential competence are controlled. To answer, we model *Approval* separately for Democrats, Republicans, and Independents as shown in Table 2.8, excluding the month of each major presidential event and the month after.[27] The most interesting feature of this table is that with the economy and presidential party controlled (and major events excised), Democratic and Republican approval follow entirely different trajectories. Democratic *Approval* is a function of lagged Democratic *Approval* but not lagged Republican *Approval*. Similarly, Republican *Approval* is a function of lagged Republican *Approval* but not lagged Democratic *Approval*.

For further diagnostics, we turn to the residuals from the Table 2.8 equations, the deviations of the observed values from the equation predictions. To the extent residual *Approval* is dominated by competency perceptions alone, the three sets of partisan residuals should be quite positively correlated, just as we see for the movement of Democratic and

27 For maximum efficiency, these three equations are estimated using Zellner's "seemingly unrelated regressions." For a nearly duplicate exercise, we can substitute the president's party and the opposition party for Democrats and Republicans.

# Performance

Table 2.8. *Approval Equations for Three Partisan Groupings*

|  | Democratic Identifiers | Independents | Republican Identifiers |
|---|---|---|---|
| Intercept | −8.55[a] | −13.45[a] | 2.12 |
|  | (−3.27) | (−5.33) | (0.89) |
| Democrats' Approval$_{t-1}$ | 0.84[a] | 0.26[a] | −0.05 |
|  | (20.58) | (6.60) | (−1.25) |
| Republicans' Approval$_{t-1}$ | 0.01 | 0.31[a] | 0.83[a] |
|  | (0.29) | (7.03) | (19.93) |
| Independents' Approval$_{t-1}$ | 0.04 | 0.40[a] | 0.11 |
|  | (0.62) | (6.64) | (1.99) |
| Economic Performance | 0.13[a] | 0.14[a] | 0.08[a] |
|  | (4.62) | (5.10) | (3.30) |
| Vietnam Deaths | −0.69 | −2.40[a] | 0.30 |
|  | (−0.53) | (−2.08) | (0.27) |
| President's Party ($D = 1$, $R = 0$) | 5.27[a] | 1.60 | −6.88[a] |
|  | (2.71) | (0.85) | (−3.90) |
| $R^2$ | .95 | .90 | .97 |
| Standard Error of Estimate | 4.50 | 4.34 | 4.07 |

*Note*: Estimates are via "Seemingly Unrelated Regression." $N = 382$. Event months and months immediately after event months are not included. $t$ values in parentheses.
[a] $p < 0.05$.

Republican *Approval* following major presidential events. To the extent that it is dominated by policy concerns, the residuals for Democrats and Republicans should be negatively correlated as Republicans and Democrats move in different directions. The reality is a mix of the two. Much of the residual variation is due to unmeasured causes of perceived presidential competency, perceived equally by Republicans and Democrats. But some is policy-related, spurring Democrats and Republicans to react differently.

The evidence is this: Residual *Approval* for Democrats and that for Republicans correlate with each other at a positive but mild .33. For a reference point, we have the residual *Approval* of a neutral panel, people who call themselves Independents. The residuals for Independents correlate at .53 with both Republican and Democratic residuals, suggesting that much of even the residual variation is due to public evaluations of presidential competence shared by all partisan groups. The lower .33 correlation between Democratic and Republican residuals is further indication that Democrats and Republicans evaluate presidents differently.

## Policy and Approval: Further Discussion

Fundamental to our understanding of presidential politics is the postulate that the president's policy stands ought to matter – that agreement between presidential policies and public opinion enhances *Approval*, while disagreement undermines it. Yet for a variety of reasons, this connection between presidential policy and *Approval* is difficult to observe at the macro level. At best, we can see indirect outcroppings of the policy response when we see differential responses by Democrats and Republicans or between liberals and conservatives, with their different policy agendas.

How then are we to understand the discrepancy? One possible conclusion is, of course, that the postulate is simply wrong. But this view is deeply embedded in the understanding of politics we bring from the tradition of spatial models, and it is shared with journalists who comment on politics and politicians who act on it. It is not merely *our* theory that fails.

An alternative view is that the effect exists in the hypothetical world of politically naive presidents, but is obscured by strategic behavior in the real world of politically adept ones. Instances of presidents promoting highly unpopular programs are censored by the acts of presidents who are highly strategic politicians. *If* presidents (and their advisors) were politically naive, they would propose sets of policies of varying appeal, some pleasing and some offensive to public sentiment. We would then observe that the pleasing policies drove up *Approval* and the offensive policies drove it down, a "policy" effect. But presidents are anything but naive, and thus they tailor their proposals to emphasize those that can achieve public support – and deprive us of the opportunity to observe public reaction to unpopular policies.

Why should we expect such skill at anticipating the consequences of policy? There are two reasons. One is that the presidency is an extraordinary selection process that winnows out fools and lightweights in politics, leaving us as actual presidents an astute group of people of extraordinary skill at anticipating public response (and with on-the-job training at error correction). A second is that presidents have unique agenda control. More than all other political actors, they can decide what to decide. That allows them to put their anticipatory skill to good use, deciding both what to propose and when to propose it.

We get occasional glimpses of what a presidency might be without such control. Lyndon Johnson was committed by his own words and deeds to winning a war in Vietnam that could not be won at acceptable political cost. Once underway, the war forced the president to set policy again and again, when, as McNamara (1995) tells us, all of the options on the table were dismal. Johnson repeatedly chose unpopular policies when their alternatives were thought to be even worse. George Bush, facing a runaway budget deficit after decreeing, "No new taxes," illustrates the same dynamic, where events prevent the president from choosing only positions known to have public support. His choice to raise taxes probably did him great harm. In hindsight, it is easy to forget that the alternative – a collapse of public belief in the ability of the U.S. government to manage its affairs – might have been worse. The same can be seen in the Iran hostage crisis of the Carter presidency. Without agenda control, presidents may be no less calculating, but calculation is not efficacious when events force the president's hand.

## CONCLUSION

For over 50 years, Gallup and other polling organizations have been collecting data on how American citizens believe the president has been handling his (and someday her) job. For most of that time, political scientists have analyzed this flow of data to figure out what accounts for the president's *Approval* rating. Much is known. Most of the time a president's popularity is the predictable function of some simple variables, time, the economy, and (at least *post facto*) important presidential events. Of dominant importance, the president must appear competent and in control, although policy issues lurk mysteriously in the background.

We conclude on a humble note, observing that the president's *Approval* rating can comprise more or less than what is imputed by those who follow the numbers. We have assumed that the responses meant exactly what the question asked. The subject was "the president" and no one else. The object of evaluation was "handling his job" and nothing else. But we know enough of survey respondents to know that this can't always be the case.

We know two things in particular that call into question our tidy interpretation of presidential approval. One is that ordinary citizens, particularly those most distant from the daily life of inside-the-beltway politics, do not share in the sharp distinctions drawn by professional observers of politics. Thus, "the president" might mean to many "president and first lady," "president and administration," "president and government," "president as leading Democrat (or Republican)," and so on. Many Americans are not aware of divided government, when it exists. Relatively few are comfortable with the idea that presidents can lose a competition with a congress controlled by their own party. Thus "the president" might mean George W. Bush, acting in his official capacity. But it might also connote "that mess in Washington," or the skill and courage of U.S. armed forces in combat, the talent of American Olympic athletes, or even the vibrancy of the corporate economy. "The president" is a symbol for all of these things to different sets of citizens.

A second, related, thing we know about citizen response to surveys is that diffuse attitudes get expressed in response to specific questions. It stretches the point, but only by degree, to note that a citizen upset by garbage collection, service by the local phone company, crime, traffic, or any number of other ills may choose to express his or her frustration on "the president," presumed manager of everything. We like to think that survey respondents censor their feelings, listening carefully to questions and apportioning their dispositions only to appropriate objects. Imagine a hypothetical citizen "mad as hell at the mess in Washington" saying to him- or herself, "Well, the question asks specifically how President Bush is handling his job. . . . I should wait until they ask me about government in general to express my views." This is not a likely outcome.

Thus we must conclude that presidential approval means both more and less than it seems to mean. Congressional foes of the president should not take unmitigated pleasure at declining presidential ratings, for they probably connote declining approval of government as well. (Thus an opposition that chooses a course of conflict and divisiveness can probably drag down the president's public standing, but risks taking itself down with the presidency.) And it is probably much less a barometer of specifically presidential skill than we commonly take it to be, but much more a barometer of how things are going at the moment.

How skilled a particular individual is in "handling his job," seen as a kind of personnel evaluation, should have little consequence beyond its immediate relevance to retaining that person in the job at reelection time. But approval as a more diffuse barometer will be seen to have more general consequences. One of notable import, to be seen later, is a generalization to the president's party – with increases in the president's standing leading more citizens to "think of themselves" as belonging to the president's party (or the reverse).

It is not notably controversial to assert that presidential approval is a barometer of how things are going in Washington and on Main Street. In Chapter 3, we ask whether we have got the tense right, deemphasizing "how things are going," or "how they have gone," in favor of "how they are expected to go." Much of what we have seen in this chapter tends to confirm existing theories of public response to presidents. Much of the next chapter should be seen as a challenge to standard views.

# 3

## Expectations and Political Response: The Character of Intelligence of the American Electorate

About 20 years ago economists began considering the then radical notion that economic actors – producers and consumers – took into account information about the likely future course of the economy in their daily decisions. That simple assumption, that rational actors necessarily act on all that they happen to know, produced the rational expectations revolution. Granting that one assumption had implications that swept aside essentially all of macroeconomic theory as it then existed. The macroeconomic theory of an earlier day presumed that the economy could be manipulated – most particularly by government – and that producers and consumers would then respond to that manipulation *after it happened*.

The idea that people use all of what they know quickly implies that (1) some of what they know is about the future, informed speculation about the likely course of events and (2) they use that knowledge. That means that people should foresee that part of the future that happens to be readily predictable, and the full rationality postulate implies that when they know it, they should act on it. They should, that is, act on expectations, which of necessity implies that action anticipates predictable events; it does not follow them. The older theories of government intervention were caught in a logical trap. If government action was a sensible response to the conditions that existed, then it should be almost fully predictable. If predictable, then economic actors should foresee it, act on their expectations, and then do nothing in response to the application of what had been predicted.

As applied to financial markets, rational-expectations theory was quick to win acceptance, for its postulates seemed reasonable in the high-stakes world of stocks and bonds, and its predictions of hypersensitivity to information flows was essentially a description of long-known facts of market behavior. (Not surprisingly, those who sell advice that claims to give investors the edge that the rational-expectations efficient market thesis holds to be impossible were and are considerably more reluctant in the matter.) Elsewhere, in the economics of "main street," acceptance was slower and more grudging. But the rational expectations paradigm gradually pushed aside its competitors. But even there it gradually emerged into dominance, requiring reformulation of the older views to fit the new one. It would be wrong to claim that the controversy was easy, quickly settled, or that it is over, but the dominance is so nearly complete that the modern debate is principally around the edges, identifying, for example, the sorts of economic behaviors that seem not to demonstrate full information use.[1]

One reason that the rational expectations view emerged as quickly as it did is that its micro foundation was the rationality postulate that is essential to the core theory of microeconomics. When macroeconomists began to think about the implications of full rationality, they were doing what microeconomists had always done. So, rational expectations unified the disparate strands of micro- and macroeconomics. The assumption of full rationality was easier because most of the residents up and down the academic hallway already assumed it. But that is clearly not the case in political science, where the assumption of rationality applied to politics is open to hot contests. But that raises a quandary. How can it be that consumers are rational actors, but citizens are not? Citizens and consumers are the same people. (And if we talk about the subset of citizens who vote, then they are a selection biased toward the upper end of the distribution of knowledge, education, and information within the set of consumers.) Thus it would appear that if rational expectations is right for economics, then it must also be right for politics (or that it must be wrong for both). We can have two spheres in which people bring different amounts of information, see choices as involving different stakes, and perhaps even develop different habits of decision. What we can't have is a citizenry that thinks about the consequences of its acts in one sphere, but acts heedlessly in another.

---

1 Among political scientists the issue is occasionally seen as a fight between political rather than scientific positions. Since rational expectations denies the effectiveness of government interventions in the economy, it is argued to be a conservative doctrine, undercutting the Keynesian position often advocated by the political left. We disagree with this view in two senses, first that we should even take into account political implications in the discussion of whether or not a scientific explanation happens to be true or not, but second also because rational expectations is an "equal opportunity" destroyer of economic theories. The view is equally effective in denying the efficacy of monetarist and supply side views favored by conservatives. Indeed, the perspective is most devastating as applied to the Friedman monetarist view, which emphasizes a predictable money supply as a key economic policy. The most predictable outcomes are those least likely to be effective in the rational expectations view.

## Performance

In this chapter, we confront that conflict over rationality in citizen behavior. We shall take seriously the implications of a full rationality postulate as applied to particular behaviors. We examine these particular behaviors, approving the president or not and forming expectations about the national economy, because they make it possible to push rational expectations into making specific predictions about political behavior. We shall develop tests that push those implications into clear empirical claims. We can't know at the end whether the inference from these tests applies *only* to the particular behaviors. But what justifies the research is our belief that forming economic expectations is not sui generis political behavior. Its distinctiveness is that it lends itself to a clean test.

Our focus in particular is the rational-expectations claim that people make efficient use of the information at their disposal. To structure future analyses we can think of that claim in two parts. The easier of the two is that all relevant information is used. We can observe situations where we know a priori that information is relevant to evaluation and ask whether it is used, that is, whether it helps predict the evaluations that are reached. The stronger claim is that information is used efficiently, that is, that it is weighted somehow in proportion to its true value. If, say, datum "a" is twice as important as datum "b," then the person who weights "a" and "b" in any proportion other than 2/1 does not make optimally efficient use of the information at hand. We shall find a situation where we can observe this optimal weighting issue as well.

This is a tall order. Five decades of research on political behavior have painted a portrait of voters who know next to nothing and prefer to think about issues other than politics. That in the aggregate people use information efficiently seems a staggering claim in such a context. That is nonetheless what we are going to assert. Part of the discrepancy between the micro evidence of information holding and the macro efficiency claim is reduced by understanding exactly what the efficiency claim does and does not mean. It is a common misunderstanding of rational expectations that it claims that actors *have* all the information relevant to a decision.[2] It does not. The claim is merely that people *use* what they do have efficiently. Rational information use thus remains a possibility even when one concedes that most citizens hold relatively little information about economics and politics. It is still a stretch.

---

2 A complete information property is produced for aggregate markets. If all individual buyers and sellers use what they know, then market prices come to reflect all of what is known. But this is an emergent property. It does not require individual actors to know all.

## Expectations and Political Response

We ask the reader to humor us for a while. We are going to assume some things that may not be easily believed (for example, that the electorate is well informed in the aggregate) and use those assumptions to leverage some empirical predictions about politics and economics. We will then use those predictions to reflect back on whether the assumptions are as off the mark as they might at first seem.

### MODELS OF THE ECONOMIC VOTER

In the political science literature, the model of the economic voter has undergone considerable evolution. In an earlier day (for example, Key 1966), citizens were understood to respond to *personal* economic conditions, as typified by the phrase "voting one's pocketbook." But the psychology of the response was not mapped much beyond the general notion of stimulus and response. Personal prosperity made people feel good about the incumbent while personal adversity made them feel bad. Whether this response was instrumental or affective was rarely at issue. One could imagine the response of the economic voter as purely an emotional reaction, void of any cognitions about the economic future. (On affective reactions to the economy, see Peffley 1985; Conover and Feldman 1986.)

The rationality of evaluating political leaders based on the state of one's pocketbook is limited by the fact that for most people, most of the time, government activity has little to do with one's *personal* economic circumstances. For the discerning citizen, a far better criterion by which to judge the government's contribution to one's personal prosperity is the current state of the economy itself. Just as a rising tide lifts all boats including one's own, so one's economic status can be affected when the overall economy surges and declines. Indeed, the weight of evidence shows that political evaluations do respond more to the perceived national economy than personal economic circumstances. For instance, as Kinder and Kiewiet (1979, 1981; Kiewiet 1983) have shown convincingly, voters react more to their perceptions of the national economy – what they call "sociotropic voting" – than to their personal pocketbooks.[3]

When people evaluate their personal pocketbooks or the economy from looking backwards in time toward the recent past, they are evaluating retrospectively. Retrospective evaluations, however, can form the basis for evaluations of the future. As Fiorina (1981) has forcefully

---

3 Our earlier work (MacKuen et al. 1992) focused partly on the personal vs. sociotropic issue, with the result of decisive support for the sociotropic. Here we simplify matters by excluding the personal measures from the outset.

argued, the retrospective voter can use current economic circumstances to form expectations about the economic future under the current incumbent. In this sense, the retrospective voter is also prospective. This version of the economic voter uses personal experience or the current health of the economy as a signal of the incumbent's economic competence, which will affect the nation's and the voter's economic prosperity in the future.[4]

Whether it is guided by their own pocketbooks or by their perceptions of national conditions, the behavior of instrumentally retrospective voters is roughly in accord with the economists' model of "adaptive expectations." (For a discussion, see Alt and Chrystal 1983.) According to the adaptive-expectations model, people modify their expectations about the future by extrapolating from a weighted average of current and recent values. An important limitation of this version of the economic voter, however, is that although prospectively oriented, the voter is myopic. Unable to look beyond current conditions, the myopic retrospective voter does not react to the future implications of current policy, or even to economic forecasts. Easy to fool, the myopic economic voter is a crucial ingredient in most models of the political business cycle (for example, Nordhaus 1975; Tufte 1978).

Rational-expectations theory changes everything. The heart of rational expectations is the notion that decision makers incorporate all available information, responding to events and conditions when they are anticipated rather than waiting until they occur. Applied to economic voting, rational expectations would result in an electorate that responds to messages about the future economy rather than one that extrapolates only from current conditions. In the aggregate, we can imagine an electorate guided by the same intelligence as the economic forecasters. (For useful introductions to rational expectations theory, see Shaw 1984; and Sheffrin 1996. On rational expectations and public economic perceptions, see Alt and Chrystal 1983; Chappell and Keech 1985; Beck 1991; Haller and Norpoth 1994; Clarke and Stewart 1994; and Krause and Granato 1998.)

Figure 3.1 highlights three different models of the electorate's economic judgments of the president. The pure-retrospections model holds that people assess the president in terms of the economic past without regard for what the future is likely to hold (trace path *ac*). The connection here may be more emotion than cognition – vengeance and reward rather than instrumental behavior.

---

4 For convenience, and following convention, we use the language of personal self-interest to describe the voter's motivation. In doing so, we do not deny the desirability or the possibility of altruistic motivation – preferring good economic outcomes for others.

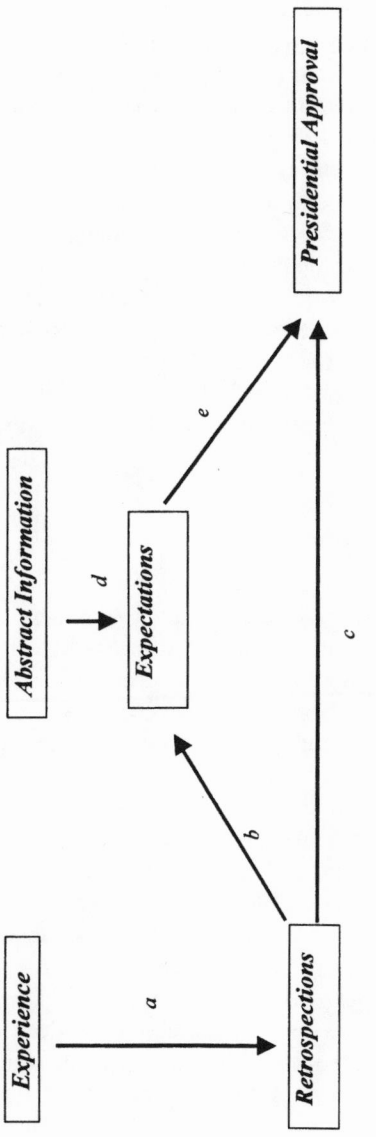

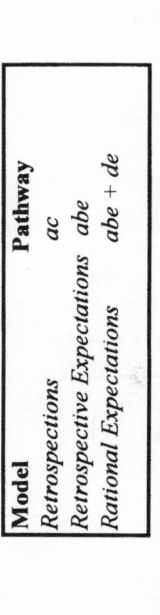

| Model | Pathway |
|---|---|
| *Retrospections* | *ac* |
| *Retrospective Expectations* | *abe* |
| *Rational Expectations* | *abe + de* |

Figure 3.1. Three Models of the Incorporation of Economic Information into Presidential Evaluation

## Performance

The second model, expressed by Fiorina (1981), says that people care about the future, but they rely on past experience as a guide for what the future holds (path *abe*). This is an expectations view, to be sure, but one that limits understanding of the future to extrapolation from current trends. We endorse this understanding – as far as it goes.

The third position, the one we propose, suggests that people *also* use information beyond past experience to make judgments about the future (path *abe* + *de*). That is, people take advantage of current information about the future to judge the president. We call this "rational expectations" because people use all the information they have at hand. Shifts in presidential approval respond to retrospective judgments but only in proportion to how the past guides the future. We simply argue that when information is learned about the economic future beyond what is known by extrapolating from the past, people use this information rather than throw it out.

## Rational Expectations for Real People

The argument of this chapter is that when citizens evaluate the president in terms of the economy, they do so using rational expectations. The electorate incorporates its information about the future when evaluating the president. But more than this, the electorate gives proper weight to current conditions and its expectations of future economic change when it anticipates the state of the economy on the horizon. This rationally anticipated expectation of the future economy is the one mass economic perception that drives presidential approval.

In the economics literature, it is now accepted that economic actors' expectations of future conditions are based on more than simple extrapolations from the recent past. In its simplest form, this rational expectations argument can appear obvious to the point of being vacuous. Why would people *not* use any relevant information at hand for making forecasts? Still, in the political science literature, the application of this idea to the world of ordinary voters has met resistance and indeed has been treated with incredulity (e.g., Norpoth 1996). In part, this resistance to the idea that citizens use information about the future may be attributed to the conditioning of political scientists to perceive the typical individual citizen as holding virtually no information to process.

Indeed, when it comes to *political* information, the impoverishment of the U.S. electorate has been well documented (e.g., Delli Carpini and Keeter 1996). Surveys also show that many Americans tune out economic discussions, perhaps even more than they tune out politics. When asked to estimate the inflation rate or unemployment rate, many respondents can offer no more than wild guesses (Conover, Feldman, and

Knight 1986). When asked to forecast the economic future, many survey respondents show even less capability. As Conover, Feldman, and Knight (1987, p. 579) summarize their findings, "In effect, economic forecasts reflect more a combination of hopes and political guesses about the future than they do an awareness of current economic conditions and an awareness of how the economy functions."

How could the electorate reward and punish its president based on an informed economic outlook when in fact the typical voter holds little information about the economy? This situation is one of many where the macro-level behavior of the electorate does not match the micro behavior of the typical citizen. The explanation for this seeming paradox can be summarized in three main points. First, citizens are exposed to much free or accidental information about the economy, emanating in large part from observable indicators and expert commentary. Thus, the average of economic perceptions (although not necessarily the average citizen's perception) is reasonably informed. This is our second point. Individuals may stray from the consensus forecast about the economic future, but their errors cancel out, leaving only the message from the informed signal. Third, when people form expectations about the future economy, they incorporate their learned information along with their knowledge of the recent past rather than throw it away. Thus, in the final analysis, when evaluating the president as prospective voters, they respond to new information about the economic future as well as retrospective clues.

When we posit that people act rationally, we mean it in the sense of Popkin's (1991) phrase, "limited information rationality." Most people are not economists or financiers and do not explore deeply the nature of the economy. Yet, people *are* everyday producers and consumers and therefore engage in learning during the course of their economic lives. Real estate agents, sales representatives, small business owners, individual investors, job seekers, and many others have incentives to develop informed expectations about the future. Equally, people planning the purchase of a home, car, or appliance; or choosing among employer pension options; or saving for their children's college tuition will find it worthwhile to anticipate inflation, interest rates, and their own income stream.

Further, the institutional division of labor in our political economy often makes it unnecessary to energetically pursue economic information in order to obtain some understanding. Financial agents, investment houses, bond traders, and fund managers spend large sums of money to anticipate the near and distant economic future. Much of this information filters down to the mass media and then to the mass public. When a network economics correspondent stands before the canyons of Wall Street to report on the day's news, the reporter sends a clear signal to the viewers: Financiers see a rosy or a dark future. In this way, the intelligence applied to the making of money gets translated – in simplistic form – to the wider public.

Of course, some will know more and some will know less. And ordinary people will process information more slowly than financial markets. And they will occasionally make (collective) mistakes. The matter at hand is not whether ordinary people know everything about the economic future. Instead, the question is whether they (rationally) use what they know or (irrationally) ignore it. When people hear talk of upcoming layoffs at work, they do not remain unconcerned because the previous quarter was fine. Similarly, we suggest, people would not ignore economic forecasts on the grounds that the economic change has not yet been directly experienced.

In their daily lives, citizens are exposed to a continuing flow of news, even if they do not actively seek it. Like tomorrow's weather, daily life exposes people to conversations about the economy. These, we believe, are effective means of diffusing reports from sophisticated analysts, through the mass media, and down to the street level. It is quite important that we not make extravagant claims about the individual citizen. The key element of our postulate is our belief that acquiring economic news is *easy*. A metaphor helps here. Imagine that we survey citizens and ask them about tomorrow's weather, "Do you expect it to be a nice day?" Most will be able to answer, and we would expect a fairly strong consensus. This is not because meteorological genius is widespread in the population. In part, people will generally know tomorrow's weather because they can extrapolate from today's. But they use other information as well to achieve a consensus forecast. This consensus forecast is obviously a reflection that most have been exposed either to the same news reports or to each other. They care enough to remember in a loose sort of way the tone of the predictions. Under aggregation, these street forecasts will focus in on the signal, the consensual part of the response, and it will turn out to be roughly the same signal we could obtain by averaging the day's (expert) forecasts. None of this required great feats of understanding. This is our view of citizen response to economic forecasts. Many individual citizens come to know whether or not tomorrow's economy will be an economic "nice day."

Of course, even if economic information is more widespread than one might initially think, the diffusion of information is far from universal. Many citizens – sometimes, perhaps *most* citizens – remain blissfully ignorant of widely reported economic conditions. For the typical individual at the *micro* level, economic perceptions may be more noise than signal. Analysis at the *macro* level reduces the noise to acceptable levels.

Whatever bizarre, confusing, or personally biased perceptions individual citizens bring to the evaluation task, in the aggregate all that idiosyncratic variation is self-canceling. The aggregate of individual expectations then becomes a quite orderly response to the flow of economic news. This is *necessarily* the case. The only way that net citizen perceptions could vary from the main path of economic news is for citizens to *innovate* understandings of the economy and then widely – almost universally – diffuse those innovations among themselves. Such coordinated action is hard to imagine.

We are prepared to argue not only that the public's collective forecasts of economic conditions contain elements of economic intelligence. We also argue that these collective forecasts provide the pathway by which people alter their judgment about the president's economic performance. When the economy affects the public's level of presidential approval, the innovations stem from new information about the quality of the economic future rather than simply new information about the recent past.

EMPIRICAL CHALLENGES: ARE EXPECTATIONS RATIONAL?

The claim of efficient information use, as we noted in the introduction to this chapter, can usefully be thought of as two claims. The easier of the two is that all relevant information is employed in evaluative processes. Given an optimal weighting of two pieces of relevant information, that is, the claim is that neither has an effective actual weight of zero. The stronger claim, and the harder one to test, is that given that same situation, the actual weights are the optimal ones. We structure our analysis in the four sections to come around the two claims. First in test 1, we will revisit the evidence of predicting presidential approval from economic expectations. We ask whether expectations are employed in evaluating the president, the easy claim. Then, in test 2, we ask how expectations are formed, how the electorate combines perceptions of current prosperity with relative expectations of change to come to formulate expectations of actual (i.e., absolute) conditions a year in advance. This again is the easy claim, whether or not both relevant pieces of information are employed in the production of expectations. Then we switch to the harder claim, that the public uses economic information *efficiently*. In test 3, we ask whether the electorate makes efficient use of economic information to predict actual prosperity a year in advance. Finally, in test 4, we switch back to approval and ask whether people use the same sort of efficiency to evaluate the president.

Before beginning the four tests we deal briefly with consumer sentiment and its components.

## Performance

### Consumer Sentiment and Its Components

Our empirical analysis offers a time-series analysis of the connections among (1) objective economic indicators, (2) aggregated economic cognitions, and (3) presidential approval. The economic cognitions are the *Index of Consumer Sentiment* (*ICS*) and, crucially, its components. The *ICS* and its components have been measured as part of the Survey of Consumer Finance by the University of Michigan's Survey Research Center since 1953. The *ICS* responds to the national economy (Katona 1964, 1975) and usefully augurs the economic future as well (Fuhrer 1988; Matsusaka and Sbordone 1989). *ICS* components have previously been shown to predict *Presidential Approval* (Shapiro and Conforto 1980). Of particular advantage here is that the individual items composing the *ICS* are similar in format to the economic items used in the National Election Studies. (See Lewis-Beck's [1988] innovative analysis of individual-level *ICS* data.) Exploiting the aggregate measures of these variables, we can learn something about the aggregate psychology by which the economy affects politics.

In the Survey of Consumer Finance, respondents are almost always asked to evaluate national business conditions, comparing the current situation both to the past and future. They answer similar questions with respect to personal finances as well. In Table 3.1, we list five of the resulting time series that will be used in our analyses.

The wording of the questions suggests clear-cut measures of pocketbook and sociotropic as well as retrospective and prospective evaluations.[5] Each item (and each index as a whole) is scored on a 200-point scale representing the net balance of positive and negative opinion, with 100 representing the neutral point.

Some of these indicators will play bit parts in analyses to come, some starring roles. Most of our emphasis will focus on the first two, *Expectations*,[6] our standard measure of how good or bad business conditions will be one year ahead, and *Relative Expectations*, a variant that focuses not on what conditions will be but on how they compare to the current

---

5 Also available, but not exploited in this analysis, are measures of current buying conditions and a five-year variation on the *Expectations* question. The latter we have previously used (in MacKuen et al. 1992), but its extreme collinearity with (one-year) *Expectations*, $r = .96$, makes it redundant.

6 A note on usage: we shall employ *Expectations*, (capitalized, italicized to distinguish it from the generic expectations) always to stand for the Michigan series of expectations for year ahead (absolute) business conditions. We follow the common time series practice of dropping the subscript $t$ for the current value of the series. Thus *Expectations* implies *Expectations at time t*. When we consider lags and leads, we shall be explicit in our notation.

Table 3.1. *Indicators of Consumer Economic Evaluations*

| Variable | Type | Time Horizon | Question Wording |
|---|---|---|---|
| *Business Conditions Indicators* | | | |
| Expectations | Business Conditions | Year Ahead | Now turning to business conditions in the country as a whole – Do you think that during the next 12 months we'll have good times financially, or bad times or what? |
| Relative Expectations | Business Conditions | Year Ahead | How about a year from now? Do you expect that in the country as a whole business conditions will be better, or worse than they are at present, or just about the same? |
| Retrospections | Business Conditions | Year Ago | Would you say that at the present time business conditions are better or worse than they were a year ago? |
| *Family Finance Indicators* | | | |
| Personal (Relative) Expectations | Family Finance | Year Ahead | Now looking ahead – Do you think that a year from now you (and your family living there) will be better off financially, or worse off, or just about the same as now? |
| Personal (Relative) Retrospections | Family Finance | Year Ago | Would you say that you (and your family living there) are better off or worse off than you were a year ago? |

economy, better, worse, or about the same. The distinction turns out to have revealing empirical consequences.

Note the symmetry across four of the questions – two retrospective questions about relative economic change in the past, one personal, one "sociotropic," and two prospective questions about relative change in the future. Only *Expectations* asks about the level of prosperity – one year in the future. A challenge before us will be the lack of a direct assessment of the *level* of prosperity today, only whether things have been getting better or worse.

The Survey Research Center has asked the consumer sentiment questions on a quarterly basis since 1954 and on a monthly basis since 1978. We analyze the quarterly means from 1954 through 1996. Except for occasional missing entries, these data provide an almost continuous series spanning 43 years.

## Performance

The paths of our aggregate measures are highly correlated in our time series. Periods of prosperity lead to generalized good feelings, while recessions affect current and prospective evaluations of self and society. Yet the extent of this covariance is not overwhelming. The different series react differently to economic stimuli by taking different paths through time, with the expectations series leading their retrospective realizations.

Our macro-level analysis allows us to investigate the net responses of the national electorate rather than individual voters. A compelling advantage of macro-level analysis is that idiosyncratic sources of variation in economic judgment cancel out. Judgments whether the economy will improve or falter, for example, may be too noisy for worthwhile analysis at the individual level. But their noise cancels out in the aggregate, to provide the powerful measure of collective judgments of the economic future. Moreover, these data from economic surveys are decidedly free of the problem of political response rationalization that plagues micro-level analysis. On balance, the aggregated time-series data set we examine here offers an important degree of inferential leverage that individual-level survey evidence cannot provide.

For a first test of the information claims of rational expectations, we take up the evidence of the impact of expectations on presidential approval. This is the sort of evidence that first led us to consider that a rational expectations account of political behavior might be plausible in MacKuen et al. (1992). Here we extend the data series from that early exercise and repeat the essential evidence for the many readers who have not seen the original.

### Test 1: Presidential Approval

For our quarterly time-series analysis of *Presidential Approval*, we model quarterly *Approval* as a function of lagged *Approval* (at quarter $t - 1$) plus current values of our economic variables of interest. To guard against spurious effects and improve the precision of our estimates, our *Approval* equations also include a number of standard controls, for which we do not present the actual coefficients. These include dummy variables for presidential administrations, Vietnam deaths (for the Johnson presidency), Watergate, the Iran hostage crisis, the Gulf War, and a modest series of important events.[7] The dummies for administra-

---

7 Our strategy here is to use our post hoc knowledge of external disruptions to *Approval* to improve model specification so that the explanations of interest are not forced to try to statistically account for movements they did not cause. Our "events" series is relatively slim, since we sought to include only events that left a major impact on the quarter's average reading, and not just the temporary spike

tions are particularly useful to control for the fact that different presidents start out their terms with different starting values for the economy. We want to compare popularity levels as a function of the economy *within* presidencies rather than across them. By giving different intercepts for different presidents, the presidential dummies in effect allow us to assess whether individual presidents' popularity varies as a function of relative economic prosperity within the president's term.

We proceed in two steps. First, we ask whether consumer sentiment carries the signal of events in the real economy into political evaluation of the president. Second, we will decompose the amalgam of consumer sentiment into its retrospective and prospective elements and ask which is the more important predictor of response to the president.

*Consumer Sentiment and the Objective Economy.* We first set up a base equation predicting approval from objective economic variables. Column 1 of Table 3.2 shows coefficients for the inflation rate and the quarterly change (first difference) in unemployment level, plus the controls for presidencies and presidential events (not shown). As expected, both inflation and unemployment change show significant negative effects on approval.[8]

Column 2 of Table 3.2 introduces the composite *Index of Consumer Sentiment* (*ICS*), which has a decidedly significant impact on *Approval*. Moreover, introduction of the *Index* wipes out the direct contributions of the economic variables. The important inference is that *Consumer Sentiment* is an intervening variable between the objective economy and *Approval*.

of a transitory rally point. Positive events (+1) include the Geneva Summit, 1955:3; Cuban Missile Crisis, 1962:4; Moscow treaty, 1972:2; Paris treaty, 1973:1; *Mayaguez* incident, 1975:2; Camp David Accords, 1978:4; assassination attempt, 1981:2; the Grenada invasion, 1983:4, and the Panama invasion, 1990:1. Two negative events (−1) are Nixon's pardon, 1974:4; and Iranscam, 1986:4. Also, quarters 1973:2–4 are coded as −1 events due to Watergate; Carter's Iran Crisis is coded +2 for 1979:4; 1 for 1980:1; and −1 for 1980:2. The Gulf War is coded +2 for 1991:1. The event effects in the *Approval* equations are in the range of +8 points and highly significant.

8 Unemployment change and inflation rates are the variables most often used in the analysis of approval. Another candidate, growth in real disposable income, makes a significant contribution to the approval series, but only if unemployment change and inflation are omitted from the equation. Growth in the Index of Coincident Indicators offers some improvement over unemployment change and inflation alone. The Index of Coincident Indicators is a comprehensive index that includes employment statistics among its components.

Table 3.2. *Presidential Approval by Economic Conditions and Consumer Sentiment*

| Independent Variable | Approval | | | |
|---|---|---|---|---|
| | (1) | (2) | (3) | (4) |
| Approval$_{t-1}$ | 0.86$^a$ | 0.78$^a$ | 0.84$^a$ | 0.79$^a$ |
| | (21.50) | (19.50) | (21.05) | (19.75) |
| Inflation | −0.28 | 0.01 | | |
| | (−1.75) | (0.06) | | |
| Change in Unemployment | −1.96$^a$ | 1.53 | | |
| | (−2.20) | (1.49) | | |
| Consumer Sentiment | | 0.32$^a$ | | 0.29$^a$ |
| | | (6.40) | | (4.83) |
| Index of Economic Performance | | | 0.20$^a$ | −0.03$^b$ |
| | | | (5.03) | (−0.49) |
| Combined Significance of Inflation and Unemployment Change ($p$) | .0054 | .33$^b$ | | |
| Adjusted $R^2$ | .892 | .911 | .899 | .910 |
| N | (157) | (148) | (157) | (148) |

Note: $t$ statistic in parentheses. Data are quarterly, 1954–1996. Approval estimations include (additional but not shown) variables controlling for political events, Vietnam war, and administration dummy variables. Each column represents a separate regression equation, each with approval as the dependent variable.
$^a$ $p < 0.05$.
$^b$ Test based on coefficients with wrong sign.

A more dramatic demonstration is shown in the estimates of columns 3 and 4. Column 3 shows a highly significant "effect" on approval by quarterly readings of the *Index of Economic Performance*. (Recall from Chapter 2 that this index is a composite of 13 economic indicators weighted to give the maximum prediction of *Consumer Sentiment*.) Measured quarterly, this index correlates at 0.86 with the *Index of Consumer Sentiment*. As column 4 shows, when *Consumer Sentiment* itself is in the equation, the *Index of Economic Performance* loses its significance. Clearly, objective economic indicators affect *Approval* because they affect what people think about the economy.

The objective economy affects *Presidential Approval* by affecting perceptions of the economy, and these perceptions are captured by the *Index of Consumer Sentiment*. But the index comprises several items, which even in the aggregate correlate imperfectly with each other. Our next task is to ascertain which of the indicators that compose the index are the crucial intervening variables between the economy and approval.

Table 3.3. *Predicting Presidential Approval: Three Models*

| Independent Variable | Approval | | |
|---|---|---|---|
| | Pure Retrospections | Adding Expectations | Only Expectations |
| Approval$_{t-1}$ | 0.82[a] | 0.79[a] | 0.80[a] |
| | (20.50) | (19.75) | (20.03) |
| Retrospections | 0.06[a] | −0.01 | |
| | (6.01) | (−0.50) | |
| Expectations | | 0.11[a] | 0.10[a] |
| | | (3.67) | (5.02) |
| Adjusted $R^2$ | .893 | .901 | .911 |
| Standard Error of Estimate | 3.81 | 3.66 | 3.62 |
| N | 143 | 143 | 153 |

*Note*: $t$ statistic in parentheses. Data are quarterly, 1954–1996. Approval estimations include (additionally but not shown) variables controlling for political events, the Vietnam War, and administration dummy variables.
[a] $p < 0.05$.

We now know that *Consumer Sentiment* taps aspects of the public's economic perceptions that are relevant to determining *Presidential Approval*. But which aspect or aspects are most relevant: Is response based on citizens' collective reading of the current economy? Or could the driving force be the public's collective expectations about the nation's economic future? In this section, we examine the statistical evidence.

In Figure 3.1 we laid out three competing stories of how citizens process experience into evaluations: (1) using pure retrospection, (2) forming expectations based solely on retrospection, and (3) forming expectations that also incorporate novel information about conditions not necessarily "experienced," but relevant to forecasting the future economy. Here we explore the three models and take up evidence relevant to testing them.

The pure retrospections formulation has citizens observe economic conditions and decide to reward or punish the incumbent for them. It is "pure" in the sense that it requires no thought of the future. If conditions are good *now*, reward. If not good, punish. It is accordingly simple to operationalize. Our measure *Retrospections* (how good are business conditions compared to a year ago?) captures the essential notion. The first column of Table 3.3 is a preliminary test of pure retrospection. It models *Approval* as a function of lagged *Approval*, *Retrospections*, and the additional specification variables (not shown). The key result is the significant effect of *Retrospections*. Pure retrospection fares well in this preliminary test; evaluation of the current state of the economy clearly does influence *Approval*.

But the issue is not whether retrospective evidence matters. It matters for all three models. The question is whether it matters to the exclusion of future orientations. That requires additional specification. In the second column, we add *Expectations* (how good will the economy be next year?) to the estimation. Here we have immediate evidence that pure retrospection is wrong. *Expectations* has a strong and significant impact on *Approval*. In the presence of *Expectations*, the effect of *Retrospection* disappears from the model, its coefficient wrong-signed and nonsignificant. *Retrospection* matters, but the pure retrospection formulation is clearly wrong; the effect works through *Expectations*. Because the effect is wholly encapsulated in *Expectations*, removing *Retrospection* from the model slightly improves the fit (see column 3). Economic retrospections matter *only* because they influence expectations.[9]

But we have two models that assert that expectations matter. The retrospective expectations account holds that they matter because citizens form expectations from the evidence of retrospection. In this account, *Retrospections* and *Expectations* are essentially the same variable; the latter includes the former with some random fluctuation on top of it. If this were the case, if, that is, expectations carried no systematic signal other than the influence of retrospection, then our statistical expectation is that the two variables should share more or less evenly in the explanation of *Approval*. Clearly they do not.[10] The rational expectations model asserts, in contrast, that expectations do carry an additional signal, that is, the informed speculation about the future economy that arises not from direct experience, but is instead the result of economic forecasts. It is the model most decisively supported by this evidence.[11]

---

9 We model the effect of current rather than lagged *Expectations* on *Approval*. This would lead to biased estimates in the presence of a reverse causal flow from *Approval* to *Expectations*, for instance, if popular presidents had the gift of convincing people that prospects were better than they were. This hypothesis of reverse causality receives no support from the standard Granger test. When *Expectations* (or any other component of *Consumer Sentiment*) is regressed on lagged *Expectations* and lagged *Approval*, lagged *Approval* is decidedly nonsignificant. For further discussion, see MacKuen, Erikson, and Stimson (1992).

10 The data clearly support the rational expectations view here, but a model of expectations based upon retrospections alone would not fare badly. We will present evidence separating the two in analyses to come.

11 In MacKuen et al. (1992) and in earlier versions of this analysis, we entertained regression "races" where large numbers of factors were allowed to affect *Approval*. The "race" evidence consistently supports the rational expectations conclusion we report here. We also have examined alternative specifications of

## Expectations and Political Response

The bottom line of this first test is this: Given information about the economic present and future, citizens use both in assessing the president. The easy test is easily passed.

### Test 2: The Origin of Expectations

If presidential approval is closely tied to the electorate's expectations about the economy, where do these expectations come from? Our next challenge is to offer a fuller accounting of the sources of aggregate business expectations. A beginning of an answer is that people are embedded in a rich system of social communication. The social communication network is full of information not only about the past and the present, but also about the future. Any encounter with the nightly news will subject the viewer to the bullish or bearish views of politicians or Wall Streeters or economic correspondents. The news stories tell of new developments, sometimes citing inflation or unemployment numbers, but more often describing a war, a drought, a strike, a currency fluctuation, or the daily rise and fall of the stock market. Almost inevitably, such events are read as good or bad omens. While the particulars of such accounts may fail to register in the public's consciousness, our evidence suggests that the general sense of optimism or pessimism seeps through the system in politically important ways.

The experts who translate the economic numbers into good times and bad times attend to more than the standard news. In the business of looking ahead, they absorb news that is critical to professional forecasting but often of little direct interest to the general public. Their translations convey their sophisticated understanding to all. Without trying, the public is exposed to the best information about the economic future that exists: Merely by noting that most forecasters say good (bad) times are ahead, the public becomes subject to the causal influence of the professionals' more esoteric tools.

If this story fits the truth of the flow of economic news, it follows that we should find some of the innovations in expectations flowing from early indicators of the economic future, such as the Commerce Department's *Index of Leading Economic Indicators*. This *Index* measures the economic winds that are not otherwise apparent from current measures such as unemployment and inflation. We do not assert that the public monitors the *Leading Indicators* directly, nor do we believe that the *Index* comprises the entirety of economic intelligence. Rather, changes

the equations in Erikson, MacKuen, and Stimson (2000). The evidence consistently supports the dominant role of *Expectations*. We have excluded this evidence for brevity.

Table 3.4. *Explaining Components of Consumer Sentiment*

| Independent Variables | Dependent Variable | | |
|---|---|---|---|
| | Expectations | Economic News | Expectations |
| Inflation | −1.52[a] | −1.05[a] | −0.61 |
| | (−4.57) | (−2.39) | (−1.33) |
| Change in Unemployment | −4.32 | −12.23[a] | 10.72[a] |
| | (−1.34) | (−2.55) | (2.90) |
| Growth in Leading Indicators | 0.53[a] | 0.89[a] | 0.36[a] |
| | (3.31) | (4.94) | (2.25) |
| Personal Retrospections | | | 0.22 |
| | | | (1.57) |
| Economic News | | | 0.33[a] |
| | | | (4.71) |
| Expectations$_{t-1}$ | 0.77[a] | | 0.69[a] |
| | (15.40) | | (13.80) |
| Economic News$_{t-1}$ | | 0.52[a] | |
| | | (7.43) | |
| Adjusted $R^2$ | .893 | .780 | .888 |
| Standard Error of Estimate | 11.14 | 12.02 | 7.07 |
| N | 111 | 102 | 109 |

Note: *t* statistic in parentheses. Data are quarterly, 1954–1988.
[a] $p < 0.05$.

in the *Leading Indicators* provide a rough and consistently available measure of shifting expert forecasts. When the *Leading Indicators* influence the forecasters, that influence should find its way into ordinary people's views.

We test this thesis with a series of regressions, shown in Table 3.4, modeling quarterly *Expectations* and (for comparison) other *ICS* components. On the right-hand side, these equations include (1) lagged levels of the dependent variable, (2) the usual suspects of unemployment change and the inflation rate, plus (3) the annualized quarterly *growth* in the *Index of Leading Indicators*. Because the current version of the *Index* incorporates the *Index of Consumer Expectations* (Hertzberg and Beckman 1989), we are limited to the pre-1989 version, which was uncontaminated by direct measures of consumer expectations. Thus, this one analysis is limited to the years 1954–1988.[12]

12 The quarterly measure of leading indicators used here is lagged one month. For instance, for quarter 4 we use months 9, 10, and 11. (The growth measure is the average of three three-month growth readings, and is scaled as quarterly growth.) The time adjustment is to make the relevant time frame of leading indicators com-

## Expectations and Political Response

We predict *Expectations* in Table 3.4, column 1. In this equation, the contribution of inflation is significant, while that of unemployment change is in the expected direction but not significant. Bouts of inflation, of course, increase individual economic uncertainty and thus reduce confidence in the future. More to our point, however, current unemployment is not seen as a harbinger of the long-term economic future. The *Index of Leading Indicators*, meanwhile, shows a statistically significant effect, just as our social communications model predicts.

We have argued that the electorate develops its economic expectations from the economic forecasts available in the mass media. To test this proposition, we can exploit another item from the Survey of Consumer Finances that we have hitherto ignored. Most *Consumer Sentiment* surveys include an item asking respondents' perceptions of recent economic news:

*During the last few months, have you heard any favorable or unfavorable changes in business conditions? What did you hear?*

Aggregated, this measure of *Economic News* is the net balance of positive versus negative news about the economy during the quarter. The question has a retrospective flavor that should prompt responsiveness to reports of current conditions (people out of work or back on the job, inflation at the supermarket) as well as reported revisions in economic forecasts. According to Tims, Fan, and Freeman (1989), this aggregate measure is strongly responsive to the actual valence of economic news reported in the media. Column 2 of Table 3.4 shows the *Economic News* equation. Provocatively, this measure is very strongly responsive to growth and decline of the *Index of Leading Economic Indicators*. Thus, it appears that the economic news people remember is about the future more than the past.

When people make judgments about the current or future economy, they must rely almost entirely on two sources of information: their personal experience and the available economic news. We now have a survey-based measure of each: *Personal Retrospections* measures the aggregate sense of personal economic well-being within the electorate. *Economic News* measures the direction of economic news that people report hearing. We can incorporate each as an independent variable in our equations predicting *Expectations*. The results are shown in Table 3.4, column 3.

parable to the other quarterly indicators. The monthly index is not public knowledge until late the following month. Monthly readings of current indicators are also reported on a delayed basis, but their measurement supposedly represents the experiential basis of economic information. The *Index of Leading Economic Indicators* is a proxy for available forecasts.

## Performance

As expected, *Economic News* makes a significant contribution to *Expectations*. Including *Economic News* removes some of the direct effect of *Leading Indicators* (compare column 1), as if economic forecasts affect expectations by passing through the *Economic News*. Further, neither unemployment change (wrong sign) nor aggregate *Personal Retrospections* contributes to *Expectations*. Even inflation, which can be directly experienced by all, shows no statistically significant effect. Collectively, people do not seem to make a connection between their current standard of living and the economic future. Instead, they judge the future based on what they are told in the mass media.[13]

The electorate acts as if it develops sophisticated expectations based on economic forecasts rather than current economic conditions. This follows because, in the final analysis, the electorate bases its expectations on what is reported in the news. And the news reports what the future holds.

*The Quality of Expectations.* The traditional retrospective view of the political response to the economy holds that people update their presidential evaluations from ongoing observation of the economy *as* it happens. This view is incomplete in one important respect. Our contrary view is that when people evaluate the president they also incorporate updated forecasts of the economy *before* it happens. Stating the distinction this way focuses attention on the quality of expectations. Put simply, can people foresee upcoming economic change with any meaningful accuracy? Can the electorate collectively foresee likely outcomes any better by gazing into the fuzzy future than it can by simply extrapolating from the relative clarity of the recent past? Our answer to that is yes.

To understand this answer, it is helpful to remind ourselves that the mass perception that drives approval is not *relative* expectations ("will times get better or worse?") but rather expectations about the *level* of prosperity. Expectations of the level of prosperity at some future time must be a combination of the perceived prosperity today, plus expectations of economic growth between today and the future time. In this section, we examine the variable we call *Expectations*, defined as the

---

13 We could also insert *Retrospections* on the right-hand side of the *Expectations* equation. When this is done, *Retrospections* are decidedly not significant while its close correlate, *Economic News*, retains its statistically significant stature. We should generally be cautious about interpreting coefficients for survey items on the right-hand side of the equations predicting ICS components. The dependent variable and the independent variable are likely to share the same survey error (oversampling of optimists or pessimists).

expected *level* of prosperity one year ahead. Let us label the level of prosperity experienced at time $t$ as simply $P_t$. *Expected* prosperity four quarters ahead is then the experienced prosperity today plus the expected change over the following four quarters, or simply:

$$E(P_{t+4}) = P_t + E(P_{t+4} - P_t) \qquad (3.1)$$

We see that $E(P_{t+4})$ has two components, the foundation of experienced prosperity at time $t$ plus the expected change over the following year. In this section, we examine these two components. First, we evaluate the quality of the electorate's expectations of relative change over the following year, *Relative Expectations*, the equivalent of $E(P_{t+4} - P_t)$ in our new terminology. Second, we analyze the foundation of experienced prosperity $P_t$. Because the *Consumer Sentiment* surveys ascertain retrospections of the economy only in the form of *relative* change and not the *level* of prosperity, estimating $P_t$ presents something of a challenge. Yet estimating $P_t$ is of particular interest for several reasons. We want to know how much $P_t$ is updated from realizations of economic change that depart from their advance expectations. Second, we want to know how much the citizenry discounts economic change from the past when it forms its perceptions of $P_t$. Finally, we want to see how accurately $E(P_{t+4})$ matches actual $P_{t+4}$. In other words, how much accuracy regarding the economic future does the electorate gain by estimating the future prospectively as $E(P_{t+4})$ rather than a simple retrospective extrapolation from observed $P_t$?

*Relative Expectations.* How accurate are the electorate's aggregate forecasts of economic change? Using the *Relative* measure of *Expectations*, we can assess how well *expected* growth for the following year corresponds to the amount of economic growth that actually occurs. Table 3.5 presents the correlations of objectively measured economic change with its advance expectation and, for comparison, its retrospective recall. Our objective indicator is per capita income growth, measured over four quarters (*One-Year Income Growth*).[14] We relate *One-Year Income Growth* over the previous four quarters to *current* retrospections of the past year and to *lagged* economic expectations measured one year before. All measures of expectations and retrospections are of *relative* conditions (better vs. worse), with a one-year perspective forward or backward in time. We ask, how well does the electorate predict the eco-

14 Per capita income growth is the ideal criterion variable because it is virtually uncorrelated from year to year. As a result, the log of per capita income behaves as a unit root variable. The next growth rate cannot be predicted from its current value.

Table 3.5. *Correlations Between Income Growth, Retrospections, and Expectations*

|  | Last Year's Income Growth | Next Year's Income Growth | N |
|---|---|---|---|
| Personal Retrospections | .54 | .25 | 169 |
| Business Retrospections | .64 | .24 | 149 |
| Personal Expectations | .39 | .37 | 159 |
| Relative Expectations | .19 | .45 | 154 |
| Expectations | .46 | .34 | 164 |
| Five-Year Expectations | .39 | .32 | 161 |
| Economic News | .57 | .41 | 145 |

*Note*: Based on quarterly data, 1954–1996. Income Growth is for quarters $t - 4$ to $t$ or quarters $t$ to $t + 4$.

nomic future, relative to the accuracy of its collective retrospections about the recent economic past?

The correlations between expectations and the actual readings of *One-Year Income Growth* are positive. They are of modest magnitude, suggesting that the electorate may not be able to see the economic future any better than, say, economists. These correlations of personal expectations and business expectations with future growth are more impressive when viewed in the context of the surprisingly modest correlations between retrospections (personal or business) and actual income growth recently experienced. Income growth is more accurately perceived when it has already occurred than when it is merely expected, but the difference is not overwhelming.[15]

The far from perfect correlations between the objective and subjective versions of the recently experienced economy indicate that the subjective economy is somewhat different from the one objectively measured by income growth. If the perceived and objective economies are different, perhaps the public is better able to predict its future *subjective* economic state a year ahead than its *objective* state in one year. This conjecture is confirmed: Both sets of current expectations for change from $t$ to $t + 4$

15 For both *Expectations* and *Retrospections*, the public responds as if it takes the one-year horizon seriously. When *Retrospections*, for example, is regressed on per capita income growth for quarters for quarters $t - 4$ through $t$, all quarterly readings are statistically significant. When the reading for quarter $t - 5$ is added, it is not significant. More interesting, when *Relative Expectations* is regressed on income growth for each of the next four quarters, each measure is statistically significant. The reading for the fifth quarter forward, however, is not.

predict their retrospective counterparts measured one year in the future (looking backward at experienced change, $t$ to $t + 4$) better than they predict objective *Income Growth Next Year* (from $t$ to $t + 4$). In fact, aggregate personal expectations actually predict year-ahead personal retrospections better than does the objective economy as measured by the experienced per capita income growth for the year (.68 vs. .54). And business expectations predict future business retrospections almost as well as per capita income growth (.57 vs. .63). In other words, if one knows the income growth for a year's interval, and knows public expectations a year earlier, the two variables are about equally useful for predicting the amount of economic change actually perceived by the public.[16]

## Current and Future Prosperity, as the Electorate Sees It

The driving force of presidential approval is not expected economic *change* but the expectation of the future *level* of prosperity, reflected in *Expectations*. Good times in the future are a function of future growth, but also a function of the size of the foundation of current prosperity. Thus, *Expectations* has a built-in retrospective component. One's perception of the goodness or badness of the economic times next year (and beyond) must depend in part on what is known about economic

---

16 Below we test whether *Expectations* are rational, balancing retrospective and prospective components efficiently. At this juncture, we can ask whether *Relative Expectations* are rational. To do this, we assume that *Relative Expectations* comprise the public's forecast of *Next Year's Income Growth*. The empirical question is whether aggregate expectations of the next year's economic growth are generated efficiently from the information that people hold. We assume people know three pieces of information: their individual estimates of current *Retrospections* and *Personal Retrospections* plus the *Economic News*.

For the test, we regress *Next Year Income Growth* on *Relative Expectations* and compute residuals. These residuals are the forecast errors, which we regress on the three predictors. The results are decidedly nonsignificant, meaning that we tentatively *accept* the rational expectations conclusion. The theoretical argument is that when the electorate forms expectations as a weighted composite of subjective *Retrospections*, *Economic News*, plus other intangible considerations, the electorate chooses efficient weights for the best prediction. Even when objective economic indicators (unemployment change, *Leading Indicator* growth) are entered as predictor variables, one cannot obtain an impressively significant explanation of forecast errors. In other words, once public short-term expectations are taken into account, it is a challenge to round up other variables that collectively add significantly to the prediction of future income growth.

times today, which is itself an accumulation of economic change from the past.

Earlier, Equation 3.1 defined this foundation as $P_t$ in

$$E(P_{t+4}) = P_t + E(P_{t+4} - P_t),$$

where the economy is expected to be in four quarters $(E(P_{t+4}))$, that is, a function of where it is perceived to be now $(P_t)$ and expectations of relative movement, for better or worse, over the coming year $[E(P_{t+4} - P_t)]$. Now we are ready to exploit measured consumer attitudes to empirically estimate each of the components of Equation 3.1.

Two of the terms have empirical indicators: *Expectations* stands in for $E(P_{t+4})$ and *Relative Expectations* measures $E(P_{t+4} - P_t)$. There is no direct measure of perceived current prosperity, $P_t$. That would require a survey question of the form, "How good is the economy now?" when what is actually asked is a comparison to the previous year.

If we knew last year's prosperity, then we could control its contribution to the evaluation of current business conditions "compared to a year ago." That suggests an estimation strategy. Since we have these relative evaluations going back almost five decades, if we incorporate all of them into our estimate, we effectively control the influence of comparison of present to past.

Thus, although we lack a direct measure of perceived current *Prosperity*, we can manufacture one as a weighted average of retrospections past and present, weighting so that more recent perceptions of change count the most. We model *Expectations* $[E(P_{t+4})]$ from *Relative Expectations* $[E(P_{t+4} - P_t)]$ and current *Prosperity*. We create *Prosperity* as an index of weighted retrospections, past and present. Our weighting scheme discounts the past by .73 every year.[17]

We observe the estimated prosperity, along with *Expectations*, in Figure 3.2. The figure shows the time series of estimated *Prosperity* and *Expectations*, starting with 1961.[18] Clearly, *Expectations* serves as a leading indicator of perceived prosperity, which traces the same path with a delay of a quarter or two. The two variables correlate at .82 con-

---

17 *Prosperity* is a weighted function of prior innovations in retrospections. Thus, for example, the value for 1960 would be the current innovation plus .73 times the innovation from 4 quarters previous, plus $.73^2$ times the innovation 4 quarters before that, and on backward in time to our 1952 beginning point. For more detail on procedure, see Erikson, MacKuen, and Stimson (2000).

18 We start with 1961 to allow several quarters to go by before we use the weighted cumulative variables. Although their pre-1954 contributions cannot be factored in, after 28 quarters their theoretical contributions would be so lightly weighted as to be safely ignored.

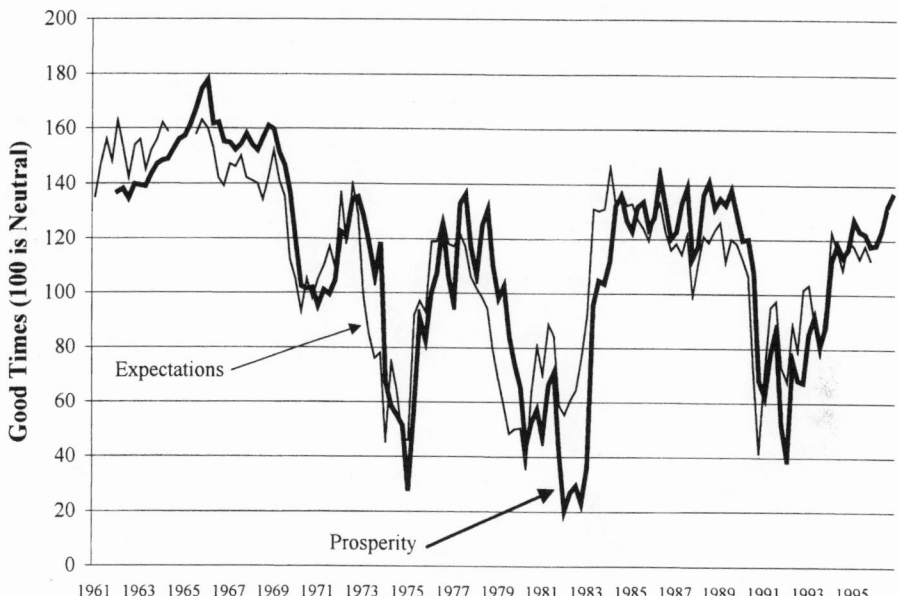

Figure 3.2. Expected Year-Ahead Prosperity and Estimated Prosperity

currently and .84 when *Expectations* is measured one quarter ahead of perceived realizations.[19]

Now we can estimate our *Expectations* equation. Our goal in doing so is to observe the two key coefficients on current prosperity and expected relative change over the year. We wish to know (1) whether both sorts of information are used in forming expectations, and (2) whether the electorate uses them efficiently or instead engages in some nonrational discounting (which implies wasted information). The first question is easily answered in the first column of Table 3.6, where both current prosperity and relative expectations are seen to weigh heavily in forming (absolute) expectations for the year-ahead economy. The very clean fit ($R^2 = .95$) and very strong significance of each term leave no room for doubt. Equation 3.1 is a tautology. What we learn from the empirical estimation of it is that the components behave as they should.

---

19 Because of its discounting of the past, *Current Prosperity* does not correlate with objective prosperity measured as *Logged Per Capita Income*. However, it does correlate with cumulative weighted *Per Capita Income Growth*. The weighting scheme that maximizes the correlation with *Prosperity* ($r = .74$), weighs each quarter's income growth .84 times the previous quarter's, as if the electorate discounts the economic past by .84 each passing quarter.

Table 3.6. *Predicting Expectations and Actual Outcomes: Are Expectations Weighted Appropriately?*

| Term | Indicator | Predicting Year-Ahead Expectations: $E(P_{t+4})$ | Predicting Actual Outcomes: $P_{t+4}$ |
|---|---|---|---|
| $E(P_{t+4} - P_t)$ | Relative Expectations | $1.11^a$ (27.75) | $1.18^a$ (7.38) |
| $P_t$ | Prosperity (Cumulated Retrospections) | $0.56^a$ (56.01) | $0.61^a$ (12.20) |
| Intercept | | −9.59 (1.93) | $−132.50^a$ (−46.99) |
| $R^2$ | | .946 | .628 |
| Standard Error of Estimate | | 7.28 | 26.0 |
| N | | 141 | 137 |

*Note:* $t$ statistic in parentheses. Data are quarterly, 1961–1996. Approval estimates include (additionally but not shown) variables controlling for political events, the Vietnam War, and administration dummy variables.
$^a$ $p < 0.05$.

Neither *Current Prosperity* nor *Relative Expectations* is an adequate predictor of *Expectations* for whether the economy will be (absolutely) good or bad. The tautology requires that they work in tandem, and that is what we observe.

## Test 3: Are Expectations Formed Efficiently?

The equation doesn't tell us how to answer our second question. It has no parameters for the two components and thus no standard against which to measure our observed parameters. How big should the weight on current prosperity be? How big the weight on relative change? What we know is that expected change has about double the influence of current prosperity in our estimates (1.11 compared to 0.56). Is that ratio the right one? To get leverage on that issue we perform a second regression in which we predict year-ahead *Prosperity* $(P_{t+4})$ using the same two variables.[20] Our purpose is to observe the relative weight on *Expectations* when removing the psychological element from assessment of future prosperity.

The result, in the second regression of Table 3.6, is striking. It produces nearly the same parameters as the first and the same 2 to 1 ratio

---

20 Our measure here is the same series from which we estimate $P_t$, except with a four-quarter lead.

(1.18 compared to .61) of future to current appraisals.[21] Whatever the perfect weight may be, this one is best in the sense of predicting actual outcomes. Any other ratio would err by weighting either current or future too heavily. Thus we conclude that the public uses the information it possesses about current and future economy efficiently. *Rational Expectations* requires efficient information use. We observe efficient information use. Thus the *Rational Expectations* view of the world looks right, at least for this question.

We know now that information about the future economy is used efficiently, at least by one limited test. But does this efficiency matter, or is it an increment meaningful only to theory? To address this question, we need to ask how much the electorate gains by using information about the future over what could be known from simple retrospection.

The electorate's gain from this collective rationality can be seen from the following calculations. First, we note that *Prosperity$_t$* statistically accounts for but 48 percent of the variation in *Prosperity$_{t+4}$*. Thus, a simple persistence forecast predicts less than half the variance in the experienced economy one year ahead. *Expectations$_t$* explains 68 percent of the variance in *Prosperity$_{t+4}$*, so that current expectations predict about two-thirds of the variance in the experienced economy a year ahead. Thus, taking expectations into account offers a 42 percent improvement (20/48) over simple retrospections. Put another way, the gain from expectations is a full 38 percent of the distance (20/52) between retrospective extrapolation and perfect foresight. Efficiency matters; it produces notably better judgments.

### Test 4: Does Approval Reflect Efficient Information Use?

We now see that retrospective economic change makes a powerful contribution to the expectations that govern presidential approval. As the electorate updates its estimates of the expected quality of the economy in the foreseeable future, it takes into account not only the changing relative expectations but also shifting retrospections that represent actual realizations of the economy (as *experienced*). Once each new time period results in new realizations, expectations from the past leave no statistical trace in current *Expectations*.[22] This is as it should be. Just as

21 Other analyses, not shown, employ disposable income either on the left-hand side at $t + 4$, the right-hand side at $t$, or both in place of the Estimate $P_t$. The same result, the roughly 2 to 1 ratio of coefficients, obtains in each of these analyses.

22 For instance, if lagged *Relative Expectations* is cumulated in the same manner as retrospections, the cumulation does not add significantly to the prediction of *Expectations*. Past errors in expectations are corrected by subsequent retrospections.

Table 3.7. *The Prediction of Approval Decomposed into Present and Future*

| Independent Variables | The "Standard" Model Repeated | Predicting from Current and Future Components |
|---|---|---|
| Approval$_{t-1}$ | 0.80[a] | 0.81[a] |
| | (20.03) | (20.25) |
| Expectations | 0.10[a] | |
| | (5.02) | |
| Relative Expectations | | 0.10[a] |
| | | (3.33) |
| Prosperity | | 0.05[a] |
| | | (20.01) |
| $R^2$ | .907 | .907 |
| Standard Error of Estimate | 3.67 | 3.71 |
| N | 129 | 129 |

*Note: t* statistic in parentheses. Data are quarterly, 1961–1996. Approval estimates include (additionally but not shown) variables controlling for political events, the Vietnam War, and administration dummy variables.
[a] $p < 0.05$.

the electorate takes into account more than retrospections when developing expectations about the economic future, it does not ignore the instances when past expectations about short-term change turn out to be wrong. Thus, we need not worry that a government could continually fool the public with a stream of economic forecasts that is rosier than the realizations. Even if the public believes the next forecast of better times, it factors in the realizations from the past when estimating the net quality of the economic future.

The public's expectations of the future economy are based on both a foundation of the current economy (with recent inputs weighted the highest) plus expectations of future change, which are more accurate than we might have thought. The significance for *Presidential Approval* is that the public incorporates its partial knowledge of the future when it collectively evaluates the president based on the economy. Let us return to the *Approval* equation once again. First we reestimate our standard *Approval* model as a function of *Expectations* for the 1961–1996 period (see Table 3.7).

Our *Expectations* measure is a significant predictor of *Approval*. Next, we break *Expectations* down into the two key components of the previous section: *Relative Expectations* and (current) *Prosperity*. The earlier analysis showed a 2:1 ratio of the two components, predicting either year-ahead expectations or actual year-ahead prosperity. For the most efficient result, we expect the same ratio of 2:1 when these two variables are employed to predict *Approval*. This is the result in Table 3.7. Thus we see that the electorate weighs the past and expectations efficiently when assessing the president. These expectations present an advantage over simple extrapolation from the economic past. When the electorate evaluates the president based on expectations of the future, the electorate gives appropriate weight to the foundation of the retrospective past and its expectations regarding economic change.

### CONCLUSIONS: A FARSIGHTED ELECTORATE?

We have presented a theoretical and empirical case for the U.S. electorate using rational expectations when judging the president's economic performance. Voters respond in terms of their expectations of the future level of prosperity. These expectations efficiently weigh retrospective and prospective knowledge of the economy. The prospective information adds an appreciable increment to the information about the economic future for evaluating the president.

That the public uses rational expectations rather than simple retrospections strikes some observers as preposterous at first. Yet we know that the public, as an aggregate, uses both previous experience and novel information in order to judge the economic future. This hardly seems startling when we notice that the public, as consumers and producers, constitutes the economy. The rational expectations proposition is that the same people, empowered with an understanding of political economics beyond a simple projection of the past into the future, use all the information at hand. When making political judgments, people do not discard the information they use when they make economic judgments but instead use it to make sense of the political world.

Understanding that expectations lie at the core of political evaluations forces a new view of the political economy. When citizens are retrospective, their politics are grounded in reality – personally experienced or observed in others. When citizens act on expectations, they rely on an informed imagination. This transformation of the base of politics, from reality to imagination, suggests a serious reconsideration of the role that information – and information production – plays in the polity.

First, think about the potential for political actors to manipulate economic and political outcomes. We might imagine such perversities as the president who maintains approval by continually convincing the electorate that prosperity is around the corner even as the economy actually declines, or the reverse, a president who is pilloried for negative economic forecasts even as the economy continues to prosper. We do not envision perverse scenarios such as these for two reasons. First, if such patterns existed, they would be manifest in the data. We would find extended periods when expectations persist in one direction even though their trailing retrospections go the other. We find no such patterns. While one quarter's innovation in economic expectations may be wrong in one direction, the next quarter's innovation may err in the opposite direction. As these innovations accumulate, the errors cancel out to produce an accumulation of expectations that closely matches accumulated realizations. Second, and more importantly, when the electorate modifies its approval in response to a forecast that later proves to be mistaken, the electorate will eventually correct its evaluation in accordance to reality. In other words, the electorate responds both to the immediate surprise of revised forecasts and to the gradual surprise of errors in past forecasts.

Further, because the electorate is farsighted rather than myopic, it is less easily fooled by the kinds of short-term fiscal or monetary strategies that supposedly give rise to political business cycles of the sort where presidents overheat the economy for short-term political gain (e.g., Nordhaus 1975; Tufte 1978). Recent work on the political business cycle, in fact, assumes that the electorate enjoys the necessary sophistication to take into account the motivations of political leaders (Rogoff and Sibert 1988; Alesina and Rosenthal 1995). Beyond the question of strategic manipulation, we must understand that even voters with farsightedness are at the mercy of the quality of the available information. For the electorate to properly evaluate presidential performance, a requirement is that economic forecasts be accurate and readily available. Our research suggests these conditions are met, but that the hold may be fragile.

Intriguing is the possibility that the electorate evaluates presidents on the basis of expectations that are self-fulfilling – as if consumer confidence by itself boosts the economy.[23] When expectations are self-fulfilling, judgments based on those expectations will always appear to be sound even when they represent little more than fantasy. For the practical policy maker, self-fulfilling expectations are two-edged: It is possible to effect economic and political change by affecting expectations alone. But political actors may, on the other hand, be unable to effect

---

23 Economists have long debated the role of consumer expectations in predicting economic growth. The empirical demonstration of a causal link from expectations to economic growth faces a special challenge. This is because residual effects of consumer expectations – unaccounted for by economic "fundamentals" – may be an artifact of omitted variables. For recent claims that consumer sentiment either affects (or uniquely predicts) the economic future, see Fuhrer 1988 and Matsusaka and Sbornone 1989. Whether causal agents or not, consumer expectations are often thought to predict economic change. Witness the Commerce Department's inclusion, starting in 1989, of the Survey Research Center's Index of Consumer Expectations (of which our *Expectations* is a part) as a component of its revised *Index of Leading Economic Indicators*.

real change when expectations discount current acts. (For a thoughtful discussion and evidence on the matter, see Alt 1991.) For the political theorist, the matter is more profound: If political judgments are self-sustaining, by what standard can one measure the wisdom of democratic decisions? By what standard can one measure success?

Although we have presented evidence of an impressive economic intelligence on the part of the U.S. electorate, it is worth repeating that this result depends on the power of aggregation. As individuals, voters show no strong talent for economic forecasting. Massive biases and seemingly random errors swamp whatever accuracy is present in individual forecasts (Conover et al. 1987). When these weak forecasts are aggregated, however, the noise cancels out to leave only a signal surviving. The process of aggregating information is not unlike the process that leads a large jury to reach an accurate verdict in situations when individual jurors may not (Grofman and Owens 1986; Miller 1986).

Our results do suggest one reason to offer special praise for the individual qualities of American voters. This is the electorate's choice of economic signal to guide its political judgments. Instead of judging presidents retrospectively, based on economic conditions as they happen, voters respond prospectively to the likely economic future. While evidence of prospective behavior is limited to the evaluations of the economy and the president (and thus does not directly address matters of policy and voting), it suggests richer possibilities in the political system than are often assumed. When politicians know that people care about the future, they will act accordingly. Thus, while a myopic electorate produces short time horizons for politicians, a farsighted electorate may reward policies that extend beyond the next election. The fact that the aggregate public listens to, and moves in accord with, an informed elite analysis empowers that public to make collective political judgments quite beyond the individual talents of its members.

### Is It Just Economic Expectations?

We have seen that economic expectations are formed as predicted from the rational expectations theory. The evidence is very strong. Now the issue at hand is this: Have we observed the *only* case in which citizens are forward looking in their behavior? Or is the formation of beliefs about the future economy just the best empirical testbed for a phenomenon that is ubiquitous in the life of the polity? We believe the latter is the case, and so we must ask what is special about the evidence we have observed.

What is crucial about the economic expectations case is not that it involves economics or that we have good measures (although both help). What permits the analysis is the fact that the expectations formed from observation and experience sometimes differ from expectations based upon informed forecasts. Because they sometimes differ, it becomes possible to separate out the information and ask which sort matters and by how much. That is what we have exploited.

Is it ever the case outside of economics that citizens have information about the future that diverges from the information of experience? Imagine the following illustration as a sort of thought experiment. Voters in multicandidate elections such as the typical early stages of American presidential primaries face a situation that requires strategic calculation. A vote for the most preferred candidate will sometimes simply contribute to that candidate's victory and therefore effectively transmit the voter preference into governance. But often it will be the case that the most preferred candidate has little chance of winning at later stages, so that voting for him or her might inadvertently contribute to an outcome that violates the voter's preference. Thus voters will need to think about both who they prefer and whether the vote will have undesirable consequences if the preferred candidate is not ultimately elected. This is just a standard strategic voting scenario. Voters will have an information set containing knowledge about the viability of the preferred candidate from performance in other previous contests. But if they attend at all to media reports, they will also be exposed to forecasts of later success and failure. These forecasts, just like those of economics, will be based on leading indicators that have predictive value (e.g., polls in states with later primaries, analysis of candidate funds availability, and so forth). This will be novel information to most voters, who, like the consumers that they are, are not professionals.

In this scenario, we, along with campaigns, candidates, and pundits, expect the same result. We expect, that is, that ill-informed voters will in the aggregate act as if informed by strategic calculation, and that expectations – the fruit of expert calculation – will influence behavior. We thus venture the hesitant conclusion that rational expectations will be apparent in politics whenever the future differs from the present and whenever it is possible through informed speculation to have some purchase on that future.

*Approval* varies. Its ups and downs make for bright or dreary presidencies, happy or unhappy White Houses, probably for strong or weak ones. But it is stationary in the long view; its excesses up or down get corrected. But we ask if they also leave a permanent trace. To answer that question, in Chapter 4 we look at partisanship, a matter of standing decisions, not momentary evaluations. Partisanship will turn out to be related to *Approval*, capturing its fast dynamics and holding them in a more permanent reservoir of attitudes toward the parties.

# 4

## Macropartisanship: The Permanent Memory of Party Performance

In early 1973, Richard Nixon and his Republican Party both were riding high. The past November, Nixon had been reelected in a record landslide. Then, as the first major act of his second term, Nixon concluded a peace treaty to end the Vietnam War. The political image of the day was of American prisoners of war returning to the United States, kissing American soil on landing, and praising the president of the United States for their return. This is about as good as it gets for political leaders. Nixon's 65 percent *Approval* rating in the February Gallup Poll showed that most Americans approved of Nixon's presidential performance. Meanwhile, while Nixon enjoyed this pinnacle of success, about one in four Americans answered "Republican" to Gallup's query, *"In politics as of today, do you consider yourself a Republican, a Democrat, or an Independent?"* This was the normal "party identification" response for the Nixon years to that point.

Then on March 6, 1973, awaiting sentencing on what was expected to be the end of the peculiar incident of the break-in to Democratic Party headquarters at the Watergate complex, James McCord said in open court that the break-in was orchestrated by high government officials whose role was subject to a continuing cover-up. Thus began the most important presidential scandal in American history. Before it ran its course, ending in Nixon's resignation in August 1974, Watergate would be an almost unimaginable nightmare for Nixon's party. In partisan terms, the political damage was entirely one-sided. The guilty parties were all Republicans, and each, before he went down, was publicly defended by other Republicans. And it sat at the center of American politics, week after week, month after month. In the end, almost everyone turned on Richard Nixon. In the final days, only family members would step forward to defend the president.

Watergate was a time of disillusion and despair, affecting Republicans most of all. It is hard to imagine a series of events that could do more to discredit and disable a political party than having its leader turned out of office in public humiliation. Thus we might expect that many millions of Americans, whose disgust with Nixon was not in doubt, would turn away from his party and could no longer "consider themselves" Republicans. Let us look at the poll numbers at the time of Nixon's resignation.

Judging from the Gallup poll, most of those who had approved of Nixon in February 1973 withdrew their support by summer 1974. By the time Nixon was poised to resign, his approval rating had plunged to a near-record low of 24 percent, indicating that he had lost the support of about 60 percent of his onetime supporters. The impact on partisanship, however, was much less severe. The more than 25 percent who claimed Republican identification in early 1973 reduced to about 22 percent when Nixon left office. (See Figure 4.1.) By our best estimate, the drop-off of Republican identification during the Watergate period was 3.7 points, or a loss of about 15 percent of the party's early 1973 identifiers.

The post-Watergate drop-off in Republican identification was real, not a statistical artifact. And it was not trivial. But we must be impressed that this deeply embarrassing and long-lasting scandal left the partisan sentiment of 85 percent of the Republicans intact. That tells us something of great importance about the permanence of party ties, that this worst possible party disaster eroded the loyalties of only a relative few. At least for some partisans, some of the time, partisanship must run far deeper than an evaluation of how well the party has performed lately. Nothing else would have mitigated this disaster for the Republicans. No small number of citizens must have said, in effect, "I *am* a Republican, no matter how bad things are for my party."

Now, let us look at the same political statistics from a different perspective. The major drop in Nixon's popularity had consequences that, though obviously major, were short-lived. Once Gerald Ford ascended to the presidency, the public had a new president to evaluate on the basis of his own actions rather than those of his predecessor. Meanwhile, the small drop in Republican partisanship, while going virtually unnoticed at the time, had lasting consequences for the political future. Throughout the latter half of the 1970s, the Republican Party remained in public disfavor, not only losing the adherence of a significant fraction of its former adherents, but also (judging from opinion polls) gaining dangerously few new adherents among young voters. The consequences could be seen not only in Democrat Jimmy Carter's capture of the White House in 1976 but also in the extraordinary Democratic dominance below the presidential level in the elections of 1974, 1976, and 1978. That Republican fortunes began to reverse starting in 1980 shows that partisan

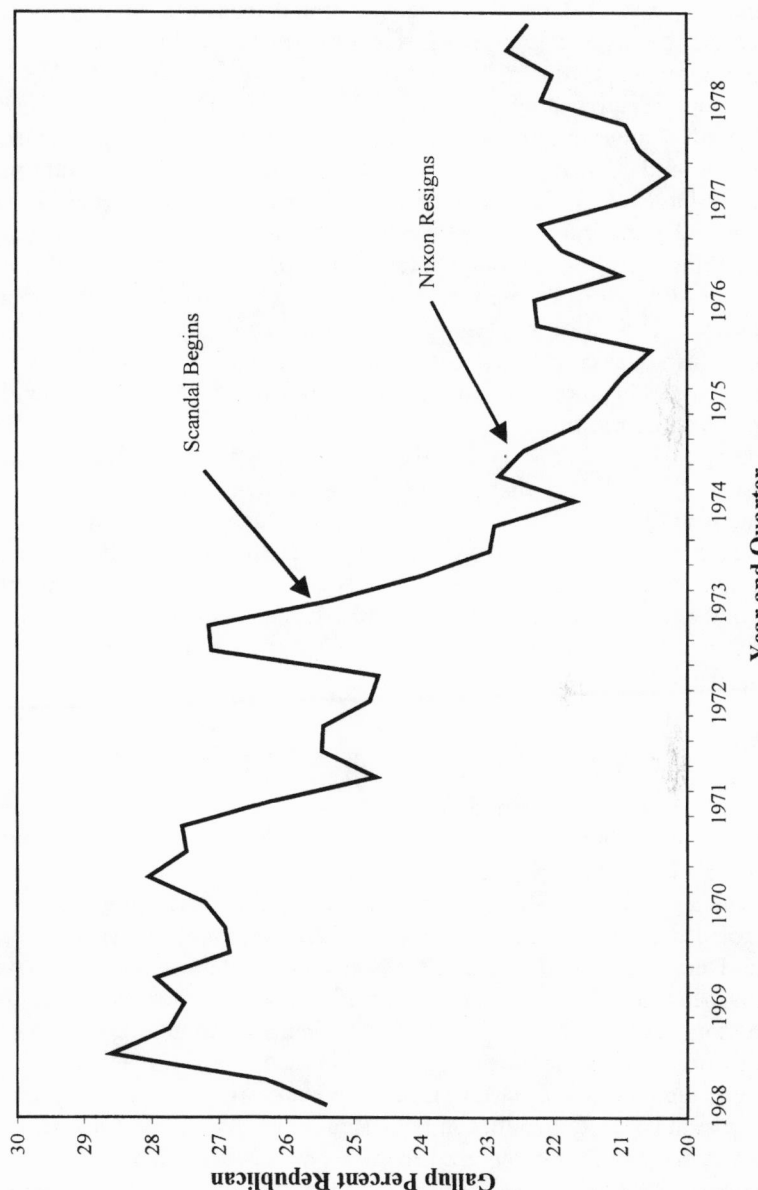

Figure 4.1. Gallup Republican Macropartisanship, 1968–1978

111

success is always subject to change generated from the latest political events. Former Republicans eventually returned to the fold, but not until they saw reasons to do so.

The post-Watergate drop in Republican support is not the largest short-term change in partisanship on record. The record for short-term change would probably be the Republican surge around the time of Reagan's landslide 1984 victory. Although some of this surge turned out to be long lasting, fueled by the economic recovery of the time, much of it dissipated once the campaign ended. Indeed, many shifts in U.S. partisanship turn out to be the temporary response to momentary political excitement. This, too, tells us something important about partisanship. At least for some citizens, at least some of the time, partisanship is in a state of flux. This requires that some citizens are *not* anchored by standing partisan commitments.

From our argument so far, partisanship can be a bedrock, impervious to challenge, or it can change in small but enduring fashion, or it can fluctuate in large but temporary deviations. Our starting point for the analysis to come is that all these perspectives are true – if not for the same voters then for different subsets of the electorate. The macro phenomenon we believe is a blend of the three. Thus, we shall develop micro-level models for each and ask what results when we aggregate the blend of the three.

## MACROPARTISANSHIP AND MACRO POLITICS

To distinguish macro-level partisanship from micro-level partisanship, we apply the label *macropartisanship* to the national aggregation of partisanship. The aggregate partisan division has long been understood to serve as a baseline expectation of electoral outcomes. Different regions and locales, of course, take on different partisan colorations: Some are more Democratic and some more Republican. Similarly, there have clearly been different partisan eras in U.S. political history, with Republican domination after the turn of the twentieth century, Democratic domination during the midcentury, and a much more competitive era at the turn into the twenty-first century. In theory, then, we can aggregate the division of party loyalists in the country (and corrected for turnout) to predict what would be the outcome of an election in which the short–term, election-specific factors were balanced to produce an expected "normal vote" (Converse 1966).

Suppose the national-level "normal vote" is constant for long periods of time. It would be important for (at least) four reasons. First, it provides analysts a baseline against which to measure historical events. When Dwight Eisenhower won two consecutive presidential elections in the 1950s, the electorate chose a Republican popular leader as president but did not change its fundamental partisan Democratic orientations. These "deviating elections" (Campbell 1964) arose from important elements associated with the Eisenhower promise and performance, the public's judgments about Stevenson, and the failures of the prior Truman administration. In the same way that occasionally a Democratic city or state elects a Republican mayor or governor – in reaction to scandal or to personality or to some other specific factor – the nation as a whole occasionally deviates from its long-term preferences and chooses a president from the minority party. Contemporary observers, then, can understand that the mere deviation does not imply a fundamental shift in the electorate's preferences.

Second, the partisan vote informs politicians about the future. Because the Democratic Party had a "normal vote" advantage of about 53–47 percent, strategists from both parties understood what they had to do to compete in national elections. Republicans knew that in order to win an election they needed to secure a palpable short-term advantage such as picking a popular war hero (Eisenhower) or a candidate who could appeal strongly to the middle ground of independents in the electorate (as Richard Nixon). On the other hand, a permanent advantage allowed Democrats to pursue a policy agenda that accorded with their genuine preferences rather than adopt policies exclusively for electoral advantage. Politicians' electoral and policy-making strategies depend enormously on their understanding about the political lay of the land.

Third, when partisanship anchors people's votes, it also stabilizes the political system. That is, when people have attachments toward the parties they will find it less tempting to jump at novel appeals offered by flash candidates or parties. Clearly important for the development of new democratic systems (for an early discussion, see Converse 1969), the citizen foundation for the party system strongly affects the sorts of party choices that are presented to the electorate. In the U.S. presidential election of 1992, for example, candidate Ross Perot presented an enormously attractive candidacy that pulled voters from both partisan camps as well as mobilized millions of independents. However, his chances for success were seriously constrained by the partisan orientations of the greatest part of the electorate (Zaller 1995).

And finally, a partisan vote provides a vehicle for system memory. While electoral choice often reflects the politics of the moment – issues and events that appear and then disappear – partisan ties embody more enduring divisions in the public's preferences. When the Democratic Party enjoyed its ascendance during midcentury, it did so because the electorate had accepted the main message of the New Deal, and that fundamental decision persisted for decades in setting the tone of U.S.

politics. *Macropartisanship*, then, suggests itself as a candidate for smoothing out the oscillating fortunes of political events to produce a more predictable, and perhaps a more deliberative, public judgment. When electoral outcomes are rooted in more fundamental factors, we expect a politics driven by enduring interests and judgments rather than by the passions of the moment.

At least this was *Macropartisanship* as it was understood by *The American Voter* authors of the 1950s and 1960s (Campbell et al. 1960). If *Macropartisanship* changes with ordinary political events, the scandal of Watergate, or the economic fortunes of each administration, then it no longer represents a stable system feature that anchors the politics of an era. Instead, we ask how to conceive of a dynamic *Macropartisanship* in terms of how it affects the strategies and outcomes that characterize a changeable political system.

In our Watergate example, the political parties acted as though the scandal's consequences would be meaningful and enduring. The Republicans, most notably under the leadership of William Brock, reinvigorated the national party, developed and adopted the tools of modern-day campaigning, and set about rebuilding the state-level party to regenerate a cadre of candidates (Sabato 1988; Aldrich 1995). The Democrats, in the opposite fashion, treated their surplus partisan advantage as fresh political capital to draw on, pressing for further liberal policies despite an increasing public dissatisfaction with governmental activism (see Chapters 8 and 9). Each party's leadership treated the macropartisan consequences of Watergate not as a transitory phase but instead as an enduring feature of their political system. Of course, during the Reagan presidency the G.O.P. regained its competitiveness. Was this resurgence evidence that Watergate was indeed a temporary deviation – one that would necessarily disappear into the mists of history with the passage of time? Or were the parties right in believing that *Macropartisanship* had changed permanently, subject to a reversal only by future historical events?

To answer these questions, we turn to our evidence on *Macropartisanship*. We shall establish that *Macropartisanship* changes continuously over time, that it changes meaningfully in accord with the parties' performance in office, and that that those changes produce both transitory and permanent consequences. In the end, we shall conclude that *Macropartisanship* is truly an important feature of the political system. Contrary to the earlier conventional wisdom, *Macropartisanship* is not a singular constant but instead generates a critical moving mark that incorporates ongoing history. We shall conclude that our understanding of the political system is thus transformed.

But first, rather than moving directly to the macro evidence, we consider the micro models that dominate current thinking about *Macropar-*

*tisanship* and show how they need to be rethought before approaching the macro consequences.

## MICRO MODELS

The foundation for our study of *Macropartisanship* is the wealth of science on micro-level partisanship. In the voting literature, partisanship has a central place as perhaps the most important variable in the understanding of why voters vote the way they do. About two-thirds of Americans align themselves with the Democrats or Republicans, with most of the rest calling themselves Independent. Without knowing any further attributes of an election contest or the voters themselves, one can confidently predict that most Democratic identifiers will vote Democratic, and most Republican identifiers will vote Republican. In some way or another, one's partisanship is a proxy for how one would vote if presented with a new electoral decision. That much we know. Yet there is surprising disagreement regarding the psychological foundations of *micro*-level partisanship. By some interpretations, different micro-level theories force different macro-level predictions. These possible implications of macro-level findings regarding the correct micro-level model only add to the controversy about the nature of partisanship.

Much of what is written about partisanship can be understood as an unsuccessful attempt to shoehorn diverse and contradictory behaviors onto a single micro model. Evidence of permanence and stability points to a formulation of self-identification, the classic *American Voter* model of party identification. Evidence of partisan change in response to the current context of politics points to a partisan choice as a continuous process of reevaluation, as in Fiorina's (1981) "running tally." Much ink has been spilled in the contest for dominance between the two sorts of approaches. We do not intend to referee the contest, but rather to begin by taking seriously all the conflicting evidence to conclude that both sorts of micro model are correct for some citizens, some of the time. Then, as we turn to macro data, we will ask not which model is most likely to have generated the data, but what *mix* of models is culpable.[1] We begin by entertaining the *American Voter* model of identification.

### Partisanship as Permanent Commitment

The authors of the influential book *The American Voter* (Campbell et al. 1960) are largely responsible for the interpretation that holds party

---

1 This mixed micro models approach to the macro data is similar in spirit to DeBoef (1994).

identification to be a permanent commitment that rarely changes. The basic idea, rooted in reference group theory, had individuals projecting themselves into the public space through the party symbols and then defining a part of themselves in that projection. The key evidence, as Campbell et al. saw it, lay in the accumulation of survey research that revealed the pervasiveness and stability of people's party identifications. When early researchers attempted to discern political learning from within the family, for instance, the one attitude with a clear consistency from parent to offspring was party identification (Hyman 1959; Campbell et al. 1960; Jennings and Niemi 1968, 1974). Even citizens lacking political sophistication generally identified with the Democrats or Republicans (Campbell et al. 1960). When researchers discovered the general instability of attitudinal responses from panel surveys, they found that a major exception was the relatively consistent responses to the party identification question (Converse 1964; Achen 1975; Converse and Markus 1979).

Party *identification*: So often used in sequence, the two words "party" and "identification" roll off the tongue automatically – so much so that we have stopped noticing the second word. Usage has evolved toward treating the whole as meaning some amalgam of ties toward party. This usage shift has gone so far that it is now common for scholars who explicitly reject the idea of identification to continue to use the term. But it is useful for model building to return to the starting conception and take *identification* to mean exactly *identification*.

What, we ask, would be the behavior over time of the citizen who defines him- or herself in part by sense of attachment to party? On a scale of commitment from the indifferent to the profound, self-identification clearly pushes in the latter direction. Much of what we think of ourselves is constant for a lifetime – and we expect this of party identification. In many ways, people's attachment to the party system resembles their orientation to automobiles. In some parts of the country, perhaps most famously in the pickup truck world, there are "Chevy" people and "Ford" people. A Chevy person likely comes from a family of Chevy owners, perhaps wears a cap with the bow-tie emblem on its crest, pulls for Chevy drivers at Daytona and Indianapolis, argues the merits of Chevys over Fords at the drop of a hat, and surely feels proud of this orientation. Similarly, a Democrat votes Democratic at every election, cheers whenever Democrats score points in the Beltway's daily political tournament, argues for Democratic positions in policy debates, and cares deeply if the Democrats win or lose an election. Like our Chevy people, partisan identifiers not only prefer one side to the other but also begin to identify themselves as at one with the contestants.

But identification stops just short of lifetime commitment in this model. We must allow for the possibility that events can alter partisan self-perception. We might require these to be events of great drama, impact, and duration, as nothing short of this combination should have the power to break the strong chemical bond of self to party. A careful reading of *The American Voter* shows that its authors recognized that some people's party identifications would be rearranged by the events of the day, some of the time. As the idea of a stable party identification took hold, however, observable mass change in partisanship was deemed to be quite unlikely, except via conversion scenarios so dramatic that they must be labeled as realignments.

### Partisanship as Standing Choice

Imagine another sort of citizen who asks about the parties not, "Is it mine?" but, "Is this the best party?" These citizens do not project themselves into the party system as participants, joining the fray and playing the game, but instead reflect on the promise of the parties and choose the most appealing side. They consider the parties' past histories, current performance, and prognosis for the future. They make a standing choice, one that they constantly update as new evidence comes to bear. Our car consumers, rather than identifying with Chevrolet or Ford (or Dodge or Toyota), choose the automotive brand with which they have had good experience. Perhaps starting with Chevrolets, this sort of driver reacts to a bad experience and tries another make – say, a Toyota. And, with a few good years of experience, these people begin to develop a positive orientation toward Toyota. Not to the point of wearing a Toyota cap, or arguing for Toyotas in bars, or rooting for Toyota race car drivers – not to the point of thinking of themselves as part of the automotive battles. But they do develop a sense that Toyota is the best alternative and will stick with that decision when they come to another automotive purchase – until they have experience to the contrary.

This aspect of partisanship has its intellectual roots in the work of Key (1966) and, more recently, Fiorina (1977, 1978, 1981). Citizens make substantive decisions about their political allegiances and then modify those decisions as the evidence warrants. Importantly, though, these partisans weigh information as it comes in, formulate a conclusion about the parties, and then go forward. Fiorina described this process as a "running tally" where citizens continuously consider the parties' current performance and update their comparative evaluation accordingly.[2]

---

2 Part of the confusion about Fiorina's position is the question of whether the "running tally" discounts events of the past or not. In his major pieces, Fiorina himself does not take a definite position. We take advantage of this distinction here referring to people who form long-lasting evaluations as having made a "standing

## Performance

Partisans thus store their past experience with the party system through their attachments to the party symbols – consciously or even unconsciously.[3]

### Partisanship as Momentary Support

Finally, many citizens associate themselves with a party only in the sense that they react to current events. Far from a psychological commitment, or even an association derived from past evaluations, this attachment reflects the specifics of today's decision. In terms of our automobile public, this partisan orientation is akin to the buyer who comes to each car purchase anew, picks up a copy of *Consumer Reports*, and chooses the car that gets the highest value rating in that particular year. While being a Chevy or Toyota person in only the most literal sense, this buyer's brand attachment incorporates only the elements implicit in the current choice. Things will begin anew tomorrow. In politics, this part of partisanship is much closer to a party "supporter" who, when saying "I'm a Republican," means that he or she is supporting the Republican candidate today. When the personalities or the issues change, this person's partisan orientation will change as well.[4]

Survey researchers force respondents to answer the "party identification" question in terms of how they think of themselves, intending to tap long-term *identification*. But our "supporters" would be more comfortable answering a question about their current assessment of one party or the other as better able to govern at the moment. *Support*, like approval, may wax and wane, driven by short-term indications of success and competence.

choice." Those who change their "running tally" according to current conditions and essentially forget the past we call "party supporters." See below.

3 These assessments need not be explicitly conscious, of course, and may instead represent a form of "on-line" processing (Lodge, Steenbergen, and Brau 1995) in which people alter their summative party assessments as they go along but never really store in accessible memory the particulars that influence their judgments. Thus, partisanship might carry political experience without anyone actively understanding why. Partisanship would thus be a repository of rational, but not consciously rational, judgment.

4 This idea of "supporter" as partisan is prevalent in the politics of Western Europe – where the party system has been more fluid. This distinction was most clear in the 1950s when American researchers tried to import the idea of party identification directly to the politics of France, Italy, and Germany. Note ahead that a considerable portion of the dynamics are indeed driven by the "supporter" mentality.

118

## Macropartisanship

### From Micro Models to Macro Expectations

These models of partisanship lend themselves to different expectations regarding how *Macropartisanship* moves over time. For an electorate composed of partisan identifiers of the *personal commitment* mold, stability in the aggregate follows from individual stability. We would expect a *Macropartisanship* that moves only in a very narrow range and then with glacial tempo. Except for periodic crises so profound as to rearrange partisan perceptions, aggregate partisanship should be a constant. The millions of Republicans whose identification survived the Watergate scandal are anecdotal evidence of identification at work.

The notion of a stable macro-level partisanship receives a certain validation from some known facts. From the beginning of scientific polling in the 1930s into the 1980s, Democrats led Republicans in party identification, on average by a ratio of about 3 to 2. At least until the 1980s, it was generally thought that any variation around this average was too slight and too trendless to be of much significance. This persistent Democratic advantage had to come from somewhere, and that somewhere was the previous "realignment" of the 1930s when voters responded to the searing national depression and Franklin Roosevelt's New Deal: They divided on the basis of social class with the poor tending to be Democratic and the rich tending to be Republican. This new division resulted in a Democratic advantage that seemed a constant feature of American politics.[5]

But the evidence we now have in hand suggests otherwise. When we observe the flow of *Macropartisanship*, we see a series that *varies* and that *varies systematically* over time. We turn to this evidence.

### MACROPARTISANSHIP OVER TIME: THE EVIDENCE

Figure 4.2 graphs *Macropartisanship*, 1953–1996, as annual readings of the percent of partisan identifiers who call themselves Democrats rather

---

5 According to political historians, the 1930s realignment was the fifth major political alignment in U.S. history (Burnham 1970; Clubb, Flanigan, and Zingale 1980; Sundquist 1983). (Previous realignments occurred in the 1820s, 1850s, and 1890s.) Each realignment results in a new "party system," so that the fourth realignment of the 1930s ushered in a "fifth" party system. Since previous realignments were separated by only 30–40 years, an obvious challenge has been whether the United States was entering a still new realignment and still new "sixth" party system.

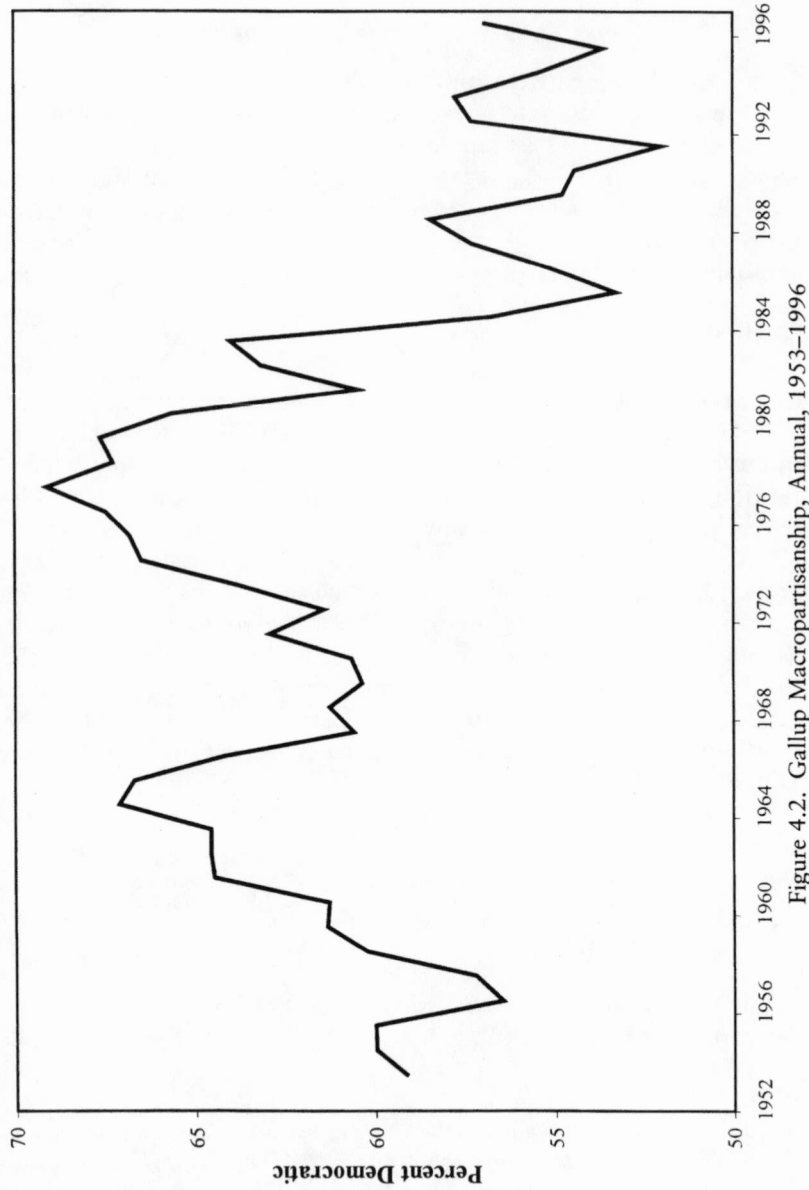

Figure 4.2. Gallup Macropartisanship, Annual, 1953–1996

than Republicans in Gallup polls.[6] The graph depicts continuous movement, with several identifiable peaks and valleys. Two major Democratic peaks (Republican valleys) coincided with the Democrats' electoral triumphs in 1964 (Johnson over Goldwater) and 1976 (Carter over Ford). Each was followed by a less clearly defined Democratic valley (Republican peak) corresponding roughly to the Nixon and Reagan eras. Besides these major cycles, the graph shows lesser periods of turbulence, defined by local maxima and minima of lesser magnitude. Taking a closer look at the movement of the series, we observe the following patterns:

- During the Eisenhower era (1953–1960), the Democrats held at a fairly steady state in popularity, but this lead was not without its oscillations. For instance, the Democrats had a minor rise starting in 1958, corresponding to the time of the economic recession and a dip in Eisenhower's approval.
- During the Kennedy-Johnson years (1961–1968), the Democrats first surged to new heights and then fell back. The major rise corresponded with the Democratic landslide victory in 1964. The later decline coincided with the increased U.S. involvement in Vietnam. As Johnson's popularity declined, so did the Democrats'.
- During the Nixon-Ford years (1969–1976), the Democrats gained again, with a particular surge starting in 1973, corresponding to the economic recession and the Watergate revelations.

---

6 Here our *Macropartisanship* measure comes from the full set of Gallup surveys conducted over the quarter century. *Macropartisanship* is calculated as the percent Democratic of the two-party identifiers in each survey. That is, we eliminate independents from the calculation. In theory this decision might matter, but in practice is of little consequence. To the extent that we want to infer dynamics we want to be sensitive to sampling error. Fortunately, averaging over 4,000 respondents per quarter, our readings have a statistical reliability of 0.98.

The series notably changes when Gallup changed from an in-person survey to a telephone survey – for reasons that baffle, the telephone surveys are slightly more Republican (Hugick 1991) – and we have adjusted the latter surveys to conform with the former. Since Gallup in-person surveys use standard sampling techniques and produce partisanship estimates similar to those of other survey houses, we take them to be the standard against which the telephone surveys are measured. The latter use proprietary, i.e., secret, sampling methods geared to produce low-cost results. We observe 26 quarters where Gallup surveys of both types exist and note that the telephone surveys are 3.12 points lower in the computed two-party estimate of Democratic proportion. This difference is quite significant. Left undisturbed it creates a "trend" toward Republicanism that is clearly a method artifact, one which appears in neither in-person or telephone surveys by themselves – and for no other survey house – but emerges from the method effect when the two are spliced together as a single series. To assemble a series with no such trend artifact, we adjust each of the telephone surveys by the amount of the observed bias.

- Following Carter's election in 1976, the Democrats were near their zenith in *Macropartisanship*. Forecasting naively from trends at the time, one might have predicted the extinction of the Republican Party. Instead, the Republicans made major gains leading up to Reagan's defeat of Carter in 1980.
- The Reagan years (1981–1988) at first saw Democrats regaining lost ground during the 1982–1983 recession. Then, as the economy recovered, 1984–1985 saw a precipitous drop in Democratic fortunes. Here was the Republican shift we noted earlier. At the end of the Reagan years, the Democrats recovered slightly – possibly as fallout from the Iran-Contra investigations.
- The Bush term started with Republican gains. By *Macropartisanship*'s measure, Democratic fortunes reached a nadir in early 1991, corresponding to Bush's successful waging of the Gulf War. Then, as the economy soured (setting the stage for Clinton to beat Bush), Democratic fortunes increased somewhat only to decline again once Clinton took office. But as the perceived economy improved later in Clinton's first term, so rose his popularity and, along with it, Democratic identification.

Knowing that *Macropartisanship* moves is only part of the story. We also know that it moves in accord with political news that reflects the success and failure of the incumbent presidential party. When the economy goes well and the president's performance is widely approved, the presidential party benefits; when things go badly, the presidential party suffers.

The main course of the evidence is apparent in Figure 4.3. Here we see the responsiveness of *Macropartisanship* to *Presidential Approval* and *Consumer Sentiment* – separated out by presidential administration, Eisenhower through Clinton I. Each is presented on a separate metric.[7]

The data bear close inspection. While the precision of a mathematical representation has yet to be demonstrated, the plausibility of modeling partisanship as a function of economic well-being and presidential

7 In Figure 4.3, MICS (the *Michigan Index of Consumer Sentiment*) and *Presidential Approval* are scaled in standard deviation units, while *Macropartisanship* is scaled in 1.5 standard deviation units. This calibration allows approximately identical variances to the change scores in the three variables. Each series is depicted as centered around the within-administration mean, with the approval series centered two units higher than MICS and *Macropartisanship* centered two units higher than approval. (All this rescaling is for illustrative purposes in this figure only – not in the data analysis to follow.)

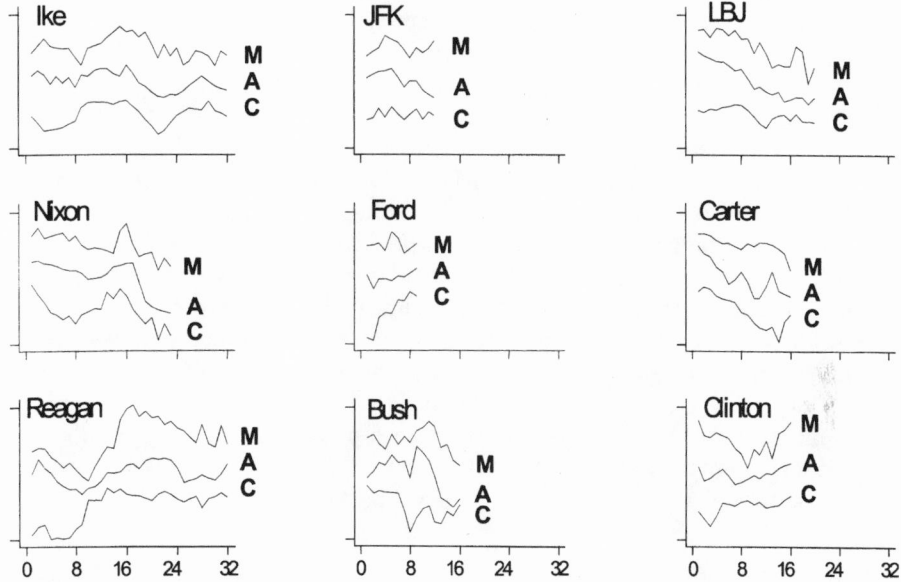

Figure 4.3. Consumer Sentiment, Presidential Approval, and Macropartisanship over Nine Administrations

approval is apparent. The relationship is evident to the naked eye. We take up the statistical description in a later section of this chapter.[8]

This evidence on dynamics gives the lie to the expectation that *Macropartisanship* remains stable over time – subject only to perturbations of the random sort. We can now eliminate one simple understanding of partisanship: the notion of party identification as a permanent personal commitment fails to account for the historical series – at least not by itself. Instead, we must shift our focus from stability toward

---

8 Standard Granger exogeneity tests shows no evidence of causal sequencing from *Macropartisanship to Consumer Sentiment* or *Presidential Approval*. (When lagged *Macropartisanship* for the president's party is included in the *Approval* equation, it is decidedly nonsignificant.) What this causal ordering at the macro level says about individual psychology at the micro level is less certain, due to the hazards of making individual inferences from aggregate data. The Granger test does tell us that when *aggregate* party identification shifts due to exogenous causes, it does not alter *collective* opinion of the president. But, as noted in Chapter 2, Democrats and Republicans tend to divide strongly in terms of approving the president. We surely expect that *individual*-level changes in partisanship can affect presidential approval.

dynamics – toward exploring the character of macropartisan political change rather than ignoring it altogether. In doing so, we revisit our understanding of the micro-level processes.

We tread carefully. Despite the palpable movement in *Macropartisanship*, so obvious by visual inspection, the validity of this demonstration has been surprisingly controversial. Advocates of the "stable partisanship" orthodoxy are spirited in their denial (Miller 1991; Abramson and Ostrom 1991; Green, Palmquist, and Schickler 1998).

To hear the critics, it would seem that *Macropartisanship* does not really move at all, but if it did show real movement, it would consist of short-term variation unconnected to political and economic events. Some of the critics' motivation could be fear that evidence of macro movement undermines the foundation of micro-level stability. In truth, the implications of a variable *Macropartisanship* have been overdramatized. While knowledge of micro-level partisanship informs our understanding of *Macropartisanship*, the fact of macro-level movement presents little threat to existing theories of micro-level partisanship.

### INDIVIDUAL PARTISANSHIP: A REFORMULATION

Here we set aside the conflicts over competing models and start from scratch to think through partisan ties, almost as if the matter of partisanship were newly discovered. Our strategy is in three parts. First we develop a model of individual partisan ties based upon reasonable postulates. We ask what factors are likely to produce a tie between citizen and party. Rejecting a single answer requires us also to think about how combinations of factors interact. Then we ask what happens when we switch levels of analysis, how individual party dispositions become *Macropartisanship*, and what changes and biases arise from the act of aggregation. This leads us at last to a formulation that may be tested with macro data, and that test is the centerpiece of our analysis.

Before we begin, it is helpful to free ourselves of the complications of usage of "party identification." We wish to start with no preconceptions about the character of party ties and with an abstraction, not a measurement system. Party identification is entangled in both a particular measure, the NES 7-point scale, and – more importantly – in a conception of *identification* rooted in *The American Voter*.

### A Micro Model of Partisan Disposition

Imagine that each citizen has a latent link to the parties that may be conceptualized as a score somewhere on the continuum between total association with one party and total association with the other. Let 1 be the president's party and 0 be the "out" party. Then each citizen *i* has a *party disposition PD* at time *t*:

$$0.0 \leq PD_{it} \leq 1.0 \tag{4.1}$$

where $PD_i$ might be the probability of voting for one party as opposed to the other – or the probability of arguing for the party or contributing to the party or claiming association with the party.[9] We wish to think about what happens to $PD_i$ as *t* varies, that is, to know the dynamic path of party ties.

The beginning, of course, is to ask where the party disposition comes from in the first instance. We let the root of party ties be any of the processes commonly postulated, as each no doubt is for some citizens some of the time. Thus the party tie may come from childhood socialization, from cues given by the social environment, from intellectual choice based upon policy or ideology, from momentary preferences that arise from response to particular politicians or particular events, or even from happenstance such as when a young person registers for the first time and discovers a need to designate a party. These possible processes run the gamut of intellectual and emotional commitment, from intense to trivial. We expect the strength of $PD_i$ to be similarly variable across citizens.

We posit, more specifically, that each citizen bears the mark of processes that tend to build cognitive and affective ties to a party. Although the net effect of each will sometimes be zero, we posit that each citizen is an amalgam of:

- *Parental (and Peer) Socialization:* People inherit a disposition. Because the inheritance may occur at an age before choices based upon reasonable understanding are possible, the socialization process can be a quite pure inheritance, devoid of rationale and even rationalization.
- *Social Context:* In adulthood, men and women develop attachments similar to those of their families, friends, and local traditions. The social environment structures information flow so that people

9 We offer this as a bare-bones representation, understanding full well that a rigorous model would need further complexity. As an alternative, calibrate $PD_{it}$ as a function of $p_{it}$, an *open-ended* degree of Democratic vs. Republican partisanship. As a probability of, say, voting Democratic, $PD_{it}$ would be a function of $p_{it}$ in the form of an S-shaped probit (or logit) curve. All statistical modeling of partisanship in a linear model would be conducted in $p_{it}$ (see Erikson et al. 1998) while we discuss the polar $PD_{it}$ here for heuristic purposes. We only mean to sketch out a minimal outline.

naturally hear news consistent with their friends' or newspaper's party. And when social ties are more important than politics, then people may uncritically adopt the party of their community, their church, or their country club.

- *Identification:* Those who inherit a disposition to favor a party may or may not come to think of themselves in terms of party. "I *am* a Democrat (or Republican)" is something different and more than merely "I prefer that party" or "I usually vote for it." Usually joined with the socialization and social communication processes that often produce it, identification may nonetheless be separable, and we choose for clarity to keep it so.

- *Ideology, Core Values, and Policy Preferences:* People may assess their views, compare the two parties, and choose to become associated with the one that is in accord. This is an intellectual process that will sometimes be a rationalization of a disposition on the basis of inheritance or identification, but may occur without them as well. Much of the contemporary political discussion about the Democrats moving to the center or Republicans to the right reflects this basic understanding that the parties attempt to woo voters on ideological, value-oriented, or policy grounds.

- *Evaluation of Performance:* People may also choose on the basis of the ability of the parties to manage government – to provide for peace and prosperity. In lieu of other commitments, citizens may keep score on party success and failure and then choose the party that has a better success rate.

- *Idiosyncratic Events:* Last of all, we allow for the possibility that some citizens may not inherit a party tie, identify with a party, care about policy or ideology (or if they do, know where the parties align), or evaluate outcomes, but *still* develop a party disposition. While the processes that might come into play would probably not be truly random – for example, a youngster might develop a tie to the party of a favorite teacher or school chum – the cause would appear so to the observer.

It will be important to note, when we turn to macro-political dynamics, that these various causes of disposition are not so equal as our list might imply. Most of our scientific understanding about partisan dispositions stems from years of research in political psychology. Appreciating how citizens perceive and experience the political world is, of course, a matter of real interest. And much of our science has focused on how some people, rather than others, develop dispositions toward one party and not the other. This is cross-sectional variation.

## Macropartisanship

But in this book we are interested not in the political psychology of individuals but in how the politics of the political system register in the strategies and actions of politicians and the electorate. When we adopt a macro-political perspective, we focus on how politicians can anticipate a public response to their actions and then how that public response might translate into electoral consequences. In particular, we shall examine both the *dynamics* and the *aggregation* of partisan dispositions.

### Equilibrium and Dynamics

First we ask about dynamics. Start with a notion of an expected level of partisanship – one that is driven by all the relevant factors that we have discussed. We expect that a partisan disposition $PD_i$ will remain stable when it is in harmony with all those factors. Someone born a Democrat, married to a Democrat, committed to liberal policy activism, and living in good times during a Democratic administration will have a $PD_i$ of nearly 1.00. A similar citizen, now married to a Republican, may change to something more like 0.75. The point is that we want to posit a partisan disposition that is consistent with and sustained by the citizen's social, intellectual, and political state. Call this $PD_i^*$ with the star indicating that the partisan disposition is in equilibrium.

We now postulate a flow of information about politics to the citizen as he or she witnesses successive regimes over time. The information flow will be of positive and negative news about the preferred party as it and its opposition govern, take positions, make policy, and so forth, across time. The positive news will reinforce ties, and the negative news will undermine them.

Citizens, we believe, will encounter two sorts of stimuli. Some of these will prove transitory, such as attraction or repulsion to particular candidates or response to particular events that define politics for the moment, but then fade from memory. Such stimuli will move the citizen to $PD_i'$, a temporary deviation, at time $t$. $PD_{it}'$ is a *transient*, an effect that gradually decays to zero as its cause recedes in time. And then as the particulars fade from memory and influence, $PD_i$ will return to its long-term equilibrium level before it was disturbed at $t$:

$$PD_i = PD_i^*, \text{ when } PD_{it}' \rightarrow 0.0, \qquad (4.2)$$

where $PD_i^*$ is again the *equilibrium* party disposition for individual $i$.

Other stimuli will produce changes that are not transitory but instead fundamental. When the citizen encounters evidence of success and failure, competence and incompetence, he or she may form conclusions from the evidence that alter the foundations of partisanship.[10] Having observed, for example, that party $R$ is a skilled manager of the national economy at time $t$, the citizen may judge that the fundamental character of the party has changed. This conclusion will endure unless and until it is refuted by newer evidence about the fundamentals. In this case, the new party disposition at time $t$ becomes a new $PD_{it}^*$, a new equilibrium level that will persist indefinitely. (The double subscript on $PD_{it}^*$ indicates that the equilibrium is no longer a constant for all time, but instead responds to political economic stimuli.)

We shall be interested in what types of stimuli are associated with changes in equilibrium party disposition and what types with the transitory component in partisanship. In particular, we shall be interested in matters of policy and performance.

It is noteworthy that most of our equilibrating mechanisms that operate at the micro level – *inheritance, social context, identification,* and *ideology* – remain constant over long periods, or even for a lifetime, and are thus incapable of producing ebb and flow in partisan dispositions. And much of the change will be either inconsequentially idiosyncratic or of a glacial nature. Some individuals will rebel against their parents, others will marry outside their family party, others will change social class or adopt different reference groups, others will move into different neighborhoods or communities or across regions, and so on. But much of this individually important change will occur independent of party politics – for example, when individual Republicans marry into Democratic families or individual Democrats join the upper class – or reflect party politics only vaguely and gradually – for example, when people migrate toward the conservative Sun Belt, they marginally change partisan orientations away from the Democracy and toward the GOP. The net impact of these changes cannot account for the ebb and flow of *Macropartisanship* we saw in Figure 4.2. And because these changes are so distant from the year-to-year practice of party politics, they produce little political impact.[11]

---

10 Such conclusions are a natural fit to theories of on-line processing of political information (Lodge, McGraw, and Stroh 1989). If the citizen does not attend to facts, theories, indicators, and arguments, but instead remembers only the bottom line, for example, "Republicans are better at running the national economy," then we should expect such memories to be permanent.

11 Surely, over the course of generations these class transformations, mass migrations, and regional metamorphoses will have enormous long-term consequences. Contemporary electoral politics of class, race, and region surely look very different than they did at mid-twentieth century and the parties' strategists surely pay heed. The difference is that most politicians necessarily live from election cycle to election cycle – adopting a time horizon of years and not decades – and develop

128

## Macropartisanship

On the other hand, parties produce outcomes that notably do shape the dynamics of party politics. The parties alternate in office and alternate success and failure. And so to the extent that citizens base their party dispositions on evaluation of performance, they are reasonably likely to switch parties from time to time. And some of that party switching will reflect changes in equilibrium disposition and, thus, have long-term consequences for the party system. We want to know how much of change represents mere transient fluctuations in party support and how much is permanent. Understanding this is crucial for understanding the role of *Macropartisanship* in the political system.

Whether it is *possible* for such permanent effects to exist is indisputable. Whether real events in the life of the polity ever have this character then becomes an empirical issue. It is not an issue that we can settle at the micro level, because our abstract notion of individual dispositions does not correspond to any available data on individual party dispositions as they evolve continuously over lengthy time spans. But we will see that macro implications of permanent disposition effects will emerge under aggregation, and we will be able to deal with the issue at the macro level. We turn now to thinking about the macro characteristics of our simple micro model.

### Aggregation: Individual Partisan Dispositions Become Macro Dynamics

If we aggregate all the individual partisan dispositions $PD_{it}$, we get $\overline{PD}_t$, the mean over all individuals at time $t$. Since we lack sensitive measures of $PD_{it}$, the continuous underlying disposition, we will instead turn to a closely related aggregate, the percentage of all citizens choosing the Democratic Party, given a dichotomous choice between Democrats and Republicans. Call it $M_t$, for *Macropartisanship* at time $t$. That is:

$$M_t \cong \overline{PD}_t \qquad (4.3)$$

It looms large that $M_t$ is a *macro* measurement. We want to understand that the dynamic behavior of the composite $M_t$ will not necessarily be the behavior of the "typical" individual. This is true both because $M_t$ incorporates the behavior of different individuals and because $M_t$ reflects social as well as individual-level phenomena.

For instance, we expect that people will be anchored by the "equilibrium mechanisms" already noted. Individuals with a strong parental

political strategies accordingly. The way that long-term and election cycle strategies blend together is a matter of some interest.

partisan legacy, whose friends and community support the inherited partisanship, and who have come to identify with the party, will maintain their partisan disposition even in the face of contradictory evidence about the party's performance in office. On the other hand, those with only weakly operating equilibrium mechanisms – whose parents cared little for politics, whose social circles disdain political conversation, and who feel unattached to the party system – will more likely alter their dispositions to match the environment. Similarly, those with contradictory "cross-pressuring" mechanisms – Democratic parents and a conservative ideological perspective, for example – may equally find their dispositions susceptible to new information. Thus, we might normally expect that deeply rooted partisans would be unlikely to shift their orientations and shallow-rooted partisans would be more likely to do so. Or, in the aggregate, we expect that the dynamics of *Macropartisanship* will reflect the mindsets of the marginal rather than the committed partisans.[12]

Alternatively, the sorts of politics that change an individual's partisan disposition will also change the social-political environment as well. When party performance fluctuates or when politicians effectively alter the issue agenda, then the character of elite political discussion – in salons and in the media – will locate the political impact in institutions beyond the ken of ordinary people. When conventional wisdom changes, so too do the ideational equilibrium mechanisms that sustain $M_t$. And further outside individual psychology, social interactions can produce equilibrium mechanisms that support macropartisan change. When any single individual is moved, so will be his or her friends and neighbors – and their views will simultaneously reinforce the initial change in disposition (e.g., MacKuen and Brown 1987). This mutual interdependence can produce nonlinear dynamics and emergent phenomena. We do not now know how all this works in practice – this is a matter for sustained examination of micro-macro connections. But we do want to be sure that when we form mental images of how the electorate moves over time we keep in mind that we should be thinking of subtle, heterogeneous, and interdependent social and psychological processes.

12 In a more rigorous way, we expect that the relationship between any "fundamental" and a partisan disposition will take on something like an S-shaped (or logistic) functional form – with the greatest marginal impact concentrated among those whose prior disposition was neutral. Thus, the dynamics associated with a change in any single factor will be felt mainly by those held in place by weak or conflicting equilibrium mechanisms. Further, there may be "strong partisans" who are little interested in public affairs – their allegiance is strong not because it is based in the fundamentals but because it is unchallenged. Presumably, if these people happen to encounter contradictory evidence their partisan dispositions will be susceptible to change.

# Macropartisanship

## Two Mixed Processes

Our observed aggregate $M_t$ now can be seen to be a mixture of partisan dynamics of two sorts, the transient $PD_i'$ and the moving equilibrium $PD_{it}^*$. Here we ask what sort of time series results from aggregating individuals, each of whom mixes the two sorts of response. The outcome is two hypothetical series:

$$M_t^* \cong \bar{P}_t^*$$
$$M_t' \cong \bar{P}_t' \tag{4.4}$$

where each of the macro series $M_t$ acquires the properties of the individual series $PD_t$. $M_t^*$ becomes *Equilibrium Macropartisanship*, the level to which *Macropartisanship* returns after being disturbed by some transient. Because it represents the permanent memory of partisan change, it can be expressed as a unit root series:

$$M_t^* = M_{t-1}^* + u_t \tag{4.5}$$

where $M_t^*$ is a cumulation of all the changes in partisan dispositions from previous times, and $u_t$ is a perturbation at $t$.[13] Every time someone switches sides, that is, the series will reflect that switch in a new equilibrium level. This equilibrium will have no tendency to revert to a mean; but is itself the reversion point, the level of *Macropartisanship* to which the series will return when disrupted by a transient effect. This is the behavior we would expect of an aggregation of individual partisanship if individual partisanship were a matter of enduring but changeable *standing choices*.

We expect $M_t^*$ to be the carrier of the message of political success and failure. When parties do well or badly in the business of running government, the track of mass evaluation should be seen in the altered equilibria represented by $M_t^*$. When we turn to modeling *Macropartisanship*, this is the component in which we expect to find permanent effects of economic evaluations and *Presidential Approval*.

$M_t'$, in contrast, is a transient (autoregressive) series of temporary deviations from $M_t^*$.

$$M_t' = \phi M_{t-1}' + v_t, \text{ where } 0.0 \leq \phi \leq 1.0 \tag{4.6}$$

$M_t'$ shows the effects of political events ($v_t$) that influence partisan dispositions, but impermanently. Driven by routine economic or foreign policy success or failure to scandals, disasters, or whatever involves the

---

13 The model is a random walk time series. "Random walk" is a term often misunderstood outside the ranks of time-series analysts. Its only random component is the input at time $t$; the series is otherwise highly determined.

party system at the moment, the character of $M_t'$ shows the influence of the political environment while memories of recent events are still fresh.

Insofar as it represents movement away from equilibrium conditions, we may think of $M_t'$ as deviation. It is the relatively short-term disruption of partisanship that is responsive to the events of the moment. Unlike $M_t^*$, which we can think of as the flow of new *conclusions* that one party is better than the other, $M_t'$ is as transient as the passing series of events that draw public attention. $M_t'$ represents a real response to real events, and therefore not "error" in the common usage of that term. But it is an equilibrating response that seeks a mean (of zero) in the long run. After the events that move it are gone from memory, so too is the response.

All this is hypothetical. Beginning with hypothetical individual dispositions and continuing into the aggregations producing macro-level partisan movement, we have merely postulated responses and examined consequences. What then of the measured time series *Macropartisanship*? It is clearly neither of the simple components, but a mixture:

$$M_t = M_t^* + M_t' \qquad (4.7)$$

Our measured series then consists of a component that taps the new equilibrium level of partisan dispositions plus a component that is a temporary disruption from equilibrium.

Here is where we stand. We have a theory that accounts for the movement of two hypothetical series, the permanent $M_t^*$ and the transient $M_t'$. To test the theory we have $M_t$, a mixture of the two. To estimate the separable components we need leverage in the form of causal associations. We will find such leverage in citizen response to the economy and in *Presidential Approval*. We will use the leverage to estimate an error correction formulation, which becomes an explicit representation of our theory.

## THE ENDURING IMPACT OF POLITICAL AND ECONOMIC PERFORMANCE

We contend that *Macropartisanship* represents the cumulative memory of *Equilibrium Macropartisanship* plus short-term movement around this equilibrium. *Equilibrium Macropartisanship* $(M_t^*)$ represents the long memory of political and economic news. When the (political or economic) times cast favor on the presidential party, the presidential party gains. When the times cast disfavor on the presidential party, the presidential party loses. These gains and losses accumulate without decay, so that each new shock leaves a permanent trace on the partisan record. Their accumulation represents the running tally of party performance.

## Macropartisanship

In this section, we set about the task of actually measuring the equilibrium values of *Macropartisanship* ($M_t^*$). We have seen that *Macropartisanship* tracks *Presidential Approval* and *Consumer Sentiment*. However, it is not that the levels of *Approval* and *Consumer Sentiment* themselves cause the increased support – as if *Macropartisanship* begins to reflect the prosperity and presidential popularity of the moment. Rather, the accumulation of political and economic news that causes changes in *Presidential Approval* and *Consumer Sentiment* also causes changes in *Macropartisanship*. We see this by reconfiguring the relevant independent variables as the accumulation of quarterly innovations to the *Approval* and *Consumer Sentiment* series. The distinction is that the cumulative innovations incorporate new inputs in *Approval* and *Consumer Sentiment*, but not their decay. In statistical terms, we model the political and economic causes of *Macropartisanship* as the composite of two integrated series (cumulative innovations) rather than two stationary series (*Approval* and *Consumer Sentiment*). In theoretical terms, the cumulation of economics and politics represents a permanent system memory rather than a transient condition. We want to know the extent to which *Macropartisanship* represents the permanent as opposed to the transient.

We keep this exercise as simple as possible. First, we regress *Approval* on lagged *Approval* (omitting presidential transition quarters) and *Consumer Sentiment* on lagged *Sentiment*, and collect the residuals.[14] Then, we regress current *Approval* residuals on current and lagged *Consumer Sentiment* residuals, and collect a second set of residuals, which are now purged of *economic* effects. These are the *Political Innovations*.[15] The *Consumer Sentiment* residuals are the *Economic Innovations*. These two new series constitute the surprises – the changes in the political or economic climate not anticipated by the previous levels of *Approval* and *Consumer Sentiment*. We cumulate the two sets of innovations starting at zero in 1953:1, adding for Democratic administrations and subtracting for Republican administrations. (For the political cumulation, the unobserved political innovation for the first quarter of each presidential term is set to zero.)

We can now formulate a representation of *Macropartisanship* that incorporates the possibilities of *both* enduring change and transient change. With an encompassing model, we can test to see whether either

14 The regression of approval on lagged approval is: $A_t = 3.791 + 0.917A_{t-1}$. The *Consumer Sentiment* regression is: $MICS_t = 8.993 + 0.897MICS_{t-1}$.

15 The political innovation $A_t$ is the residual from: *Approval Innovation*$_t$ = 0.450 + 0.429$E_t$ + 0.161$E_{t-1}$ where $E_t$ is the economic innovation, the residual from the *Consumer Sentiment* equation.

or both components are important by examining the coefficients associated with each. If either the transient or the enduring part of change turn out to be unimportant, our empirical estimates will tell us so.

We choose the increasingly familiar error-correction model,[16] where current change has two components: one due to current inputs, and one due to a reequilibration or a return to a sustainable value. In our application, the first part is straightforward: People react to political and economic information. The idea of the second part is that if prior *Macropartisanship* $M_{t-1}$ were out of equilibrium – for example, if people overreacted to good news – then people would move back toward the partisanship that is consistent with their psychological and social environment, hence error correction.

The observable dynamics are thus an explicit function of two elements: (1) a transient response and (2) an equilibrium that has the potential to be dynamic itself. More formally, we write change in *Macropartisanship* as a function of economic and political news and a correction of prior deviations from *Equilibrium Macropartisanship*. The short-term dynamic is

$$\Delta M_t = b_E E_t + b_A A_t - d(M_{t-1} - M_{t-1}{}^*) + u_t \qquad (4.8a)$$

where $\Delta M_t$ is change in *Macropartisanship*, $E_t$ and $A_t$ are current economic and political approval innovations; $M_{t-1}$, macropartisanship at $t - 1$; and $M_{t-1}{}^*$, equilibrium macropartisanship. Note the role played by the error-correction component $-d(M_{t-1} - M_{t-1}{}^*)$: If the last deviation is positive, then $\Delta M_t$ goes down; if negative, then $\Delta M_t$ goes up. We simultaneously estimate lagged *Equilibrium Macropartisanship* $M_{t-1}{}^*$ as a function of the fundamentals:

$$M_{t-1}{}^* = c_0 + c_E CumE_{t-1} + c_A CumA_{t-1} \qquad (4.8b)$$

where $CumE_{t-1}$ and $CumA_{t-1}$ are the *cumulative* economic and political approval innovations.

This formulation produces a critical test in the coefficients $c_E$ and $c_A$: If they are both zero, then we infer that *Equilibrium Macropartisanship* $M_t{}^*$ is a constant – as was assumed to be the case years ago – and the effects of political and economic news on *Macropartisanship* are transitory rather than permanent.[17] If, on the other hand, we see important

---

16 The classic formulation of this model is by Davidson et al. (1978) and its use is now commonplace (e.g., Bannerjee et al. 1993, and Hendry 1995). Beck (1991) provides an instructive discussion of ECMs in political science.

17 That is, when $c_E$ and $c_A$ are zero, then it follows that $M_{t-1}{}^* = c_0$ in (4.8a) and, thus, that $\Delta M_t = c_0 + b_E E_t + b_A A_t - dM_{t-1} + u_t$ by substitution. This latter form produces an elementary first-order transient – a simple autoregressive scheme. Thus,

Table 4.1. *An Error Correction Model of Macropartisanship as a Function of Economic and Political News, 1953–1996*

| | Equilibrium Macropartisanship Component | Change in Macropartisanship Component | Summary Statistics for Full Model |
|---|---|---|---|
| Cumulated Economic News | 0.17[a] (4.68) | | |
| Cumulated Political News | 0.13[a] (4.39) | | |
| Constant | 64.17[a] (45.53) | | |
| Economic News | | 0.05[a] (2.01) | |
| Political News | | 0.11[a] (3.87) | |
| Error Correction to Equilibrium Partisanship | | −0.20[a] (−4.53) | |
| Adjusted $R^2$ | | | 0.17 |
| Standard Error of Estimate | | | 1.71 |
| N | | | 175 |

*Note*: Quarterly macropartisanship data from the Gallup series. The entire model is estimated using Nonlinear Least Squares. $t$ values in parentheses.
[a] $p < 0.05$.

coefficients in this part of the model (4.8b), then we understand that $M_t^*$ varies over time and varies as a function of political and economic news.

The empirical analyses, produced in Table 4.1,[18] show that change in *Macropartisanship* is indeed a function of *both* the short-term news about politics and economics as well as the long-term cumulation of that news. Especially important, we see that the coefficients associated with the permanent reaction of *Macropartisanship* to the political

if the coefficients in the equilibrium *Macropartisanship* part of the model vanish, then the *full* model reduces to a simple autoregression. Here we estimate all the parameters of the full model (including both components) using nonlinear least squares – thus relying on the virtues of full specification estimation.

18 The estimates for equations 4.8a and 4.8b are obtained by algebraically substituting the latter into the former and using a nonlinear least squares algorithm. Alternatively, one could use a two-step procedure (Engle and Granger 1987): estimate equation 4.8b and then substitute the estimated $M_{t-1}^*$ into equation 4.8a, all in OLS. Although there is a lively literature on whether the two-step or one-step procedure is preferable, the matter is moot here. The two-step estimate correlates with our one-step estimate at .998.

economy, $c_E$ and $c_A$, are decisively nonzero (look at the coefficients 0.17 and 0.13 in the first column). *We conclude that the Equilibrium Macropartisanship is a dynamic function of the political and economic environment.*

But these numbers are modest – suggesting that when the public changes its evaluations of the economy or the president's performance, only about one in six or seven will thence change their fundamental partisan dispositions. The impact is small but enduring. We see that when party performance affects *Macropartisanship*, it does so in ways that are hardly perceptible but that have substantial consequences for the future because they cumulate over time.

Figure 4.4 graphs observed $M_t$ along with the $M_t^*$ equilibrium values. With $M_t$ and $M_t^*$ correlated at .77, over half the variance in $M_t$ is accounted for by $M_t^*$, the moving long-term equilibrium. Meanwhile, the residuals (standing for $M_t'$) reveal a pattern of systematic short-term variation. Most of these temporary surges center around landslide national elections, for instance, a Democratic gain in 1964 and a Republican bounce in 1984.[19] We begin to understand more about what constitutes a temporary deviation from the long-term path. And, looking at the solid line, we also understand that varying party performance has produced substantial and politically significant dynamics in *Equilibrium Macropartisanship* over the past half-century.

### The CBS News/New York Times *Macropartisanship Series*

Because of its frequent surveys extending back to the early 1950s and before, we rely on the Gallup poll as our primary source for the measurement of *Macropartisanship*. It is worth pondering whether our result is robust – whether it would survive a wholly different data set and partly different time period. Gallup's question wording is not exactly identical to the more standard wording used by other survey houses, including the biennial National Election Studies and CBS News/*New York Times* (CBS/NYT).[20] For that purpose, we employ the measure of partisanship

---

19 These election-year temporary movements were first noticed by Converse (1976) who properly concluded that these shifts represented something other than the enduring partisan dispositions that proved so important for the study of party identification. Our analysis suggests that this conclusion was correct – as far as he took it.

20 Gallup asks people, "In politics today, do you think of yourself as a Republican, Democrat, Independent, or what?" while the more traditional Michigan item asks, "Generally speaking, do you think . . ." Some researchers (Converse 1976; Abramson and Ostrom 1991) have speculated that this difference in framing the

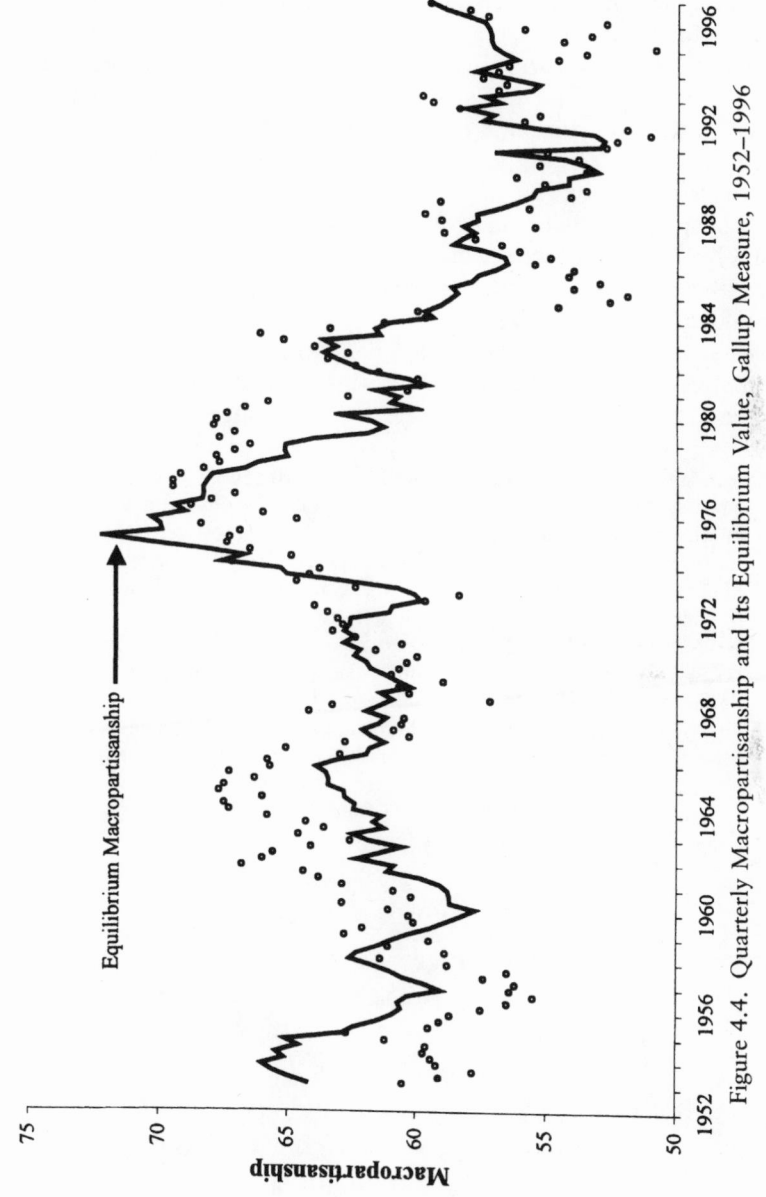

Figure 4.4. Quarterly Macropartisanship and Its Equilibrium Value, Gallup Measure, 1952–1996

137

produced by the CBS News/*New York Times* consortium. Available in usable form for the 21-year period from 1976 to 1996, the CBS/NYT measure permits a parallel analysis with a different dependent variable. This parallel analysis frees us from the limitations of a single survey house and, in particular, from the Gallup "in politics today" language that some say denies legitimacy to a Gallup-based measure of *Macropartisanship*.

We again estimate an error-correction model, this time for the CBS/NYT data, and for comparison, we also reestimate the Gallup model for the same time period.[21] Consistent with the CBS/NYT "generally speaking" question asking respondents for their party identifications over a broader time frame, the CBS/NYT measure seems slightly less responsive to current news and sticks closer to the long-term cumulation

partisanship question makes a substantive difference. They suggest that the wording "generally speaking" taps a more stable partisan vein than Gallup's "in politics today." And they argue that the latter tempts responses in terms of short-term voting choice rather than long-term partisan attachment. The result, they say, is that a series with the "generally speaking" wording would show less movement and indeed present an entirely different time series. The CBS News/*New York Times Macropartisanship* series provides a test of this argument because these surveys use the familiar Michigan "generally speaking" format. We do find modest support for the conjecture: the differences in the series are in the direction expected – although the differences are not quite statistically significant. More important, as we show below, fears that question-wording makes a major difference for substantive inferences are not validated by the evidence. (See also MacKuen, Erikson, and Stimson 1992 and Bishop et al. 1994.)

21 For CBS/*New York Times*, the estimated dynamic parameters are:

$$\Delta M^C_t = 0.019 E_t + 0.096 A_t - 0.536 (M^C_{t-1} - M^C_{t-1}{}^*)$$
St. Err. = (0.053) (0.048)  (0.098)

and the equilibrium parameters are:

$$\Delta M^C_{t-1}{}^* = 64.52 + 0.174 CumE_{t-1} + 0.156 CumA_{t-1}$$
St. Err. = (1.83) (0.031)  (0.026)
Adj. $R^2$ = 0.254; SEE = 2.281; $N = 83$

For Gallup, the dynamic estimates are:

$$\Delta M^G_t = 0.029 E_t + 0.127 A_t - 0.294 (M^G_{t-1} - M^G_{t-1}{}^*)$$
St. Err. = (0.039) (0.035)  (0.070)

and the equilibrium equation is:

$$\Delta M^G_{t-1}{}^* = 64.29 + 0.221 CumE_{t-1} + 0.143 CumA_{t-1}$$
St. Err. = (2.50) (0.044)  (0.035)
Adj. $R^2$ = 0.265; SEE = 1.168; $N = 83$.

of economic and political experience. More important, the estimates for *Equilibrium Macropartisanship* are almost identical for the two series (see Figure 4.5). To the extent that the question wording matters for assessing individual-level partisanship, it seems to affect the measure of the transitory component rather than equilibrium component of partisanship. The fundamentals seem to come through strongly despite the wording differences.

### The Predictive Power of Equilibrium Macropartisanship

We have modeled *Macropartisanship*'s response to cumulative innovations in *Consumer Sentiment* and *Presidential Approval* by positing a permanent memory of political and economic shocks. We test the assumption of permanence against models that allow inputs from the past to decay over time, and it does very well – much better than the alternatives. (See the Appendix to this chapter.) In political practice as opposed to scientific theory, though, the precision of this assumption matters little. Real politicians, having a relatively short time horizon, will formulate the same strategies whether the impact on partisanship dissipates or grows by a factor of 0.01 per quarter or not. The essential point is that part of the impact of politics and economics on *Macropartisanship* is enduring rather than transitory.

We can put this inference to a more critical test by using our theory to do some forecasting. The best proof lies in the ability of *Equilibrium Macropartisanship or $M_t^*$*, the sum of political and economic history, to predict future *Macropartisanship*. We ask which is the stronger predictor of future *Macropartisanship*: (1) its current values of *Macropartisanship* as observed in surveys or (2) the current values of $M_t^*$ as estimated from cumulative political and economic news?

To proceed, we regress future *Macropartisanship* on both current *Macropartisanship $M_t$* and our estimate of current *Equilibrium Macropartisanship $M_t^*$*. We repeat the exercise for extended lead times to see if one measure or the other works better for predicting the distant future rather than merely one quarter ahead. The coefficients, shown in Table 4.2, provide the evidence. As each estimate represents the effect of (1) current *Macropartisanship* or (2) estimated *Equilibrium Macropartisanship* controlling for the other, we gain a strong sense of each component's predictive power. We compare the terms for $M_t$ and $M_t^*$ in each pair of columns. For example, for predicting the one-quarter-ahead future in the Gallup series, the power of $M_t$ is about twice that of $M_t^*$ (compare 0.70 with 0.35 in the first row, first two columns). Note that this first comparison, however, is the only one clearly "won" by $M_t$ – as the time horizon goes out beyond the next quarter or two, $M_t^*$ is the

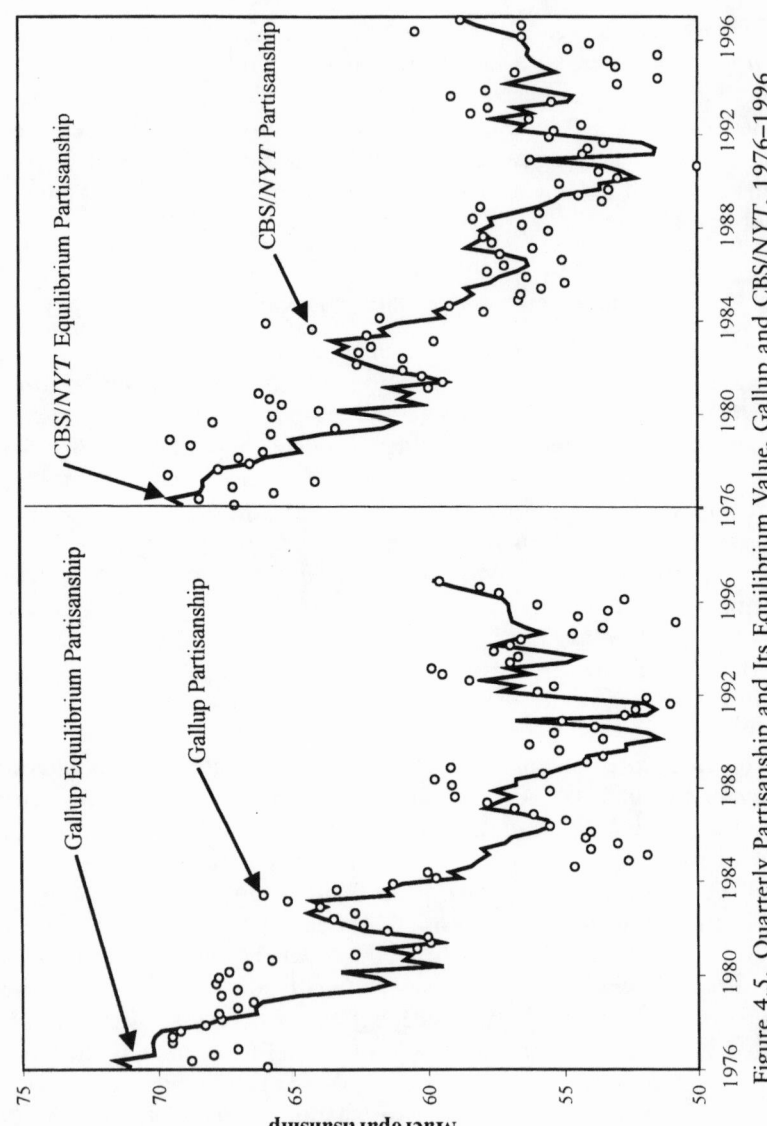

Figure 4.5. Quarterly Partisanship and Its Equilibrium Value, Gallup and CBS/*NYT*, 1976–1996

140

Table 4.2. *Regressing Future Macropartisanship on Current Observed Macropartisanship ($M_t$) plus Current Equilibrium Values of Macropartisanship ($M_t^*$), 1976–1996*

| Dependent Variable | Gallup | | CBS News/ New York Times | |
|---|---|---|---|---|
| | $M_t$ | $M_t^*$ | $M_t$ | $M_t^*$ |
| $M_{t+1}$ (N = 83) | 0.70[a] | 0.35[a] | 0.49[a] | 0.50[a] |
| | (9.43) | (3.57) | (5.08) | (4.49) |
| $M_{t+2}$ (N = 82) | 0.55[a] | 0.50[a] | 0.31[a] | 0.67[a] |
| | (6.20) | (4.22) | (3.05) | (5.75) |
| $M_{t+3}$ (N = 81) | 0.38[a] | 0.65[a] | 0.23[a] | 0.74[a] |
| | (3.49) | (4.47) | (2.15) | (6.12) |
| $M_{t+4}$ (N = 80) | 0.24[a] | 0.78[a] | 0.26[a] | 0.67[a] |
| | (1.95) | (4.84) | (2.41) | (5.41) |
| $M_{t+5}$ (N = 79) | 0.04 | 0.96[a] | 0.19 | 0.71[a] |
| | (0.30) | (5.62) | (1.61) | (5.12) |
| $M_{t+6}$ (N = 78) | −0.12 | ·1.01[a] | 0.09 | 0.77[a] |
| | (0.60) | (5.34) | (0.69) | (5.45) |

*Note*: Each row represents a pair of regression equations (one for Gallup and one for the CBS/*New York Times* series) for a prediction of $M_{t+L}$ at different "lead" times. The entries are regression coefficients, with $t$ values in parentheses.
[a] $p < 0.05$.

decisive "winner." And beyond four quarters, the coefficients for $M_t$ are statistically insignificant: There is no information in actual *Macropartisanship* beyond that of the fundamentals captured in $M_t^*$. As we might expect, $M_t^*$ is an even more decisive winner for the CBS/NYT series, the one with a less transitory wording component.

Thus the test to see which best predicts future *Macropartisanship* is conclusive. To know the current equilibrium represented by the cumulative shocks to *Consumer Sentiment* and *Approval* is more important than knowing the current value of *Macropartisanship*. The equilibrium value represents the fundamentals; any current deviation from this value will be short-lived. Moreover, the fundamentals provide stability, correlating at 0.97 with its lagged values. *Equilibrium Macropartisanship* looks very much like the type of partisan division about which we normally think – it is both changeable and enduring at the same time.

### INDIVIDUAL PARTISANSHIP AS AN INTEGRATED SERIES

If *Macropartisanship* is integrated, cumulating experience over time, the same should be true of its components – individuals' partisan dispositions. Indeed, the available evidence is unambiguously supportive. The panel analysis by Green and Palmquist (1994) confirms this expectation for individual voters when measurement error is properly taken into account. By our computations (Erikson et al. 1998), their mean estimate of the autoregression of "true" partisanship (the micropartisanship that averages out as macro-level *Equilibrium Macropartisanship*) is virtually 1.00.

### The Polarization of Partisanship with Aging

Now if any time series is integrated, then its variance must increase over time. Thus, if individuals' partisanship is integrated, we expect the variance of partisanship to increase with age. That is to say that over time individuals will move away from their initial partisanship rather than homing back onto their family heritage – weak partisans may become stronger partisans or even switch sides, but they will not necessarily go back to their beginnings. Substantively, we expect that any individual who has experience with a party in office will react to the experience, that is, to change the standing choice rather than inevitably return to the original disposition.[22] Thus, we expect older voters to be more polarized in their partisanship than the young. Is this prediction fulfilled?

Figure 4.6 depicts the variance of the National Election Studies (NESs) party identification scale by age, pooling all NES respondents 1952–1996. Confirming our expectations, the youngest age groups have. the lowest variances – consistent with the usual expectation that new voters are not very partisan as they start out adulthood. As successive age cohorts respond to the party's performances over time, the variance of partisanship continues to steadily expand, even into old age, with septuagenarians marked by twice the partisan variance of the youngest voters.

This pattern of increased polarization was first noticed by Converse (1976) with the argument that people *strengthen* their partisan inclinations over time – perhaps as a function of such mechanisms as selective exposure to, and perception of, political information and the biases of social-political stratification. The life cycle evidence suggests that when

---

22 Suppose that the time series of individual partisanship were stationary rather than integrated. Then, an individual's partisanship would vary around an equilibrium value that would be constant over the lifetime, rather than evolving.

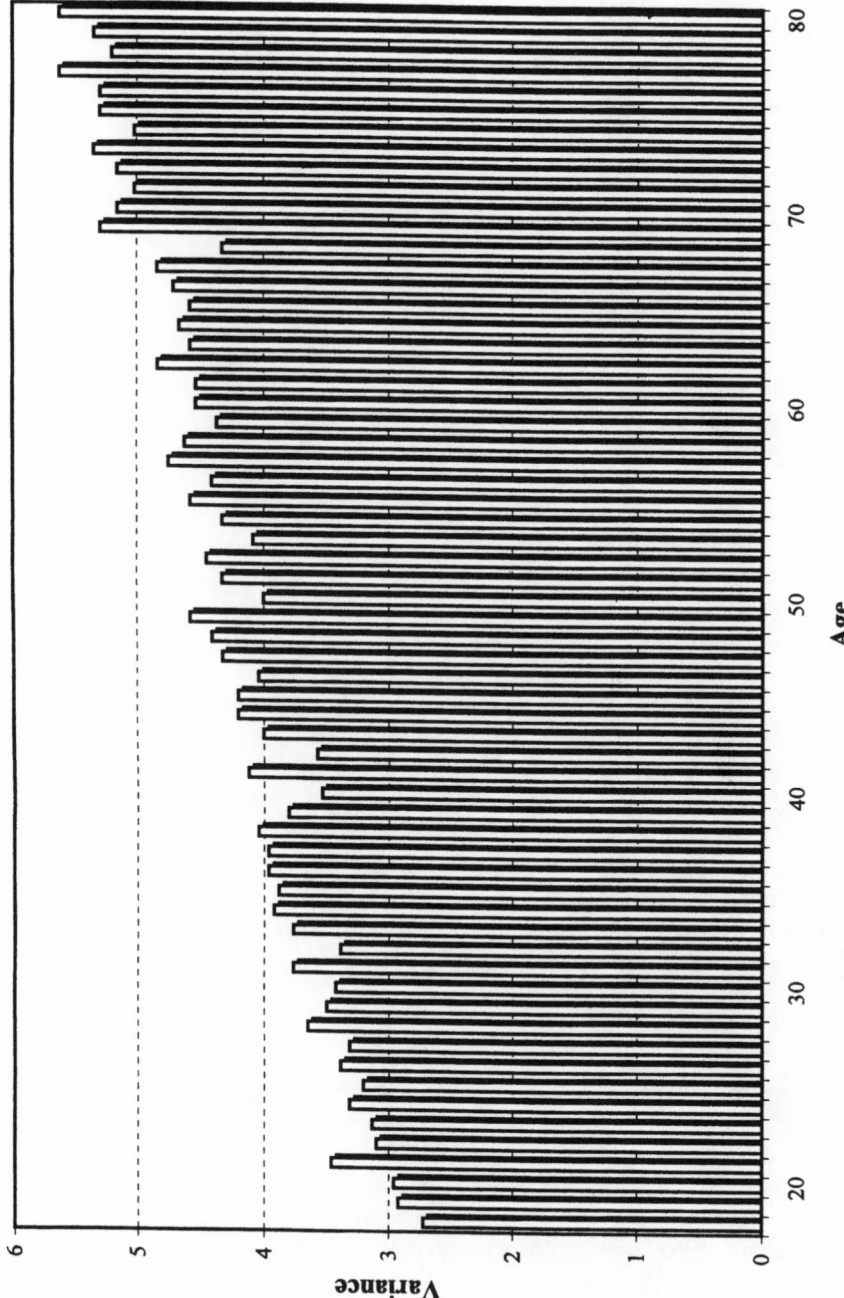

Figure 4.6. The Variance of Partisanship over the Life Cycle (Combined NES Data, 1956–1996)

people respond to the political world, they do so in ways that store the memory of those events over time – whether they merely strengthen their dispositions or whether they also occasionally switch we cannot say. In abstract terms, the implication is that individual partisanship, rather than reverting to its initial conditions, incorporates historical events.

## Generational Continuity

We can also observe evidence of the integrated component of partisanship from the behavior of political generations over time. Of special interest are the pre-depression generation and the immediate post-depression generation, distinguished from one another by their coming of political age just before and just after the Great Depression. Both generations lived through the depression and were affected by it. But only the pre-depression generation was affected by the earlier political climate of the 1920s.

The *American Voter* authors (Campbell et al. 1960) noticed that even as late as the 1950s the pre-depression generation continued to be more Republican than the post-depression generation who followed. As we show in Chapter 5, this partisan difference between the two generations persisted into the 1980s, when both groups were well into their senior years. Their partisanship was different even though their political histories were almost identical. The one exception was the older group's early exposure to pre-depression political stimuli. If there were no permanent component to partisanship, the influence of the pre-depression period would have long decayed and the two generations would be alike politically. Put another way, the excess Republicanism of the pre-depression generation shows that partisan memory can persist over the full span of adulthood. Just as contemporary voters will be affected over their lifetimes by politics today, the politics of the 1920s and even before held an impact on the elderly electorate of the late twentieth century.

## Macro Dynamics and Micro Stability

*Macropartisanship* is dynamic at the aggregate level, with much of the movement traceable to economic and political performance. At the same time, the evidence that party identification is stable at the micro level is also compelling. Thus, the truth to be confronted is that partisanship is stable among individuals but unstable in the aggregate. How can we reconcile macro-level dynamics with micro-level stability?

According to the careful panel analyses by Green and Palmquist (1990, 1994), people's *true* partisan dispositions change very slightly over time relative to others' with most of the *observed* change being measurement error. Because this is change relative to the mean partisanship, it represents idiosyncratic personal circumstances rather than national forces. For system-level analysis, we are interested not in change relative to the mean but in change in the mean itself. Is it plausible for the mean to move sufficiently to account for the observed change in *Macropartisanship* if the amount of idiosyncratic change (around this moving mean) is slight?

The answer turns out to be yes. When measured on a common scale, the partisan response to national forces captured by *Macropartisanship* has only a fraction of the variance observed at the micro level. "Small" micro movement on the order estimated by Green and Palmquist is quite consistent with the "large" macro movement we observe. The calculations that underlie this statement are complicated and presented in detail elsewhere (Erikson et al. 1998).[23] The intuition, however, is simple: A given amount of change can look minor at the micro level but major at the macro level. For instance, we can measure aggregate partisanship in NES surveys as either the mean 7-point scale position or as *Macropartisanship*. When we overlay the two, one point on the 7-point scale is equivalent to a whopping 24 points of *Macropartisanship*. What looks small on the former scale looks large on the latter. Thus, the perceived inconsistency between macro-level movement and relative stability at the micro level is a statistical illusion. The fact of macro-level movement should not challenge the view that party identification is highly stable at the individual level.

### PEASANTS, BANKERS, AND MACROPARTISANSHIP

In Chapter 3 we modeled *Presidential Approval* as a function of the public's economic assessments. With *Approval* being a relatively short-term phenomenon, it mirrors current and recent expectations about prosperity. As if the electorate were bankers, current innovations in presidential evaluation were shown to be based on rational expectations about future national prosperity. Voters, it would seem, evaluate the president based on their expectations of the future economy rather than personal economic circumstances. Party identification, we have

---

23 According to the estimates in Erikson et al. (1998), the true relative variance in partisanship *change* using the Green and Palmquist assumptions is 19 times the variance of the change in the equilibrium component of *Macropartisanship*.

now verified, is also influenced by the perceived economy. Are voters "bankers" when they change their partisan dispositions, or are they "peasants"?

We have two reasons for reservations that the banker model – so clearly confirmed for *Approval* – would carry over to *Macropartisanship*. First, changing one's approval of the president is easy compared to changing parties. Whereas one might change one's presidential evaluation on the basis of nothing more than informed speculation about the future of the general economy, this is an insufficiently strong motivation for partisan conversion.

Second, we know that *Macropartisanship* differs from *Approval* in that it is influenced by the permanent accumulation of perceived economic (and political) shocks rather than mainly by shocks of recent vintage. If shocks accumulate without forgetting, a reasonable expectation is that people absorb perceived changes in economic realizations rather than perceived changes in expectations.

We put theory to the test. From the *Index of Consumer Sentiment*, we separate out the two distinct components of pocketbook realizations or *Personal Retrospections* (aggregated perceptions of whether family fortunes improved over the past year) and *Business Expectations* (one-year forecast of business conditions). Then, we repeat our error correction model (ECM) exercise with *two* economic components plus the political component (the *Approval* shocks purged of the variance of the two types of economic shocks). We obtain the estimates in Table 4.3.

The result is clear. *Equilibrium Macropartisanship* $M_t^*$ is driven by aggregate pocketbook considerations and the political component of approval, but not business expectations. (Compare the first column's 0.12 with an insignificant −0.02.) Partisan self-identification, quite unlike approval of a president, is a matter of personal experience rather than informed speculation. Thus, while economic expectations can affect a president's popularity, any long-term effect on *Macropartisanship* depends on whether the expectations are followed by their realizations.[24]

---

24 Besides *Business Expectations* and *Personal Retrospections*, the *Index of Consumer Sentiment* contains additional ingredients that can be added to the mix. When the models containing the various combinations of cumulative economic effects are examined, it is clear that retrospections dominate over expectations and that personal pocketbook considerations dominate sociotropic ones. In some equations, cumulative sociotropic indicators have negative signs. One could make a statistical case that a party builds success by presiding over an economy where people collectively share the illusion that they are personally better off relative to others.

Table 4.3. *An Error Correction Model of Macropartisanship as a Function of Retrospections, Expectations, and Politics, 1953–1996*

| | Equilibrium Macropartisanship Component | Change in Macropartisanship Component | Summary Statistics for Full Model |
|---|---|---|---|
| Cumulated | 0.12[a] | | |
| Retrospections | (0.02) | | |
| Cumulated | −0.02 | | |
| Expectations | (0.02) | | |
| Cumulated Political | 0.11[a] | | |
| News | (0.02) | | |
| Constant | 61.89[a] | | |
| | (1.50) | | |
| Retrospection | | 0.03 | |
| Innovations | | (0.02) | |
| Expectation | | 0.02 | |
| Innovations | | (0.02) | |
| Political News | | 0.12[a] | |
| | | (0.03) | |
| Error Correction to | | −0.27[a] | |
| Equilibrium | | (0.05) | |
| Partisanship | | | |
| Adjusted R-Square | | | .22 |
| Standard Error of | | | |
| Estimate | | | 1.74 |
| N | | | 174 |

*Note:* Quarterly macropartisanship data from the Gallup series. The entire model is estimated using Nonlinear Least Squares. Standard errors in parentheses.
[a] $p < 0.05$.

## MACROPARTISANSHIP AND MACRO POLITICS

We started this chapter with the "standard" views of partisanship – positing that partisanship was either a matter of stable personal identity or that it shifted constantly to reflect the politics of the moment. These pictures represent different qualitative portraits of the political psychology involved in how citizens relate to the party system. As normally interpreted, these models produce a political system with a fixed equilibrium value around which party politics revolves. For the post–World War II generation, that equilibrium was thought to be a mildly Democratic plurality – one that might ebb and flow with short-term political happenstance – but one that generated a politics where the Democrats might reasonably expect to win elections as long as they could match the candidate and issue appeals of their opponents.

## Performance

We know that the fundamental picture is quite different. Instead of a single long-term equilibrium around which partisan politics centers we see that there exists no such stable entity. Politicians cannot reliably expect that the overall distribution of party loyalties will home in on any particular value. Accordingly, neither Democrats nor Republicans can count on any baseline expectation about electoral outcomes. While the parties surely retain large numbers of loyal identifiers (who are extremely unlikely to switch sides), there remain sufficient numbers of citizens who take on a "standing choice," which is derived from the performance of the parties in office. Thus, the best guess about some future's partisan distribution is not a system-level constant (say, 53 percent Democratic), but instead the current *Equilibrium Macropartisanship*. And that equilibrium is rooted in the fundamentals of party performance. Finally, of course, we also know that while current *Equilibrium Macropartisanship* is our best guess about the future, we also understand that the actual values will depend entirely on the course of political events between now and then.

Thus, the idea of a system-level "normal" vote takes on new meaning. There is no partisan constant that anchors the political system – no such absolute stability exists. Instead, the system is characterized by core uncertainty – as the baseline of electoral politics derives wholly from the historical path of party politics. For system theorists, and for electoral politics, this is an entirely radical re-conceptualization of partisanship and its macro consequences. Rather than homeostatic, macropartisanship is path dependent.

Further, while the idea of a fixed-point equilibrium now seems incorrect, we should not give up on the idea that *Macropartisanship* anchors the party system. After all, we find that the movement in $M_t^*$ (*Equilibrium Macropartisanship*) is slow. That is, when dramatic political events occur, they do affect people's partisan dispositions in permanent ways, but even large events actually change the dispositions of only a smallish number of people. It takes sustained good or bad times in order to generate a shift of, say, 5 to 10 percent of the public. Thus, in ordinary times politicians can reasonably expect that the *current* level of *Equilibrium Macropartisanship* will be stable for the foreseeable future. They may plan their political strategies, their trade-offs of current policy choices against future electoral consequences, and their schemes for personal ambition with a reasonable expectation that the fundamental baseline will be pretty similar over the predictable time horizon.

But crucially, they must also realize that the baseline, as embedded in *Macropartisanship*, is subject to change. And that change will reflect the performance of the parties in office. Parties that produce political and economic success will benefit; those that produce failures will pay.

# Macropartisanship

Further, the political memory of the system assures that parties may count on the public's "remembering" the past when elections roll around. So, in the long run, *Macropartisanship* is the summing up of the parties' performance and, thus, is only as predictable as is the success and failure of American governments.

Knowing that *Macropartisanship* is changeable and enduring merely asks the next question: Do these changes reflect the judgment of the entire electorate in a sort of ongoing national plebiscite or do they reveal concentrated changes of a different kind – say, rolling subnational "realignments" in which only a few specific sectors of the citizenry change their fundamental party dispositions? To answer this question, we must turn to data on partisanship of different subgroups of the population, as they are measured over time.

### APPENDIX: MACROPARTISANSHIP AS AN INTEGRATED SERIES

In time-series jargon, *Macropartisanship* contains a permanent or fundamental component that is an integrated series or a random walk. The integrated component $M_t^*$ is the cumulative weighted sum of the same economic and political innovations that cause *Consumer Sentiment* and *Presidential Approval*. The second component $M_t'$ behaves statistically as an autoregressive error term. It is $M_t^*$ that is of long-term importance, because when a series is a combination of an integrated and a stationary component, the integrated component dominates over the long run (Bannerjee et al. 1993). In this appendix, we present some statistical details.

### Is $M_t^*$ Integrated?

By construction, our cumulative series ($CumE_t = \Sigma E_j$; $CumA_t = \Sigma A_j$; $j = 0, 1 \ldots t$) represent the strict addition of estimated political and economic shocks. Because the shocks are statistically independent over time, the cumulated series are statistically integrated. $CumE_t$ and $CumA_t$ (and therefore $M_t^*$) all easily pass the statistical challenge of the Dickey-Fuller unit root tests; with nonsignificant $|t|$ values of 1.65, 1.57, 1.80, and 2.31, respectively, the null hypothesis of a random walk cannot be rejected for any of these variables. Dickey-Fuller tests on the residuals ($M_t - M_t^*$) produce $|t|$ values of 4.44 and 4.36, respectively, which are significant beyond the 0.01 level. Thus, standard diagnostic tests reassure that $M_t^*$ is unit-root with stationary residuals.

Of course, to construct integrated series from political and economic shocks is not by itself sufficient evidence of the correct specification for

149

the explanation of *Macropartisanship*. An alternative construction would be stationary series where effects decay geometrically ($CumE_t = \Sigma E_j \lambda^{t-j+1}$; $CumA_t = \Sigma A_j \lambda^{t-j+1}$), according to a $\lambda$ parameter between 0 and 1. In effect, we chose $\lambda = 1.00$. Other possibilities, even in the $\lambda = .99$ range, produce lower correlations between predicted and actual $M_t$. For this test, we search for the value of $\lambda$ that maximizes the $R^2$ predicting $M_t$ from the $\lambda$-specific *CumE* and *CumA* measures. We start the cumulations in 1953 and use them to predict $M_t$ for 1976–1996. Actually, the $\lambda$ that maximizes the $R^2$ is 1.002 for Gallup and 1.006 for CBS/NYT.

Thus, we model *Macropartisanship*'s equilibrium as a random walk and observe that empirically this model appears to defeat all alternatives. Still, our analysis does not depend on the knife-edge assumption that the autoregressive parameter is precisely 1.0000. If in truth $M_t^*$ is merely "near integrated" (see Banerjee et al. 1993; DeBoef and Granato 1997), then the implications would be no different for practical politics.

## Is an Integrated $M_t^*$ Statistically Plausible?

Some argue against the possibility that a bounded series such as *Macropartisanship* could be integrated or unit-root. The objection is that a random walk implies an explosive variance and a run to the boundary conditions (0 or 100%). In theory, this objection carries weight; in practice, the concern is misplaced.

First, *Macropartisanship* is an unbounded variable that is indexed as a bounded percentage due only to measurement limitations. The concept itself (the electorate's mean relative attraction for the Republican vs. Democratic Party) is unbounded. For comparison, consider the plausible argument that the stock market is unit-root. If we were forced to measure its performance as the percentage of stocks above some arbitrary value-per-unit threshold, then the truth of the statistical properties of the underlying variable would remain unchanged. In any case, we could make measured *Macropartisanship* unbounded by the simple expedient of recalibrating it by the logit transformation. Such a maneuver is unnecessary for the observed data that range from about 50 to 70 percent Democratic. $M_t$ and its logit transformation $[\log(M_t/(1 - M_t))]$ correlate at 0.9998 for the actual $M_t$ observations.

Second, $M_t^*$ avoids the calamity of a run to the 0 and 100 percent boundaries because of its slow speed of movement. In theory, the net change in a unit-root variable will have zero mean with a variance equal to $m\text{Var}(u_t)$, where $m$ is the number of periods and $u_t$ is the change over interval $t$. The variance in $\Delta M_t^*$ is a shade under 1.0, so the expected variance over $m$ quarters is about equal to the number of quarters. For instance, following a century of change, the expected variance is about

400, and the expected standard deviation is about 20. With a standard deviation of 20, half the cases are within 16 points of the mean. Thus, the median absolute value of $\Delta M_t^*$ over several runs of 100 years is a mere 16 percentage points.

Because the bounded variable works well enough and because we want to keep the measure easily interpretable ("Percentage Democratic" rather than "log of the odds that a partisan is a Democrat"), we chose to follow convention and use percentages, even though we expect an integrated behavioral process.

### The Autocorrelation Evidence

For a stationary series, the autocorrelations (correlations between current and lagged values) decay exponentially to zero. (See Chapter 2 and the discussion of *Presidential Approval*.) For an integrated series, the signature would be autoregressive coefficients near unity for all lags. For a combined series (e.g., $M_t^*$ plus $M_t'$), the signature would be autoregressive coefficients that decays exponentially not to zero but to the proportion of the variance "explained" by the permanent component. This is the case with *Macropartisanship*. By 12 to 15 quarters, the autoregression coefficients converge not to zero, but to .50, the proportion of the variance "explained" by $M_t^*$.

151

# 5

---

## *Decomposing Partisan Change*

In Chapter 4, we analyzed *Macropartisanship* as the aggregate partisanship of the entire electorate. When *Macropartisanship* moves, however, voters do not all move in tandem. Some groups may undergo more partisan change than others, or even move in opposite partisan directions from each other. Moreover, with some entering the electorate and others exiting, the very composition of the electorate is always changing. Every 60 years or so, the population of adult citizens gets entirely refreshed as new citizens replace the old. We should not mistake the shifting partisanship of different generations for partisan conversions among a constant set of citizens.

We have not had much to say about demographic divisions or changing electoral composition thus far. Indeed, the consistent strategy of our enterprise is to ignore differentiations of all kinds and ask what we can learn by focusing solely on variations that occur over time. That is what we have done with partisanship in the previous chapter. Although we have stopped short of asserting the point, the implicit message of that chapter is that distinctions are unnecessary, that the movements that matter happen to the whole electorate over time, not only for certain demographic groups or certain political generations.

An alternative view is that not only does partisan movement vary by group or generation, but indeed that by focusing on such distinctions we can explain the movements we ascribe to the whole electorate. Thus, for example, the Republican resurgence of the 1980s is a descriptive fact. But how we understand that fact would be different if it turned out to be the case that the national movement was entirely accounted for by a particular region or a particular generation.

In this chapter, we dip beneath the surface of national politics to find out how much of the macro movement in *Macropartisanship* is accountable in terms of selected demographic groups or in between-generation differences rather than movements over time. Doing so requires that we employ a different style of analysis and that we turn to data that are rich in individual variations. We ask how much the demographic divisions of North versus South, white versus black, and men versus women contribute to the partisan changes we have seen rippling over time. And we ask how much different partisan perspectives of different age cohorts (generations) contribute to the net partisan change. We know at the outset that we will see differences along these lines. The interesting question is how much. Their accounting enriches our understanding of the partisan movement over time that we have observed.

### The CBS News/New York Times *Measure of Macropartisanship*

So far, most of our discussion of *Macropartisanship* has been based on the Gallup poll's quarterly readings, 1952–1996. Our discussion in Chapter 4 also touched on a second measure, based on the polls jointly conducted by CBS News and the *New York Times*, 1976–1996. Unlike the Gallup surveys, the CBS/*NYT* surveys are available for analysis at the micro level of the individual poll respondent. The CBS/*NYT* surveys include measures of race, region, gender, and age, allowing a rather complete tracking of *Macropartisanship* across racial, regional, and gender categories and by political generation.

We can, as we will see, compare the partisanship of white and African American respondents on a nearly quarterly basis for over 21 years. For the same time span we can compare the partisanship of women and men. And we can examine the important distinction between the South and the non-South, as we track the trek of southern whites from the Democratic to the Republican party over the 21-year span of our analysis.

Most important, the CBS/*NYT* surveys allow a fine-grained analysis of different age groups as they enter and leave the electorate. Starting in 1980 (alas, not for the 1970s), the CBS/*NYT* surveys ascertained respondents' ages in exact years. This allows us to take a far more precise accounting than hitherto possible of generational differences in partisanship. Tracking generations allows us to separate out partisan movement due to the electorate's changing composition from partisan movement due to party conversions by established voters.

In our focus on macro aggregates, we have ignored these sorts of individual-level and group-level phenomena. Our task in this chapter is to flesh out the subnational movements in order to understand more fully the structures that underlie the macro system's dynamics. We want to know how much we lose in the translation of individual political psychology into macro politics – and begin to develop explicit linkages between the two levels of analysis.

This challenge sets the agenda for the remainder of this chapter. Traditional partisan theory stemming from *The American Voter* would argue that most aggregate movement must be due to the behavior of newly socialized voters rather than the conversion of established voters. Thus we will examine the relative contributions of replacement and conversion to *Macropartisanship* change. It has also been argued that the major shift in the Republicans' favor over the past decade is due simply to southern whites finally locating their proper ideological home within the Republican party. Thus we will examine regional differences in *Macropartisanship* over time. Along the way, we also examine race and gender as sources of *Macropartisanship* difference.

The chapter closes with an exploration in what we call "political archeology," where we use CBS/NYT surveys to infer the *Macropartisanship* of an earlier era. Much of a cohort's partisanship can be traced to its exposure to events in its years of initial political awareness. Thus to focus on the partisanship of older generations allows a glimpse into the partisanship of the electorate of the past, including the prepoll era. And finally, this focus on the partisanship of youth informs our speculation about the partisan future of our own era.

## REPLACEMENT, CONVERSION, AND MACROPARTISANSHIP

All macro-level movement is necessarily composed of change at the individual level. Part of this individual-level change consists of individual replacement, as some citizens enter and others exit the electorate. New members may be more Republican than exiting voters they replace, for example. Other individual-level change results from change by individuals themselves, for instance when an individual converts from Democratic to Republican. All aggregate movement can be accounted for (exactly) as either replacement or individual change.

The relative importance of individual replacement and individual conversion depends on the time interval. Over a calendar quarter or two, almost all aggregate change will be accounted for by individual conversion among a constant set of individuals rather than be the product of exit and entry. Over a few decades, about half of the electorate will be replaced, but it is an open question whether new partisans are appreciably different from those they displace.

Replacement occurs when new (mainly young) citizens enter the eligible electorate and other (mainly older) voters die off. The *American Voter* school has singled out new voters as a major conduit of partisan change. The theory is that new voters respond the strongest to contemporary partisan trends or shocks, for the reason that they lack the strong partisan commitment that established voters possess. Thus we have a model of aggregate change due to the shifting partisan imprint on newly hatched voters, while old voters die off, taking with them their partisan imprints from the time of their entry into the electorate. In this way, aggregate partisan change can occur even with people maintaining their initial party identification throughout their political life cycle. This life-cycle model has even been used to explain the major Democratic gain of the 1930s realignment era. The literature on the New Deal realignment includes a lively dispute between those who argue that new voters accounted for most movement (Anderson 1979) and those who claim there was major partisan conversion among established voters of the time (e.g., Erikson and Tedin 1981; Sundquist 1983).

By no stretch of the imagination could the dynamics of voter replacement even come close to accounting for the amount of movement in *Macropartisanship* observable over one or two quarters. Still, there is reason to believe that younger voters are more receptive to contemporary partisan trends, and that people become more resistant to partisan change as they progress through their political life cycle. The most plausible model would have responsiveness or resistance to partisan shocks as a matter of degree, depending on the person's location in the political life cycle. Like first-time voters, established voters respond to new partisan forces. But the responsiveness may decline gradually with age. Perhaps we can detect evidence that generational replacement does account for some of the long-run trends in *Macropartisanship*.

To directly observe the relevance of generational differences to *Macropartisanship* movement, we turn to the CBS/NYT series. Beginning in 1980, CBS News/*New York Times* respondents were coded according to exact age in years. This allows the tracing of *Macropartisanship* by specific age cohorts. For illustrative purposes, we choose three separate age cohorts, which we describe by their age in 1980, the first year of the series. The "young" cohort comprises people who were 18–29 years old in 1980 and 34–45 when our series ends 16 years later in 1996. The "middle-aged" cohort is formed by people who were 30–54 in 1980 and 46–70 16 years later. The "old" cohort is made up of those 55–72 in 1980 and 71–88 16 years later. This older cohort represents voters who had come of political age (then, 21 years old) between 1929 and 1947, the New Deal generation.

Figure 5.1 presents the *Macropartisanship* of the three generations in the CBS/*NYT* surveys, 1980–1996. As predicted, the young cohort moves the most over this span. In 1980, on the eve of the Reagan era, all three age groups were similar in their partisanship, each scoring about 65 percent Democratic in *Macropartisanship*. Over the next 16 years, both the middle-aged and the old cohort shifted about 5 percentage points more Republican. But by far the largest movement is by the young cohort, shifting 15 percentage points to become virtually evenly divided between Republicans and Democrats by the end of the Reagan years –

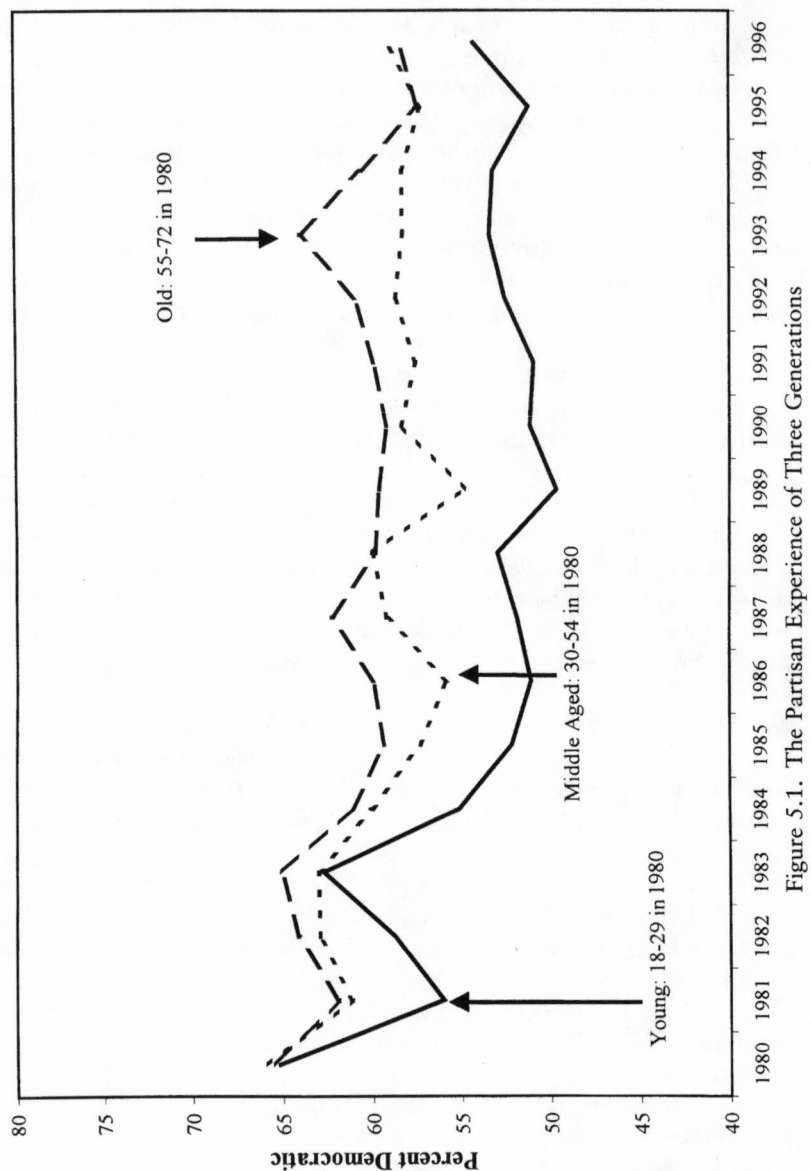

Figure 5.1. The Partisan Experience of Three Generations

but then, more than older cohorts, moving back toward the Democrats in the 1990s.

By the endpoint of our analysis (1996), our oldest cohort reached the advanced age range of 71–88. This old cohort is the "realignment" generation that came of political age in time to cast its first presidential votes in the FDR era. It followed another famous political cohort – the pre-realignment generation that came of political age before the Great Depression and New Deal. In various analyses of NES data going back to the 1950s, this pre-realignment cohort remained disproportionately Republican as if its entry into electoral politics in the 1920s and before produced resistance to the Democratic temptations of the New Deal era and beyond.

The CBS/*NYT* surveys present sufficient data on this pre-realignment cohort for a cursory analysis. We consider the group born 1900–1907, who were 73–80 at the start of our analysis period, 1980. Because its numbers were ravaged by mortality in the 1980s, we conclude our analysis of this group in 1988. Figure 5.2 compares this pre-realignment cohort with our slightly younger post-realignment cohort, for the years 1980–1988. Note that the older of these two cohorts remained decisively less Democratic, even as the two groups were advancing through old age. Thus, we see the effects of early socialization. At the same time, we also observe that this older pre-realignment generation was far from being one-sidedly Republican. As this most Republican of cohorts entered the twilight of its political life, it contained slightly more Democrats than Republicans. Obviously, its partisanship, though tempered by early Republican socialization, bent considerably in the Democratic direction during its lifetime. In this pattern, we see testimony to the permanence of early socialization *and* the permanence of reactions to subsequent political history.

Since the pre-realignment generation was more Republican than average, its gradual departure from the political scene worked to the advantage of the Democrats. But as this pre-realignment generation approached extinction, the net Democratic gain came to an end. Reversing partisan fortune, Republicans began to gain as young Republican voters replaced old post-realignment Democrats.

By 1989, a still new "Reagan" cohort developed, of people who came of voting age during the eight Reagan years. Figure 5.3 picks up the partisanship of this new group of young voters for 1981–1996, comparing them with the exiting pre-realignment voters, 1980–1988. The new Reagan generation starts out even more Republican than the exiting pre-realignment generation that it replaced. The pre-realignment generation, so noted for its Republican tendencies, represented the partisan memory from before the depression through the era of Democratic dominance

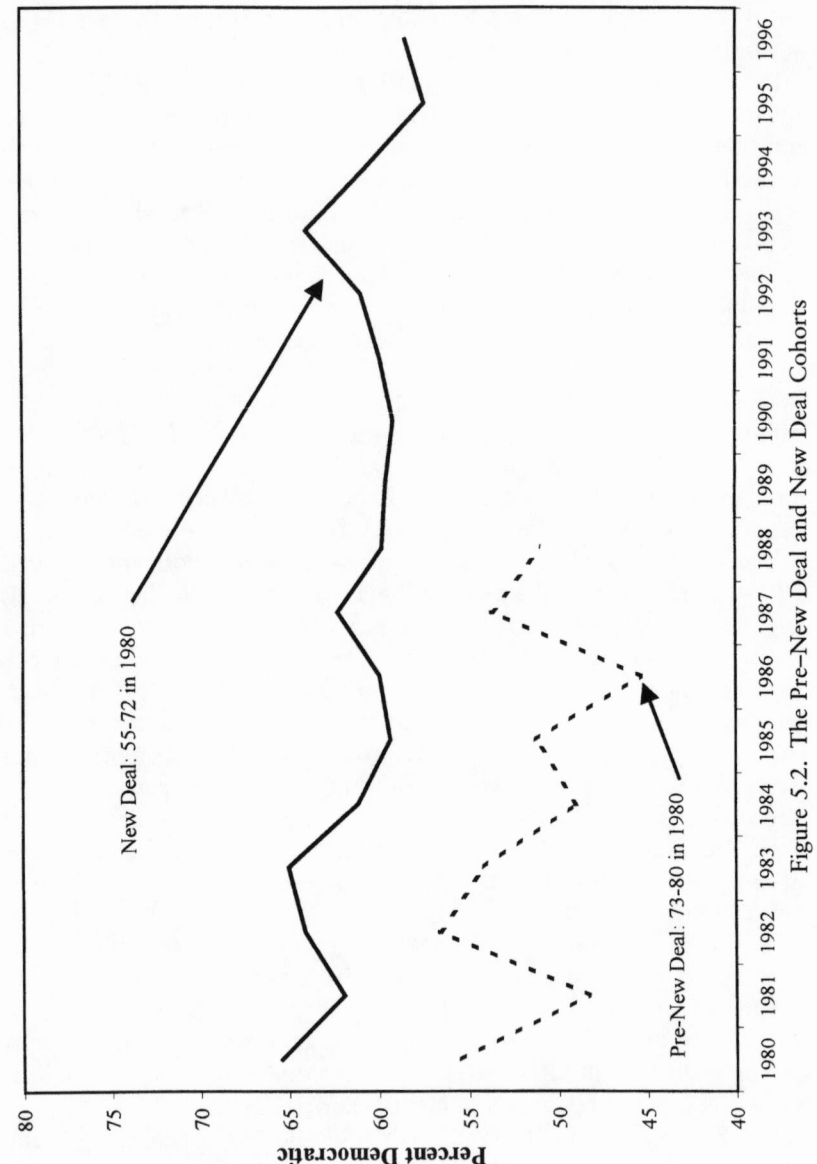

Figure 5.2. The Pre-New Deal and New Deal Cohorts

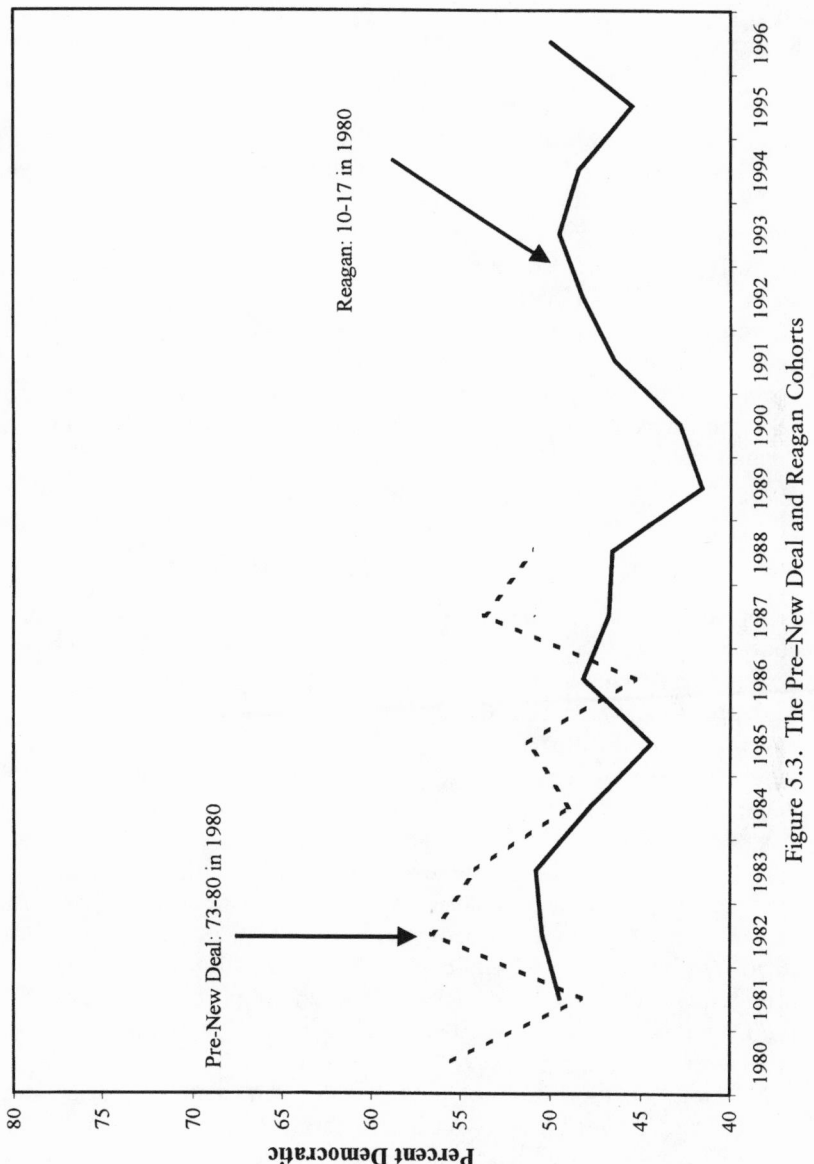

Figure 5.3. The Pre–New Deal and Reagan Cohorts

and into the Reagan era. The Reagan generation learned its partisanship from the politics of the Reagan era, with little influence from prior history.

As one final illustration of generational differences in partisanship, Figure 5.4 compares the Reagan cohort (coming of age 1981–1988) with the previous young cohort (17–29 in 1980). The time series runs from 1981 to 1996. At the start of this brief time series, the Reagan cohort was even more Republican than our "young" cohort starting out in 1980. By 1992, both cohorts became slightly more Democratic. Meanwhile, a new "Bush" cohort grew up, becoming eligible to vote during the four-year Bush administration. Starting in 1993, the first year of the new Clinton administration, the three groups of "young" voters showed similar partisanship, with some small but clear Democratic gains. The newer Bush cohort entered the electorate more Democratic than the Reagan cohort; meanwhile, the Reagan cohort and the slightly older group moved slightly more Democratic.

## *Generational Change and* Macropartisanship *Change*

From our analysis of age and partisanship it is clear that young voters contribute disproportionately to *Macropartisanship* movement, and that potentially, replacement of old cohorts by the new can affect long-term *Macropartisanship* trends. But by how much? The temptation is to forecast the partisan future from contemporary trends especially among the young. One should beware, though, that far more than the predictable demographics of age, the greatest source of partisan change is the unpredictable course of political events.

Consider, for instance, prognostications around the time of the Gulf War in 1991. Noting partisan trends, especially among young people, the press was beginning to report initial rumblings of a new Republican majority. Instead, the Democrats made steady gains (winning two presidential elections along the way), although by the mid-1990s the Democratic edge was far below what it was during the Democrats' glory years.

An even better example of how one might misread the future from extrapolating from today's youth was the state of partisanship in the mid-1970s. In 1977, with a Democratic president and a decisively Democratic congress, the Democrats appeared poised to dominate U.S. politics for years to come. They not only held a partisan lead of two to one, but also had the demographics of age apparently working in their favor. The downtrodden Republicans received little strong support from new or young voters, and their strongest age group was the dying pre-realignment generation. In actuality, of course, in a few short years,

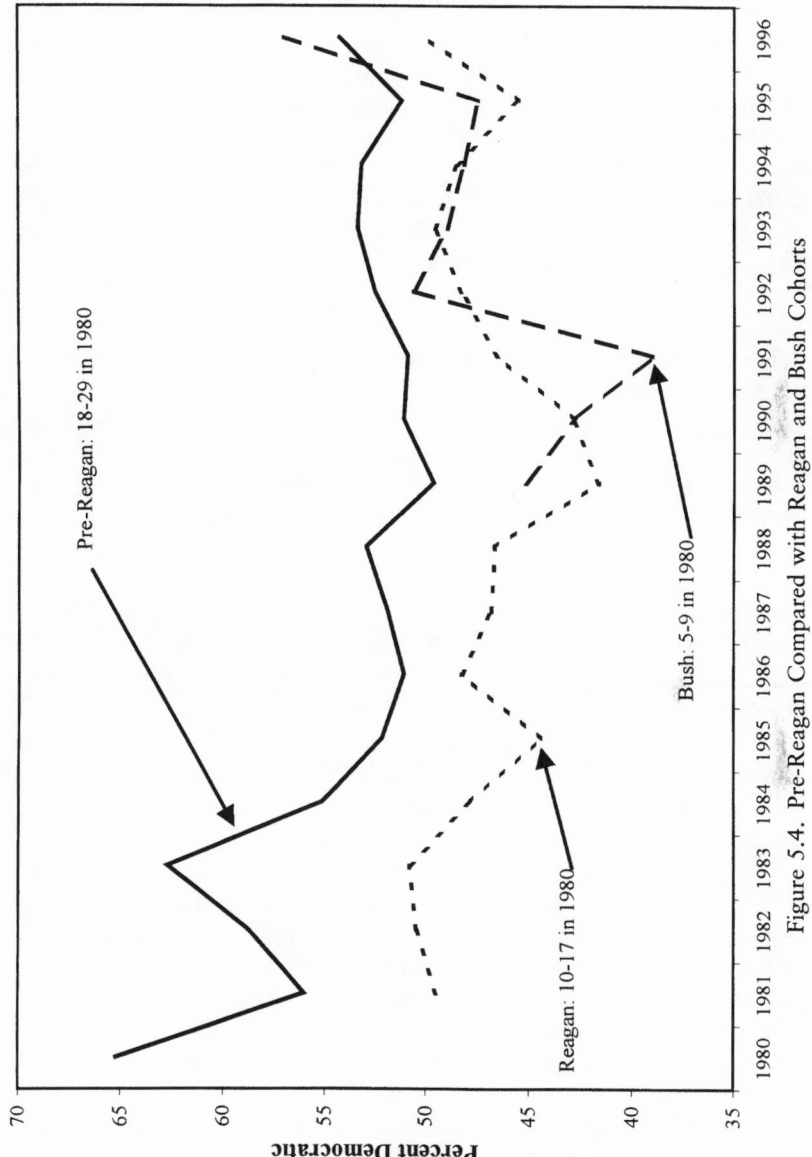

Figure 5.4. Pre-Reagan Compared with Reagan and Bush Cohorts

all age groups moved Republican (in varying degrees), and the Reagan era began.

In the final analysis, how much of the change in *Macropartisanship* is accounted for by generational change as opposed to conversion? For the 16-year period of our CBS/NYT analysis, we can estimate the net partisan conversion for citizens who were adults for the entire period. The difference between this estimate of net conversion and the overall net change in *Macropartisanship* must by definition equal the net change from the second source, generational change.

The goal is to compare the partisanship in 1980 and 1996 of people who were adult citizens for the time period. Except for immigration and delayed citizenship, all citizens 36 years of age or older in 1996 were eligible voters (18 or older) in 1980. However, we cannot know which citizens in 1980 survived until 1996. What we can do is weight 1980 respondents by their probability of surviving 16 years and record the 1980 partisanship of 1980 respondents weighted by these survival probabilities. The difference between the net partisanship of these two samples (1980 weighted; 1996, 36 or older) provides the estimate of conversion-induced change over the period.[1] For the period 1980:1 to 1996:3, our quasi-panel of citizens went from 62.8 to 56.2 percent Democratic, for a Democratic decline of 6.4 points of *Macropartisanship*. Thus, we obtain assurance that conversion of established voters contributed to the long-term Republican gain. The net *overall* change 1980:1 to 1996:3 (63.1% to 54.4%) was a Democratic loss of 8.7 points. Thus, the net Republican gain was only 2.3 points greater than it would have been if the 1980 electorate had remained constant. This leaves little room for generational replacement as a source of major aggregate change, even over a span of 16 years including the Reagan presidency.

Of course, the amount of replacement-induced change depends on both the length of time and the exact time interval examined. During the pre-1980 period, replacement dynamics favored the Democrats. Over the period 1952–1980, new voters were relatively Democratic while the die-offs were mainly from the disproportionately Republican pre–New Deal pre-realignment generation. Using NES data and a similar methodology

1 The mortality weights are derived from 1996 respondents to the CBS News/*New York Times* surveys. For respondents 35 and older, the relative frequencies of birth years provide the (relative) expected frequencies of survival for 1980 respondents. In this way, the 1980 and 1996 quasi-panels share the same distribution of birth years. Strictly speaking, the expected frequencies are only frequencies and not probabilities. Thus, we know the relative survival rates of the birth cohorts to each other, but not the actual probabilities of survival. As a result of this limitation, we cannot estimate the exact proportions of the 1980 electorate who did and did not survive 18 years.

to that just described, we estimate a 5.5 percentage point discrepancy between the Democratic gain over the 28 years from 1952 to 1980 when measured for all voters (63.4% to 64.5%), and for a quasi-panel of constant voters (68.1% to 63.7%). While citizens who were present from the 1950s through the 1970s drifted slightly more Republican, this trend was offset by young Democrats replacing older Republicans.

We have seen that young voters are more responsive to partisan trends, just as traditional partisan theory suggests. And we observe cycles both in the partisan trends of the moment and in the partisan trends among the generation dying off. Even so, the net change in *Macropartisanship* that is produced by the dynamics of replacement amounts to a surprisingly small shift. New generations may differ from those exiting. But the amount of change is not nearly as large as that found in the shifting partisanship of surviving voters. If we want to learn what moves *Macropartisanship*, we must focus mainly on what causes citizens to realign their own partisanship, not what causes one generation to differ from another.

### Aging and Partisan Change

As we have noted, students of partisanship disagree on the mechanisms of partisan change. At one extreme, all partisan change could be due to generational change. If this were the case, all partisan movement at the macro level would be due to the varying partisanship at entry by new voters. Voters would enter with a partisan imprint derived from political events during their formative years, and would never change. At the macro level, each generation would maintain a constant partisanship over its lifetime. The alternative mechanism is conversion. Each crop of new voters would respond exactly as established voters (no more, no less) to the politics of the times and would continue to respond to the political winds throughout their lifetime. At the macro level, each generation would reveal a mild partisan distinctiveness over its lifetime as a function of entry conditions, but would also change with the times. At issue then is how the amplitude of the partisan response varies with age. Is this amplitude strong in youth but then severely dampened? Is it constant through the political life cycle? Or is the answer something in between? The answer is important for what it tells us about the sources of partisan change in the past and perhaps into the future.

Our analysis has clearly shown the presence of conversion. Yet, consistent with the generational story, we also see clear evidence that partisan change is amplified early in political life. Political forces generate more partisan change among the young than the old. In this section, we attempt to depict more exactly the relationship between age and the partisan response.

163

## Performance

We have seen that as a new cohort enters the electorate, its partisanship differs to some degree from its predecessors. As each cohort matures, it responds to period effects representing the response to the immediate political environment. The magnitude of this period effect is, as we have seen, a function of age. The older the voter, the less the response to the immediate political environment. We ask, what function describes this process, whereby the amplitude of the partisan response declines with age?

In most studies of voter cohorts, both periods and cohorts are conceptualized in terms of election cycle intervals of two or four years, or even larger. Exploiting the large $N$ of the CBS/NYT pooled sample, we have been able to slice time even more finely than usual – to observe cohorts over periods measured in the units of specific years. Moreover, we are able to highlight cohorts not simply by their entry election year (at two- or four-year intervals) but by their initial year of eligibility. In this way we can take into account the effects of aging where the magnitude of the response to period effects depends on exact age in years. In short, we can model a cohort's aggregate partisanship as a function of the cohort's year of entry plus the accumulation of period effects from the time of entry onward, where the amplitudes of the year effects are determined by the cohort's age in years. (We start the adult life cycle at age 18, even though before 1972 most citizens were ineligible to vote until age 21.)

More formally, we model cohort partisanship as a function of the cohort's partisanship at age 18 plus cumulative year effects modified by age:

$$M_{kt} = \Gamma_k + \sum_{y=k}^{t} \lambda_{age} u_y \qquad (5.1)$$

Here $k$ is the year any cohort entered the electorate, $M_{kt}$ is cohort $k$'s *Macropartisanship* in year $t$, $\Gamma_k$ is the beginning partisanship for cohort $k$ at entry, and the summation over the political events $(u_y)$ from entry to the present represents the cumulation of experience in partisanship. Note that the yearly effects are weighted by $\lambda_{age}$, which is a function of the cohort's age at the time. In our data, we start in 1980, so we have:

$$M_{kt} = \Gamma_{k,79} + \sum_{y=80}^{t} \lambda_{y-k+18} u_y \qquad (5.1a)$$

where $\Gamma_{k,79}$ is cohort $k$'s *Macropartisanship* in 1979, and (by arithmetic) age $= y - k + 18$.

We estimate the parameters of Equation 5.1a where the units of analysis are cohort years, for example, $M_{1966,1985}$ represents the 1985

## Decomposing Partisan Change

*Macropartisanship* of respondents born in 1948 and turning 18 in 1966 (and 21 in 1969). To estimate how age amplifies the partisan response, the appropriate dependent variable is $\Delta M_{kt}$, the cohort's change in *Macropartisanship* from one year to the next. Our independent variables are year dummies representing year effects, multiplied by a measure of $\lambda_{age}$, the amplification parameter. We searched for the plausible function for $\lambda_{age}$ that explains the most variance in $\Delta M_{kt}$ and found that the best model to describe responsiveness as a function of age is one where the amplitude declines by a proportion of 0.02 each year of age (after 18 – the year of entry). More precisely,

$$\Delta M_{kt} = 0.98^{(age-19)} u_t \qquad (5.2)$$

where $\Delta M_{kt}$ = the change in *Macropartisanship* for cohort $k$ from year $t$ – 1 to year $t$ and the year effect is normalized so that $\lambda = 1$ for 19-year-olds.[2]

We now have learned that a cohort's responsiveness to new political and economic shocks declines by about 2 percent per year of political maturity.[3] It means that a cohort's partisanship is only about two-thirds as responsive to current political events as it was to events 20 years earlier. After 40 years, a cohort loses about half its original responsiveness. Thus, seniors respond less markedly to current performance than youngsters, but they *do* respond substantially. This is merely a matter of degree. Overall, though, because the permanent component of partisanship never decays, an older cohort's *Macropartisanship* becomes a function less of the contemporary era and more and more a function of political events long ago.

### RACE, REGION, AND MACROPARTISANSHIP

Can we identify certain groups that are most responsible for the long-term movement of *Macropartisanship*? This question invites an investigation of two special (and intertwined) cleavages that divide Americans, race and southern regionalism.

---

2 An alternative model with a slightly lower $R^2$ posits that the amplitude declines with the inverse of age. Although this alternative model may have superior intuitive appeal, the exponential decay model we employ is easier to manipulate in our "archeological" calculations below. The model of equation 5.2 was chosen because it predicts year-to-year of cohort change with a higher adjusted $R^2$ (0.11) than plausible alternatives. For the modeling exercise, we observe cohort-year partisan change for two separate cohort-year subsamples, representing the same cohorts one year apart. We weigh these observations by $(N_1 N_2)^{1/2}$ where $N_1$ and $N_2$ are the sample sizes for the cohort in successive years.

3 For instance, if 30-year-olds move 10 units more Democratic one year, then 31-year-olds move 9.8 units the same year.

# Performance

As the United States has become noticeably more Republican over the past decade or so, one group that has decidedly resisted the new partisan trend is African Americans. It follows that if we separate out white Americans for special analysis, in percentage terms their partisan movement must be greater than for Americans as a whole, where all racial groups are included.

As demonstration, Figure 5.5 presents separate trends in *Macropartisanship* for white and black Americans. The data are from the CBS/*NYT* series, 1976–1996. The figure shows a black-white gap in partisanship that makes the size of the *Macropartisanship* shift over time seem microscopic by comparison. As the figure shows, blacks who take partisan sides tend to be Democrats by almost 9 to 1, with no noticeable Republican gains. For whites, however, the decline in Democratic allegiance takes on crucial importance. Whereas in the 1970s, white Democrats outnumbered white Republicans by 3 to 2 or better, beginning in the mid-1980s, the Republicans have held a slight plurality among whites.

One may venture that racial issues (civil rights legislation, affirmative action, etc.) have been a source of the increasing racial divide. Given the history of race relations in the South, we could expect a regional division in terms of the degree of partisan response among whites. As whites polarize in opposition to black gains, the greatest white sensitivity we would expect to find in the South.

Due to the history of race relations after the Civil War, the white South was predominantly Democratic in voting and party identification, even well into our current time series. As the Democratic Party became more identified with civil rights, especially in the 1960s, the white South's longstanding identification with the Democrats became an anomaly. To some, it seemed only a matter of time until the white South shifted Republican to become consistent with its conservatism. Over the past few decades, the Republicans have made major gains in the South in terms of electoral politics, and this gain has accrued almost entirely from among the white electorate. Scholars have debated the reasons for this Republican claim on the white South. The question is whether the source is "racial politics" (Carmines and Stimson 1989; Huckfeld and Kohfeld 1989; Edsall and Edsall 1991) or some more benign form of conservative ideology (Abramowitz 1994).

Not surprisingly, this Republican gain is found not only in terms of election outcomes but also in terms of our *Macropartisanship* indicator. Observing the distinct southern partisan trend, Miller (1991) went as far as to assert that virtually all the Republican gains from the 1980s accrued from whites in the South. While this claim is certainly overstated, we can see an exaggerated change in *Macropartisanship* for whites in the South when compared to the comparable change for nonsouthern whites.

166

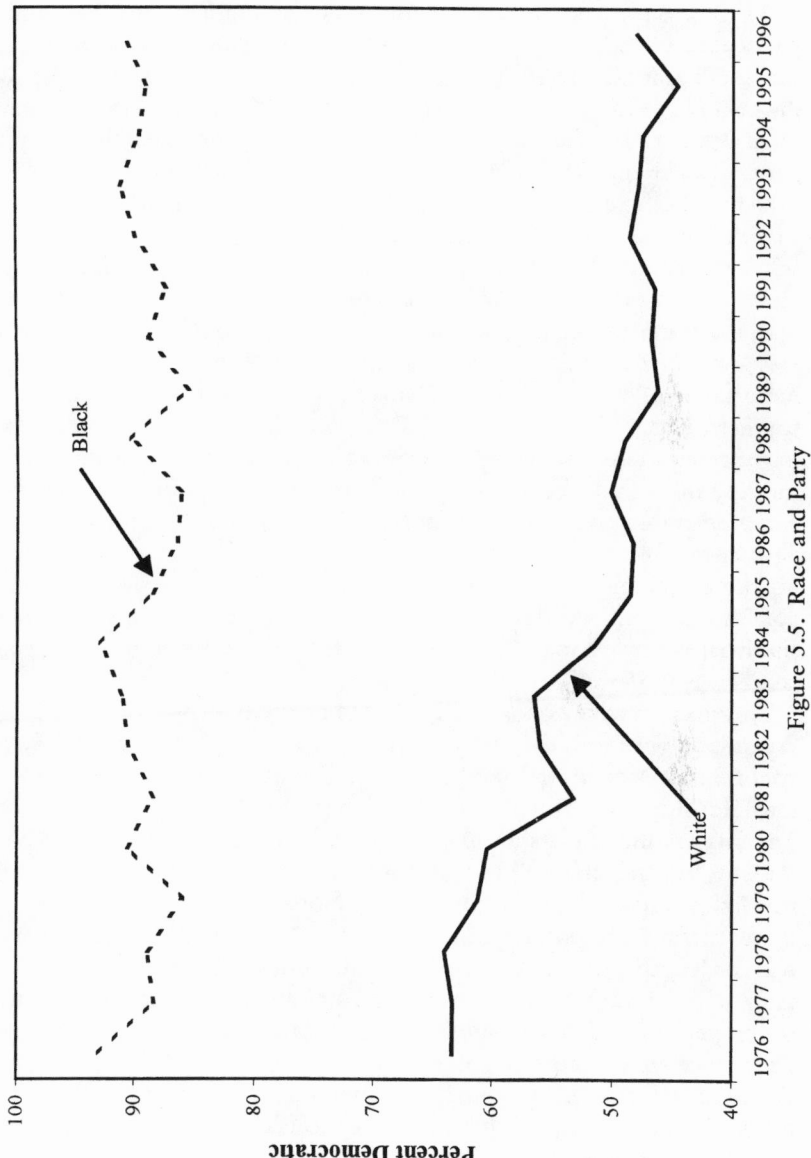

Figure 5.5. Race and Party

167

## Performance

Figure 5.6 presents the basic comparison of southern and nonsouthern whites in the CBS/*NYT* series. Republican gains were strongest in the South but clearly evident in both regional groups. At the start of the time series in 1976, about 60 percent of northern white partisans were Democrats rather than Republicans. Democratic strength was even stronger in the South, as about 70 percent of white southern partisans called themselves Democrats. Twenty years later, at the end of our series, slightly less than half of the partisans, North and South, called themselves Democrats. For all practical purposes, the regional gap in the party identification of white voters had disappeared.

In the previous section, we showed that the Republican gains of the 1980s and 1990s came disproportionately from younger age cohorts. The importance of the generational change is readily seen in the growth of southern Republicanism. Figure 5.7 displays the partisan change of different generations (among whites), South and non-South. Whichever way the data are sliced, the most dramatic drop in Democratic identification occurred among the youngest cohort (18–29 in 1980) of southern whites. At the start of the time series in 1980, this young cohort scored almost 60 percent Democratic in *Macropartisanship*. By the early 1990s, the partisan division reversed to 60 percent Republican. Meanwhile, older southern whites changed little. Even in the late 1990s, the older white southerners (55–72 in 1980) persisted as solidly Democratic.

This comparative cohort analysis does not fully explain the declining South–non-South *Macropartisanship* gap. In none of the three southern cohorts did Democratic partisanship decline as fast as for the South as a whole. Since the parts do not add up to the total, something is missing. The missing ingredients are the exiting older cohort, heavily Democratic in the South, and the extremely Republican Reagan-era cohort, even more Republican in the South than the North.

An obvious question about the Democrats' slide in the South is, where will it all end? Has the regional shift stopped, or will it continue apace until a Republican dominance among southern whites makes the South a one-party Republican region? Perhaps the trend toward a regional divergence with a more Republican South has now ebbed. However, the greater Republicanism among young southern whites than among young northern whites suggests that the Republicanization of the white South is still evolving.

### GENDER

Race, region, and age form a trilogy of accounts of partisanship in the United States, pretty much unchanged for 50 years. They are the old standards of party analysis. In most of the half century distinctions

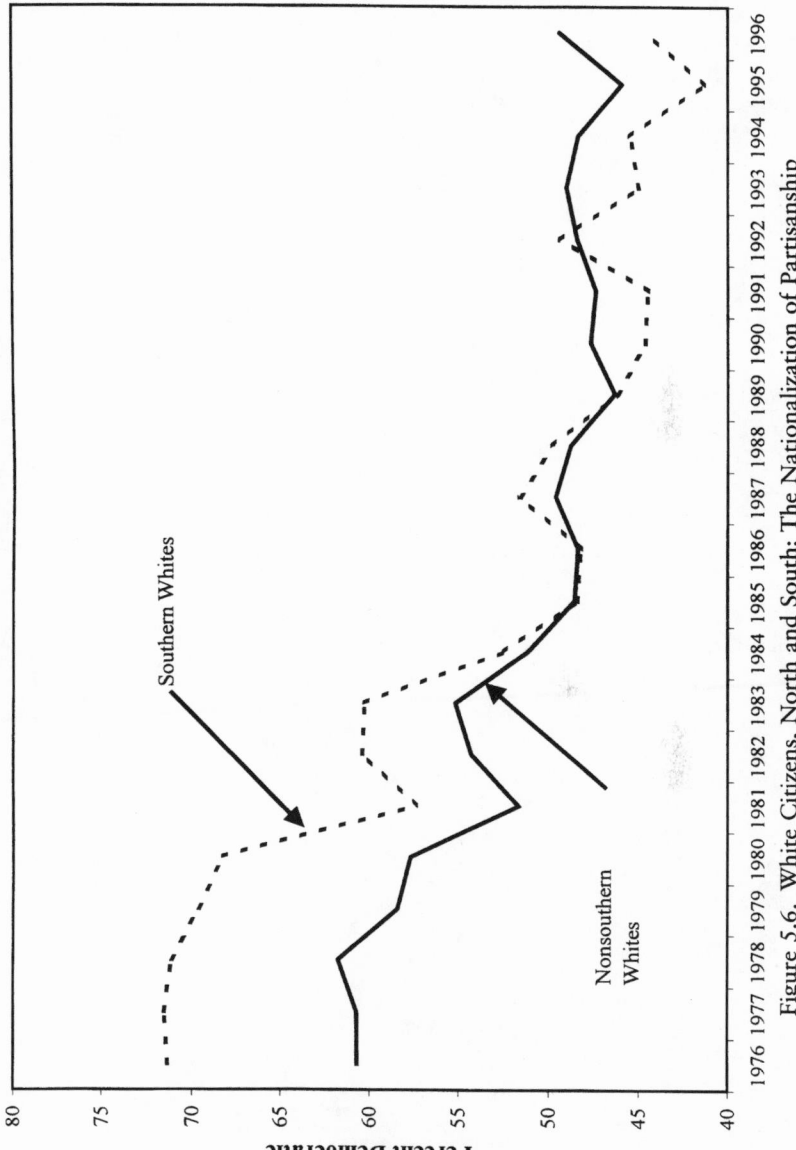

Figure 5.6. White Citizens, North and South: The Nationalization of Partisanship

169

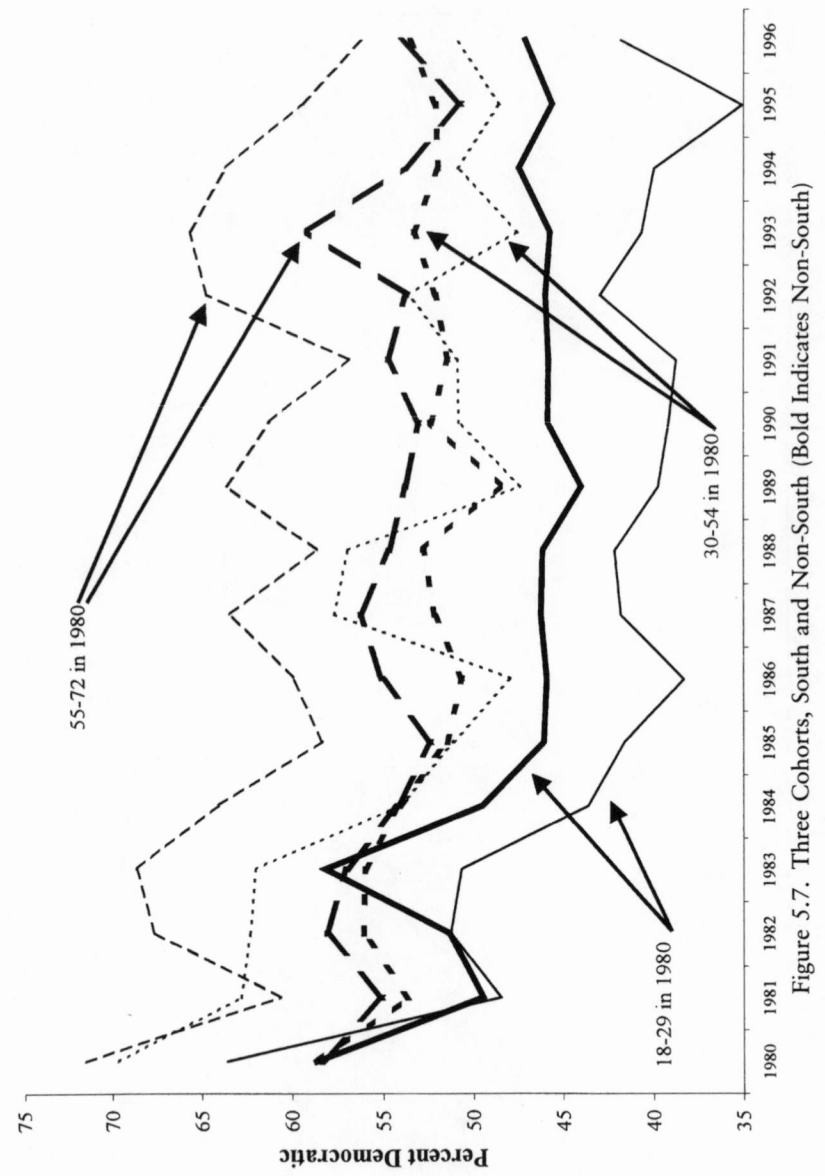

Figure 5.7. Three Cohorts, South and Non-South (Bold Indicates Non-South)

between men and women, on the other hand, are unusual. The early-century debates about suffrage took place in an environment in which both sides shared the idea that given the franchise, women would behave remarkably differently than men in politics. That consensus was proven wrong by the experience of actual women voters, who surprised the political experts by engaging in politics pretty much the same as men had done before (though see Brown 1991). That produced a new consensus, opposite the old one, that political behavior was undifferentiated along gender lines.

In the 1980s it began to be noticed that men and women were responding differently to the presidency of Ronald Reagan. Reagan was appealing to men, even across party lines, while women were much less impressed. The difference came to be called the "gender gap." It became the subject of speculation among campaign professionals and moved into the popular spotlight. With the question usually framed as "Why are women different?" – that is, with an implicit assumption that male response to Reagan was somehow normal, and therefore the difference to be explained was in women's behavior – all the usual stereotypes about gender differences (attitudes toward women's role, war and peace, and so forth) were tried as explanations.[4] All failed. To the degree that gender differences in responses could be explained, it was the more mundane social and economic differences that had some power to account for the gap: More economically marginal for a host of reasons (that include, but go beyond, gender discrimination), women in low-paying, low status, insecure jobs responded as men did in the same economic strata; that is, they disapproved of Reagan's low-tax, small-government policies and the deprivations of a slow-growth economy that accompanied them in the early 1980s.[5]

---

4 Popular commentary to this day often continues to misconstrue the evidence. Thus, for example, the gender gap is often portrayed as a problem for the Republican Party. If only women would vote like men, the pundits say, then Republicans would do better. But in simple logic, it is equally the case that if only men would vote like women, then the Democrats would do better! Kaufmann and Petrocik (1999) argue that the focus on women is fundamentally misguided, that the gender gap is mainly the creation of men moving toward the Republican Party while women's attachments have remained nearly constant.

5 It needs also to be asked why this differential response was relatively new in the 1980s. For women had always been more economically marginal. What was new (beginning on a large scale only in the previous decade) was the norm that virtually all women were in the workforce. As more and more working women were heads of households, the economic effects of government policy more and more differentiated between male and female head-of-household families, rather than the more politically benign differentiation between incomes of husbands and wives.

But we now know that the gender gap was more than a response to a single president. As we press the issue further, persistent gender differences can be found in virtually all politically relevant attitudes. And that includes partisanship. We plot the *Macropartisanship* of men and women in Figure 5.8, and show that there is differentiation between the sexes in party disposition and that it is not merely an artifact of the 1980s or of Ronald Reagan.

The pattern of Figure 5.8 is clear. With a little mental smoothing, the gender gap in *Macropartisanship*, barely discernible is the late 1970s, shows a pretty steady growth over the whole period. That it reaches maximum size in the last year of the series suggests that growth may still be under way, that we are witnessing dynamics that have yet to run their course. Larger for the Bush presidency than for Reagan, the gap in partisan dispositions is larger still for Bill Clinton.

Why this growing gender differentiation? One means to answer the question is to see if the gender gap can be explained by other things we know about voters. We can model the choice of party as a function of variables available from the CBS/NYT surveys and then ask whether gender makes a further and unique contribution. Using what we have, for many explanatory variables come and go and are not available for the whole series of studies, we model individual partisanship (with probit analysis) as a function of race (black and white only), ideology (self-declared liberalism vs. conservatism), and income. Then we add gender to the equation and ask whether it makes a significant contribution to predicting partisanship. The answer is that it does. The coefficient on gender in this fully specified model is about two-thirds what it is all alone as a predictor.[6]

The gender effect is large. Is it also growing? To assess that we repeat the modeling exercise, but this time doing it year by year. This permits us to look at gender as an independent effect and learn whether it is growing. The answer is that it is. Small and nonsignificant (occasionally wrong-signed) in the early years, the estimated gender coefficient grows steadily stronger in a fashion that is more nearly linear than what is seen in Figure 5.8. Thus we can say that the larger gender differences of the 1990s are *not* the result of growing differences in income, ideology, or race. Within the severe limits of what the data can tell us, it appears to be the case that gender is a cause of partisan dispositions *in and of itself*.

6 This estimation, which we do not report, is probably biased against the gender thesis by the inclusion of ideology as a predictor. To the degree that gender causes ideology and then, in turn, partisanship, the analysis gives all the explanatory credit to ideology and fails to capture a gender effect.

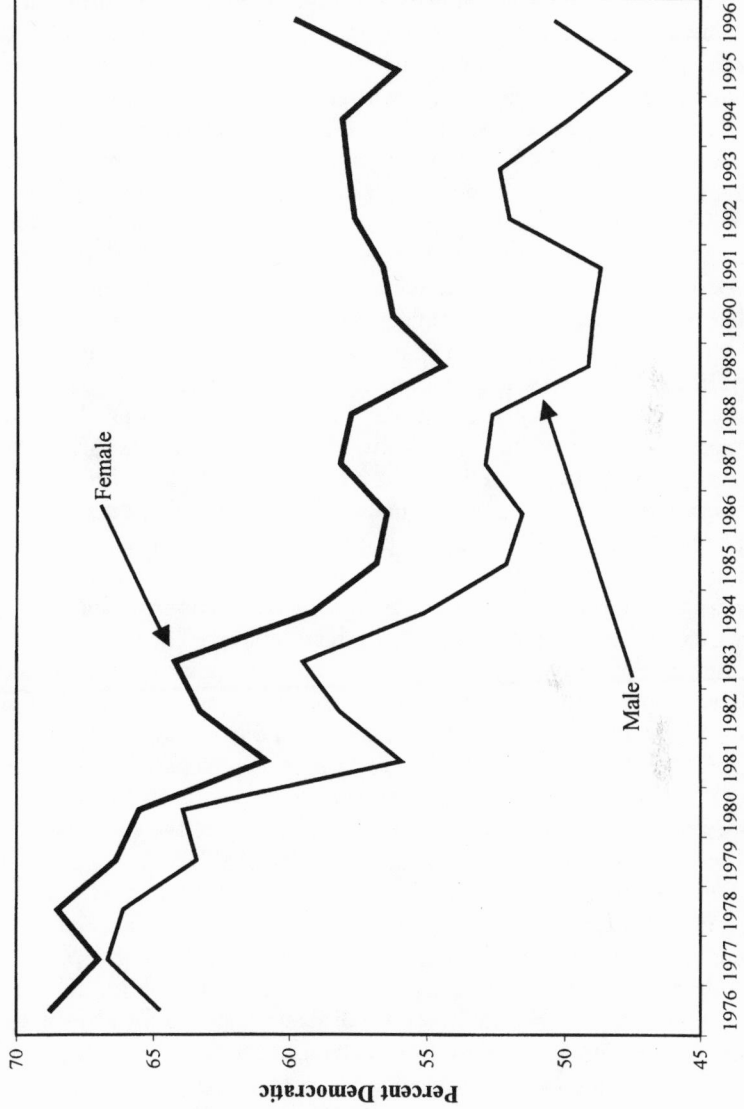

Figure 5.8. Persistent and Growing Gender Differentiation in Macropartisanship

Why then should the effect grow? We suggest, but stop short of declaring, one further factor. When the gender gap first came to public awareness in the 1980s, it could not have been produced by a self-conscious, gender-identity party selection. It wasn't known before then which party was favored by men and which by women, and therefore no one could have acted on that knowledge. But since gender differentiation became known, many millions of young people have come of age and faced a choice between the parties. They, unlike earlier generations, can know from popular commentary that the G.O.P. is the "male" party and that the Democrats are more attractive to women. Given that gender identity is at the very center of self-concept and that gender identity is under stress in the crucial adolescent years, which are also prime time for choice of partisan identity, it is not unlikely that large numbers of men and women could reinforce their gender identities by choosing the gender-correct party identification. We know that young men who are insecure in their gender identity are likely to wrap themselves in macho symbols, for example, guns and pickup trucks. Is it not also likely that they will identify with the "male" party in politics? And the same goes for young women.

We can get a little bit of evidence (far from confirmation) for this thesis by examining party choices by birth cohort. Those who came of age before the 1980s could not have considered gender in their choice of party (but could, of course, have changed subsequently). Those who came of age during the Reagan years made a party choice when the idea of gender differences in politics was in play. And those who have come of age subsequent to Reagan may have seen (we don't know directly) gender as an established fact of politics. If this were the case, we should see distinctive changes in the gender gap by birth cohort. We examine that possibility in Figure 5.9.

Figure 5.9 provides some support for the gender-identification thesis.[7] There we see in the pre-Reagan cohort the modest (about 4-point) difference between male and female choices characteristic of the period before the 1980s. Those who came of age roughly during the Reagan years are substantially more aligned by gender, with about a 10-point difference. Thus they are more differentiated along gender lines than is

7 The reader should be warned that cohort analysis of surveys spread over a 20-year span have the effect of selecting respondents not only by when they were born but also by when they were surveyed. The younger cohorts could not have been surveyed in the early years and some of the older pre-Reagan cohort would not have survived long enough to be interviewed in the later years. Thus the observed differences include both generation and time of interview effects, which are not easily disentangled.

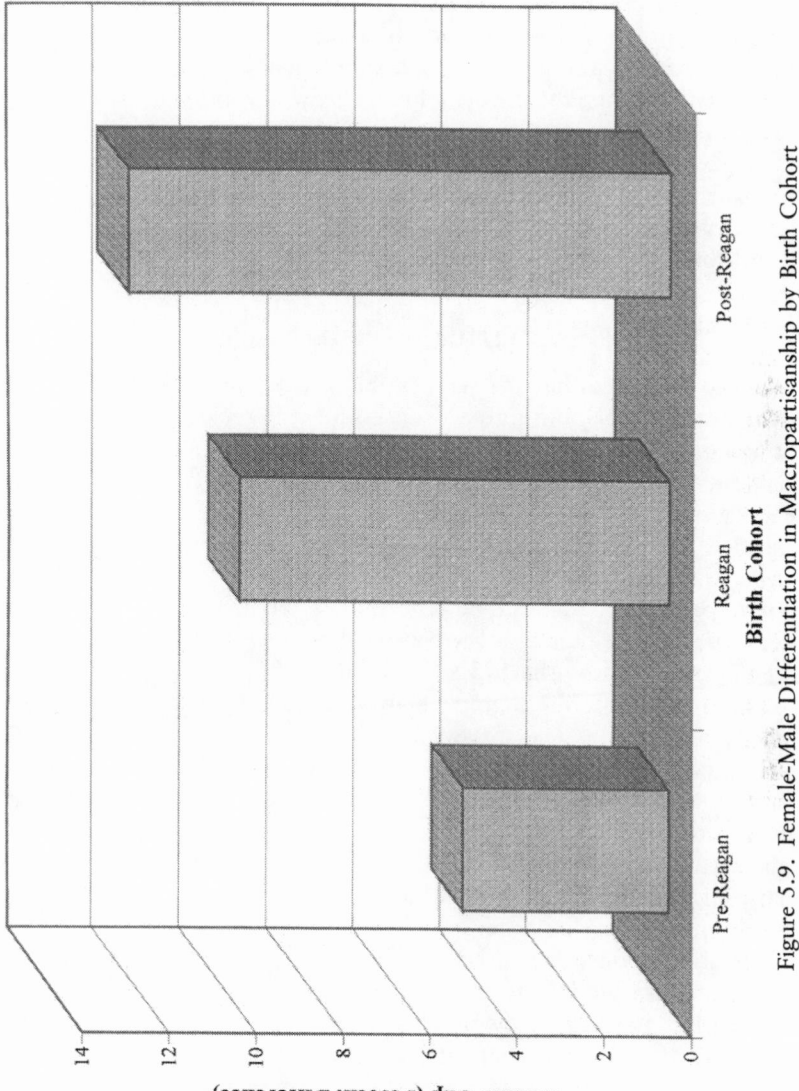

Figure 5.9. Female-Male Differentiation in Macropartisanship by Birth Cohort

the whole electorate, even at its maximum. And the group that comes after Reagan completes the story. It is the most differentiated group in the electorate, at about 12 points. If subsequent generations match these two recent cohorts, the gender gap will grow beyond what we have seen to date. And, of course, it is also possible that the newcomers will exceed the current youthful generation.[8]

Gender has moved from a position of irrelevance to American political behavior to one of now substantial import. The possibility exists that it may become central.

### POLITICAL ARCHEOLOGY

We have used the CBS/*NYT* surveys' massive volume of partisanship data to understand the shifting partisanship of different generations for the period of the surveys, 1980 to 1996. These rich data also provide potential clues about the partisanship of an earlier era. The partisan differences among the older birth cohorts tell us something about partisanship forces that forged the cohorts' partisan leanings during their youth. Of special interest is what this recent survey evidence reveals about the era before partisan change can be observed directly from voter surveys. The era of particular interest is the period of partisan realignment extending from the 1920s into the 1930s.

By all accounts, the amount of partisan change we observe directly from post–World War II surveys must be dwarfed by the partisan change that occurred between the 1920s and 1930s. We can follow the historical traces of this change from the changing pattern of party fortunes seen in election returns of the time. But, because the surveying of party identification did not begin in earnest until the post–World War II period, we have virtually no record of the party identification (or the *Macropartisanship*) of the earlier time.

We ask: If pollsters had been asking national samples of respondents for their party identifications in the 1920s and 1930s, what would this time series look like? How large was the magnitude of the realignment shift compared to the contemporary *Macropartisanship* movement we directly observe? And was it a gradual or a punctuated evolution?

We call this an exercise in political archeology. Archeologists study the prehistoric period for indirect clues regarding such matters as early

---

8 From the post-Reagan cohort we can identify a small number of respondents who came of age roughly during the Clinton first term. At about 47 percent Democratic, they were similar to the Bush cohort in entry partisanship. But here we are running out of numbers for reliable estimation. This estimate is based on only 760 respondents and is therefore subject to considerable sampling fluctuation.

human life, the origins of biological species, and major climatic change. One of their goals is the understanding of the major shifts from one pre-historic era to another, which were due perhaps to such things as sudden and profound changes in the climate. The political analogy is the sudden shifts of partisanship during periods of realignment. Analogous to the prehistoric nature of even the most recent change of geological era, even the last realignment of the 1930s is "prehistoric" in the sense of being before the days of survey research.

To understand the changing division of partisanship during the New Deal realignment, we must resort to indirect evidence. Pressing the archeological analogy further, our chief evidence is akin to the rings of ancient and fossilized trees that reveal the climatic conditions of their time. Our "tree rings" are the distinct signatures of partisan differences by birth cohorts among older voters who experienced the politics of the realignment era as adults.

This quest is hardly original with us. The *American Voter* authors were the first to find historical meaning in the division of partisanship according to birth date. From examining the relationship between age and partisanship in the 1950s, they found that people born before about 1910, who were first eligible to vote for president in 1932, were far more Republican than those born later. They inferred that political shocks of the realignment period had a far greater impact on new voters of the time than on established voters who were voting before the depression began. It should be clear, though, that the established voters at the time of the depression were not immunized from partisan conversion. At the time they must have been one-sidedly Republican. They could not have held totally firm in their Republican identification, given that by the time they were surveyed in their old age, they had shifted in the Democratic direction to the point where they had become about equally divided between the two parties.[9]

As a preview of our archeological findings, Figure 5.10 offers a styl-ized presentation of the relationship between birth date and partisanship for two different years, 1980 and 1996. Each graph depicts partisanship by one-year age categories from 18 through 80, where all estimates are based on the estimated year and cohort effects as discussed earlier in this chapter rather than cohort-year subsamples, which are subject to

---

9 Andersen (1979) took the archeological quest a step further by inferring the earlier partisanship of contemporary NES respondents from their self-reports of conversion. Even with this adjustment for recalled change, more reported partisans from the 1920s were Democrats than Republicans. Niemi, Katz, and Neuman (1980) show that survey respondents greatly underestimate their own conversions, thus accounting for this discrepancy.

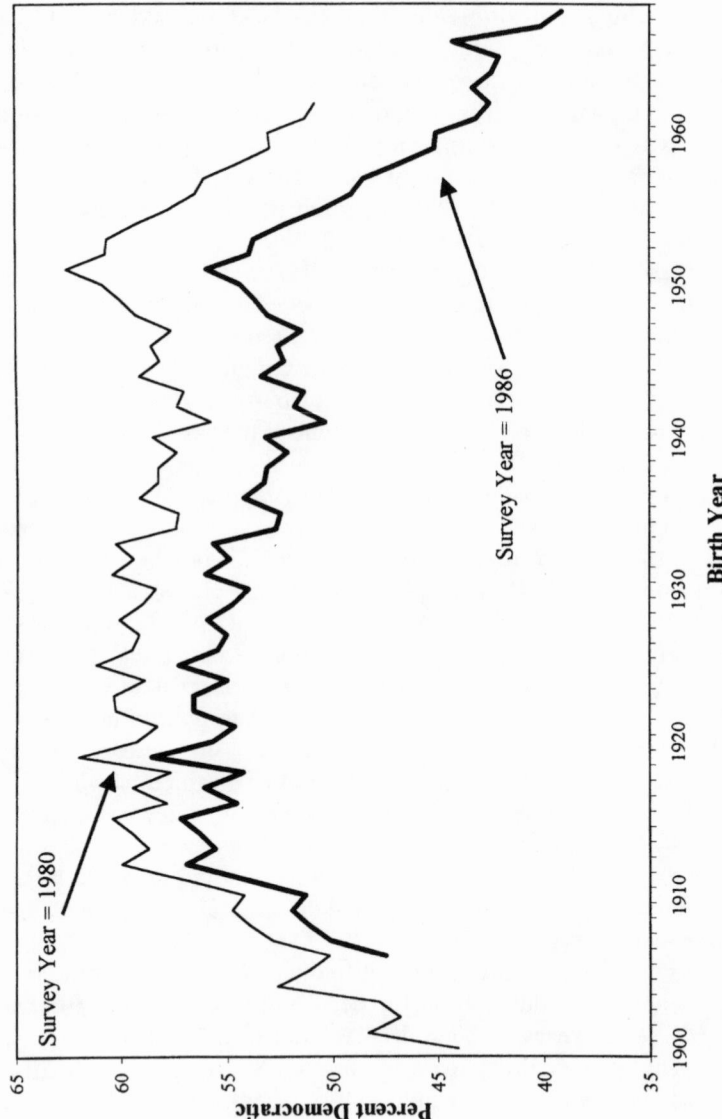

Figure 5.10. Partisanship by Birth Year, 1980 and 1986

178

considerable sampling error.[10] The gap between these overlaid distributions represents the cumulative effect of events between 1980 and 1996.
*All* birth cohorts became more Republican over this 16-year period as
part of the *Macropartisanship* shift, with younger citizens showing the
most movement. That statement summarizes much of what we learned
about age and partisanship earlier in this chapter.

For our current interest in retrieving the historical record of earlier
partisanship, our attention centers on the slopes of the graphed relationships between birth date and partisanship. The biggest cliffs in the
slopes are around the 1910 birth date, just as the *American Voter* authors
found. We can slice this evidence in a different way, by observing different birthday groups over time during the 1980s and 1990s. Figure
5.11 presents the smoothed time series for four different birth cohorts,
born at intervals 10 years apart. These are examples of our "tree rings."
Note that people born in 1920 and 1930 – who came of political age
after the consolidation of the New Deal realignment – vary only slightly
from each other in their partisanship. People born in 1910 – and who
came of political age at the height of the depression – are noticeably more
Republican. And the partisan gap is even wider between this 1910 cohort
and the earlier one born in 1900. Profound forces must have been at
work during the realignment period to generate such relatively massive
generational differences that persist to this day.

Why is the archeological record of early partisanship preserved in this
manner? It is preserved because partisanship is long memoried. As we
saw in Chapter 4, *Macropartisanship* has a long-term component that is
integrated (no forgetting) and a short-term component that disappears
in a matter of years if not quarters. The short-term component (often
associated with particular elections) dissipates quickly, leaving no trace
in the cohort record. The long-term component represents the fundamentals of partisanship, the moving equilibrium of *Macropartisanship*.
Each cohort has its own moving equilibrium, representing the cumulated
history of its partisan shocks.

By making some plausible assumptions, it is possible to make inferences about the partisanship of age cohorts as far back as early in
the twentieth century from our knowledge of these cohorts in the contemporary era (i.e., 1980–1996). Three assumptions guide this
archeological inference:

1. The history of each contemporary cohort consists of an entry
   socialization plus cumulative year effects, consistent with our
   notions of an integrated partisanship.

10 The exact smoothing exercise is described below.

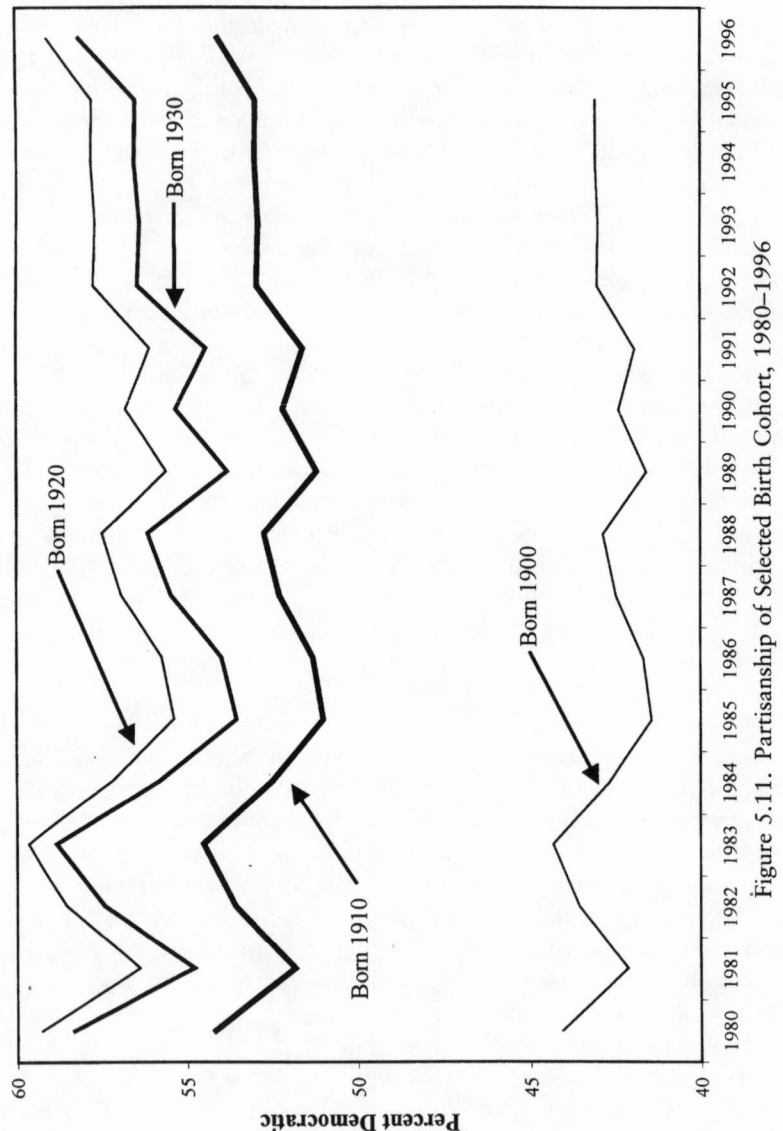

Figure 5.11. Partisanship of Selected Birth Cohort, 1980–1996

2. Effects accumulate as the sum of $\lambda_{age}u_y$, where the $u_y$ are year effects and the $\lambda_{age}$ are age-related amplitudes, which we have estimated to be $\lambda_{age} = .98^{age-19}$.

3. The unobserved amplitudes of year effects during adolescence increase linearly from 0 at age 13 (no attention) to 1.00 at age 19.

With these assumptions, and our knowledge of contemporary cohort differences, it is possible to trace any cohort's *Macropartisanship* for prior years of the cohort's adulthood. The details of this methodology are presented in the appendix to this chapter.

## Tracing the Early Partisan Record

Figure 5.12 shows the results of our simulations, in the form of the estimated partisanship of newly enfranchised voters, by year, 1912–1996 (21-year-olds pre-1971, 18-year-olds 1971–1980). For 1980–1996 we observe the partisanship of 18-year-olds directly from our modeling of CBS/NYT survey data.[11]

For years 1912–1920, the trajectory of entry partisanship is a wobbly line, due to the limited data in CBS polls for people born in the 1890s. But by our estimates, these cohorts were considerably more Republican than the generation entering in the 1920s. Put another way, young voters of the 1920s, roughly evenly divided in partisanship, were more Democratic than their elders. The full composite of pre-depression voters in the 1920s probably was far more Republican than our monitoring of young voters of the time would suggest. If this inference is correct, it also follows that the 1920s was a time of change in *Macropartisanship*. This follows from our assumption that cohort changes reflect partisan conversions at the time. Just as Republican gains of the Reagan era among the young were reflected (with lesser amplitude) in *Macropartisanship* generally, so too the Democratic gains among the young around the time of the depression – and seemingly earlier – should have been reflected in Democratic gains in *Macropartisanship* generally throughout the same era.

By the mid-1930s, the Democratic surge leveled off with entry voters decidedly more Democratic than Republican in partisan identification, in a range of about 2 to 1. Democratic identification among entry voters held steady at a roughly constant plateau from the 1930s to the early 1970s, consistent with the steady-state partisanship of that era. Then in the 1970s, Democratic identification among entry voters plunged

---

11 That is, the estimates are derived from the estimated year and cohort effects, not the actual survey marginals.

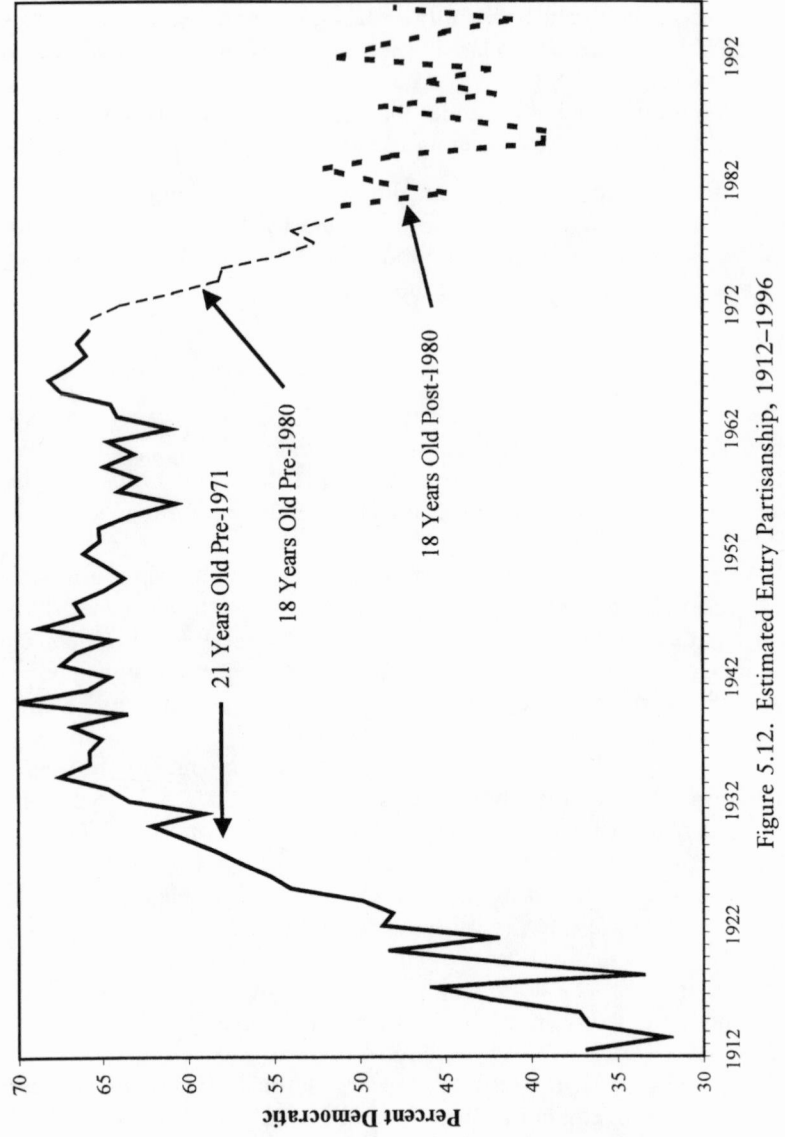

Figure 5.12. Estimated Entry Partisanship, 1912–1996

dramatically, not leveling off until the 1980s. Since the mid-1980s, entry voters have been almost evenly divided between Democrats and Republicans. This pattern is in general accord with our expectations.

We can take this exercise one further step by simulating the movement of earlier cohorts from their entry point to their partisan division at the end of our series in 1996. Figure 5.13 simulates these trajectories for the three cohorts newly eligible for the elections of 1920, 1940, and 1960. (The light line in the background is the entry level for all cohorts from Figure 5.12.) The movements are the accumulations of the imputed year effects, where the amplitude declines .98 per year. For instance, the class of 1920 starts out at about 50-50 in partisanship, becomes modestly more Democratic, and then gradually more Republican again. We see the class of 1940, at the height of the New Deal, start very Democratic and become gradually less so, even as it persisted into the 1990s as one of the most Democratic cohorts. The 1960 cohort (the Eisenhower children), starts out less Democratic than the 1940 cohort and moves to Republican at a faster rate.

### Evaluating the Model

Like all exercises that infer past attitudes from contemporary cohort differences, our modeling exercise is subject to the hazards of oversimplified assumptions. Our key assumption is that at any point, people in all age groups 19 and older respond in the same way to partisan forces of the time, but with an age-dependent amplitude. Similarly, we assume that adolescents go from zero response at age 13 to the adult maximum at age 19, with the slight decline thereafter. The simulations are dependent upon reasonable estimates of cohort differences and the parameters that govern the process. Moreover, since the parameters of the simulation were estimated from contemporary (1980–1996) data, we assume that the "rules" that govern cohort partisanship today also governed the process even during the depression realignment and before.[12] Note, for

---

12 One possible violation of the rules is that for some periods youthful voters and their elders may respond differently to the same political events. This may explain the peak of simulated youthful Democratic partisanship in the late 1960s and early 1970s – in between the two peaks of Democratic *Macropartisanship* in the early 1960s and again in the mid 1970s. The youthful generation that mobilized for McGovern in 1972 probably was more Democratic than the short-term forces for older voters would suggest. The result is that our model exaggerates the Democratic year effects around the time of the early seventies. And the simulated bubble of unusually Democratic support among the sixties generation, while probably accurate, exaggerates the nature of the Democratic decline among the more "normal" entry cohorts who followed.

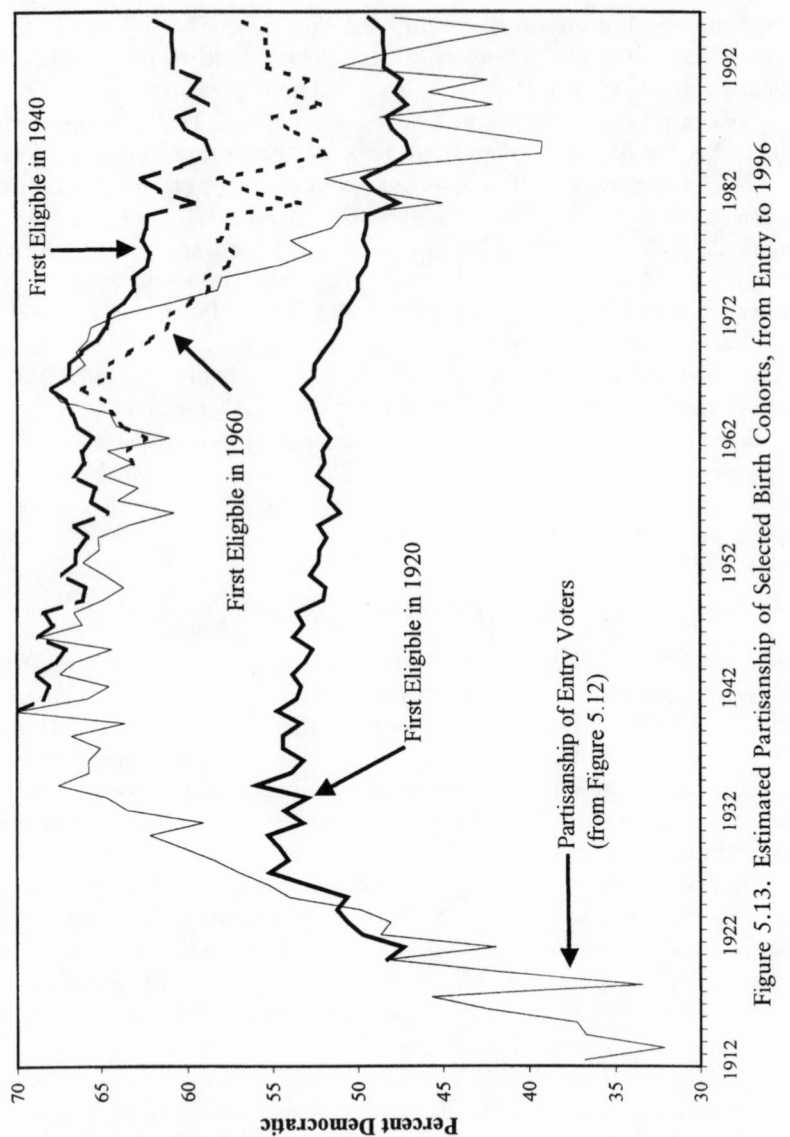

Figure 5.13. Estimated Partisanship of Selected Birth Cohorts, from Entry to 1996

184

instance, that we assume that partisan influence peaks around age 19 as citizens reach political maturity, even when citizens were first eligible to vote at age 21.

Redoing the simulations with variations in the assumptions shows that the results are robust to reasonable tinkering. For years when surveys are available, we also have the hard facts of empirical validation. The estimates for the 1950s through the 1970s track very well the cohort-year partisanship observed in NES surveys.

If there is a surprise in the simulations, it is the projection that the Democratic gains of the New Deal era began earlier than generally understood – well before the advent of the depression and New Deal themselves. The basic fact that drives this inference is the partisan differential in the 1980s and 1990s by birth year for cohorts who came of political age before the 1929 depression. If people who came of political age, say, in 1927, were more Democratic than those who came of age, say, in 1926, the probable cause is a differential in their preadult socialization with the younger group getting an increased dose of Democratic socialization at the point of entry that the older group lacked. But questions must remain. Was the socialization of newly minted voters really moving more Democratic in the mid-1920s? Or was the partisan differential among 1920s cohorts something that developed only later by a process we do not understand?

One lesson from our simulations is that the partisan movement of youth in the 1920s and 1930s is the mirror image of that observed in recent decades. Starting in the 1970s, recent entry cohorts have moved Republican at a pace not dissimilar to the pace of Democratic movement in the 1920s and 1930s. Have the evolving Republican gains of recent decades matched in magnitude the Democratic gains from earlier? Or is there some aspect of the comparison that we are missing?

We see from our archeological adventure one obvious forecast for the future. That forecast is for a likely Republican gain in *Macropartisanship*, as the post-1960s generation of partisans displace the more Democratic generations that came before. At the limit, the electorate should become no more than slightly Republican, because that is the partisan tendency of recent entry cohorts. But another factor is that the political winds that drive *Macropartisanship* can always change and change in either partisan direction. When the winds move, they move slowly, but their effects accumulate. In short, apart from the displacement of one political generation with another, the partisan future is impossible to forecast.

# Performance

## CONCLUSIONS

We have argued that *Macropartisanship* is the agent of memory that carries past experiences of the electorate into the future, a fundamental contention of the previous chapter. We began this chapter by asking what we could learn by looking at distinctions between different sorts of Americans: black and white, South and North, young and old, male and female. That there are distinctions along these lines is, except partially for gender, well known and long established. But the real issue that concerns us here is whether or not knowledge of distinctions alters the story we tell of American politics.

To be sure, age and generational replacement plays a role in the evolution of the electorate. The electorate is composed not of one set of continuous citizens, but of different generations or birth cohorts who enter and leave the electorate at different times. When political events favor one party over the other, the response is generally felt among all birth cohorts, with the strongest amplitude among the young. This differential response produces part, but only part, of the changes we observe.

During the Reagan era, Republicans made their greatest gains among the youth and Democrats lost disproportionately as the older New Deal generation started to disappear. Similarly, in the period from 1952 to 1980 a similar generational replacement was at work – this time working for the Democrats. But in neither case does the generational phenomenon account for the major bulk of the change – it is obvious that the main dynamics were due to surviving individuals switching their partisan dispositions.

Similarly, we see a dramatic movement toward the G.O.P. in the white South. Some of this transformation is generational – with newly entering younger southerners being the most ready to adopt the G.O.P. and older southerners, remaining loyal to the Democracy, slowly exiting the lists. But the transformation of the southern and white electorates between 1980 and 1996 occurred *in addition to*, rather than in place of, reactions to the macro politics of the era.

Further, men have clearly drifted toward the Republicans while women have remained more Democratic. In the years since 1980, it appears that gender has become an important, perhaps a central, component in forming partisan dispositions. This change, similarly, arose independent of the ebbs and flows of party fortunes – reactions to which were evident in both genders.

And finally, as the "exception that proves the rule," African Americans remained almost impervious to the fluctuations in the parties' fortunes. Throughout the era, they held steadfast in their loyalties to the Democrats. This extraordinary constancy depresses responsiveness of the elec-

186

torate to events of all sorts. It affects the parameter estimates on events, but doesn't alter our understanding. A subgroup that is unusually loyal to one party simply doesn't contribute much longitudinal variance.

The crux of the issue is whether or not the macro and longitudinal story is fundamentally altered by knowledge of micro distinctions. In general, we would answer in the negative. It is clear that the Republican growth in the 1980s, for example, cannot be understood solely as a phenomenon of the South. Or of the male diaspora. Or the replacement of New Deal seniors with Reagan youngsters. All these factors were important, to be sure. But almost all Americans responded, for example, to the bad news of the Reagan recession and even more to the good news of the subsequent recovery, to the Iran-Contra scandal, and to the economic fortunes and misfortunes of Clinton and Bush. To find one subgroup where, for whatever reason, the response was sharper is not a convincing denial that it did not happen everywhere. Young and old, northerners and southerners, men and women all reacted to the macro-political performance of the parties, shifting their partisan dispositions to reflect success and failure.

*Changing Focus*: For four chapters now we have pressed what we know about how the electorate responds to the events of politics, in particular those events that reflect well or badly on the party in power. These are matters of *performance*, that is, success or failure in producing outcomes desired by all. For most of the rest of this volume we now turn away from performance to our second major focus, on *policy*. We now wish to think about government and the electorate in terms not of ends, but means, the "how" of politics, not the "what."

In the next chapter, we conceptualize policy preferences as *Public Policy Mood*, the moving preferences of the electorate for more or less government over time. In Chapter 7, we turn to national elections, asking how policy and performance combine to produce victories for one party or the other. Then in Chapter 8, we take up the matter of representation, asking how, when public preferences change, government responds in acts of policy making. And in Chapter 9, we look to policy as a cumulative phenomenon, asking how it responds to preferences and how preferences in turn respond to policy.

In the pages to come, we take up our conception of public opinion as a moving set of preferences for government action.

APPENDIX: RECONSTRUCTING THE PARTISAN PAST

In order to retrieve estimates of cohort-year partisanship from the prepoll era, we need a key to translate contemporary partisan differences among cohorts into "period effects" from the cohorts' formative years. If one birth-year-specific cohort is 5 points more Democratic than people born a year earlier, for example, what inference should we make about the two cohorts as they approached political maturity? Solving this puzzle makes it possible to estimate partisanship for any observable cohort for any year during the cohort's adult lifetime.

In year $t$, each cohort's partisanship is the sum of age-amplified year effects, summing backwards through time:

$$M_{kt} = \sum_{y=1}^{t} \lambda_{age} u_y$$

$$= \sum_{y=1}^{t} \lambda_{y-k+18} u_y$$

(5.3)

where $M_{kt}$ = the *Macropartisanship* in year $t$ for the cohort turning 18 in year $k$. The $u_y$ shocks are a combination of parental influences (cumulating through the childhood years) plus direct cohort experience that starts with the onset of politicization.[13] The series starts in mythical year $y = 1$. In this way, an age cohort's *Macropartisanship* represents a continuous record of partisan evaluation, with some years weighted more than others. This series has no definite starting point. In theory, we could sum backwards indefinitely, so that a cohort's partisanship today incorporates a collective response to events not only during its adulthood and attentive youth but also during the attentive years of the parents and grandparents. The transmission across generations represents political learning ("socialization") during childhood. During childhood, the collective cumulative partisan verdict of the parental generation is passed on – presumably with a somewhat muted amplitude – from one generation to the next.

Define $\gamma_{kt}$ as the difference between the *Macropartisanship* of adjacent cohorts $k$ and $k - 1$ in year $t$: $M_{kt} - M_{k,t-1}$. We focus on $M_{kk}$, the difference between the *Macropartisanship* of 18-year-olds and 19-year-olds in year $k$. It follows from Equation 5.3 that $\gamma_{kk}$ will be:

$$\gamma_{kk} = M_{kt} - M_{k-1,t} = \sum_{y=0}^{t} (\lambda_{t-i-18} - \lambda_{t-i-19}) u_y$$

recalling that $k$ = the birth year +18. Adjacent cohorts differ in partisanship as a function of their differential exposures to the stream of

13 In principle, we would include family influence spanning generations, as each cohort is influenced to some degree by ancestral families and their responses to the partisan influences of the time. We assume these historical influences greatly fade, starting at a mythical year 1.

partisan influences over time. Some of the terms are known. We have estimates of the $u_y$ for 1980 and beyond. We know that for ages 19 and above, $\lambda_{\text{age}} = .98^{\text{age}-19}$. We do not know the pre-1980 $u_y$ or the pre-19 $\lambda$s. But as described next, we use some reasonable assumptions about the pre-19 $\lambda$s to derive estimates of the unobserved $\gamma_{kk}$ and then the $u_y$. The ultimate result is the estimate of prepoll cohort partisanship $M_{kt}$.

Consider cohort $k$ turning 18 in year $t$ and the previous $k - 1$ cohort, 19 years old in year $t$. How could their partisanship differ? We can start with an assumption about the two cohorts' partisanship early in adolescence, just before the two cohorts pay attention to politics but when they hold partisan beliefs based on parental transmission. In this starting year, which we set for purposes of discussion to be year $k - 6$ or when cohorts were 12 and 13 years old, the two cohorts are alike in partisanship. That is, we assume that for any year, 12- and 13-year-olds hold approximately identical partisanship. Then, between ages 14 and 19, their respective $\lambda$ amplitudes increase from 0 (no attention) to 1 (the responsiveness of 19-year-olds).[14] Thus, the partisanship of cohorts $k$ and $k - 1$ in year $t$ (when 18 and 19, respectively) can be accounted for as follows:

$$M_{kt} = M_{k,t-6} + \lambda_{14}u_{t-4} + \lambda_{15}u_{t-3} + \lambda_{16}u_{t-2} + \lambda_{17}u_{t-1} + \lambda_{18}u_t$$

and

$$M_{k-1,t} = M_{k-1,t-6} + \lambda_{14}u_{t-5} + \lambda_{15}u_{t-4} + \lambda_{16}u_{t-3} + \lambda_{17}u_{t-2} + \lambda_{18}u_{t-1} + u_t$$

Since $M_{i,i-6} = M_{i-1,i-6}$ by assumption, the cohort difference at ages 18 and 19 is a function of the difference in the intervening year amplitudes:

$$
\begin{aligned}
M_{kt} - M_{k-1,t} = \gamma_{kk} \\
= \lambda_{14}(u_{k-4} - u_{k-5}) + \lambda_{15}(u_{k-3} - u_{k-4}) + \lambda_{16}(u_{k-3} - u_{k-2}) \\
+ \lambda_{17}(u_{k-2} - u_{k-1}) + \lambda_{18}(u_{k-1} - u_k) - u_k \\
= -\lambda_{14}u_{k-5} + (\lambda_{14} - \lambda_{15})u_{k-4} + (\lambda_{15} - \lambda_{16})u_{k-3} \\
+ (\lambda_{16} - \lambda_{17})u_{k-2} + (\lambda_{17} - \lambda_{18})u_{k-1} + (\lambda_{18} - 1)u_k
\end{aligned}
$$

where $\gamma_{kk}$ denotes the one-year partisan difference between cohort $k$ and its predecessor in year $k$ when the $k$th cohort's age is 18. Note that if $\lambda$ increases linearly from age 13 (0) to age 19 (1), or if $u_y$ is constant from year $t - 5$ to $t$, then the cohort difference $-\gamma_{kk}$ is simply the mean $u_y$ years $t - 5$ to $t$. Even if these conditions do not hold, $-\gamma_{kk}$ is a rough average of the $u_y$ from $t - 5$ to $t$ so that the accumulation of the $-\gamma_{kk}$ from years

---

14  Note that our theoretical argument requires the absence of year effects for the starting age, which in our discussion is year 13.

$t - 5$ to $t$ should strongly approximate the accumulation of the $u_y$ over cohort $k$'s adolescence.

The key is that the partisan difference between two age-adjacent cohorts reflects the older cohort's extra year of experience. More generally, the partisan gap between any two cohorts reflects the extra partisan experience held by the older cohort but not the younger – that is, experience during the adolescent years. The practical implication is that we can estimate a moving average of year effects centered around year $y$ as the partisan gap between 18- and 19-year-olds *a few years later*, when the two cohorts emerged from their differential adolescent experiences.

One final complication is that for pre-1980 years, we do not observe the $\gamma_k$ partisan gaps of 18-year-olds versus 19-year-olds. But we do observe the partisan gap between cohorts $k$ and $k - 1$ in year $t$, where $t$ can be 1980 or later. Define this observed gap as $\gamma_{kt}$. Utilizing the rule that $\lambda$ declines by .02 per year of age,

$$\gamma_{kk} = \gamma_{kt} - .02(M_{k+1,t} - M_{k+1,k+1}) \tag{5.4}$$

and

$$M_{kt} - M_{kk} = .98(M_{k+1,t} - M_{k+1,k+1}) + u_k \tag{5.5}$$

We assume that the correspondence between the moving average of year effects and the age 18–19 partisan gap is that $u_{k-3} = -\gamma_{kk}$. In other words, the gap between 18- and 19-year-olds represents the average shock when the older cohort was age 16. We start by using the observed $-\gamma_{80,80}$, $-\gamma_{81,81}$, and $-\gamma_{82,82}$ gaps as estimates of $u_{77}$, $u_{78}$, and $u_{79}$. Next, equation 5.5 is used to infer $\gamma_{77,77}$, $\gamma_{78,78}$, and $\gamma_{79,79}$. Then Equation 5.4 is used to infer $u_{74}$, $u_{75}$, and $u_{76}$. The iterations continue until we estimate the $u_{it}$ as far back as 1910.

Our interest is not in the exact $u_{kt}$ estimates, which must remain highly smoothed moving averages. The final step is to subtract the age-amplified $u_{kt}$ from the observed $M_{i80}$ cohort partisanship in 1980. The result is the estimation of *Macropartisanship* for each cohort year, 1910–1996. These estimates are based on knowledge of how the amplitude of the partisan response declines with age during adulthood and a reasonable argument that the partisan gap between cohorts aged 18 and 19 reflects the greater salience of recent politics among the older cohort.

We assume here that the 18- versus 19-year-old cohort gap reflects partisan effects on average three years earlier. This choice of three years can be only a guess. Fortunately, the choice of one, two, or three years makes appreciable difference for the estimates of past partisanship reported here. If we estimated the $u_t$ from the $\gamma_{ii}$ one or two years ahead instead of three, the results would be little different from the results reported here.

# PART II

---

## *Policy*

# 6

## Public Opinion

Politics is about choice. So far, we have focused exclusively on matters of performance, that is, the successful provision of good times, tranquility, and clean government. But performance on matters about which all agree is only one part of the democratic experience; the polity also wants to make choices about which there is disagreement. We want to know how citizens affect such decisions.

Clearly, the democratic public's role involves more than simply evaluating how well government achieves the goals agreed upon by all – peace, prosperity, and probity. Much of politics is about choosing *among* goals that are not shared and, when goals are shared, choosing from conflicting choices the best path to the common goal. The public can do more than pass judgment on the size of the pie. It also has a voice in how it should be divided. These are matters of preference, and generally of conflicting preferences. Democratic elections decide whose preferences should prevail and whose should not. Those preferences – what they are, what they mean, how they arise, and how they move over time – are the focus of this chapter.

Governments choose between alternative sets of public policy. Citizens have preferences over at least some of these choices. In this chapter, we shall look at preferences in the usual way, as respondent reports in answer to questions posed in survey research. Then we will conceptualize them in longitudinal terms, as a force that flows – and can be measured – over time. And then we will look beneath those flows and find a common theme that unites them.

Our measure of the public's net preferences over time is the construction labeled *Policy Mood* (Stimson 1991, 1999). *Mood* is our best effort at measuring the public's movement regarding support for government programs or movement on the liberal-conservative continuum. This chapter describes the measurement of *Mood* and presents a preliminary investigation of what moves *Mood*. *Mood* is a pivotal variable in the chapters that follow, as the electorate's *Mood* influences its behavior at the ballot box, and the anticipation of this effect influences politicians. By entering *Mood* into the system of equations, we see that the public's role in politics is more than the evaluation of government competence. The public also guides the direction of government policy.

## POLICY PREFERENCES: MICRO AND MACRO

What do responses to survey questions about public policy choices mean? We need some answers to that question before we can take up the related quandary of the meaning of changes in policy preferences over time. It is instructive to begin with the instrument, the survey question itself. And for illustration it is handy to have one concrete example at hand.

Beginning in 1973, the General Social Survey has posed a battery of questions to a national sample of respondents beginning with the following lead-in:

*We are faced with many problems in this country, none of which can be solved easily or inexpensively. I'm going to name some of these problems, and for each one I'd like you to tell me whether you think we're spending too much money on it, too little money, or about the right amount. Are we spending too much, too little, or about the right amount on . . . ?*

followed by a varied list of national priorities. One of these is *". . . improving the nation's education system?"*

What, we ask, does a response to such a question mean? What does it tell us about the respondent's preferences? The naive answer with which the survey tradition began was that the respondent had thought about the particular controversy, had formed a preference on it, and was reporting that preference.

Such a view fares badly with the evidence of several decades of survey research. That evidence includes numerous demonstrations of response instability over time, the best known being Converse (1964). Such instability could be evidence of remarkably fickle judgments of public-policy questions. The better explanation, we have come to believe, is that survey questions do not present the same stimuli to different respondents or to a single respondent at different times. Zaller and Feldman (1992; Zaller 1992) characterize the survey response process as sampling from a host of competing considerations, any one of which might yield an answer to the question. Presented with a question on which no programmed response is available, where the real state of mind is ambivalence, the respondent does a brief search of his or her views that might be relevant, chooses one that comes to mind, and applies it to the issue at hand. Not a settled view on the issue, the respondent report is a function of which set of attitudes was drawn first. Given a different context, for example, previous questions that focused on one or another aspect and "primed" that attitude set, different responses would have been reported.

For our illustration, such considerations might include (1) a set of attitudes toward "government" or the federal government, the implicit focus of the question, (2) attitudes toward "spending," the action in question, or (3) attitudes toward "the nation's education system." Other sorts of attitudes are also possible. The point of the Zaller-Feldman view is that a respondent might produce three (or more) different responses, depending upon which set of attitudes is primed. Americans, in general, value education, and are willing to commit resources to "improve" it. But the same citizens generally dislike public spending, and are willing to compromise policy goals to limit it. And, a matter of less consensus, the American public is ambivalent about "government" itself, with many harboring deep suspicion of all government activities. Thus our typical survey respondent may at one time announce support for improving education, at another opposition to spending, at another support or opposition for a federal government role. And all these reports can be genuine.

### Interpretation: Cross-Sectional

Given a particular result on our illustrative question from a single survey cross section, what then can we learn about the relevant attitudes? We will learn little from such a design about attitudes toward government itself. The problem is that government is implicit in all *public* policy issues. In many it is named explicitly. Since we do not have a set of *non*-governmental public policy preferences for comparison, we have no leverage to identify "government's" contribution to preferences. Our tradition is to ignore it, to presume that an item on government spending on education is about spending or education. We can assume that attitudes toward government matter or that they don't, but we can't learn which is the case from a cross section.[1]

---

1 Attitudes toward government do imply a commonality of response to preference questions, which predicts that a single dimension of support or opposition should structure responses to at least a subset of preference questions. That can be observed, in principle, in a factor analytic framework, where we expect a "government" factor. Common factors are generally found in factor analytic designs, but don't settle the issue both because we tend to disagree about what in fact is common and because the strength of common components is subject to interpretative disagreement of a half-full, half empty nature.

## Policy

We can (and regularly do) learn about the other considerations that might generate the response. We can compare questions about the same goals, for example, "improving the nation's education system," that do and do not involve spending. Equally, we can compare spending for different purposes, such as education, welfare, national defense, or whatever. We can assert with confidence, for example, that spending on education elicits more public support than spending on welfare.

Imagine a set of issues that is tapped at multiple times with different cross sections. What can we learn from this design? Aggregation over time obviously does not change the nature of the survey response. But it does tame its huge random variation. Response to a particular question will still be a mixture of competing considerations, but in lieu of systematic changes in context, that mixture will tend to be the same over time.

Importantly, the attitudes toward government itself now become identifiable. Such attitudes lead to a clear prediction that responses to all policy-preference questions will tend to move in parallel over time. If respondents are reacting to government itself, and if these reactions change over time and experience, then we should see this in common movements across policy questions. A public that approves government activity will produce relatively liberal, that is, progovernment, responses and one that disapproves will produce relatively conservative ones. And this should be true wherever government is implicated, which is in nearly all public policies.[2]

Covariation over time is the key to identifying which sorts of considerations are driving response to preference questions. We can imagine scenarios in which, for example, education questions covary with other education questions, where education spending covaries with other sorts of spending, or where all sorts of policy preference covary. The three scenarios would provide remarkably different interpretations of what it is that these measured preferences tell us about the structure of mass opinion. What kind of covariation is to be found is an empirical matter.

The data from which these questions are best settled are all of the repeated survey items that assess policy preferences. These are the result of thousands of individual studies by numerous survey organizations in the period of our focus. The full set of policy-preference data present thorny methodological difficulties, all a result of the immense irregular-

2 The foreign policy domain will be seen to be a prominent exception. Attitudes toward how the United States ought to deal with other nations seem to have no commonalty with attitudes in support or opposition to government. Other exceptions will also be found.

196

ity with which particular controversies arise and are measured by survey research. We shall deal with these difficulties in due course, but lest they become distracting, we start with an illustration that allows us to ignore them for the moment.

For illustration, we take up a mere four items that have the virtue of having been asked by a single organization at (almost) the same times. One of these is the education spending issue already discussed. For diversity of content, we add a GSS measure (originally posed by the Gallup organization) on whether a police permit should be required for gun ownership. A third item is spending of a very different sort, for national defense. Because we expect it to move contrary to domestic spending, it is coded in the opposite direction: opposition to spending is considered the liberal position. An item on spending to aid cities is the final choice.

For each time each item is asked, the public's net response is coded as the percentage of all responses that are liberal (pro spending for cities and education, pro gun control, anti defense spending) divided by the percentage that are either liberal or conservative. Thus neutral responses, along with the usual unusable missing responses, do not enter the calculation. The result is shown in Figure 6.1.

The figure simply graphs the net liberalism of the responses to the four items over time. Each of the four items traces a general path from early liberalism to strong conservatism – in relative terms – centered around 1980 and back to liberalism in the 1990s. This pattern is most dramatic in the case of defense spending (Bartels 1991), but can be seen in all four series. Since each series follows this common path – as do many, many others – it would appear that much of their variance is in common. To illustrate that common movement, we simply take the average for each year of the four series and graph it in Figure 6.2 as a band of two standard deviations (one on each side of the average) moving over time. When the four original series are overlaid on the common band, it is quickly seen that most of the variation is within the common band. We could do a decent job predicting each of the four from the common movement or from each other. If, say, attitudes toward requiring police permits for gun ownership successfully predict net attitudes toward federal education spending, then the two must share something in common.

Statistical evidence of common movement is correlation. And correlations among multiple items may be summarized by principal components analysis, which represents the $N$-dimensional space of $N$ items with $N$ axes, constructed to represent evidence of common variance. For the four-series illustration, the first such component accounts for a variance of 2.77, 69 percent of the total (4.0). For the case at hand, such evidence

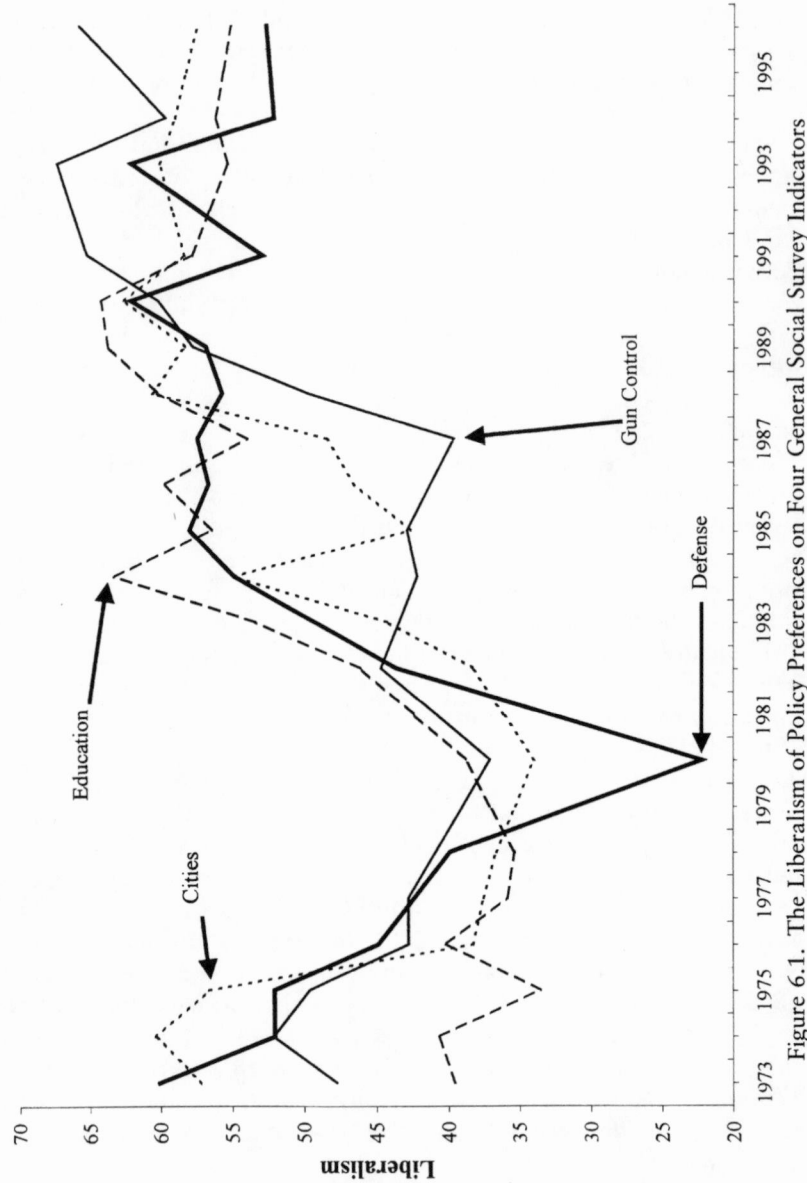

Figure 6.1. The Liberalism of Policy Preferences on Four General Social Survey Indicators

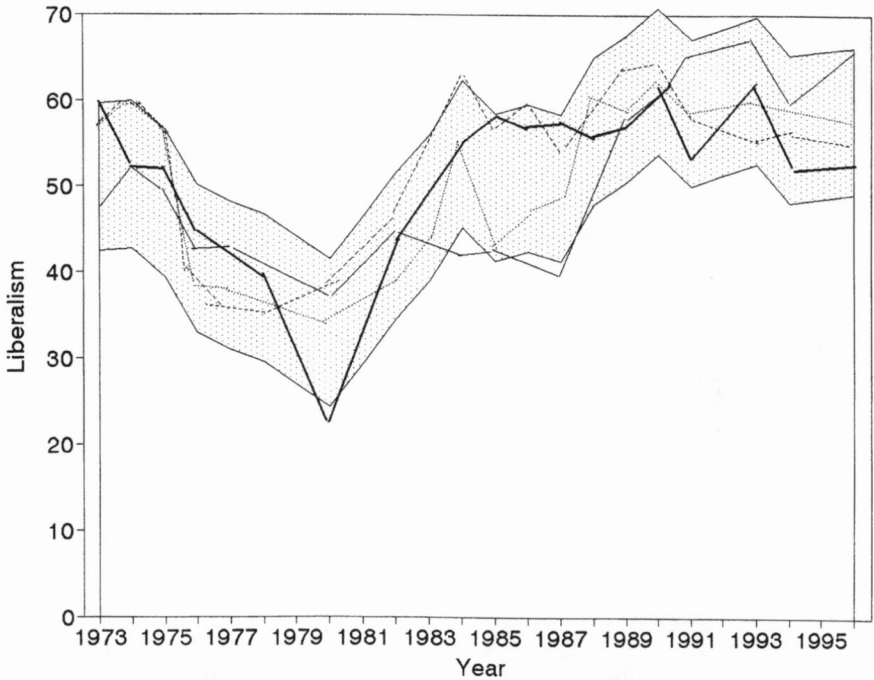

Figure 6.2. Four Individual Indicators and a Band of Their Common Components

is consistent with an interpretation that each of the four series is an indicator of the one underlying concept, liberalism.

The model for such a conception is seen in Figure 6.3. The variance of any variable can be decomposed into reliable and error components. Within the reliable category, it can be further decomposed into common (or shared) variance and specific (or unique) variance. Common variance is variance shared with all other variables. It begs for parsimonious explanation in terms that are as general as the set of variables. Specific variance is understood to be the causal result of something real that is not shared with other indicators. If attitudes toward education spending moved in response to some event peculiar to education – imagine, for example, a controversy over declines in national test scores – then such movement would be genuine, not one of the myriad forms of "error." We can readily imagine limiting cases where the movement of policy preferences might be all in common or all unique. The assumption that longitudinal variance is specific to policy domains (if not to particular indicators) is widespread. We shall emphasize the opposite,

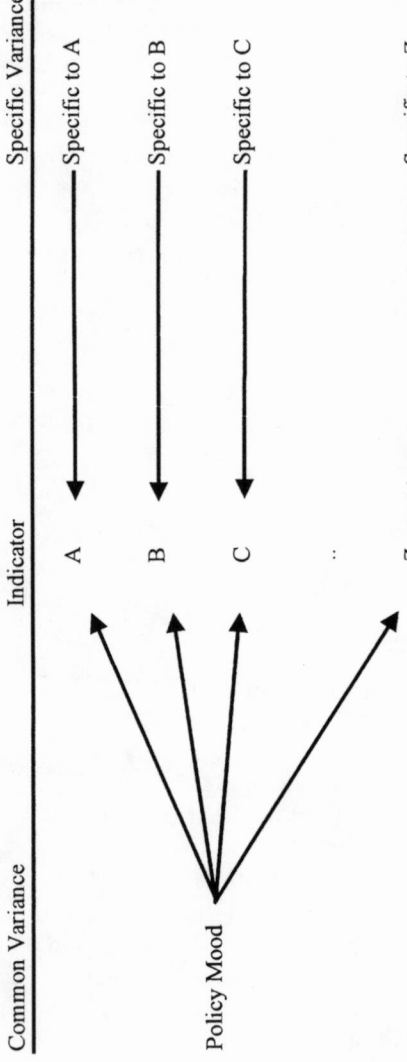

Figure 6.3. A Common Factor Model of Item Longitudinal Variance

the view that global attitudes toward government move preferences across policy domains. The empirical issue becomes estimating the incidence of each.

The basis for such estimation is the record of measured policy preferences. That is an extremely large universe of data. Given our focus on change over time, that unwieldy universe becomes restricted to measured preferences repeated (on national cross sections) over time. It is further restricted to rule out foreign policy preferences, which we know from earlier analyses to move separately from the domestic policy sphere. It is restricted by necessity to survey results that are in the public domain, ruling out an unknown quantity of work ordered by corporations, interest groups, and political parties and candidates for private use, but never released. But within these limits we use everything that we know exists, all repeated questions that ascertain domestic policy preferences for national cross sections by all survey houses, both academic and commercial.[3] These amount, for analyses to come, to some 133 series of varying length comprising 1610 separate questions.

How then do we move beyond illustration to estimate a model such as that of Figure 6.3 for all available policy-preference indicators? There is no problem with the principal components technology, in one or another of its flavors. This sort of estimation is what it is designed to do. The problem is the data. They fail the first requisite of principal components, that we have a set of variables for analysis. What we have instead is a set of domestic policy-preference series where at best, half of all time units (years here) are represented with real values and the rest are unobserved. Many series are measured only four or five times. Across the universe of domestic policy-preference series, about one-fourth of all years are measured, and three-fourths missing.

With so many observations unavailable, it is not beyond reason to make some strong assumptions about missing cases and proceed. For example, with the National Election Study preference series we could assume that missing odd years resembled the even years before and after. But the bigger problem is that all series are missing on at least one end of the time span, and most are missing on both. Extrapolation on a massive scale to periods never observed quickly becomes an exercise in modeling data, not observing the world. One common way around such

---

3 It would be foolish to claim that we have succeeded in acquiring everything that exists in our universe. But the more limited claim we can assert is this: everything we find we use. Finding survey results is greatly facilitated by the Roper Center for Public Opinion Research, which archives survey results. We have everything we can locate from that source plus other materials, such as National Election Study results, not archived by Roper. See Page and Shapiro (1992) for an excellent treatment of the historical survey record.

problems, the pairwise estimation of a full correlation matrix, is also not possible. Many of the correlations, representing associations between series that are never measured in the same periods, are undefined.

We have had to proceed instead to design a means to extract common dimensions from irregular series. The starting point of such an approach is to abandon the idea of analyzing "variables," which we do not have, and turn instead to the data that we do have. What we do have is a very large number of series, each covering multiple (but not all) time points of interest. The metric of each is unique, unavoidably entangled with the peculiarities of question wording. But the *ratios* of (liberalism) values between one time and another *are* meaningful. If we observe that, say, 55 percent of respondents take the liberal position on education spending in one year and 60 percent do so in a later year, then we are not stretching the interpretation very far to assert that the latter year is more liberal than the former on this measure. We can express this change as a ratio: 60/55. We still don't know whether education spending is a good measure of "liberalism," but that can be learned from systematic analysis of the covariation of such ratios between series.

With ratios as the unit of analysis, it now becomes straightforward to build scales that average across series. The raw series have no known expectation, and any attempt to combine them runs afoul of the biases introduced when some are missing.[4] The ratios, on the other hand, all have an expected value of 1.0, and so an average of $k$ such ratios out of $N$ series (where $N - k$ are missing) is an unbiased approximation of the unattainable average of all $N$. That is how we shall proceed.

The mechanics of extracting common dimensions from these huge sets of ratios we will not explain in detail here (but see Stimson 1999; Chapter 3 and Appendix). Suffice it to say that these mechanics are designed to approximate a principal components solution (and in the limiting case of no missing values do produce a principal components solution). Our goals are to examine the common variance of a correlation structure, to decompose it into dimensions and characterize the importance of each, and then to construct scales of the derived latent concepts. When completed, the result will not be very different from the average of our four illustrative series; but it will have worked for the general case and for the universe of policy preference data.

4 Imagine, for example, that we attempted to measure liberalism with two items, one on education spending, where an average of 80% prefer more to less spending, and one on welfare spending, where preferences are reversed. So long as both indicators are available, all is well; their average is driven only by the over-time changes we wish to observe. But any period in which the education measure is available and the welfare measure missing will veer wildly toward liberalism. And an equally large conservative bias results from the reverse case.

## THE FIRST DIMENSION OF PREFERENCE:
## DOMESTIC POLICY MOOD

We begin with a one-dimensional solution, imposed by our prior theory about the role of global attitudes toward government. A first question about such a solution is how much of the observed variance is in fact common to the latent dimension. The answer is that about 38 percent (37.8) of all variance in observed policy preferences is common to this first dimension, to be called domestic *Policy Mood.*[5] The remaining 62 percent is either issue-domain specific; item specific, that is, a function of question wording specifics; or error. Most of the major controversies of American politics align themselves with this common dimension. Among them are taxing, domestic spending of most kinds, racial equality, welfare, environment, gun control, defense spending, and fiscal policy. What these diverse issues have in common, with the exception of gun control, is a single underlying disagreement over the scope of government activity, and in particular, federal government activity. These are, of course, the issues that have regularly divided the two political parties in modern American politics. Democrats (and liberals) have advocated more expansive government (except in defense), where Republicans (and conservatives) have preferred less.

Figure 6.4 displays our estimates over time of *Mood*, the latent variable underlying policy responses in opinion surveys. These estimates are scaled on average like the raw data from which they are derived. Thus, we may say, in a rough and ready fashion, that the mean value of 60.65 implies that over 60 percent of Americans who gave nonneutral responses choose the liberal response options over the period. The graph then looks much like common understandings of periods of American politics, with notable liberalism in the 1960s and notable conservatism in the 1980s. But it is different, too. The buildup to liberalism that we see has its roots in the Eisenhower Administration and is already in decline by the mid-1960s. The buildup to conservatism is the same story, starting earlier and peaking earlier than common perceptions. Commentators on public opinion, by this account, are slow to recognize movements. They are "discovered" and become part of the popular culture not while they are happening, but after they have happened.[6]

5 The variance explained calculation is an eigenvalue estimate for the common dimension divided by the total variance of the issue matrix. These are similar to their principal components analogue, except for being weighted by the number of periods each series contributes to the solution.

6 A story that fits the evidence is this: Conventional wisdom is highly inertial. It takes so long for enough evidence to come in to convince most observers of an impor-

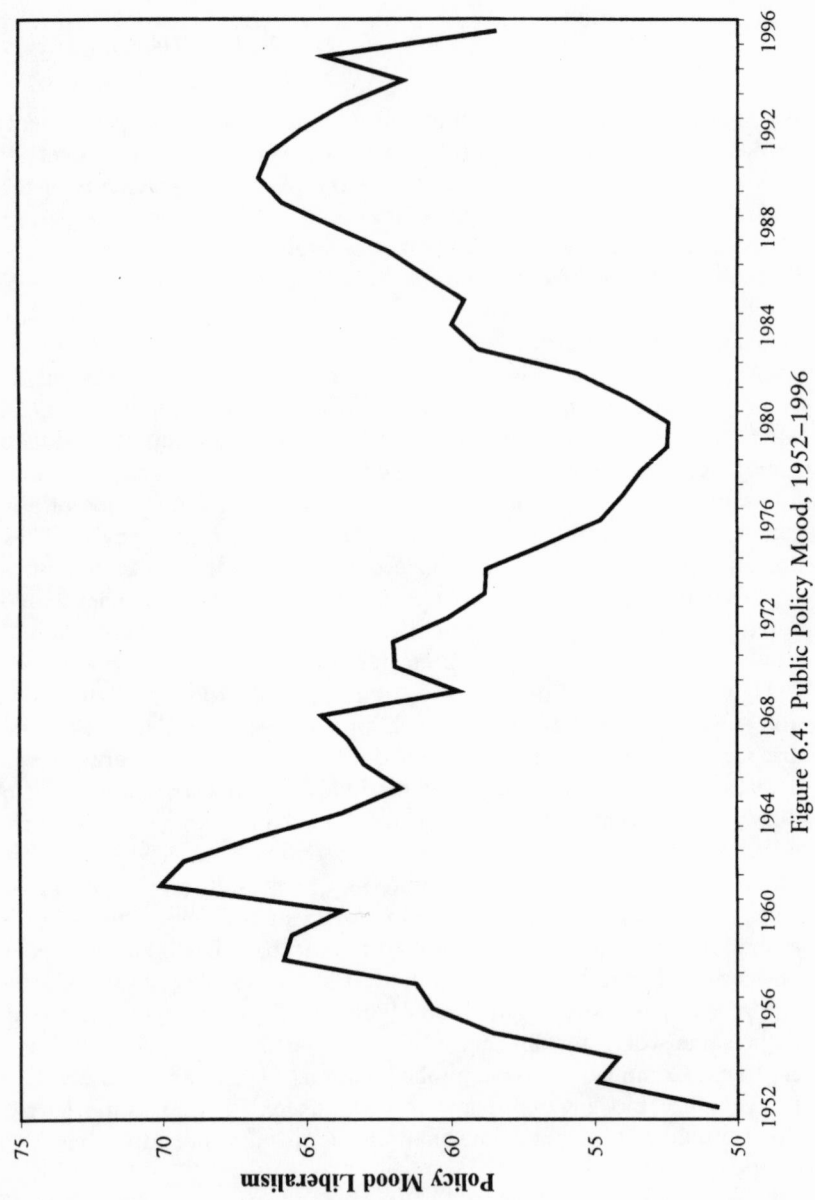

Figure 6.4. Public Policy Mood, 1952–1996

In an era in which we have come to accept as normal antipathy toward every aspect of government – which is just another way to say conservatism – it will strike many as more than strange that six out of ten Americans should choose liberal positions on domestic issues where but four are on the conservative side. That is nonetheless a fact. Not a function of our scaling methodology or any special assumptions about which issues matter and which don't, that is roughly the number one would get by simply taking the average response over thousands of domestic policy-preference questions posed over the last four decades of survey research.

This fact is also more than a little inconsistent with the self-image of the American public, which is about the reverse of these numbers. Of the two-thirds of all citizens who are willing to choose ideological labels, self-described conservatives always outnumber self-described liberals. Pressed to account for this discrepancy, we return to our understanding of multiple conflicting considerations in public opinion (Zaller and Feldman 1992; Zaller 1992). Questions that ask people whether government should do more or spend more to solve problems appear to focus concern on the problems. Considerations about the quality of education, the beauty of the natural environment, and so forth, seem to come to the fore and produce liberal responses. The same people, when asked to think about whether government is too large or spends too much, say "yes." Considerations having to do with the abstraction "government" tend to produce antigovernment conservative responses. As always, from the ambivalence point of view, "Which set of responses is the right one?" is the wrong question; they are both right. The American public wants government to do more than it is doing to solve public problems. And it wants government to be smaller, spend less, and be less intrusive. Contrary though they are to those of us who think these conflicts should be faced and resolved, one way or the other, the views are genuine. They are real public opinion, not some artifact of the way we assess opinion.

## Mood: A Second Dimension?

Not all issue responses move when *Mood* moves. Issues that fail to align themselves with this policy mood dimension are mainly of two sorts, matters of crime and punishment on the one hand and abortion rights on the other. Prominent on the list of preferences that lie outside policy mood are items on the death penalty, treatment of convicted criminals,

tant shift in public opinion that the "trend" all come to agree upon has already reversed course when its existence comes to be established.

and numerous and diverse treatments of the abortion controversy. Added to the pool are shorter series (hence less satisfying evidence) on birth control and affirmative action.

Our primary understanding of public preferences, that they are dominated by attitudes toward government, leads us to expect structure from a single dimension of preference. But do other dimensions also matter, generating common movement across policy issues? Here we set aside that understanding of a single dimension and let the data speak. Our question is this: After domestic *Policy Mood* has explained what it can of the movement in preferences across the gamut of individual issues, is there anything still systematic in the data? To address the question, we again merely extend the normal approaches of dimensional analyses to this special case. Specifically, we proceed by estimating the first dimension as before and then regressing each of the individual issue series on it, one at a time, to find their residual variation not shared with policy mood. Then that residual variation is subjected to similar analyses to see whether or not another coherent organizing dimension arises from the data.

There is, in fact, a second coherent organizing dimension. Thus we need to ask how coherent is it, both absolutely and relative to *Mood*, and then what it is and what it means. Here we are in a more exploratory temper. Since Scammon and Wattenberg (1970), most analysts (which is to say, most cross-sectional analysts) have posited a second, social or moral dimension to attitudes. This proves to be an elusive concept, for the understanding is focused on *the* one social issue of the day, and these sorts of individual issues have had little staying power. There seems most of the time to be *a* social issue important to political discourse, but not the same one, for example, in successive presidential elections. In its very statement, this is a residual concept; the social issue is an important controversy that doesn't have to do with the standard scope of government debate.

The whole idea of dimensions, it is worth noting, is different in longitudinal data than in the psychological traits conception that produced dimensional technology. To be correlated with another time series means to be in phase, to move up and down synchronously. To be orthogonal means the reverse, to be out of phase, asynchronous. Thus any dimension of preference that emerges from this analysis might still be called liberalism and conservatism, but it will be – mathematically must be – an out-of-phase variety of the species. That out-of-phase relationship may be seen in Figure 6.5, where the *Policy Mood* dimension of opinion is as before and now joined with the weaker second dimension of preference. Because the true mean and variance of this second dimension are

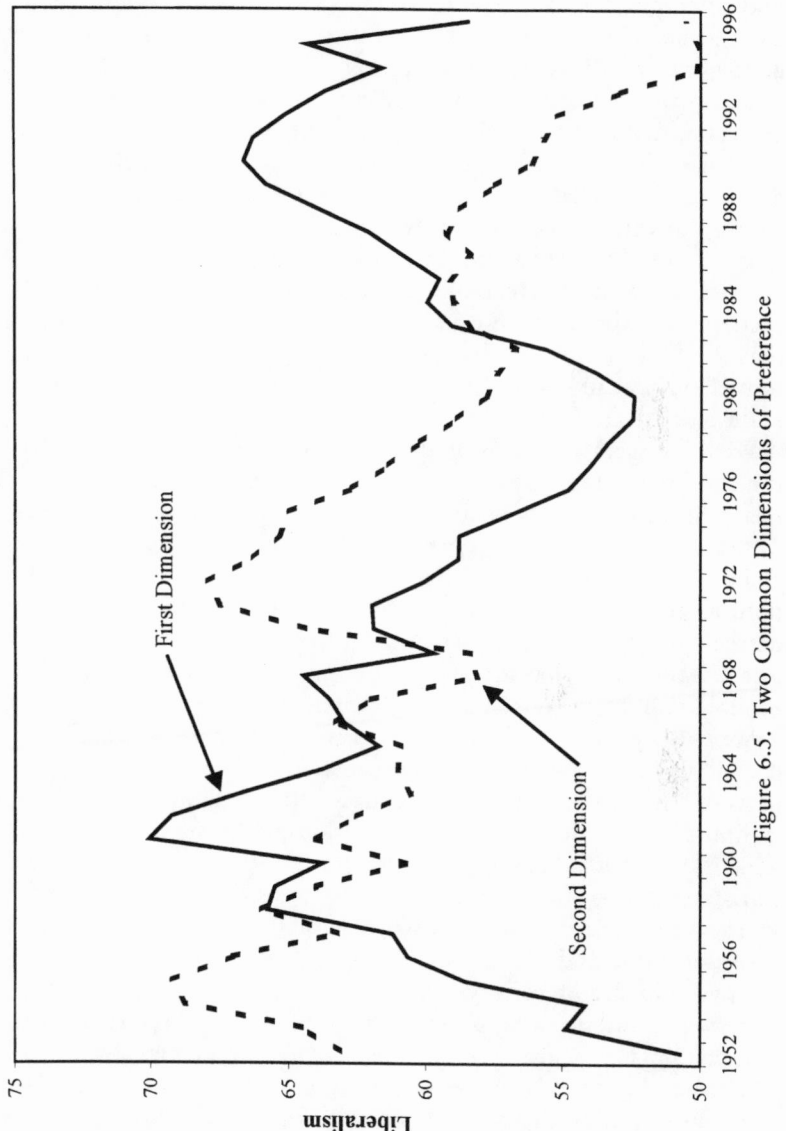

Figure 6.5. Two Common Dimensions of Preference

207

underidentified, the series is set to the same mean as *Policy Mood* and its variance is set as a fraction of the first dimension standard deviation in proportion to its explanatory power.

The movement of this second dimension is less distinctive, less clearly associated with common understandings of American politics. It builds to its liberal crest during the Vietnam War years, although preferences about the war itself are not included in the analysis. It moves pretty steadily toward conservative views thereafter, a trend never more than modestly reversed. If the opinion forces underlying this observed residual dimension of preferences is less distinctive, in part it ought to be. It accounts for about 16 percent of the variance across preferences – less than half the strength of the *Policy Mood* dimension. As a weaker force (and presuming that it is real), it ought to have had more subtle influences.

We learn what a dimension means by observing its content. That we can determine simply by observing which of the preference measures correlate with the dimensions and how strongly they do so. The 133 series in the analysis, including some mere scraps of series, are too much for comprehensive display. And the strength of correlations is comparable only when the length of series is. To deal with both these issues, we present the correlations of series with derived dimensions in Table 6.1. The selection criterion for the table is simply length of series; all series available for 15 or more years are included.

We can see from Table 6.1 that (as we asserted earlier) *Policy Mood* cuts across a wide swath of domestic issues. It is associated with issues of how big government should be, how much it should tax, how much it should do. And it has weaker associations with issues like gun control, which less clearly belong in the size-of-government domain. We also learn something from what fails to be associated with a dimension. *Policy Mood* is clearly *not* associated with abortion preferences or with issues of crime and criminals, both of which produce correlations that are trivial in size or negative.

Some of these issues assert themselves on the second dimension, labeled, albeit without great confidence, "Social Compassion." Here we find issues that seem to share the attribute of sympathy (or lack thereof) for some social group. Most distinctive are attitudes toward criminals. Items on the death penalty (for murderers) and on treatment of (generic) criminals load strongly. Shorter series (not in the table) on aiding the poor, privacy, consumer protection, and expanded health care also seem important. These are not "the social issue" as commonly understood. What then are they? Do they have in common anything more than their residual standing? It would appear that they are in a sense the human side of the liberal versus conservative debate. Much of the standard scope

208

Table 6.1. *Correlations of Issue Scales with Two Dimensions of Mood*

| Item | Years | First Dimension | Second Dimension |
|------|-------|-----------------|------------------|
| Taxes too high | 28 | 0.90 | 0.35 |
| Gun control | 24 | 0.57 | −0.52 |
| Harsh treatment for criminals | 24 | −0.02 | 0.56 |
| Spend on cities | 23 | 0.83 | −0.03 |
| Spend on education | 23 | 0.70 | −0.72 |
| Spend on environment | 23 | 0.91 | 0.11 |
| Spend on welfare | 23 | 0.62 | 0.29 |
| Spend on health care | 23 | 0.74 | 0.54 |
| Death penalty | 22 | −0.43 | 0.78 |
| Spend on race | 20 | 0.91 | −0.15 |
| Abortion if . . . can't afford | 19 | −0.44 | 0.23 |
| Abortion if . . . defect | 19 | −0.50 | 0.03 |
| Abortion if . . . mother's health | 19 | −0.24 | −0.20 |
| Abortion if . . . not married | 19 | −0.33 | 0.03 |
| Abortion if . . . unwanted | 19 | −0.18 | −0.28 |
| Abortion if . . . rape | 18 | −0.23 | −0.32 |
| Spend on defense | 18 | 0.78 | 0.44 |
| Death penalty | 17 | 0.40 | 0.55 |
| Do more . . . health care | 17 | 0.59 | 0.58 |
| Spend on defense | 17 | 0.66 | 0.31 |
| Urban renewal | 17 | 0.08 | 0.30 |
| Aid minorities | 16 | 0.56 | 0.45 |
| Provide jobs | 16 | 0.50 | 0.70 |
| Approve unions | 15 | 0.53 | 0.46 |
| Busing | 15 | 0.76 | −0.75 |
| Do more . . . education | 15 | 0.88 | 0.58 |
| Equalize wealth | 15 | 0.45 | 0.70 |
| Open housing | 15 | 0.63 | −0.88 |

of government debate, the main dimension, has to do with government activities that distribute benefits widely. Programs for the elderly, education, environmental protection, and so forth, directly benefit the families of Americans of all economic standing. These programs appeal to voters' self-interests. The second dimension, in contrast, seems heavily to involve programs for (and sympathy for) those from backgrounds "deprived" by middle-class standards. The appeal here is not self-interest, but charity,[7] thus our interpretation of this weak second dimension as the

7 Because the groups benefited are neither large in number or regular in voting habits, little but charity could explain how such programs gain majority support.

social compassion side of liberalism, support for (or opposition to) sympathetic treatment of others.

Such interpretations may reach too far. Clearly much of the content that we ascribe here to two dimensions is shared by the same people at the same times. The two series are out of phase because the technique forces them to be so; all in-phase variation is credited to the main dimension. If pressed to state what we know – as opposed to how our intuitions make order out of a huge array of correlations – it would be that there are two identifiable dimensions, the first much stronger than the second.[8]

If we pressed the data further, which we shall not do, the remaining candidate not associated with the two main dimensions is the abortion controversy. Because of its political importance, this issue is one of the best measured and most often measured policy-preference debates. At about 10 percent of the entire domestic policy data base, it is notable that this debate fails to align with either dimension. The number and quality of measures make it likely that such a cluster would dominate a variance-decomposition exercise. That it does not is clear evidence that abortion is an exception, an issue all by itself that does not move with others.[9]

8 Entertaining the possibility that we might have shorted the "social issue" domain by forcing the dimensional solution to fit data for the full time span, when social issues are often conceived as relatively new additions to the political agenda, we have repeated the analysis for the period 1970 to 1996. The result is essentially unchanged. The first dimension is nearly identical to the full period estimate. The weaker second dimension is similar to its original estimate. Dimensional analyses, it must be said, can be no better than the data they operate on, and American survey research has not done a good job of representing issue conflicts over religion, e.g., prayer in schools or the teaching of creationism or of what is now labeled "family values." Since the focus of these concerns is often more on private behaviors than on public policies, particularly national public policies, that is an expected result.

9 An analysis of the abortion items by themselves shows that they are highly associated with one another, as would be expected, and that the limited movement back and forth between pro-choice and pro-life positions appears to be responsive to events specific to the abortion domain. Pro-choice sentiment was increasing until the 1973 *Roe v. Wade* decision that legalized most abortions, which set off movement toward the pro-life position, which in turn was reversed at the time of the Supreme Court's later *Webster* decision (accompanied by numbers of state actions intended to make abortion more difficult, which set off movement back toward the pro-choice position). This response to events specific to the policy domain is a model case of the pattern we postulated would hold for other issue sets, if in fact they had been independent. Abortion passes the test all other issues failed.

## WHO MOVES WHEN MOOD MOVES? GETTING BENEATH THE AGGREGATE RESULTS

We now have in hand a measure – perhaps two of them – that we can use to represent the concept of mass policy preference (or just public opinion). We have learned some basic facts about it from the dimensional solution. We will learn much more when we examine its causes and consequences in major analyses to come. All these results are, and will be, at the macro level. But one important kind of understanding of this macro phenomenon is to be found beneath it, by knowing something about the behaviors of the individuals who compose mass electorates, one at a time. That is our task here.

To get to those individuals, we cannot just disaggregate this aggregate level concept, *Policy Mood*. Although every datum on which it rests was gathered from individuals, they were gathered from thousands of different surveys. For some of these surveys, the data are available from public archives such as the Interuniversity Consortium for Political and Social Research or the Roper Center. But for many others they are not.

To observe *Mood* change by type of individual, we turn to one particularly useful set of studies, the General Social Survey (GSS) series of the National Opinion Research Center (NORC). The GSS studies, which are separate annual cross sections spanning 1973 to 1996, provide a useful test bed for looking at macro and micro behaviors. Many GSS items figure prominently in our measure of *Mood*. And the design provides especially valuable comparability of samples, procedures, and items over time. It is not a panel survey; individuals interviewed in one study do not reappear in a later one. Thus, simple individual-level analysis of change is not possible. But it does permit us to use what we know about individual characteristics, race, education, party identification, and so forth, to trace attitude movement of similarly situated individuals over time.

Our goal is to produce an analogue to our macro-level concept, *Mood*, which may be assigned to particular individuals in the GSS studies. That will then permit between individual analyses. To produce such an analogue we begin with the policy-preference questions that are repeated over time. A number of such questions, or sets of them, are repeated several times. But only the spending priorities questions (of which we have already seen examples) span the full 24-year series. That limitation is potentially a great one. For we can't know a priori that these relatively narrow policy controversies move in tandem with other preferences, and thus whether we have a valid measure of preferences. This *potential* limitation, we will quickly see, is not a real one.

## Policy

To build our analogous measure, we perform a principal components analysis of this set of seven policy preferences[10] on all GSS respondents, 1973–1996. The analysis yields an obvious single factor solution where the common dimension is associated with about 32 percent of the total variance. The pattern is what would be expected, positive association with all domestic policy spending preferences and negative association with defense spending.

We use the principal component solution to construct an individual level "factor score" measure of *Policy Mood* for the period covered by the GSS. That permits us to address two questions of some importance: (1) Does the narrow selection of items we have used track the broader concept *Policy Mood?*, and (2) Does the method of estimation – aggregate principal components analogue versus actual principal components on individual data – matter? To address both questions separately, we use the aggregate methodology on the same GSS questions as annual aggregates (percentage liberal). With content thus controlled we can answer the method question by examining the dimension estimated by both methods. The data (see Figure 6.6) leave no doubt about the answer. *Mood*, estimated from aggregate data from all survey houses and a huge variety of questions and formats, correlates at .95 with the individual-level analogue for GSS respondents, aggregated up to annual averages. That association across methods is actually stronger than the comparable correlation (.89) between *Mood* and a subset estimated from only the GSS items as annual aggregates. We conclude that we may assign computed scores to the GSS respondents whose preferences they represent with great confidence and that our macro concept *Mood* is a meaningful individual attribute. That permits us to move on to individual analyses that illuminate our understanding of the macro concept. Before doing so, we pause to lay out a set of common understandings for how observed properties of aggregate public opinion data might arise from differing individual views.

### Three Stories About Aggregation

When we observe macro behaviors, such as systematic movements in policy preferences, and wish to ascribe them to individual-level

10 Preference items available in all studies are spending priorities for environment, health, urban aid, education, aid to minorities, military, and welfare. Varied wordings of these items are not used. The analyses are of all GSS respondents with complete responses to the seven questions, some 17,139 individuals out of 35,284 total. The huge loss of cases results mainly from the fact that beginning in the mid-1980s these question forms are posed only to randomly selected half (sometimes one third) samples, with others getting varied wordings.

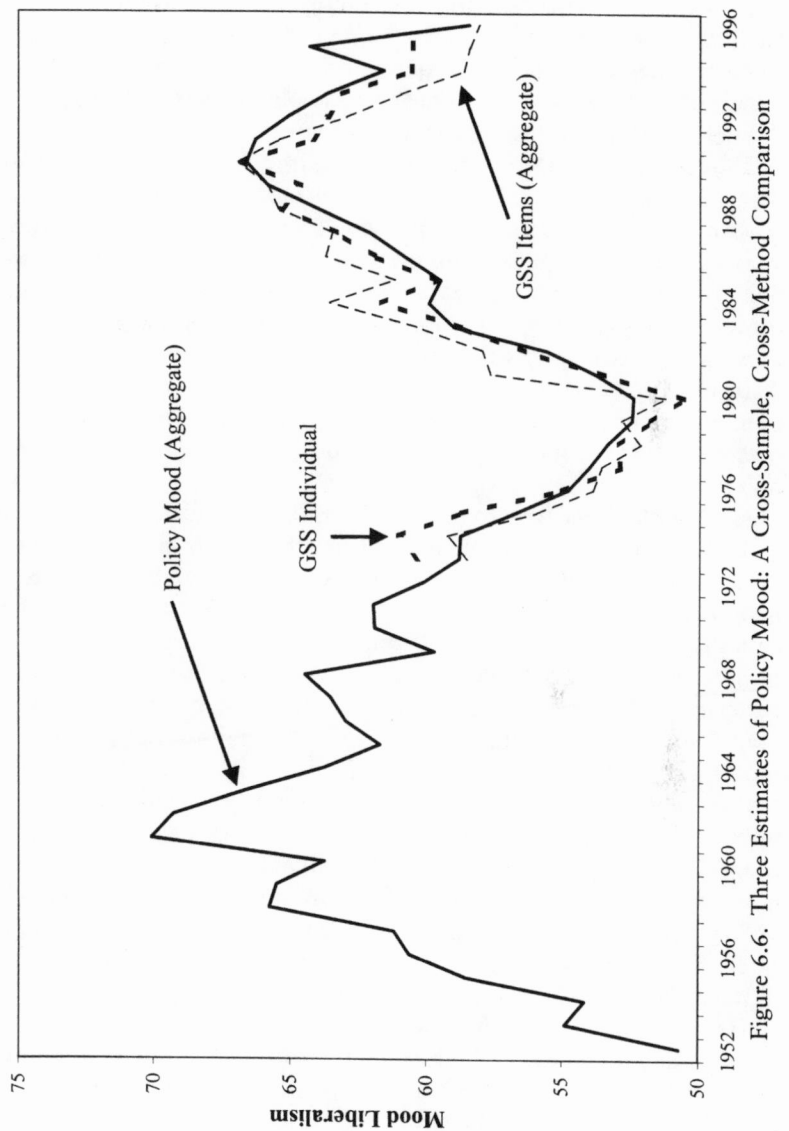

Figure 6.6. Three Estimates of Policy Mood: A Cross-Sample, Cross-Method Comparison

213

behaviors, there are three sorts of common stories we can tell. Each connects what we know about individuals to what we observe in the aggregate, but they make different assumptions about the process and yield remarkably different conclusions about the meanings to be ascribed to public opinion shifts. We take them up here.

The simplest of the stories we'll call the *baseline* model; that is, the micro-level change underlying the macro change is essentially the same for all citizens. At its simplest, a macro opinion shift of $x$ points arises from an electorate in which each citizen moves $x$ points. For more realism, we allow individuals to vary in their opinion movements, some more, some less, and assert that the macro movement arises from a distribution of individual movements, randomly distributed around a central tendency that is identical to the macro opinion change. When *Mood* moves, the change occurs among all segments of society and largely independent of the content of original opinion holding.

A plausible alternative to the baseline model postulates that mass electorates are mainly inert, not moving at all. Rather, macro-level movements arise from an *opinion elite*, a refined segment of the electorate that is atypically informed about and interested in public affairs. The opinion elite story has macro variation arising from a mass component with little or no variation around a flat mean plus a small elite segment with highly patterned movement. The usual mathematics of aggregation gain tell us that in such a scenario the macro signal would faithfully mirror the elite movement, while mass opinion cancels itself out.

If this elite scenario were true, what consequences would flow? On the one hand, if a small elite generated *Mood*, this elite could vote its ideology. If so, political change would be driven by the changing views of a volatile elite. On the other hand, the standard view holds that elites are firm both in their policy preferences and their partisan commitments. If elites were volatile in their policy preferences but stable in their partisan behavior, macro movements in preferences would be of small consequence to politics. In a world where most citizens do not move (systematically) at all, and where those who do move have prior commitments to one or the other side in politics, aggregate changes in policy preferences might connote little.

A second alternative to the baseline model turns the opinion elite conception upside down. This *peripheral voter* model looks to the least informed and involved segments as the "dynamic element" of opinion change. In this view, it is citizens atypically *un*informed and *un*involved, not anchored in place by stable motivation, who account for change. If part of politics is merely fashion, sets of views that come to be conventional wisdom by repetition (e.g., on TV), then those who don't care

214

much about politics or lack commitment to a motivated point of view should be most susceptible to these fashionable political views. This peripheral voter explanation also tends to discount the importance of macro-level movements. It holds that most do not change at all; it disparages those who do. Fashion and fad are real enough and can have important short-term impacts, but those who follow fashion in politics will predictably move on to other views.

The three stories are ideal types. We do not expect any to be fully accurate. With the same concept measured at both levels, we have unusual leverage here to find out precisely which sorts of individuals appear to have produced the aggregate opinion change. We know that *Mood* moves systematically over time. Our challenge here is to account for it in terms of the types of people who experienced similar opinion changes.

The General Social Survey presents few opportunities for measuring elite, mass, or peripheral standing in politics, lacking in particular the sort of political knowledge questions that have proven so useful for this task in the National Election Series.[11] What we do have for the purpose is respondent education, ordered for this analysis into four standard groups, "Less Than High School," "High School Graduate," "Some College," and "College Graduate." We also have the "Gallup-Thorndike Verbal Intelligence Test" for some, but not all, of the GSS studies. This, unlike its name, is a measure of respondent vocabulary knowledge. It ought to complement the formal education measure by tapping an important product of exposure to education. In this battery of 10 items, respondents are presented with a word, presented as something not generally known, and urged to "guess" which of five synonyms is a correct match to it. That produces a vocabulary scale from 0 to 10, which we will collapse into five groups for analysis.

These two measures are good indicators of general social standing. They do not, however, tap anything specific to the political sphere. Thus well-educated respondents with rich vocabularies may be quite uninterested in politics and far from "elite" in the political sense. And the converse is also true; the poorly educated who, for one reason or another, have been drawn into unusual political activity, are likely to be more informed and sensitive than these measures gauge. These are rough and ready indicators, which capture some, but not all, of the distinctions that are important for the political dimension of social standing. They are the best we have.

---

11 The NES has a more basic failing for this analysis; it lacks continuity of policy-preference measures. See Luskin (1987) and Zaller (1992) for treatments of the concept of political sophistication.

## Policy

Our question is: "*Who moves when mood moves?*" We wish to know what sorts of people contribute to the observed aggregate-level change. To answer that question we stratify the electorate by our two measures. This allows us to observe groups of GSS respondents moving through time. We wish to know which groups contribute to observed aggregate movement. In the concrete terms of this analysis, we can now restate the three models of aggregation. The "opinion elite" conception leads us to expect strong and systematic movement only from the best educated in the two senses, and little from the lesser educated. The naive "baseline" conception leads us to expect movement from all groups of more or less the same direction and magnitude. The "peripheral voter" conception leads us to expect most of our aggregate pattern arising from movements at the bottom of the education scale, with greater stability (i.e., flatness) at the top. These expectations may be tested against the data of Figures 6.7 (education) and 6.8 (vocabulary). In both figures we have imposed a three-period moving average on the series for smoothing.[12]

Of the three models of aggregation, we can see quickly that one, the peripheral voter conception, is just wrong. The overall shift of preferences forms a "V" pattern around 1980, essentially an average of the four (or five) groups. The least educated and lowest vocabulary respondents contribute less to the overall pattern than do the others; they cannot be its driving force. Elite status by our two measures is associated with contributing more to the common movement. The preference changes in these groups (college graduates, best vocabularies) are sharper and larger than for all others. But on balance, the opinion elite model does not square well with the two figures. That conception of aggregation has most movement coming from a relative handful of "elite" respondents, where all others are essentially flat. What we see instead in Figures 6.7 and 6.8 is that all groups are moving in tandem. The elite groups move more, and thus contribute a little more than their proper numeric share to the aggregate. But they do not by any means dominate the process.

12 The patterns are fully present and visible without smoothing. But the zigs and zags of year-to-year movements in these small subsamples makes the systematic movement harder to see. Our practice throughout the GSS analysis is to graph the results as a 24-year continuous time series by using linear interpolation for the missing (1979, 1981, 1992,1995) years. We know from other studies that each of these years lies in fact between the years before and after. We depart from this practice in the case of the vocabulary test, where there are large gaps between administrations – a crucial one, 1979–1981, missing what is elsewhere the conservative high of the series. Here we graph the short series on a discontinuous time scale.

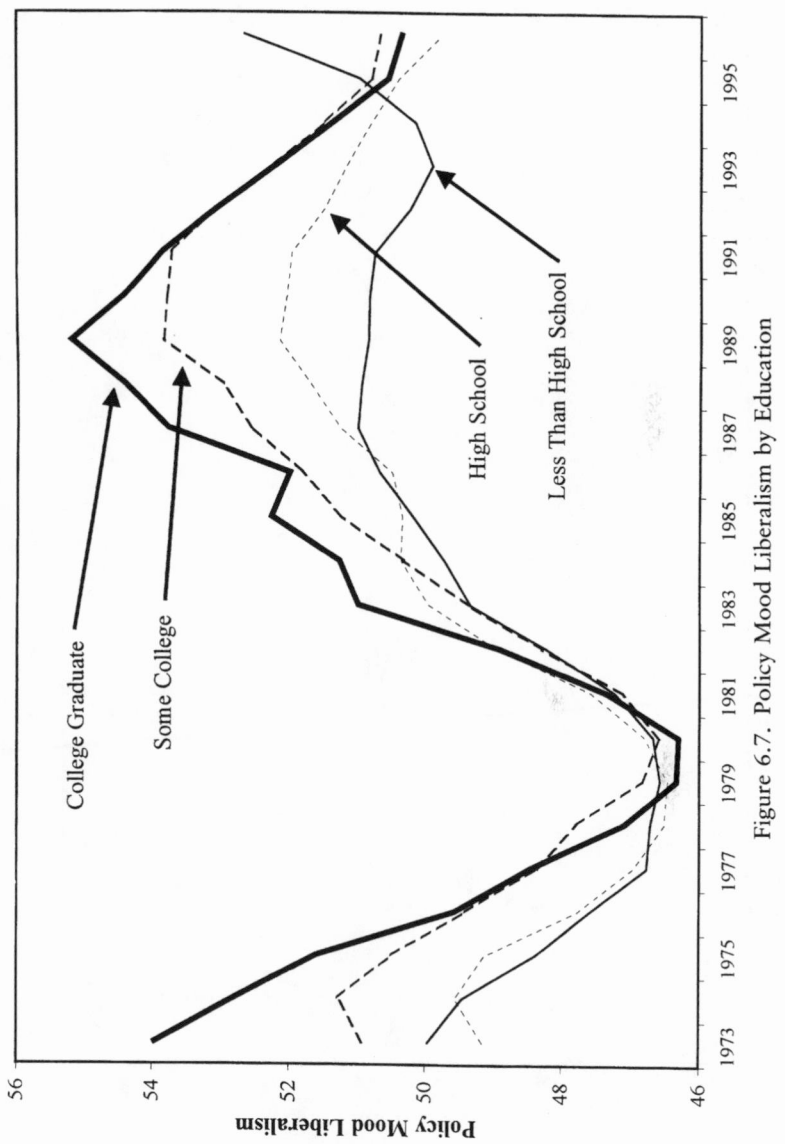

Figure 6.7. Policy Mood Liberalism by Education

College Graduate

Some College

High School

Less Than High School

Policy Mood Liberalism

217

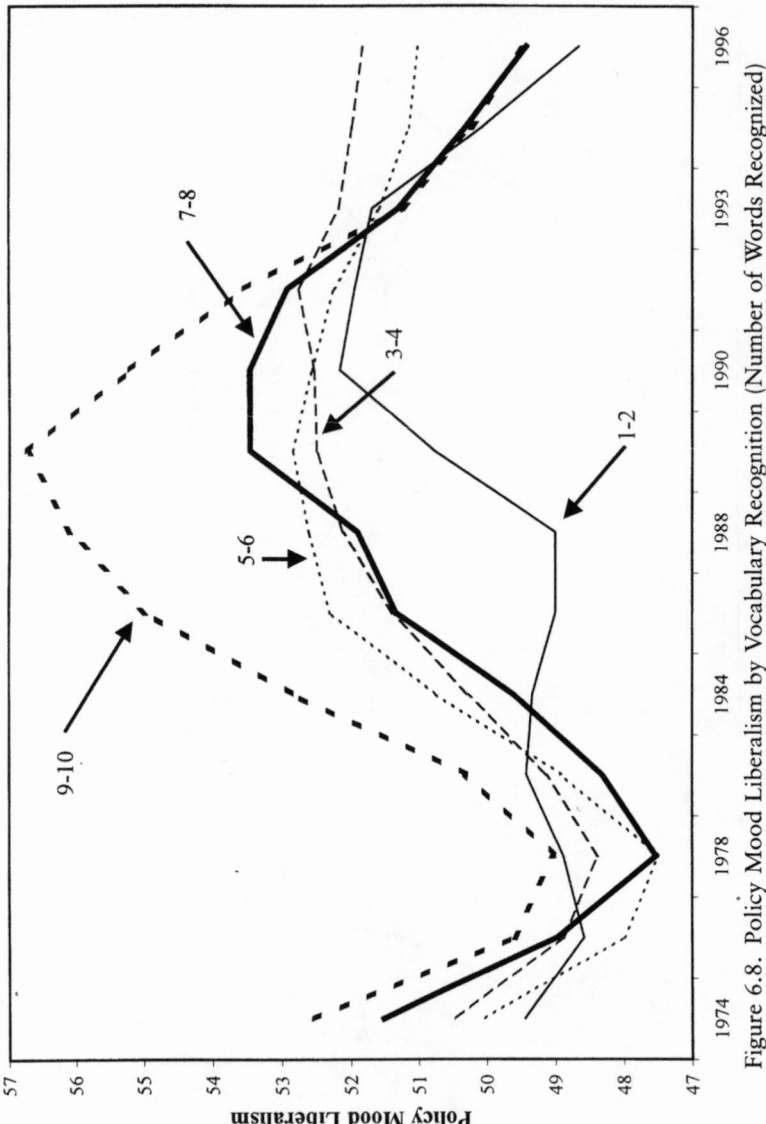

Figure 6.8. Policy Mood Liberalism by Vocabulary Recognition (Number of Words Recognized)

We conclude that the best account of where observed preferences arise is the naive one; that is, aggregate preference moves because the preferences of most individuals are also in motion. The better educated move more than do others, but movement seems to come from all strata of American society. This uniformity of preference change across individuals points us to search for uniform explanations for the phenomenon, to responsiveness to real events and conditions as cause, and to single-source channels of communication as mediation. We take up this explanatory challenge later in the chapter.[13]

## HOW MUCH DOES MOOD MOVE?

We see that *Policy Mood* varies. The question then is, how much? That question appears to have a simple factual answer. We can say that it has a range of about 18 points from its liberal extreme of 70.1 in 1961 to its conservative extreme of 52.4 in 1980.[14] It has a standard deviation of 4.45. But how much is that? In comparative terms, its variance is slightly greater than *Macropartisanship* but considerably less than that for *Approval*. It looks substantial in Figure 6.4. But graphic displays aren't always to be trusted on the issue of a variability of a time series. If, for example, we had displayed the series in its full, theoretically possible, range (0 to 100), it would "look" less substantial. What is or isn't "substantial" then seems more subjective, a function of how much variation we expected to see. That makes the "how much?" question a more difficult, more subtle, matter.

We gain some interpretative leverage by thinking about what the scale numbers mean. A one-point increase in *Mood* conservatism, for instance, will be produced when, on average, the opinion-giving respondent shifts to a 1 percent greater probability of choosing the conservative response option *for every available survey question*. So we might say that the 1961–1980 18-point movement amounts to, when averaged over individuals and items, an increase of 18 percent in the probability of choosing conservative options in 1980 than in 1961.[15]

---

13 For an extensive analysis of *Mood* as an individual-level concept, see Stimson (2001). That analysis explores how mood varies within the categories of standard political behavior explanatory variables such as race, region, gender, income, and party identification.

14 The year 1952 is actually the global conservative extreme point of the series. But as a beginning point estimated with very little data, we lack confidence in the estimate and focus instead on 1980.

15 Of course, they aren't exactly the same people, but a little interpretative license will help authors and readers on this point.

# Policy

It is worth emphasizing that these opinion movements apply not to one policy preference, but to all policy preferences. The estimates are an average across all issues. Thus a one-point movement implies a one-point movement on every domestic policy preference at the same time. Or if some issues do not follow the global pattern, then other movements must be even larger to produce the observed result. It is relatively easy to think of events that might move millions of people to change views on a single issue. And thus we come to think of double digit percentage changes in issue preferences as not surprising, hence not all that important. But the evidence here is of global movement. To explain why millions of people are shifting all of their domestic policy preferences is a matter of great consequence.

Another way to appreciate the movement in *Mood* is to compare it to the distribution of micro-level liberalism among citizens, measured as cross-sectional *Mood*. Consider the distribution of scores to a micro-level composite index of policy liberalism, where the measure is the respondent's "percent liberal" to a battery of policy items, weighted in proportion to their contribution to *Mood*. A reasonable guess is that the standard deviation of this index would be less than 20 percentage points, as responses would cluster around the mean position, with very few answering conservative or liberal to almost all items.

This exercise provides a frame of reference for aggregate *Mood* movement. An 18-point *Mood* movement might be about one standard deviation if *Mood* were measured cross-sectionally. Imagine a normal distribution of cross-sectional *Mood* in the 1960s and another in 1980, where the variance stays the same but the mean moves one standard deviation. When a normal distribution shifts one standard deviation, the average percentile movement is 26 percentile units, with the greatest shift in the middle of the range. Thus, assuming the *Mood* movement 1961–1980 was a standard deviation, a citizen at the median liberalism score in 1961 would, by 1980, be as conservative as the person at the 14th percentile of liberalism in 1961. Similarly a 1961 liberal at the 86th percentile of liberalism would, by 1980, be no more liberal than the median citizen of 1961.

This discussion relies on no more than informed speculation about the cross-sectional variance of *Policy Mood* within the electorate. But we can do better. We can exploit once again the GSS survey items that tap spending preferences 1972–1996. Recall that we have a factor score computed from seven items that tracks the global measure of *Mood*. For each year of the GSS surveys, we can observe the cross-sectional distribution of factor scores. We can then follow these distributions over time.

This movement of the distributions is shown in Figure 6.9. The lines are the liberalism scores of 10 percentile cut points – the 5th through the

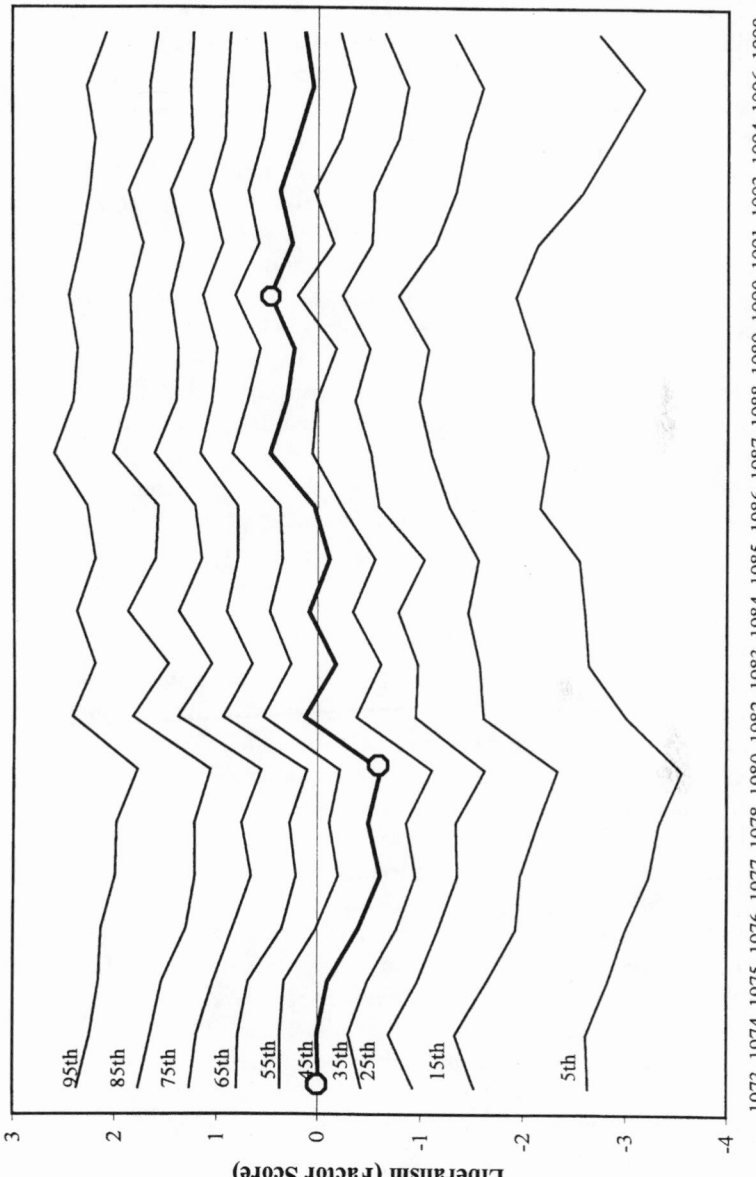

Figure 6.9. Estimated Movements in Public Policy Mood at 10 Percentile Divisions of the Electorate

221

95th. To get some sense of the movement, concentrate on the 45th percentile voter, slightly more conservative than average, who was essentially neutral on *Mood* in 1973. (See the dark line and the circle that marks its starting point.) By 1980, this voter, as did all others, moved rightward. Then, during the Reagan-Bush years 1980–1990, overall *Mood* rose to its leftmost peak. How much change was this? Our 45th percentile voter moved from a conservative to a liberal preference. Notably, the voter had now shifted to the position that the 65th percentile voter held in 1980 – that is to say, a moderate liberal. On average, between 1980 and 1990 voters became as liberal as their counterparts 20 percentile units to the left had been in 1980.[16]

Does *Mood* move enough to matter? The answer would seem to be a clear yes. A reasonable inference, consistent with what we now know from micro-level studies, is that if policy moderates become conservatives and then become moderates again, the electoral climate would change. Thus, our expectation is that *Mood* changes contribute to the electoral climate, affecting both elections and policy making. In later chapters, we will find that these expectations are correct.

## IDEOLOGY AS SELF-IDENTIFICATION

Our *Mood* concept – ideology, in other words – is a composite measure, a weighted average of survey responses to many different policy issues. This contrasts with the most common measure of the electorate's ideological preferences, the distribution of respondents' *self-reports* of their identification as liberal, moderate, or conservative. In this section, we compare the trend over time in *Mood* with the trend indicated by the familiar ideological self-identification measure.

The self-identification of ideological preference bears an obvious resemblance to *party* identification. To compare with our measure of *Macropartisanship* (the distribution of Democrats among Democratic and Republican identifiers), we estimate macro-level ideological identification as the frequency of self-identified "liberals" among identified liberals and conservatives. It is known that aggregate ideological identi-

16 From 1980 to 1990, the global measure of *Mood* became 14 points more liberal. Earlier we speculated that the 18-point movement, 1961–1980, represented a one standard-deviation movement of opinion. If 18 points is one standard deviation, then a 14-point movement is .78 standard deviation of movement. Indeed, the mean movement of the GSS series from 1980 to 1990 is exactly .78 standard deviation of factor score liberalism. Our speculation has clearly been on the right track. When a normal distribution shifts .78 standard deviation, the average percentile change is 21 percentile units, the approximate 1980 to 1990 change shown in Figure 6.9.

fication (*Macro-Ideology*) is essentially unrelated to *Macropartisanship* or other obvious stimuli (Box-Steffensmeier, Knight, and Sigelman 1998). But is it related to *Mood*?

As we will see, the clearest trend in ideological self-identification is a growing preference for the conservative rather than liberal label. However, the word *liberal* was once in greater fashion than it is now. Its root is the word *liberty*, reflecting that liberalism once stressed political freedom from state oppression. In European usage, political *liberalism* continues to mean *less* government. In the United States, the meaning underwent some evolution. Early in the twentieth century, political liberalism began to mean a generous concern for the plight of the less fortunate in society. When politicians spoke the ideological language, they generally embraced the idea of being a liberal. For instance, in the crucial 1932 presidential election, both President Hoover and his successor Franklin Roosevelt called themselves liberals. Once in office, President Roosevelt commandeered the term liberal as a positive term for his New Deal agenda. *Liberal* quickly took on a clearer meaning as *government involvement* to help the poor. New Deal opponents became labeled as *conservatives* (Rotunda 1986).

Until about 1971, national surveys only rarely included items ascertaining self-identified ideological preferences. Between 1939 and 1965, there may have been no more than nine national surveys that asked respondents straightforwardly to choose between a liberal and conservative identification. About an equal number of surveys asked respondents to choose between hypothetical liberal and conservative political parties. With either variation in the question, the reported ideological division was almost always very close to a 50-50 split (Erskine 1964; Robinson and Fleishman 1984). Ideological polling was too sparse to discern any trends. Whether it was the late New Deal era, the McCarthy period, or the liberal ascendancy of the Kennedy-Johnson years, people divided about evenly between liberals and conservatives.

Then, starting some time in the 1960s, ideological identifications turned decidedly conservative. No national survey today would show anything close to the even liberal-conservative split typically found over 30 years ago.[17] The exact timing of the change cannot be documented because during the period 1965–1969, in the heart of the turbulent 1960s, no national survey of which we are aware ascertained the nation's

---

17 A direct comparison is difficult, however, because the early ideological items did not offer respondents the "middle-of-the road" or "moderate" option that most contemporary survey questions about ideological preference include. When given a chance, a plurality of respondents will often choose the middle option instead of a conservative or liberal self-label.

ideological preferences in any direct manner. By the time the monitoring of ideology resumed in 1969, the change was already well underway. Instead of an evenly divided electorate in terms of ideological preferences, conservatism gained ascendancy. Since the early 1970s, it has been a question not of whether conservatives outnumbered liberals but by how much.

By 1971, pollsters were ascertaining ideological preference with sufficient frequency to generate the start of an observable time series. Surveys were also offering a third choice of "moderate" or "middle-of-the road." The exact question varies from survey house to survey house, and even within a house over time. To be sure that observable trends are not artifacts of shifting question wording, we adjust our estimates for variation in wording. Our trend line, shown in Figure 6.10, represents the percentage of liberals of ideological identifiers over 25 years, based on 580 separate surveys. We adjust for question-wording effects by presenting annual means corrected to reflect the question-wording of the CBS/*New York Times* polls.[18]

Figure 6.10 starts the ideological series in 1971, when ideological preferences already had begun their conservative tilt. The figure shows that the conservative trend continued through the seventies, reversed somewhat during the eighties, and then accelerated in the nineties. In the early seventies, conservatives were "winning" by about 55 to 45. By the mid nineties, the typical margin was more like 65 to 35.

We have on our hands a puzzle. Measured by *Mood*, opinion is generally liberal, in the sense that when averaged over many survey items, more people give the liberal than the conservative position on specific policy. But in self-declared ideology, Americans since at least 1970 have seen themselves generally as conservative. This combination of facts supports the adage that Americans are "operationally liberal" but "philosophically conservative" (Free and Cantril 1968).

Not only is ideological identification more conservative than *Mood*, but, at least at first glance, the two trend lines seem to be unrelated in their movement over time. How could there be two indices for ideological trend spotting that look so different in their short-run movement – a variable curve for *Mood* with peaks and valleys of liberalism and a

---

18 CBS/*NYT* asks: "How would you describe yourself on most political matters? Generally speaking, do you think of yourself as liberal, moderate, or conservative?" We adjust for question-wording effects by regressing percentage liberal (of identifiers) on 24 dummies for years (for year effects) and 19 dummies for variants on wording (for wording effects), with the CBS/*NYT* wording as the base. For each year, the estimated mean is simply the equation intercept plus the coefficient for the year dummy.

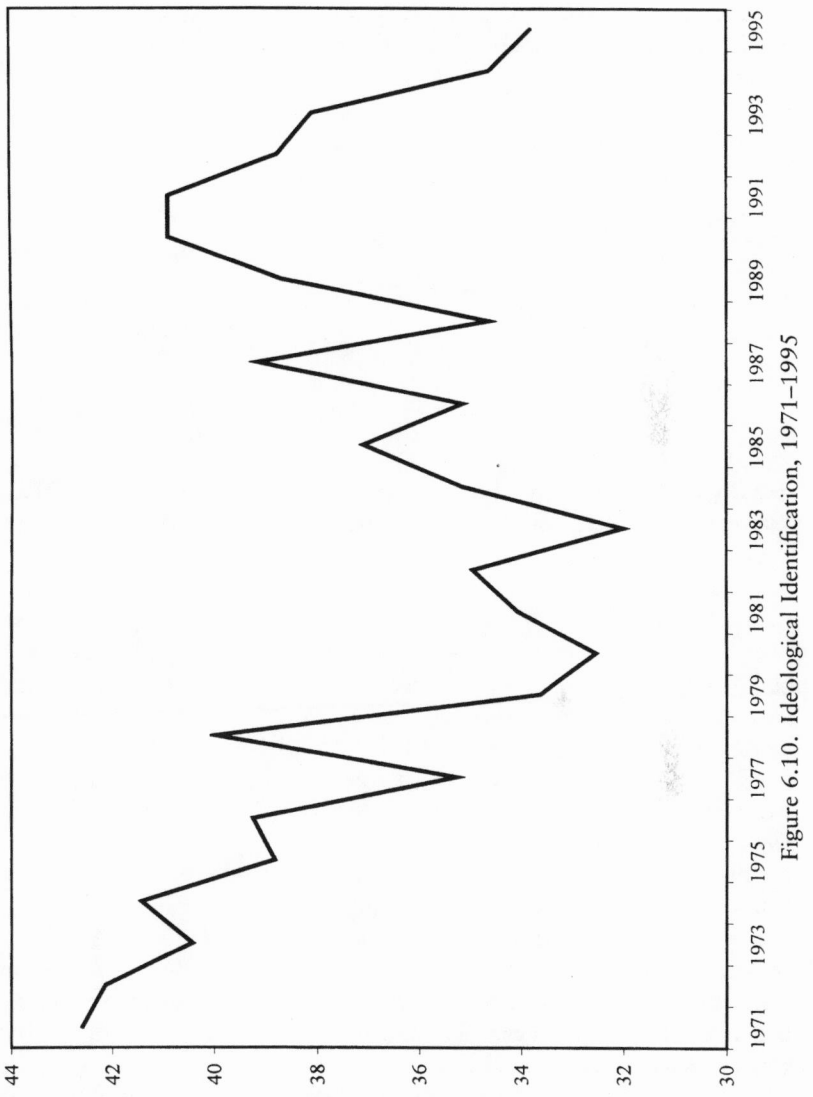

Figure 6.10. Ideological Identification, 1971–1995

Liberals as Percent of Ideological Identifiers

225

## Policy

Table 6.2. *Predicting Mood from Ideological Self-Identification and Mood*

| Variables | Coefficient | $t$ |
|---|---|---|
| Ideological Identification$_{t-1}$ | 0.32 | 1.73 |
| Mood$_{t-1}$ | 0.31[a] | 3.00 |
| Years Since 1971 | −0.30[a] | −3.49 |
| Constant | 12.19 | 1.95 |
| Adjusted $R^2$ | .77 | |
| Standard Error of Estimate | 1.40 | |
| N | 24 | |

*Note*: Data are annual observations, 1971–1993.
[a] $p < 0.05$.

steadily conservative trend for identification? *Mood* reflects the varying answers to concrete policy questions over time. But whatever the current trend in policy choices may be, preferences for ideological labels become increasingly conservative.

Much of the explanation for the increasing preference for the conservative ideological label must be a shifting threshold of what passes for liberal and what passes for conservative. Holding constant policy preferences, many of today's conservatives would have called themselves moderate or liberal at an earlier time; and many of today's moderates would have once called themselves liberals. And as we will see, *Mood* and ideological identification are not as statistically unrelated as it would seem at first glance.

Adjusting for the linear trend toward increasing conservative identification, *Mood* and identification actually track very well for the 1971–1994 period. This is shown graphically in Figure 6.11. Trend-adjusted, macro-level identification correlates at 0.57 with *Mood* and 0.65 with *Mood* lagged one year. The latter may not seem very impressive, until one realizes that identification also correlates with its own lagged values at no more than 0.65.

Quite clearly, macro-level ideological identification reflects the same currents as *Mood*. If we regress macro-level ideological identification on lagged *Mood*, a counter (years since 1971) for the trend, and lagged identification, we get the equation shown in Table 6.2.

To predict macro-level ideological identification, one is better off predicting from *Mood* and time than from lagged ideological identification. Like any survey indicator, ideological identification has its unique source of variance independent of *Mood*. But ideological identification clearly

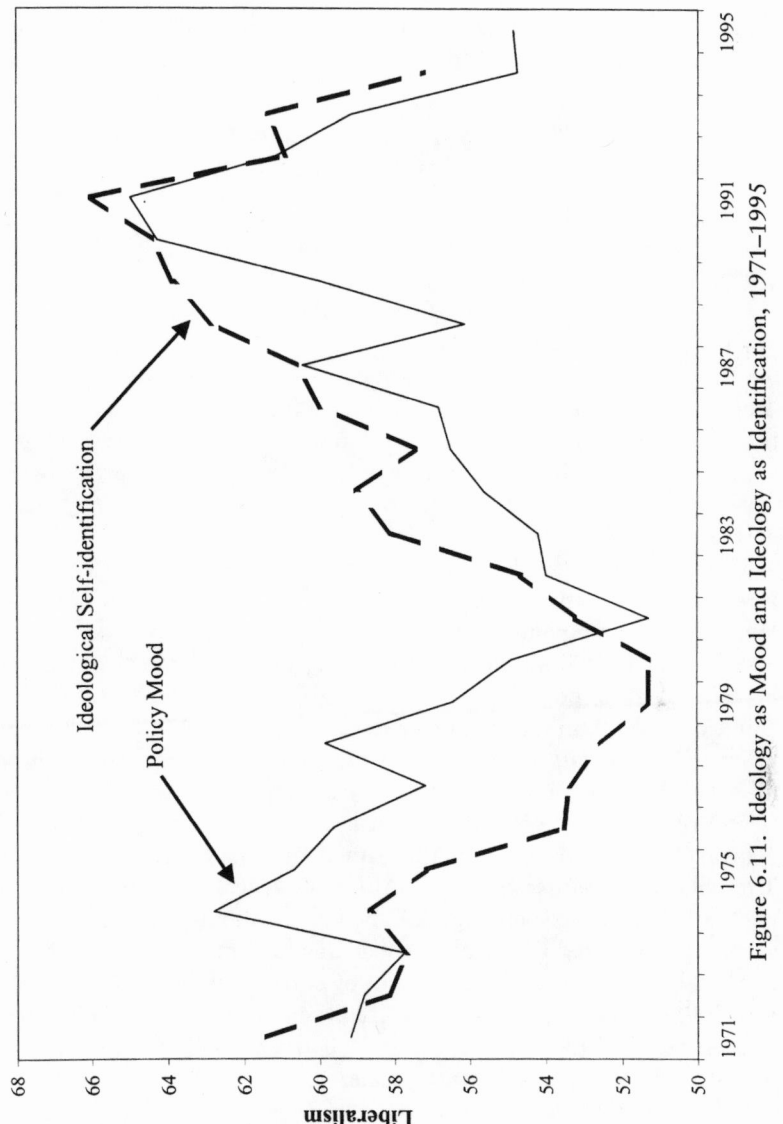

Figure 6.11. Ideology as Mood and Ideology as Identification, 1971–1995

227

shifts in response to the same variables that affect policy preferences in general, as reflected in *Mood*.[19]

### Policy Mood and Self-Identification: Macro Match and Micro Mismatch

The neat longitudinal covariation we have just seen sets the stage for a look at individual-level covariation of the two sorts of ideology, self-designation and policy preference. Again, making use of the GSS cumulative studies, we look at the policy preferences of self-styled liberals, moderates, and conservatives. To simplify interpretation, this time we drop the defense spending indicator – which moves opposite the others – and scale the other six (all spending) indicators as 1 for "too little" spending, 0 for "about right," and –1 for "too much." Then it is a simple matter to add them together, producing a domestic spending preferences scale ranging from –6, "cut everything," to +6, "increase everything."

The spending issues at hand are the mainstream of American liberalism in the domestic sphere, such as health, education, welfare, cities, race, and environment. Thus, we comfortably expect liberals to advocate greater spending, conservatives less, and moderates something in between. This expectation is wrong. In Figure 6.12, we graph the distributions of domestic spending preferences of the three ideological groups. The message of the figure is that the three groups are discernibly different from one another – but *only* discernibly different.

The reality of Figure 6.12, often noted in scholarly treatments, but contrary to popular beliefs, is that Americans like government spending. They like more rather than less. Although generic "government spending" and "domestic spending" are the villains of much political rhetoric, spending connected to social goals elicits much more approval than disapproval. The three ideological groups sort themselves out a bit. Their median preferences align as expected. But the overlap is much more impressive than the divergence, and all three center themselves in the liberal, pro-spending, end of the scale.

We summarize those distributions of preference in Table 6.3. There we break the scale into three natural portions favoring, on balance, more spending, less spending, or the same. If advocating more domestic spending is liberal, as it certainly is in the national political dialogue, then all three groups would be classified as liberal. "More" is the modal choice (61.0%) even of self-described conservatives. Only about

---

19 Meanwhile, *Mood* does not respond to lagged ideological identification. Although *Mood* contributes to ideological preferences, the reverse is not true.

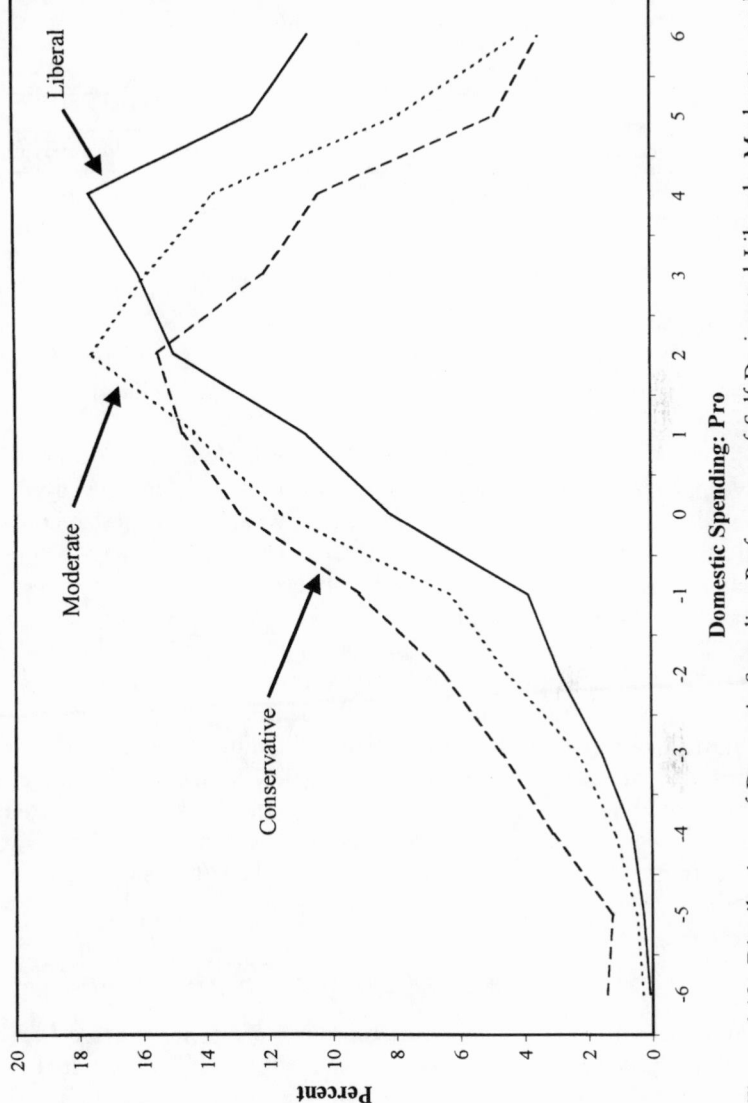

Figure 6.12. Distributions of Domestic Spending Preferences of Self-Designated Liberals, Moderates, and Conservatives

# Policy

Table 6.3. *Domestic Spending Preferences Among Self-Designated Ideological Groups, 1973–1996*

| Domestic Spending Preference | Self-Designation | | |
| --- | --- | --- | --- |
| | Liberal | Moderate | Conservative |
| More | 82.6% | 73.3% | 61.0% |
| Neutral | 8.2% | 11.6% | 12.9% |
| Less | 9.3% | 15.1% | 26.1% |
| Total | 100.1% | 100.0% | 100.0% |

*Source*: Cumulative General Social Survey.

one-fourth (26.1%) of all conservatives take the expected anti-spending position.

Most liberals by identification are liberal in preference. Most conservatives by identification are *not* conservative by preference. And while the evidence we have presented, limited by what was available consistently over time, concerned only spending issues, this pattern is much broader. On numerous other domestic concerns, most conservatives do not take "conservative" positions.

We know, from Conover and Feldman (1981), that self-identified liberals and conservatives do not bring quite the same meanings to the terms. We surmise that many self-identified conservatives think the term "conservative" means "prudent," "thoughtful," "practical," "patriotic," or some similarly positively valenced stance. For some, it probably codes "white." Some, no doubt, guess what it means. The result, for whatever reason, is confusion. Large numbers of Americans like to think of themselves as conservative while they support liberal policies.

## WHAT MOVES POLICY MOOD?

We have seen that *Mood* moves. According to our summary evidence from aggregating the survey evidence, the electorate's liberalism had two peaks – in the 1960s and again briefly in the early 1990s. A more conservative *Mood* prevailed in the early 1950s and the late 1990s – at the beginning and end of our series – and in around 1980. But why these differences? And why the subtler differences from year to year that mark the *Mood* series? If the electorate could turn more liberal or conservative from one year to the next, what could be the cause?

One hypothesis is that *Mood* moves in response to partisan performance. For instance, the public's *Mood* could be influenced by the presidential party's performance in the economic and other realms. Republican successes and Democratic failures would lead voters to think more of conservative ideas and less of liberal ones. The reverse would be true of Democratic successes and Republican failures. This idea, however, receives no support from the data. As measured, for instance, by *Presidential Approval* or economic prosperity, success does not bolster the support for the policies associated with the party in power.

From micro-level research arises a related hypothesis – that *Mood* follows from *Macropartisanship*. Among individual survey respondents, ideological preferences and party preferences are strongly related, especially among the more ideologically sophisticated (Erikson and Tedin 1995; Knight and Erikson 1997). In aggregate terms, the same people who are conservative tend to be Republicans. Does it follow that *Macropartisanship* drives *Mood* or perhaps vice versa? The answer from the data is clearly negative, as *Mood* and *Macropartisanship* follow different trajectories and rarely are found in phase. In fact, the time-series correlation is clearly negative. When Democrats are strong in party identification, liberalism is more likely than not to be in retreat. We treat this negative relationship more as coincidence than directly causal. As we will see in Chapter 7, the negative *Mood-Macropartisanship* correlation is capable of masking the effects of each variable. We return to it in Chapter 11, speculating further about its source.

Rather than *Mood* responding simply to retrospective performance in the manner of *Macropartisanship*, the more promising place to look is to the policy needs of the voters. Voters become more liberal when circumstances dictate a liberal approach and more conservative when circumstances dictate a conservative approach. Much of this discussion we reserve for Chapter 9, where we show the influence of past policies on *Mood*: When policy becomes more liberal, *Mood* turns conservative. When policy becomes more conservative, *Mood* turns liberal.

One connection between perceived policy need and policy choice is between economic need and *Mood*. But how would the economy affect *Mood*? One could imagine good times causing liberal *Mood* as people perceive they can afford greater government services (Durr 1993). But one could just as easily expect bad times to cause liberal *Mood*, as economic hardship causes people to ask for government help. Neither of these hypotheses is supported by the data. Rather, as we will see, the economic circumstances that affect *Mood* are the mix of potential economic maladies. Unemployment, we will see, pushes *Mood* in a liberal direction. Inflation, on the other hand, drives *Mood* conservative.

# Policy

## Mood *and the Economy*

How would inflation and unemployment affect *Mood*? We know that when unemployment increases, demand for government activity (i.e., *liberalism*) follows. When the employment rate improves, the demand weakens. We also know that prosperity sometimes fuels inflation, which fuels demand for government austerity (i.e., *conservatism*). Economists have often described (but less so these days) an unemployment-inflation trade-off, the "Phillips Curve,"[20] where government policy making will work toward reducing either unemployment or inflation, but not both. (For a good discussion, see Hall and Taylor 1993.)

Considerable evidence exists that a differential response to the unemployment-inflation trade-off is a major source of division between Republican and Democratic policy makers (Hibbs 1987; Alesina and Rosenthal 1995). Policy makers within both parties see both inflation and unemployment as undesirable, of course, but they place different weights on the desirability of correcting one versus the other. Democrats place greater weight on stimulating employment; Republicans place greater weight on guarding against inflation. For any decision maker, the exact trade-off will depend also on the circumstances, the urge to expand the governmental role increasing in proportion to the worry over unemployment, and the urge to retreat increasing in proportion to inflation.

Thus, we can think of a policy-making elite that shifts its ideological *Mood* in response to the degree of unemployment and inflation. Could we not imagine the same *Mood* shifts by the public at large? To test this idea, we regress annual *Mood* on lagged *Mood*, the annual inflation rate and the annual percent change (first difference) in unemployment, 1956–1996.[21] We do the analysis two ways. First, to ensure a conservative inference about the economic effects, we use a version of *Mood* that is unsmoothed.[22] Our concern here is that the smoothing process might get in the way of a clean examination of causation. But the smoothed measure both has better qualities and is a superior match to the *Mood* concept. The distinction, we shall see, does matter, but either analysis supports the same inferences.

20 The concept of a long-run trade-off of unemployment and inflation is now seen by economists as naive. Any trade-off is for the short term. For instance, an expansion of inflation would cut unemployment in the short term, but unemployment would eventually equilibrate to its "natural" rate.

21 We have also measured unemployment as the deviation from the "natural rate" of unemployment. The results are little affected by the distinction.

22 The *Mood* estimation algorithm normally employs exponential smoothing during the estimation process. See Stimson (1999) for details.

232

Table 6.4. *Mood by Inflation and Unemployment Change, 1956–1996*

| Variables | Unsmoothed Mood | Smoothed Mood |
|---|---|---|
| $Mood_{t-1}$ | $0.38^a$ | $0.67^a$ |
| | $(2.72)$ | $(6.64)$ |
| Inflation Rate$_t$ | $-0.78^a$ | $-0.47^a$ |
| | $(-3.67)$ | $(-2.99)$ |
| Change in Unemployment$_t$ | $1.10^a$ | $0.77^a$ |
| | $(2.30)$ | $(2.34)$ |
| Constant | $41.57^a$ | $22.01^a$ |
| | $(4.55)$ | $(3.27)$ |
| Adjusted $R^2$ | .58 | .80 |
| Standard Error of Estimate | 2.95 | 2.03 |
| N | 41 | 41 |

$^a$ $p < 0.05$.

The result in column 1 of Table 6.4 shows that liberal *Mood* is positively affected by unemployment and negatively by inflation, just as predicted. Both coefficients are highly significant. A one-point movement in inflation produces almost an 0.8 movement toward conservatism in *Mood*. A one-point increase in unemployment produces a larger, 1.1-point, increase in liberalism. The nature of the domestic economy is thus a major contributor to our understanding of the politics of mass preferences.

The unsmoothed version of the *Mood* estimate has zigs and zags – particularly in its first decade, where data are neither rich nor numerous – which hide its own persistence and attenuate observed relationships with other variables. To see that effect, we perform the same regression in the second column of Table 6.4, this time on a smoothed dependent variable. What we see from this analysis is that the more persistent *Mood* translates the economic effects somewhat differently. The two economy coefficients are each about two-thirds their unsmoothed size – still highly significant – with effects that now show more of a distributed lag. The substantially increased coefficient on the lagged dependent variable now carries more of the effects of the previous year – including the previous year's economy – into the current year's *Mood*. In this formulation, the current year's economy gives up about a third of its effect, but gives it up to the previous year's economy.

To visualize how strong the connection really is, we first generated a short-term "prediction" based solely on the inflation and unemployment

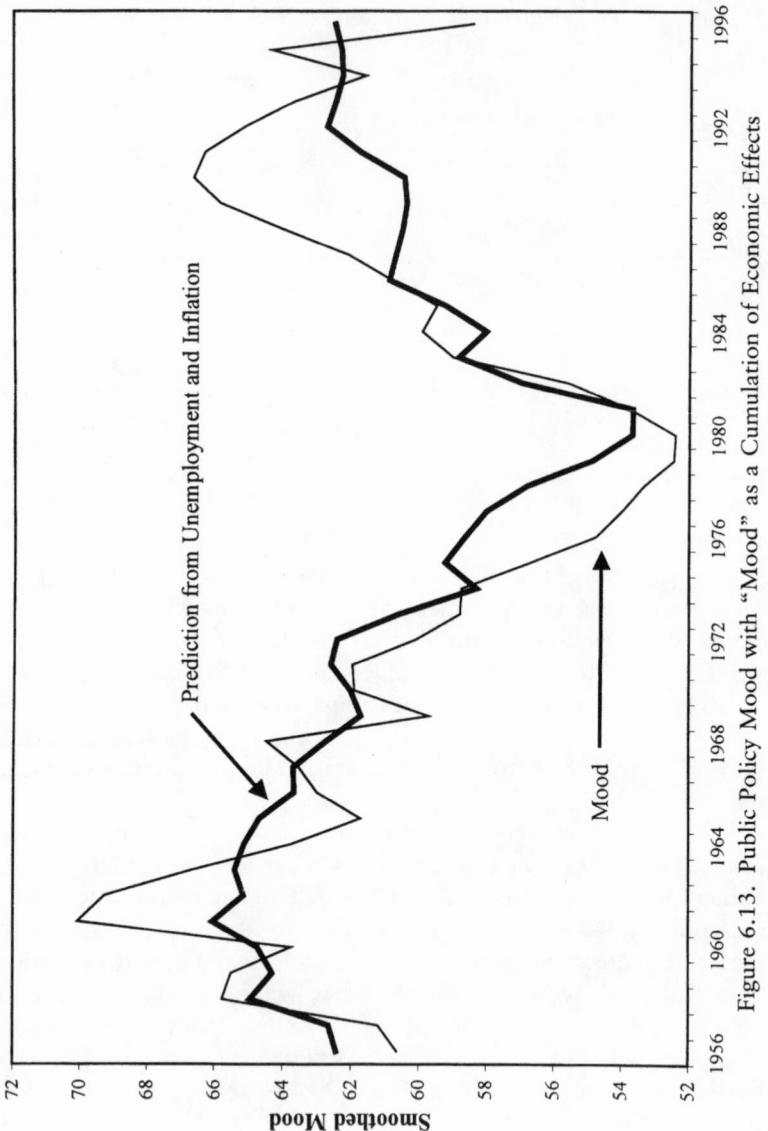

Figure 6.13. Public Policy Mood with "Mood" as a Cumulation of Economic Effects

234

components of the Table 6.4 (not including lagged *Mood*).[23] This short-term prediction correlates at .72 (.73 smoothed) with observed *Mood*. We then created a cumulative prediction variable representing the accumulated effects of inflation and unemployment to *Mood* over time. Using the series mean as an estimate of *Mood* in year 0 (1955), we start in year 1 with the short-term prediction, including the estimated intercept. For later years, we add the current "short-term prediction" (including intercept) and the cumulate past values of "short-term" predictions, weighting the previous year's accumulation by 0.38 (0.67 smoothed), which is the estimated rate at which *Mood* persists from its past values. The result is Figure 6.13. The cumulative predictor represents the running tally of cumulative unemployment minus inflation, each weighted properly by their regression coefficients. The resultant correlation is a very high .79 (.83 smoothed). By a dynamic model involving unemployment and inflation, we succeed in explaining about two-thirds of the variance in *Mood*. This is not yet everything that can be explained, but it is a powerful piece of it.

### SUMMARY

This chapter has brought *Policy Mood* into our discussion of the macro polity. We have seen that the public has relatively stable preferences for more or less government, that these preferences move over time in a coherent fashion, and that much of their movement can be explained. We have seen that *Mood* is predictable from the state of the economy. Not a simple matter of degree of prosperity or generic economic performance, it is the *kind* of performance that matters. Erring toward too much inflation produces conservatism as a correction. Erring toward high unemployment produces liberalism as a response. Economic performance, conceived as better or worse, success or failure, we have long known influences evaluations of the competence of political actors. That was the story from the first half of this book. Now we know something more. We know that citizen preferences move toward the left or right as a function of economic performance, differentiating between employment and price stability. This is *political* economy.

In later chapters, we will explore *Mood* as a cause of political and policy outcomes, asking how preferences shape the outcomes of elections and how they factor into government decisions about public policy. Our

---

23 *Predicted Mood = 1.11 × Change in Unemployment − 78.42 × Inflation.*

understanding of democratic processes requires citizen preference to play a starring role, and we will see that it does. We will also show that *Mood* reacts to policy as well, just as it reacts to the economic needs of the moment. In Chapter 7, we turn to the matter of elections for public office.

# 7

---

## *Elections*

We have asked how the public evaluates presidents, how it forms ties to political parties, and how it decides upon a mix of most preferred polices. In five previous chapters we have produced a large stock of answers to these queries, and we have left doubts hanging here and there. Pushed to defend these matters – *Approval*, *Macropartisanship*, and *Mood* – as subjects of inquiry, we might briefly argue their inherent importance, the pleasure of knowing why and how they move. Ultimately, however, our recourse would be this: they matter for election outcomes in the United States. For elections are the central issue of democratic governance. If we are going to understand politics, then we must understand elections. That is the sole business of this chapter.

But how should we approach the topic of elections? For chapter after chapter we have ignored the differences and distinctions among Americans and asked how much we could learn from studying the electorate as a unit and, in particular, a unit with interesting variation over time. We have dealt with evaluation, identification, and preferences not as individual choices, approve or disapprove, Democrat or Republican, more environmental control or less, but as barometers of a unitary electorate. *Approval*, *Macropartisanship*, and *Mood* we treat as barometers of how the electorate thinks about things and where it is. When we do so, we lose the power that differences and distinctions bring to analysis. But we also lose the distortions of that powerful, but often uninteresting, variation. This abstraction has allowed us to connect the pieces of American politics that are usually disconnected in micro analysis, to observe connections that cannot be observed in the study of individual attitudes and behaviors.

This is how we shall proceed again with elections. Instead of simply looking at voting – Democrat, Republican, other, or nonvoter – we shall ask what proportion of its votes the unitary electorate chooses to

237

allocate to the two major parties. In this case, there is a literature on election forecasting that operates on the same unitary electorate assumption. But we wish to go beyond that literature, with its intense focus on macroeconomic performance, to address also the individual voting behavior literature, typically associated with the Michigan voting behavior tradition, and also the impact of policy views on voting, usually mainly a micro-level concern.

We begin with three different stories that purport to explain voting and elections, one focusing on the psychology of candidate evaluation as its central theme, one on macroeconomic performance, and one on party and voter issue positions and the calculus that connects them.[1] Largely, but not wholly, in separate literatures, these accounts differ substantially in emphasis. But they are not mutually inconsistent. Not denying the central tenets of alternatives, they tend rather to deemphasize them. *The American Voter* (Campbell et al. 1960), and with it much of the subsequent voting behavior tradition, begins with a complete causal system, one that leaves room both for competence in managing the government and for policy agreement and disagreement to work their influence on the ultimate vote. But the strategic choice to begin analysis with attitudes most proximate to the vote and then work backwards in the "funnel of causality" leaves most of the emphasis on the psychology of candidate evaluation, not on rational reward and punishment for incumbent success and failure or calculating which party's proposals are more in line with voter policy preferences.

The Downsian spatial distance approach to policy views similarly has a role for incumbent competence and evaluation of candidate character in updating the credibility of proposals. It does not deny these things, but its emphasis on rational calculation is elsewhere. The "economics and politics" story, and particularly its variant emphasizing election forecasting, has been limited heretofore by the availability of indicators. The set of good time-series indicators is rich in measures of economic

---

1 A fourth tradition, dominant in campaign press reporting, emphasizes the quality of the campaign as a central feature of success and failure. Electoral success is often attributed to "running a good campaign," while failure is virtually always attributed to a bad campaign. Insofar as this is understood as a matter of pure political skill in the technical sense, knowledge of how to organize people for action, we think it is wrong. High levels of skill are typically available on both sides, the differential never likely to be particularly large. But the hypothesis can never be disconfirmed, because success (and anticipation of success) always makes campaigns look "good," with the opposite result for failure.

## Elections

Table 7.1. *Three Standard Stories of Voting and Elections:*
*Theory and Indicators*

| Story | Main Components | Indicators |
|---|---|---|
| Economic Voting | Rational Retrospection | Objective Economic Indicators, Consumer Confidence |
| Candidate Evaluation | Individual Psychology "The Person" of the Candidate | Net Candidate Evaluation (from ANES "likes and dislikes") |
| Policy Voting | Prospective Policy Calculation Minimizing Spatial Distance | Policy Mood, Party Platforms |

performance, but poor in candidate evaluation (with the occasional appearance of presidential approval, but no comparative candidate indicators). Measures of the public's policy position relative to the parties have not existed at all, and so the Downsian calculation goes unnoted in this literature.

In this chapter, we will draw out the main themes of these three stories (and do injustice to attempts in each to reconcile with the others), treating them as caricatures of the three main-line approaches. From the Michigan voting school, we abstract the psychology of candidate evaluation. From the rational choice tradition we look at a macro version of the idea that voters choose parties based upon the closeness of their positions to the voters' own. And we draw on retrospective economic voting from the forecasting literature.

We lay out the three components in Table 7.1, a beginning of a roadmap of analyses to come. In it we summarize the stories, the main components of micro theory that they require or entail, and the macro indicators that we will use to represent them.

*The Plan of This Chapter*: The three stories of Table 7.1 set up our basic analytic strategy. We take up each of the three, first the economy, then candidate evaluation, and then policy preference, digressing along the way to reintroduce *Macropartisanship* as a means to carry the memory of these three influences to the scene of election day. In each case, we will develop macro indicators and ask how well they predict presidential election outcomes. Then we put them all together, addressing in particular the question of how substitutable they are for one another. Last, we take this presidential scheme and employ the

239

# Policy

appropriate pieces of it that work to predict the outcomes of elections for the House and Senate.

## MICRO MODELS

Election outcomes are aggregations of individual vote choices. Thus, the literature on individual voting is the source of micro models. From this literature, we extract three familiar accounts, (1) that citizens vote to reward or punish incumbent governments for the goodness or badness of the times, (2) that citizens respond to alternative candidates, liking some and disliking others, voting for those they like, and (3) that citizens compare their preferences for mixes of public policy to the choices offered in the election and choose parties and candidates closest to their preferences. We give here a brief account of each, necessarily highly abstract and simplified.

- *Reward and Punishment*: In this model, most associated with political economy research, citizens observe past success and failure and then vote for or against the incumbent party to reward or punish it appropriately. This could be rational evaluation as in Fiorina's (1981) account of retrospective voting. But the same behavior, voting on the "goodness of the times," is considered evidence of the absence of sophisticated understanding of politics in *The American Voter* (Campbell et al. 1960). Its hallmarks in either case are retrospection, instead of consideration of the choices offered by current candidates, and focus on measurable outcomes, which in effect becomes mainly macroeconomic performance.
- *Candidate Affect*: Originating from the "funnel of causality," the most proximate attitudes as final explanation of vote choice in *The American Voter*, that is, candidate affect – the degree to which the voter "likes" one candidate more than another – emerges as a powerhouse predictor of the individual vote. Although the "funnel" leaves room for a panoply of factors to influence that "liking," the emphasis of the original Michigan school is on pure affect, just "liking." This formulation, invented to explain the success of the grandfatherly war hero Eisenhower, whose views were largely unknown, emphasizes pure personal attractiveness as a central component. Consistent with campaigns dominated by image advertising, this model is usually associated with scholars who disparage the sophistication and rationality of typical voters. As best elaborated in Stokes (1966), the emphasis is on "pure" affect, attitudes that do not derive from rational evaluation or calculation.

240

- *Policy Preference*: In this model, most often associated with Downs (1957), the voter observes the policy stances offered by competing candidates and chooses the candidate whose stance is most in line with the voter's own. Fully prospective, the key issue being future behavior projected from current promises, this view requires a view of the voter as a rational actor. This choice between alternative policy sets emphasizes what candidates will do in office (policy) as opposed to how well they will do it (outcomes).

## Macro Interpretation

We shall be brief here to get on to the analysis. We merely note that what elections mean is profoundly the consequence of choice between competing micro models. Any interpretation of outcomes as messages from the electorate in particular requires some expression of policy-preference voting. The issue was well joined in the 1980 presidential contest where the moderate liberal incumbent Jimmy Carter was decisively beaten by the quite conservative Ronald Reagan. If our micro model is *reward and punishment*, then the message of the election is that Carter ought not to have gone into an election season with a recession on his hands, nothing more. If the model is *candidate affect*, then we conclude that Reagan, the person, was just more attractive to voters than Carter, the person. But if we entertain *policy-preference* voting, then the outcome must indicate a preference for more conservative policies.

What elections mean is a matter of great consequence and, accordingly, of considerable controversy. We endeavor here to sort through the macro-level evidence to arrive at an answer, to discover what mix of these simple behaviors is most consistent with observed outcomes.

## The Micro-Macro Mismatch

If it is obvious that election outcomes are the aggregate of votes, then we would expect general similarity between both the explanations offered and the variables of empirical analysis at the two levels. That is definitely not the case. Micro analysis (i.e., "voting behavior") consistently emphasizes partisanship and the attitudes that are filtered by pre-existing partisanship as key components of the explanation of the vote. Around that, generally agreed-upon core matters such as candidate traits, policy preference, and evaluation of incumbent economic performance come into play in important but lesser roles. This is textbook voting behavior.

## Policy

Students of macro elections read a different textbook. Largely concerned with forecasting elections, the macro literature also has one key explanation that dominates all else; it is macroeconomic performance. As if voting and elections were wholly different topics, neither shares much with the other. The key explanation of micro voting studies, partisanship, does not even appear in the forecasting models. And, almost in parallel, the key explanation of macro elections, economics, is usually peripheral in voting studies. And not infrequently, it is altogether omitted.

This discrepancy gets little notice. Perhaps that is because scholars usually work on one level or the other, but not both. Not only are economists such as Ray Fair key players in the forecasting literature, but political scientists who visit the topic are also rarely associated with the study of individual voting. We, the three authors, are outliers in this. Each of us has scholarly roots in voting behavior and of course our current enterprise focuses at the macro level. We take it as a special challenge to come to terms with the discrepancy. And, to tip our hand in advance, we will end up supporting the micro-level claim for the central importance of partisanship. And to that story we will add a claim that looms large at neither individual nor macro-level empirical work (but is central to political theory): that the fit of voter policy preferences to party issue positions is fundamental to understanding election outcomes. Before we get there, we will visit alternative stories that look so good that they could easily *seem* to justify an end to the search.

### EXPLAINING THE PRESIDENTIAL VOTE

As a maturing quantitative social science responded to serve a general curiosity about the electoral future, electoral forecasting emerged in recent years as a popular novelty. Forecasting models typically incorporate indices of the national economy and perhaps presidential approval plus other indicators that are observable in advance of the election.[2] Yet even with the best of statistical models, national elections become predictable only as the election approaches. And even with late information

2 The economist Ray Fair (1978, 1982, 1996) is in the forefront of those who insist that the elections can be explained by economic conditions without resort to political variables. Political science forecasters usually include political variables such as presidential approval, which can be observed in advance of the election. See Lewis-Beck and Rice (1982), Abramowitz (2000), Holbrook (2000), and Wlezien and Erikson (2000).

242

from the eve of the election, forecasters risk embarrassment from the occasional grand mistake.[3]

Our interest here is the *explanation* of election outcomes, a task that is often best performed after the election, when the range of relevant variables can be known. Yet prediction and explanation go hand in hand. Forecasting is meaningful only if the predictor variables reflect actual causes of the vote rather than lucky guesses (Lewis-Beck and Tien 2000). For predicting in advance or explaining after the election returns are in, the pursuit is the same: to find a fundamental set of variables that determine the electorate's collective decisions.

Understanding the forces that influence election outcomes is important for politicians as well as the idly curious. Politicians know that their behavior affects their electoral success. By understanding the electoral consequences of their actions, elected leaders and their challengers are able to take actions to enhance their electoral success. By so doing, they also satisfy the voters' needs. Conversely, when politicians are unable to anticipate the voters' collective response to their actions, the burden falls solely on the electorate to obtain the desired result at the ballot box rather than via politicians' anticipatory behavior.[4]

This chapter examines the series of U.S. national elections between 1952 and 1996. We start with 1952 because that is the earliest we can rely on regular aggregations of the relevant survey data and other indicators. Over the 1952–1996 period, congressional elections were conducted every two years, yielding 23 observations for analysis. Presidential elections, conducted every four years, attract far greater attention. Alas, between 1952 and 1996, we have a scant 12 observations of presidential elections for statistical analysis.

With only a few national elections to analyze, any statistical results must remain tentative and open to rival interpretation. In any case, our chief objective is not to forecast so much as to foster the understanding of the variables that drive elections. We begin our search for explanation with the matter of macroeconomic performance.

3 Fair's regression model, with several variables, picked the winner of all 19 presidential elections 1916–1988. Then in 1992, it forecast Bush over Clinton by the margin that Clinton actually defeated Bush. How a model based on the economy could forecast Bush's reelection poses an interesting statistical question. Whereas Bush's defeat is predictable from most simple models based on economic growth, Fair's model was overburdened by too many irrelevant variables.

4 Political actors are not the only ones who benefit from anticipating elections. Because different parties enact different policies when in office, economic actors also have an incentive to anticipate election outcomes. Uncertainty about the next election can have important consequences for the economic system. See Alesina and Rosenthal 1995.

# Policy

It is a commonplace observation to state that the economy affects presidential elections, now a cornerstone of the accepted wisdom of political science. Statistically, this fact can be summarized by statements such as that "the correlation between the incumbent party vote and election-year growth in per capita income is .70." The exact indicator could be a different choice such as growth in GDP, or perhaps the preelection change in the unemployment rate. And the time span for observing the economic change may vary. But with a variety of measures and time spans, the statistical answer is roughly the same. Any of several reasonable economic indicators will statistically explain about half – or perhaps more – of the variance in the incumbent party vote.

We will choose one indicator to illustrate the now standard connection of economic performance to election outcomes. But the reader should understand that we could easily have chosen others. The relationship is robust, and "good times" are pretty much "good times," no matter what the measurement strategy.

## Objective Macroeconomic Indicators

*Per Capita Income Growth* is our primary measure, in part for its intuitive appeal. From a statistical perspective, this variable is ideal because each quarterly reading is statistically independent of those before. The correlation between current and lagged disposable income growth is –.03, essentially zero. Thus, as a voter observes income growth over a presidential term, change in each of 16 quarters contributes in roughly equal proportions to the overall growth. But do voters weigh them equally? As Hibbs (1987) has shown, a compact way to estimate the electorate's temporal perspective is to impose the orderly assumption that voters discount the past with an exponential decay – where each quarter's economic outcome is weighted by some constant $\lambda$ $(0.0 \leq \lambda \leq 1.0)$, times the quarter following. If $\lambda = 1$, voters weigh all quarters equally. If $\lambda = 0$, only the last quarter matters. As did Hibbs, we find $\lambda = .80$ to be a reasonable approximation.[5] With $\lambda = .80$, cumulative income growth does not forecast the next election very well until the eve of the election

---

5 Hibbs searched across possible $\lambda$ values for the one that best predicts the incumbent party vote. His estimate is a $\lambda$ value of .80. Our estimate, based on updated data and three additional election cycles, is very close at .81. Because of the small difference, we stick with Hibbs's round value of .80. The meaning of this estimate is a best guess that voters weigh each quarter 1.25 times the one before. Over 16 quarters, the final quarter is weighted 32 times the first of the series.

year. Then, starting about quarter 12 of the four-year electoral cycle, the cumulative effects come into focus. After 15 quarters, the correlation between cumulative income growth and the incumbent party vote is .70, meaning that cumulative income growth explains almost half the variance in the vote. Figure 7.1 presents a graph of the relationship between cumulative quarter 15 income and the incumbent party vote. Note that in this bivariate relationship, the presidential party's vote is expected to exceed 50 percent when per capita income grows at an annual rate of 1 percent or higher. The lesser standard of *any* positive growth rate is insufficient for the presidential party to enjoy a positive expectation of victory.[6]

*Leading Economic Indicators* do even better than *Disposable Income*. Cumulated over the term at $\lambda = .90$ (Wlezien and Erikson 2000), the *Leading Indicator* series represents the sum of economic growth shocks measured a quarter or two before they happen. Cumulated *Leading Indicators* predicts the vote best, with a handsome correlation of .84, when measured in quarter 13 at the *beginning* of the election year. This result is interesting because the index early in the election year anticipates *actual* economic conditions later, at the time of the electorate's collective decisions. Evidence both that economic performance is very important and that some part of citizen reaction to the economy is forward looking, the *Leading Indicator* series maximizes our ability to call elections from objective economic indicators.

All of the objective measures of economic performance share a common problem in predicting political outcomes; the political translation of them is not constant over the long time of our analysis. As economic performance varies over the long term between comparatively good times and comparatively bad ones, our evaluation of the indicators varies also. During good times, for example, the 1960s or later 1990s, annual income growth of, say, 2 percent is mildly disappointing. But in other decades, that same growth rate would have represented substantial success over the prevailing expectations of the times. This limitation inheres not in the hypothesis that economic performance matters for election outcomes, but in the *indicators* of performance themselves. We turn now to subjective measures of optimism and

6 The election that is the biggest outlier is 1952, where after 20 years in power the Democrats did noticeably worse than expected based on the economy alone. Our estimate of the correlation between cumulative income and the vote is slightly less than Hibbs's even though Hibbs's cumulation and ours correlate at .95. Hibbs used earlier versions of income growth and corrected for OPEC shocks, which we ignored. With $\lambda$ equaling 1.0 so that income growth cumulates without any decay, then income growth correlates only at 0.59 with the presidential vote.

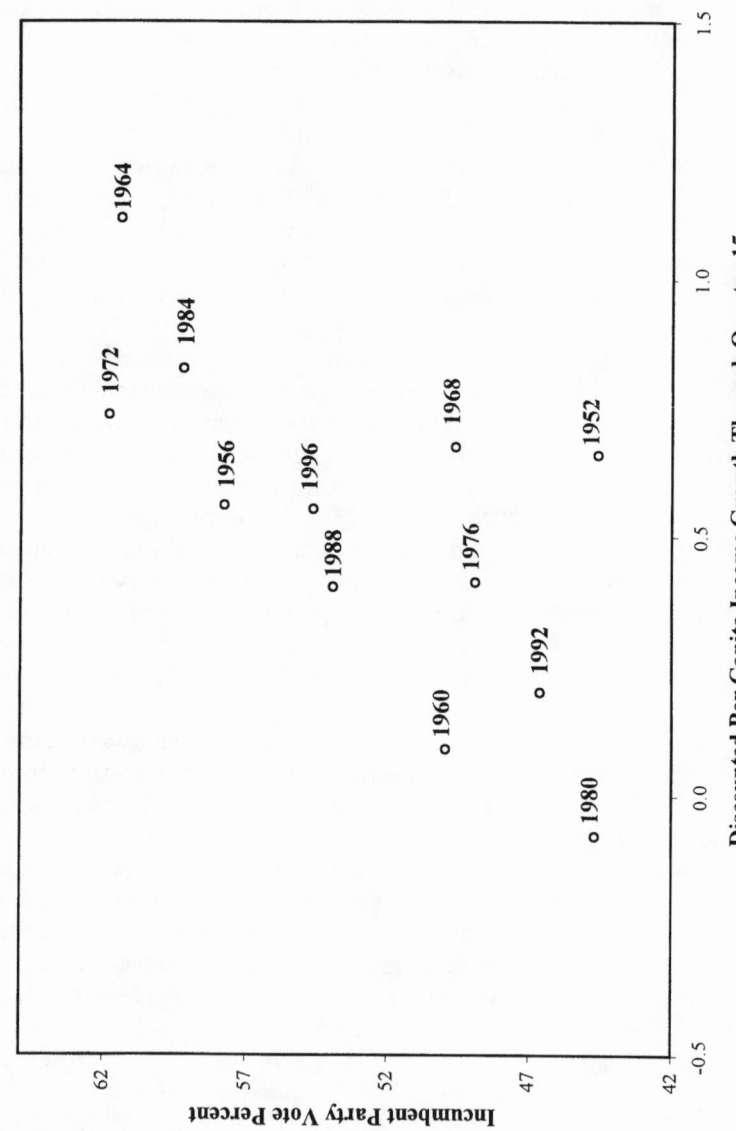

**Discounted Per Capita Income Growth Through Quarter 15**

Figure 7.1. Presidential Vote by Cumulative Per Capita Income Growth

pessimism that have the virtue of being self-calibrating to the expectations of the times.

## *Subjective Evaluation: Consumer Sentiment*

To influence the vote, economic indicators must first influence public perceptions of the economy. Thus, a measure of perceptions themselves should short circuit this causal flow and be strongly correlated with the vote. The Michigan *Index of Consumer Sentiment* and its components are just such direct measures. Mean *Consumer Sentiment* over the year before the election correlates unspectacularly with the incumbent party vote at .64. But just before the election (at quarter 15), *Consumer Sentiment* correlates at an impressive .82 with the vote.[7] Close to the vote in time and in causal proximity – where citizen evaluation of the economy is the final step before political translation – the *Index* should be a good predictor of response to the economic competence of incumbents, and it is.

We might want to expand the analysis of *Consumer Sentiment* and the vote to extract information regarding which of the *Consumer Sentiment* items best predicts the vote. If *Business Expectations* constitute the best predictor, then presidential voting is consistent with Chapter 3's story of voters as future-oriented "bankers" when deciding whether to approve the president's performance. If *Personal Retrospections* predicts best, then presidential voting is consistent with the Chapter 4's partisanship story of retrospective pocketbook voters. Retrospections shows the higher correlation (.814 vs. .705 with the incumbent party vote, 1956–1996), and therefore is the nominal winner of this race. The interpretation of the lower correlation between expectations and the vote is muddled, however, by the likelihood that electoral expectations fuel economic expectations. When voters expect the in-party to be sacked because of a lagging economy, this expectation of an incumbent loss can enhance economic optimism.

## *The Economy and the Vote: A Summary*

Our "best" measures of the objective economy are either cumulative leading indicators measured early in the election year, or cumulative income growth, just prior to the election. Each is a strong predictor of consumer sentiment late in the campaign, which in turn predicts the vote. While economic information appears particularly important if measured

7 Due to missing data for the third quarter of 1952 (quarter 15 of the election cycle), fourth quarter *Consumer Sentiment* is substituted for 1952.

## Policy

late in the electoral cycle, our investigation shows no evidence that economic voting is particularly forward looking. If it were, we would find significant predictive power from late (quarter 14 or 15) leading indicators. Lacking such evidence, we cannot claim a strong prospective element to election-day voter decisions, which is a notable contrast to our assessment of the prospective character of the economy's effect on presidential approval in Chapter 3.

At best, the economy "explains" somewhat over half the variance in the incumbent party vote. "Over half" is a lot, guaranteeing that economic prosperity is the most important vote predictor. Considerable variation in the vote is left to be accounted for by other explanations. We turn to this task shortly.

### Political Business Cycles?

The sensitivity of the electorate to economic change late in the electoral cycle suggests the possibility of a reactive political business cycle (Nordhaus 1975; Tufte 1978). The political business cycle (or PBC) is a familiar if controversial idea. The theory is simple in its most basic form: Voters give extra weight to the degree of prosperity just before the election. To take advantage, presidents stimulate short-term economic growth for the run up to the next presidential election. They get reelected, and an economic cooling ensues but is forgotten at the next election.

A limitation to PBC theory is that presidents have very limited authority over fiscal and monetary policy. Thus, presidents can do little to manipulate the timing of economic growth even if they want to. Empirical studies find little evidence of concentrated economic growth spurts late in the electoral cycle. (For reviews, see Keech 1995; Alesina and Rosenthal 1995.)

Over the 12 election cycles leading up to the presidential elections of 1952 to 1996, there is no discernible pattern of economic gain late in the cycle. Figure 7.2 shows this. On average over these 12 election cycles, logged (real) income grew in a strictly linear pattern rather than with a late spurt just before the election. This graph also reveals the electorate's role in rewarding and punishing for economic performance. In the six instances where the incumbent party won, economic growth did spurt near the end of the cycle. In the six instances where the incumbent party lost, growth waned late in the cycle.[8]

---

8 But while presidents cannot do much to manipulate objective economic performance, they perhaps can manipulate subjective impressions. Suzuki (1992) reports

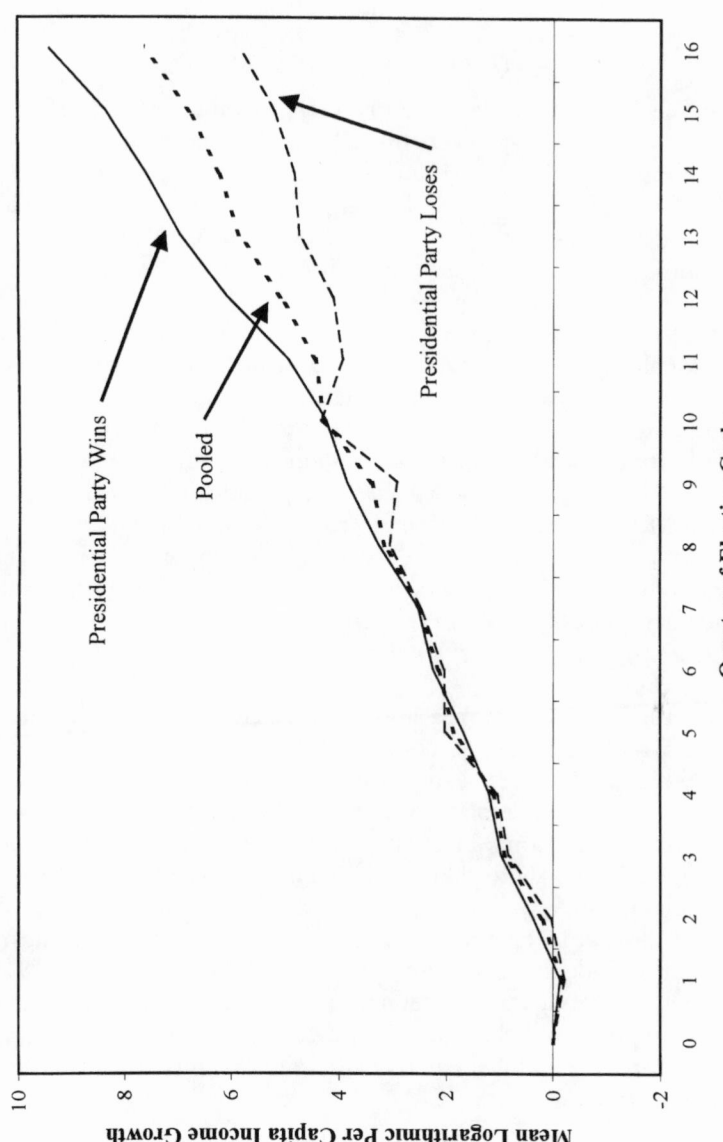

Figure 7.2. Income Growth over the Election Cycle, 1949–1996

# Policy

## STORY 2: CANDIDATES

One of the first discoveries of early voting studies was the electoral relevance of the candidates' vote appeal independent of party identification. For instance, *The American Voter* authors (Campbell et al. 1960) explained the preference of a Democratic electorate for Republican Dwight Eisenhower in his two victories over Democrat Adlai Stevenson (1952 and 1956) as due to Eisenhower's unusual popularity. The nation simply "liked Ike."

As evidence accumulated for multiple elections, it became clear that the personal appeal of the candidates was crucial to other elections as well. Using NES measures of respondent "likes and dislikes" regarding the candidates, sophisticated multivariate analyses indicated that unusual unpopularity of the challengers was responsible for Johnson's landslide win over Goldwater in 1964 (Stokes 1966) and for Nixon's landslide win over McGovern in 1972 (Popkin et al. 1976). Although interpretations vary between analyses, the importance of pure personal attractiveness (and unattractiveness) is a constant in American election commentary. We ask, how can that effect be measured and is the hypothesis true?

*Measures*: We have two measures of the electorate's affect toward the candidates in presidential elections. One is the president's *Approval Rating*, which we measure as the mean rating over the final three months of the campaign.[9] The second is the *Index of Net Candidate Advantage*, derived from the National Election Studies' open-ended questions about what the voters like and dislike about the candidates. Following Stokes' (1966) original analyses of these items, we consider only likes and dislikes that deal with the *personal* attributes of the candidates and not policy, political ideology, or party competence. Following Tufte (1978), we construct the index as the net sum of candidate 1's likes and candidate 2's dislikes minus the sum of candidate 1's dislikes and candidate 2's likes. For the incumbent party vote, we set candidate 1 to be the incumbent party candidate.

intriguing evidence that for reasons not attributable to objective economic indicators, consumer economic expectations rise late in the electoral cycle. This statistical regularity is puzzling. Do presidential administrations successfully spin positivity about the economy from thin air? Or do expectations rise even under bad times because the election provides the hope of defeating the incumbent president?

9 In three election years (1964, 1972, 1976), Gallup chose not to measure third quarter *Approval*. For these years, values were interpolated.

Table 7.2. *Correlations Between Measures of Candidate Affect, Economic Conditions, and the Incumbent Party Vote, 1952–1996*

|  | Consumer Sentiment | Income Growth | Presidential Approval | Net Candidate Advantage |
|---|---|---|---|---|
| Index of Consumer Sentiment |  |  |  |  |
| Cumulative Growth in Per Capita Income | .75 |  |  |  |
| Presidential Approval | .78 | .45 |  |  |
| Net Candidate Advantage | .35 | .24 | .77 |  |
| Incumbent Party Vote | .80 | .70 | .85 | .71 |

Having excluded respondent references to party, policy, and economic performance from the face content of our measure, it would seem that *Net Candidate Advantage* would be a measure only of the personal, that is, a mix of beliefs about candidate traits and personality and simple emotional response. But we know at the outset that one measure of response to candidates, *Presidential Approval*, is driven by factors quite apart from personal response. Thus even the apparently purely personal content of the candidate evaluation measure is likely also to incorporate content not in the literal words survey respondents use. For this reason, we look at the evaluation measures in the context of what we already know about economic assessment.

Table 7.2 presents the correlations among *Presidential Approval*, *Net Candidate Advantage*, two economic measures, and the incumbent party vote. One economic measure is cumulative income growth ($\lambda = .80$) through quarter 15. The other is subjective opinion, measured as *Consumer Sentiment* in quarter 15 (quarter 16 for 1952). By itself, *Presidential Approval* is a strong predictor of the vote ($r = .85$). In general, presidents (or their party's candidate) can expect to win if the president's *Approval* in quarter 15 is 50 percent or better. One reason why *Approval* predicts so well is that it reflects the economy. As measured by consumer sentiment, subjective economic perceptions are highly correlated with the vote, but even more highly correlated with approval. This is as we should expect because as we saw in Chapter 3, *Approval* responds strongly to *Consumer Sentiment*.[10] *Net Candidate Advantage* is the purest measure of perceived candidate competence. However, with the

10 *Approval* responds more to *Expectations* than to retrospective economic opinion, and this is reflected by the fact that quarter 15 *Approval* correlates best with quarter 15 *Expectations* measures.

251

Table 7.3. *Regressing the Incumbent Party Vote on Candidate and Economy Measures*

| | (1) Per Capita Income Growth, Approval | (2) Income Growth, Net Candidate Advantage | (3) Index of Consumer Sentiment, Approval | (4) Consumer Sentiment, Net Candidate Advantage |
|---|---|---|---|---|
| Presidential Approval | 0.30[a] | | 0.26[a] | |
| | (4.66) | | (2.65) | |
| Net Candidate Advantage | | 7.05[a] | | 6.02[a] |
| | | (3.81) | | (3.64) |
| Cumulative Income Growth | 7.56[a] | 10.55[a] | | |
| | (2.71) | (3.70) | | |
| Consumer Sentiment | | | 0.23 | 0.40[a] |
| | | | (1.41) | (4.64) |
| Intercept | 33.48[a] | 45.68[a] | 19.21 | 15.39[a] |
| | (10.96) | (27.33) | (1.81) | (7.66) |
| Adjusted $R^2$ | .82 | .76 | .72 | .82 |
| Standard Error of Estimate | 2.67 | 3.04 | 3.30 | 2.63 |

*Note:* $t$ ratios in parentheses. Approval, ICS, and Cumulative PGIG are measured for third quarter of the election year.
[a] $p < 0.05$.

economy controlled (see Table 7.3), *Net Candidate Advantage* predicts the vote at least as well as *Presidential Approval*. So we consider the two side by side.

We wish to know the degree to which these subjective reactions to presidents and presidential candidates bring in novel sources of evaluation or merely reflect the health of the economy. We can imagine either (1) that personal evaluations of the candidates are what they seem to be – that voters notice whether candidates are sincere, religious, trustworthy, and the like, and care about these attributes – or (2) that economic success is everything, and that these apparently unrelated criteria are merely the warm glow of it (or, of course, the less warm glow of failure). The four regressions of Table 7.3 answer the question in favor of the view that personal attributes matter a good deal, independently of economic success. In each regression, the candidate variable makes a significant addition to the prediction of the vote.

We can also see a difference between the contributions of *Approval* and *Net Candidate Advantage*. *Approval* appears to absorb the economic effects, while adding only modestly beyond the economic effects to the vote prediction. *Net Candidate Advantage*, on the other hand, makes a strong contribution that is quite independent of the economic variables. The single "best" equation predicts the vote from *Net Candidate Advantage* plus *Consumer Sentiment* – two independent sources of voter attitudes measured in independent surveys.

The predictive power of income growth alone, about .50, is moved to the .80 range by the addition of evaluations variables (see columns 1 and 2). The predictive power of *Consumer Sentiment* alone (adjusted $R^2$ of .64) does not rise much with the addition of *Presidential Approval*, but zooms to .82 with the addition of *Net Candidate Advantage* (column 4).

We have now come a long way in explaining the presidential vote. Using two measures of electoral attitudes, the *Index of Consumer Sentiment* and the candidate likes and dislikes composing the *Index of Net Candidate Advantage*, we explain 82 percent of the variance in the presidential vote.[11] Two implications may seem to follow from this result. One is that our task is largely complete, that there are marginal benefits at best from pursuing the predictions of elections much further. The second implication follows from the nature of the predictive variables. If elections are decided by little more than the degree of perceived prosperity and by voter evaluations of the personal attributes of the candidates themselves, we have a narrow, almost apolitical, interpretation of presidential politics. There would seem to be no room for voter evaluations of policies or even for party identifications to matter.

In truth, our task is far from complete. Election outcomes are *not* just a matter of economic conditions and candidate affect. Based on the analysis that follows, both *Macropartisanship* and the electorate's relative proximity to the candidates on the liberal-conservative dimension affect elections considerably. In the final analysis, these political factors will prove the decisive ones.

## INTRODUCING MACROPARTISANSHIP

So far, our modeling of the presidential vote has followed the traditional path found in the literature. With considerable predictive success, our equations have modeled the *incumbent party* vote as a function of the economy and candidate affect. In this and the following sections, we start fresh, modeling the *Democratic* vote as a function of political variables:

11 The same explained variance obtains using *Cumulative* Income Growth plus *Approval*. This second entry loses the battle of the "R squareds" on a technicality when the coefficient is computed to the third decimal place.

Table 7.4. *Correlations Between the Democratic*
*Presidential Vote and Macropartisanship, 1952–1996*

| Time of Measurement in Election Year | $M_t$ Measured | $M_t^*$ Equilibrium | $M_t'$ Transient |
|---|---|---|---|
| Quarter 1 | .10 | .04 | −.01 |
| Quarter 2 | .21 | .10 | .11 |
| August | .45 | .25 | .36 |
| September | .56 | .26 | .62 |
| October | .54 | .27 | .65 |

*Note:* $N = 12$ for $M_t$, 11 for $M_t^*$ and $M_t'$ (1952 omitted).

*Macropartisanship*, *Mood*, and the party positions. We start by observing what happens when we model the presidential vote strictly as a function of *Macropartisanship*.

*Micro*-level party identification is often depicted as the starting point of the voting decision, how one would vote in the absence of information beyond party affiliation. Thus, aggregate-level *Macropartisanship* is a plausible starting point for the collective vote decision by the electorate as a whole. In fact, this may be the main reason why the movement of *Macropartisanship* generates so much interest and controversy. If *Macropartisanship* were electorally irrelevant, its statistical behavior would attract little attention.

At the same time, we know that much of the recent history of presidential elections reveals outcomes that are major departures from *Macropartisanship*. The early voting studies by the *American Voter* authors commented upon the electorate's willingness to deviate from its Democratic tendencies to vote Republican for Eisenhower for president. More recent elections have shown a continued variability of the presidential vote that requires explanation in terms of deviations from *Macropartisanship*. Indeed, early voting studies indicated macro-level partisanship to be essentially a constant, so that the baseline for the "normal vote" (Converse 1966) would be a steady but slight Democratic edge of about 54:46.

If it is a constant, *Macropartisanship* cannot contribute to the explanation of the vote across elections. But we now know that *Macropartisanship* does vary and varies systematically with accumulated economic and political forces. Our task here is to see whether the variation in *Macropartisanship* serves as an electoral predictor after all, thus perhaps justifying the general interest in the movement of this concept.

Table 7.4 presents the correlations between the Democratic presidential vote and *Macropartisanship* in each of the first two quarters of the election year and monthly from August to October. The table also shows the correlations with *Macropartisanship* subdivided into its *Equilibrium* and *Transient* components. As explained in Chapter 4, we break down *Macropartisanship* as a combination of *Equilibrium Partisanship*, due to accumulated political and economic shocks, and *Transient Partisanship*, representing temporary fluctuations of the moment beyond those traced to cumulated political and economic shocks. Operationally, the *Transient* component is simply the difference between observed *Macropartisanship* and its estimated long-term value.

Table 7.4 shows that *Macropartisanship* increases its power as an electoral predictor during the run-up to the election. Measured for the first quarter of election years, *Macropartisanship* is virtually uncorrelated with the vote. By the fall campaign, a clearly positive correlation emerges, although with unimpressive values no higher than .56. The *Transient* component correlates the strongest with the presidential outcome, as it reflects the issues that stir excitement during the campaign. We see only weak correlations between the vote and *Equilibrium Macropartisanship*, representing the permanent cumulation of political and economic shocks that enter the electorate's collective partisan memory.[12] On its face, this collective memory evidently has little bearing on the collective vote decision. We see this clearly from regressing the vote on the two partisan components measured in October of the election year in Table 7.5.

*Macropartisanship* accounts for but one-third of the variance in the vote, with most of the predictive power via its *Transient* component. To the extent that partisanship predicts elections, the crucial factor is not the electorate's partisan memory but rather a temporary influence on the vote that has no lasting consequence.

Or so it would seem. We resist as implausible the idea that people would align in stable and predictable partisan divisions in terms of what they call themselves, yet these alignments would have no bearing on the vote. We know that party identification predicts vote decisions at the micro level. In the next section, we will see that that it does at the macro level as well.

---

12 To measure *Equilibrium Macropartisanship* for monthly data, monthly estimates are prorated from quarterly estimates. Monthly measures *of Transient Macropartisanship* are derived as the difference between observed and *Equilibrium* values in the usual way. Monthly estimates during the fall campaign average over 5,000 cases, making monthly estimates feasible. The one exception where monthly estimation required prorating from surrounding months was (surprisingly) 1992. Unfortunately, all available Gallup readings for October 1992 were based on unusable samples of registered or likely voters rather than general population surveys.

Policy

Table 7.5. *Predicting Presidential Election Outcomes from Two Components of Macropartisanship*

| Independent Variables | Percentage Democratic Vote Dependent |
|---|---|
| Intercept | 25.27[a] |
| | (0.75) |
| Equilibrium Macropartisanship | 0.40 |
| (October) | (0.73) |
| Transient Macropartisanship | 0.87 |
| (October) | (1.08) |
| Adjusted $R^2$ | .325 |
| Standard Error of Estimate | 5.57 |

*Note: t* in parentheses.
[a] $p < 0.05$.

STORY 3: POLICY PREFERENCES AND PARTY POSITIONS

It is truly important to know if matters of public policy affect election outcomes. We now know that economic performance matters. But we know much less about whether, or how much, policy preferences of the sort described in Chapter 6 determine elections. In this chapter we examine a simple model and the data supporting it to provide an answer.

According to the common understanding of how issues affect the vote, as exemplified by Downs' (1957) spatial model, candidates and parties gain votes by maximizing their proximity to voters on the liberal-conservative dimension. In its most elementary form, this means that (1) candidates and parties move to the center of the public's preferences (usually the "median voter") and (2) when the public's preferences change from year to year, the parties follow accordingly. Spatial models get much more complex and subtle when considering multiple dimensional issue spaces (for example, Enelow and Hinich 1984; Hinich and Munger 1994) and alternative rules of citizen choice (most interesting, "directional" voting, Rabinowitz and Macdonald 1989). In the spirit of our macro modeling, however, we shall keep things simple by aggregating across issue domains to the single liberal conservative dimension and we shall examine only the most common voting rule, proximity, in which voters choose candidates most similar to themselves. Our simplification concentrates on the central notion that the policy preferences of voters and the policy promises of parties both matter for elections. Despite the importance of this proposition, it has not been subject to serious macro-level testing. In this section we take on that task.

Measuring the contribution of policy choices to the vote presents a special challenge. We assume that policy preference is represented by a single left-right or liberal-conservative dimension. We have a global measure of the electorate's opinion on a liberal-conservative scale, the electorate's *Policy Mood* introduced in Chapter 6. We could simply ask (as in Stimson 1999) whether *Mood* predicts election results, assuming that the positions of the Democratic and Republican candidates (and parties) are largely fixed over time. Given the parties' ideological differences on public policy, the expectation is that the greater the demand for liberal policies (liberal *Mood*), the more Democratic the voting. As we will see, this prediction is borne out well enough even when we assume that party positions remain constant.

We would like to do more. We would prefer to measure the temporal oscillations in party policy positions on the liberal-conservative dimension. Toward this end, we are fortunate to have quadrennial measures of party positions on the left-right scale, borrowed from Budge and Hofferbert's and McDonald's work on party manifestos and platforms (Budge and Hofferbert 1990; McDonald, Budge, and Hofferbert 1999). These authors coded U.S. party platforms for left-right content, with each party's platform scored as percent liberal minus percent conservative statements.[13]

Using these data, we can measure the net electoral advantage accrued by the parties due to their policy promises. On the *Mood* dimension, all the voters to the liberal side of the Democrats and to the conservative side of the Republicans choose easily enough – leftists vote Democratic and rightists vote Republican. Those *between* the two parties split their votes – the hypothetical voter exactly halfway between the two parties marks the dividing line (being equally close to the two parties, this voter is indifferent). We can calculate this indifference point as the mean of the two parties' positions. For example, if the Republicans are at 50 and the Democrats at 80, the dividing line is 65: Voters "above" 65 (that is, more liberal than 65) vote Democratic, and those "below" vote Republican.

13 The data were collected by the Manifesto Research Group for what has become known as the Comparative Manifesto Project (Budge, Robertson, and Hearl 1987). The update through 1996 in the United States was supplied to us through Ian Budge. Note that these data calibrate the liberal/conservative content (or agendas) of the party platforms and thus represent something akin to a "directional" rather than a "proximity" measure of party positions. While we use the proximity formulation throughout this chapter, the theoretical result that *for party choice* proximity and direction are indistinguishable (Macdonald et al. 1998) allows us to combine these data types.

## Policy

The mean of the parties' positions thus serves as an indicator of how the parties' strategic policy stances will affect elections. With the Democrats to the left of most voters, we expect the Democrats to win votes in proportion to their movement toward the center, thus in the conservative direction. By the same logic, the Republicans on the right should gain votes by moving to the center, thus in the liberal direction. Similarly, moves to the extremes will diminish each party's appeal. Thus, *liberal* movement by either party shifts the dividing line between Democratic and Republican voters further to the *liberal* side of the voter distribution: The result is fewer people with a Democratic preference and more with a Republican preference. Overall, combining party positions and *Mood*, the best electoral scenario for the Republican Party is a conservative electorate wooed by relatively liberal parties, so that the electorate sees a moderate Republican Party best representing its views. The best electoral scenario for the Democrats is a liberal electorate wooed by relatively conservative parties.[14]

Our expectation is not that voters generally read party platforms, of course, but rather that the content of the platforms reflects the tone of the party's presidential campaign. But we must ask: Do the latest platforms really represent where the parties and candidates are positioned? Our answer is, no, not quite. Platforms rather are the parties' *current* assertions of where they stand. Yet, our analysis in Chapter 3 showed that citizens use information grounded in the past as well as novel information of a more speculative sort, that they rationally develop expectations from all the information available. Applying this principle to voters' choosing presidential administrations, we expect them to weigh both information from the past along with the latest platform promises. The question is how we operationalize prior history. Here, we approximate the experience of past promises with a smoothed version of prior platforms – understanding that past promises reflect past realities because parties *do* more or less follow up on their promises (Ginsberg 1976; Pomper and Lederman 1980; Budge and Hofferbert 1990; McDonald, Budge, and Hofferbert 1999). Thus, where the parties stand in the eyes of the electorate will incorporate both the present platform and past platforms. In the end, while the parties are able to use the platforms as a vehicle for altering the image of where they stand, they can alter that image only slowly over time.

---

14 Actually, the idea that moderation wins votes does not require that the median voter is ideologically in the middle between the two parties. As long as the Democrats stay to the left of the Republicans, either gains voters by moving toward the other's position.

To produce measures that capture the dynamics of rational updating we offer a second, smoothed, measure of party position as the exponentially weighted moving average of current and past platform positions.

$$Position_t = \alpha Platform_t + (1.0 - \alpha)Position_{t-1}$$

starting from our first measure of platforms, for 1948, which we treat as $Position_{t-1}$ for 1952, the first year of our series.[15] For the $\alpha$ parameter we choose .20, a number that suggests that parties can be only partially successful at reinventing their appearance with each new platform.[16] To distinguish between them we shall refer to the current assertion of position as *Platform*, and the smoothed estimate of perceptions as *Position*.

Figure 7.3 shows the ideological scores for the two parties, 1952–1998, both the "current" *Platforms* as measured and "smoothed" *Positions*. For each election, the Democrats, of course, are to the left of the Republicans (i.e., higher on the graph) while both parties score more conservatively over time. Importantly, each party shifts its policy appeals considerably over our period, with the Republicans moving from a

15 In effect, the 1948 *Platform* scores serves as a proxy for the earlier platforms of the New Deal Era. Note that this formulation weighs the present platform more than any single instance of the past (prior platforms get discounted exponentially as they recede into the distant past).

16 More exactly, the $\alpha = .20$ parameter gives one-fifth weight to current platforms compared with past positions. An $\alpha$ of 1.0 would mean that only the current platform matters. An $\alpha$ of zero would mean a constant party stand (rooted in the 1948 platform) independent of year-to-year strategic adjustments. Such would be the naive expectation that the parties merely stand at opposite ends of the political spectrum, without any important dynamics. Our empirical analysis, which follows, indicates a maximum fit parameter of something like $\alpha = .50$ – but with only 12 cases (and fewer degrees of freedom) such an estimate cannot mean much. We can only say that the true value likely lies between the extremes of zero and one.

Our choice of the value $\alpha = .20$ is driven as much by a theoretical plausibility constraint. We have very strong theory that suggests that the two parties will approach the median (or mean) voter in their attempt to maximize votes but that they will not actually cross over the median. That is, we expect the parties to bracket the voters' ideal point. Beyond theory, we have examined the American National Election Studies issue scales for 1972–1996, creating a smoothed combination of the major issues tapped by the surveys, to see that indeed the mean voter preferences lie in between the more conservative Republicans and the more liberal Democrats. For our data, it turns out that an $\alpha$ of something less than .21 is necessary to meet our constraint. We choose .20 as a reasonable approximation.

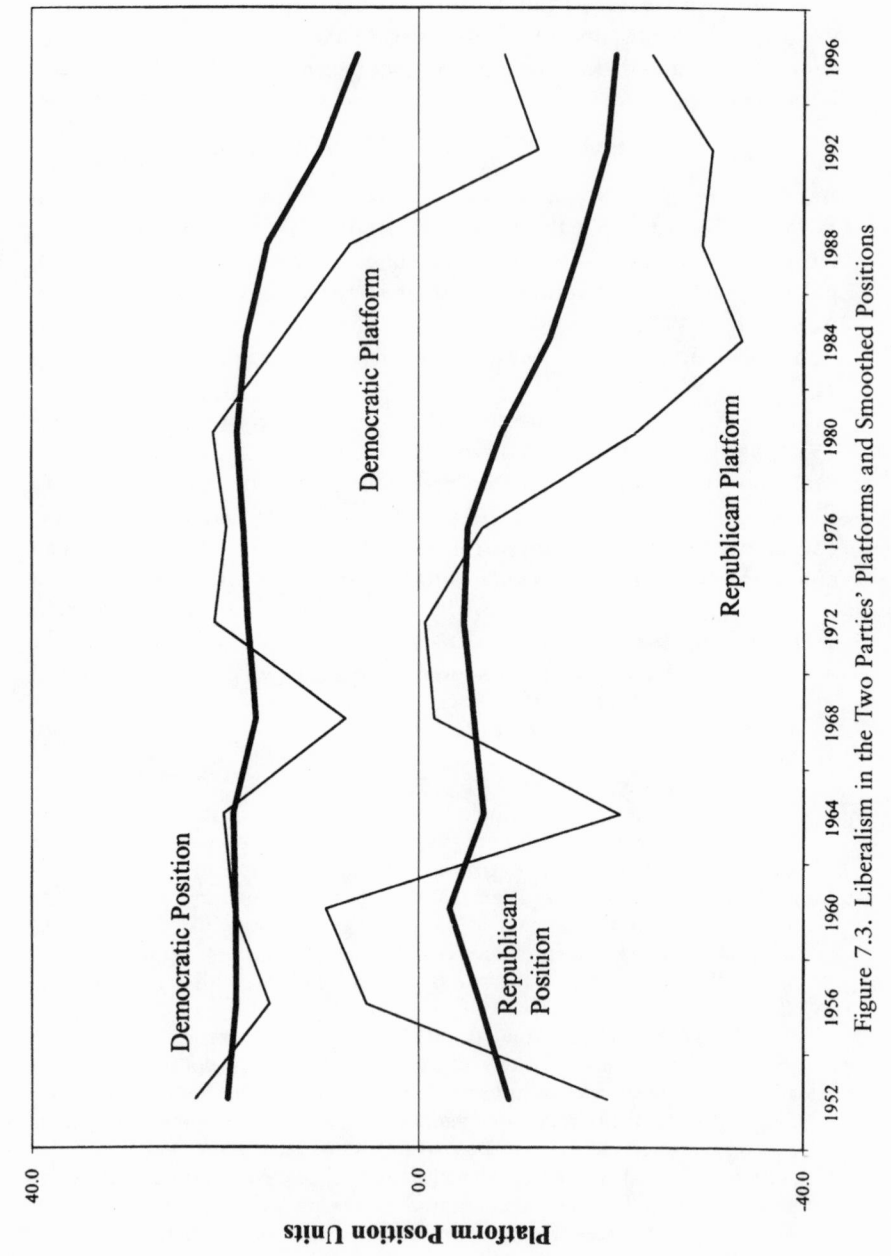

Figure 7.3. Liberalism in the Two Parties' Platforms and Smoothed Positions

moderate to a very conservative stance in the 1980s, and the Democrats becoming more centrist during the century's last decade.[17]

Spatial theory (Downs 1957) holds that voters choose the candidates and parties that are closer to them in an issue space. At the macro level the theory implies that the party closer to the midpoint of the electorate's policy preferences is advantaged. Is this true, we ask? We now have a specification that allows putting these ideas from spatial theory to test. We measure the electorate's collective preferences by *Policy Mood*. We measure the net electoral advantage due to party policies as the mean of the Democratic and Republican *Platform* scores – the mean being the cutting line that divides Democratic and Republican voters. Call this *Platform Midpoint*. To be explained is the Democratic percentage of the two-party vote. Our expectation is that liberal *Mood* increases the Democratic vote while liberal *Platform Midpoint* decreases it. Table 7.6 presents the estimated effects of *Mood* and *Platform Midpoint* on the presidential vote, 1952–1996. Column 1 shows the predictive power of the two variables standing alone on the right-hand side of the equation. The result is interesting. As indicated by the negative adjusted $R^2$, *Mood* and *Platform Midpoint* together predict the vote worse than would be expected by chance. Thus, our first analysis suggests that issue proximity does not matter after all. But so far, we have been modeling the effects of policy considerations and partisanship separately, without controlling for the other.

To find evidence that presidential elections are affected by the parties' relative closeness to the voters, we introduce *Macropartisanship*, measured in October of the election year. As shown in column 2 of Table 7.6, controlling for *Macropartisanship* on the cusp of the election changes everything. All three coefficients (*Macropartisanship*, *Mood*, and *Platform Midpoint*) are highly significant, with the expected signs, and together explain 92 percent of the variance in the Democratic presidential vote. This is a level of predictive power considerably higher than that provided by any combination of economic indicators and attitudes toward the candidates. It tops even the

---

17 Statistically, the platform time series are difficult to explain by other variables. Although there is at least a hint that parties enact more moderate platforms given adverse *Macropartisanship*, there is little evidence that party platforms respond to *Mood*. Correlations between smoothed *Position* and *Mood* are –.13 for Republicans and –.24 for Democrats. In terms of current platform scores, they are .10 for Republicans and –.45 for Democrats. The negative correlations for Democratic platforms reflects the Democrats' conservative platform tilt in the 1990s when *Mood* was relatively liberal. Platforms may be written more to satisfy party constituents than to win general elections. But they have, as we will see, important electoral consequences.

Table 7.6. *Regressing the Democratic Presidential Vote on Mood, Platform Ideology, and Macropartisanship, 1952–1996*

| | (1) Mood and Observed Platforms | (2) Macropartisanship Added | (3) With Party Position | (4) Without Platform or Position |
|---|---|---|---|---|
| Policy Mood, Election | 0.36 | 0.90[a] | 0.91[a] | 0.92[a] |
| Year (% Liberal) | (0.88) | (6.96) | (7.81) | (3.23) |
| Party Platform Midpoint | −0.15 | −0.32[a] | | |
| (Liberalism) | (−0.82) | (−5.93) | | |
| Party Position Midpoint | | | −0.78[a] | |
| (Liberalism) | | | (6.77) | |
| Macropartisanship | | 1.41[a] | 1.46[a] | 1.15[a] |
| (% Democratic), | | (10.14) | (11.53) | (3.98) |
| October | | | | |
| Constant | 26.07 | −90.00[a] | −90.49[a] | −75.05[a] |
| | (1.05) | (−6.86) | (−7.50) | (−2.59) |
| Adjusted $R^2$ | −.02 | .92 | .93 | .60 |
| Standard Error of | | | | |
| Estimate | 6.64 | 1.89 | 1.69 | 4.14 |

*Note*: t ratios in parentheses. N = 12 elections, 1952–1996.
[a] $p < 0.05$.

prediction one can make on election eve from the *final* Gallup poll (adjusted $R^2 = .90$).

There is more. We have measured party issue *Positions* not only from the content of the current platforms but also incorporating platforms past, as an exponentially weighted moving average of platforms past and present. In column 3, we introduce the measure of party *Position* in a similar *Position Midpoint*, to go along with *Mood*, and October *Macropartisanship*. The result is much the same, with a marginal improvement in the model, as the adjusted $R^2$ rises from .92 to .93.[18]

In the last column of Table 7.6, we estimate the effect of *Mood* and *Macropartisanship* again, this time dropping the party measures altogether. These estimates reassure that the contributions of *Mood* and *Macropartisanship* do not require the importing of party positions into

18 As further verification, we divide smoothed *Position* into its two components, (smoothed) *Republican Position* and *Democratic Position*. The two coefficients are −.23 and −.50, both negative as expected.

the model. By themselves, these variables account for 60 percent of the variance, and are highly significant. Their coefficients suggest that 1 point of each is worth about 1 percent of the vote, just about the maximum effect one could expect. But equally important, a comparison of the last two columns indicates that the parties' ideological stances matter enormously.

We now wish to approach the proximity[19] issue more directly. To this point we have used the midpoint of the two parties' *Platforms* and *Positions* to lever the logic of which party was closer to the median voter. That did provide a clean test of the prediction of spatial theory, and we have seen that test passed with flying colors. What this approach lacks, however, is a direct measurement of the proximity concept. Such a direct measure is more readily interpretable, but requires assumptions we have not had to impose up to now. That is the logic of our presentation, presenting first the indirect test that required no special assumptions. Now as we proceed to the direct appraisal, the reader can be confident from the result *already known* that we have not "cooked" a relationship between proximity and the vote by heroic assumption.

### Policy Proximity and Presidential Elections: A Closer Look

Ideological positioning of the parties matters. We have shown that the U.S. electorate votes more Democratic when its *Mood* is liberal and when the party platforms are conservative. We would like to do more, and track the left-right positioning of the party positions relative to the electorate over time.

We first want to align *Mood* and the *Party Positions* on the liberal-conservative scale. While we can translate the metrics, we need to center the distributions so that they line up properly. As a likely approximation, we set the mean of the two *Party Positions* to that for *Mood*. We assume that the two parties are equally adept at matching the policy views of the American political center over the near half century of our analysis (but not necessarily in any particular electoral contest).

---

19 We use the term "proximity" because it is standard in the spatial theory literature. At the macro level, however, we can not discriminate between a true proximity formulation and the directional theory of Rabinowitz and Macdonald (1989) and Macdonald, Rabinowitz, and Listhaug (1998). Either could produce the macro result we observe, and so our result has nothing to say about which is the preferred theory of individual voter choice.

## Policy

The trick now is to place the parties' *Positions* in the same metric as public *Mood* in order to understand how close the parties are to the median voter – to generate a measure of party distance. Here we use the scalar information in Table 7.6 where we see how the metric of both *Mood* and *Position* translate into presidential votes. Since Table 7.6, column 3, suggests that 0.91 unit of *Mood* liberalism has the equivalent electoral impact of 0.78 unit of *Position* conservatism, we reconfigure *Position* in *Mood* units and compute the difference. For each party, *Distance* is the separation from the "median voter" or the absolute value of the difference between the two:

$$\text{Party Distance}_t = |(0.78/0.91)\text{Party Position}_t - \text{Mood}_t|$$

where $(0.78/0.91)$ is the translation of *Party Position* into *Mood* units. This tells us, in *Mood* units, how close each party is to the decisive voter.

We can now place the parties in our issue space. Figure 7.4 shows, on the same scale, the histories of the (rescaled) Democratic *Position* and the Republican *Position* as well as *Mood*. Implicit in the figure are the *Party Distance* scores – the vertical gap between the parties' *Positions* and *Mood*. In the 1950s and 1960s, we can see that the G.O.P. took moderate stands while the Democrats consistently stood on the liberal side of the spectrum. In the early years, a conservative electorate rewarded the Republicans' moderate positions, but when the public started to demand more liberal policies in the 1960s, the Democrats' steadfast liberalism started to work for them. When the public turned rightward in reaction to the Great Society, the relative moderation of the G.O.P. under Nixon and Ford produced large policy proximity advantages for the party, with clear electoral implications. Up until 1980, the dominant portion of the dynamics was associated with changes in public preferences rather than in the parties' stances. Then, of course, the Reagan Revolution pushed the Republicans firmly toward the right, so that by 1984 both parties stood at some distance from the public's ideal point. Finally, under Clinton's leadership, the Democrats moderated substantially so that they reaped considerable support during the 1990s. All of this is reasonable enough – it accords with common understanding of our era's politics – and, happily, the picture reinforces our confidence in our proximity measures.

Next, we can construct the election specific measure (Democratic) *Proximity Advantage*$_t$ by taking the *difference* between the Republican and Democratic *Distances*, with the larger score for the Republicans marked as a "plus" for the Democrats. That is:

$$\text{Proximity Advantage}_t = \text{Republican Distance}_t - \text{Democratic Distance}_t$$

264

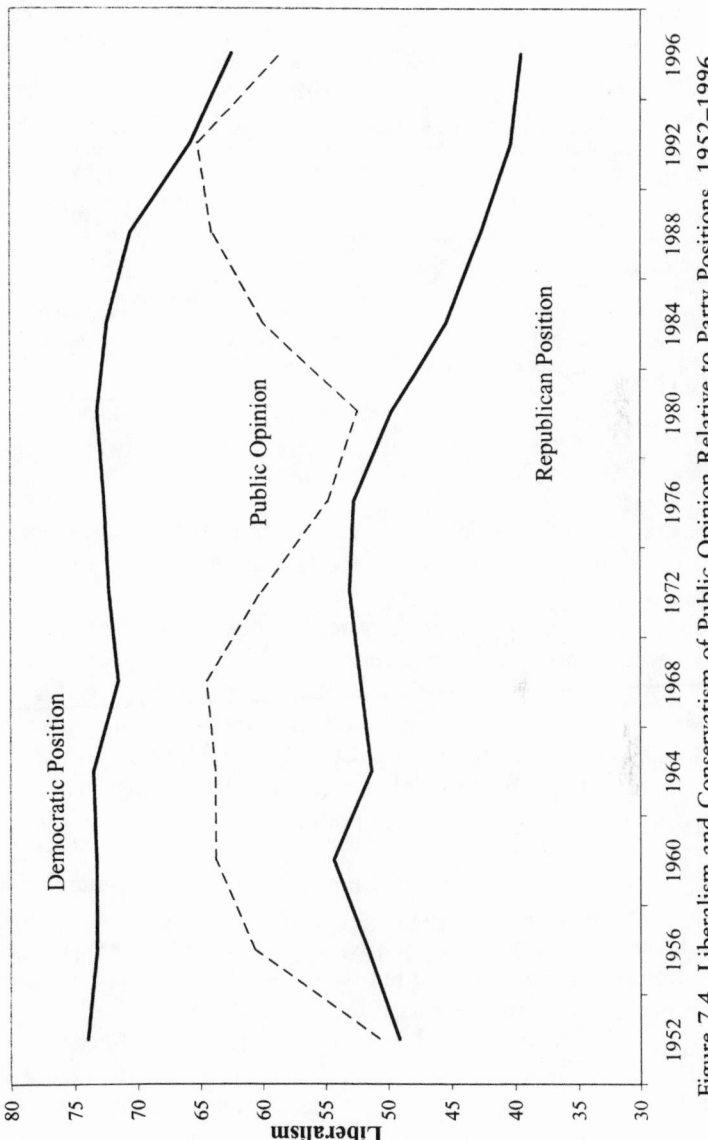

Figure 7.4. Liberalism and Conservatism of Public Opinion Relative to Party Positions, 1952–1996

# Policy

Table 7.7. *The Direct Effect of Party Issue Proximity to the Electorate on the Democratic Vote Share (Controlling for Macropartisanship), 1952–1996*

| | |
|---|---|
| Policy Proximity Advantage (Republican Distance minus Democratic Distance in Mood Units) | $0.45^a$ (11.03) |
| Macropartisanship (% Democratic), October | $1.46^a$ (12.23) |
| Constant | $-38.77^a$ ($-5.45$) |
| Adjusted $R^2$ | .94 |
| Standard Error of Estimate | 1.60 |

*Note*: $t$ ratios in parentheses. $N = 12$ elections, 1952–1996.
$^a$ $p < 0.05$.

Note that when the Republicans are farther away from the median voter than the Democrats, the Democrats gain an advantage, and vice versa, of course.

Now we are ready to put the question directly: Is the party closer in issue space to the median voter thereby advantaged in election outcomes? The answer, given in Table 7.7, is quite dramatically "yes." *Proximity Advantage* is now measured in *Mood* units and scores the relative Democratic advantage over the Republicans. For each party, a single point of movement toward the political center, again controlling for *Macropartisanship*, is worth .45 percentage point of the presidential vote. And, of course, a move toward ideological purity similarly costs .45 of the vote. That is an effect of huge consequence, leveraging so many points of movement in the outcome between parties that its absence would change the outcome of many American presidential elections. Its statistical properties approach the limit of what is possible in such a restricted sample, but it is the substantive message that most matters.

Figure 7.5 provides a sense of policy's import for U.S. elections. Here the *Proximity Advantage* scores implicitly illustrated in Figure 7.4 are translated into a percentage of the vote that was determined by movement in the public's preferences and in the parties' positions. To be sure, these exact numbers come from our assumptions about structure and equivalence. Nevertheless, they do provide a strong suggestion of how matters of public policy have affected the vote. Ignoring 1952 (we are cautious about the measure for that year's *Mood*) we see a modest advantage to one side or the other during the 1950s and 1960s. But in 1976 and 1980, the G.O.P. reaped huge advantages of 7 and then 8 percentage points of the vote – when the public turned rightward toward

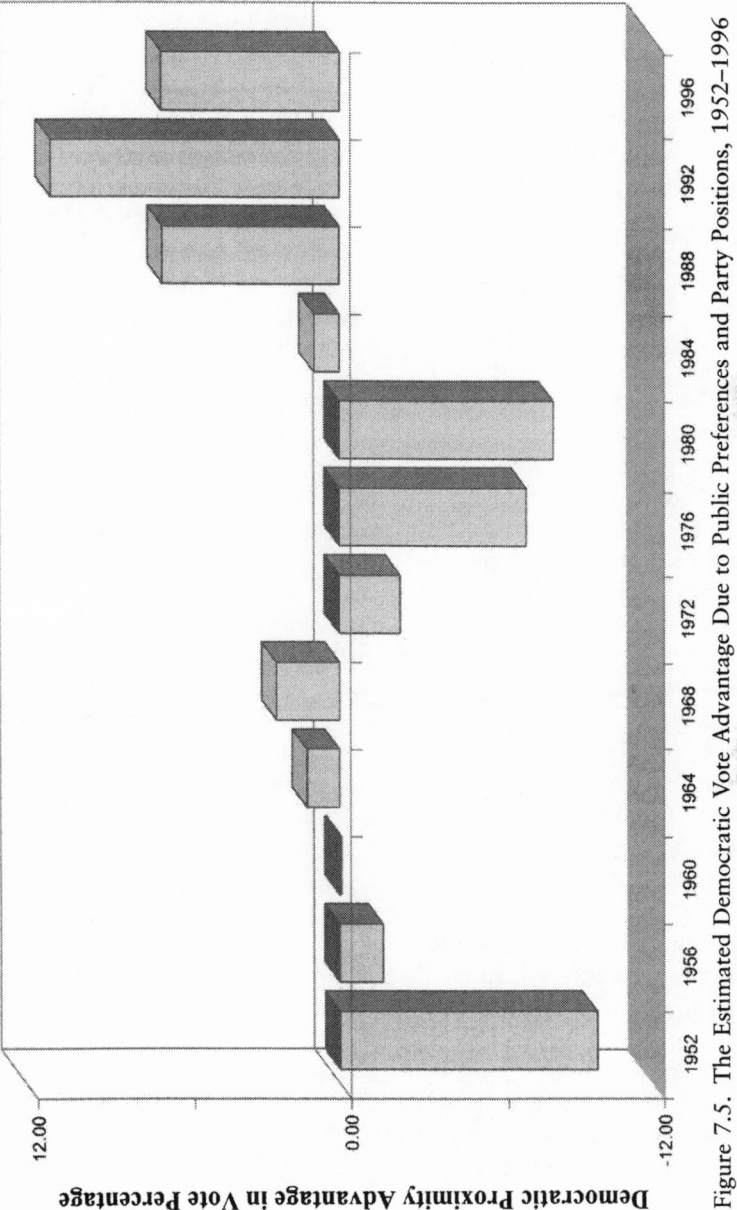

Figure 7.5. The Estimated Democratic Vote Advantage Due to Public Preferences and Party Positions, 1952–1996

the Republicans and the Democratic platforms remained consistent in their liberalism. And rather quickly thereafter, with the rush to hard conservatism in the G.O.P. and the move to moderation by the Democrats, the Democrats generated windfalls of 7, 11, and then 7 points. Clearly, party proximity to the center is a powerfully important determinant of American election outcomes. Excepting only *Macropartisanship*, the contribution of which is necessary to observe this powerful effect, it has no rival.

## The Joint Influence of Macropartisanship and Policy Proximity

We have seen now that the public's policy preferences matter for presidential election outcomes and that party platforms matter as well. The Downsian policy distance calculus appears to correctly model the behavior of the macro electorate, so that the party closer to the median voter in its policy stands gains electoral advantage. But that is not all. We also see for the first time strong evidence that *Macropartisanship* is a dominant predictor of the vote.

This important pair of results came about only by estimating each while controlling for the other. The independent variables are correlated in a way that masks their effects in the absence of the control. October *Macropartisanship* correlates at −.44 with annual *Mood*, .40 with (smoothed) *Position Midpoint*, and −.54 with the combined index of *Proximity Advantage*. In short, the controls are necessary because parties produce their most ideologically extreme platforms when strong in terms of party identification, as if parties spend their electoral capital (*Macropartisanship*) on platform commitments for their ideological activists.[20]

Given the fact that both partisanship and policy proximity have been ignored in forecasting studies, their massive contribution to predicting the vote presents a surprise. Yet this predictive power is precisely that finding we would expect by extrapolating from micro-level analysis. In

20 By this argument, the stronger the party's long-term electoral standing (best measured by *Equilibrium Macropartisanship*), the more the party will cater to its ideological wing in the next election and at platform writing time. We see possible evidence of this from the −.65 correlation between October *Equilibrium Macropartisanship* and *Proximity Advantage*. Even more impressive is the −.79 correlation between *Proximity Advantage* and *Equilibrium Macropartisanship* in quarter 12 of the electoral cycle (one year before the election), at the time when parties are formulating their electoral strategy. Add to the statistical mix the fact that *Platform* ideology is virtually uncorrelated with *Mood*, as if parties are indifferent to public opinion at platform writing time.

micro-level studies, party identification and policy proximity dominate as predictors of the vote. The macro-level implications may have been ignored because for so long it was commonly assumed that aggregate levels of partisanship and left-right preferences were essentially constant over time. We have seen that both assumptions are wrong. The evident macro-level effects of partisanship and ideological proximity escaped detection as long as the relevant macro-level indicators went unmeasured. Here, we were able to apply measures of both macro-level opinion and party positions, along with the crucial ingredient of *Macropartisanship*.

The joint influence of *Macropartisanship* and *Policy Proximity* is illustrated by the two panels of Figure 7.6. The first panel shows predictions (from the equation in Table 7.6, column 3) assuming zero *Proximity* scores. That is, the thin line reflects the impact of *Macropartisanship* alone, with *Proximity* effects neutralized. Although the correlation is modest, we see that, with one exception, electoral change is in the same partisan direction as the change in *Macropartisanship*.[21]

Panel 2 repeats the information of panel 1, adding the prediction from *Macropartisanship* and *Policy Proximity*. The prediction is as good as one could expect. When the prediction from *Macropartisanship* alone errs, incorporating the information for ideological proximity leads to an improved – if not near perfect – prediction. We would not see the excellent fit from either explanation acting alone. Both are necessary to provide the excellent fit.

### Macropartisanship and the Vote: A Closer Look

Not to be lost, given our preoccupation with *Policy Proximity*, is the resurrected role of *Macropartisanship* for the prediction of presidential voting. What should we make of the evident "effect" of *Macropartisanship* on the vote? To the extent that it is due to the *Transient* component, it may reflect only late presidential deciders temporarily identifying with the late-gaining party. This is of no lasting consequence. But to the extent that it represents the persistent effect of *Equilibrium Macropartisanship*, then inputs to *Macropartisanship* are permanent. Moreover, because the measure of *Equilibrium Macropartisanship* is based on the cumulation of political and economic inputs (see Chapter 4), the time

---

21 The exception is 1988–1992. The correlation in levels may look larger than its .44 value would indicate, because the correlation in first-differences is a relatively strong .77. Partisan change predicts electoral change better than the level of *Macropartisanship* predicts the vote.

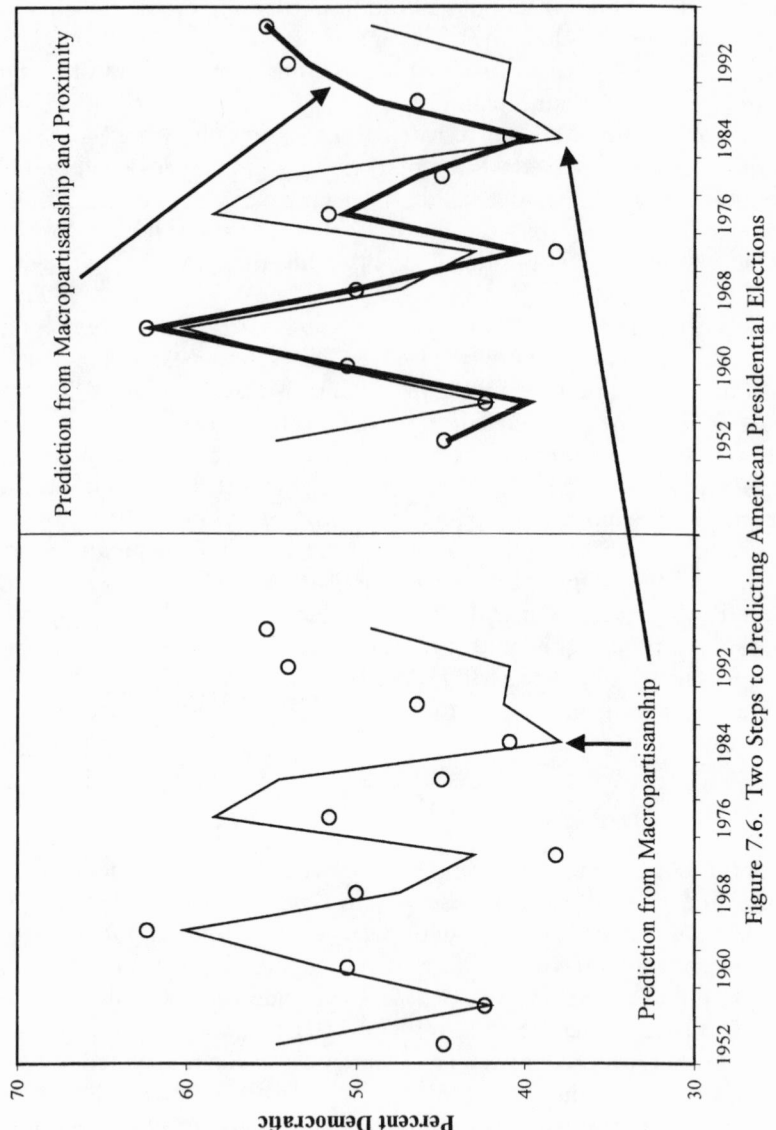

Figure 7.6. Two Steps to Predicting American Presidential Elections

270

Table 7.8. *Partisanship and Proximity Model of the Presidential Vote, with
Macropartisanship Measured at Different Times*

| Dependent Variable: Democratic Percentage of Two-Party Vote | Macropartisanship Measure | | | | |
|---|---|---|---|---|---|
| | Quarter 1 | Quarter 2 | August | September | October |
| Policy Proximity Advantage | 0.55 | 0.57[a] | 0.54[a] | 0.49[a] | 0.50[a] |
| | (2.14) | (2.69) | (4.08) | (4.34) | (9.62) |
| Equilibrium Partisanship | 1.62 | 1.70 | 1.97[a] | 1.78[a] | 1.71[a] |
| | (1.77) | (2.22) | (3.61) | (3.83) | (8.23) |
| Transient Partisanship | 0.49 | 1.07 | 0.89 | 1.25[a] | 1.32[a] |
| | (0.75) | (1.69) | (2.63) | (3.28) | (8.75) |
| Constant | −51.45 | −57.02 | −71.75[a] | −59.82[a] | −53.93[a] |
| | (−0.92) | (−1.22) | (−2.16) | (−2.12) | (−4.29) |
| Adjusted $R^2$ | .14 | .31 | .65 | .74 | .95 |
| Standard Error of Estimate | 6.29 | 5.62 | 3.99 | 3.47 | 1.58 |

*Note*: *t* ratios in parentheses. N = 11 elections, 1956–1996.
[a] $p < 0.05$.

ordering for direction of causality from partisanship to vote cannot be
challenged.

This is demonstrated in the regressions of Table 7.8, which explain the
vote from *Policy Proximity* and the two components of *Macropartisanship* (*Equilibrium* and *Transient*). They differ only in the time within
the election year when *Macropartisanship* is measured – from the first
quarter to October of the election year.

As we change *Macropartisanship*'s measurement date from early to
late, two patterns emerge. First, if we look only at the coefficients for
*Proximity* and *Equilibrium Macropartisanship*, the coefficients are
remarkably stable and similar to those of Table 7.6. This stability holds
even as the percentage of the variance explained zooms from virtual zero
to 90.[22] Second, as the election approaches, *Transient Macropartisanship*
increases its predictive power. This is crucial, because incorporating late

22 When *Macropartisanship* is measured at different times but not broken down into
its two components, estimation is slightly less precise. This is expected because
without being separated out, *Transient Macropartisanship* acts as measurement
noise. The stability of the estimates based on pre-October readings of *Macropartisanship* are most wobbly when we include the 1952 observation which was not
usable for Table 7.5. For 1952, pre-October measures of *Macropartisanship*
behave as outliers. The economy heated late in 1952, perhaps the cause of a late
surge in Democratic partisanship that fell short of keeping a Democrat in the
White House.

*Transient Macropartisanship* sharpens the statistical power of the other variables.

Despite our modeling success, we see that elections are very unpredictable a few months in advance of the election. Even knowing the *Party Positions* and *Mood* for the year, plus the two *Macropartisanship* components of the moment, our forecasting ability is limited until the month before the election. The variable that makes the difference as the election looms closer is *Transient Macropartisanship*. Both volatile and essentially uncorrelated with the other variables of the model, *Transient Macropartisanship* is electorally irrelevant early in the election year. As the election approaches, however, it absorbs otherwise unaccounted-for causes of the actual vote. These otherwise unaccounted-for causes explain a considerable share of the outcome. The resultant increase in explanatory power helps to increase the statistical power of the other variables of greater interest.

Thus, in summary, the model fits so well and *Proximity Advantage* reveals its importance because *Transient Macropartisanship* accounts for much of the extraneous variance in the vote. At the same time the relevance of *Transient Macropartisanship* to prediction should strike a note of caution for the goal of election forecasting. Only a modest portion of the vote is knowable from *Policy Proximity* and from the "fundamentals" emanating from party performance in the economic and political spheres (*Equilibrium Macropartisanship*).[23] Other forces, absorbed by *Transient Macropartisanship*, also matter.

UNRAVELING THE CAUSAL SEQUENCE

This chapter has produced major models of the presidential vote, each impressive in explaining the presidential vote. First, we have a combined

23 It is instructive to further break down October *Equilibrium Macropartisanship* into $M^*$ at the start of the current administration and $\Delta M^*$, the change during the current administration. With *Position Midpoint*, *Mood*, and *Transient Macropartisanship* in the equation, both long-term partisanship components are significant with similar coefficients. One implication is that $M^*$ at the end of one election cycle carries over to affect the next election. But suppose we now delete *Position Midpoint* and *Mood* from the equation, retaining the two $M^*$ components plus *Transient Macropartisanship*. Now, the coefficient for $M^*$ at the start of the administration dissipates and in fact is slightly negative – as if any partisan advantages at the start of a term get spent, perhaps on policy consumption. (See Chapter 9.) Meanwhile, a two-variable equation with $\Delta M^*$ and *Transient Macropartisanship* explains two-thirds of the variance, with both coefficients highly significant.

Table 7.9. *Competing Models of the Presidential Vote*

| Dependent Variable: Democratic Percentage of Two-Party Vote | (1) Consumer Sentiment, Net Candidate Advantage | (2) Macropartisanship Proximity | (3) Combined Models |
|---|---|---|---|
| (Consumer Sentiment − 100) | 0.38[a] | | 0.13 |
| × Party, Quarter 3 | (4.35) | | (1.29) |
| Net Candidate Advantage | 6.47[a] | | 1.45 |
| | (3.69) | | (0.70) |
| Presidential Party (Democrat | −33.48[a] | | −11.90 |
| 1; Republican −1) | (4.27) | | (−1.29) |
| Policy Mood, Election Year | | 0.91 | 0.67[a] |
| (% Liberal) | | (7.81) | (3.04) |
| Party Position Midpoint | | −0.78[a] | −0.55 |
| (Liberalism) | | (−6.76) | (−2.33) |
| Macropartisanship, October | | 1.46[a] | 1.12[a] |
| | | (11.53) | (3.12) |
| Constant | 50.02 | −90.49 | −56.50 |
| | (60.16) | (−7.50) | (−1.75) |
| Adjusted $R^2$ | .84 | .93 | .92 |
| Standard Error of Estimate | 2.64 | 1.69 | 1.85 |

*Note:* $t$ ratios in parentheses. $N = 12$ elections, 1952–1996.
[a] $p < 0.05$.

model starting with the familiar economic influence on the incumbent party vote, supplemented with voter response to the candidates. Second, we account for the vote from the closeness of party positions to the electoral center and electoral partisanship. Because both models work quite well, they must offer similar predictions. And they do; correlations between the predictions of various versions of the two models average in the .85–.90 range. The competing models, each unique in its story about electoral success, predict each other's predictions about as well as they predict the vote. How can this duplication of predictions from separate explanations occur?

The dominant model that encompasses all others is the one with the best prediction of the vote – based on *Macropartisanship* and the two components of party proximity, *Mood* and *Position*. Table 7.9 illustrates. Column 1 selects for repetition the strongest of the "economy plus candidates" models, here converted to predict the Democratic rather than the incumbent vote. As before (Table 7.3, column 4) the model successfully explains 84 percent of the vote. Column 2 repeats Table 7.7's result,

# Policy

with *Macropartisanship* and the proximity components accounting for 93 percent of the vote. The question is, what happens when the models are combined? One might expect a dicey outcome, with six independent variables (including party control), considerable multicolinearity, and only 12 cases.

Column 3 presents the verdict. The coefficients for *Consumer Sentiment* and *Net Candidate Advantage* lose all claim of statistical significance. Meanwhile, the coefficients of the "partisanship and proximity" model hold their magnitudes and their statistical power. Similar comparisons result, substituting other versions of the "economics and candidate" model or entering single economic or candidate indicators one at a time. In all instances, the combination of *Macropartisanship* and *Proximity* decisively trumps the alternatives.

Although the effect of the economy "disappears" in this analysis, the economic effect is not spurious. In the language of causal modeling, the economy's impact survives as a combination of an indirect effect (via other variables) and a small (but nonsignificant) direct effect. From the little we can tell based on 12 observations, the indirect effect is dispersed in several directions. The economy, we know from Chapter 4, translates slowly into *Equilibrium Macropartisanship*, the permanent record of electoral politics, but also gets reflected in *Transient Macropartisanship* late in the campaign. It also predicts mildly (but not significantly) the closeness of *Mood* and *Party Position*, as if a good economy encourages in-party *Proximity*.[24]

By this analysis, the mechanism of economic effects is quite different from that assumed in the literature. Instead of voters observing the economy and responding independent of their partisan and ideological leanings, voters change their partisan and ideological leanings in response to the economy. Some independent direct effect is reserved, but this residual is better reflected by short-term *Macropartisanship Change* than by the observed economy.[25]

---

24 We must stress that the data are far too sparse to support any serious decomposition of effects. At best, we have suggested paths that add up to a whole. For instance, we can observe that Quarter 15 *Cumulative Income Growth* correlates at a positive .42 with *Transient Macropartisanship* measured for the in-party. With 11 cases, however, this correlation is far from significant. Moreover, if the three variables of the Table 7.9 column 1 equation are used to predict each of the column 2 variables, none of the coefficients or equations are significant. Still, in combination, the three variables of column 1 collectively predict 88 percent of the variance in the *vote predictions* of the column 2 variables.

25 At the micro level, economic perceptions often survive as vote predictors even with the imposition of controls for party identification and policy proximity. Yet whether these direct "effects" are real or rationalizations is a subject of de-

While an electoral impact for economic conditions survives our analysis (albeit in modified form), the diagnosis for candidate affect is less certain. When *Net Candidate Advantage* is added to the explanatory variables in the dominant equation (Table 7.9, column 2), its coefficient is not significant. But does *Net Candidate Advantage* indirectly affect the vote via an influence on *Macropartisanship* and *Mood*, or is its correlation with the vote spurious? We suspect the latter. *Net Candidate Advantage* is affected by *Party Position* as extremism causes less liking for a party's candidate.

Candidate popularity in part reflects the degree of extremism reflected in party platforms. Popular candidates win, but in part because popular candidates represent popular parties and, especially, because the degree of ideological extremism affects candidate popularity. If candidate affect as represented by *Net Candidate Advantage* influences the vote at all (rather than serving as only an electoral symptom) it would be by causing late breaks in *Macropartisanship*. An interesting indication of a possible causal flow from candidate affect to late partisanship is the increasing correlation between *Net Candidate Advantage* and the transient component of *Macropartisanship* as the election season progresses.[26] Still, the data are too limited for a conclusive verdict.

Our statistical analysis has turned the tables on the usual discussion of forecasting elections. Our evidence suggests that political variables – partisanship and ideological proximity – are the most proximate causes of the vote. The economy is present as a cause, but the economy does its work on the vote in large part via influencing political variables. Prosperity moves the political variables in a positive direction for the party in power, and these factors in turn influence the vote. If the party in power is the Democrats, for example, prosperity causes a Democratic surge in *Macropartisanship* and a positive view of Democratic candidates. Similarly, good times under Republican presidents foster Republicanism and attraction to Republican candidates. Bad economic times, of course, would produce the opposite set of results.

---

bate. Some part must be rationalization, since the magnitude of the observed micro-level effects often exceed what is possible, given the macro-level zero-order relationships between ICS components and the vote. In micro-level analysis, the notion that economic perceptions affect party identification has some support. See Fiorina (1981).

26 The correlations between *Net Candidate Advantage* and $M_t'$ are .23, .46, .67, and .69 for $t$ of quarters 1, 2, 3, and October, respectively. A statistical case can be made that candidate affect influences *Transient Macropartisanship* starting in quarter 3, while the economy's influence takes hold in October.

*Policy*

With 12 cases, this argument has been pushed to its statistical limit. But there is a certain attraction to the fit between theory and data. Part of the stuff of politics is that ideologues of the right and left each believe that their partisan side is correct. For the pragmatic general public, the relevant evidence is whether one side, when given power, brings more prosperity than the other. Even though presidents possess but limited control over the economy, the public takes economic performance as crucial evidence for scoring partisan debates. This should be no surprise, given the importance of the economy to people's lives and the ease of observing its condition.

### PARTISANSHIP, IDEOLOGY, AND THE PRESIDENTIAL VOTE: RECONSTRUCTING ELECTORAL HISTORY

If our analysis is correct, the electorate responds to both its partisanship and its policy proximity to the presidential candidates. Let us then take into account the fact that Democrats have the edge in party identification, yet Republicans more than hold their own in presidential elections. If the Democrats are more popular *and* the parties are equidistant ideologically from the electorate (mean *Proximity*, that is, is zero), how could it be that the Republicans have scored greater electoral success? How do we add up the effects properly for a successful electoral accounting?

The obvious answer is that the Republicans are more successful on other grounds – perhaps at offering bread and circuses to the enchanted masses, or perhaps simply in offering stronger candidates on nonpolicy grounds. The one difficulty with this obvious conclusion is that it does not register with our measure of *Net Candidate Advantage*. Although by this index Republicans offer the more attractive candidates (NES respondents historically have said nicer things about them), *Net Candidate Advantage* does not even have the correct sign when entered into regressions with October *Macropartisanship* and *Proximity*. Thus, if Republicans have run the best candidates, we are not measuring candidate effects very well.

A second nominee for the obvious answer is that the Republicans in fact might actually be closer to the voters on the issues. If Democrats outnumber Republicans and neither party has the edge on nonideological grounds, then maybe the Republicans actually hold the edge on *Proximity*. In other words, perhaps the mean *Proximity* score is not zero as we have assumed, and we should rescale Figure 7.4 by pushing the Republicans closer to the voters and Democrats farther away. This answer would not necessarily be cause for Republican rejoicing, however,

276

because it would mean that a Republican issue advantage was spent early in the time series. By the 1990s, Republicans had moved so far in the conservative direction as to nullify any argument about an issue advantage.

Before conceding an issue advantage to the Republicans, it is worthwhile asking, why are there more Democrats if Republicans are favored on the issues? In Chapter 4, we accounted for *Macropartisanship* from economic and political shocks, which, as far as we can tell, are independent of ideology or *Mood*. The ebb and flow of party fortunes seems largely governed by perceptions of competence. But does it necessarily follow that the long-term Democratic competitive advantage results solely from greater competence? The long-term Democratic lead in *Macropartisanship* is traced to the New Deal era, when a Democratic advantage was forged, on competence to be sure but also from the electorate's collective preference for Democratic over Republican policies.

One possible scenario is as follows. With more Democrats than Republicans, the public gives the initial policy edge to the Democrats. What then are the Republicans to do? At least early in our time frame, the Republican solution was the adoption of presidential policy stances (reflected by platforms) closer to the voters' than the Democrats could or would muster. Later in our time frame, as the electorate became more Republican, the Republican platforms tilted toward more consistent conservatism. But the Democrats moved in the conservative direction too, by an even bigger margin. By the 1990s, when much of the Democratic edge in partisanship was lost, the Democrats had positioned themselves closer to the electorate and reaped presidential rewards.

Finally, we should not forget congress. To understand the historic Republican success in presidential elections, we must take into account the even greater (until recently) Democratic success in congressional elections. A popular if controversial interpretation is that some voters try to achieve a global ideological balance by voting for one office conditional upon knowing party control of the other. This balancing theory is most commonly used to explain presidential party midterm loss, with moderate voters giving extra support to the out-party as an ideological balance to the president (Alesina and Rosenthal 1995). Balancing, of course, can work both ways. Some of the otherwise unexplainable Republican presidential success leading into the 1990s might be traced to voter willingness to elect Republican presidents to block a Democratic congress, just as a newly Republican congress may have encouraged voters to reelect Bill Clinton in 1996.

# Policy

## ACCOUNTING FOR THE CONGRESSIONAL VOTE

So far our discussion of national election outcomes has focused entirely on presidential elections. Congressional elections are held every two years, providing an additional electoral barometer with twice the number of readings. It would be impossible to summarize the vast literature on the national congressional verdict, most of which deals with either economic effects or midterm year losses by the presidential party. Here we touch on these topics, while introducing *Macropartisanship* and *Mood* to the congressional discussion.

When we introduce the totality of potential influences on the national congressional verdict, represented by the partisan division of House and Senate seats, the statistical results share a lot in common with our analysis of the influences on the presidential vote. The economy, as measured by *Consumer Sentiment*, influences the outcome, but indirectly via *Presidential Approval*. As a summary indicator of the presidential parties' performance success, *Approval* translates to the congressional level. But similar to the verdict for presidential elections, *Approval*'s influence is largely subsumed when *Macropartisanship* (along with *Mood*) is taken into account.

Our House equations predict the partisan division of seats (variously, the percentage for the presidential party or the Democratic Party). Our Senate equations predict the partisan division of the small number of seats (about 33) contested for the specific election year, ignoring seats determined at earlier elections. By concentrating only on Senate seats contested at the moment, we see far greater responsiveness to national forces in Senate elections than the House. The reason, of course, is that House outcomes tend to be insulated from national forces by one-party districts and a strong incumbency advantage. Senate constituencies (states) are by far the most competitive from a partisan standpoint and hence display a stronger seat swing per shift of the national vote. One other difference between our House and Senate equations is that for the prediction of House seats, it helps considerably to control for the lagged seat division in the previous congress. For the Senate, lagged seats are of no substantive or statistical significance, and thus are discarded for the equations presented. Lagged Senate seats are unimportant whether measured as the division of contested seats one election past (as an indicator of partisan trends) or three elections past (as an indicator of the net incumbency advantage among the current candidates).

Table 7.10 presents regressions predicting the *presidential*-party seat division in House and Senate elections, with an eye toward understanding the contribution of key performance measures, the economy, and

Table 7.10. *Regression of Congressional Seats on Consumer Sentiment, Approval*

| | Presidential Party Percentage of House Seats | | | Presidential Party Percentage of Senate Seats | | |
|---|---|---|---|---|---|---|
| | (1) | (2) | (3) | (4) | (5) | (6) |
| Consumer Sentiment, Quarter 3 | 0.18 (1.98) | −0.09 (−0.81) | | $0.51^a$ (2.25) | 0.04 (0.11) | |
| Presidential Approval, Quarter 3 | | $0.26^a$ (3.31) | $0.22^a$ (4.09) | | 0.47 (2.09) | $0.49^a$ (3.30) |
| Percentage of Seats, Previous Election | $0.85^a$ (4.18) | $0.76^a$ (4.60) | $0.78^a$ (4.84) | | | |
| Presidential Election Year Dummy (Yes is 1) | 4.28 (1.92) | $6.34^a$ (3.34) | $5.68^a$ (3.35) | 0.09 (0.02) | 4.71 (0.98) | 5.02 (1.31) |
| Presidential Party (Democrat 1, Republican 0) | 0.23 (0.06) | 4.01 (1.16) | 3.12 (0.96) | 7.95 (1.81) | $11.77^a$ (2.65) | $11.95^a$ (2.98) |
| Constant | −13.02 (−1.07) | −1.62 (−0.16) | −7.18 (−0.93) | −3.72 (−0.20) | 9.01 (0.49) | 10.79 (1.24) |
| Adjusted $R^2$ | .819 | .884 | .886 | .258 | .371 | .403 |
| Standard Error of Estimate | 4.11 | 3.30 | 3.26 | 10.21 | 9.41 | 9.16 |

*Note*: *t* ratios in parentheses. N = 23 elections, 1952–1996.
$^a$ $p < 0.05$.

*Presidential Approval.* The first three columns show equations predicting House seats, while the latter show equations predicting Senate seats. The equation in column 1 shows an almost statistically significant effect for economic perceptions, in the form of quarter 3 *Consumer Sentiment,* suggesting that the economy may be of some modest importance in House elections. Column 4 shows a larger and significant effect for Senate elections. But that is before incorporating *Approval.* With *Approval* in the equation (columns 2 and 5), the *Consumer Sentiment* coefficient loses its significance and (for House seats) displays the wrong sign. With or without *Consumer Sentiment* in the equation (columns 3, 6), *Presidential Approval* makes a larger and highly significant contribution. Approval of the president serves to predict congressional outcomes because *Approval* is a general proxy for the performance aspect of voters' partisan evaluations, including economic perceptions. Translating the coefficients for seat percentages into seats won, each point of *Approval* is worth about one House seat (.22 × 435) and about .15 of a Senate seat (.0049 × 33).

## Policy

Next, we turn to the simultaneous testing for *Mood* and *Macropartisanship* effects. Here, we switch from the presidential party's seat percentage to the *Democratic* seat percentage as the dependent variable. We predict both House and Senate seats from *Mood* and *Macropartisanship* plus lagged seats (for the House only) and a midterm variable.

One modification here is a different choice of *Macropartisanship* measure than for presidential elections. For presidential elections, the measure that works best and makes sense is *Macropartisanship* observed in October just before the election. This measure reflects both the equilibrium component and a transient component, which matter with virtually identical coefficients when used separately to predict presidential voting. Much of the influence of *Macropartisanship* in presidential years is the soaking up of other effects by the transient component of *Macropartisanship*. Congressional elections, interestingly, seem unaffected by this transient component, as if national partisan forces in congressional races are immune to the short-term excitement of the presidential contest.[27] For this reason, our measure of *Macropartisanship* applied to congressional elections is *Equilibrium Macropartisanship* measured for the third quarter of the election year, or $M_t^*$.[28]

The results are shown in Table 7.11. Column 1 shows the basic House equation. Both *Mood* and *Macropartisanship* $(M_t^*)$ are highly significant.[29] According to the equation, every point of *Equilibrium Macropartisanship* translates into 1 percent of the seats. Put another way, a 1-point fundamental movement in *Macropartisanship* accrues about four new House seats for the gaining party. The equation also says that every point of *Mood* movement yields about a .63 percentage point movement of seats, or, that every *Mood* point is worth about 2.5 added seats to the advantaged party.

Column 3 shows an even stronger result for the basic Senate equation, with *Mood* and *Macropartisanship* each highly significant. Together with the midterm variable, they account for almost three-fourths of the variance of the partisan seat division. Every point of *Macropartisanship* or *Mood* is worth about 2 percent of contested Senate seats. Translated from percentages to numbers won or lost, each three

---

27 For instance, October $M'$ correlates at $-.06$ with the congressional vote, while October $M^*$ correlates at $.50$ with the congressional vote.

28 For 1952, we substitute $M^*$ measured at 1953:1.

29 *Macropartisanship* and *Mood* pass the $.05$ threshold of statistical significance given any reasonable measure of *Macropartisanship*.

Table 7.11. *Regression of Congressional Seats on Mood, Macropartisanship*

| | Democratic Party Percentage of House Seats | | Democratic Party Percentage of Senate Seats | |
|---|---|---|---|---|
| | (1) | (2) | (3) | (4) |
| Policy Mood, Election Year | $0.57^a$ (3.45) | $0.43^a$ (2.38) | $2.17^a$ (6.56) | $1.92^a$ (4.65) |
| Equilibrium Macropartisanship, Quarter 3 | $0.99^a$ (4.69) | $0.72^a$ (2.87) | $2.39^a$ (5.27) | $2.16^a$ (3.82) |
| Midterm$^a$ | $-4.89^a$ (−4.56) | $-5.25^a$ (−3.52) | $-7.79^a$ (−3.98) | −5.70 (−2.09) |
| Democratic Percentage of Seats, Previous Election | $0.69^a$ (4.98) | $0.73^a$ (5.26) | | |
| Presidential Approval/ Presidential Party Interaction | | 0.11 (1.87) | | 0.10 (0.75) |
| Presidential Party (Democrat 1, Republican 0) | | −5.59 (−1.78) | | −7.33 (−1.03) |
| Constant | $-77.63^a$ (−3.67) | $-54.82^a$ (−2.20) | $-222.20^a$ (−5.26) | $-192.85^a$ (−3.49) |
| Adjusted $R^2$ | .725 | .769 | .731 | .730 |
| Standard Error of Estimate | 2.92 | 2.80 | 6.36 | 6.37 |

*Note*: Midterm = 1 if midterm with Democratic president, −1 if midterm with Republican president, and 0 for presidential year. $t$ ratios in parentheses. $N = 23$ for congressional elections, 1952–1996.
$^a$ $p < 0.05$.

points of *Macropartisanship* or *Mood* is worth about two additional Senate seats.[30]

Columns 2 and 4 of Table 7.11 show the fate of *Presidential Approval* when *Macropartisanship* and *Mood* are in the equation. For both House and Senate, the *Approval* coefficient shrinks to statistical insignificance. Evidently, much, though certainly not all, of the competency effect captured by *Approval* is indirect, captured by *Macropartisanship*. Since

30 Following any one election, the net partisan division of all 100 senators reflects *Mood* and *Macropartisanship* over three successive elections. We can predict 78 percent of the partisan variance for 100 seats from pooling the forecasts for the three relevant election years.

*Policy*

the *Macropartisanship* measure here is *Equilibrium Macropartisanship* ($M_t^*$ at quarter 3), the competency effect is largely absorbed in the permanent component of *Macropartisanship*.

Finally, we note the importance of the midterm effect for the prediction of House and Senate elections. The persistently negative coefficient for this variable signifies that at midterm each party is better off *not* controlling the presidency. This result is often interpreted as evidence of ideological balancing on the part of the electorate (Erikson 1988; Alesina and Rosenthal 1995).

CONCLUSIONS

Even if they are not always predictable much in advance of the actual vote, election results generally can be explained in terms of certain fundamental laws of politics. One rule is that the economy matters, but the exact mechanisms by which the degree of prosperity influences voters are open to debate. Popular candidates help their cause, which is no surprise. And *Macropartisanship* matters, so that readings of partisan change carry real electoral consequences. Finally, the electorate's current taste in policy and ideological direction matters. Our measure of *Mood* is of considerable electoral importance, particularly in presidential contests, but also in congressional contests.

In general, our evidence regarding the effects of *Macropartisanship* and *Mood* pushes the upper bounds of plausible outcomes. This result naturally works to strengthen the case that these variables matter. It may also work to generate controversy. Could the apparent evidence be so strong that we overstate the case?

Actually, this chapter has presented two converging stories. One is about economics and the vote; the other about politics and the vote. Importantly, the electoral predictions from economic conditions closely correspond to the predictions based on the political indicators. This chapter has suggested a resolution: Good economic times (and other signs of good management) make all political attitudes more favorable to the in-party and push them in the opposite direction under bad times. In this way, both economic and political explanations of the vote may be of equal validity.

Our story is a positive one for democratic accountability. When the votes are counted at the aggregate level and the partisan verdict determined, the public holds its leaders accountable both in terms of managing the economy and other aspects of governing, but also in terms of the public's demand for future policy change, measured by *Mood*. This provides the leverage for policy representation. With elections determined by the electorate's aggregate policy choices, politicians have reason to anticipate public preferences and enact the desired policy changes before they feel the voters' wrath at the polls. This aspect of the representation process is the subject of the next two chapters.

# 8

## Public Opinion and Policy Making

Does public opinion exert much influence on public policy? At least at first glance, the answer would be a resounding "no." Most voters are inattentive to the details of public policy (see Delli Carpini and Keeter 1996, for the most thorough review), a sad fact known since at least *The American Voter* (Campbell et al. 1960). If one were to generalize from the typical voter depicted in micro-level studies of public opinion, the macro-level electorate would seem incapable of setting the course of public policy. Moreover, it would be implausible that politicians would anticipate that the electorate could do so. Innovations such as Johnson's Great Society, Reagan's conservative agenda, or Clinton's measured moderation must find their source somewhere other than the demand of public opinion.

But the first glance does not provide the correct perspective, under-estimating as it does the concentrated energy of *informed* opinion. Is it possible that public opinion could be an important engine of public policy in the American democracy? We argue in the affirmative. We know that the public's *Policy Mood* moves systematically over time (Chapter 6) and is a major factor in national elections (Chapter 7). In its liberal phase, the public elects more Democrats; when conservative, it elects more Republicans. All it takes for a policy response then is for the parties to put their ideologically distinct agendas into law when elected, a matter we test next. But the direct action of elections is not the only spark. Rather than simply pursue their ideological agendas and await passively for the electoral verdict, politicians can *anticipate* the electoral effects of public opinion and adjust their policy-making behavior in advance. In this way, the electorate can achieve policy satisfaction with a minimum of electoral turnover.

This chapter and the next address the response of policy to public opinion. The question of this chapter is, "How does public policy respond to movements in public opinion?" Then, Chapter 9 advances

284

the question to address the dynamics of policy and public opinion, that is, how each moves the other over time.

In order to address these questions, we first must tie down the concept of public policy. We wish to relate policy to the *Mood* of the American electorate, which is scored for its left-right content on a global set of policies. In effect, we want to assess the degree to which the left-right (or "ideological" in political shorthand) tendency of the public's *Mood* directs the left-right content of national policy. It is imperative, therefore, that similar to the measurement of *Mood*, we score policy by its left-right content on a global scale, reflecting all relevant substantive areas of national policy.

But what is meant by policy? When we ask, "what is policy?", the answer closest to common usage is that *policy is the sum total of laws and regulations regarding the particular set of issues.* Thus (federal income) tax policy, for example, is essentially the Internal Revenue Code, the regulations and court decisions that implement it, and the culture of enforcement. What is important to note about this concept is that it is highly cumulative, the result of a long stream of decisions over time. Tax policy is not made anew each year. Even the massive reforms that come at multiyear intervals leave most of the code untouched.

In a complex society, it could not be otherwise. Governments lack the capability of enacting whole new policies every year. And even if they could do so, genuinely new policies – as opposed to incremental shifts in old ones – would present such radical dislocations that the social order could not accommodate them.

This conception of policy as a cumulation of past decisions has an important implication for any attempt to understand the flow and dynamics of policy; most of it cannot be accounted for by current factors, such as public opinion, because most of it is not itself current. Thus we need to think instead not about policy, but about policy *change*, which we shall define as current revisions to policy.

*Policy* and *policy change* in our conception are analogous to the time-series concepts of *level* and *difference*. *Policy Change*, that is, is the first difference of *Policy*:

$$Policy\ Change = Policy_t - Policy_{t-1}$$
$$= \Delta Policy_t$$

and *policy* equally is the cumulation of *policy change*. Policy incorporates its own history, responding to current factors only at the margin.

## Policy

When public opinion affects policy, the response is in stages. The most immediate response is one of policy activity by political elites. *Policy activity* is our conception of the day-to-day action in Washington, for example, voting on proposals in congress. Activity becomes policy only if it meets the constitutional requirements for law making. Coordinated action that commands majorities large enough to overcome constitutional choke points becomes *policy change*. Other activity is just action; the translation is contingent.

At the other end of the process, policy generates *policy consequences* for people's lives. Putting the parts of the chain together, we expect (with some delay) for people to get the policy consequences that they ask for.

Policy consequences are the most slippery of all, since it is difficult to separate out the contribution (good and bad) of governmental intervention upon people's social and economic fates. The liberalism or conservatism of government policy making, for instance, plausibly affects the degree of income inequality in society. The level of income equality is driven in some part by the degree to which the government attempts to take more from some and give more to others. But government does not *control* the outcome in question, which results from nonpolitical aspects of the social and economic structure. Government policy may influence income inequality, but only at the margin.

We see that policy can mean the sum of policy enacted over time; it can mean the changes to policy that engage the national debate. And it can mean the consequences of policy in terms of the effects on people's lives. Because the wheels of policy making grind slow, it is a challenge (but, as we will see, not an impossible one) to trace policy changes and their consequences to public opinion. The easiest link to observe in the chain of connections between opinion and policy is at the beginning of the process – the link between opinion and the actions of politicians as they go about making policy.

In this chapter, the question we ask is, what is the effect of public opinion on the *policy activity* of national elites? We explore both the indirect effect – as opinion causes electoral change, which causes change in elite behavior – and the direct effect as elites engage in rational anticipation. Our analysis follows the paradigm of our 1995 article, "Dynamic Representation" (Stimson et al. 1995), updated to include the important political changes of the 1990s. Then in the next chapter, we examine the dynamics of the policy system, as *Mood* causes change in policy (as measured from major changes in national legislation), which feeds back on public opinion.[1]

---

1 We address policy consequences only indirectly. Inflation and unemployment levels are two policy consequences that receive considerable attention as dependent vari-

Now we begin our consideration of how policy making and policy move in response to the flow of normal politics. Our strategy is to begin with a simplistic static model of the individual policy maker, an abstraction of presidents, members of congress, bureaucrats, and the like. This will prove not very illuminating – we need to beg the reader's patience for the exercise. Then, with the static concepts in hand, we ask what happens under dynamics, in particular, under the dynamics of a system in which public opinion moves over time. Last, we deduce the macro-level consequences of the individual behavior to build a macro model of policy making.

Here we take two approaches. Proceeding formally we demonstrate (in an appendix to this chapter) that elected officials necessarily follow the signal of public opinion change. For the less mathematical reader we appeal to intuitions about the decision problem of the politician.

## A MICRO MODEL OF POLICY-MAKER RESPONSE TO OPINION CHANGE

Start with a politician facing a policy choice. With both preferences over policy options and a continuing need to protect the electoral career from unwanted termination, the elected official will typically need to balance personal preference against electoral expediency. We presume that politicians have personal preferences for and against particular policies, and also that they value reelection. Then for each choice, we can define (1) a personal "ideal point" in the space of policy options and (2) an "expediency" point, the position most likely to optimize future reelection chances. The personal ideal point may be the politician's considered policy preference, or it may represent the demands of the politician's core supporters and contributors, or it may stand for the latent threat of a possible intraparty challenge in a primary or caucus: This ideal point reflects a choice over outcomes independent of the electorate's wishes. The expediency point, in contrast, derives from the general election voters. It might be the constituency's median voter or some similar construct – we are not concerned here about particular rules – all that

---

ables affected by political variables. Several studies have compared unemployment and inflation under Democratic and Republican rule for evidence that the party in control matters. (Hibbs 1977; Beck 1982; Alesina and Rosenthal 1995; Alesina, Londregan, and Rosenthal 1993). These studies typically find that Democrats are more likely to reduce unemployment and Republicans are more likely to reduce inflation. See also our discussion in Chapter 6. In that chapter, we discussed unemployment and inflation, not as consequences directly but as inputs feeding back on *Policy Mood*. See Chapter 6 and ahead to Chapter 9. On the consequences of party control for redistributive policy generally, see Hibbs and Dennis 1988.

matters is that the politician have a *perception* of the most expedient position.

The static choice then weighs policy preference and electoral security. Politicians who highly value policy formulation or who feel safe at home choose policy over security; those who face competitive challenge in the next election lean toward expediency and security. There is a stochastic element that derives from the fact that individual actors have little agenda control; they can optimize only over *available* choices. Therefore we expect each actor to have a *distribution* of acceptable positions. For expediency, politicians who serve conservative constituencies will be drawn to the right, and those serving liberals will be drawn to the left. Similarly, politicians' preferences may vary, but most often in contemporary American politics Democrats will be arrayed with ideal points to the left of most expedient positions and Republicans similarly to the right. This is a commonplace view of practical politics.

In this static model, electoral turnover stems from events that overwhelm the margin of safety that the politicians select. Campaign finance, personal scandals, challenger tactics, the framing of electoral choice – all affect outcomes. The victims come both from those who take electoral risk by pursing policy and also from those who ignore personal preference and concentrate solely on reelection: What matters is the force of electoral events relative to the politician's expectations. Here these factors should run independent of policy preferences: Conservative surprises and liberal surprises will cancel each other. In the static case, election outcomes provide little systematic influence over public policy.[2]

### Adding Dynamics

To breathe life into this system, let us put it into motion to see its aggregate and dynamic implications. We know from Chapter 6 that public opinion – global attitudes toward the role of government in society – moves over time. Now, the changes in personnel will prove systematic: Rightward shifts in public opinion will replace Democrats with Republicans, and leftward shifts, Republicans with Democrats. Or rather,

---

2 This verbal sketch represents what is surely a more complex process at equilibrium. Some politicians will, of course, make mistakes or take principled policy stands. Folklore, however, suggests that most share in their appreciation of the electoral imperative and act upon it. Our assumption about the independence of electoral surprises, policy preferences, and politicians' professional sophistication is, to be sure, a simplification. One notable exception is, of course, the surprise implicit in fluctuating macroeconomic conditions that translates into the electoral fortunes of the president's party in congress (Jacobson 1997).

surprises in such public opinion shifts will generate partisan change because they overcome politicians' safety margins in a systematic way. They occur across the board and produce a policy signal that stands out against the background noise of local politics. Cross-sectional representation becomes dynamic representation. Changing policy by shifting politicians and their ideal points, that is, *turnover*, is the standard electoral connection.

Turnover from elections works most transparently with politicians who are neither well informed – until hit on the head by the club of election results – nor strategic. But that does not look at all like the politicians we observe. The oft-painted picture of members of congress, for example, as people who read five or six daily newspapers, who work 18-hour days, who leave no stone unturned in anticipating the electoral problems that might arise from policy choices, does not suggest either limited information or naivete.

We explicitly postulate the reverse of the dumb and naive politician: (1) that elected politicians are rational actors, (2) that they are well informed about movements in public opinion, and (3) that they agree with one another about the nature of those movements. Here we examine each of these postulates as they play in our dynamics.

*Postulate I: Rationality*: Political scientists tend to emphasize calculation and strategic thinking when we talk about rationality. Borrowing from rational expectations economics, we wish to stress another dimension. Rational actors make decisions in the present, but the utility they maximize lies wholly in the future. And except as evidence for inferences about the future, the past has no importance at all. The political import of that future orientation is that *all is anticipation*. In particular, if politicians are rational, the only elections that ought to influence their calculations are those to come in the future.

Thinking about future elections then, by postulate, is of great importance but is also extremely difficult. Politicians face a serious information problem – which becomes a desperate information problem as they push the problem out two, three, or four elections into the future – they cannot know *who* their opponents will be and they cannot know *what* issues will be raised.[3]

---

3 This focus on anticipation as the quintessential behavior of elected politicians has much in common with Arnold's (1990) statement about the congressional side of government. Note that, given the enormous personal commitment required for launching a political career, politicians must plan on winning a *sequence* of elections before the expected rewards exceed the costs (Erikson 1976). Thus, they must make judgments about a series of future moments, not merely the next press

# Policy

*Postulate II: Well Informed:* Given those difficulties, and the presumption that public policy preferences matter, what sort of information about preferences would be most valuable? Almost anything about specifics has an exceedingly low probability of being relevant. Because public preferences only rarely crystallize on specifics, this sort of information, even if relevant, is exceedingly difficult to know.

For anticipating an uncertain future, trends in global sorts of preferences, such as whether more or less government is desirable, offer the greatest promise. At that level, public attitudes are real, they are knowable, and they are likely to be relevant to the electoral future. We postulate that politicians do attend to this information by the numerous mechanisms, personal and social as well as formal, that are open to them.[4]

*Postulate III: Consensus:* The community of politics – by which we mean not only politicians, but also journalists, commentators, academics, and others – talks incenssantly about where public opinion is going. This talk is both face-to-face, as in the dialogue of the cloakroom, and public, as when people in the Washington community swap sequences of ideas with one another, using statements and responses from the *Washington Post* or from the "talking heads" on the *Jim Lehrer Newshour* or the political shows on cable television as a kind of bulletin board. The end result is a public opinion that carries clarity probably beyond its genuine ambivalent character. Were beliefs about the fundamental direction of public opinion of a random or conflicting character, then the force of opinion would be neutralized. To the degree that consensus arises on the direction of opinion change, the net effects of common beliefs can become large.

Elected politicians, we believe, sense the mood of the moment, assess its trend, and anticipate its consequence for future elections. Changes in

conference. A House member or a senator must anticipate the electoral climate over a two- to six-year time horizon. Clearly, savvy politicians will pay more attention to climate change than to the swirl of day-to-day weather patterns. They must look for trends, not momentary movements.

4 Note that politicians rely on several sources of information about the public's policy judgments, including opinion polls, constituency newspapers, chats with ordinary voters, monitoring mail, "lobbying" efforts, and comparisons with other Washington politicians. Politicians also have conversations with close friends and supporters, their *personal* constituencies (Fenno 1978), whose views may genuinely alter the politicians'. Furthermore, politicians may be influenced, again genuinely, by changes in the "intellectual" climate, which also, simultaneously, change public judgments. As Kingdon (1973) suggested some time ago, personal views and strategic positions may become indistinct in some politicians' minds.

opinion, correctly perceived, will lead politicians to revise their beliefs about future election opportunities and hazards. Revised beliefs also imply revised expedient positions. Such strategic adjustment will have two effects: (1) It will dampen turnover, the conventional path of electoral influence, and (2) it will drive policy through rational anticipation.

When politicians perceive public opinion change, they adapt their behavior to please their constituency and, accordingly, enhance their chances of reelection. While still susceptible to surprises of unusual magnitude or suddenness, politicians who anticipate the public's movement will reduce the impact of public opinion change on their own careers by shifting their positions to satisfy shifts in public preferences.

This sensitivity to change we have termed *rational anticipation* – it is supremely rational for career politicians to anticipate public opinion change whenever possible. Importantly, in our world of savvy politicians, this rational anticipation also produces a dynamic representation in politics without the need for actual electoral defeats. Politicians modify their behavior, that is, alter their support for liberal and conservative policies, to accommodate changes in public opinion and thus produce a clear dynamic linkage between what the public wants and what politicians provide.

This anticipatory behavior does not exhaust the possibilities. For other actors also anticipate the effects of future elections on the current behavior of elected officials. Those who advance policy proposals – bureaucrats, lobbyists, judges, and citizens – are concerned with what can be done successfully, be it an administrative act, a judicial decision, or a legislative proposal. And other politicians, those who pursue a leadership role or advocate particular policies or those who craft party programs for future elections,[5] may choose to push ahead of the curve – to multiply the effects of even marginal shifts in opinion by anticipating others' reactions.

### Macro Model

When we aggregate over our micro politicians, each making strategic decisions weighing policy preference against expediency, what we expect

---

5 The importance of party-centered rational anticipation is becoming increasingly well appreciated. We now understand that on many major issues (but not all), the party leaderships and rank-and-file cooperate to establish a party stance that will serve them well in future elections. See current discussions of party government, and especially *conditional* party government (Rohde 1991; Cox and McCubbins 1993; and Aldrich and Rohde 2000a, 2000b).

to emerge is a net shift toward the direction of expediency calculations, i.e., public opinion. Since we presume perceptions of expediency to be consensual, these small strategic adjustments will not cancel one another. Instead they will tend to move in the same direction – following the same public opinion signal – at any given time. What we will see, that is, is a modest shift in the entire distribution of preferences and positions, left to right or right to left. That entails a shift in the central tendency of policy decisions and hence:

$$Policy_t = f(Opinion_{t-1})$$

Elections serve to replace one set of policy makers with another. That personnel turnover in turn revises the distribution of ideal points. Thus policy outcomes will depend also on election outcomes:[6]

$$Policy_t = f(Elections_{t-1})$$

Policy, we postulate, is often dynamic. Most obvious in the case of budgetary incrementalism, the action at any given time will often have a dependence upon previous actions:

$$Policy_t = f(Policy_{t-1})$$

Last, as we saw from Chapter 7, election outcomes will often be responsive to public opinion:

$$Elections_t = f(Opinion_t)$$

Collecting all these expectations and assuming linear relationships, we have the simple equation system:

$$Policy_t = \alpha Policy_{t-1} + \beta Elections_{t-1} + \gamma Opinion_{t-1} + e_t$$

$$Elections_{t-1} = \pi Opinion_{t-1} + e_{t-1}$$

with priors:

$$\alpha > 0.0$$

$$\beta > 0.0$$

$$\gamma > 0.0$$

$$\pi > 0.0$$

To summarize, $\alpha$, the parameter on previous policy, implies a positive relationship between one year's policy and the next, all else equal. The $\beta$ parameter on previous elections implies that personnel turnover matters; for example, Democrats will typically enact more liberal poli-

6 Elections also are sometimes a peculiarly relevant signal about public opinion.

cies than Republicans. Rational anticipation, the direct effect of public opinion on policy, is modeled in parameter $\gamma$. The final parameter, $\pi$, in the elections equation captures the effect of public opinion on elections.

## MEASUREMENT

Before we can estimate models of policy making, we need to pay some attention to measurement issues. In particular, we need to think about measures of policy making itself. For often as we write about it, there is no conventional measure of policy itself. Much of this owes to our tradition of particularism, of seeing the output of government as a myriad of policies, each a totally independent response to particular issues. We shall assume the reverse, that under all the particulars and details, governments move in coherent directions and much of this can be understood in the common left versus right terms of the American political dialogue.

A study of policy particulars in the traditional manner can never yield an inference that they are variations on a common theme. Particulars lead to particularism. But those who study the outputs of presidents and congresses (Poole and Rosenthal 1997) do find coherent directions beneath the particularism, and we shall proceed in this direction.[7]

### The Measures: Policy Change

How then do we begin to get measures of left versus right directions in policy making? What we observe is decisions, such as congressional votes, not quite "policy." Our view is that each decision involves policy change at the margin. The issue as it is typically confronted is: "Should we move current government policy in more liberal – expansive – directions or in more conservative ones?" What we observe is who votes how. We see, for example, a particular vote in which the liberal forces triumph over conservative opponents. We take such a vote to mean that in fact the (unobserved) content of the vote moves policy in a liberal direction – or resists movement in the conservative direction.

This is a direct analogy to public opinion as we measure it. We ask the public whether government should "do more" or "spend more" toward some particular purpose. We take the responses "do more," "do less," "do about the same" to indicate the preferred direction of

---

7 This is in the spirit of our work on public opinion, where the dimensionality of the issue space is a more empirical question, and where we find but one or two dimensions. It would be odd if public attitudes toward government moved in a left vs. right track while government dealt independently with the particulars of every situation.

policy change. In each case, direction of change from the status quo is the issue.

Measuring this net liberalism or conservatism of global policy activity seems easy enough in concept. We talk about some congresses being more or less liberal than others as if we knew what that meant. But if we ask how we know, where those intuitions come from, the answer is likely to be nonspecific. The intuitions probably arise from the fuzzy processing of multiple indicators of, for example, congressional action. And if none of them by itself is probably *the* defensible measure, our intuitions are probably correct in netting out the sum of many of them, all moving in the same direction. That, at least, is our strategy here. We will exploit several indicators of annual congressional policy activity, each by itself dubious. But when they run in tandem with one another, the set will give more confidence than its members individually.

*Congressional Rating Scales*: Rating scales are a starting point. Intended to tap the policy behaviors of individual House members and senators, scales produced by groups such as Americans for Democratic Action and Americans for Constitutional Action are now available for most of the period in question. Neither of these is intended to be a longitudinal measure of congressional action. And from a priori consideration of the properties such a measure would need, this is not how we would derive one.[8] But if scales move similarly across chambers and scales from different organizations move in common over time, then we begin to believe that whatever it is they are measuring is probably global liberalism or conservatism of roll-call voting. Thus, as a measure of Net Group Rating, we take the yearly average of the House's (or Senate's) ADA score and (100 minus) the ACA/ACU score.

*Congressional Roll-Call Outcomes*: The strength of the rating scales is their cross-sectional validity; they discriminate liberals from moderates from conservatives in any given year. Their weakness is longitudinal validity. We are less confident that they discriminate liberal from moderate from conservative congresses. For greater face validity, we turn

8 The essential problem is year-to-year comparability of roll calls – or lack thereof. If, say, an ADA scale aggregated for all members increases from one year to the next, we can't know for certain whether (1) the second congress was more liberal, or (2) the ADA picked an easier set of votes to scale in the second year. Having multiple indicators is thus important because different "rating houses" are unlikely to have identical motives in shifting the liberal-conservative anchor points for their scales. Of course, it is important that the different rating houses are interested in a similar common dimension. For reassuring evidence on the matter, see Smith, Herrera, and Herrera 1990.

to the roll calls themselves as measures of policy making. A quite direct measure is the answer to the questions: "On ideological votes, who wins? ... and by how much?" Provided that we can isolate a set of roll calls that polarize votes along the left versus right main dimension of American domestic politics, measuring the degree of, say, liberalism is as easy as counting the votes. If we know which position on the vote is liberal and which is conservative, then all that remains to be done is to observe who won and by how much (and then aggregate that roll-call information to the session).

We exploit the cross-sectional strength of the rating scales (specifically ADA) to classify roll calls. For each of the more than 27,000 roll-call votes in both houses from 1956 to 1996, we classify the vote as left-right polarized or not (and then in which direction). The criterion for the classification as polarized is that the vote must show a greater association with member ADA scores than a hypothetical party-line vote for the particular members of each congress. The intuition of this criterion is that we know we are observing a left-right cleavage when defection from party lines is itself along left-right lines, conservative Democrats voting with Republicans, liberal Republicans voting with Democrats. Although the party vote itself might be ideological, we can't know that it is. One measure of the net liberalism of a session (for each house separately) is then simply the median size of the liberal coalition (on votes where the liberal and conservative sides are defined). A second approach to the same raw data is to focus on winning and losing, rather than coalition size.[9] In this set of measures, we simply count the percentage of liberal wins. We are observing quite directly, then, who wins, who loses, and by how much.

To get a sense of how legislative policy activity has moved over the years, look at Figure 8.1, which presents our three measures for the House of Representatives.[10] It is clear that each indicator (wins, coalition size, and ADA-ACA ratings) contains both a common component

9 This speaks to concerns such as Riker's (1962) size principle, which would suggest that gains on one or the other side would not result in larger coalitions, but rather ratchet up the content of votes so that "better" votes could be won by minimum winning coalitions. Recent research (Mouw and MacKuen 1992) shows that the party leaderships and presidents do, in fact, alter their political agendas to accord with political circumstances and with the strength of their coalitions. Thus, from a theoretical point of view, it is critical that we include both wins and coalition size. (Empirically, as we shall see, this subtlety matters little for our aggregate analyses.)

10 To keep the eye on systematic movement, we have smoothed the graphs by taking a centered three-year moving average for each series. Note that we smooth only in this graph: We use the measured data for the statistical analysis.

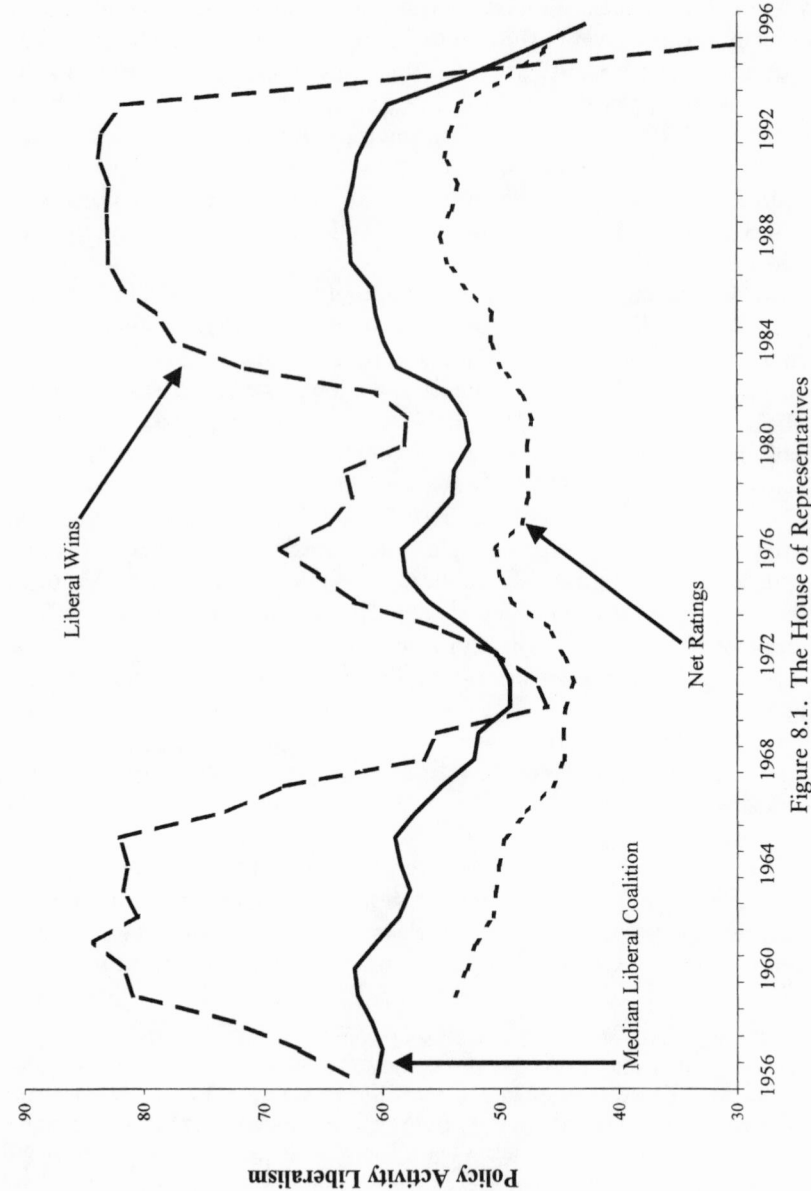

Figure 8.1. The House of Representatives

and an idiosyncratic component. The lines move together, with a bit of zig and zag around the main flow. The panel for the Senate (Figure 8.2) carries a similar message. Peaks of liberalism came during the early 1960s and late 1980s with conservatism at its height around 1980. While thus similar in outline, the patterns are not quite identical.

*Presidential Policy Liberalism*: The beginning point of dealing with the presidency is noting the near impossibility of direct measures of presidential liberalism from what presidents say and do. While we have an intuition about various acts and speeches, any attempt to quantify that intuition, to extract acts from the context of actions, quickly becomes hopelessly subjective. The alternative is to look instead at presidents through their quantifiable records of interacting with the legislature and judiciary.

We know how often particular members of congress support and oppose the president. And we can measure the liberalism of individual members in several ways. The most convenient of these is ADA scores, which are present for the entire period, as other comparable indicators are not. And we know that ADA ratings are very highly correlated with other ratings when available – positively or negatively – so that they can serve as a useful instrument of the underlying concept.

How then to combine these different pieces of information? A first approach is to ask the question: "How liberal were the regular supporters of the president each year?" and then adopt that standard as a reflection of what the president wanted from congress. That, however, is confounded by shared partisanship between president and member. We expect members of the president's party to be more likely to be regular supporters – independent of ideological agreement with the president's program. To deal with shared party ties as a confounding factor in presidential support, we opt instead to focus on presidential support within party. The strategy is to first divide each party into support and opposition groups based upon whether member presidential support is above or below the average for the party. The mean ADA rating of each party's "support" group is then an estimate of the president's ideological position. The opposition groups similarly measure the reverse. The measurement question then may be reduced to how such separate estimates are to be combined. For a summary measure of presidential position, we perform a principal components analysis of the eight indicators (support vs. oppose by party, by house). That analysis shows decisively that each of the eight taps a single underlying dimension. Such a dimension is estimated with a factor score, rescaled (to mean 50, standard deviation 10) to approximate the ADA scales from which it was derived (see Figure 8.3).

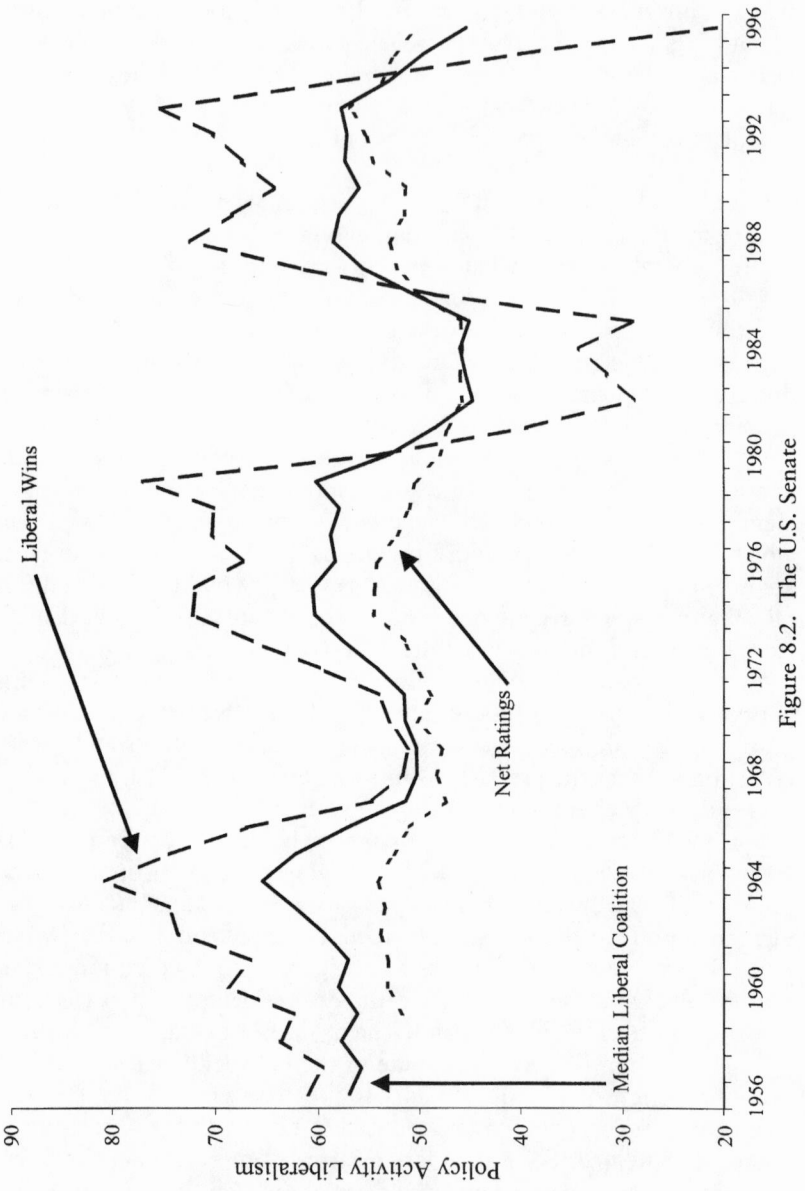

Figure 8.2. The U.S. Senate

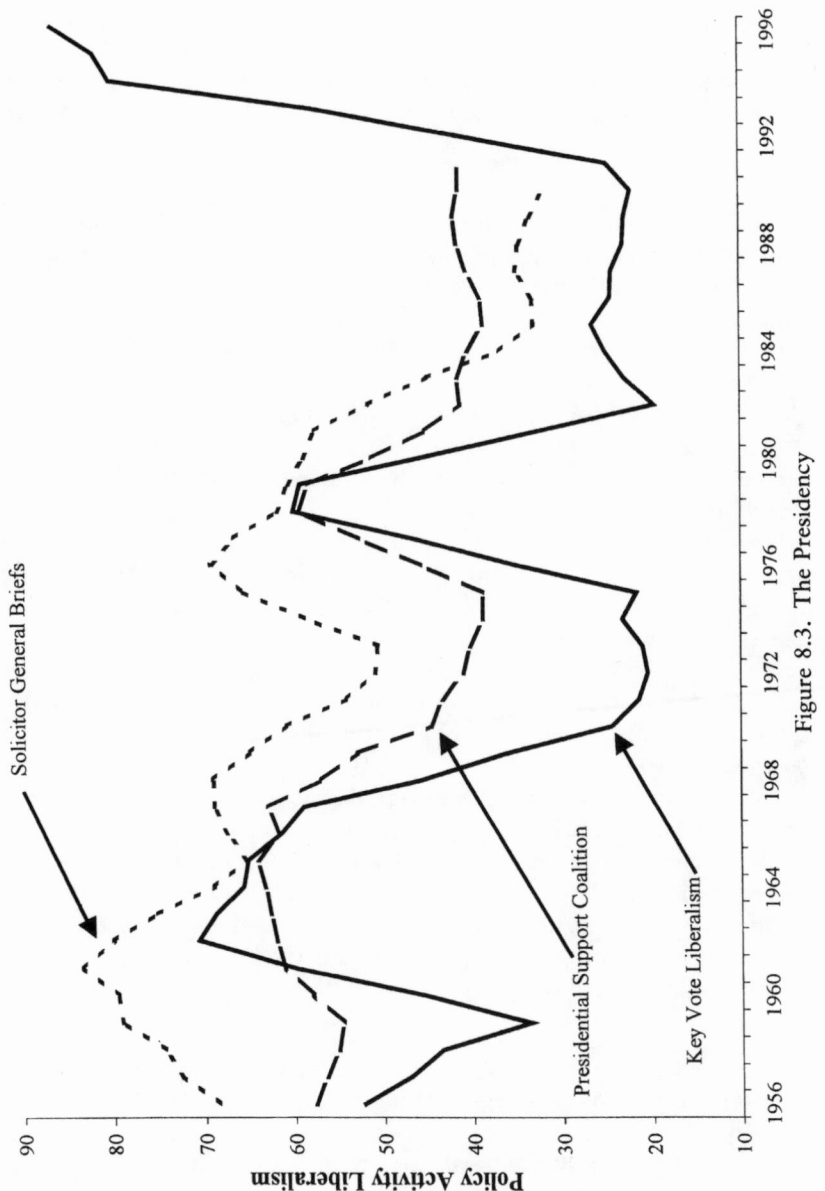

Figure 8.3. The Presidency

## Policy

For a second legislative presidential position measure, we simply take the recorded presidential position for the *Congressional Quarterly* "key votes" and compute the percentage of presidential stands each year that are liberal, where again the votes are classified by polarization with individual ADA ratings.

*Presidential Interaction with the Court*: With less regularity and on a quite different set of issues, presidents make their policy views known to the U.S. Supreme Court. The mechanism for doing so formally is the amicus curiae brief filed by the presidency's designated agent to the courts, the solicitor general (Lee 1986; Segal 1988; Salokar 1992). On over 700 occasions from the 1953 through 1989 terms, the solicitor general went on record with the Court, arguing that the holdings of particular judicial decisions ought to be affirmed or reversed. About 90 percent of these briefs take positions on cases that are themselves classifiably liberal or conservative.

We employ the solicitor general briefs data as leverage to measure presumed presidential position on judicial issues. Using the direction coding from the Spaeth Supreme Court data base for the case and our knowledge of whether the solicitor general argued to affirm or reverse,[11] we code each of the briefs as to direction: liberal, conservative, or nonideological. It is then an easy matter to produce aggregated annual scales as the percentage liberal of the ideological positions taken.

A quick comparison of the presidential series with the legislative series (in Figures 8.1 and 8.2) suggests less coherence in the presidential measures. Much of the discord comes from the solicitor general series (which we retain, nevertheless, for its substantive value). Note also that the presidential series is typically more conservative than the two congressional series – as we might reasonably expect from the historical party control of the two institutions.

*Supreme Court Liberalism*: For data we have the Supreme Court data base for the period 1954–1996. Using the Spaeth Supreme Court data base coding of direction of cases, we content classify the majority position in individual cases as liberal, conservative, or neither, and from that the lifetime liberalism or conservatism of individual justices is readily derived. We have chosen three major case categories, civil rights and lib-

---

11 We are grateful to Jeff Segal for aiding our task by providing his solicitor general data. We have supplemented the Segal data to fill out the time period under analysis.

erties, criminal procedure, and economics,[12] the number a compromise between separating matters that might in principle produce different alignments and grouping broadly enough to have sufficient cases in each for reliable annual measures.

For each measure, we construct a time series that consists of the percentage of votes cast by the justices on the liberal side of the issue, whichever that is, for the year. This focus on justice decisions, rather than aggregate outcomes of the Court, appears to produce a more moderate measure over time than the alternative. This is in the spirit of Baum (1988), who argues that the liberalism of the Warren Court and the conservatism of the Burger Court both tend to be overestimated from outcome (that is, which side won or lost) measures. Further, we concentrate on the two-thirds of the cases in which the Court reverses the decision of a lower court – those cases for which the Court's policy preferences are decisive.[13]

We examine the three domains in Figure 8.4. There we see mainly that the issue domains move pretty much in tandem. All domains show the famous liberalism of the Warren Court in the mid-1960s and the conservative reaction of the Burger Court. Most show a modest rebound of liberalism beginning in the early 1980s. (The final movement toward a conservative stance in the economics realm is based upon very few cases and is of smaller significance therefore than meets the eye.)

The pattern of more substantive notice is that the criminal procedure cases produce no liberal rebound in the 1980s. This is an interesting exception, for public attitudes toward crime and criminals are themselves an exception to the growing liberalism of the 1980s (Stimson 1999). This is a case where the conservative message – "the solution is more punitive law enforcement" – is still dominant.

### The Input: Mood and Party Control

Our key public-opinion indicator, of course, is the *Policy Mood* of the electorate, measured with a one-year lag. A second set of indepen-

---

12 Civil rights and liberties includes the data base categories civil rights, first amendment, due process, and privacy. Criminal procedure is one category alone. Economics includes unions and economics.

13 Caldeira, McGuire, and Smith (1997) argue that the subset of cases in which the Court affirms lower court rulings reflects unusual case selection motivations and therefore submerges the usual ideological patterning of votes. An examination of such cases as a time series confirms the conjecture; such a series shows none of the ideological patterning that all observers agree is typical of particular Courts and eras. Accordingly we select for analysis reversals only. This considerably sharpens the evidence of ideology over what we reported in an earlier analysis (Stimson et al. 1995) of the same issues.

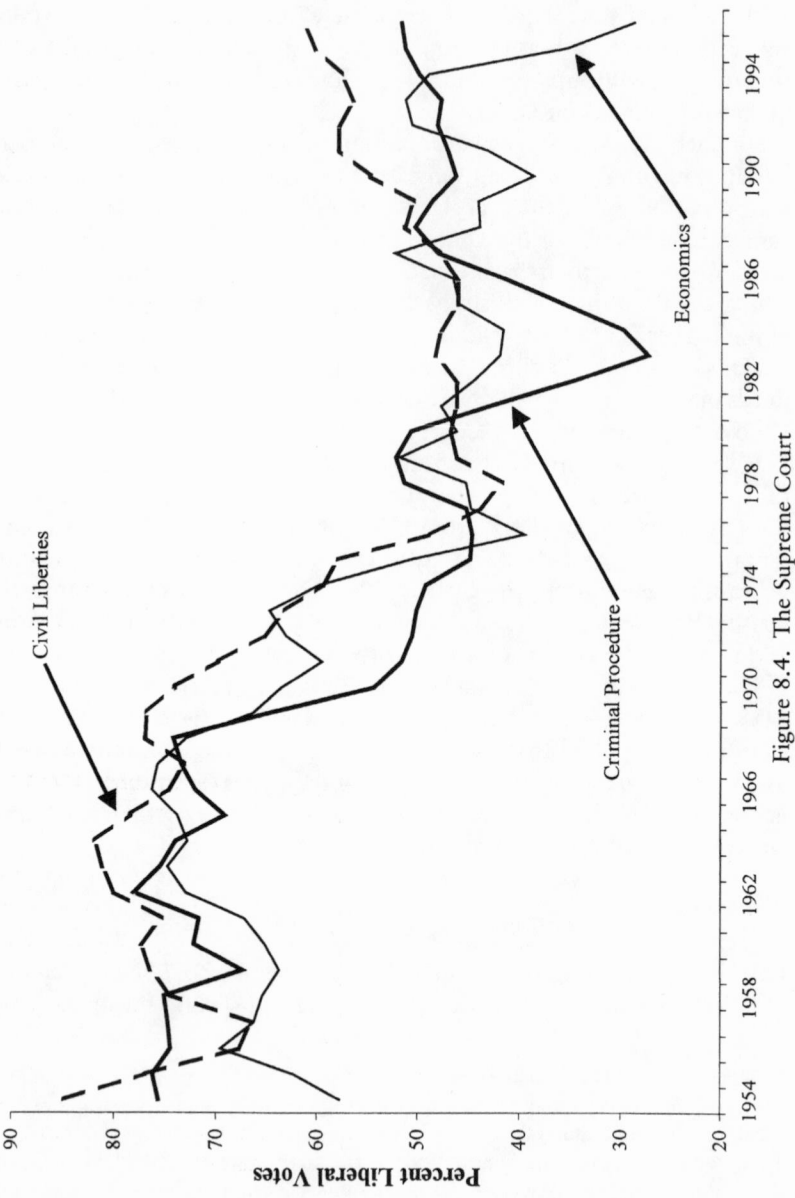

Figure 8.4. The Supreme Court

302

dent variables measure relative Republican versus Democratic control of the institutions of national government. Varying by the focus of analysis, the party control concept is tapped by indicators such as the party of the president and the Democratic percentages of the U.S. House of Representatives and U.S. Senate. We also include a party control variable, scored 1 when the Democrats organize the chamber and zero otherwise. Democratic percentages in the two houses measure partisan seat turnover (which follows different paths in the two houses) and thus capture what is probably the main carrier of the electoral message – the introduction and disappearance of personnel in the body. Real changes in real people clearly indicate changes in the houses' policy preferences. Further, they also hammer home the partisan electoral message to incumbents who, cleverly or otherwise, escaped electoral judgment.

## ESTIMATION OF MACRO MODELS

To recapitulate, we have put forward a static micro model of how policy makers choose between alternative courses. We have derived an important dynamic implication from that model – that policy makers ought to observe shifts in public opinion, anticipate their future electoral consequences, and shift slightly within their range of possible positions. We have seen as an aggregate consequence that the distribution of positions across policy makers ought to shift with opinion change. We have derived a statistical model of opinion influence on elections and election and opinion influence on policy making. And we have produced measures for all the key concepts in that model. Now we are ready to proceed to estimate parameters in the model.

We pose the question: "Do opinion and election changes influence the course of policy making?" Our analytic strategy leans heavily on the use of multiple indicators for our dependent concept, policy making. That requires us to adopt an estimation methodology that can cope with estimating a dynamic latent concept from a set of observed indicators. We choose the DYMIMIC setup of the Kalman filter for this task.[14] Like a combination of principal components analysis and regression, it estimates both the underlying dimension of a set of indicators and a structural model relating dependent to independent variables. Unlike that combination, it does everything in one step and with particularly robust time-series properties. Drawing its measurement metric from the first dependent indi-

---

14 The technical reader can consult Engle and Watson (1981) and Watson and Engle (1983) for original development of the DYMIMIC setup, Beck (1990) for its introduction to political science, and Kellstedt, McAvoy, and Stimson (1995) for its application to this problem.

cator, structural coefficients from the DYMIMIC estimator may be interpreted as if they were from a regression. The DYMIMIC setup also provides also some additional information about the contribution of each of the measured indicators to the latent dependent variable.

With the 40 years between 1957 and 1996 as our units of analysis, we estimate the model for each of the national governmental bodies and then, in a summary mode, for government itself. Given our focus on public opinion, we will estimate two statistical models for each analysis. The first, reduced form model is bare bones empiricism; we wish to ask the question, "Does public opinion move policy making?" and observe an answer relatively free from the influence of our assumptions about causal processes. Here we simply ignore the intervening influence of elections and personnel turnover, focusing on opinion alone. Because we have left out some of what we know, these estimates will not have desirable properties. Then we focus on how public opinion interacts with election turnover to produce policy change, our full model. This allows us, along with the earlier election analyses of Chapter 7, to lay out a reasonably complete system of opinion influence on policy making, including both the direct route through rational anticipation and the indirect route through electoral turnover. We begin with that part of government intended to be most representative of public views.

### The House of Representatives

The House of Representatives is by name and constitutional tradition an obviously appropriate target for our representation theory. Contemporary conventional wisdom, however, suggests that modern practices might make the House less than fully responsive to public opinion. It is widely believed – particularly by those who propose to cure the disease with term limitations – that the modern House is insulated, beyond the public's ability to move. (For thoughtful discussion on this matter, see Fiorina 1989 or Jacobson 1991.)

We begin with the simple reduced form specification, where only public opinion and previous policy making (and a control for Vietnam, discussed below) are allowed to predict current policy making. In this model, we exclude our measure of partisan composition, one of the possible pathways to responsiveness, in order to assess the total effect of opinion on policy, without regard to electoral mediation. This first analysis (see column 1, Table 8.1) fails to show an opinion effect. Because we can find such an effect when the time series stops with 1994, we suspect that we have a specification failure, a model that is ill-fitting because an important source of variance is omitted. This likely culprit is party control. Thus, we estimate a reduced form model with the dummy vari-

Table 8.1. *Policy Activity in the House of Representatives: Reduced Form and Full Models*

| Variables | Reduced Form | Reduced Form with Party Control | Full Model |
|---|---|---|---|
| | | Model | |
| Dynamics $(Y_{t-1})$ | $0.59^a$ | $0.19^a$ | 0.12 |
| | (4.89) | (2.11) | (1.54) |
| Mood$_{t-1}$ | 0.36 | $1.21^a$ | $1.28^a$ |
| | (0.96) | (5.84) | (6.72) |
| Cumulative | $-0.32^a$ | $-0.62^a$ | $-0.61^a$ |
| Vietnam | (−2.10) | (−7.47) | (−8.25) |
| Casualties | | | |
| Democratic Party | | $51.76^a$ | $48.93^a$ |
| Control (Dummy) | | (6.29) | (5.49) |
| Percentage | | | $0.45^a$ |
| Democratic | | | (2.05) |
| Constant | 7.43 | $-65.16^a$ | $-88.97^a$ |
| | (0.39) | (−4.07) | (−4.57) |
| Number of Cases | 41 | 41 | 41 |

| Measurement Model (Communalities) | | | |
|---|---|---|---|
| Percentage Liberal Wins | .89 | .96 | .98 |
| Median Liberal | | | |
| Coalition Size | .99 | .94 | .91 |
| Net Group Ratings$^a$ | .80 | .74 | .69 |

*Note*: Scored as average of ADA and ACA/ACU rating reflected in the liberal direction. *t* values in parentheses.
$^a$ $p < 0.05$.

able for Democratic control in column 2. Here we uncover a strong effect; each 1-point movement in *Mood*[15] produces about 1.2 units of change in the same direction in policy making. Public opinion matters for House policy; the question is how?

We know (from Chapter 7) that movements in public opinion are only modestly associated with House election outcomes. The strong association we have just seen cannot therefore arise solely from membership turnover effects. We may then ask how public opinion affects House policy. A clear alternative arises from understanding that members of the House may be so adept at reelection because they practice so well

---

15 To keep causal ordering straight, public opinion is measured from year $t - 1$ in all analyses. We take up the matter of feedback from policy to opinion – the reverse causal ordering – in the next chapter.

rational anticipation. When we estimate a full model that includes the percentages of Democratic seats in the House and public opinion, we see both as highly significant. Each additional Democratic percentage point (that is, about 4 House members) produces about 0.45 percent liberalism in policy; each point shift in public opinion produces an additional (and distinct) 1.28-point shift in policy. Note two things. First, the election turnover force on policy is only marginally connected to public preferences (it represents shifts in partisanship, midterm effects, and other factors). Second, and most important, the rational anticipation connection is very powerful. It produces a direct, one-to-one connection between percentage shifts in public opinion and percentage shifts in public policy. House members do not wait for elections to hear the public's message; they anticipate it and produce the appropriate response.

The measurement results in this case – the communalities in the lower portion of the table – suggest little variation in indicator validity.[16] The estimated latent dimension of policy making is correlated – correlation is the square root of the communality – at about .9 or more for all three indicators. We turned to multiple indicators because we weren't confident that any of the indicators by themselves properly tap policy liberalism. This result suggests that we could have been, that each by itself is a pretty good measure of the concept.

Initial analyses with the standard model were ill-behaved as a result of unusually conservative policy outcomes during the Vietnam War period, which we take to be a direct result of the war's first claim on national priorities. We have therefore added a control for this effect to the House model, cumulative American deaths in Vietnam, a measure of the intensity and priority of the war in American politics. This effect, each 1,000 deaths moving policy about half a point rightward, produces the good model fit and crisp coefficient estimates we had earlier failed to see.

We have also entertained models (for both House and Senate policy change) in which the president plays an agenda-setting role. These become complicated by the fact that there are at least two offsetting effects of presidential policy leadership. We expect, for example, a Democratic president to produce a more liberal agenda. But a rigorously liberal presidential agenda also makes it likely that liberals will win less often

16 The communalities are estimated from the (squared) empirical correlations of the indicators and the state variable. They can be interpreted, in a standard "factor analytic" way, as keys to the substantive meaning of the common dimension. However, we refrain from leaning on a validity interpretation because in these models the communalities seem to be dominated, instead, by the relative measurement reliabilities of the indicators.

– because the proposals are tougher – and by smaller majorities when they do. Including presidential party in the models shows these confounding patterns, with usually small and nonsignificant effects. We do not report them, because we believe they would be improperly interpreted. A valid assessment of presidential agenda setting would require measures of the content of the presidential agenda, which is well beyond the scope of this analysis.

## The U.S. Senate

By conventional standards, the U.S. Senate should look very different. The Constitution engineered the Senate with the intent to make it a more deliberate body than the House; its six-year terms should make it less reactive to public opinion. Yet, political reality emphasizes that senators, compared to their House colleagues, enjoy at best a very modest reelection advantage. While required to seek reelection only one-third as often, their state-level constituencies generally are more electorally competitive than House districts. As we saw in Chapter 7, Senate elections may be the most responsive of all to public opinion, as the 33 or so electoral verdicts each election year shift in response to the public's *Policy Mood*.

The straightforward "reduced form" version of the test (in column 1 of Table 8.2) shows a clear and strong relationship between public opinion and Senate policy making. Every point change in public preferences yields 1.03 points in policy. Thus, the Senate reflects clearly public opinion. We next ask: By what route does this force penetrate the institution?

The Senate, as we have seen, exceeds the other elected branches of the national government in its electoral responsiveness to public opinion. This strong electoral connection produces a corresponding influence on public policy. The Senate Policy Activity model (in column 2 of Table 8.2) indicates that the partisanship of each new senator contributes about .63 points to policy change – and party control by itself has a massive effect. Notice also that when we control for the electoral connection, no statistical evidence remains for a direct public opinion effect. Thus, contrary to the usual expectations, it is the Senate rather than the House that works like a textbook representation mechanism – Senate elections are responsive to public opinion, and then the new membership produces policy outcomes consistent with the Senate's party composition but otherwise independent of the electoral *Mood*.

Why should this be so? Part of the answer must be that senators are so regularly replaced by electoral defeat that they have little opportunity to be out of step with current public opinion. Since, as we saw in Chapter

307

# Policy

Table 8.2. *Policy Activity in the U.S. Senate: Reduced Form and Full Models*

| Variables | Model | |
|---|---|---|
| | Reduced Form | Full Model |
| Dynamics ($Y_{t-1}$) | 0.47[a] | −0.08 |
| | (4.76) | (−1.19) |
| Mood$_{t-1}$ | 1.03[a] | −0.13 |
| | (3.09) | (−0.52) |
| Percentage Democratic | | 0.63[a] |
| | | (2.74) |
| Democratic Party Control (Dummy) | | 34.77[a] |
| | | (7.84) |
| Constant | −31.97 | 8.14 |
| | (−1.57) | (0.53) |
| Number of Cases | 41 | 41 |
| Measurement Model (Communalities) | | |
| Percentage Liberal Wins | .96 | .99 |
| Median Liberal Coalition Size | .97 | .90 |
| Net Group Ratings[b] | .61 | .57 |

*Note*: $t$ in parentheses.
[a] $p < 0.05$.
[b] Scored as average of ADA and ACA/ACU rating reflected in the liberal direction.

7, Senate elections regularly screen out those whose views are out of line and select those who are in line, there is relatively little room left for direct response to opinion. The evidence of the reduced form analysis is that the Senate is highly responsive to the climate of opinion. What we do not see for senators is direct response to opinion change.

The six-year term is one of the more obvious differences between House and Senate. We might surmise that senators feel free to ignore public opinion for most of their term, taking it seriously only in the last year or two as the reelection challenge looms (e.g., Thomas 1985). But if we can see clearly that such behavior tends to get them in trouble, why shouldn't they see it at least equally well? That seems too thoughtless for a group of people we know to be exceptionally goal-oriented. But the longer Senate term has more subtle consequences as well. One of these is that the uncertainty associated with projecting today's public opinion into the future, high under the best of circumstances, becomes extreme when that future is as far off as six years. Changes in today's opinion are a relatively strong signal for how one might cope with the November of this year or next. For the November five or six years hence, the signal is much weaker. In two chapters to come (9 and especially 10) we will see that projecting uncertain information into the future of more than a year or two will regularly fail.

But rational actors don't ignore even weak or uncertain information. To explain why they might do so we need something on the other side of the ledger, something that might outweigh a weak signal. For that, we suggest that it is useful to think about the senator's relationship with his or her base supporters (Fenno's [1978] "personal constituency") and with in-party supporters (the "primary constituency"). Both have been vital to electoral success. And their enthusiasm – and not merely acquiescence – will be necessary for future success.

In contrast with the preferences of a future electorate, the supporters' policy views can be understood with near certainty. In normal American politics, the political bedfellows from the senator's party will be committed ideologues of the left or right, depending upon party. So the pull of public opinion in one direction will often engage the counterpull of the party base. Early in the senator's term, it seems likely that the counter will be the stronger force. Without the need from an impending election, it should be hard to justify following opinion shifts when they lead away from the senator's stance. And thus senators are likely to give more weight to the uncompromising attitudes of supporters than to the general public. (House members would do the same in the same situation, but they are never without the threat of impending election; it is omnipresent.) As reelection nears, senators should behave like House members. But with only a third of the Senate exposed in any given year, this responsiveness could be lost in statistical noise.

### The Presidency

Presidential policy positions contain a bit of subtlety around a pattern of brute simplicity. The latter is that presidential position varies to an extraordinary degree with presidential party; Democrats are liberal, Republicans conservative. This is not the sort of pattern that merits much modeling attention. Our goal here is to model out the brute simplicity (with a presidential party dummy variable) in order to see the subtlety. That allows us to observe variations both within party and from year to year within a presidency.

We begin by examining the simplest, but perhaps the most fundamental, relationship. The first column in Table 8.3 shows the reduced form equation, where we model presidential policy liberalism on previous policy liberalism[17] and on public opinion. Here we pay no attention to process, but instead ask the question: "Is presidential liberalism

17 We make no special provision for transitions.

# Policy

Table 8.3. *Presidential Policy Activity: Reduced Form and Full Models*

|  | Model | |
| --- | --- | --- |
| Variables | Reduced Form | Full Model |
| Dynamics $(Y_{t-1})$ | $0.93^a$ | $0.26^a$ |
|  | (15.42) | (4.80) |
| Mood$_{t-1}$ | $0.80^a$ | $0.51^a$ |
|  | (4.06) | (2.36) |
| Presidential Party |  | $33.03^a$ |
|  |  | (11.57) |
| Constant | $-39.01^a$ | $-11.79$ |
|  | (-3.21) | (-0.86) |
| Number of Cases | 41 | 41 |
| Measurement Model (Communalities) | | |
| Key Vote Liberalism | .92 | .97 |
| Presidential Support Coalition | .73 | .46 |
| Solicitor General Amicus Briefs | .25 | .05 |

*Note*: $t$ in parentheses.
[a] $p < 0.05$.

associated with opinion change by whatever route?" The answer, clearly, is yes. Here we see that each point change in opinion produces about .80 point presidential liberalism.

We know from earlier analyses that presidential elections turn, in part, on public opinion (measured by *Policy Mood*). Given the party differences in presidential behavior, the electoral connection itself produces representation of a sort. Here we wish to pursue the more subtle issue of public opinion influence on the presidency beyond the elections that produced the incumbents. In the analyses to follow, presidential party captures the electoral turnover route to representation, and public opinion represents the rational anticipation effect. Also included is the usual dynamic term (presidential liberalism of the previous year). The estimation also produces measurement models for the congressional key vote liberalism, the presidential support coalition series, and the solicitor general amicus brief series.

The result, in the second column of Table 8.3, provides support for the obvious party effect – Democratic presidents are about 33 points more liberal than Republicans. Of more interest, the coefficient estimated for public opinion shows a quite substantial effect, even after controlling for presidential party. Now we see that even taking into account the huge party differences among presidents, movement in public preferences also produces corresponding movement *within* presidencies. The estimated coefficient on preferences, 0.51, implies movement in either direction by about half the size of public opinion change. We will see in Chapter 9 that opinion movement is typically contrary to the ideological persuasion of a president; that is, liberals and Democrats produce opinion movements toward conservatism, and conservatives and Republicans do the reverse. Thus, the flavor of public opinion influence on presidencies is to induce moderation as the term wears on.

The measurement analysis in Table 8.3 provides the communalities of the indicators. They provide a rough idea of the overall "fit" of the model to the empirical measures. Here, the communalities (.97, .46, and .05 in column 2) suggest that the indicators of presidential liberalism derived from the president's interactions with congress are closely tied to the latent concept, the solicitor general series much less so. That is an expected result because the two congressional indicators of presidential position are more reliably estimated than the judicial materials permit. There is nonetheless some association ($r = .25$) between estimated presidential liberalism and the judicial positions scale.

### The Supreme Court

Faithfully representing public opinion is no part of the mandate of the Supreme Court of the United States. The Court is to be governed by the Constitution and the law, but not by public opinion. Scholars have, however, long suspected otherwise (Dahl 1957; Adamany 1973; Funston 1975; Casper 1976; Barnum 1985; Gates 1987; Marshall 1989; Caldeira and Gibson 1992). For the Court deals in public business and is made up in the main of men and women whose careers have led them to be sensitive to how the public wants its business done.

Once on the Court, justices will also have reason to monitor public opinion. We see two main reasons. First, justices care deeply about substantive outcomes. They also share policy-making authority with elected politicians. When competing with politicians, justices must consider the possibility that their decisions will be overridden or indifferently enforced. They compare the policy outcome that obtains when they choose their "ideal point" and engage political opposition against the outcome likely when they compromise in an effort to avoid active political opposition. Thus, justices who wish to exert authority over the direction of American life will anticipate actions of the other branches of government. Further, institutionally minded justices will want to avoid public defeat and the accompanying weakening of the Court's implicit authority: They will compromise in order to save the institution (Murphy 1964). All this implies paying some attention to what the public wants from government. But "paying some attention" is some distance from

Table 8.4. *Justice Liberalism as a Function of
Public Opinion and Presidential Party at the Time
of Confirmation*

| Variables | Individual Justice Liberalism |
|---|---|
| Mood | −0.09 |
| | (−0.12) |
| Presidential Party Dummy | 21.36[a] |
| (Democrat = 1) | (3.17) |
| Constant | 44.10 |
| | (0.93) |
| Number of Cases | 20 |
| Adjusted $R^2$ | .35 |

*Note*: $t$ in parentheses.
[a] $p < 0.05$.

the immediate concern public opinion demands of elected officials. And so the representation we expect of the Court is respect for the general contours of public expectation, but not the omnipresent finger in the wind we expect of the elected branches.

The Court lacks a simple election pathway to opinion influence, but we think its more complicated composition does reflect the ebb and flow of public sentiment. The composition mechanism is not directly electoral, of course, but instead reflects a blend of congressional and presidential politics. When presidents decide whom to nominate and Senates decide whom to confirm, both will reflect their own policy preferences (their ideal points) and also their sense of what the public will accept. Thus, the nomination-confirmation process embodies the electoral and the rational anticipation mechanisms built into the presidency and the Senate. Here we examine the conditions of American politics during the confirmation years of 20 justices. We regress the individual justice lifetime liberalism scores (percentage liberal) on *Mood* for the confirmation year and on the party of the appointing president.

The message of Table 8.4 is clear. The party of the president matters a lot, as we would have expected. Confirmed nominees are over 21 points more liberal if the appointment is made by a Democratic president. *Mood* at the time, however, does not matter. Its trivial coefficient (−0.09) is nonsignificant and carries the wrong sign. *Mood* matters because we have seen that it has much to do with who is the president. What we learn from this analysis is that there is no additional effect. (And the same conclusion would be reached by analysis of the *Mood* of the presidential election year rather than the year of the confirmation.)

Table 8.5. *Supreme Court Policy Activity: Reduced Form and Full Models*

| Variables | Model | |
|---|---|---|
| | Reduced Form | Full Model |
| Dynamics ($Y_{t-1}$) | 0.90[a] | 0.26 |
| | (17.00) | (1.68) |
| Mood$_{t-1}$ | 0.43[a] | 0.90[a] |
| | (2.85) | (4.00) |
| Court Composition (Justice Lifetime | | 1.15[a] |
| Liberalism) | | (4.68) |
| Constant | −20.80[a] | −70.86[a] |
| | (−2.57) | (−4.26) |
| Number of Cases | 43 | 43 |

| Measurement Model (Communalities) | | |
|---|---|---|
| Civil Liberties | .84 | .82 |
| Criminal Procedure | .78 | .74 |
| Economic | .60 | .63 |

*Note*: $t$ in parentheses.
[a] $p < 0.05$.

As with the other branches, we begin our look at the Court with the basic representation question, "Do Court decisions reflect changes in public opinion?" The answer shown in Table 8.5 is that they do. Movements in public opinion predict movements in Supreme Court outcomes in the following year, with a significant coefficient of 0.43. This is a weaker translation of opinion into outcomes than we have observed in the elected branches, very much what we would expect. But in absolute terms it is strong. That almost half of every point of opinion change becomes policy change indicates a far more responsive Court than most would suspect.

Again, there exist two main channels: composition and rational anticipation. We assess the Court's composition through our measure of the lifetime liberalism of the serving justices for a particular year. This should mediate the preferences of presidents and Senates into Court outcomes. Thus we can ask whether the Court follows public opinion entirely through the nomination and confirmation process as Norpoth and Segal (1994) assert, whether it responds to public opinion directly, as Mishler and Sheehan (1993) claim, or whether it is a combination of both. The full-model specification, in column 2 of Table 8.5, shows that Court composition dominates; liberalism in justices produces liberalism in decisions by a slightly more than one-to-one translation. The processes that influence who serves on the Court – one of which, indirectly, is public opinion – in turn influence outcomes. But introducing a control for composition, far from driving out the evidence of direct response to public opinion, actually considerably enhances it. The coefficient on opinion more than doubles over the reduced form model, where composition is not taken into account. Both of the pathways show powerful effects. The founders' intentions notwithstanding, the Supreme Court of this analysis is strongly responsive to the public. Although we posit a quite different model of opinion flow, our results weigh in to the controversy over opinion and the Court on the side of Mishler and Sheehan.[18]

### A Summary Analysis of Governmental Responsiveness

For a final summation of dynamic representation, we slice across the institutional structure of American politics, returning to the familiar questions, (1) "Does public opinion influence public policy?", and (2) "By what process?" Our combining the policy activity of the four institutions is, of course, a fiction – a single national public policy is not the average of independent branches. We "average" across different branches to provide a rough answer to a rough question. Here we select two indicators from each of the four prior analyses, President, House, Senate, and Supreme Court, and then estimate representation as it works on the American national government as a whole.[19]

The estimates of Table 8.6 sum up the dynamic representation story. The first column produces a bare-bones model that posits policy activity as a simple and direct function of public opinion. While this representation misses much, it has the virtue of answering the first question without complication. And the answer is yes: Public opinion influences public policy. We see that each point change in public opinion produces about a fifth of a point (0.18) change in the overall policy activity of the federal government. The result passes statistical muster ($t = 2.2$) and produces clear evidence that public opinion matters.

18 Figure 8.4 would seem to justify an assumption that our three policy domains are really a single common dimension of liberalism and conservatism. If that is the case, then the content of the three can be combined, here as an average weighed by number of cases, for a single measured dependent variable. Doing so with an ordinary least squares regression reproduces these findings almost exactly.

19 We have forced the "variance" of each of the measures to be equal and fixed the scalar translations of the indicators to unity. This trick corrects for a tendency for the estimation to track the Senate (the most opinion sensitive institution) and ignore the rest.

Table 8.6. *Estimations of Global Representation*

| Variables | Model Reduced Form | Full Model (with Vietnam) |
|---|---|---|
| Dynamics ($Y_{t-1}$) | 0.77[a] | 0.20 |
| | (8.64) | (1.90) |
| Mood$_{t-1}$ | 0.18[a] | 0.36[a] |
| | (2.15) | (4.16) |
| Composition | | 0.88[a] |
| | | (5.91) |
| Cumulative Vietnam Deaths | | −0.23[a] |
| | | (−7.05) |
| Constant | 1.13 | −29.67[a] |
| | (0.17) | (−3.37) |
| Number of Cases | 41 | 41 |

| Measurement Model (Communalities) | | |
|---|---|---|
| Senate Percentage Liberal Wins | .39 | .34 |
| Senate Median Liberal Coalition Size | .43 | .37 |
| House Percentage Liberal Wins | .26 | .29 |
| House Median Liberal Coalition Size | .15 | .17 |
| Presidential Key Vote Liberalism | .37 | .27 |
| Presidential Support Coalition | .60 | .46 |
| Supreme Court, Civil Liberties | .41 | .25 |
| Supreme Court, Economics | .29 | .14 |

*Note:* $t$ in parentheses.
[a] $p < 0.05$.

We turn, as usual, to a richer model. As a proxy for composition of government, we average across institutions (percentage of Democrats in the two houses, presidency dummy, and percentage of liberals in the Court).[20] We may now compare the turnover and rational anticipation linkages.[21] As can now be seen clearly, both composition and opinion are unquestionably important for policy making. Each percentage point of Democratic (or liberal) composition produces nearly a full point (0.88)

20 The composition indicator is the first principal component of the four measures, scored to be comparable to the percentage Democratic congressional composition measures already employed. Like our more natural composition measures, this summary measure is in turn a function of its previous value ($\beta = 0.57$), *Macropartisanship* ($\beta = 0.64$), and public opinion ($\beta = 0.35$).
21 As with the earlier House models, the effects emerge more clearly under control for the distinct policy making of the Vietnam era.

of policy. And equally, a unit of public opinion change produces a rational anticipation response of over a third (0.36) of a point in policy activity. It is through elections and the anticipation of elections that public opinion drives governmental decisions.

Public opinion is substantially important. Combining the two paths, each point movement in preferences produces an electorally linked policy response (0.50 = 0.57 × 0.88) and a direct rational anticipation response (0.36) totaling 0.86 points in public policy. That is to say, there exists nearly a one-to-one translation of preferences into policy, where policy and preferences are measured in familiar percentage liberal terms.

We get a better sense of the historical dynamic by examining Figure 8.5. Plotted here are measures of public opinion, public policy, and predicted policy. The first (in the light solid line) is public opinion, with its liberal peaks during the early 1960s and late 1980s and its conservative peak around 1980. The dark solid line represents policy – a simple average of our eight policy indicators. Without much work, it is clear that the two series are basically similar: Policy reflects the timing and range of public opinion change.

Yet, the two paths are not identical. *Policy Activity* turned much more conservative during the late 1960s and early 1970s than the public demanded. And then, contrary to the continuing turn to the right, *Policy Activity* temporarily shifted leftward under Carter's leadership. Although we predict a rightward movement following Republican seizure of control of congress in the 1994 elections, the actual effect – seen in the average indicator series – is considerably more dramatic. Now look at the small dots that show predicted policy (the "state" variable taken from the last equation of Table 8.6). The fit is exceptionally strong. More important, one can see that the model now can account for the otherwise surprising conservatism just before 1972 and the liberalism of the late 1970s – by including the Vietnam War and the composition variables. Thus, while the main part of policy moves in accord with public preferences, significant deviations can and do occur. Those deviations seem explicable, but not by public preferences. Public opinion is powerful, but not all powerful.

Figure 8.5 takes us back to where we started, public-policy preferences, and forward to the end of the story, the liberalism and conservatism of American government *Policy Activity*, 1956 to 1996. The point is that the two are a lot alike.

## THE DYNAMICS OF INSTITUTIONAL RESPONSE

While we now know that national institutions reflect public opinion, we need to know more before we understand the character of dynamic rep-

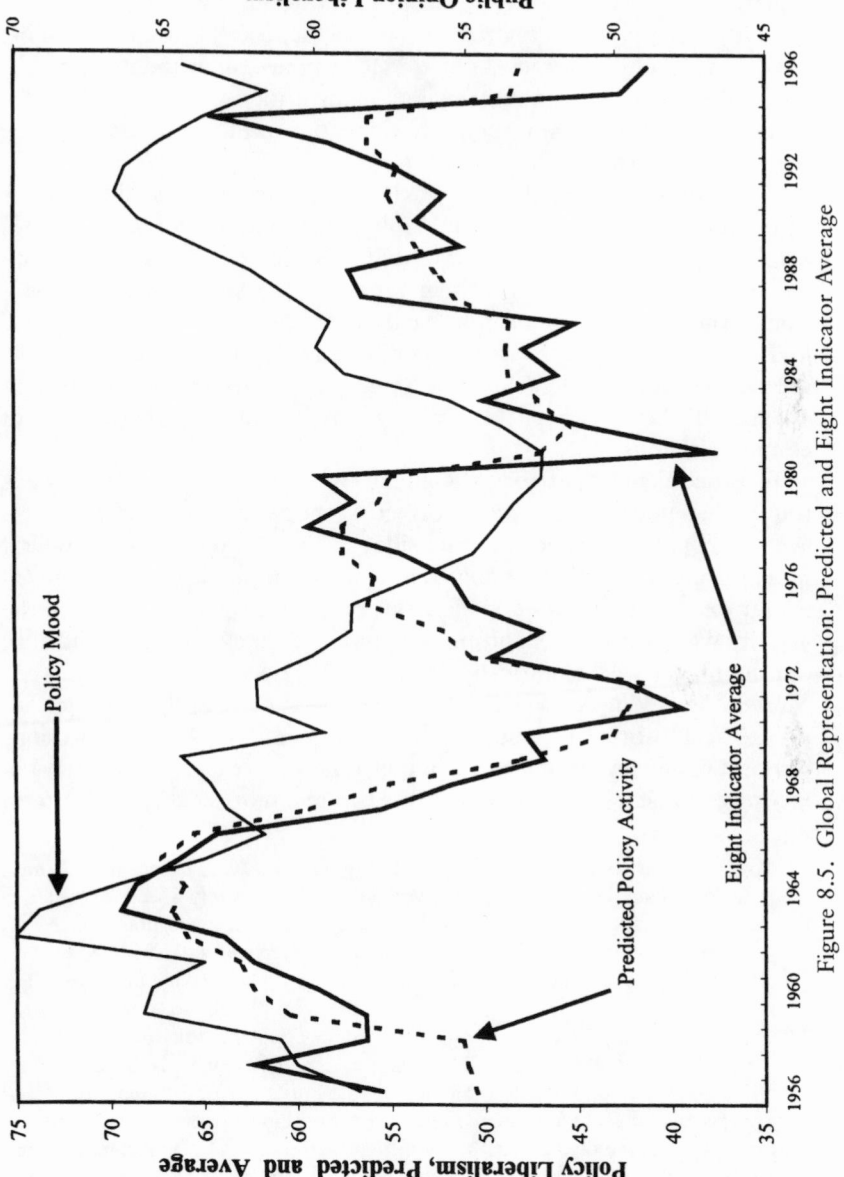

Figure 8.5. Global Representation: Predicted and Eight Indicator Average

resentation. In particular, we want to know about the speed and nature of that response. These matters are, of course, central to understanding the character of democracy. In fact, much of the debate about the checks and balances built into the federal Constitution centers around the ways that governmental response to "passions of the moment" might be tempered.[22]

We concentrate on how quickly American political institutions respond to changes in the public's policy preferences. Our analyses thus far show that *Mood* and *Policy Activity* are closely connected – both directly through rational anticipation and indirectly through composition – and that this connection varies by political institution. And we know the timing of composition – by consulting the periodicity of the relevant electoral cycles. But how rapidly does government respond to changes in *Mood* when those changes represent mere harbingers of coming elections?

To proceed, we construct a Kalman Filter analysis that is analogous (but not identical) to the error-correction model we used in Chapter 4. We model policy (on the left-hand side) as a function of previous policy, previous public opinion, and current changes in public opinion (as well as our exogenous variables).[23] For our purposes, we concentrate on the alacrity with which the institutions respond to changes in preferences. In our setup, we ask, empirically, how quickly do discrepancies between $Mood_{t-1}$ and $Policy\ Activity_{t-1}$ disappear, or, substantively, how quickly do political institutions adjust to the public's signals? Do the institutions respond within a year or two or do they take a more measured approach, ignoring momentary fluctuations to generate a more coherent long-term

22 This recalls a famous interchange between George Washington and Thomas Jefferson. When Jefferson asked over the breakfast table why a second legislative chamber had been created, Washington asked, "Why did you pour coffee into your saucer?" "To cool it," Jefferson answered. "Even so," said Washington, "we pour legislation into the senatorial saucer to cool it." (Quoted in Sundquist 1992, p. 27.)

23 This format is similar to (but not identical to) the popular Error Correction Mechanism (Davidson et al. 1978). We do not assume that our variables are cointegrated (they are not integrated) but merely that *Policy Activity* responds to *Mood*. For specification purposes, we include the relationship between current *Mood* and *Policy Activity*, knowing that the coefficients are not, by themselves, meaningful. Because the contemporary relationship combines a positive representation effect with a negative policy reaction effect (see Chapter 9), the coefficient for current opinion will necessarily be seriously attenuated – and misleading. For this reason, the full estimation models are not shown: Table 8.7 produces only a set of calculated dynamic parameters. Note that for our inferences, the underlying statistical distributions are not normal, so standard $t$-tests will mislead. Standard errors are given to provide a sense of precision.

Table 8.7. *The Dynamics of American Political Institutions*
*(Kalman Filter Estimates)*

| Parameter | Model | | | |
|---|---|---|---|---|
| | President | House | Senate | Supreme Court |
| Error Correction Rate | 0.87 | 0.86 | 0.77 | 0.44 |
| | (0.06) | (0.11) | (0.12) | (0.16) |
| Time for Complete Reaction | | | | |
| (Years) | 3.4 | 3.5 | 3.9 | 6.9 |

*Note*: Standard errors in parentheses.

path? Do the institutions vary in their response, some acting more quickly than others?

Our empirical estimates are shown in Table 8.7. These numbers, the error-correction rates, represent the proportion of the discrepancy between *Mood* and *Policy Activity* that is eliminated by the next year. For the presidency (in column 1), about 87 percent of any gap between the public's demand and the president's *Activity* is "corrected" within a year – implying a fairly dramatic response. Comparing institutions, we see that the House (0.86) and Senate (0.77) evince similarly speedy reactions. This means that the *Policy Activity* of these institutions quickly adjusts to opinion change – with the bulk of the adjustment being almost immediate. Even the Supreme Court, without any direct electoral motive, evinces responsiveness though somewhat more moderate in pace. We estimate that about 44 percent of the discrepancy is "corrected" in a year, a reaction about half that of the electoral institutions.

Another way to characterize these dynamics is to calculate (theoretically) how long an institution will take to absorb completely a change in opinion. We present "settling points," the time frame for 99 percent of the correction, in row 2 of Table 8.7. For the presidency, the House, and the Senate, we see that any change in *Mood* is fully processed within four years – the period of a single presidential administration. And the Court takes a bit longer, nearly seven years, to accomplish the task – clearly a more deliberate speed than the elected branches but perhaps surprisingly quickly nevertheless.

Thus, it is clear that politicians not only respond to opinion but that they do so with considerable urgency. All this makes sense when we remember that politicians have every reason to detect and absorb any dissatisfaction the public expresses. This sensitivity is least, of course, for the Court. But for the presidency and the House, especially, a shift in *Mood* yields an almost immediate shift in *Policy Activity*. Hardly indifferent, these politicians are keen to pick up the faintest signals in their political environment. Like antelope in an open field, they cock their ears and focus their full attention on the slightest sign of danger.

To be sure, these analyses have focused on a political response in terms of *Policy Activity*. When our politicians sense change, they react as quickly as possible. But before concluding too much, we must ask whether the immediacy in response that we see for *Activity* will be evident in the shaping of the overall trends of government policy. The Madisonian constitutional design, with separated institutions and complex interactions, was meant to temper the consequences of policy making rather than political activity. This is the subject of the next chapter.

## SOME REFLECTIONS ON AMERICAN POLITICS

The past four decades of U.S. history show that politicians translate changes in public opinion into policy change. Further, the evidence suggests that this translation varies by institution, both in the mechanisms that produce the link and in the nature of the dynamics.

Most important, dynamic representation – the thesis that government policy making responds over time to movements in public opinion – finds strong support. Our work indicates that when the public asks for a more activist or a more conservative government, politicians oblige. The early peak of public opinion liberalism during the early 1960s produced liberal policy; the turn away from activism and the steady move toward conservatism was similarly reflected in national policy; and the recent 1980s upsurge of public demand for action was also effective (with the exception of the Court). To be sure, other things matter, too. We have modeled a late 1960s shift rightward in policy – beyond that driven by public opinion – as a function of the Vietnam War's dominance over domestic political agendas. In addition, we produced the shift leftward during the years of the Carter presidency – a shift contrary to the prevailing movement in public opinion – as a coincidence of compositional factors.

While we are confident that the basic result holds, we know that we do not yet fully understand movement in public policy. Nevertheless, the main story is that large-scale shifts in public opinion yield corresponding large-scale shifts in government action.

The link between opinion and policy is undoubtedly more complicated. While concentrating on policy response to opinion, we have had little to say of the reverse, that opinion is to be understood as a reaction to policy. That is a matter to be taken up in the next chapter.

Beyond the basic result, we can say that American national institutions vary in the mechanisms that produce responsiveness. It is the Senate and not the House of Representatives that most clearly mimics the eighteenth-century clockwork meant to produce electoral accountability. When comparing the effectiveness of turnover and rational anticipation, we find that for the Senate (and also for the presidency) the most important channel for governmental representation is electoral replacement. Equally responsive, however, is the House of Representatives. Its members employ rational anticipation to produce a similarly effective public-policy response – without the overt evidence of personnel change. The Supreme Court appears to reflect public opinion far more than constitutionally expected, but, in comparison, it is the institution that responds least.

Finally, the dynamics prove interesting. Each of the electoral institutions translates public opinion immediately into *Policy Activity*. That is to say, when politicians sense a shift in public preferences, they act directly and effectively to shift the direction of public policy. We find no evidence of delay or hesitation. The Court, not surprisingly, moves at a more deliberate speed. Understanding politics well, the constitutional framers were correct in expecting short-term politics to be a fundamental part of dynamic representation.

The U.S. government, as it has evolved over the years, produces a complex response to public demands. The original constitutional design mixed different political calculations into different institutions so that no personal ambition, no political faction, no single political interest, and no transient passion could dominate. We now see the founders' expectations about complexity manifest in contemporary policy making. Constitutional mechanisms harness politicians' strategies to the public's demands. In the end, the government combines both short- and long-term considerations through both rational anticipation and compositional change to produce a strong and resilient link between public and policy.

## APPENDIX: MODELING REPRESENTATION: FROM THE INDIVIDUAL LEGISLATOR TO THE AGGREGATE

We start with the postulate that the politician's decision problem is to obtain satisfaction from pursuing his or her preferred policy while at the same time ensuring reelection by acting expediently. Denote the utility of the preferred policy as $U(P)$ and the utility derived from the probability of reelection as $U(\Phi)$. The politician derives utility from winning, normalized to equal one times the probability of winning, $\Phi$.

### Modeling a Static Single Choice

In the mode of formal modeling, let us assume that the expedient position represents the median voter on the left-right dimension. The

321

# Policy

median voter's attraction to the politician is a probabilistic function of the proximity of politician and voter.[24] Our politician places relative weights on the values of reelection and policy maximization. The problem to solve is, in the language of economics, maximizing $U$, the "objective function," with its competing goals of reelection and policy satisfaction:

$$U = U(\Phi) + U(P)$$

Subscripts for the individual ($i$th) politician are omitted for clarity. The solution lies in picking a position, $X$, from the range of options available, for which $U$ is a maximum.

Start with $U(\Phi)$, the utility derived from the probability of reelection. Generically, the politician makes the following assumption about the vote plurality ($V$) at the next election:

$$V = \lambda - \gamma(M - X)^2 + e \qquad (8.1)$$

where $V$ is the politician's vote margin as the percentage of the major-party vote minus 50 percent, $\lambda$ is the expected vote plurality given the expected positions of the median voter and the likely opponent, $\gamma$ is the parameter for the voter's responsiveness to ideological proximity, $M$ is the median voter's preferred position, $X$ is the politician's actual record (on a left-right scale), and $e$ is a random disturbance term with standard deviation $\sigma$.[25] The politician is punished, that is, as a quadratic loss of choosing $X$ that deviates from $M$. The politician cannot know $e$ (or therefore $V$) in advance, but has an expectation for $V$:

$$\hat{V} = \lambda - \gamma(M - X)^2$$

where $\hat{V}$ is the expected vote plurality (as a percentage point lead) as a function of choice of $X$.

The part of Equation 8.1 that is outside the politician's control is $\lambda + e$. The $\lambda$ term represents expectations of known forces such as constituency partisanship and the impact of the next opponent. The stochastic term $e$ represents the politician's uncertainty. The expected probability of winning the next election is the cumulative normal density at $\hat{V}/\sigma$, which we label $\Phi\hat{V}$. Meanwhile, the politician's policy preferences, $U(P)$, also matter:

24 Our candidate does not maximize the expected vote but rather the probability of winning. Given the uncertainty in the model, maximizing the vote and maximizing winning are not the same thing. Conceptually the problem of maximizing the probability of winning is greatly simplified if we summarize the electorate by one pivotal voter (at the median) as opposed to a distribution of voters.

25 The electorate's expected attraction to the opponent's position is fixed as part of $\lambda$.

322

$$U(P) = \omega(S - X)^2$$

where $S$ is the politician's preferred position and $\omega$ is the weight the politician places on ideological consumption relative to reelection. Choosing $X$ that deviates from the politician's ideal point, $S$, thus also produces a quadratic loss. Thus we have the two utilities and the problem is now to maximize their sum:

$$\begin{aligned} U &= U(\Phi) + U(P) \\ &= \Phi\hat{V} + \omega(S - X)^2 \end{aligned} \qquad (8.2)$$

Equation 8.2 is maximized by taking the first derivative with respect to $X$, setting it to zero (where the function reaches its maximum), and solving for $X$.

$$\begin{aligned} dU/dx &= -2\gamma(X - M)(2\pi)^{-\frac{1}{2}}\exp\left\{-\frac{1}{2}\left(\hat{V}/\sigma\right)^2\right\} - 2\omega(X - S) \\ &= -2\gamma(X - M)(2\pi)^{-\frac{1}{2}}\exp\left\{-\frac{1}{2}\left(\frac{\lambda - \gamma X}{\sigma}\right)^2\right\} - 2\omega(X - S) \end{aligned}$$

where $(2\pi)^{-\frac{1}{2}}\exp\left\{-\frac{1}{2}\left(\hat{V}/\sigma\right)^2\right\}$ is the normal density at $\hat{V}/\sigma$. The right-hand quantity will be zero when:

$$X = \frac{(2\pi)^{-\frac{1}{2}}\exp\left\{-\frac{1}{2}\left(\hat{V}/\sigma\right)^2\right\}\gamma M + \omega S}{(2\pi)^{-\frac{1}{2}}\exp\left\{-\frac{1}{2}\left(\hat{V}/\sigma\right)^2\right\} + \omega} \qquad (8.3)$$

Policy behavior thus is a weighted average of constituency and personal preferences. The weight the politician gives to constituency preferences over the politician's own is governed by the constituency's responsiveness to policy ($\gamma$) and the politician's own weight to policy ($\omega$), where the effect of $\gamma$ is magnified by the constituency's perceived marginality, the normal density at $\hat{V}/\sigma$.

### Aggregate Dynamics

The case we care about here is the aggregate, not one individual decision on one issue, $X$, but the sum total of decisions $\overline{X}$. This aggregate result is now a function of the combined constituencies of all politicians, which have an aggregate median voter $\overline{M}$. What changes in the dynamic case is that $\overline{M}$ becomes $\overline{M}_t$, the position of median voters *in motion* as

# Policy

*Policy Mood* shifts over time. We assume that $M$ is uncorrelated with parameters $\gamma$ and $\omega$, and $S$ is uncorrelated with the normal density at $\hat{V}/\sigma$ and $\omega$ (essentially that constituency responsiveness, the expected closeness of the vote, and the politician's concern about policy are all uncorrelated with the preferences of the median voter and the politician). If we now subscript $\overline{M}$ as $\overline{M}_t$, allowing it to change over time, then equally the solution $\overline{X}$ to the utility maximization must also change as a function of $\overline{M}_t$, becoming $\overline{X}_t$ in 8.4:

$$\overline{X}_t \cong \left( \frac{(2\pi)^{-\frac{1}{2}} \exp\left\{-\frac{1}{2}\left(\hat{V}/\sigma\right)^2\right\}_t \gamma M_t + \omega S_t}{(2\pi)^{-\frac{1}{2}} \exp\left\{-\frac{1}{2}\left(\hat{V}/\sigma\right)^2\right\}_t + \omega} \right) \tag{8.4}$$

$$\cong \alpha_1 \overline{M}_t + \alpha_2 \overline{S}_t$$

where $\alpha_1$ is the mean of

$$\left[ (2\pi)^{-\frac{1}{2}} \exp\left\{-\frac{1}{2}\left(\hat{V}/\sigma\right)^2\right\}_t \gamma \right] \Big/ \left[ (2\pi)^{-\frac{1}{2}} \exp\left\{-\frac{1}{2}\left(\hat{V}/\sigma\right)^2\right\}_t + \omega \right]$$

and $\alpha_2$ is the mean of

$$\omega \Big/ \left( (2\pi)^{-\frac{1}{2}} \exp\left\{-\frac{1}{2}\left(\hat{V}/\sigma\right)^2\right\} + \omega \right)$$

We thus arrive at an important point. $\overline{X}_t$, the aggregate of individual positions at $t$, is *Policy Activity*. $\overline{M}_t$, the aggregate central tendency across constituencies at $t$, is *Mood*. *We know, therefore, that Policy Activity is a function of Mood.*

We have a second point. The mean position of the elected politicians is also a function of unobserved $\overline{S}_t$. We know that Democratic and Republican politicians' preferences are sharply divided. *Thus the party division in the House or Senate becomes a proxy for member preferences.*

# 9

A *Governing System: Laws and Public Opinion*

Dynamic representation implies a system in which the public's political demands produce a quick and palpable response in the institutions of national government. By the usual standards of representative democracy, this is evidence for good democratic government. In this chapter, we wish to push further by examining the governing system more closely – in a theoretically ambitious way. We extend the argument to a more rigorous measure of fundamental policy change (rather than *Policy Activity*) and thus further strengthen the dynamic representation story. Equally important, we close the loop by exploring the way that the public adjusts its political demands according to the changing nature of governmental policy. In a real sense, we outline the character of a governing system in which the public and the politicians act and react to each other to produce an evolving public policy that suits both the public's tastes and its view of real-world circumstances.

The previous chapter depicted dynamic representation in terms of observable political actions. By taking positions, casting roll calls, filing briefs, and engaging in other visible behavior, national political leaders respond promptly to public opinion. It should be clear, however, that such actions are not the same as government policy. At best, the kinds of actions we have examined correspond approximately to the sum of actual policies that affect people's lives. At worst, these actions could be but a political sideshow of opportunistic posturing, quite independent of real policy making. We must move from action to policy. Action is relevant to policy change – but it is not quite policy.

To measure the content of actual policy changes, it is necessary to observe the laws in the form that passes both houses of congress and survives the scrutiny of a veto-wielding president. In addition, we want matters of consequence, changes that have impact over the years. In this chapter, we measure the liberal versus conservative content of federal policy directly – and then estimate its responsiveness to national public opinion.

Next, having established that changes in public opinion produce changes in policy, we ask if the reverse is also true, if the public's preferences are a dynamic result of earlier changes in policy. This will lead us to posit a dynamic system between opinion and policy, where changes to either opinion or policy feed back to the other at later times. We estimate a model of such a system, which we employ to simulate long-run consequences of moving either opinion or policy for system dynamics. In the end, we shall see self-government rather than mere representation.

## THE GOVERNING SYSTEM AS A THERMOSTAT

Imagine a cast of characters, say, a departmental faculty, sharing an old office building. Given the heating system, they must agree on an overall temperature for the entire building. Each member has a different preference for room temperature, with tough-minded conservatives preferring cold in the winter to encourage self-reliance and soft-skinned liberals wanting heat so that people may doff their sweaters and share equally in a communally generated warmth. Together, they choose the appropriate room temperature (by voting for a building engineer to handle these matters). If the temperature rises above the agreed-upon norm, the real conservatives will continue to say "too hot" and the truly soft-skinned liberals will continue to say "too cold." But the middle types will switch from "about right" to "too hot" and the engineer will properly turn the furnace down. Similarly, should the temperature drop, the extremists will continue to complain in their usual manner, but now the centrists will say "too cold."

Two mechanisms must be in place for this governing system to work. First, the engineer must want to please the collective judgment – to shift the furnace settings in reaction to the messages from the building residents. And second, the residents must pay attention to the current temperature and (at least as a collectivity) give negative feedback so that the engineer can readjust the furnace to avoid overshooting. The first system, in which the dynamic relationship between people's demands and the engineer's furnace control, seems well established in the previous chapter in the form of dynamic representation. It is the second system, the one that relies on people monitoring the environment and sending back the appropriate commands to the engineer, that will serve as the focus of this chapter.

As a secondary question, we ask whether the building residents merely monitor the building's internal temperature or whether they also watch the furnace settings. It makes sense for building residents to watch the temperature. But they need not delay their response to the engineer's activities until the change in temperature is felt. Rather they can immediately voice their response to the anticipated temperature change at the time when the engineer adjusts the furnace.

In addition to the current furnace settings, the residents of our mythical building must respond to the shocks of changing circumstance. In the short term, the demand for heat will be tempered by the warmth or the chill of the current outside temperature. And over the long term, tastes can change. Over time, the building may get more conservatives or more liberals and produce a different collective choice about what is the "proper" temperature. Alternatively, in the long run, styles of clothing may change so that people are less eager to wear jackets or hats indoors. We would observe a secular trend toward liberalism when, in fact, the basic character traits and philosophical arguments about the settings would remain the same. In politics, we ask whether preferences for public policy have changed over the years and how the political system has responded to these long-run developments.

Our underlying model of the governing process is similar to the model proposed by Christopher Wlezien (1995, 1996), with more distant roots found in the systems models of Easton (1965) and Deutsch (1963). The Wlezien model posits public opinion to be a thermostat for government actions. The idea is that when government policy is too liberal for public tastes, public opinion demands more conservative policies. Similarly, when policy is too conservative, opinion asks for more policy liberalism. Government decisions then respond to this popular demand for ideological adjustment. The result is a reduction in electoral pressure and a restoration of equilibrium between public preferences and government policy.

Thus, we expect not only that public officials read liberal or conservative signals from the cacophony of polls and other indicators of the public mood, but also that the public mood responds to the character of public policy. In this way, the polity has a chance to govern itself in a reasonable fashion. Should the public not adjust its demands in accord with actual policy, the elaborate governing mechanism embodied in dynamic representation will serve little useful purpose. It is as though the best engineers in the world devised an elaborate steering mechanism for an automobile – only to find an inattentive driver veer off the side of the road.

Wlezien tests his model using budgetary data. The greater the public demand is for domestic (or defense) spending, the greater is the increase. Similarly, the more the spending, the less the demand is for more. As measures of public opinion, Wlezien employed GSS survey items concerning more or less spending on specific government services. These items, while not identical to our *Mood* indicator, are in fact major components of our *Mood* index.

In this chapter, we investigate the role of our *Mood* indicator as a thermostat for federal policy. If officials are responsive, then when *Mood* becomes liberal, policy should *shift* in a liberal direction. Similarly, the more liberal the run of policy making, the more *Mood* should shift in a conservative direction.

## IMPORTANT LAWS AS PUBLIC POLICY

Thus, we want a measure of governmental policy that encapsulates the major shifts in the way that the government manages the political economy. This measure should emphasize substance over symbolism – in the sense that we want an indicator of the sorts of programs in place that affect people's lives rather than the sorts of activity comprised mainly of hot air and smoke. In addition, we want a measure that emphasizes longish-term changes because the public is likely to discount (or at least should discount) the furor of politics of the moment. In sum, we want a measure of what acute observers would mark as major shifts in American governmental policy over the years.

One possible policy measure is the index of annual liberal-conservative *Policy Activity*, which formed the basis for our analysis in Chapter 8. Our *global* measure of *Policy Activity* serves this purpose, measuring as it does the *Policy Activity* by congress and the president for the given year. As we saw in Chapter 8, the activity that makes up this index is highly responsive to the public's liberal-conservative *Mood* and responds quickly, with most of the response occurring within one or two years of the *Mood* shift.

But our measure of *Policy Activity* does not necessarily reflect major policy innovations. To be sure, it includes (in one form or another) important matters as well as the trivial. However, we understand the bulk of policy activity to comprise relatively minor matters, for example, failed policy attempts or only partial successes, and symbolic plays before the mass audience. Much political activity goes into the production, and the reformulation, of novel policy ideas well before any actual change is effected. In addition, the most visible political fireworks revolve around the most controversial of issues. Not surprisingly, the press concentrates its attention on the battleground as defined by issues that may be won or lost. But these political battles typically do not constitute major policy programs but instead represent matters at the cutting edge of the current definition of conflict.[1] Rather than measure policy by inferring it from political activity, we propose to measure policy more directly.[2]

Policy at any one moment is the sum of laws in force at that time. This sum of laws represents an accumulation over many years. With the important exception of budgetary appropriations, which last but one year, congressional legislation is cumulative. That is, congressional policy represents the sum of past and current legislation. The content of early legislation persists unless explicitly revised or legislated (or, alternatively, "sunsetted") out of existence.

In theory, we can sum the ideological content of congressional legislation. For any bill that passes congress without a successful presidential veto, we could score its degree of ideological impact (liberal vs. conservative) and add this impact to that of previous legislation. For any year or congressional session, we could provide a summary score of the net ideological movement for the time period. We could then add this score to the cumulated score from prior years, for an overall cumulative score. With this information, we could then examine the dynamic relationship between opinion, reflected in *Mood*, and policy.

A complete endeavor of this sort is beyond the scope of our investigation here. How could we discern the ideological content of every law? Instead of searching or even randomly sampling all legislation, we begin with an already compiled list of laws deemed to be of major importance by observers at the time. Dealing with a modest number of highly visible laws, it becomes possible to code the ideological content of legislation as liberal, conservative, or neutral in ideological direction.

As our data base, we use the list of important legislation supplied by David Mayhew (1991) and updated through 1996 in an independent effort by Jay Greene. Mayhew, in *Divided We Govern: Party Control, Lawmaking, and Investigations, 1946–1990* (1991), reminds us that public policy is often determined in particularly crucial public laws.

---

1 The *Congressional Quarterly's Key Votes*, for example, are picked in large part because they are controversial. Often, especially on major legislation, the *politically interesting* vote will take place on an ambitious amendment when the final passage will seem a foregone conclusion. Alternatively, the ADA and ACU often pick strenuous tests of ideological commitment when they select their roll calls. While useful as a measure of political strength or illustrative of coalition strategy, these amendments and ideological tests typically do not involve the heart of the major policy change.

2 To use our thermostat analogy, *Policy Activity* represents the public debate among the building engineer and his staff as they prepare their response to public demands. The building residents would not respond with demands for less or more heat unless and until the change in settings actually occurs.

## Policy

These are occasions where both houses of congress and the president concur on major changes of direction in the activities of the federal government. In Chapter 8, we used as statistical fodder thousands of roll-call votes on congressional legislation. Here we take a last look at about 200 public laws identified as having had particularly crucial consquences. We ask whether policy as measured by these laws follows the same course as the more routine matters we have examined to this point.

For his list of important laws, Mayhew conducted two "sweeps." In sweep 1, he identified legislation that was considered important by observers at the time. In sweep 2, he identified legislation that passed relatively unnoticed but was later considered to be important (for example, the Delaney Amendment). Mayhew counted some legislative acts as exceptionally important (e.g., passage of Medicare). For our analysis, we coded the content of Mayhew's laws from 1953 through 1990, the last year studied by Mayhew. For 1991–1996, we coded from an updated list of important laws constructed by Jay Greene, following Mayhew's protocols.[3]

To code liberal or conservative direction, we first eliminated all legislation dealing with foreign or defense policy. We also eliminated legislation with an impact more local than national (e.g., Alaska statehood) and all agricultural bills. Since we were interested in measuring ideological movement as seen by the public, we excluded laws on Mayhew's list that were deemed important upon later analysis (sweep 2) but not seen as important at the time (sweep 1).

From the remainder, we coded the content based on our judgment whether the law was seen by contemporary observers as moving policy in a conservative or a liberal direction. Thus, we eliminated many laws where the ideological direction was ambiguous at the time, or (as with many tax bills) the mix was an ideologically ambiguous trade-off. The residue of this culling is a measure of the net ideological change in policy for the year or biennium. Obviously, our judgment is subjective, with some close calls whether to include or exclude a particular law. However, our belief is that the analysis we report does not depend in any crucial way on minor coding decisions. Readers who disagree with our measure may find reason to invent their own.

Liberal legislation is counted +1, and major conservative legislation is counted −1. Exceptionally important legislation (by Mayhew's judgment) is double-counted as +2 or −2.[4] Our measure of *policy innovation* then

3 Following Mayhew's procedure for his later year of analysis, Greene's update relies on the year-end reviews of congressional accomplishments in the *New York Times, Washington Post,* and *Los Angeles Times.*

4 Using our judgment for the post-1990 observations, we also double-counted the 1993 budget bill and 1996 welfare reform bill.

is the sum of liberal minus conservative legislation for the year or for the congress. Our measure of current *Policy* is the cumulation of policy innovations, starting with our base year of 1953 through the current year.

The laws forming our *Laws* index are shown in the appendix to this chapter. This table contains 124 items. Reflecting the evolution of legislation, far more important new laws are coded as liberal than as conservative. Thus, variation in policy innovation represents mainly the pace of new liberal legislation. On an annual basis, the largest net score is +15 for 1965, at the height of the Great Society frenzy. The lowest is a seemingly reactionary −4 for 1981 at the start of the Reagan revolution.

For congressional output, the natural unit is not the year but the biennium. The biennia, of course, correspond to particular congresses elected every two years. Switching to the biennium as the unit of analysis truncates the number of cases by half, but helps to put law-making dynamics into statistical focus. This switch also allows us to exploit the sketchy *Mood* data from the early 1950s, which we have hesitated to do in our annual analyses. Smoothed over biennial readings, *Mood* is a more reliable indicator.

Figure 9.1 traces the time series of our *Laws* index – our policy innovations. For comparison, it shows the index of *Policy Activity* and *Mood* measured on a biennial basis.[5] At the eyeball level of analysis, *Laws* moves in rough correspondence to lagged changes in *Mood*. In general, *Laws* tracks Chapter 8's measure of *Policy Activity* except during the Nixon-Ford years – when *Laws* suggests a liberalism not found in the activity measure.

Figure 9.2 cumulates the *Laws* index scores to produce a measure of governmental policy – arbitrarily starting the series at 0 before the count begins for 1953–1954. The count for this first biennium of the Eisenhower administration (and a Republican congress) was a net score of −1. Since then, net policy innovation has been positive for almost every biennium. Thus, the cumulative liberalism of federal policy grows over time. The state of government policy in the 1990s represents an accumulation of many liberal major laws and very few conservative major laws that passed since the 1950s. Viewed this way, it is clear that the battles between liberals and conservatives are not over which types of legislation to pass. Rather, the key battles are over the pace of liberal

---

5 On a biennial basis, the *Laws* index and the index of *Policy Activity* correlate at 0.40. Laws correlate with lagged *Policy Activity* at 0.41. $Laws_t$ correlates more strongly with *Policy Activity* as cumulated from time $t$ backwards over a series of biennia.

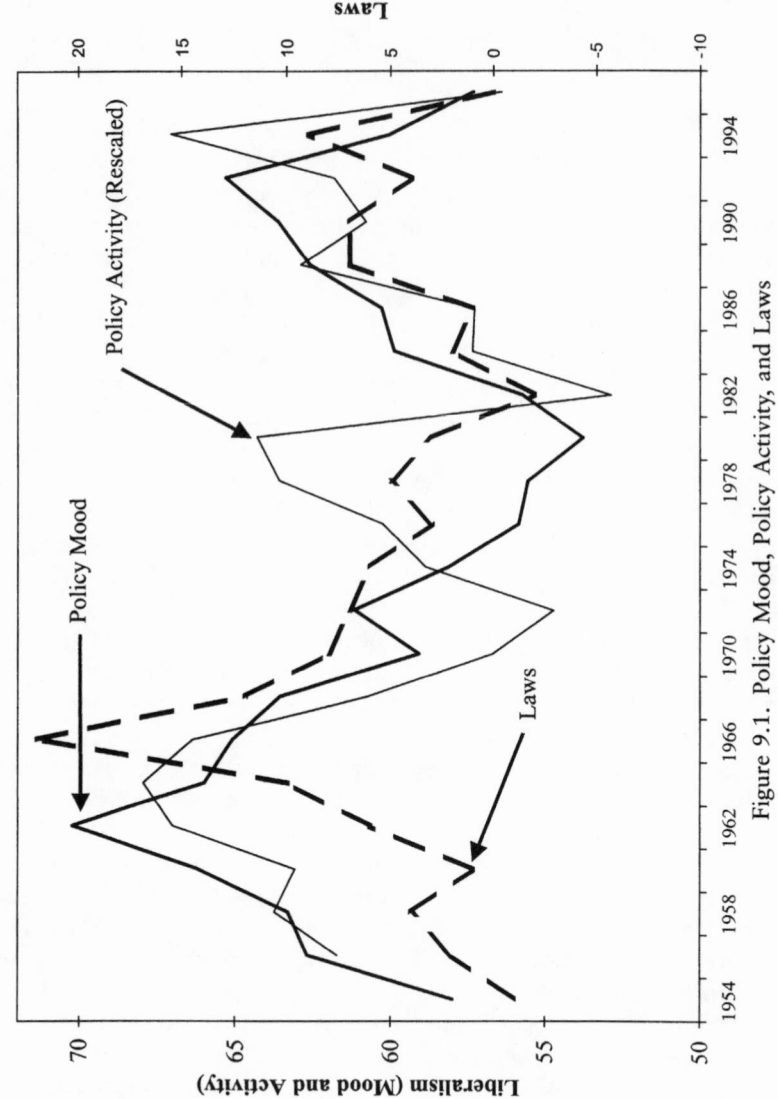

Figure 9.1. Policy Mood, Policy Activity, and Laws

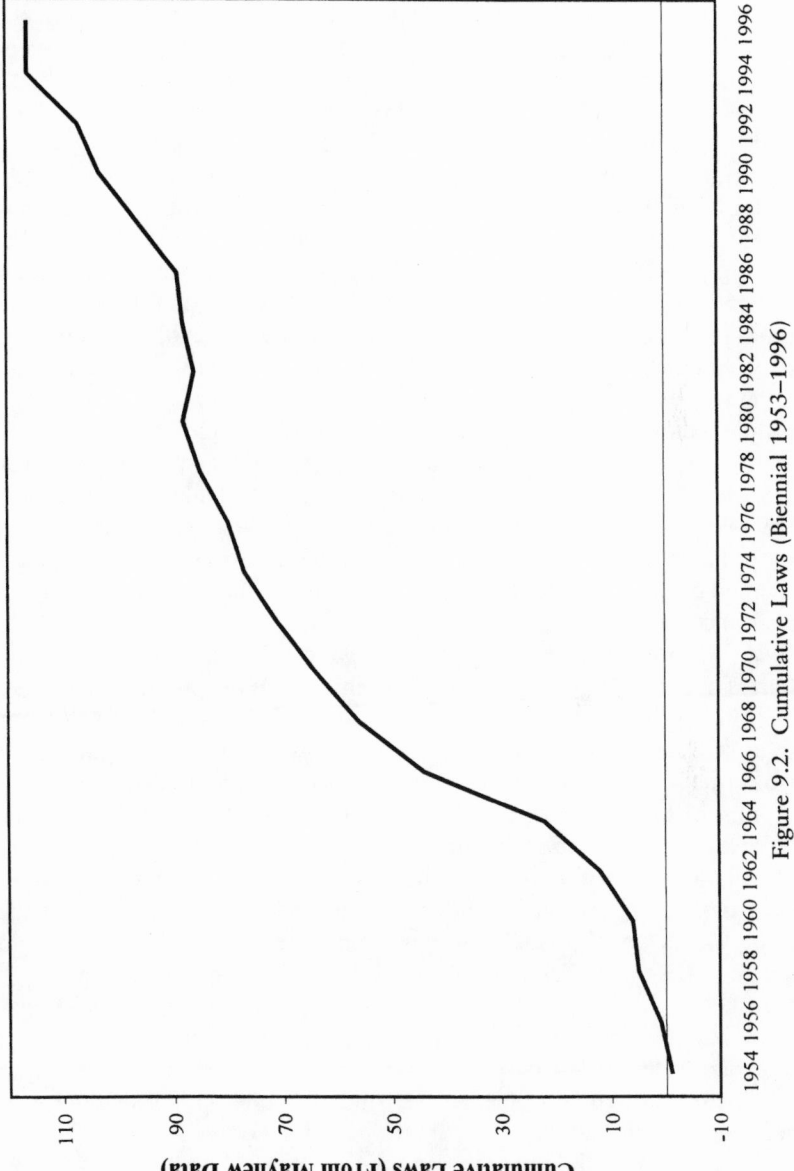

Figure 9.2. Cumulative Laws (Biennial 1953–1996)

333

legislation, with very few outright reversals of liberal policies from the past. The early Reagan years provide the one period where the exception proves the rule.

This general expansion of the governmental role is familiar to all and worth keeping prominently in mind. While the day-to-day and year-to-year politics reflect arguments about the scope of governmental policy, it is absolutely clear that the complexity of government (in institutions and regulations) has grown steadily over the past half-century. Of course, this may be perfectly understandable given the increasing complexity of late twentieth-century America: A constant public philosophy would produce increasing government simply because the evolving nature of societal conditions demand it. Many of the new laws tweak current programs and regulatory schemes to reflect changing circumstances in people's daily lives – when the government required the granting of family leave for medical emergencies, it reacted to the move toward two-earner households and the changing character of family life. Other new laws emanate from changing sensitivities about what constitutes subject for policy. When the government decided to regulate access for the handicapped or fund toxic waste cleanups or mandate the portability of health insurance, the role of government expanded.

By our measurement, government policy has become increasingly liberal over the years. But this need not imply that the public has changed its public philosophy much at all. A straightforward view would suggest that the only way this increase in government could occur would be if it reflected an increasingly liberal public. But instead, think of this history as the reflection of a (more or less) constant public philosophy applied to changing conditions. The result would be a more liberal government policy (in the sense that government engages in activities that it would not have considered in the 1940s), but at the same time a government policy that represented a stable political and ideological system. For example, consider the steering mechanism of an automobile. The driver may steer left or right of center and make constant corrections to keep going straight down the road. However, if the road itself curves to the left, a steady-state correction will produce a general leftward movement over time. The alternative, of course, is crashing into the weeds.

Thus, a more telling way to view the state of policy is as an accumulation *relative* to the long-term trend. Between 1953–1954 and 1995–1996, policy accumulated as an average (net) 5.85 new liberal laws per biennium. Figure 9.3 documents federal policy through time by this standard. The scale arbitrarily begins at zero for 1951–1952. It then adds for each biennium the net policy innovation while subtracting out the trend – that is, the 5.85 average innovation. On this time-adjusted scale,

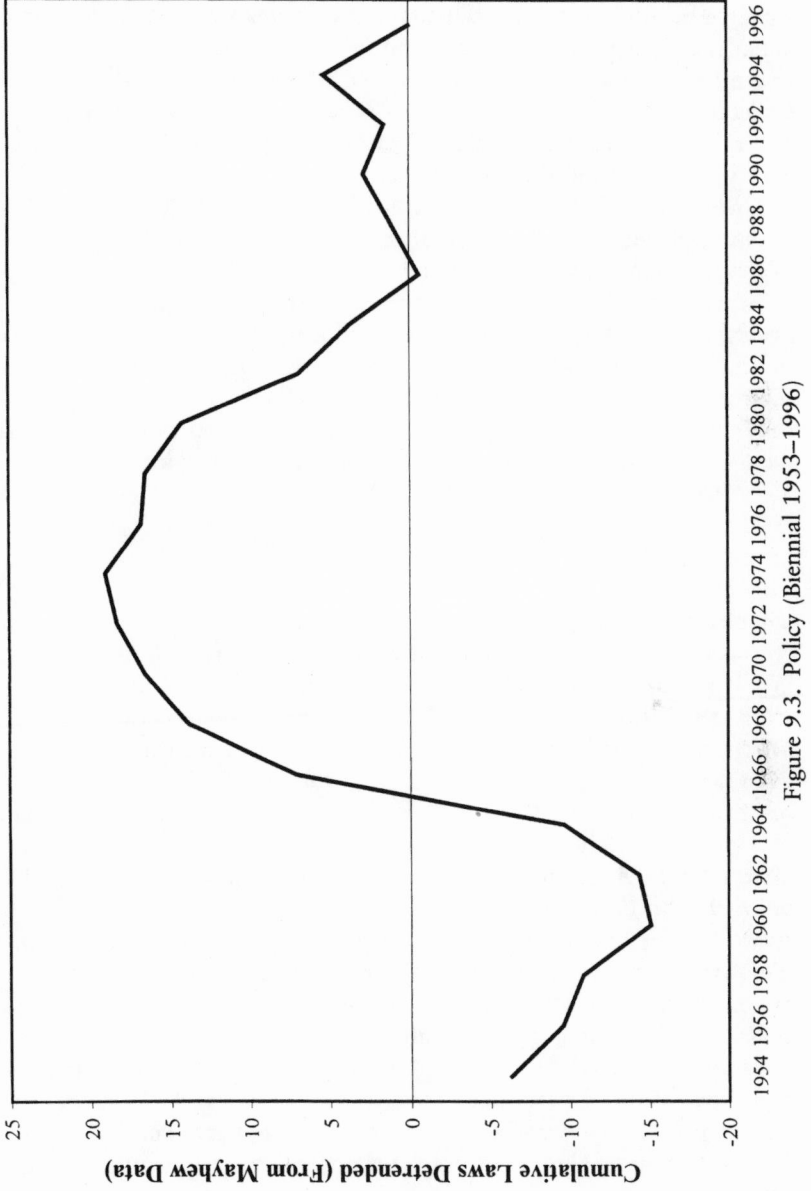

Figure 9.3. Policy (Biennial 1953–1996)

# Policy

*Policy* liberalism increases whenever the average of 5.85 is exceeded.[6] What makes Figure 9.3 so powerful is that it allows us to see policy at any time in comparison to the long-term liberal trend that is driven by societal conditions. Relative to this trend, the figure shows a surge of liberalism during the 1960s, a decline in the 1970s, and a slight growth beginning in the late 1980s.

This detrended measure of what we shall call *Policy* has decidedly different implications for representation and governance than do *Laws* and *Policy Activity*. The latter two reflect current movement, while the former reflects the current state. In our thermostat metaphor, *Laws* and *Policy Activity* represent the adjustments to the furnace setting while *Policy* represents the setting itself. This setting is the ultimate focus of thermostatic demands. A rational public will react to the temperature that can be expected once current changes in the setting are fully implemented rather than wait until the temperature change kicks in.

## THE EFFECT OF OPINION ON POLICY

The analysis of the dynamic representation link is now reasonably straightforward – here accomplished using ordinary least squares regression (OLS). We examine how opinion affects *Policy Activity* (as in Chapter 8) as well as *Laws* and *Policy*. Our units are congresses, 1953–1954 through 1995–1996. Our key independent variable is *Policy Mood*, measured by biennium, lagged one biennium earlier.

Table 9.1 shows the initial results. In the first column, we repeat the scheme of Chapter 8, this time with biennia and with a single measure of "global" *Policy Activity*. As before, *Policy Mood* (lagged) clearly affects *Policy Activity* – for every point shift in opinion, we get a 1.19 point shift in *Policy Activity*, controlling, of course, for previous *Policy Activity*. This much we have seen already. The second column mimics the same analysis, this time substituting *Laws* for *Policy Activity*. Here, we see that *Mood* drives *Laws*. The final analysis shifts to our *Policy* measure (that is, cumulated *Laws* detrended). Here, again, it appears that the product of the political process, *Policy*, reflects the ebb and flow of *Mood* over time. Thus, we get the dynamic representation result for *Policy Activity*, actual *Laws*, and cumulative *Policy*. The dominant inference of Chapter 8 holds for different measures of government action.

---

6 We detrend the *Cumulative Policy* index by first scoring *Laws* as a deviation from the mean of the observed series and then cumulating. The detrended series rises slightly over time because *Laws* scores are higher late than early in the series.

Table 9.1. *Policy as a Function of Mood*

| | Dependent Variable | | |
|---|---|---|---|
| | (1)<br>Policy Activity$_t$ | (2)<br>$\Delta$Policy$_t$ (Laws$_t$) | (3)<br>Policy$_t$ |
| Policy Mood$_{t-1}$ | 1.19[a]<br>(2.54) | 0.62[a]<br>(2.99) | 0.93[a]<br>(3.86) |
| Policy Activity$_{t-1}$ | 0.14<br>(0.61) | | |
| Laws$_{t-1}$ | | 0.30<br>(1.69) | |
| Policy$_{t-1}$ | | | 1.11[a]<br>(11.45) |
| Constant | −26.63<br>(−1.04) | −34.23[a]<br>(−2.78) | −56.74[a]<br>(−3.83) |
| Number of Cases | 20 | 22 | 22 |
| Adjusted $R^2$ | 0.31 | 0.46 | 0.87 |
| RMSE | 7.74 | 3.83 | 3.98 |

*Note:* Biennial data, 1953–1996. Each column is a separate regression, with the dependent variable labeled at the top of the column. Policy is cumulative laws, detrended. *t* values in parentheses.
[a] $p < 0.05$.

A close look at Table 9.1 also shows that biennial scores on the *Laws* index are essentially unaffected by either lagged *Laws* or lagged cumulative *Policy*. The latter we can see by converting the dependent variable in the equation of column 3 from *Policy$_t$* to *Laws$_t$*, which is the same as the first difference *Policy$_t$* − *Policy$_{t-1}$*. We obtain

$$Laws_t = -56.74 + 0.11 Laws_{t-1} + 0.93\ Mood_{t-1} \qquad (9.1)$$

The *Laws$_{t-1}$* coefficient near zero (and statistically insignificant) suggests an even more streamlined equation:

$$Laws_t = -41.89 + 0.77 Mood_{t-1} \qquad (9.2)$$

We will treat Equation 9.2 as our basic equation translating *Mood* into *Laws*. We can elaborate on the *Policy* model, as we did in Chapter 8, to see if the route from *Mood* to *Policy* runs through replacement or rational anticipation. First, we need to show that party control over the governing institutions affects *Policy*. For this demonstration, we simply regress change in *Policy* (the *Laws* score of the biennium) on lagged *Policy* plus dummies for Democratic control of each of the House, Senate, and presidency. Table 9.2, column 1, shows the expected result. Control of any of the institutions seems to yield from three to

## Policy

Table 9.2. *Policy as a Function of Mood and Party Control*

|  | Dependent Variable = $\Delta$Policy$_t$ (Laws) | | | |
|---|---|---|---|---|
|  | (1) | (2) | (3) | (4) |
| Democratic House$_t$ | 2.97 | | | |
|  | (0.77) | | | |
| Democratic Senate$_t$ | 4.73 | | | |
|  | (1.75) | | | |
| Democratic President$_t$ | 4.27[a] | | | |
|  | (2.23) | | | |
| Democratic Party Control$_t$ | | 4.19[a] | 2.72[a] | 2.28[a] |
|  | | (4.14) | (2.32) | (2.10) |
| Policy Mood$_{t-1}$ | | | 0.47[a] | |
|  | | | (2.10) | |
| Mean Policy Mood$_{(t-1,t-2)}$ | | | | 0.62[a] |
|  | | | | (2.92) |
| Constant | −2.64 | −3.31 | −28.62[a] | −36.78[a] |
|  | (−0.86) | (−1.48) | (−2.34) | (−3.17) |
| Number of Cases | 22 | 22 | 22 | 22 |
| Adjusted $R^2$ | .380 | .434 | .516 | .590 |
| RMSE | 4.12 | 3.92 | 3.62 | 3.40 |

Note: Biennial data, 1953–1996. Each column is a separate regression, with the dependent variable labeled at the top of the column. Policy is cumulative laws, detrended. Change ($\Delta$) in Policy is simply Laws. Democratic Party Control is the number of the three institutions controlled by Democrats. Mean Policy Mood$_{(t-1,t-2)}$ is the mean Mood of the previous two biennia. $t$ values in parentheses.
[a] $p < 0.05$.

four additional liberal laws per biennium. The estimates for the individual institutions, however, are not sufficiently precise to allow us to say any one institution is more important than another, or, for that matter, that any single institution is important at all. However, a joint statistical test on party control ($p < 0.02$) shows that, as a set, they *are* important.

Because we cannot reliably estimate the impact of the institutions separately, and because proposals need the support of all three to become law, we combine them into a single index of *Party Control*. The index simply sums the number of the institutions that are controlled by the Democratic Party. The index ranges from zero in 1953–1954, when Eisenhower had an agreeable Republican congress, to 3 in the periods of Democratic rule: the 1960s under Kennedy-Johnson, the late 1970s under Carter, and in 1993–1994 during Clinton's first biennium. This simplification (column 2) makes clear that *Party Control* matters statistically, with each institution the Democrats control adding about 4.19 new liberal laws.[7]

Now we examine the dynamic representation theoretical result by combining *Party Control* with *Policy Mood*. Because public opinion affects election outcomes and *Party Control*,[8] we know from Chapter 8 that it can affect public policy through *composition* as well as through *rational anticipation*. When the public is in a liberal *Mood*, they are likely to elect Democrats to office. And we know that Democrats, once in office, produce liberal *Laws*. The question is whether public opinion matters directly as well as indirectly.

Our analysis confirms *Mood's* dual influence over *Policy*. The pattern in column 3 echoes the now familiar dynamic representation story. New *Laws*, or policy change (as well as *Policy Activity*), reflects the power of public opinion *both* through the composition of the national political institutions and through politicians' rational anticipation. Consider first composition, independent of *Mood*. For *each* additional institution controlled by the Democrats, the policy consequence is an average of 2.72 additional liberal *Laws* per biennium. The estimated difference between Republican and Democratic control in Washington is about eight liberal *Laws* – a substantial difference given the long-term average of 5.85 *Laws*. Also consequential, though, is the persisting impact of *Mood* independent of composition; about three-fifths of the overall impact (compare 0.47 in Table 9.2, column 3, with 0.77 of Equation 9.2) is felt separately from its influence on *Policy* through electoral outcomes. That is to say, no matter which party attains nominal control over the main institutions of government, politicians pay heed to change in public opinion and produce policy accordingly.

These results of column 3 receive even greater amplification in column 4. For this equation, we measure lagged *Mood* as the average *Mood* over the previous *two* biennia rather than just the most recent biennium. There are two reasons for doing so. First, measuring *Mood* over a longer

---

7 We have experimented with various ways of combining institutional strength. For congress, counting the size of majorities or paying particular attention to the northern Democrats produces little power – it seems that gaining control over the institutional structure is critical. A straightforward multiplicative interaction – looking for special power when all three institutions are under control – produces no special insight. The simple composite, counting the number of institutions controlled, does the job as well as any more complex formulation.

8 The regression of *Party Control* on lagged *Mood* shows a regression coefficient 0.11, statistically significant with standard error of 0.03. The two variables correlate at 0.60. For a more detailed account of the *Mood-Party Control* connection, see Chapter 7.

time span helps to reduce the amount of error in measurement. Second, incorporating *Mood* over a two-biennium span allows for the delay in policy making under the United States' system of federal checks and balances. Column 4 shows that measuring *Mood* over a longer time span sharpens the statistical significance of the *Mood* effect at the slight expense of the coefficient for party control. The more precise the measure of *Mood*'s impact, the less can be attributed to the electoral response via party control.

The net effect of *Mood* on *Laws* is the combination of the direct effect plus the indirect effect from *Mood* to party control (via elections) to *Laws*. Measured as *Mood* for the previous biennium, the total effect of *Mood* on *Laws* is a regression coefficient of 0.77, or more than three new liberal *Laws* per every four points' increment in *Mood*. The scatterplot of this relationship (with its correlation of .66) is shown in Figure 9.4.[9] The most conservative legislative sessions, 1954 and 1982, followed the most conservative *Mood* periods and, similarly, the liberal 1960s lawmaking followed a period of high public liberalism. Notice that these examples anchor a more general upward swing – liberal *Mood* leads to liberal *Laws*.

So far for our discussion of major legislation, our units of analysis have been specific congresses or the biennia that encompass their tenure. A more natural unit is the four-year term of a presidency. We can ask whether the pace of legislative liberalism for different presidencies can be traced to the liberalism of public opinion. Thus, we aggregate 22 biennia into 11 presidencies. Although this is a small number of cases, we have dealt with this limitation before, as in Chapter 7 when we studied presidential elections as units of analysis.

If we check the correlation between the liberalism of new policies (*Laws*) and the liberalism of the public opinion climate (*Mood*) for presidencies without any lagging of variables, we find a rather unimpressive .43 coefficient. But we should expect policy making to respond with a lag. Suppose we lag *Mood* two years to measure it as a composite of *Mood* in the first two years of a presidency and the final two years of the previous one. The *Mood-Laws* correlation now rises to a more respectable .67. Lagging further, we measure *Mood* for the four years of the prior presidency. Now we get a very strong correlation of .84.[10]

9 With *Mood* measured as the average of the previous two biennia, the regression coefficient for total effect is 0.77, with a .71 correlation coefficient.
10 If we take quadrennial versions of Chapter 8's policy measure, we find a .58 contemporaneous correlation with *Mood*, but a lesser .30 correlation with lagged *Mood*. Behavioral policy indicators respond more currently to *Mood* than does policy as represented by the *Laws* index.

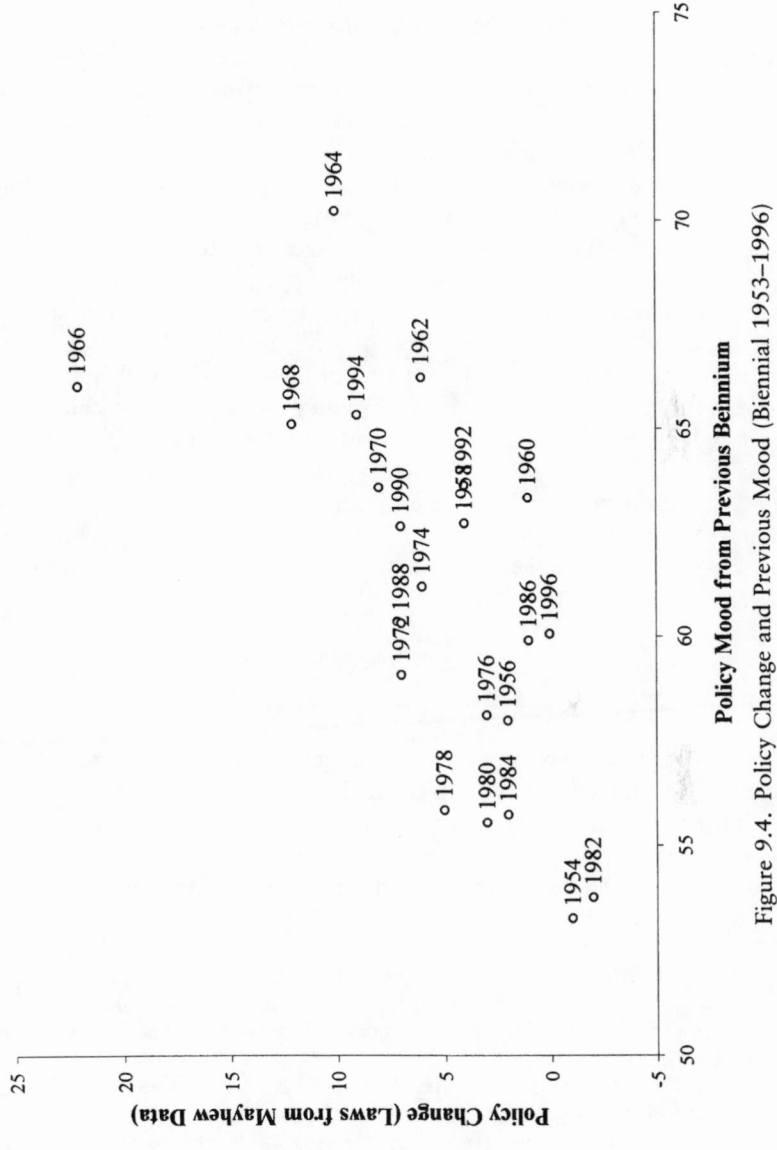

**Policy Mood from Previous Beinnium**

Figure 9.4. Policy Change and Previous Mood (Biennial 1953–1996)

## Policy

Figure 9.5 presents the scatterplot of major legislation per presidency as a function of *Mood* during the prior four-year period or quadrennium. The correlation of 0.84 is quite impressive – stronger, for example, than the correlation between the presidential vote and any economic indicator.[11] Net policy during a four-year presidential term is nearly perfectly predicted from knowing the public's *Policy Mood* during the prior four-year period. Although the statistical certainty is limited by having only 11 cases for analysis, the results could hardly be stronger.[12]

The ideological tone of policy during a presidency is a function of a public demand that is most visible during the previous presidential term. For instance, the Great Society legacy of President Johnson's full term reflects a liberal mood most evident during 1961–1964. Similarly, the energy for the conservative turn of policy during Reagan's first term seemingly came from a conservatism most evident in polls during 1977–1980.

All this confirms the dynamic representation of Chapter 8 – albeit for actual *Policy* rather than mere *Policy Activity*. What remains unanswered is whether the public is paying serious attention to what the government is doing.

### THE EFFECT OF POLICY ON OPINION

Our statistical analysis suggests a political world where elected leaders respond to shifts in public opinion. To make sense of this behavior, we posit a strong electoral connection. Politicians respond to *Mood* because they believe the demands of public opinion affect elections. Politicians anticipate *Mood*'s effect and act in advance of electoral

---

11 For a measure of *Mood* 1949–1952, we substitute biennial *Mood* 1951–1952. For other four-year periods, *Mood* is measured as the average of the two biennial *Mood* measures.

12 We can model these cases so that the sum of the *Laws* index for a four-year presidency is a function of lagged *Mood* from the previous administration plus current *Party Control* (an average for the two biennia of a presidency). The equation is:

$$Laws_t = -77.17 + 1.34 Mood_{t-1} + 3.32 Party\ Control_t, \text{ Adjusted } R^2 = .691$$

Thus we see that *Party Control* matters more in the short term (one biennium) than the longer term of one presidency, for which the coefficient is nonsignificant. Changing party control is a fast route to the restoration of equilibrium, but with parties' showing less ability to innovate as they stay in power. See the discussion next.

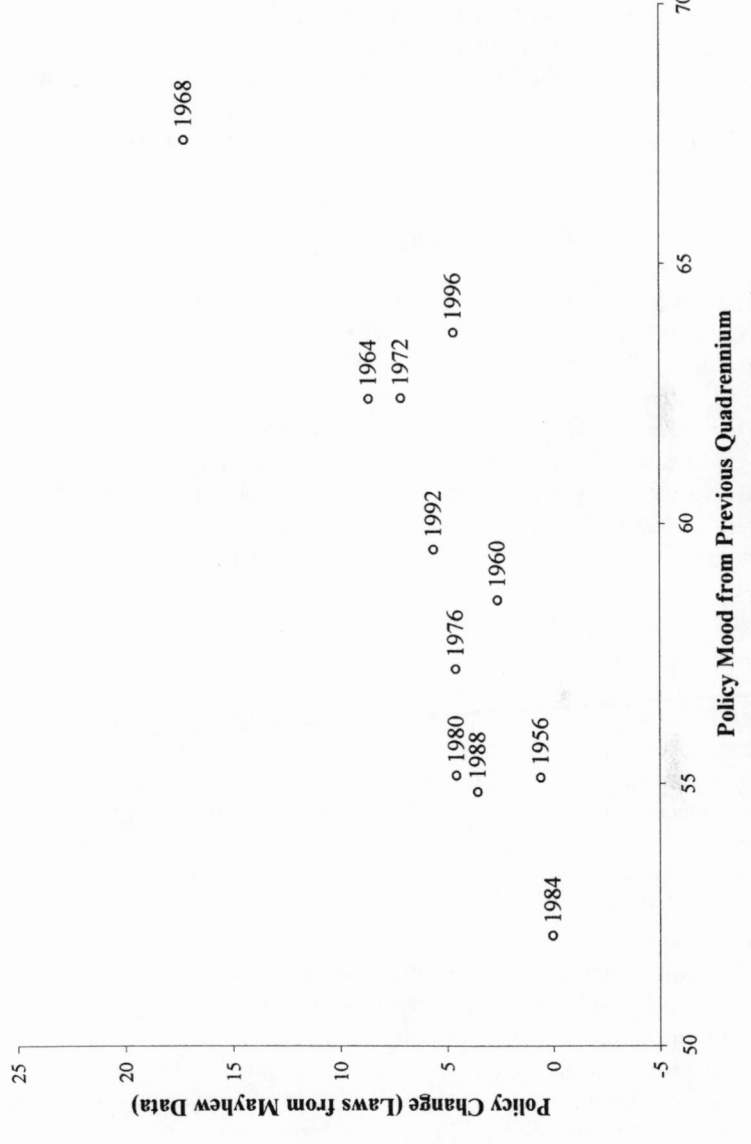

**Policy Mood from Previous Quadrennium**

Figure 9.5. Policy Change and Mood (Quadrennial)

sanctions. But for this to work, we need to find evidence that the electorate's *Mood* responds to *Policy*. Only if voters are aware of policy changes will politicians' responsiveness to public opinion do them some electoral good.

The premise is simple. When people are asked in opinion polls whether policies in certain areas should be more liberal or more conservative (or, proposed policies too liberal or too conservative), they compare their perceptions of contemporary (or proposed) policy with some ideal policy. If the policy is too liberal or too conservative, they say so.

That is to say, people hold preferences regarding their ideal mix of liberal and conservative policies. When policies are more liberal than their ideal, their policy preferences are for more conservatism. When policies are more conservative than their ideal, their policy preferences are for more liberalism. Aggregated, this is policy *Mood*. By implication, the electorate also has an ideal preference, or a preferred level of liberal-conservative policy making. We label this ideal preference the electorate's *Latent Preference* regarding the appropriate level of *Policy* liberalism. *Preference* can be conceptualized as the mean or median preferences of the electorate.

By assumption, we have the identity:

$$Mood_t = Preference_t - Policy_t \qquad (9.3)$$

where *Mood* and *Preference* are aggregates (means or medians), and where *Policy* equals the mean perception of *Policy* as errors in individual perceptions of actual *Policy* cancel out.

The electorate's aggregate *Preference* might be stable or it could fluctuate over time, due perhaps to a series of exogenous shocks. We can see immediately from Equation 9.3 that *Mood* should be negatively related to *Policy*: When *Policy* becomes more liberal, the demand for liberal policies should diminish. Do we find this pattern in the data?

Our model has *Mood* affecting *Policy* and *Policy* affecting *Mood*. Thus, operationally, we must work with lagged values on the right-hand side, predicting a negative relationship between *Mood* and lagged *Policy*. That this idea is at least plausible is readily apparent in Figure 9.6, which plots each biennium's *Mood* against lagged *Policy* from the biennium before. Clearly, the relationship is negative as the thermostatic theory suggests. The most conservative *Policy* era (during the late 1950s and early 1960s) produced the most liberal *Policy Mood*. This frustrated liberalism persisted until satiated by the flow of liberal policy making through the mid-1960s. Similarly, the most liberal *Policy* era (the late 1970s) generated the most conservative *Policy Mood*. During the 1980s, the conservative trend in *Policy* produced a liberal *Mood* backlash cumulating in the election of Bill Clinton in 1992. The overall relationship fits

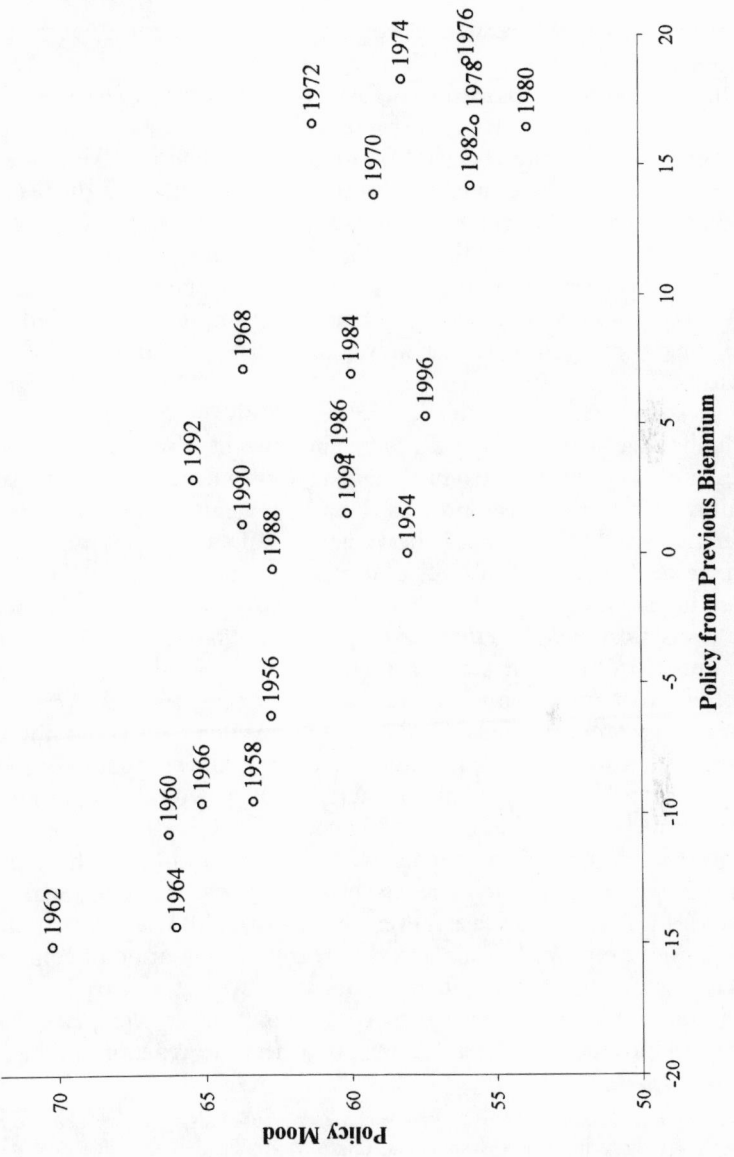

**Policy from Previous Biennium**

Figure 9.6. Mood and Previous Policy (Biennial)

the model rather nicely, with a correlation between the two measures of −.83.

The relationship described in Figure 9.6 is in terms of *levels* of *Mood* and *Policy*. An alternative is to represent the effect of one variable on another in terms of *change* scores, or first differences.[13] We mimic an experiment in which we measure *Mood* before a biennium, then subject the public to an "experimental treatment" in the form of *Policy Change* (new major *Laws*) during the biennium, and then measure *Mood* again the following biennium. Figure 9.7 shows the "before-after" change in *Mood* associated with the new *Laws*. The impressive correlation of −.63 suggests that short-term *Policy* change produces short-term change in *Mood*.[14]

This story can be examined more rigorously by estimating the size of the linkage between lagged *Policy* and current *Mood*. Here we shall be careful, as well, to introduce lagged *Mood* into the equations so as to allow dynamics in the process. Finally, we can readily examine the different sorts of *Policy* markers we have available.

In Table 9.3 we see how *Mood* responds to governmental action. Column 1 shows the case for *Policy Activity*. As expected, the coefficient that translates lagged *Activity* to opinion is negative (−0.06), but it is very small. In fact, our statistical evidence is so weak that we cannot conclude with any certainty that there is any response at all. Were we to examine the *Mood* response to *Policy Activity* alone, we could not infer any public monitoring of government. And indeed, we should not expect any. Not until *Activity* results in actual *Policy* would people reverse course and request a thermostatic change.

However, the case changes when we go to *Laws* and *Policy*. In columns 2 and 3 we see that *Mood* reacts negatively to each additional *Law* passed (−0.25) – and the case is even stronger (−0.40) when lagged *Mood* is measured over two biennia as in the regression equation of column 3. When we turn to *Policy* (rather than *Laws*), we get a sharper picture. Each additional *Law* passed – that deviates from the *long-run* public demand – produces about a quarter point negative reaction on the part

13 By examining change scores, we eliminate the possibility that we observe only a very long-term, perhaps spurious, relationship. Further, an objection to the *Mood*-lagged *Policy* correlation is that it mixes one integrated series (*Policy*) and one stationary series (*Mood*). By theory, the causal relationship should be even stronger than this correlation suggests, however, because *Preference* should be positively correlated with both *Mood* and *Policy*.

14 If the dependent variable is defined as the even shorter-term change in *Mood* from one biennium to the next, the correlation coefficient is a slightly lower −.52, which is still statistically significant. Policy change in one biennium is followed by a visible *Mood* reaction the next biennium.

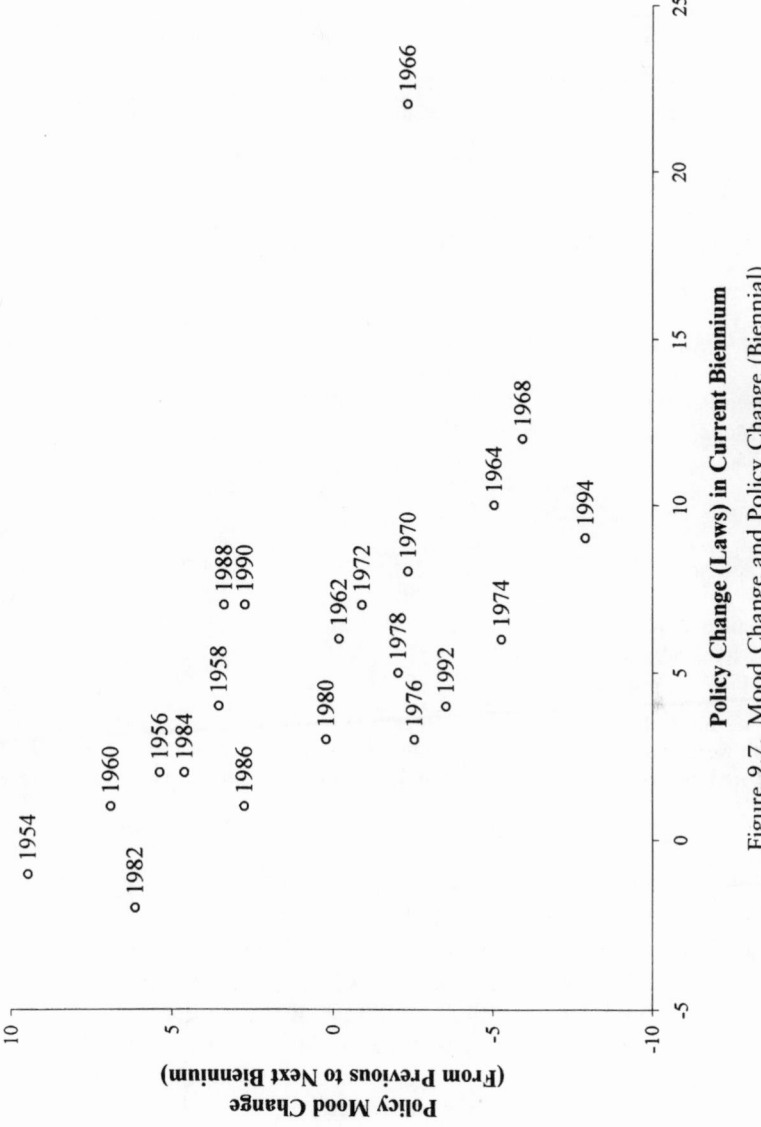

Figure 9.7. Mood Change and Policy Change (Biennial)

# Policy

Table 9.3. *Mood as a Function of Policy*

| | Dependent Variable = Policy Mood$_t$ | | | | | |
|---|---|---|---|---|---|---|
| | (1) | (2) | (3) | (4) | (5) | (6) |
| Policy Activity$_{t-1}$ | −0.06 | | | | | |
| | (−0.75) | | | | | |
| Laws$_{t-1}$ | | −0.26$^a$ | −0.40$^a$ | | | |
| | | (−2.20) | (−2.60) | | | |
| Policy$_{t-1}$ | | | | −0.22$^a$ | −0.25$^a$ | −0.17$^a$ |
| | | | | (−4.54) | (−5.64) | (−2.85) |
| Policy Mood$_{t-1}$ | 0.86$^a$ | 0.84$^a$ | | 0.39$^a$ | | 0.41$^a$ |
| | (5.04) | (5.95) | | (3.18) | | (3.68) |
| Mean Policy Mood$_{(t-1,t-2)}$ | | | 0.89$^a$ | | 0.33$^a$ | |
| | | | (4.83) | | (2.82) | |
| Inflation$_t$ | | | | | | −0.25 |
| | | | | | | (−1.16) |
| ΔUnemployment$_t$ | | | | | | 1.38$^a$ |
| | | | | | | (2.50) |
| Constant | 11.82 | 11.20 | 8.94 | 38.26$^a$ | 42.03 | 37.57$^a$ |
| | (1.27) | (1.34) | (0.83) | (5.09) | (2.82) | (5.34) |
| Number of Cases | 20 | 22 | 22 | 22 | 22 | 22 |
| Adjusted $R^2$ | .58 | .62 | .51 | .77 | .75 | .81 |
| RMSE | 2.81 | 2.61 | 2.95 | 2.02 | 2.10 | 1.82 |

*Note*: Biennial data, 1953–1996. Each column is a separate regression, with the dependent variable labeled at the top of the column. Policy is cumulative laws, detrended. Mean Policy Mood$_{(t-1,t-2)}$ is the mean Mood of the previous two biennia. $t$ values in parentheses.
$^a$ $p < 0.05$.

of the public. Whether measuring the control variable of lagged *Mood* for one (column 4) or (especially) two (column 5) biennia, the coefficient for lagged *Policy* is significant at the 0.001 level, even with the limitation of 22 cases. Now, the statistical precision is sufficient to give confidence that we have identified the nature of the result.[15]

The case is bolstered when we also control for the causal effects of the economy on *Mood*. As we saw in Chapter 6, *Policy Mood* moves in accord with a naive Keynesian view of the policy-economy causal linkage. High inflation produces public caution about expansive policy while high unemployment produces public demand for expansive policy. In column 6, we see that these empirical relationships hold up at least

15 Another more challenging mode of demonstration is to show short-term changes in *Mood* as a function of lagged short-term change in policy. The bivariate regression of *Mood* change on lagged *Laws* shows a −0.30 coefficient, which is of a magnitude consistent with the results in Table 3 and is statistically significant.

partially when we switch from years to biennia and when we include lagged *Policy* in the equation.[16] Unemployment clearly affects *Mood*. Each point increase in unemployment produces a 1.70 point liberal boost to *Mood*. The evidence that inflation causes *Mood* conservatism is now shakier, however; but that is confounded by the strong (0.78) correlation between lagged *Policy* and the biennial inflation rate – the multicollinearity makes it difficult to identify inflation's true impact.[17] The estimated impact of lagged *Policy* on *Mood* declines slightly with inflation in the equation (though it remains significant) due to the correlation of the two potential predictors.

We get another view of the same process by stepping back and looking at the sweep of policy history over presidential terms. Again, the four-year presidential term is the natural unit of American politics. Given the dominance of the presidency for setting the political agenda, proposing policy initiatives, and shaping political outcomes, we should be more than a little interested in seeing if the policy innovations (*Laws*) enacted during a presidential term meaningfully affect public opinion. Did Johnson's Great Society cause *Mood* to turn conservative? Did the Reagan revolution actually generate a liberal *Mood*?

Again, we repeat the "experimental" treatment. As a measure of policy innovation (the treatment), we use the *Laws* index for the four years of the presidential term. The dependent variable is *Mood* change from one biennium before the presidential term to the first biennium of the next. Even with only 10 administrations (down from 11 – *Mood* for Clinton II is not available for this analysis), *Laws* accounts for over half of the variance in *Mood* change.[18]

The correlation between policy innovation in one administration and before-after *Mood* change is a strongly negative –0.76, with the picture shown in Figure 9.8. The more liberal the policy stream, the more conservative is the change in *Mood*. Notably, the most liberal presidency (Johnson's full term ending in 1968) is associated with the

---

16 Both inflation and change in unemployment are measured for the span from the year just prior to the biennium to the first year of the biennium. This gives a sense of economic conditions already experienced during the two-year period.

17 At first blush, the data suggest that liberal policies may indeed generate inflation. However, it is worth noting that the liberal policies here are *not* counter-cyclic policies that might cause inflation – except through the most circuitous route. A close look at the appendix will convince that very few of the laws are directly related to inflationary stimuli. Whatever its substantive implications, this relationship creates a multicolinearity problem for our analysis.

18 The equation is:

$$Mood\ change = 5.67 - 0.47 Laws, \text{Adjusted } R^2 = .523$$

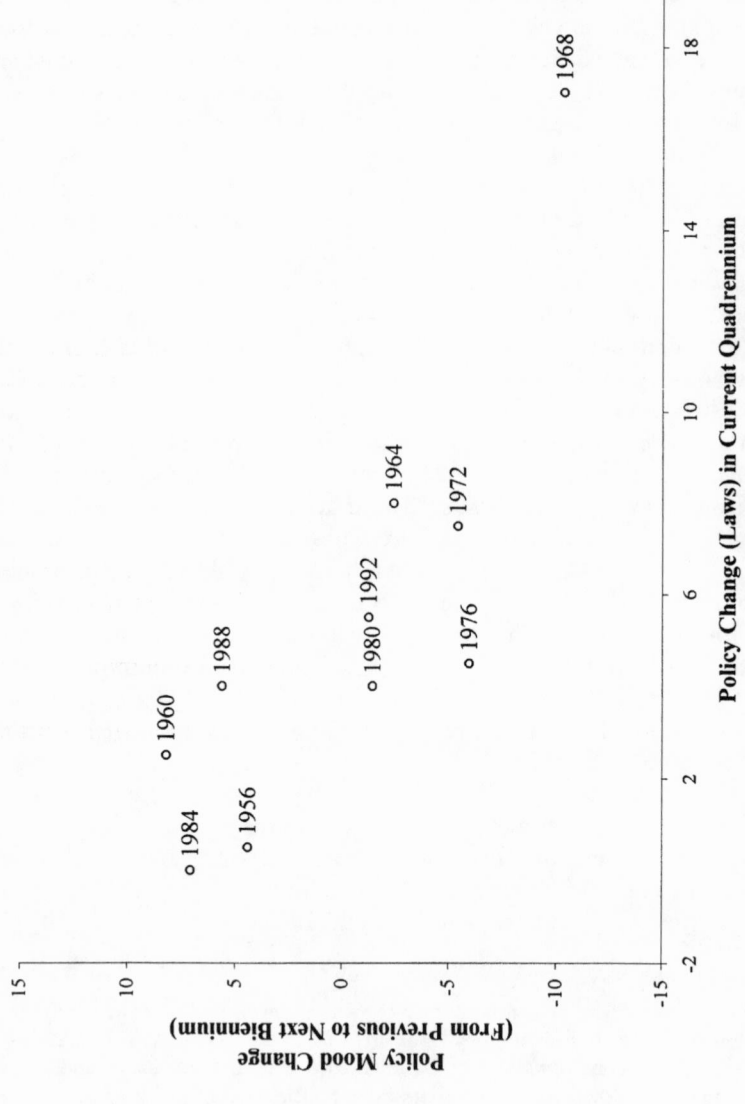

**Policy Change (Laws) in Current Quadrennium**

Figure 9.8. Mood Change and Policy Change (Quadrennial)

greatest public reaction in the conservative direction. Similarly, the conservative presidencies of Reagan and Eisenhower moved the public in the liberal direction. Note also that the less dramatic presidencies in between also generated public responses consistent with our thermostat model. From the magnitude of the coefficient, for every two pieces of liberal legislation during a presidency, *Mood* becomes one point more conservative.[19]

The evidence for a public reaction to policy seems clear. This result, of course, says much about the character of modern democracy. The conventional view about public opinion, largely studied at the individual level, suggests that people do not pay much attention to the politics in Washington. Of course, at the individual level the evidence is overwhelming. But when we turn to aggregates, to the nation as a whole, the public *does* react (and react appropriately) to policy making by the national government. Were it otherwise, American politics would run less effectively. Without public monitoring of their actions, politicians might reasonably choose to disregard the public's policy preferences, bending further to the will of more specialized interests. Even a strong dynamic representation linkage – with politicians anticipating and reacting to public opinion when they make laws – is not enough. For if public opinion does not react to actual policy making, then the system might reflect the ability of ideologicians to shape the public dialogue quite independent of reality. Or, alternatively, if the public reaction to *Policy Change* were more "positive" than "negative," getting caught up in the wave of excitement rather than urging caution about policy extravagance, the system might run entirely out of control.

## SHORT-TERM DYNAMICS

So far, this chapter has examined the time series of representation using two-year and even four-year intervals as the units. Enlarging the units in this way enhances the statistical power of the analysis. There are several reasons. First, the natural cycle of major legislation is the congress or biennium or even the presidency, not the year. Second, since major laws are somewhat rare events, their frequency is best measured over a wide time span. *Mood* also is measured with less error when scored over a wide time interval. And finally, we must take into account the pace of

---

19 We have repeated this chapter's analysis with the annual data series. While the statistical results are more noisy, the fundamental theoretical inferences are the same. *Policy* and *Mood* are linked together in a feedback system that governs the impact of exogenous influences. See the following section.

# Policy

Table 9.4. *System Dynamics in the Annual Series*

| | Dependent Variable | | |
|---|---|---|---|
| | Laws$_t$ | Laws$_t$ | Mood$_t$ |
| Mean Mood$_{(t-1,t-2)}$ | 0.30[a] | 0.18[a] | 0.60[a] |
| | (3.05) | (1.99) | (4.82) |
| Policy$_{t-1}$ | | | −0.13[a] |
| | | | (−2.69) |
| Democratic | | 1.79[a] | |
| Party Control$_t$ | | (3.51) | |
| Constant | −15.24[a] | −12.11[a] | 25.13[a] |
| | (5.91) | (−2.28) | (3.31) |
| Time Points | 43 | 43 | 43 |
| Adjusted $R^2$ | 0.16 | 0.35 | 0.55 |
| RMSE | 2.74 | 2.42 | 3.10 |

*Note*: Annual data, 1952–1996. Mean Mood$_{(t-1,t-2)}$ is the mean Mood for the prior two years. $t$ values in parentheses.
[a] $p < 0.05$.

the representation process in the Madisonian government. For public opinion to result in actual legislation takes time, through no fault of the public or its leaders.

In this section, we explore what we can learn by moving to an annual time frame. Our using the biennial readings gave us more statistical power because they smoothed out a good deal of measurement error. And they served their purpose in presenting a clear case that policy and mood are intertwined. But to model the dynamics we want to examine the relationships over the shorter term – year-to-year – so that we do not miss something due to the biennial time aggregation.

The first step is a mere replication of the prior results, this time for annual data. Table 9.4 gives the results, substituting annual for the biennial data series. Here we model current *Laws* as a function of the average of the prior two years' *Mood*.[20] A point shift in mood yields 0.30 new law (column 1) and the statistical tests on the coefficient give confidence in our inference. Dynamic representation holds. A turn

20 We use the *average* of the prior two years' *Mood* (rather than merely the single prior year's input) as this trick yields noticeable statistical leverage. In essence, this model allows the effects of a shock to mood to resonate directly in the other for two years' time. Theoretically, we expect such effects to be spread out over the two-year election cycle in American politics. The messages of two years ago will affect current politicians' lawmaking through both composition and rational anticipation.

to rational anticipation and composition, by introducing *Party Control* (in column 2), produces the same story as well. Both terms are important – with the rational anticipation effect slightly more modest (0.18) and at the margins of statistical significance. And the public feedback loop works as well. As with the biennial data, modeling current *Mood* as a function of prior *Policy* shows that the public does react to government: A law-deviation from the long-run demand for policy yields a −0.13 change in mood (column 3). In all, the story is the same as before.

With the similarity between the annual and the biennial time frames, we can examine the link between *Policy Activity* from Chapter 8 and the current *Laws*. Recall that *Policy Activity* includes many political votes not associated with major legislation – perhaps partisan infighting or symbols designed for electoral purposes – but we suspect that it also includes partial efforts that lay the groundwork for serious policy consequences. With this in mind, we expect that *Policy Activity* should foreshadow *Policy*.

We can test this expectation by assessing the *Activity-Policy* connection. Since *Policy Activity* must add up before it weighs in consequentially, we construct a measure of weighted *Policy Activity History* that reflects previous activity, each year in the past being weighted less and less.[21] Regressing *Laws* on *Policy Activity History* (see Table 9.5, column 1) demonstrates statistically that there is a clear linkage between prior politics and current laws. More interesting, when we add *Policy Activity History* to our more fully specified model, we see that history matters even when controlling for *Mood* and *Party Control*. In column 2 of Table

---

21 For *Policy Activity*, we need a clean empirical measure. Focusing on the three elected branches, the presidency, the House, and the Senate, we take *Presidential Key Vote Liberalism*, *House Liberal Wins*, and *Senate Liberal Wins* (see Chapter 8). In order for *Activity* to turn into *Law*, these three must be coincident for success – so our measure treats each as a quasi-probability measure (running from 0 to 1) and multiplies the three together to produce the probability of a liberal law. Call this *Pr(Liberal)*. Then, to capture the idea that the past counts – previous committee activity is important in laying the groundwork for bills before they get to the floor in a subsequent session – we create a distributed lag weighting scheme. Thus, our *Policy Activity History* is:

$$PAH_t = \sum_k^t \lambda^k Pr(Liberal)_{t-k}$$

with $0.0 < \lambda < 1.0$ so that it produces a standard exponentially weighted distributed lag. We arbitrarily pick the value of $\lambda = 0.80$ to capture the main flow (0.80 is not quite optimal for fit, but it is close), not wishing to put too fine a point of precision on this analysis.

353

Table 9.5. *Laws and Policy Activity History*

|  | Dependent Variable = Laws$_t$ | |
|---|---|---|
| Policy Activity History$_t$ | 4.93[a] | 2.74[a] |
|  | (4.36) | (2.04) |
| Mean Mood$_{(t-1,t-2)}$ |  | 0.15 |
|  |  | (1.57) |
| Democratic Party Control$_t$ |  | 1.29[a] |
|  |  | (2.02) |
| Constant | −1.26 | −11.23[a] |
|  | (−1.24) | (−2.05) |
| Number of Cases | 41 | 41 |
| Adjusted $R^2$ | 0.31 | 0.39 |
| RMSE | 2.51 | 2.36 |

*Note*: Annual data, 1956–1996. Policy Activity History is a distributed lag of Prior Policy Activity (see Chapter 8). Mean Mood$_{(t-1,t-2)}$ is the mean Mood for the prior two years. $t$ values in parentheses.
[a] $p < 0.05$.

9.5 we statistically isolate *Policy Activity History* from contemporary politics (*Mood* and *Party*) and see that history continues to affect *Laws* (the coefficient is 2.74 and is statistically significant). That is to say, current *Laws* are formed not only by current political conditions but also by the political work put into play over a number of years. Consistent with the run of our analyses thus far, we see the workings of Madison's constitutional design.

Clearly, both year-to-year politics and recent history matter. In addition, we expect a mutual relationship between *Mood* and *Policy* within a given year. Politicians pay close attention to public opinion and try to minimize their deviation from the public's signals. They cannot generate new "major laws" on the spur of the moment, but they may be more likely than otherwise to pass items on the current agenda. Similarly, members of the attentive public will understand and react to major legislation passed within a given session. They may not see the results of the legislation, and they may not receive the "wisdom" of organized interests' mobilization, but they will see the news reports and the contemporary commentators' judgments. These immediate effects cannot be directly observed. Because they are simultaneous (within the annual unit of observation), we cannot model them unless we make heroic (and unconvincing) assumptions. And, to be sure, the effects should have opposite signs: *Mood* generates a positive response in *Laws*, which then generates a negative reaction in *Mood*. The net effects cancel each other out. Indeed, the contemporaneous correlation between new *Laws* and *Mood* change is virtually zero, whether measured annually or biennially. Thus, we are unable to observe an empirical relationship that we fully expect to exist – we will require outside evidence to assess simultaneity.[22]

### MOOD AS ERROR CORRECTION

We have conceptualized *Policy Mood* as the public's *relative* demand for more liberal or more conservative government action. As a *relative* demand, *Mood* is a function both of current policies and of the electorate's ideal policy preference. Although we do not observe the latter directly, we would like to infer its properties. This latent variable that attracts our attention is the electorate's net ideal policy, or the pace of liberal legislation that the public at that moment (perhaps defined as the median voter) would see as "just right." The goal is to gain a fix on the statistical relationship between what people want and what they get.

In this section, we push the data to the limit and perhaps beyond, to consider the nature of the relationship between *Policy* and the electorate's unobserved net *Latent Preference* regarding the ideal left-right mix of policies. Taking our thermostatic analogy seriously, we conceptualize this relationship in terms of an error-correction model. At equilibrium, *Policy* reflects the public's collective *Preference*. But at any point, *Policy* will deviate somewhat from equilibrium. This deviation is represented by *Mood*. When *Policy* is more liberal than *Preference*, *Mood* becomes relatively conservative. When *Policy* is more conservative than *Preference*, *Mood* becomes relatively liberal. Representation occurs with the *Policy* response to *Mood*. *The faster the response, the greater the match between Preference and Policy.*

Let us explore the implications when we entertain the assumption that *Mood* at time *t* corresponds exactly to the gap between *Policy* at time *t* and *Preference* at time *t*, so that:

$$Mood_t = c(Preference_t - Policy_t) \qquad (9.4)$$

22 We can also point to at least one directly relevant piece of survey evidence apart from the *Mood* index. In the early 1960s, Gallup frequently asked national surveys whether policies should go more "to the left" or more "to the right" politically. In several surveys in 1963 and 1964, the national responses hovered in the 50–50 range. But in 1965, as policy was decisively beginning to turn left, the Gallup sample broke 41–59 with a majority of opinion holders asking for a right turn.

## Policy

where $c$ is a scalar transformation of measurement units and *Mood* is measured as a deviation from its mean value.[23] Transposing the equation and substituting $k = 1/c$, where $k$ is the increment of *Policy* demanded per one unit of *Mood*, we can estimate *Latent Preference*, as:

$$Preference_t = Policy_t + k \, Mood_t \qquad (9.5)$$

We know $k$ only by assumption and can manipulate the imputed *Latent Preference–Policy* correlation at will by our choice of $k$. The smaller we assume $k$ to be, the stronger we make the correlation. While we cannot pretend to know $k$ with any exactitude, we can constrain its range to those values that generate simulations of the representation process that are plausible. Two criteria are particularly relevant. If $k$ is set too small, we get hyper-representation in the sense that a given increment of *Mood* generates a stronger policy response than the public desires: liberal demands, for example, would only lead to an over-correction that requires a conservative correction. If $k$ is set too large, we get *Preference* innovations responding negatively to lagged *Policy*, whereas by theory there should be no response at all. (We assume *Latent Preference* to be exogenous to *Policy*.)

A small window in the range of $k = 3$ allows both constraints to be reasonably satisfied. Thus, we illustrate the possibilities with the assumption that $k = 3$, with one unit of *Mood* translating to a demand for three units of *Policy*. This choice results in the simulated outcome that the *Policy* demand indicated by *Mood* at time $t$ takes exactly four periods (eight years) to achieve satisfaction, while allowing the desired zero response of *Preference* innovations to lagged *Policy*.[24]

---

23 By asserting that *Mood* equals the difference between *Policy* and *Preference*, we in effect assert that when measured in biennia, the public observed *Policy* without delay. The alternative would be to assume that recent *Policy* changes are observed with a partial lag, perhaps not until the policy consequences are felt. See the discussion of the following section. The assumption of no delay must not be confused with issues of voter competence. A useful analogy is voter knowledge of the economy. Individual voters may have only partial knowledge of the current economy, but that does not mean that the economy in voters' minds is the economy of years past. That would be an absurd inference. (See Chapter 3.) An inattentive voter who politically awakens would learn of contemporary *Policy*, not the *Policy* of yesteryear. In any case, this is not a knife-edge assumption. If we model *Mood* as a response to current *Preference* minus a distributive lag of *Policies* past and present, the results are similar but the presentation is more complicated.

24 At $k = 3$, the seeming *Preference* response to lagged *Policy* is slightly but not significantly negative. If we identified $k$ by the value where the lagged *Policy*-on-*Preference* "effect" is exactly zero, $k = 1.82$. At $k = 3$, the regression slope of *Policy* change $t$ to $t + 4$ on $Mood_t = 1.02$ (virtual unity) with an adjusted $R^2$ of

Figure 9.9 shows the resultant graph, of *Latent Preference* and *Policy.*[25] We have no grounds for choosing the metric $k = 3$ other than its fit to desired constraints discussed above. Actual *Policy* is drawn in the dark line and our constructed *Latent Preference* in the light line (to indicate its tentative nature). The graph clearly suggests the dynamic of *Latent Preference* leading *Policy.* In this simulation, the contemporaneous correlation between *Latent Preference* and *Policy* is a modestly positive .29. However the correlation rises to .57 when *Policy* is measured one period ahead and .77 when *Policy* is measured two periods ahead. The correlation then peaks out at .88 when *Policy* is led by three periods.

One can observe (rescaled) *Mood$_t$* as the vertical distance between *Latent Preference$_t$* and *Policy$_t$*. When the electorate's *Preference* is more liberal than *Policy*, *Mood* is more liberal than its mean value. With *Mood* and *Policy* now measured on the same scale (albeit tenuously), the regression of *Laws* on lagged *Mood* now yields an interpretation in terms of proportion of the error corrected. The original coefficient of 0.77 (Equation 9.2) is now divided by 3 to yield a rough estimate of the proportion of the gap between *Latent Preference* and *Policy* for one biennium that is closed by the *Laws* of the following biennium. With the intercept omitted by measuring all variables as deviations from their means, this equation is:

$$\Delta Policy_t = 0.26\ Mood_{t-1}(\text{IN POLICY UNITS}) + u_t \qquad (9.6)$$

By our conceptualization, the *Policy* response reduces the *Mood* gap by about one-quarter, each biennium. Although this conceptualization may appear to suggest a sluggish rate of response, the *Mood* gap does get closed in the longer run.

As *Policy* responds to *Mood*, the "error" represented by *Mood* gets corrected. We ask again, how fast? We have a test that does not depend

---

.79. Assuming the *Preference* construct with $k = 3$ is real, suppose we regress *Policy* eight years ahead on current *Preference* and current *Policy*. *Preference* would dominate this equation, as if it represents the long-term equilibrium to which *Policy* is attracted.

25 There exist other criteria for selecting a value of $k$. If the goal is to minimize the variance of *Preference*, we would choose the residuals from the regression predicting *Policy* from *Mood*. (*Preference* = $e$ in the equation *Policy* = $-k\,Mood + e$.) The trouble is that the resultant *Preference* measure would be orthogonal to *Policy*, and negatively correlated with lagged *Policy*. We could assume that *Policy* equilibrates very fast so that *Preference* and *Mood* are uncorrelated. We would then choose the residuals in the equation predicting *Mood* from *Policy*. (*Preference* = $(1/c)e$ in the equation *Mood* = $-c\,Policy + e$.) The trouble is significant overshooting of policy targets three and four periods ahead.

357

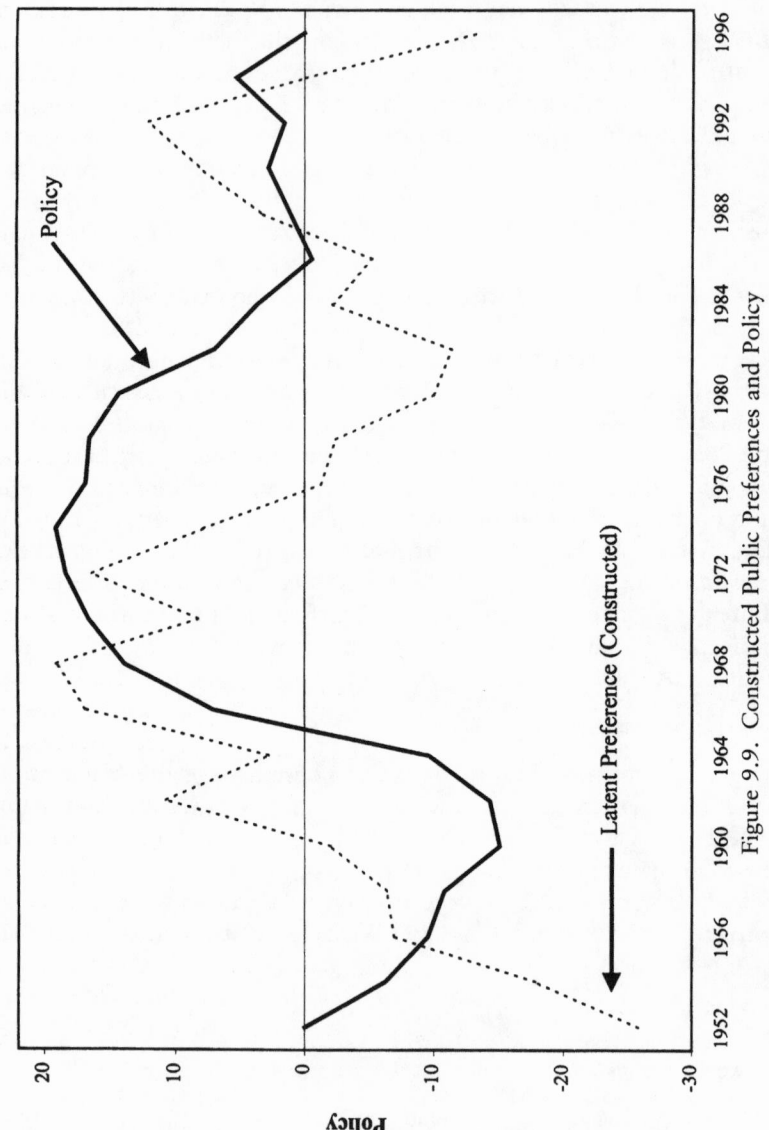

Figure 9.9. Constructed Public Preferences and Policy

on any assumptions about *Latent Preference*. Regressing *Mood$_t$* on *Mood$_{t-1}$* reveals a coefficient ($\gamma$) of 0.71. By implication, the *Mood* gap decays at a rate of $(1 - \gamma)$, or 0.29 over one period. The *Mood* gap between *Latent Preference* and *Policy* decays 0.61 over two periods ($\gamma = 0.39$), and 0.83 over three periods ($\gamma = 0.17$). By four periods (eight years), the decay is complete ($\gamma = -0.21$) and the policy demand has been fulfilled.[26]

While we cannot claim to have measured *Latent Preference* with any exactitude, we can speculate regarding its dynamics. Once again, we use the analogy of a building's occupants sending signals to the building engineer. The occupants' demands of "more" or "less" heat depend in part on the weather, which is cyclical in nature. The political analogy is the set of changing environmental conditions such as inflation and unemployment. As Chapter 6 showed, unemployment moves *Mood* liberal and inflation moves it conservative. The building occupants' demands also can vary as their set points change, either due to individuals' changing tastes or to the different tastes of revolving exiting and entering occupants. The political analogy is a shift in the electorate's net ideological set point. There would be no reason to require the set point to be cyclical movement around a constant equilibrium; it could be a random walk.

We lack the faith that would allow treating the simulated *Latent Preference* scores as if they present an observable time series. By our speculation above, *Latent Preference* is generated both by short-term conditions such as the economy and long-term changes in ideological taste. The latter is of greater importance for the long-term trends of policy making. Economic circumstances come and go, leaving in their wake transient policy changes. Ideological taste, while it may change only slowly, leaves permanent policy change in its wake. For instance, adjusted for time, *Policy* had been much more liberal in the 1960s and early 1970s than in the 1980s and 1990s. Further, the depiction in Figure 9.9 suggests that this shift was a direct result of a shift in the electorate's long-term policy preference. *Policy* changed, we submit, because the electorate's ideological preference became more conservative.

Then again, we should keep in mind that what is liberal and what is conservative is relative to the times. The *Policy* measure is adjusted for the average *Policy* change of about 5.85 new liberal laws passed per congress. Policy change over the second half of the twentieth century was a

---

26 The slightly negative autoregressive coefficient over four periods suggests that the error indicated by *Mood* at time *t* actually is overcorrected four periods later. However, since the negative coefficient is not significant, we should be cautious about claiming that the eventual correction overshoots the mark.

# Policy

pattern of an almost unrelenting expansion of liberal legislation, ending up about 100 major laws more liberal than when the half-century began. Our question is not whether this was enough or too much but whether it followed from public opinion. Did the electorate's evolving endorsement of liberal policy initiatives actually create this liberal policy growth? Or would the electorate have been just as happy to turn back the political clock? We argue for the former.

In all, it seems plausible that national policy follows directly – if gradually – from public preferences. *Mood*, we argue, represents the mechanism of adjustment, as the electorate provides signals that policy should move faster or slower (or reverse direction) in its pace of liberal legislation. This argument could turn out to be quite wrong in the details or even in the conceptualization. Yet the evidence supports the radical idea that the institutions of democracy actually provide the mechanisms for connecting public preferences to public policy.

## THE ELECTORAL CONNECTION AND MOOD-LAWS DYNAMICS

Here we take a closer look at the role of the electoral process in the *Mood-Laws* dynamic. To push forward, we shall take our modeling seriously, perhaps more seriously than can be absolutely justified, to tease out the consequences of a governing system. We want to simulate the *Policy* response to *Mood* and the *Mood* reaction – incorporating the parties' policy differences, the electorate's contribution at the ballot box, and politicians' rational anticipation of the electorate's behavior.

We start by presenting again the equation describing the effects of lagged *Mood* plus *Party Control* on *Policy Change*. Recall that *Party Control* is measured on a scale from 0 (Republican control) to 3 (Democratic control of presidency, House, and Senate). This time we illustrate by depicting *Mood* as *Policy* demand, where one percentage point of survey liberalism represents an increment of three *Laws*. With variables measured as deviations from the mean and the intercept omitted, the equation is:

$$\Delta Policy_t = 0.16 Mood_{t-1} (\text{IN POLICY UNITS})$$
$$+2.72 Party\ Control_t + u_t \tag{9.7}$$

By this formulation, the direct *Policy* response to each unit shock to *Mood* is only one-sixth of a unit. Meanwhile, each institution controlled by a party yields a change of almost three major *Laws* – independent of *Mood* and its electoral imperative. This equation suggests that if voters had to rely solely on elite anticipation for their *Policy* response, the wait would be long indeed. Even with politicians anticipating the electoral threat, the ballot box presents the quickest method for *Policy Change*. Because of their own policy preferences and those of their prime supporters, Democratic officeholders push liberal policies and Republican officeholders push conservative ones – but at an electoral cost.

According to Equation 9.7, for each congress roughly 2.7 *Laws* pivot on which party controls each of three institutions. Since each added *Mood* point represents a demand for three more liberal *Laws*, each *Policy* increment is accompanied by an electoral price of about one-third of a point of *Mood*. This is the electoral price parties pay for pursuing their own agenda. For each institution per period (congress or biennium) that a party controls, it typically "spends" enough on policy to lose almost one point of *Mood* that it would otherwise hold if the opposition were in power. It pays this price in order to pursue a political agenda that reflects the ideological preferences of its members and supporters. Over time, serving in power creates sufficient *Mood* loss to generate electoral reversal with the opposition entering power.

We want to simulate the dynamic responses of politicians and the public to political circumstance. For illustration, let us see what would happen if one party captured the presidency and both houses of congress and was able to remain in office for eight years. In an abstract sense, this is a test of what we might expect of "responsible party government" in the classic "responsible party" case – a party gains control over government and has a chance to put its policies in place. And, to keep things simple, we assume a state of equilibrium, including a constant level of preference so that *Mood* responds only to *Policy* change.[27]

Now we want to see how the *Mood-Policy* system works by separating out its components. We shall see the behavior when the electorate starts out neutral about policy (its *Mood* is zero) and the ruling party merely pursues its own agenda. Call this the agenda-only scenario – where the only dynamics come from politicians' pursuing their policy goals. Then, we shall consider the opposite, when politicians simply seek reelection and put their ideological agenda aside. Here the dynamics stem from the public's *Preferences*, or a mandate, at the start of our period. This second scenario captures the essence of Anthony Downs' (1957) and David Mayhew's (1974) election-centered politicians – who concentrate on satisfying the public at the expense of any private goals. And,

---

27 Specifically, we assume that in the long run, average *Policy* equals average *Preference*, and the parties are equally responsible so that in the long run they are in power equal amounts. These assumptions are of no substantive consequence but necessary to keep the arithmetic as simple as possible.

## Policy

finally, we shall put the pieces together, incorporating both party agendas and a response to a popular mandate.

We start the system with no mandate but a Democratically controlled presidency, House, and Senate. Using Equation 9.7, we calculate the system dynamics and illustrate them in Figure 9.10. In year 0, before the initial congress, *Mood* is zero and *Laws* are yet to be considered. In the first congress of the run, the Democrats pass four new liberal laws[28] and the public notices to generate a *Mood* of −4 (in policy, not public opinion, units). In the next congress, the Democrats' agenda spurs them to pass an additional four new liberal laws but their electoral "rational anticipation" antennae urge caution so they pass only 3.33 new laws (that is $4.00 - 0.16 \times Mood_{t-1}$). The public responds accordingly, with *Mood* reacting to −7.33. And so forth to the third and fourth congresses – each time the Democrats tempering their political urge to push liberal legislation because they are wary of an increasingly strident public reaction. Nevertheless, even after eight years they pursue their own policy at some electoral cost. In fact, the resulting *Mood* of −12 (in policy units) will translate into about a 4 percent vote loss in the subsequent election.

Now this result should not be a surprise – after all, the dynamics are driven by the parties' agenda pursuit. The party-centered policy making does diminish over time – as the electorate reacts negatively to the increasing policy legacy – but in this story the only energy comes from the governing party. Next we want to consider a very different scenario – when the public presents an ideological mandate but elects (for some reason) eight years of divided government with its neutral partisan agenda.

In Figure 9.11, we illustrate the response to a mandate of 12 – where the public's *Latent Preference* turns leftward and demands 12 additional new liberal laws. But with divided government and the parties equally balanced, ideological pressure can come only from public opinion. In year 0 (before the ideologically balanced government is elected), we see a *Mood* of 12. In the first biennium, congress responds through rational anticipation to produce two new laws, or one-sixth of the public demand. The public notices and *Mood* diminishes to 10. The politicians produce one-sixth of this demand for 10 new laws, and the public further diminishes its demand. The third and fourth congresses pass lesser amounts of liberal legislation, responding to the lessening liberal *Mood*. The new legislation further reduces the liberal demand. But even after eight years the public's mandate has not yet been fulfilled. The original request for 12 new laws still has 5.79, or about half, yet to go. The ratio-

---

28 We use round numbers to remind ourselves of the roughness of these calculations. More precisely, the effect of complete Democratic control is $3 \times 2.72 = 8.16$ new laws over complete Republican control, or about 4.08 above "average."

362

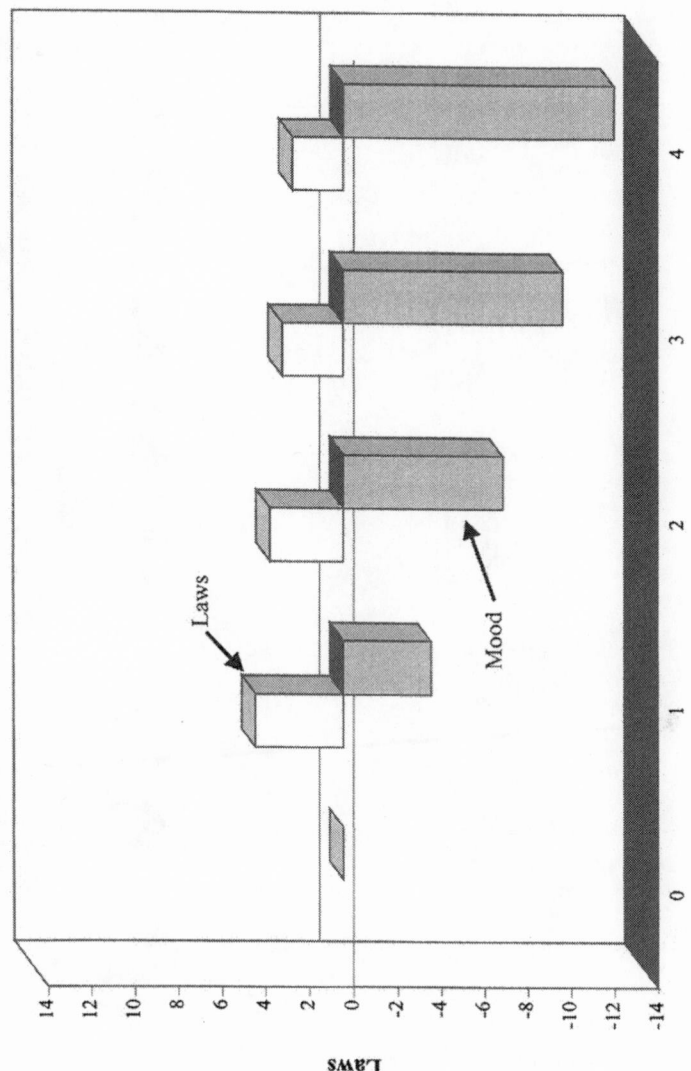

Figure 9.10. The Mood-Laws Connection over an Eight-Year Cycle: Democrats Follow Liberal Agenda with No Mandate

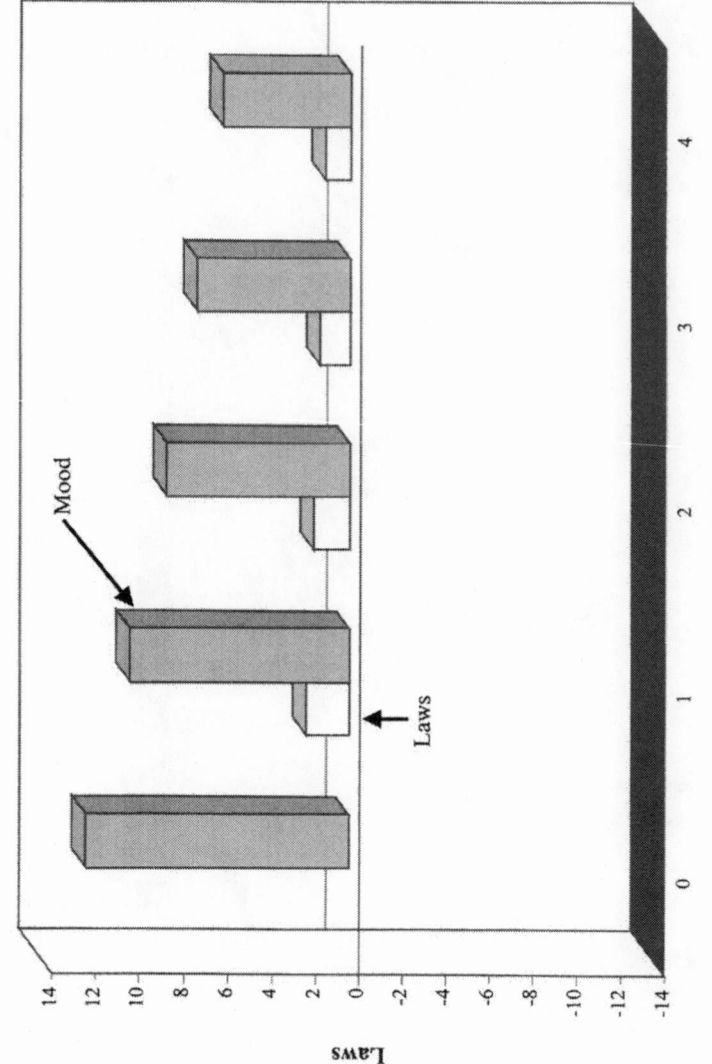

Figure 9.11. The Mood-Laws Connection over an Eight-Year Cycle: Divided Congress Follows Liberal Mandate with No Partisan Agenda

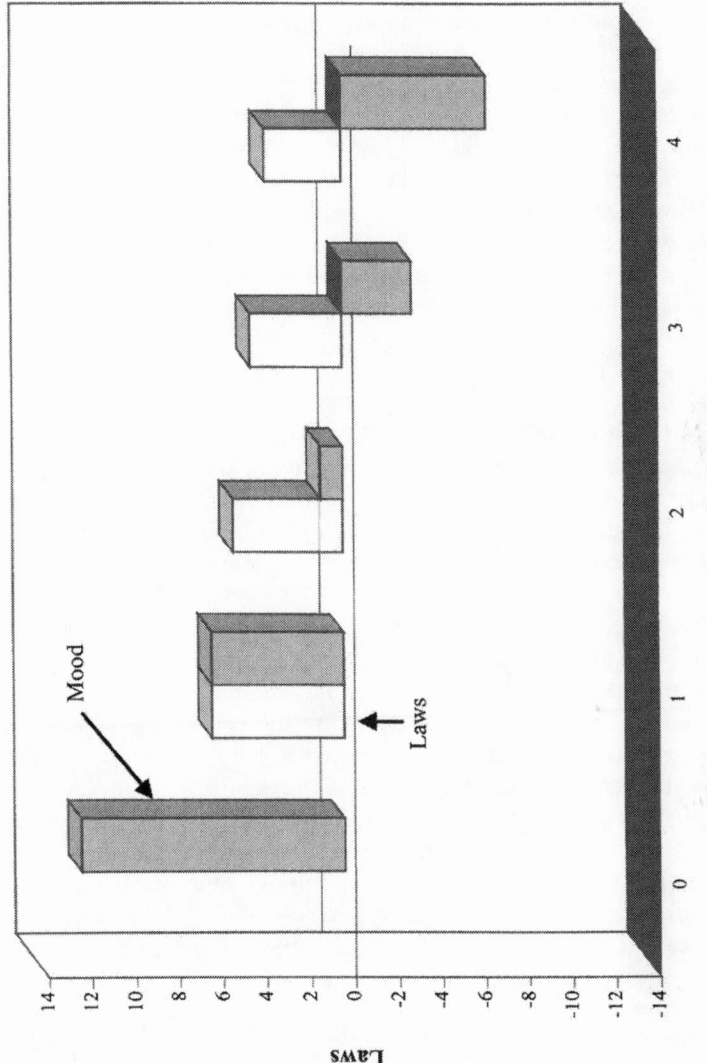

Figure 9.12. The Mood-Laws Connection over an Eight-Year Cycle: Democrats Follow Liberal Agenda with Liberal Mandate

nal anticipation mechanism seems a slow way to translate the public's preferences into public policy. As we know empirically that a surge in *Mood* should be satisfied within about eight years, rational anticipation alone turns out inadequate to produce dynamic representation.

To see how the system works, we put the two parts together, with a liberal electorate this time voting the Democrats into power for eight years. We now have both a partisan agenda and a policy mandate. In Figure 9.12 we see an initial *Mood* mandate of 12. In the first congress, the Democrats produce six new liberal laws: two laws in rational anticipation and four new laws pursuing their coalition's policy goals. *Mood* drops accordingly to 6. The Democrats then produce five major laws (four on their own and one due to electoral concerns), reducing *Mood* to 1. So, within two congresses, the *Mood-Policy* system has almost completely satisfied the electoral mandate. Unlike the situation when the only process in place was rational anticipation, a weak mechanism, we now see a quick and forceful policy response to the public's *Preferences*. Dynamic representation seems well fulfilled – mainly because the Democrats were happy, even eager, to serve the public's demands that coincided with their own party agenda.

But note what happens over the next two congresses. Democrats continue to pass liberal legislation, and the public starts to react negatively. As in the pure agenda situation, the Democratic liberal urge is only modestly moderated by rational anticipation. At the end of the eight-year tenure, the governing Democrats have produced 18.63 new liberal laws in response to an electoral mandate of 12 – and the public *Mood* now stands at −6.63. The likely electoral cost of the Democrats pursuing their goals is about 2 percent of the electorate's support in the subsequent election.

How responsive is this system to public opinion? Our example started with the public's mandate for a precise increment in liberalism. It took at least four years (one presidency) for government to produce the desired result. (If we simulated a larger mandate – an even more liberal *Mood* – it would have taken longer.) So by one standard, representation was too slow. Even with the Democrats in power, it took several years for the public's policy demands to be met. Such is the state of the Madisonian system.

In this example, we see the mechanisms in place. The exact numbers may be slightly off, the processes may be a bit quicker or slower, but the basic structure seems fairly robust. In a typical situation, an electorate that wants the government to produce policy does well to put in power the party that will avidly pursue that policy on their own. The effectiveness of rational anticipation alone will not do the job. But the ultimate cost is a string of policy products that well exceed the initial demand to the point where the electorate may have to throw out their benefactors at the next available election.

Our example shows the long-run effect of a party staying in power to be a declining ability to enact further policy that is ideologically congenial to its supporters, combined with a decline in public support due to its cumulative spending of political capital. The longer a party governs, the less it can accomplish *and* the more likely it will be replaced. The replacement provides a quick restoration of *Policy* toward its equilibrium value and the new cycle repeats the old, with a reverse of ideological direction.

Yet, not all is perfect. In an ideal theoretical world, our politicians would calculate exactly how much risk is involved in all this and produce precisely the right amount of liberal legislation that would ensure their continued reelection. Instead, with enough time in power, they exceed whatever electoral mandate that might have contributed to their election. Perhaps believing their own rhetoric, they pursue the agenda on which they were elected, and, simultaneously, they do what they believe to be the right thing for the country. Even accounting for their rational anticipation of the public's response, they nevertheless produce a policy legacy that will inevitably lead to their defeat at the polls.

In one sense, this inference should not surprise. In Chapter 8, we outlined the normal tension politicians face when they must balance electoral expediency with the opportunity to make policies that serve their constituents, their supporters, and their consciences. And, normally, we expect them to miss the electorally optimal point – leaning toward their own end of the ideological spectrum – trading off some chance for defeat against the rewards of policy making. Our analyses suggest that politicians make these trade-offs and that they are willing to pay the price.

This natural phenomenon has two consequences. First, when politicians overshoot the public's demands and run their own ideological course, they limit the public's ability to govern themselves. The only way that people can control policy is by forcibly alternating the party in power. Generally, Democrats will be more liberal than the public and Republicans will be more conservative. So the moderate voters – the ones near the middle of the ideological spectrum – face electoral choices at the extremes, either too liberal or too conservative. Given the incentives of these voters, the best course of action is to give power to a party that will pursue an agenda consistent with the public's preferences but then quickly remove that party's majority when it starts to overshoot. These marginal voters "balance" the parties across institutions and over time. Yet, because this calculus will be imprecise – the electorate guides institutional control only sporadically – the system will inevitably produce policies that either undersatisfy or oversatisfy the public's electoral mandates.

## Policy

The second consequence follows from the first. Parties alternate in power, paying close attention to the public's demands but also trying to produce policy that rewards their own preferences. The pursuit of a policy agenda produces "mistakes" that eventually catch up with them, and then the opposition will take over and follow the opposite course. This alternation of "mistakes" means that the public's *Mood*, a measure of the direction and magnitude of the government's "mistakes," will be driven *in part* by these inevitable swings in governmental policy.

An important question, one for which we have no truly satisfactory answer, is how much the fluctuations in public *Mood* that we see over the decades represent an autonomous evolution of public preferences for public policy and how much they represent the reaction to the inevitable swings in policy with changes in party control. That is, to what extent are the large movements in *Mood* driven by government policy and to what extent do they reflect genuine ideological change? By our construction, *Mood* is the difference between public preferences and governmental policy. So change in *Mood* could be generated by either component – preferences or policy – moving toward or away from the other. When *Mood* changes due to new shocks to underlying preferences, then the faster a new government with a new mandate can act, the better. When *Mood* changes only with the continual ideological overshooting of the governing party, the electorate prefers more moderation. Pursuing these issues further will inform our understanding of the role of citizen preferences in democratic government.

### DISCUSSION

From our statistical analysis, we have amassed considerable evidence of popular control of national policy. As measured by the *Laws* index, policy responds, with some delay, to the public's ideological demands as measured by the *Mood* index. In turn, ideological demand responds to policy change, albeit with some delay. That public opinion and policy respond to each other is gratifying in terms of fulfilling the expectations of democratic theory. But there are some remaining questions. How could the degree of popular control be so strong? Why are there evident delays? What are the roles of parties and elections in this process?

*Why So Strong an Effect?* In short, by our estimates, a one unit increase in *Mood* liberalism produces an immediate change of 0.77 more liberal *Laws*. Over the long run of several years, each unit change may generate up to three new *Laws*. We ask, how could changes in public opinion of such seemingly minor magnitude generate policy impacts of such force?

We believe that two factors account for this differential. The first has to do with heterogeneity in the mass public – which includes people both politically active and politically inert. Without further wallowing in individual-level data, we cannot divide the attentiveness of the public with precision. We do know, based on our analysis in Chapter 6, that when *Mood* changes, the change is seen across all social groups. So change is not solely the result of the behavior of one identifiable small elite. But within each social group, some people are more attentive than others. For those who are totally inattentive, *Mood* will not change because such people have no new information to inform their survey answers. Those who are most attentive will be most responsive to policy changes with their survey answers.

Beyond the special power of the politically attentive, we understand that the opinion-policy link is just another instance of how macro politics differs from "average" citizen behavior. Policy making is a matter of marginal power. That is, the marginal voters – those who might plausibly choose one party or the other – get special attention from savvy politicians because those marginal voters determine who wins and loses campaigns. We understand that most electoral politics is conducted in the middle range of the ideological spectrum – with relatively few politicians willing to espouse policies of the far left or far right. Voters to the left of the Democratic candidate and to the right of the Republican candidate, a substantial portion of the electorate, will find little reason to change their policy-based vote. Similarly, citizens to the left and right of the range of current policy proposals will not change their view that global policy is too conservative or too liberal (respectively). Thus, the relevant portion of the public – for whom matters of policy will be both important and decisive – is a relative few. A 1 percent shift in policy judgments will constitute a 1 percent shift in a party's fortunes at election day. When electoral campaigns prove relatively close, and where electoral consequences loom large in the minds of policy makers, we can expect that marginal shifts in *Policy Mood* will produce serious spur for policy action.

## Why Does Policy Respond with a Delay?

When we study *Policy Activity* as measured in the previous chapter, we find a strong responsiveness of annual activity to the public *Mood* as measured currently or only slightly lagged. But policy itself – as measured by the *Laws* index – appears to respond to *Mood* lagged over two and even four years. Moreover, while the quick response of the *Activity* index is best seen with annual data, the effect of *Mood* on *Laws* is best

Policy

seen when measured with a wide time band such as the biennium or even the quadrennium of a presidency.

One reason why *Laws* is best measured with a wide time band is that major laws are rare events. With an average *Laws* score of 5.85 per biennium, the average score per year is obviously only about 2 or 3. Since *Laws* scores are mainly the cumulation of liberal laws (plus the rare subtraction from conservative legislation), the score for any one year will contain considerable error as a measure of the general tone of current policy. Thus, *Laws* improves as a measure of policy liberalism as the time band expands.

But why would policy take so long to respond to opinion? This delay poses a puzzle. Changes in public opinion should get received by national politicians with speed and clarity. National politicians are professionals who stake their careers on reading public opinion correctly. That means that they will try to be well informed, that they will tend not to screen or filter messages to fit preconceived beliefs, and that they will quickly correct perceptions when they err. These things hold not because politicians are superior people, but because politics is their profession and because their stakes are very high.

Actually, we do see this quick response when the dependent variable is *Policy Activity* rather than *Policy* itself. The fuzziness of the time frame by which opinion translates into law reflects that opinion can influence policy throughout the policy-formation stage. The first stage is when new policy proposals get on the agenda. *Mood* can affect the inclination of interest groups to initiate and politicians to consider seriously a new policy innovation. *Mood* can affect the inclination of lawmakers at the crucial point of passage. And, of course, *Mood* can affect *Policy* throughout the time interval between these beginning and end points. The exact points in the policy-formation process at which *Mood* is most important are beyond our current understanding.[29] It is clear, however, that the sorts of major policy change that constitute our *Laws* and *Policy* indexes take a considerable amount of time between the origin and final passage, and they reflect years of intensive political activity. Such is Madison's legacy.[30]

29 An interesting test would be to ascertain a visible point of critical initiation for each law in the *Laws* series. We might surmise that the effect of opinion on initiation would involve a direct connection between current or very recent *Mood* and the initiation of new laws.

30 Mayhew (1991) notes that the bulk of these major laws were passed by large and bipartisan majorities. By the end of the day, enough politicking had occurred that final passage was seen as the consensual thing to do – not a matter of ideological or partisan advantage. In normal times, it takes considerable time for a major

Let us give one example of a major law that took four years from agenda stage to passage. This is the Kennedy-Kassenbaum Health Insurance Portability and Accountability Act of 1996, which made health insurance more portable. Why did this modest increment in the "liberalism" in U.S. health-care policy pass in the conservative climate of 1996, with a Republican congress? There are many reasons, but part of the story is the tracing of the bill as far back as late 1991. At that time, when the *Mood* indicator was entering a short liberal phase, federal health-care policy reentered the nation's political conscience after a long dormancy. One signal was the surprise election of Democrat Harrison Wofford in a special U.S. Senate election in Pennsylvania on the issue of expanded federal health insurance. Bill Clinton rode to the presidency in 1992 in part on the health-care issue. His 1993 health-care proposal turned out to be too ambitious, however, and failed miserably. The Republican congressional victory of 1994 reflected this perception that Clinton's proposal had gone too far. Yet the perception remained that some modest health reform should emerge from the process. The result, somewhat delayed, was the passage of Kennedy-Kassenbaum.

## Does Mood Respond with a Delay?

We have argued that *Mood* responds to policy changes with less delay than the reverse. Statistically, as far as we can tell, the response can be treated as virtually immediate. We can ask, what do citizens experience of policy change? We need to be more explicit here. We postulate that citizens observe public policy mainly as it enters into the rhetoric of proposal and counterproposal, majority and opposition, in Washington. Information flow is at its richest when policies are being changed, in the days, weeks, or sometimes months preceding decisive changes, and for a short period thereafter. News stories that begin with phrases like "Congress today . . ." are ubiquitous in the daily newspaper and the nightly news. Citizens then have a relatively costless opportunity to learn the major outlines of debate, to know something at least of the direction and scope of change.

For most policies, information flow is virtually nonexistent at all other times. Thus we reject the common presumption that direct experience of policy impacts is the stimulus of citizen response. Experience is all but unconnected in time with policy change: The citizen may not encounter

policy initiative to find its way through the congressional labyrinth and to obtain the support of both parties. In extraordinary times, of course, things do move more quickly.

policy effects directly for years after a change. And he or she often will not be in the class of people affected and thus can have no direct experience. And then he or she has almost no opportunity to observe the causal chain from policy debate, the consideration of options, to the effect experienced in everyday life. The information and inference problem here is similar to the Kramer (1983) account of citizen experience with the economy. Observing cause and effect between policy change and particular citizen experiences is difficult enough for the policy analyst. For the citizen, the task is unmanageable.

Imagine, for example, that we debate changing cost of living allowances (COLAs) for Social Security recipients, perhaps proposing that COLAs be pegged to an index slightly lower than the Consumer Price Index (CPI). Such a debate would be widely reported and experienced as rhetoric by most citizens with any but the most minimal interest and awareness. And then, some months later, a subgroup of citizens will experience the effect for the first time: an increase in the monthly check but by a few dollars less than would have been the case without the index change. Only a few will directly observe the change, and most will feel little pain. For very few, the change will be a surprise. But we suspect that virtually all will, in fact, know about the change because they experienced the policy debate and resolution preceding it. Thus, even in this instance, with a clear scenario for direct experience of policy effects in daily life, the vicarious experience of the policy debate will have been vastly more influential for the general citizenry, and probably even so for most Social Security recipients. Thus we expect citizens to respond to policy change when the change occurs. And our best evidence, albeit tentative in character, shows that they do.

### Party Control and Policy Choices

We now know that policy responds both to *Mood* and to the party control of the presidency and congress. Whenever *Mood* changes, politicians respond. They rationally anticipate the import of *Mood* for reelection and produce a policy change to head off public opinion. And the electoral process is driven in part by *Mood*, so that the party composition of the government changes accordingly.

Party control turns out to be especially important for dynamic representation in the United States. The rational anticipation phenomenon is simply not powerful enough to get the job done. Instead, the link between public preferences and policy is carried as strongly (and perhaps more consequentially) by the electorate's willingness to change party control over government. When the public wants a policy change, it is not enough that it implicitly threatens electoral consequences; rather, it must actually vote in a new president or a new Senate or House. But in changing party control, the public often gets more than it wants.

When it comes to policy choices, politicians are motivated not only by the preferences of the public but also by their own preferences. They consider the demands of their electoral allies and financial supporters, the views of their close associates, and their sense of what is best for the country. Predictably, Republicans will pursue conservative (and Democrats, liberal) policies quite apart from the implicit demands of *Mood*.

In the normal course of events, the public changes policy by both the implicit threat (enacted through rational anticipation) and by choosing leaders who will naturally, enthusiastically, and sincerely change policy in the desired direction. The likely cost, of course, is that the new leadership is likely to overshoot – producing overdoses of conservatism and liberalism. The public will react and (perhaps) enforce an electoral consequence. During ordinary times, the wobbling between Democrat and Republican, between liberal and conservative, leads to the ordinary changes in the party composition of the government. And the causal flow of public opinion gets mixed into other factors, essentially matters of performance, that also govern American politics.

However, in extraordinary times, the system's operation becomes clear to the naked eye. On the liberal side, the clear example was the 89th Congress elected in 1964. In an often documented story, the conservative coalition of Republicans and southern Democrats lost its collective majority in congress for the first time since 1938. The result of this liberal Democratic majority allied with a liberal activist president was a one-time spurt of liberal policy making. For the northern Democratic majority, the trade-off was the breaking of the legislative logjam at the expense of a long-term conservative turn to *Mood*.

A similar story could be told about the conservative revolution of the early Reagan era. An ideologically conservative Republican president allied with a Republican Senate and a House with enough conservative Democrats to coalesce with the Republican minority. The conservative policy surge – which should probably be scored at greater magnitude than our *Laws* index allows – brought real policy change but with the long-term result of a liberal turn to *Mood*.

These two instances presented the rare case of a clear ideological governing majority. Other instances include the Republican congresses at the beginning and the ends of our time series. The combination of a Republican president and Republican congress in 1953–1954 contributed to a rare conservative moment in national policy making but may have contributed to the liberal *Mood* gain of the late 1950s and early 1960s. The Republican congress elected in 1994 presented a case

373

for a conservative mandate, and certainly led to more conservative legislation than if a Democratic congress had been retained. As of this writing, the effect on *Mood* is yet to be ascertained.

In these cases, the public opinion reaction to an ideological majority – and the subsequent politician sensitivity to the reaction – tempered considerably the ability of the governing coalitions to alter the course of policy history. The Great Society and the Reagan revolution proved short-lived. In fact, it appears that *Mood*'s direct and substantial reaction against any exogenously generated policy change will govern policy toward its long-run equilibrium path.

Much of the sound and fury of American politics, much of what appear to be decade-long swings in the fortunes of ideology and party, is in reality a manifestation of a self-governing public opinion and government. And this is no mere abstraction – the system is peopled by strong-willed ambitious individuals. Given natural instincts for political power, politicians and ideological theorists and public interest organizers and newspaper columnists have every reason to read public opinion's augurs of elections to come. Equally, they conscientiously promote the virtues of their own policies and rail against the grievous excesses of their opponents. The end, then, is a regularly fueled engine that reproduces action, response, and counterresponse.

In this sense, the public opinion-policy linkage serves to keep the political system along the course set by public preferences, much as an earlier generation of "systems theorists" postulated. In normative terms, this behavior accords with Madison's vision. The governing system does respond to sustained changes in national judgment, but it responds slowly and in a stable manner.

## APPENDIX

*Laws Seen as Important at the Time, Coded for Ideological Content*

| Year | Rating | Legislation |
|------|--------|-------------|
| 1953 | C | Tidelands oil act. Turned submerged tidelands over to coastal states. |
| 1953 | L | Social Security expansion. Benefits raised; 10 million new people covered. |
| 1953 | C | Communist Control Act of 1954. Communist party outlawed. A Democratic Party move. |
| 1955 | L | Minimum wage increase. To 90 cents. |
| 1956 | L | Disability insurance. Added to Social Security. |
| 1957 | L | CIVIL RIGHTS ACT OF 1957. First since 1870s. Federal injunctive powers on voting rights. Civil Rights Commission established. |

| Year | Rating | Legislation |
|------|--------|-------------|
| 1958 | L | NDEA Act of 1958. After Sputnik, loans to college students, grants to schools. |
| 1958 | L | Social Security increase. Benefits up 7%. |
| 1959 | C | Landrum-Griffin Labor Reform Act of 1959. Curbs on union violence, corruption, power abuses. |
| 1959 | L | Housing Act of 1959. Modest compromise measure after two Eisenhower vetoes. |
| 1960 | L | Civil Rights Act of 1960. Voting rights protection, criminal penalties for bombings. |
| 1961 | L | Housing Act of 1961. Urban open spaces, middle-income housing, community facilities. |
| 1961 | L | Minimum wage increase. To $1.25. Coverage for 3.6 million new workers. |
| 1961 | L | Social Security increase. Benefits raised. |
| 1961 | L | Area Redevelopment Act of 1961. Grants and loans for economically depressed areas. |
| 1962 | L | Manpower Development and Training Act of 1962. To retrain workers with obsolete or inadequate skills. |
| 1962 | L | Drug regulation. Post-thalidomide. Tightened regulation of medical products for safety and effectiveness. |
| 1963 | L | Higher Education Facilities Act of 1963. Funds to build college classrooms, libraries, etc. |
| 1963 | L | Aid for the mentally ill and retarded. For research and treatment centers. |
| 1963 | L | Aid to medical schools. Student loans, buildings. |
| 1964 | L | CIVIL RIGHTS ACT OF 1964. Banned discrimination in public accommodations, employment, publicly owned facilities, federally funded programs. |
| 1964 | L | ECONOMIC OPPORTUNITY ACT OF 1964. Johnson's antipoverty program. Job Corps, community action programs, VISTA. |
| 1964 | L | Urban Mass Transportation Act of 1964. Federal grants. |
| 1964 | L | Wilderness Act of 1964. Set up a national Wilderness System of lands free from intrusion. |
| 1964 | L | Food Stamp Act of 1964. Program made permanent. Result of Johnson logroll with cotton and wheat interests. |
| 1965 | L | MEDICAL CARE FOR THE AGED. Medicare for the aged via Social Security. Medicaid for the medically indigent. |
| 1965 | L | VOTING RIGHTS ACT OF 1965. The major statute: federal registrars to police southern elections. |
| 1965 | L | ELEMENTARY AND SECONDARY EDUCATION ACT (ESEA) OF 1965. For the first time, broad federal aid to schools. |
| 1965 | L | Department of Housing and Urban Development (HUD) established. |

*(continued)*

# Policy

*Laws Seen as Important at the Time, Coded for Ideological Content (cont.)*

| Year | Rating | Legislation |
|------|--------|-------------|
| 1965 | L | Appalachian Regional Development Act of 1965. $1 billion for 12-state region. |
| 1965 | L | Regional medical centers for heart disease, cancer, and stroke. Federal grants. |
| 1965 | L | Highway Beautification Act of 1965. Lady Bird Johnson's project. Ban on billboards. |
| 1965 | L | Immigration reform. Ended national origins quotas. |
| 1965 | L | National Foundation on the Arts and Humanities established. |
| 1965 | L | Higher Education Act of 1965. Scholarships and insured loans for college students. |
| 1965 | L | Housing and Urban Development Act of 1965. Omnibus measure featuring rent supplements. |
| 1965 | L | Motor Vehicle Air Pollution Control Act of 1965. HEW to set emissions standards for new cars. |
| 1966 | L | Department of Transportation established. |
| 1966 | L | Clean Waters Restoration Act of 1966. Subsidies to locales to control water pollution. |
| 1966 | L | Air pollution control. Aid to states and locales. |
| 1966 | L | Traffic Safety Act of 1966. New Nader-inspired standards. |
| 1966 | L | Minimum wage increase. To $1.60, with 9.1 million new workers covered. |
| 1966 | L | Demonstration cities program. For coordinated attack on blight in selected "model cities." |
| 1967 | L | Social Security increase. 13% hike; new work-requirement (WIN) curb on welfare. |
| 1967 | L | Public Broadcasting Act of 1967. Set up corporation to aid educational TV and radio. |
| 1967 | L | Air Quality Act of 1967. Stepped-up pollution regulation. |
| 1967 | L | Wholesome Meat Act of 1967. Improved meat inspection. |
| 1968 | L | OPEN HOUSING ACT OF 1968. Ban on discrimination in sale or rent of housing. First such act in the twentieth century. |
| 1968 | L | Housing and Urban Development Act of 1968. To provide 1.7 million new or rehab units for low-income families. |
| 1968 | L | Gun Control Act of 1968. Ban on mail sales of long guns. |
| 1968 | L | National Scenic trails system established. |
| 1968 | L | National Gas Pipeline Safety Act of 1968. Set standards. |
| 1968 | L | Truth in Lending Act of 1968. Required disclosure of information to consumers in credit transactions. |
| 1969 | L | Coal mine safety act. New standards. Compensation for black lung disease. |
| 1969 | L | Social Security increase. 15% hike. |
| 1969 | L | Tax Reform Act of 1969. Said to be the most comprehensive revision of tax schedule in U.S. history. |

## A Governing System: Laws and Public Opinion

| Year | Rating | Legislation |
|------|--------|-------------|
| 1970 | L | Voting Rights Act extension. For 5 years. Coverage beyond the South. Gave suffrage to 18-year-olds (upheld by courts only for federal elections). |
| 1970 | L | Clean Air Act of 1970. Uniquely ambitious. Set specific deadlines for reduction of auto emissions. |
| 1970 | L | Water Quality Improvement Act of 1970. Aimed at oil spills, sewage. |
| 1970 | L | Ban on cigarette advertising on radio and TV. Also strengthened warning label on packages. |
| 1970 | L | Occupational Safety and Health Act (OSHA) of 1970. New on the job standards plus enforcement mechanism. |
| 1971 | L | Social Security increase. 10% hike. |
| 1971 | L | Emergency Employment Act of 1971. $2.25 billion for public-service jobs. First such plan since New Deal. |
| 1972 | L | Federal Election Campaign Act of 1972. Ceiling on radio and TV spending for ads; rigorous disclosure rules. |
| 1972 | L | Water pollution control act. Uniquely comprehensive and expensive. New standards; $24 billion to build sewage treatment plants, etc. Over Nixon's veto. |
| 1972 | L | Social Security increase. Major 20% hike, plus automatic tie of future hikes to cost of living index. |
| 1972 | L | Pesticide Control Act of 1972. Comprehensive program. |
| 1972 | L | Consumer Product Safety Act of 1972. New commission to set and enforce safety standards for consumer products. |
| 1973 | L | Federal Aid Highway Act of 1973. Opened up Highway Trust Fund to mass-transit projects. |
| 1973 | L | Comprehensive Employment and Training Act (CETA) of 1973. Reorganized manpower programs via Nixonian block grants. Continued public service employment as CETA jobs. |
| 1973 | L | Social Security increase. Two step 11% hike. |
| 1974 | L | Federal Election Campaign Act of 1974. The basic law: limits on contributions and spending, full disclosure, public funding of presidential elections, the FEC. |
| 1974 | L | Minimum wage increase. To $2.30 in 3 stages, plus coverage of 7 million new workers. |
| 1974 | L | Freedom of Information Act Amendments of 1974. Beefed up earlier act to insure public access to government records – e.g., FBI files. Enacted over Ford's veto. |
| 1975 | L | Voting Rights Act extension. For 7 years; language minorities added to coverage. |
| 1975 | L | Repeal of fair-trade laws. That is, 40-year-old state laws allowing manufacturer dealer price fixing. |
| 1976 | L | Toxic substance control act. Required chemical firms to test risky products. Banned PCBs. |

*(continued)*

# Policy

*Laws Seen as Important at the Time, Coded for Ideological Content (cont.)*

| Year | Rating | Legislation |
|------|--------|-------------|
| 1977 | L | Social Security tax increase. To raise additional $227 billion over 10 years. |
| 1977 | L | Tax cut. 3-year stimulus package. |
| 1977 | L | Minimum wage hike. To $3.35 in 4 stages. |
| 1977 | L | Surface Mining Control and Reclamation Act of 1977. New standards for strip mining. |
| 1978 | L | Comprehensive energy package. Conservation provisions; phased decontrol of natural gas prices. A shadow of Carter's April 1977 omnibus plan. |
| 1979 | L | Department of Education established. |
| 1980 | L | Windfall profits tax on oil. Carter's plan; to bring in $227 billion over a decade. |
| 1980 | L | Toxic wastes Superfund. $1.6 billion fund, largely from levies on industry, to clean up chemical dumps. |
| 1981 | C | ECONOMIC RECOVERY TAX ACT OF 1981. Reagan's plan. Largest tax cut in U.S. history; $749 billion over five years. Individual income tax cuts of 5%, 10%, and 10% over three years; indexing of tax brackets to offset inflation; cuts in corporate taxes. |
| 1981 | C | OMNIBUS BUDGET RECONCILIATION ACT OF 1981 (OBRA; GRAMM-LATTA II). Stockman plan to slash domestic spending, permanently, by revising authorization blueprints. Cuts for fiscal 1982 to total $35.2 billion. To affect disability benefits, Medicare, Medicaid, AFDC payments, subsidized housing, health programs, food stamps, unemployment insurance, CETA jobs, student loans, Pell grants, impact areas aid, school lunches, medical education, sewer grants, postal subsidies, trade adjustment assistance, small business loans, mass transit systems, highway funds, Conrail, Amtrak, and more. |
| 1982 | L | Transportation Assistance Act of 1982. $71 billion for highway construction, road repairs, mass transit. Raised the gasoline tax. |
| 1982 | L | Voting Rights extension. For 25 years. |
| 1983 | L | Martin Luther King's birthday declared a legal holiday. |
| 1983 | L | Antirecession jobs measure. $4.6 billion. |
| 1985 | C | Gramm-Rudman-Hollings anti-deficit act. Move to balance the budget by 1990 through automatic spending cuts. |
| 1986 | L | Cleanup of toxic waste dumps. Major expansion of Superfund. New standards, new taxes, $9.6 billion. |
| 1986 | L | Omnibus water projects act. First such act since 1976. $16.3 billion, 262 projects, users to share costs. |
| 1987 | L | Water Quality Act of 1987. $18 billion to sewage treatment plants, etc. Over Reagan's veto. |

378

## A Governing System: Laws and Public Opinion

| Year | Rating | Legislation |
|------|--------|-------------|
| 1987 | L | Surface Transportation Act of 1987. $88 billion for highways, mass transit. Over Reagan's veto. |
| 1987 | L | Housing and community development act. First housing authorization since 1980. $30 billion. |
| 1987 | L | McKinney Homeless Assistance Act of 1987. $443 million for shelter, health, food, etc. |
| 1988 | L | Catastrophic health insurance for the aged. Major costs to be paid for by insurance premiums. |
| 1988 | L | Family Support Act of 1988. Welfare reform. Aimed to ease taking jobs, support families of those who do. |
| 1988 | L | Grove City civil rights measure. Overturned 1984 court decision; reasserted that civil rights laws reach whole institutions receiving federal aid, not just particular programs. Enacted over Reagan's veto. |
| 1989 | L | Minimum wage hike. To $4.25 in 1991. New training wage for teenagers. |
| 1990 | L | DEFICIT REDUCTION PACKAGE. Bipartisan deal; $490 billion in tax hikes and spending cuts over five years. Fall 1990. |
| 1990 | L | Americans with Disabilities Act of 1990. To guarantee job rights and access to public facilities. |
| 1990 | L | Clean Air Act of 1990. To curb acid rain, airborne toxins, urban smog. |
| 1990 | L | Child care package. $22.5 billion; tax credits and state grants for children of working parents. |
| 1990 | L | National Affordable Housing Act of 1990. New block grants to expand stock; new HOPE program to sell off public housing projects to tenants. |
| 1991 | L | Civil Rights. Made it easier for victims of job discrimination to sue. |
| 1991 | L | Transportation. $151 billion bill to repair roads and bridges and improve mass transit. |
| 1992 | L | Cable TV. Authorized regulation of minimum cable service, over Bush's veto. |
| 1992 | L | Education. $115 billion over five years for higher education programs and made it easier for students from middle-income families to pay for college with government grants and loans. |
| 1993 | L | BUDGET DEFICIT. Deficit Reduction bill for nearly $500 billion in tax increases, spending cuts. |
| 1993 | L | Motor Voter. To allow people to register by mail, or when they apply for a driver's license or some government benefit. |
| 1993 | L | Gun Control. "Brady Bill" to require a waiting period of five business days and background check for purchase of a handgun. |

*(continued)*

# Policy

*Laws Seen as Important at the Time, Coded for Ideological Content (cont.)*

| Year | Rating | Legislation |
|------|--------|-------------|
| 1993 | L | Family Leave and Medical Leave. Family leave to guarantee workers up to 12 weeks unpaid leave to deal with newborns and medical emergencies. |
| 1993 | L | National Service. Educational grants to young people in exchange for community service. |
| 1994 | L | Crime. $30 billion crime bill bans 19 assault weapons, and allows the death penalty for dozens of federal crimes and authorizes new spending for police officers and prisons. |
| 1994 | L | Education Initiatives. Renewal of elementary and secondary education aid of $12.4 billion. An expansion of Head Start. The "Goals 2000" bill to set national achievement centers. A school-to-work transition program. An overhaul of college student loans program. |
| 1994 | L | Abortion Clinic Access. Makes it a crime to block access to clinics, damage their property, or injure or intimidate patients and staff. |
| 1996 | C | WELFARE REFORM. Ended the 60-year-old federal guarantee of cash assistance for the nation's poorest children, set a five-year limit on payment to any family, required most adult recipients to work within two years, and gave states vast new power to run their own welfare and work programs with lump sums of federal money. |
| 1996 | L | Health Insurance. Approved legislation making it easier for workers to retain health insurance coverage if they lose or change jobs and curtailed exclusions based on preexisting medical conditions. |
| 1996 | L | Minimum Wage. Raised the minimum wage to $5.15 from $4.15 in two steps and gave tax breaks to small businesses, homemakers, and others. |
| 1996 | L | Safe Drinking Water Act. Granted local government more flexibility in monitoring water quality, expanding federal aid to water suppliers, and providing consumers with more information about water contamination. Tightened regulation of pesticides, with special attention to childhood risks. Enacted a new fisheries law intended to prevent further overfishing and expanded logging on public lands. |
| 1996 | C | Same Sex Marriages. Denied members of same-sex marriages any federal marriage benefits and permitted states to ignore such marriages sanctioned in other states. |

*Notes*: L represents a liberal change in policy, and C, a conservative change in policy. Policies perceived at the time to be exceptionally important (according to Mayhew) are capitalized.
*Source*: Mayhew (1991); 1991–1996 updates by Jay Greene.

# PART III

*American Politics as a System*

# 10

## American Macro Politics: A System Model

When we explained *Presidential Approval* in Chapter 2, we did so in the way that others have done. That is, we found an election-honeymoon sequence and powerful effects of the performance of the domestic economy. In that analysis we did not predict who would be president or account for the performance of the domestic economy. We just took those as historical facts and exploited them. And the same with *Macropartisanship*: We saw that it moved in response to incumbent approval and performance and we took the party of the incumbent as historically given. John Kennedy did defeat Richard Nixon in 1960, for example, and so we assigned the White House to the Democrats for 1961 through 1964. We did explain elections (in Chapter 7), taking as given factors such as *Mood, Macropartisanship, Economic Performance,* and the like. And so on with *Policy Preferences, Policy Activity,* and, most recently, *Policy.* Each explanatory focus takes as given something else, which is itself to be explained in other chapters.

One might quickly imagine a hopeless quandary to such explanation, a grand circularity in which everything explains and is explained by everything else. Luckily, there is no such quandary; this dog chases no tails because everything in this explanatory system works on future values of the effects it produces. Thus performance produces future approval, which influences future partisanship, which influences future election outcomes. But, to stay with our example, John Kennedy's *Approval* rating does not influence the 1960 outcome. So Kennedy isn't president because he is approved, and approved because he is a newly elected president all at the same time. Our formulation, difference equations, has no contemporaneous causation.

But in a theoretical sense our dog does chase its tail. We have no statistical nightmare of causal feedback, but we do have a system where we use the convenience of taking some things as fixed and given to explain others – and then turn around in other analyses and free the one for explanation while freezing (past values of) the other. This is the traditional mode of nonexperimental research in the social sciences and elsewhere. It is a defensible means to divide the world into manageable problem sets. But proceeding in this traditional fashion prevents one from seeing the system of relationships as a system.

In this chapter, we put it all together, treating American macro politics as a system and exploring the consequences of system behavior. Systems thinking and systems language have been part of political science at least since Easton's pioneering efforts of the mid-1960s (Easton 1965). We talk comfortably about inputs, outputs, feedback, and the like. But these have been vague abstractions, not real models. Here we hope to do better, to lay out an actual working model of macro politics in America, to run the model, test it, and explore what it has to tell us beyond what we have learned from studying individual relationships in the last nine chapters.

## On Systems and Pieces

In modal social science, we abstract a piece of what we generally understand to be a larger system of relationships for study. We declare our explanatory focus a *dependent variable* and set about building theoretical and then statistical models to account for it. The ubiquitous tool of such exercises is linear modeling, in which the dependent variable is thought to be a linear composite of various exogenous influences and of random errors. In this book, that modeling technology is usually a time-series variant of ordinary least squares regression in which a lagged value of the dependent variable accounts for the systematic pull of history on the phenomenon under study.

With this familiar approach we have modeled (in chapter order) *Presidential Approval, Macropartisanship, Policy Mood*, election outcomes for the presidency and the houses of congress, *Policy Activity* in the House, Senate, presidency, and Supreme Court, the production of important public laws, and the mechanisms by which some of these things feed back at later times to many of the others. More briefly, we model social outcomes, such as the employment and inflation effects of differential party control of the White House. These effects are all statistically tractable, even though jointly endogenous, by lagged time relationships. But it is quite obvious that they *are* jointly endogenous. Almost all of the dependent variables of one chapter become inputs in another.

*Economic Performance*, for example, (measured as familiar employment and inflation outcomes) moves *Presidential Approval, Macropartisanship*, and *Policy Mood*. Each of those three influence election outcomes and policy activity. Election outcomes change party control of government. Party control of government and policy activity then change future levels of employment and inflation, bringing us back to where we (thought we) started. This is, in short, a system.

*The Cascade of Causality – An Example*: To illustrate the properties of the system we trace here the impact of a hypothetical increase in unemployment at a particular time. Later in this chapter, we will actually induce a similar effect and follow its consequences where they lead. We can answer the "what happens" question with a large number of theories of impact, supported by a larger number of regression results.

The story begins with an immediate decline of *Presidential Approval*. Then both directly and through approval, economic effects find their way into *Macropartisanship*, in this case harming the standing of the party of the White House. Already things begin to get complicated for the *Approval* effect decays in the months to come while the (smaller) influence on *Macropartisanship* is permanent.

While these first impacts of unemployment change are contingent on control of the White House, another effect is not. Increasing unemployment rates always produce liberalism in policy preferences. Thus Democrats in the White House experience offsetting effects from bad employment results and losses of presidential and party standing offset by gains in support for the party's liberal positions. Unemployment under Republican administrations produces all positive effects for Democrats. Elections for both congress and White House are next to feel the effects. They are a function of *Approval*, of *Macropartisanship*, and of *Policy Mood*, all of them carrying some of the signal of the unemployment effect. Thus, we leverage the numbers of seats in congress and probability of winning or holding the White House some periods down the road from the employment shock.

Now we will experience changes in the liberalism of *Policy Activity*. These are partly mediated by the elections effects and also partly by the direct influence of the now hypothetically more liberal *Policy Mood*. *Policy Activity*, the actions of presidents and congress of a particular time, have some permanent residue, which we shall call *Policy*. *Policy* has a permanent and cumulative character. Laws passed, for example, remain in force permanently or until some explicit counteraction. If our employment change were big enough to produce a change of party control in congress or White House, then an additional set of effects begins. We postulate that parties pursue policies that are a compromise between those preferred by their more ideological core supporters and the blander preferences of the median voter. That means that policy will usually err in the direction of the ideological position of the party. That sets off a later effect in *Policy Mood*, now contrary to the original impetus. If the unemployment shock had helped produce a Democratic White House, then it would also have produced liberal public policy and a reaction toward conservatism in public preferences – with preferences now feeling the early effects of unemployment coupled with the later adverse reaction to Democratic governance.

Party control will also influence the economic variables that in this case started the whole sequence. Democratic control of policy produces employment gains at offsetting inflationary costs. The effect has now come full circle, some periods after it started, to influence the situation which was its origin.

Now if we ask the simple question, familiar from the old path-modeling tradition, "What is the total effect of that increase in unemployment?", all our regressions won't do us much good. It isn't as simple as just multiplying through the known coefficients to get total effect. Some of the effects are contingent and some are not. Some of them influence probabilities of future events (for example, Democrats winning the White House), which have an uncertain and nonlinear translation into outcomes. And all of the cascading effects move through the system over time at differing rates. Some decay quickly. Some last forever. And some, for example, election effects, don't even begin until several periods after the cascade begins.

The bottom line is this: Even though the whole system is nothing but a set of difference equations, changes produce complicated and contingent effects as they flow into the future. In a system with Las Vegas-like uncertainty for events like election outcomes and highly complex causal feedback even for noncontingent effects, it quickly becomes impossible to anticipate the long-term effects of short-term changes. That is the essence of systems, that their dynamics become much more complicated, much less certain, than their simple linear components.

### STRATEGY

If it could be done, a multiple difference equation formulation would be an ideal representation for our system. Each single equation, such as the dynamic specifications that appear throughout this book, has an implied impulse response, the expected effect of $x$ on $y$ at $t + 1$, $t + 2$, $t + 3$, and so forth, which allows one to characterize future states of the system as a function of current values.[1] In a multiple difference equation setup, this possibility is extended to all variables that are downstream in the system, with the implied impulse response now a joint function of all the possi-

---

1 In an equation of the form $y = \phi y_{t-1} + \beta_1 x_{1t-1} + \ldots + e_t$, the implied impulse response of $y$ to a unit change in $x_1$ for $t = 1, 2, 3, \ldots k$ is $\phi \beta_1$, $\phi^2 \beta_1$, $\phi^3 \beta_1$, $\ldots \phi^k \beta_1$.

ble paths through which any $x$ can influence future values of any $y$. The virtue of this system is that it can be solved. Not a simple piece of arithmetic, it is nonetheless possible to characterize how an increment in any particular piece of an equation flows through to all other equations at later times.

That we cannot do. The problem is that we lack common case definitions that work across equation sets. Our cases are time units and we have not one, but five of them: months, quarters, years, two-year multiples, and four-year multiples. This represents not convenience or arbitrary decisions on our part, but rather the fact that frequencies are quite different across the social, economic, and constitutional phenomena we explore. At the extremes, we have economic conditions and approval, which are monthly, and presidential elections spaced one every four years. The former conditions vary frequently and can complete whole cycles, peak to trough to peak again inside a presidential term. Thus we must deal with phenomena in their natural frequencies. Consequently, we cannot put together everything we know in "simple" difference equation form.

### Statistical Simulation as Alternative

We turn instead to statistical simulation of the system. Using the computer rather than formal mathematics we can "solve" our equation system by running it and observing its outcomes. That is how we will proceed. We implement the theory and analysis of the previous nine chapters in a comprehensive system model. Beginning with the equations and parameters already seen in tables, we build a design that faithfully emulates the theory and analysis that have come before. We do so as rigidly as possible, for we wish not to explore new knowledge, change theories or measures, or in any way deviate from the claims we have already made, but rather to put them all together and see what results.[2] Thus, each equation is a column from a table, with its parameters (and standard errors) and properties (standard error of estimate) just as reported. The measures, similarly, are done just as those used for analyses. When we cross time intervals, for example, monthly to quarterly, we

---

2 Some small deviations are forced upon us. We estimate the representation processes of Chapter 8, for example, with single indicator regressions, rather than the full information Kalman filter setup used in that analysis. And when we simulate consumer sentiment, we do so only from knowledge of employment and inflation effects – which are endogenous to the model – rather than the Commerce Department's leading and lagging indicator series that we used earlier, because such indicators cannot be products of the model.

could make choices different from the aggregate series on which the analyses are based, for example using the most recent month to represent $t - 1$ rather than an average of three. We change nothing. That way our estimates retain their properties. More important, when we describe our system behavior, readers can have confidence that it is the same system already seen in the book, not one that is jury-rigged for the purpose of simulation. (Simulation has an established tradition in the field of macroeconomics. For useful discussions, see Fair 1993; Pagan 1999; and Klein, Welfe, and Welfe 1999.)

The strength of simulation as a technique is its ability to represent systems more complex than could be modeled by standard statistical estimation techniques. That is why we exploit it here. Its well-known weakness is that it is not a particularly good means of making inferences about relationships. The problem is that the very complexity that simulation models can include leaves one not knowing which of a large number of factors might account for predictive success and failure. Here we have the best of both worlds. We have already drawn our inferences about particular relationships and need not care that this technique is not well suited for the task. In that sense we are not testing any earlier assertions; they don't require further test. We don't have to choose between statistical estimation and system simulation, because we have already done statistical estimation. In this chapter we *use* what we already know; we don't need to make inferences about relationships. What we will explore is the behaviors that may arise from the system itself that would be unobserved in its individual pieces. Simulation modeling is well suited to studying complex interactions, and that is what we shall exploit in this chapter.

### THE MACRO MODEL: PUTTING TOGETHER THE PIECES

To cope with system dynamics, we turn to modeling the system itself. Our strategy is to take seriously all the theory and statistical modeling of our enterprise and put together the pieces into a system whose properties we can observe. Our means of doing so is a deterministic simulation. It is built entirely from the theory and statistical models of earlier chapters. Insofar as humanly possible, it implements what came before, adding no new assumptions or specifications. One can think of the simulation as a set of parallel difference equations complicated by the fact that we have not one time line (and set of "cases"), but rather several, each befitting the topic at hand. Thus economic outcomes move at monthly intervals, *Approval* and *Macropartisanship* in quarters, *Policy Mood*, *Policy Activity*, and *Policy* are annual, congressional elections biennial, and presidential elections quadrennial. So, this is nothing as simple as a "seemingly unrelated regressions" setup on common cases. But importantly, at its core it is still nothing but equations, estimated by regressions. But it is equations that capture the endogeneity, where change in one part of the system at one time is input to other components in later periods.

The model consists of 17 equations with 48 parameters on the political side, with two additional equations and a very large number of parameters predicting the reaction of the national economy to party control of government. Most variables in the system are endogenously determined; their values at time $t$ are the outputs of other equations at $t - 1$. Such a system is not easy to describe, nothing quite so simple as 1960s vintage path models with boxes and arrows for a set of variables measured all for the same cross-sectional case. (See the appendix for details on the equation specifications and also for more technical material.)

As a means to simplify presentation, we start with a core of three variables, *Public Opinion*, *Election Outcomes*, and *Policy Activity*, the representation model of Chapter 8. This is an arbitrary choice. It is not the core of our work; we could equally well have built the center at other loci of the model. The model represents our theory of response to opinion change through rational anticipation, grafted onto the standard electoral replacement system for opinion influence. The key concepts have the indicators of earlier chapters; *Public Opinion* is *Policy Mood*, conceived as net preference for more or less government activity across a range of domestic concerns. *Election Outcomes* are just seats in congress and indicators of party control of each house and the presidency. *Policy Activity* is tapped by summary scales of House, Senate, and presidential actions.

This allows us to put the other pieces in some context, building models of the causes and effects of the three core concepts. We break the full model into three pieces as they are joined to each of the three nodes of Figure 10.1. Beginning in model 1 (Figure 10.2) we picture the structure of influences on public opinion.

Our indicator of preferences, *Policy Mood*, is modeled as a function of unemployment (higher levels producing liberalism of preference), inflation (higher levels producing conservatism), and a negative feedback to previous policy, moving *Mood* opposite the recent flow of policy change.

Elections in our model (see model 2 in Figure 10.3) combine the influences of government performance indicators such as presidential approval and disposable income change with preferences (*Mood*) interacting with party positions on the other. *Macropartisanship* carries the

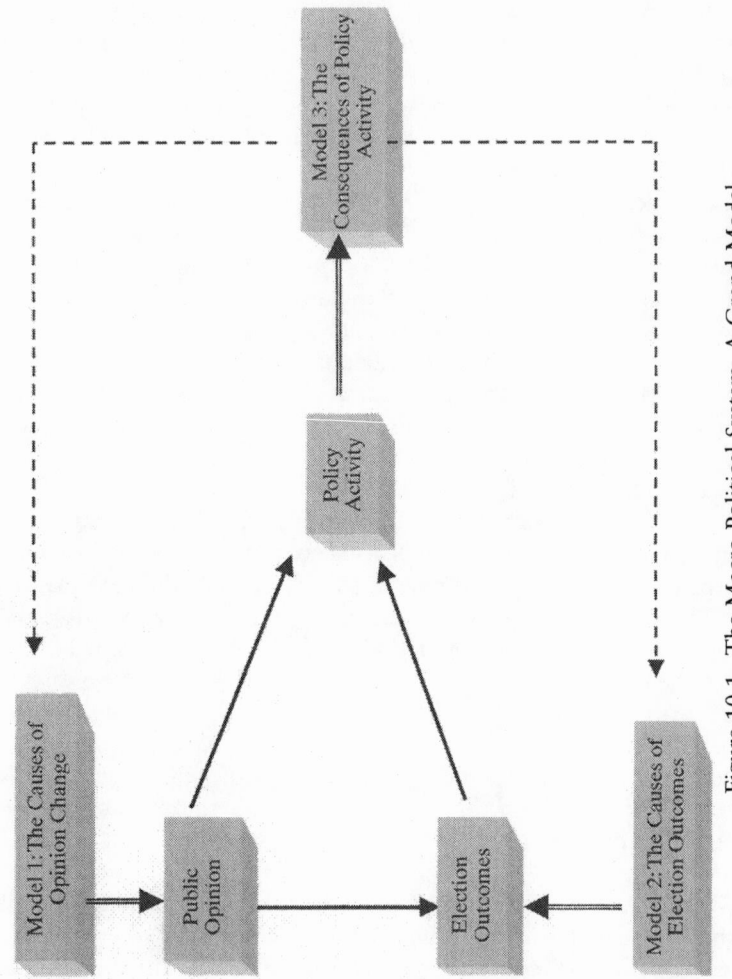

Figure 10.1. The Macro-Political System: A Grand Model

## American Macro Politics: A System Model

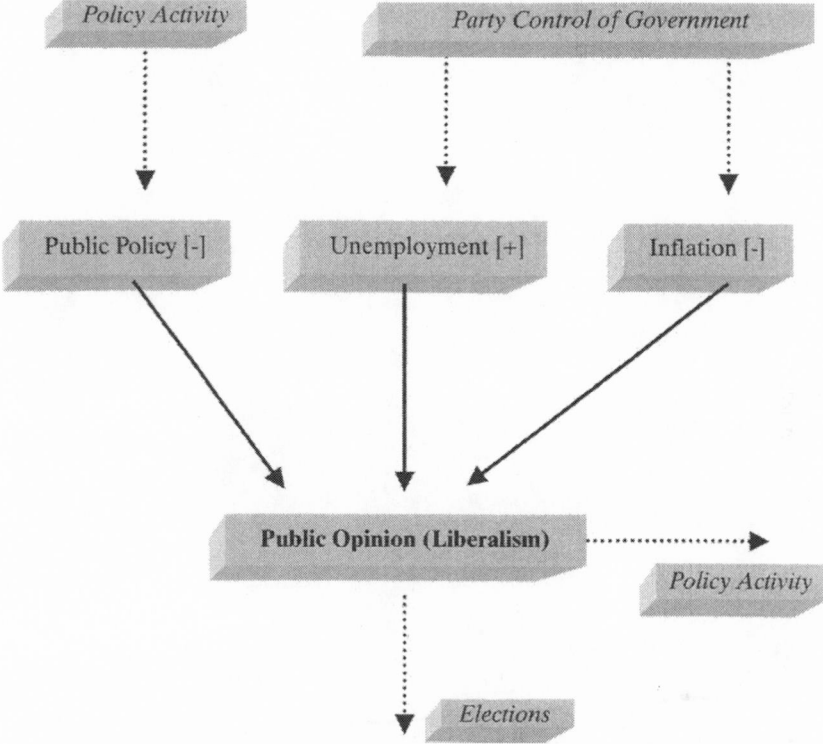

Figure 10.2. Model 1: The Causes of Public Opinion

message of the impact of events of all sorts, differing from some of its causes by being permanently memoried.

In the third and final subcomponent (model 3 in Figure 10.4) we model the flow from *Policy Activity*. A constitutional aggregation system (see below) renders *Policy Activity* (e.g., votes in congress) into policy (*Laws*). *Policy* produces delayed negative feedback to public opinion. And combined with party control of government, it produces partisan economic outcomes, greater employment under Democratic regimes, lesser inflation under Republican regimes. (See the appendix for the specifics of modeling the economic outcomes.)

Table 10.1 summarizes the basic elements of the system model. Here we present some of the key concepts and indicators of the simulation. Omitted are others, such as various pieces of the prediction of economic indicators where we make no theoretical claim, and other pieces of the model which serve mainly to tie together the elements of more

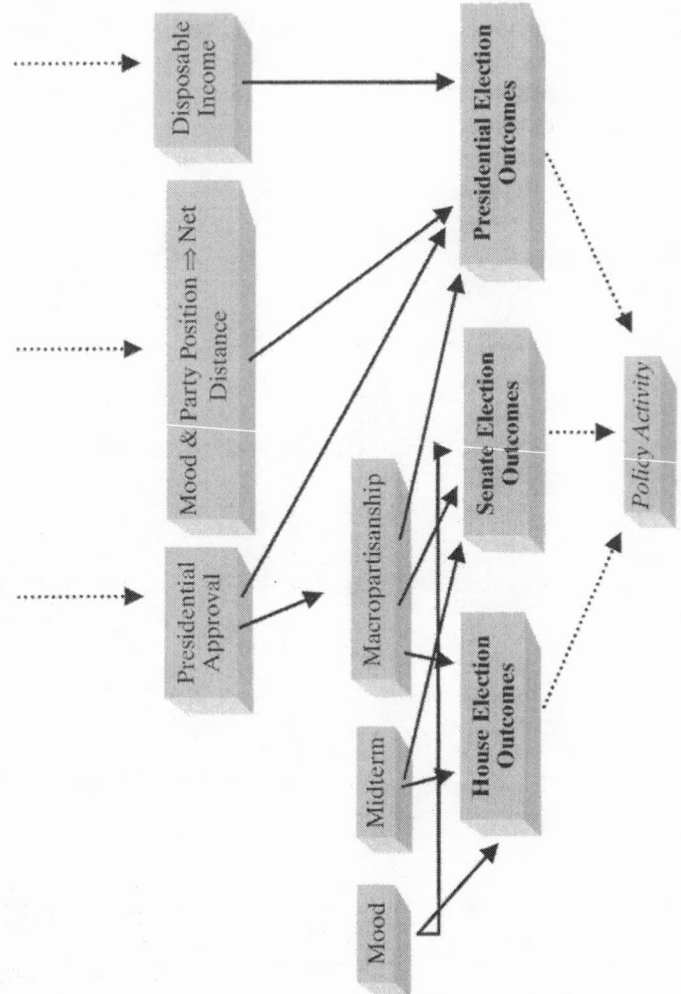

Figure 10.3. Model 2: The Causes of Election Outcomes

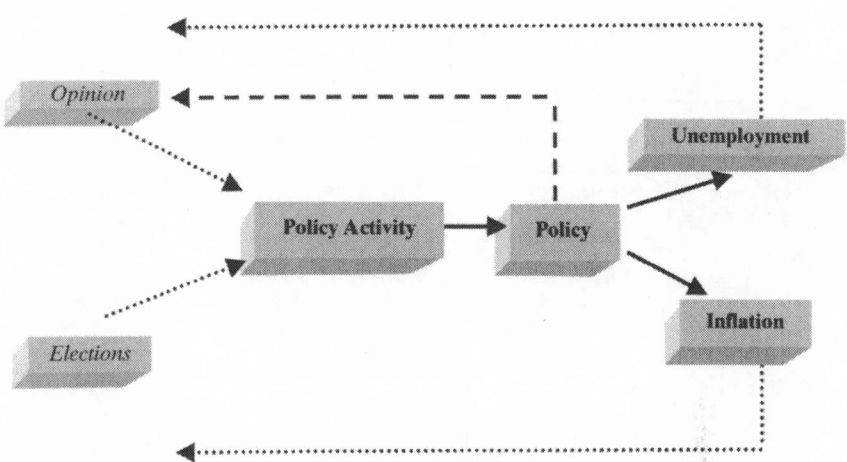

Figure 10.4. Model 3: The Consequences of Policy Activity

theoretical importance. Although we try to link each of the equations to a table in the book, this should not be read to imply exact specification. The demands of simulation differ from those of parameter estimation.

When we put the whole system together, easier on a computer than on paper, it runs. But emulating regressions does not settle all issues. Some modeling issues require structure and rules. For that we build a constitution, which parallels key features of American political structure.

### The "Constitution"

Political systems do not produce formal outcomes from statistical prediction. They have rules and procedures which we need to emulate. Some of these are easy and obvious. When we predict the Democratic proportion of the two-party vote for president, for example, we declare a Democratic win if the proportion exceeds .50 or Republican otherwise. That rule decides who occupies our electronic White House and which party controls the House and Senate.

The translation of *Policy Activity* into *Policy* presents much thornier issues. We cannot represent the process of concurrent passage of legislation by two houses of congress, followed by presidential signature. Our macro model has nothing useful to tell us of individual bills. Thus as in Chapter 9 we simulate policy activity across branches of government with a built-in dynamic to represent the complicated structure of joint consent necessary for law making.

# American Politics as a System

Table 10.1. *Basic Elements of the Simulation: Source and Model Specification Detail*

| Concept | Time Interval | Source | Right-Hand-Side Variables |
|---|---|---|---|
| Approval | Monthly | Table 2.4, Column 3 (Variation) | Lagged Approval, Honeymoon, Economic Performance[a] |
| Macropartisanship | Quarterly | Table 4.1 | Economic and Political (Approval) Innovations, Cumulated Economic and Political Innovations |
| Policy Mood | Annual | Table 9.3, Column 6 | Lagged Mood, Lagged Policy, Inflation, Unemployment |
| House Liberalism | Annual | Table 8.1 (Regression Variation) | Lagged House Liberalism, Lagged Mood, Party Control, Percent Democratic, Vietnam War |
| Senate Liberalism | Annual | Table 8.2 (Regression Variation) | Lagged Senate Liberalism, Lagged Mood, Party Control, Percent Democratic |
| Presidential Liberalism | Annual | Table 8.3 (Regression Variation) | Lagged Presidential Liberalism, Lagged Mood, Presidential Party[b] |
| House Elections (% Democratic Seats) | Biennial | Table 7.11, Column 1 | Lagged Mood, Equilibrium Macropartisanship, Midterm Dummy, Lagged Democratic Percent of Seats |
| Senate Elections (% Democratic Seats) | Biennial | Table 7.11, Column 3 | Lagged Mood, Equilibrium Macropartisanship, Midterm Dummy |
| Policy (Laws) | Annual | Table 9.2, Column 3 | Lagged Mood, Democratic Control of House, Senate, and Presidency, Policy Activity Summary |
| Presidential Elections (1) | Quadrennial | Table 7.3, Column 1 | Approval, Disposable Income Growth[a] |
| Presidential Elections (2) | Quadrennial | Table 7.7 | Policy Proximity, Macropartisanship |
| Inflation | Monthly | Appendix | Party Control of the White House, Residual Inflation |
| Unemployment | Monthly | Appendix | Party Control of the White House, Residual Unemployment |

*Note:* All right-hand-side variables are endogenously determined, except as noted.
[a] Estimated from predicted unemployment and inflation rates.
[b] Actual presidential party, not the simulation prediction, is used to predict other variables.

# American Macro Politics: A System Model

## Theory Versus History: Structure Versus Error

For the theory of this volume, times are just arbitrary markers. Thus when we model 1952, the first presidential election of our time period, we could just as well call it "time 0." But 1952 was not just an arbitrary year; it was seven years after the close of World War II and Dwight Eisenhower was not just a Republican candidate, but a hero of that war. The 1952 election marked 20 years of continuous Democratic control of the White House, and it was contested in the midst of an unpopular "police action" in Korea. These historical facts have no place in our macro theory and *should* have no place; we are not in the business of reconstructing particulars. But undoubtedly they mattered; they made 1952 something other than time 0.

History matters. All the events that are the backdrop of American politics, too specific and too idiosyncratic to have any role in systematic political theory, nonetheless leave their mark on our data. A basic decision of such a systems model then is whether it should be fully abstract, where nothing but the theoretical terms influences any outcomes, or whether it should be built on a backdrop of the events that actually did occur.[3]

The importance of the idiosyncratic suggests four qualitatively different simulation strategies:

- *Structural Simulation.* We may produce a simulation that takes a set of starting conditions (say, the observed data of the 1950s), adds the estimated structure from Chapters 2–9, and then produces subsequent outcomes, month-by-month, quarter-by-quarter, and year-by-year. In the end, we have a simulated course of American politics for the next 50 years – one that includes absolutely no new exogenous shocks to the system since its starting point. That is to say, it includes no business cycles in the economy, no Vietnam War or Watergate scandal or Oil Shock or Gulf War, no surprises in election outcomes, or no other events at all.[4]

---

3 The technical issue comes down to whether or not to make use of the actual predictive errors. They capture the intrusion of real events that are not part of the model specification. The Vietnam War and the Watergate scandal, for example, produce very distinctive patterns of residual variation. Re-creating the outcomes that actually occur is vitally affected by whether or not information from those real errors is used in subsequent predictions. If we represent history as a random draw from normal error, there is essentially no chance that it will reproduce the patterns of these decades.

4 An example of structural simulation is the simulation of the *Mood-Laws* system in Chapter 9. A limitation of this technique is that a system, with no inputs, merely returns to equilibrium.

- *Historical Structural Simulation.* Here we might take the basic structural simulation and add into the mix part of "history." This strategy acknowledges the importance of nonsystematic factors in shaping outcomes while driving the main dynamics with the system structure. The intellectual choice here is to choose which bits of "history" to reintroduce to the model.
- *Stochastic Simulation.* Rather than reintroduce observed history (in effect, correcting errors), we could add random disturbances, drawn from distributions that resemble the disturbance distributions of our estimation models. For example, in the equation for House seats, taken from Table 7.10, column 1, we estimate the House election outcome with an estimated residual (or disturbance) variance of 16.89. When we simulate House elections, we do so using the parameters and structure of the model and then add in an additional random component taken from a normal distribution (with mean zero and standard deviation of 4.11). Each such simulation, with a different set of random disturbances (or "history"), would produce a different course of political outcomes for the century.
- *Stochastic Parameter Simulation.* Finally, we understand that the parameters that we have estimated in our regressions stem from estimators characterized by their own distributions of uncertainty. The particular set of estimates that we have developed in the book depend on the particular history built into our data – and might not represent a more systematic set of relationships that would work equally well in "alternative" histories. We might augment the straightforward stochastic simulation with the additional uncertainty due to estimation of parameters to provide an array of plausible outcomes that acknowledges the known uncertainty built into the estimation process.

For the purposes of this chapter, we choose the historical structural simulation. Our understanding of politics is not sufficient to replicate a half-century using only the starting conditions and the structure. The first element we add is the exogenous economy – the large proportion of the dynamics that are independent of politics – because some of political history derives from powerful but uncontrollable economic forces. This decision seems obvious. Further, we reintroduce the Vietnam War (as in Chapter 8) simply because the war's occurrence, which had such an impact on policy, cannot be explained from the internal logic of the political system.

More interesting, and more telling, we reintroduce the historical factors that determined presidential elections. While our modeling exercise allows us to predict the popular vote in presidential elections with reasonable accuracy, we do not have the theoretical ability to correctly forecast elections that were essentially coin tosses. For example, we can predict an essential tie for the election in 1960 but cannot reliably predict the winner. In fact, of course, the election was so close that its outcome was uncertain even after the votes (outside Chicago) were counted. This phenomenon is not a function of our statistical impotence but instead a feature of the real political system. The fundamental factors that we have modeled just cannot account for the knife-edge decision about which party will win an extremely closely contested presidential vote – such as 1960 or 1968 or 1976. But these outcomes matter enormously for the subsequent operation of the political system – Democratic presidents produce more employment and more liberal policy, and their performance shapes a permanent component of *Macropartisanship*. Accordingly, we choose to reintroduce the "accidents of history" that made winners of Kennedy, Nixon, Carter, and Clinton – to ensure that the rest of the model is kept on course.[5]

## Performance

An obvious question to ask of any simulation is how well it reproduces the system being modeled. When we proceed, as we shall in this chapter, without any stochastic element, then the answer to the performance question is predictable. The quality of predicting a particular element of the system is largely determined by the quality of fit of the estimated regression model employed. Thus, models with a high $R^2$ produce good predictions; those with poor fits produce poor predictions. There is nothing to learn from observing predictive success and failure that was not already known from estimating the regressions on real data.[6] So we will have little to say about statistical prediction issues.

Now we turn to observing the system in action. Here is how we shall proceed. We have (1) real data on all elements of the system, the ulti-

5 In effect, we simply set the proper party as the winning party for each presidential election. A similar argument could be made for the knife-edge decision about which party controls the Senate and House of Representatives. For present purposes, we have chosen *not* to reintroduce these disturbances – and thus allowed ourselves to place the "wrong" party in control of the congressional institutions. In any case, the choices of which "history" to reintroduce is an intellectual one.

6 There is some slippage. When excellent model fits benefit too much from tiny sample sizes, for example, the $N = 12$ of presidential elections models, then changing the input values (or anything at all) produces results that disappoint.

mate baseline for comparison. Then we run the deterministic simulation once through, letting changes in various elements of the system influence one another. This produces (2) a set of predictions based upon real inputs. Unlike regression predicted values, $\hat{y}_t$, these predictions incorporate our knowledge of system dynamics. In Chapter 4, we use *Presidential Approval* to predict *Macropartisanship*, for example. We use the same model in the simulation, but with the important difference that it is *Approval predicted from all the things that cause it* that enters the model, not the actual historical value for a particular president in a particular month. (And the causes of *Approval* are themselves predicted from factors earlier in time and further down the causal chain.) We shall have little to say of the possible comparison of reality with predicted reality. Then we turn to "what if" questions and tinker with particular inputs to see what happens. This produces (3) "altered" predictions, outputs of the model in which inputs have been deliberately perturbed for analysis.

Our simulation projects the course of political history with starting values based on early 1950s conditions, the Vietnam War, actual presidential (but not congressional) election outcomes plus the exogenous sources of economic conditions throughout the years.

Our analysis will focus on comparisons between (2) predictions and (3) altered predictions. We will have little to say about (1) the real course of events in this chapter. Our goal is to learn what happens to our structural system when we tweak it. The reader should bear in mind, as we examine the effects of changing inputs here, that it is predictions, not reality, that are the backdrop. Sometimes the two are quite similar, sometimes not. In the second example to come, for example, our model gets a jump on history by giving control of congress to the Republicans a decade or so before it happened in the real world. That, not the real congressional lineup, will form the basis for assessing the effects of induced changes.

### SYSTEM CONSEQUENCES: EMPIRICAL APPLICATIONS OF THE MODEL

An advantage of simulation is the ability to run the system with changed outcomes and see what happens. That is also a disadvantage, because there are an infinite number of possible changes that can be induced, none of which is a straightforward hypothesis test. We can disturb any series. We can disturb it at any time. We can disturb it by any amount. And there are no rules for deciding any of these things. Thus, the analyses to come should be seen as examples that illustrate some of the system's properties. But since we cannot know what is typical or representative of shocks to our system, we surely cannot claim that these are. The best that can be said is that we learn from doing it.

We illustrate two sorts of perturbations of the model to observe its changed behavior. In the first, we change the unemployment experience of a particular time and ask how such a change flows through to the political components of our system. In the second, we start on the political side, changing an outcome of a presidential election. Unemployment is first.

### Analysis 1: Perturbing Unemployment

For this example, we start with the economy to observe how effects flow through opinion, elections, policy, and all the rest. Making some attempt at realism of magnitude, we shock the unemployment rate in June of 1959 by one point (from 5.0 to 6.0) with an ensuing decay of the shock by .90 per month. The one point is big enough to matter, but is not huge. We set it in 1959, after the second Eisenhower recession of 1958 and 18 months before the 1960 election (choosing not to emulate the Carter administration by staging a slowdown in an election year). The net effect of the shock is to preserve the recovery from the earlier recession, but dampen its size and speed.[7]

Now we can observe what ensues. In Figure 10.5, observe the middle lines. These represent unemployment as it actually occurred (the solid line) and a shocked unemployment series (the dashed line). (The scale is modified for graphical convenience, but proportions are accurate.) This effect is by construction, the source of all other changes to come.[8] The upper lines in the figure represent an emulated *Consumer Sentiment*, predicted from an empirical fit to employment and inflation levels and changes at various lags.[9] Thus, the increase in unemployment has the

---

7 This is more or less analogous to the situation of 1991, when the recovery from the 1990 recession aborted but did not lead to a new recession.

8 We do not induce Phillips Curve effects. Thus inflation rates are not altered in the model as a function of unemployment, but do respond to changes of party control.

9 Our "*Consumer Sentiment*" series is actually emulated *Consumer Sentiment*. The emulation is by taking predicted values from a regression in which actual *Consumer Sentiment* is dependent and the levels and various lags of differences in unemployment and inflation are on the right-hand side. Although the empirical difference between emulated and actual is small, there is a theoretical difference that is not. Real consumer sentiment contains the signal of perturbations in the current economy that predict a future different from the present. This is the portion of consumer expectations that cannot be predicted from current and past economic conditions. It also cannot be emulated. It is unpredictable by definition; we cannot predict the "unpredictable" part of economic experience.

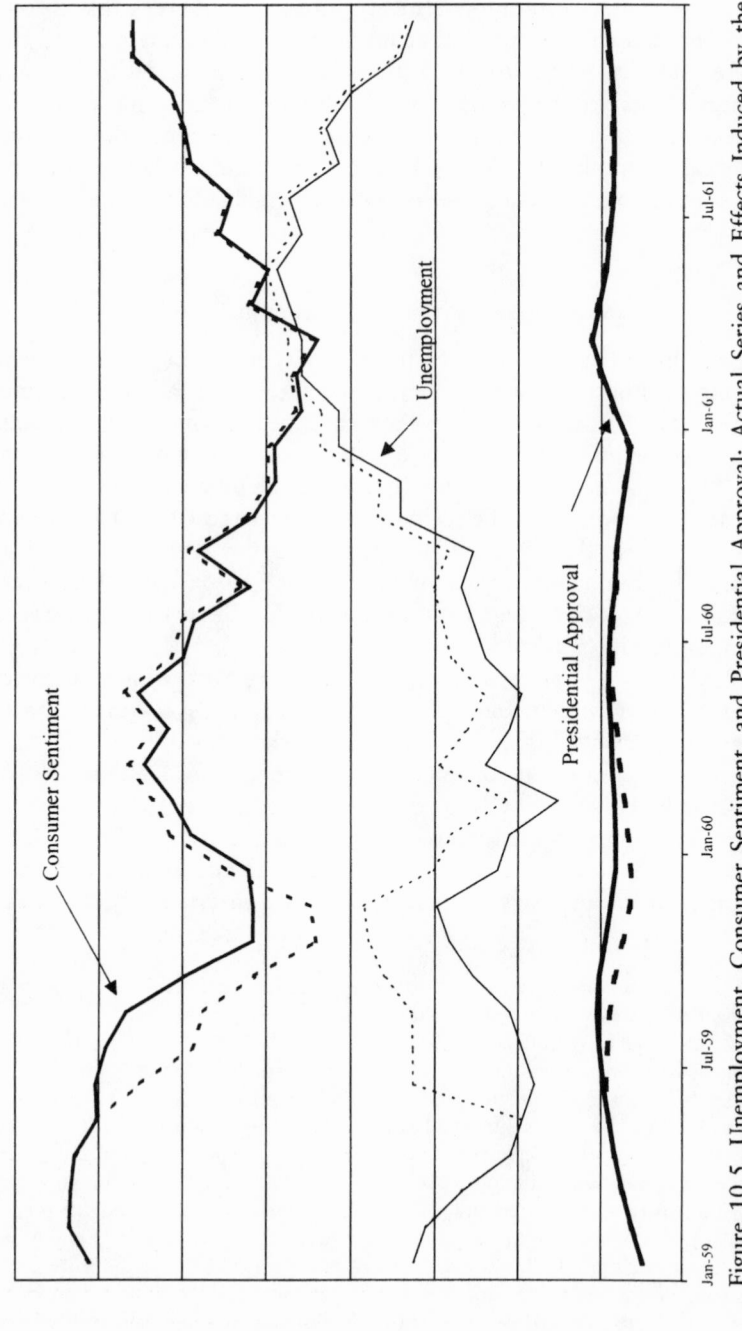

Figure 10.5. Unemployment, Consumer Sentiment, and Presidential Approval: Actual Series and Effects Induced by the Unemployment Shock (Dashed Lines Are Induced Effects)

expected effect of reducing consumer confidence in the economy in the early months after the shock. That effect is later slightly reversed, when our empirical emulation model captures the cyclicality of real economic series, producing small opposite effects at long lags.

The bottom lines of Figure 10.5 show the response of *Presidential Approval* to declining *Consumer Sentiment*, with our hypothetical President Eisenhower losing about two points from the *Approval* level he would otherwise have experienced. This effect disappears (by construction) at the 1961 transition.

In Figure 10.6, we observe how the economic and approval changes translate into (quarterly) *Macropartisanship*. There note that the effect is somewhat smaller at the outset than in the *Approval* case, but it lasts. Our *Macropartisanship* model has a permanent memory of economic and approval effects that have occurred, thus the 1959 shock persists forever. Unlike *Presidential Approval*, which resets with a transition, *Macropartisanship* carries all of its past into the future. If the graph were extended to the present, the slight induced unemployment shock would still persist.

Unemployment affects *Policy Mood* directly (as does inflation). Thus we see in Figure 10.7 a growth of liberalism in 1959 from the induced unemployment that remains above historical levels through its 1961 peak. This relatively modest increase, 2–3 points at maximum, is about 10 percent of the high-to-low range of the series. Changes in *Mood* set the stage for policy changes, to which we turn in Figure 10.8.

### Elections and Policy

Changes in unemployment, *Approval*, and *Mood* have possible consequences for elections to the houses of congress and for the presidency. For the case at hand, these consequences are small, only a seat or two in congress and no change to party control of congress or White House. This is partly a function of the decision to induce the unemployment shock 18 months before election day. Most effects are thus dissipated before elections come to the scene. But in the model generally, as opposed to this example, elections are highly responsive to other elements in the model, an important part of the general picture.

In Figure 10.8, we standardize effects to a percentage change metric to observe the flow of effects following the induced shock. *Policy Mood* in this figure is just the induced movement of Figure 10.6 in this different measurement. Following early movements in *Mood*, we can see later responses in the presidency and House that are quite large relative to the change in *Mood*. The U.S. Senate response is smaller and later, as Constitution writers intended. The line labeled "Policy Activity Summary"

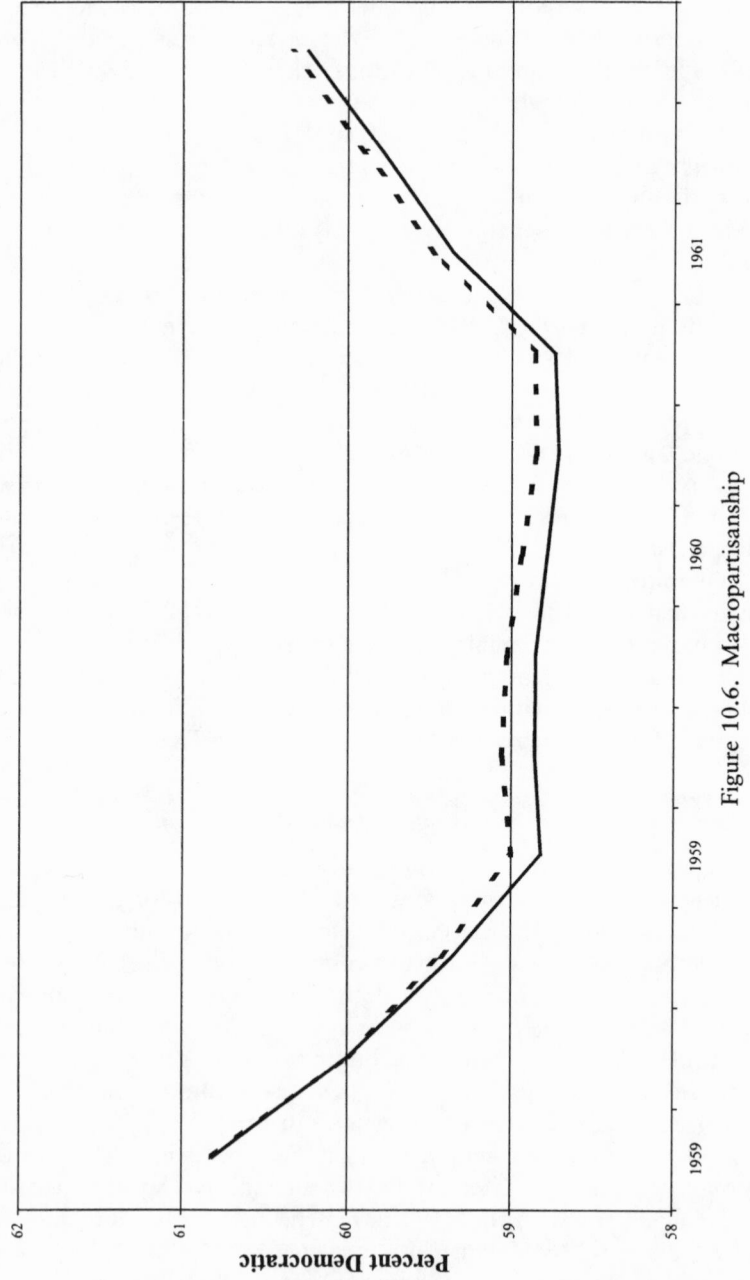

Figure 10.6. Macropartisanship

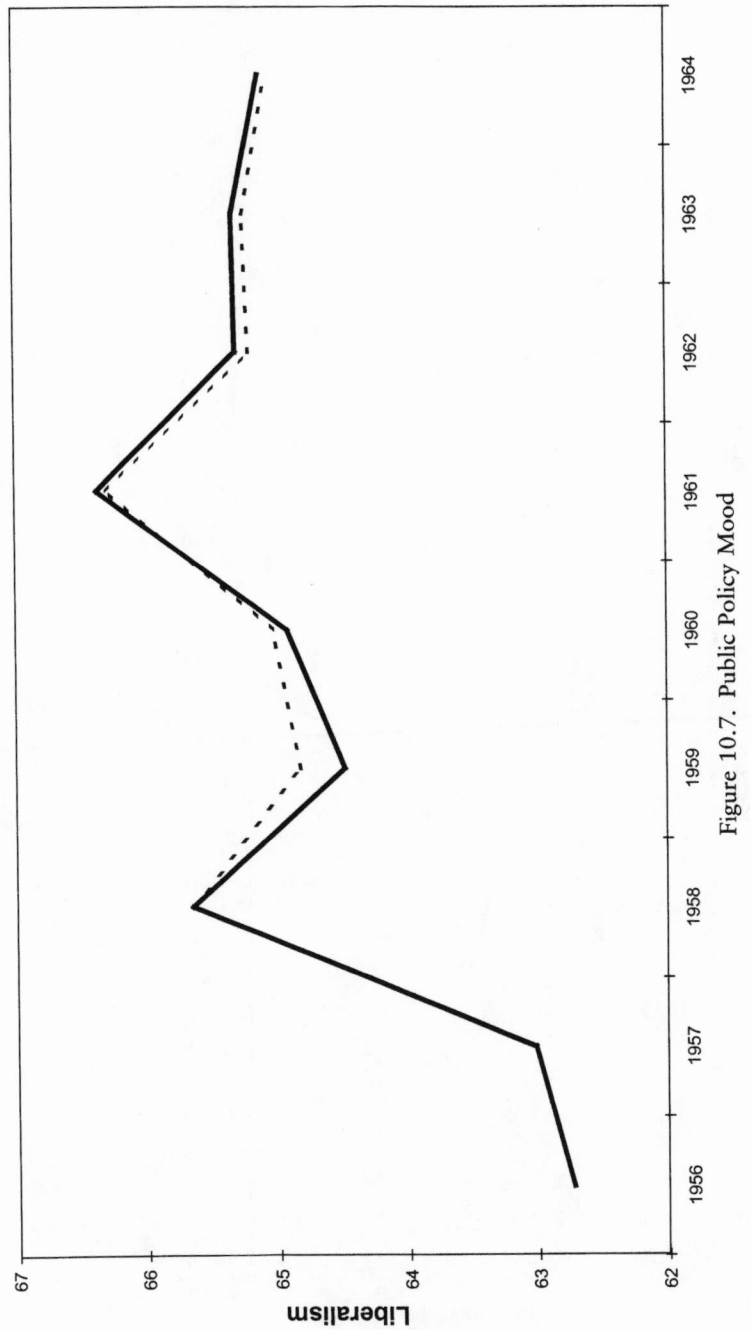

Figure 10.7. Public Policy Mood

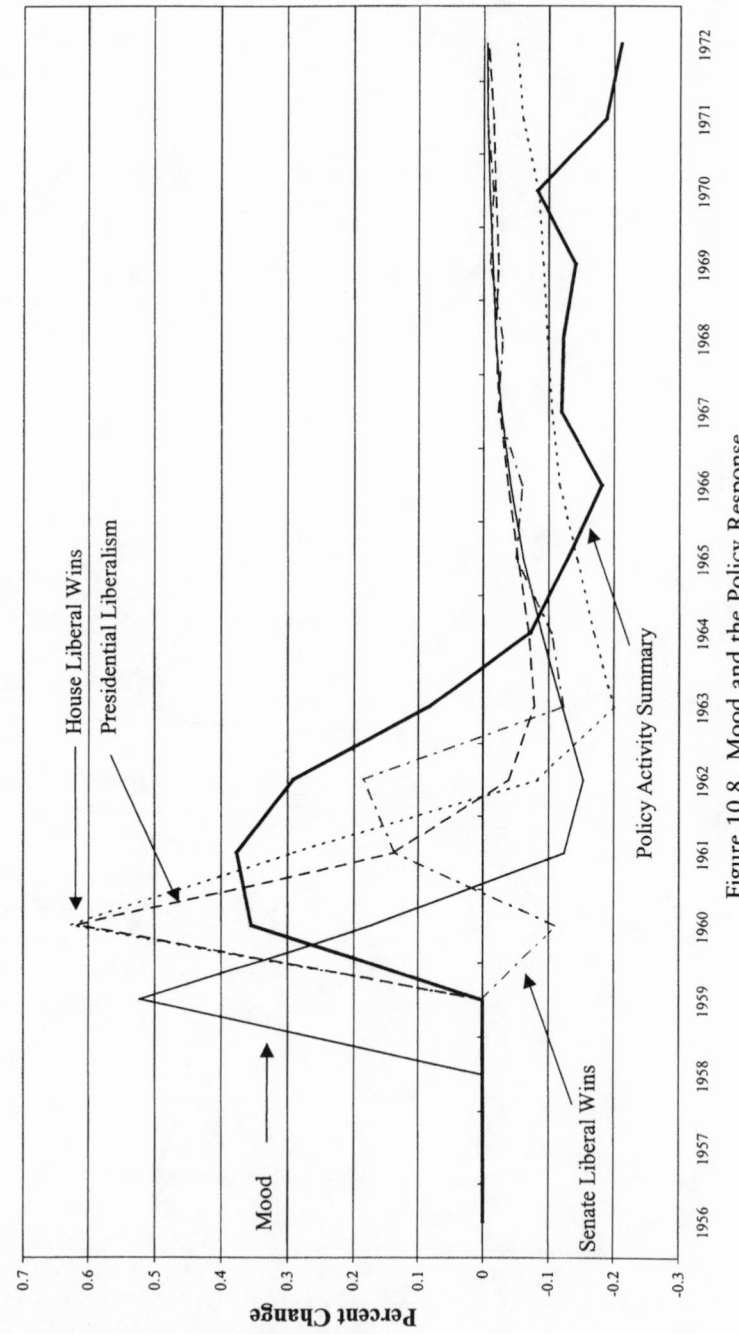

Figure 10.8. Mood and the Policy Response

House Liberal Wins

Presidential Liberalism

Mood

Senate Liberal Wins

Policy Activity Summary

Percent Change

0.7
0.6
0.5
0.4
0.3
0.2
0.1
0
-0.1
-0.2
-0.3

1956 1957 1958 1959 1960 1961 1962 1963 1964 1965 1966 1967 1968 1969 1970 1971 1972

is our constitutional emulation of the total response of the elected branches of government. Its dynamics are a mixture of those for the House, Senate, and presidency. Its response is more inertial, slower to respond to the impetus for change, but, having responded, slower also to equilibrate.

Our penultimate output, following the dynamic path of the "Policy Activity Summary," is *Policy* itself, its metric the passage of important (liberal) laws (see Figure 10.9). Based on the Mayhew "important laws" series (revised with directional coding and extended to date), our indicator captures the cumulative impact of change, with relatively rare conservative laws subtracting from the more usual pattern of increasing scope of government over time. Our induced unemployment change would have cumulated to produce something on the order of one-third of an "important" law – equivalent to several laws of the more typical scope.

*Feedback*: There are multiple opportunities for the induced effects to ripple backward in the causal chain from explicit feedback processes. Changes in party control (which are not induced in this example) feed back to economic outcomes; Democrats produce lower unemployment but higher inflation, and Republicans the opposite. Changes in *Policy* feed back to public opinion (*Mood*). But those effects are small, negative, and delayed.[10] The smallish policy consequences of our induced changes would have even smaller negative feedbacks to opinion, that is, producing more conservatism. They are too small to bother with here.

For a second illustration of the implied dynamics of our systems model we perturb a presidential election outcome. Presidential election outcomes are considered historic events in the life of the nation. The feeling of election night is that the event touches everything that matters in American politics. Here we consider changing one of those historic outcomes, choosing for our case 1980, where a different outcome is easy to imagine, and ask whether indeed it was "historic." We will see that it was.

### Analysis 2: Reelecting Jimmy Carter in 1980

Suppose the mission to rescue hostages from Iran had been a success reflecting glory on the president instead of the embarrassing failure that

10 Small, negative, and delayed are exactly the feedback attributes one would design for a stable political system. That they are all three is an empirical assertion about American politics as well as a description of our model. Feedback exists, but it is always small, always delayed, and always negative, i.e., slightly offsetting the original impetus at long lags.

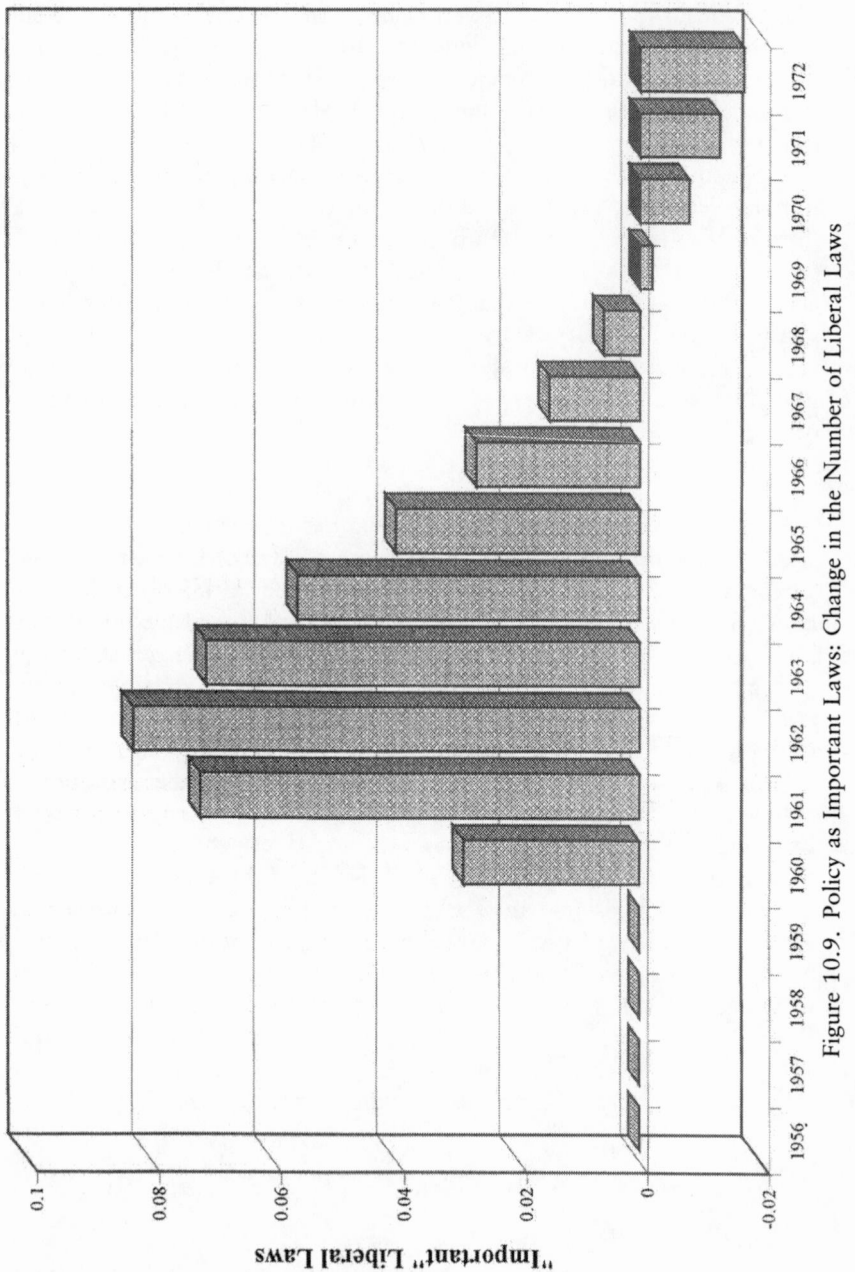

Figure 10.9. Policy as Important Laws: Change in the Number of Liberal Laws

it was. Perhaps the mini-recession of 1980 might have occurred a year earlier and left Jimmy Carter presiding over a recovery in 1980. Along with the usual advantage of seeking reelection after the first presidential term, it wouldn't have taken a lot to have changed the 1980 presidential contest into a Democratic win. Here we do so to observe what our systems model has to tell us about the impact of a presidential election outcome.

Before we start the analysis of changes induced by switching presidents it is useful to have as background a view of what actually happened in the Reagan first term. In Figure 10.10 we present three particularly relevant pieces: unemployment, a persistent problem and sometimes a crisis; inflation, problematic at the beginning and gradually coming under control; and Reagan's *Approval*, reflecting economic failures and successes.

Reagan's initial term began with historically high levels of unemployment and, after a few months in office, the employment situation worsened considerably. By late 1982, unemployment had reached almost 11 percent, a post-depression high. After that the economy picked up, becoming the Reagan recovery, a boon to Reagan personally and to the Republican Party.[11] The track of inflation was steadily downward, not unrelated to the 1982 recession. And Reagan's *Approval* follows the progress of the economy, first down and then up, but disrupted by an early 1981 surge that appeared to result from the unsuccessful attempt on his life – and his good-humored and courageous response to it. Now we can impose a Democratic president on the same external events (minus the assassination attempt) and observe how history might have been different.

*Economics*: We start examining effects with the economy. Our model of economic outcomes under Democratic and Republican Party control predicts a generally better course for our Democrat on the employment front, and generally worse on inflation. Looking first at unemployment, the indicator of Figure 10.11 – the percentage difference between model predictions for the real Reagan I term and the hypothetical Carter II – shows the generally lower levels of unemployment under Carter. At the peak of the 1982 recession (which is still a recession), the Carter unemployment is about 3 points better than the Reagan record, about 8% instead of 11%. After a good first year, Carter's inflation record is a point

---

11 The net effect of bust followed by boom was highly favorable to Reagan because many voters were willing to blame Jimmy Carter for the 1982 recession, even though it happened a year into Reagan's watch. Reagan got all the credit for the ensuing recovery.

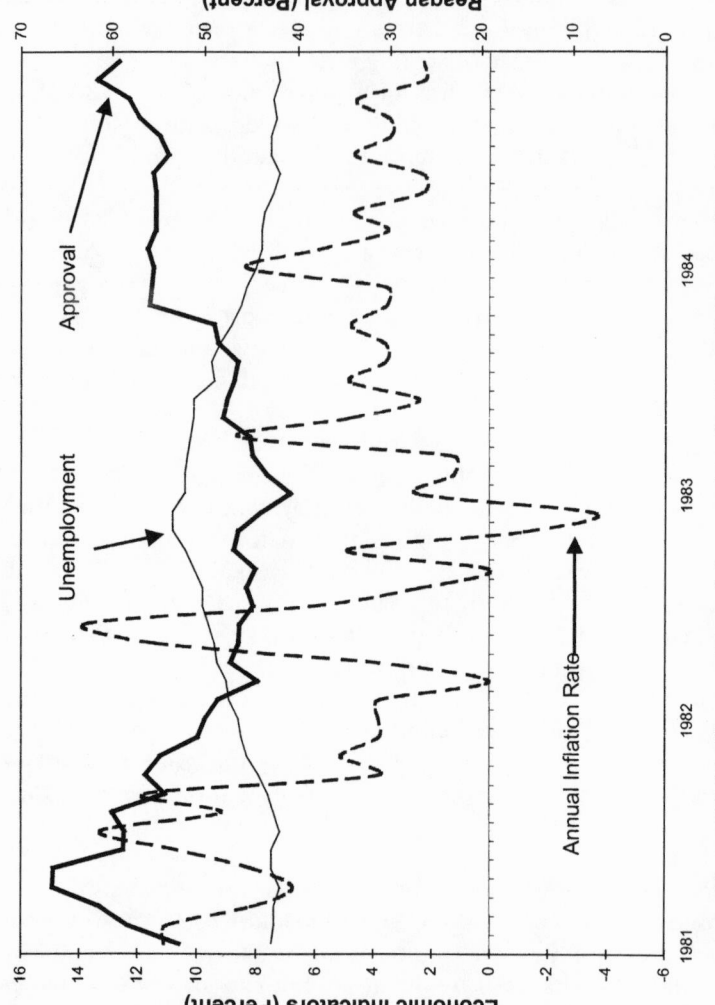

Figure 10.10. Economics and Approval in the (Actual) Reagan First Term

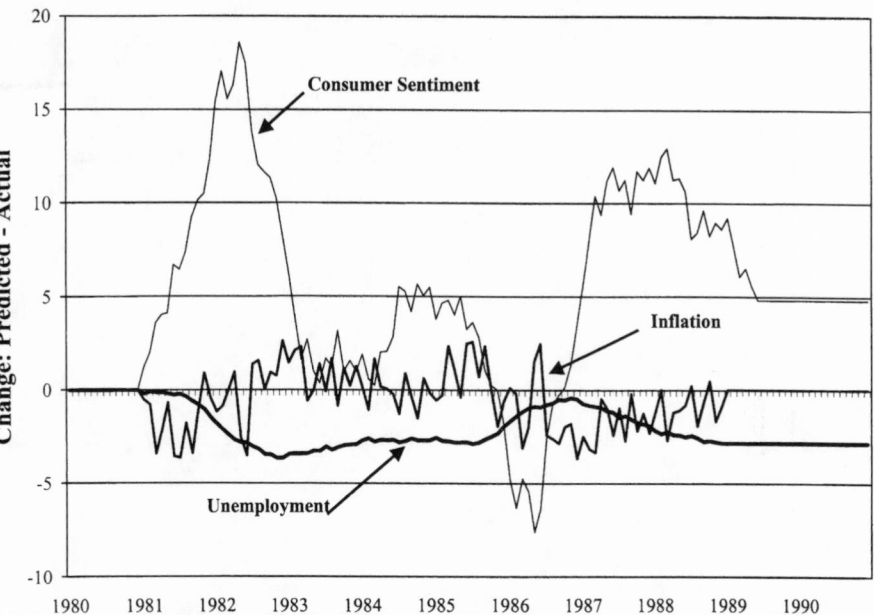

Figure 10.11. The Economic Response to Changing the 1980 Election Outcome

or two worse than Reagan's. The net result of both is that *Consumer Sentiment* is much more positive in 1981–1983 than for Reagan. This surge represents not growing confidence, but rather the absence of the steep decline under Reagan associated with the serious unemployment during the recession.

Disposable income is an amalgam of economic growth (more or less the inverse of unemployment) and of inflation. The joint effect for our hypothetical term is greater income growth under Carter II than under Reagan I (see Figure 10.12). The better employment and worse inflation combine to produce about a two-and-a-half point gain for Carter over the actual level of Reagan I. This is wholly the result of having a milder recession than actually occurred.

*Approval*: The better economic showing for our hypothetical Carter should work its way into presidential approval and, from Figure 10.13, we can see that it does. Both presidents begin the term in relatively bad economic times and with low approval ratings. The Reagan curve reacts more strongly to the 1982 recession, as should be the case. The summary story that we have seen thus far then is one of Democratic good fortune

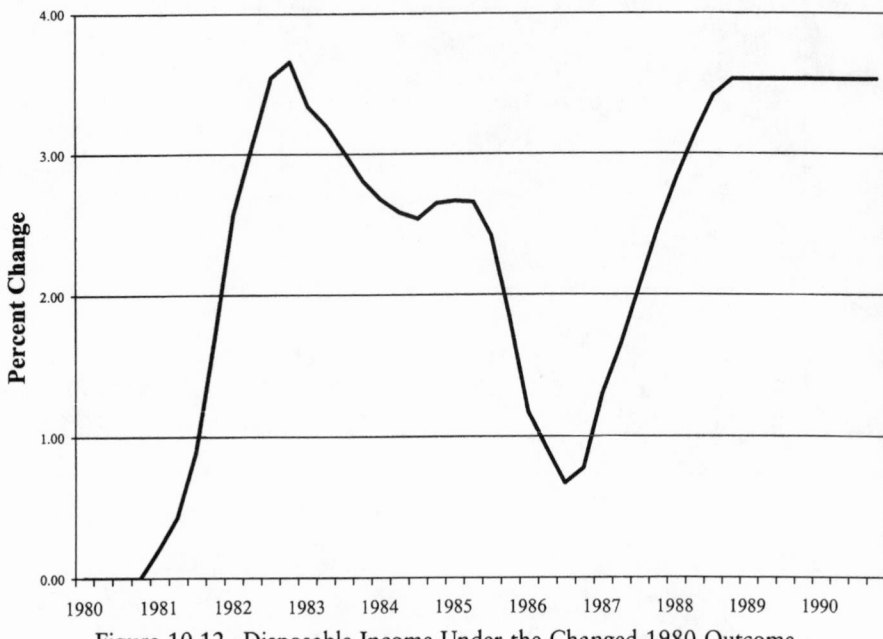

Figure 10.12. Disposable Income Under the Changed 1980 Outcome

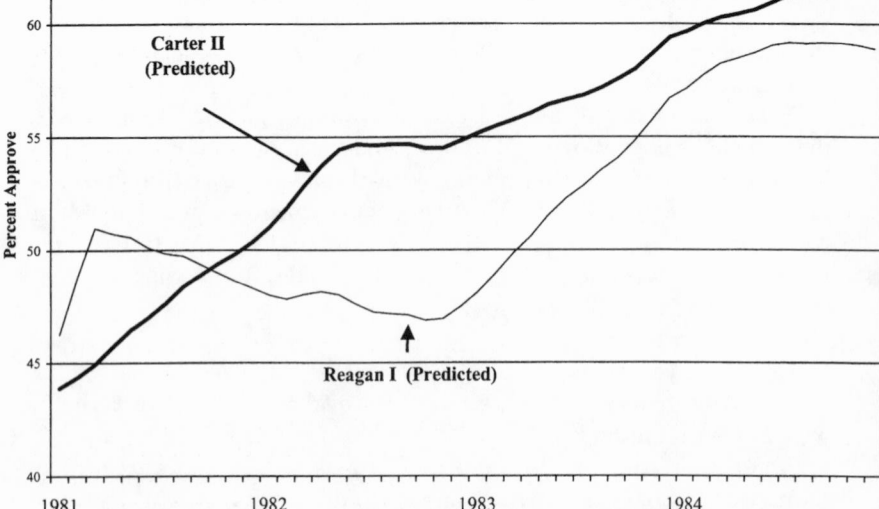

Figure 10.13. Predicted Presidential Approval: Reagan I Versus Carter II

almost wholly a function of typically stronger Democratic employment growth.[12]

*Macropartisanship*: On *Macropartisanship* it is important to note at the outset that the changes during the (real) Reagan first term are the largest on record. Following the 1983–1984 recovery, the Republicans gained more ground in partisan loyalties than ever before or since. In that context, it is easy to evaluate the pattern of Figure 10.14. The substantial cumulative gain for the Democrats in *Macropartisanship* is the result of removing the change favoring Republicans that really happened. The economic side of the story is telling. Reagan experienced a sharp and painful recession followed by a powerful recovery. Because much of the blame for the recession was successfully laid on Jimmy Carter and the Democrats, the sequence of bust and boom was very positive for the Republicans – part of the blame for bad times followed by all of the credit for recovery. Had Carter been president in 1981–1984 our model projects a more neutral outcome, blame and credit in about equal measure. Thus our simulated Carter second term experiences no net change in *Macropartisanship*, which appears in Figure 10.14 as a huge cumulative gain, relative to the Republican gains that actually did occur.

*Mood*: We have seen mainly first-order effects up to this point. When we turn to *Policy Mood*, we begin to see fairly powerful reactions set in and the story tilts in unanticipated directions. In the real Reagan first term, everything pushed *Mood* toward liberalism; high unemployment, declining inflation, and conservative policy all reinforced one another in producing liberalism. With Carter instead, all three move in the other direction: Unemployment is lower, inflation is higher, and policy is more liberal. Thus *Mood* becomes even more conservative during the term, having started from an all-time high at inauguration. (The later liberalization in Figure 10.15 occurs after the Republicans regain the White House in 1984.) This effect will now compete with Democratic gains in *Approval* and *Macropartisanship* to shape election outcomes and policy making in the early 1980s.

*Elections*: When the Reagan recession of 1982 becomes the Carter recession, on top of another one in 1980, the Democratic congressional

---

12 We note that our approval model does not discriminate between parties in assigning approval as a function of performance. Alesina et al. (1993), in contrast, argue that voters expect Democrats to do better and punish or reward relative to expectations, not to absolute performance. If that is the case, then the Carter approval gains that we predict would not have occurred.

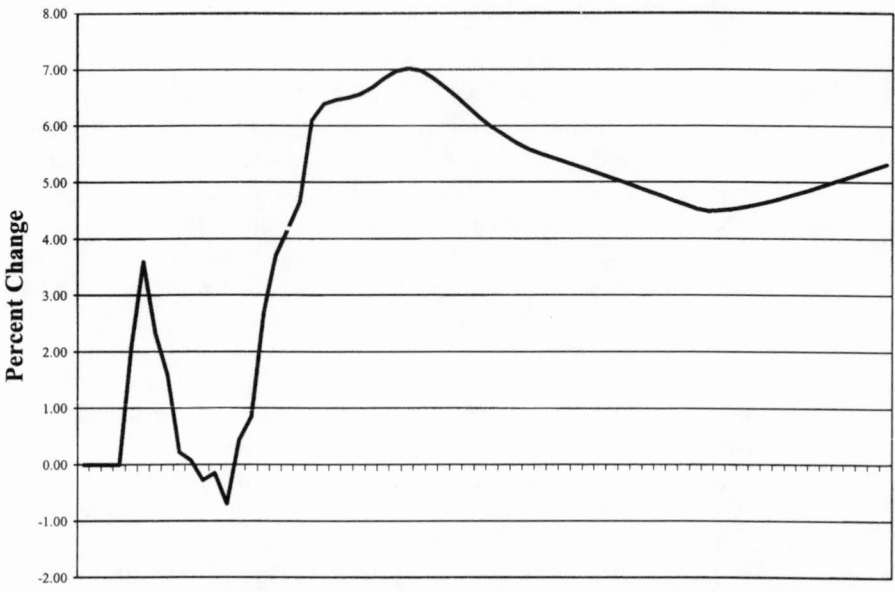

Figure 10.14. Change in Macropartisanship as a Result of the Changed 1980 Outcome

majority starts to come undone. Democrats lose 12% of their House majority – about 40 seats – in 1982 alone (see Figure 10.16). Losing another 7% in 1984, they lose their "permanent" House majority standing a full decade before it actually occurred.[13] And they never regain it once lost, all the effect simply of having succeeded in electing Jimmy Carter in 1980.

Things are simple for the House of Representatives. This year's election result is next year's party composition. The U.S. Senate, which reelects a third of its membership every two years, is a more complicated story. As election analysts, we care about this year's result, that is, the seats actually at risk. As analysts of policy making, we care about party composition, the returning base, *and* the newly elected or reelected

13 Recall that our baseline here is not reality, but the prediction of our model given the real 1980 outcome. The model, reflecting strong gains in *Macropartisanship* by the Republicans in 1984, predicts a new Republican majority in the mid-1980s, anticipating the eventual result of 1994.

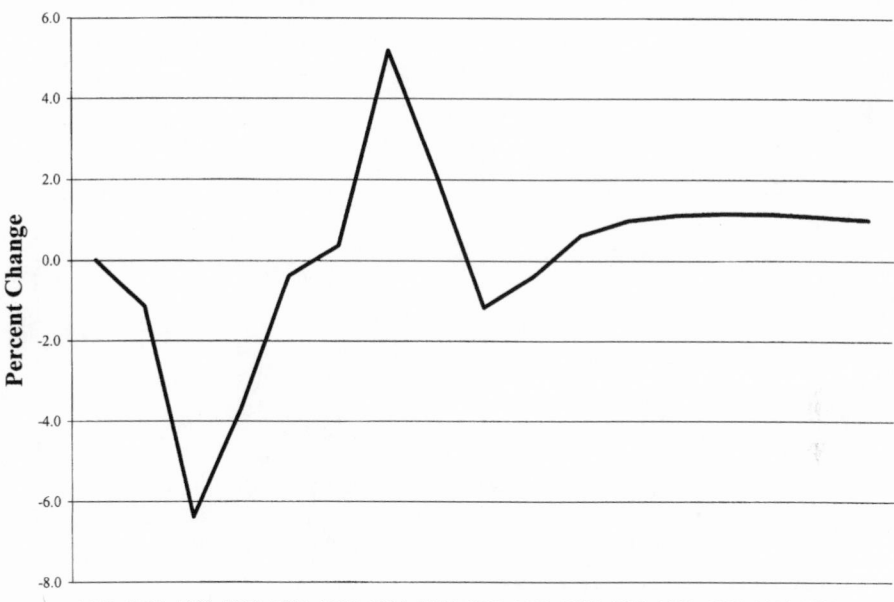

Figure 10.15. Change in Public Policy Mood Resulting from Changing the 1980 Outcome

members. We simulate both elections and composition under real conditions and with the altered 1980 outcome. Here the notable effect is that the 1982 recession, which benefited the Democrats with Reagan in the White House, produces now a loss of Democratic strength. The more gradual movement in composition (Figure 10.17) shows a Republican takeover in 1982 (which follows our failure, matched by contemporary observers, to predict the stunning 1980 Republican Senate victory). By electing Jimmy Carter in 1980, the model reverses everything, producing a combination of Democratic president and Republican congress that would have been thought an exceedingly unlikely outcome at the time. This result (and subsequent real experience) suggest that the standard and accustomed pattern was much more fragile than was thought at the time.

*Policy Activity*: Figure 10.18 is our portrait of changes in action in Washington as a function of perturbing 1980. Here the changes are large, and some would have to count as unanticipated. It is natural, almost

413

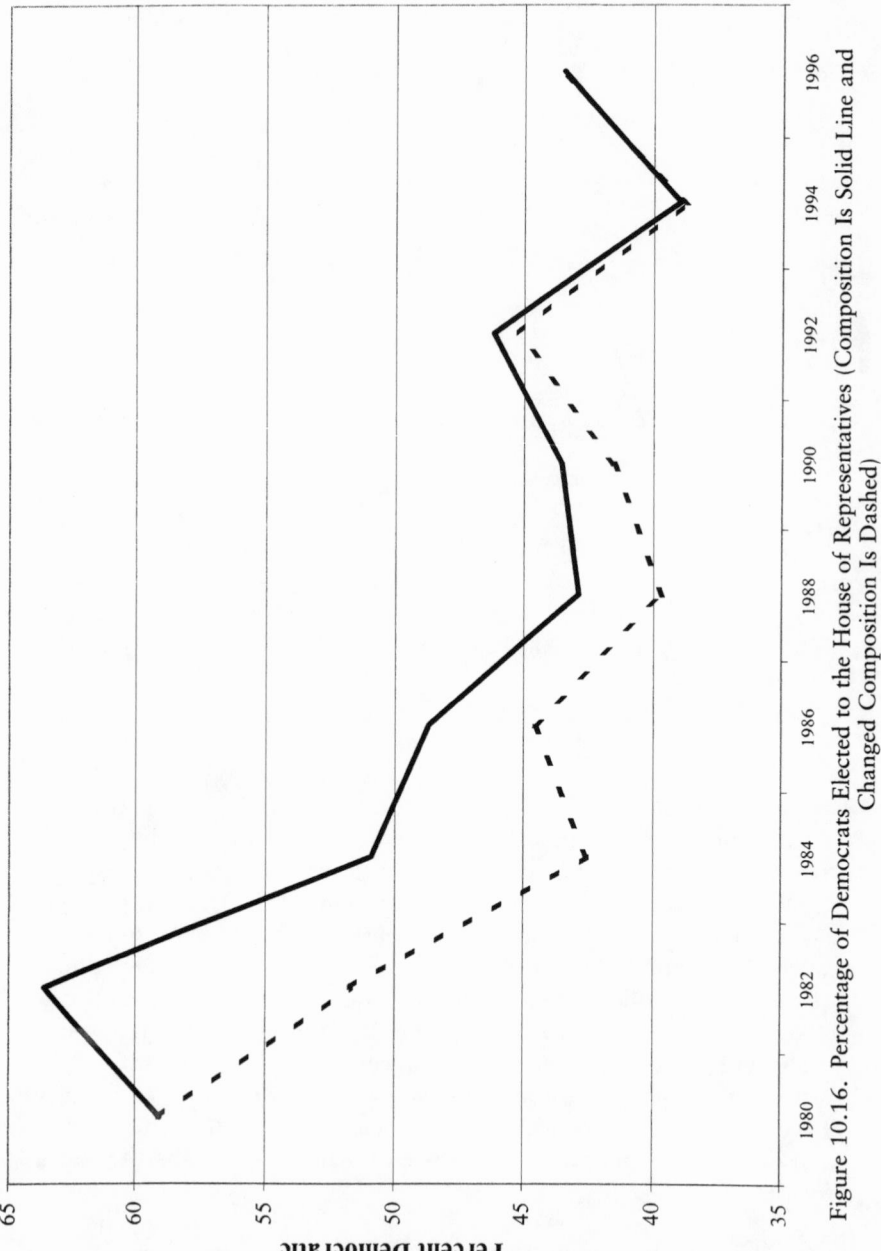

Figure 10.16. Percentage of Democrats Elected to the House of Representatives (Composition Is Solid Line and Changed Composition Is Dashed)

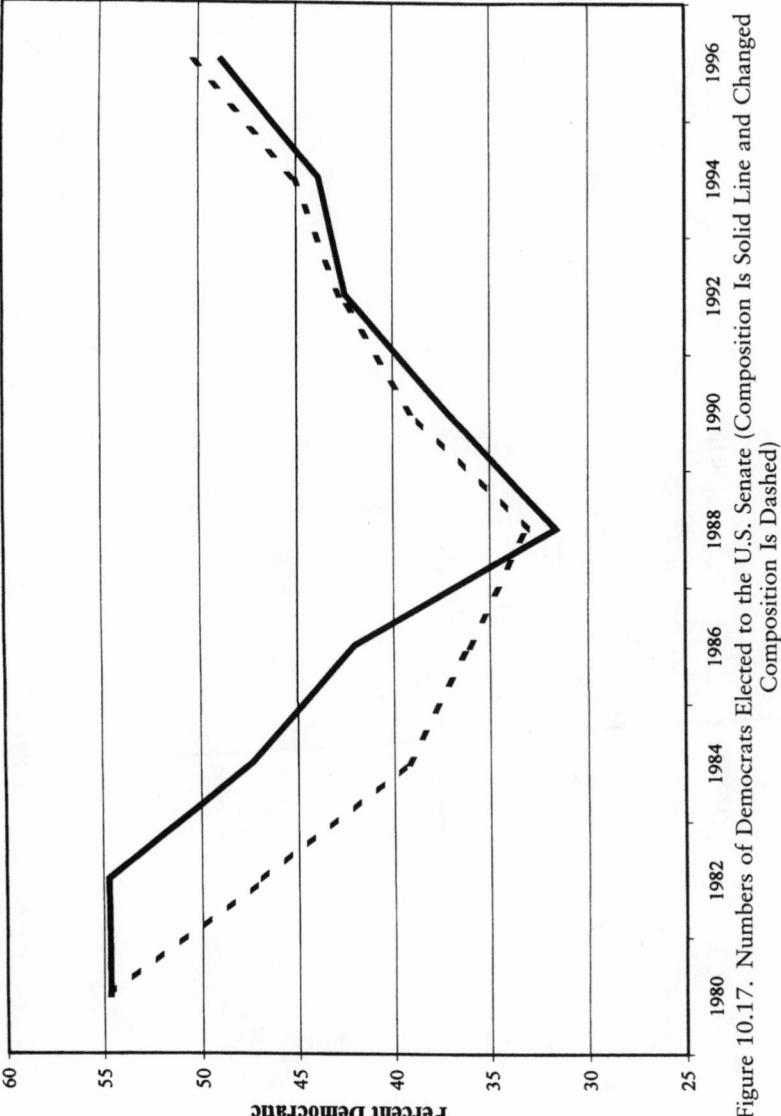

Figure 10.17. Numbers of Democrats Elected to the U.S. Senate (Composition Is Solid Line and Changed Composition Is Dashed)

415

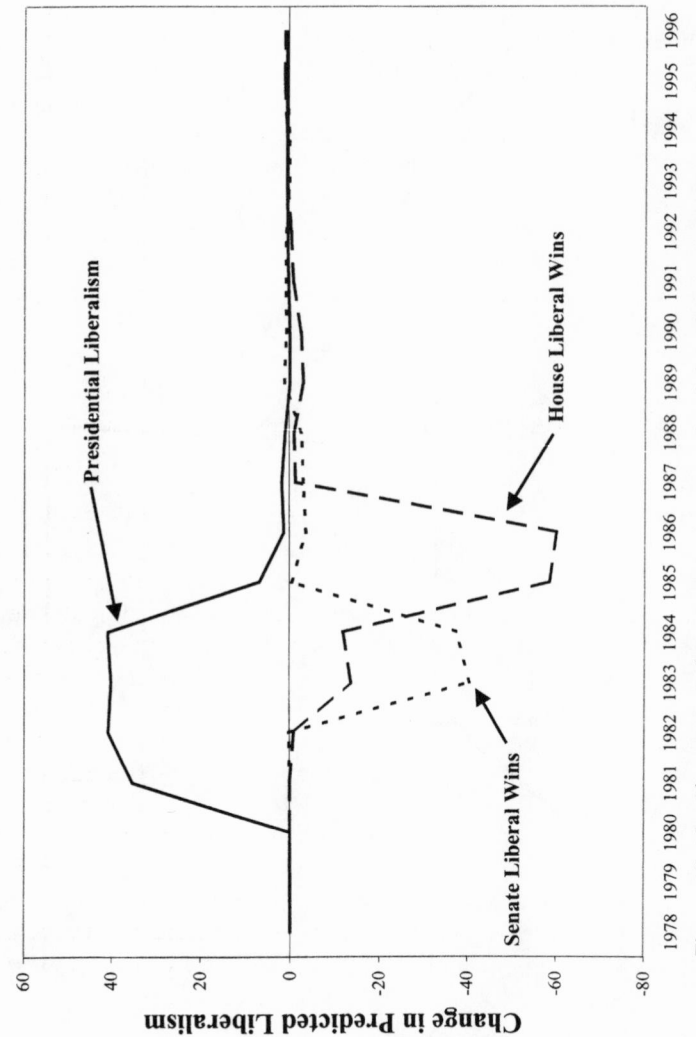

Figure 10.18. Change in Policy Activity as a Result of the Changed 1980 Outcome

inevitable, to think that parties are more likely to achieve their policy goals by winning elections than by losing them. Here we begin to see unanticipated and unintended evidence for the reverse case. Beginning with the expected effect, having Carter rather than Reagan in the White House in 1981–1984, we see the natural effect on presidential liberalism. It is the congressional response that is unanticipated. Senate and House liberalism depend upon *Policy Mood* (which in turn depends on *Economic Outcomes* and *Policy*, both of which change), party composition (percentage of seats), and party control. All three factors move toward conservatism, a function of the mood shifts and congressional election changes that we have seen previously. The effect begins to become large after the 1982 election works its changes on party composition. It gets larger still when the House is captured by the Republicans in 1984. The result is a much more conservative congress than the actual one, an effect that persists for over a decade.

*Policy*: The final result of president and congress is summarized in the Summary Policy Activity measure of Figure 10.19 (scaled on the left side). That shows the expected liberalism as a function of control of the White House in the early 1980s, which is nearly neutralized by changes in *Mood*, election outcomes, and thus party control in congress. The *Policy* indicator (independently scaled on the right), a function of *Policy Activity*, *Mood*, and party control of presidency, House, and Senate, begins with very modestly liberal response to Carter. Propelled by the early election of a Republican congress in Carter's simulated second term, it culminates in a conservative shift over time that is far from modest. *That is, the effect of electing the more liberal candidate in 1980 is to have produced much more conservative outcomes.* Here we have system causal flow that looks very different from what we might have expected from looking only at pieces of the system one at a time.

### THE LESSONS OF MODELING AMERICAN MACRO POLITICS AS A SYSTEM

These analyses are the beginning of our explorations of the systems model. For this book, they are the end. But we have much more to learn and the ambition to learn it. We have only scratched the surface of what can be done in a sustained attempt to push a systems model to produce insights. It is an activity that flows from the book and will continue after it is in press.

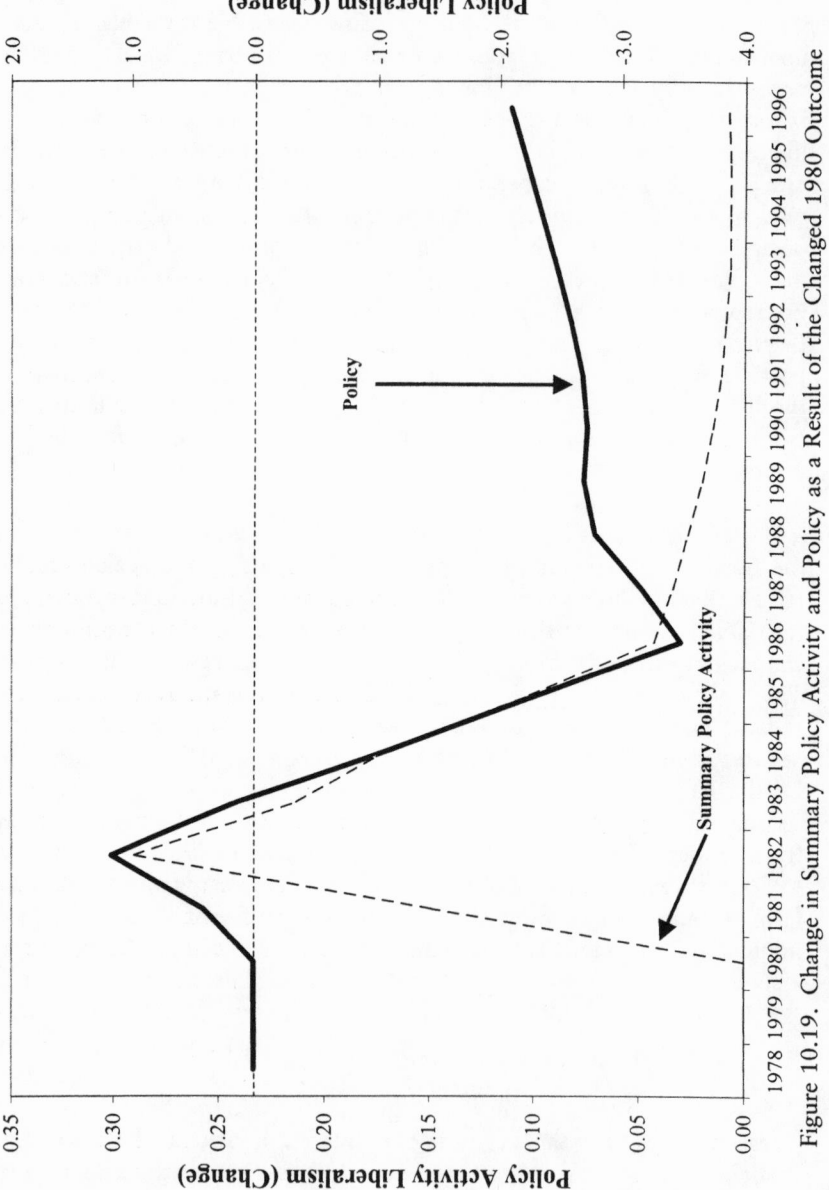

Figure 10.19. Change in Summary Policy Activity and Policy as a Result of the Changed 1980 Outcome

## American Macro Politics: A System Model

One does system simulation because it teaches lessons about system behavior that cannot be learned by simple analysis of the pieces of equation systems. It is useful therefore to ask what we have learned from this exercise, how our view of American politics differs from that of the regression analysts who began the simulation. In one sense, the most important lesson is the one we expected to learn, that the behavior of the system is much more complex – and therefore much more interesting – than one can know from component pieces. As we turn to unexpected lessons, the primacy of this first, expected, one should not be forgotten. It matters for our understanding of American politics that the first-order effects of our equations then produce a cascade of second, third, fourth, and $n$th order residual effects, some of which contradict the original impetus. The system acts like a fugue; its simple themes and variations, superimposed upon one another, cease to be simple.

### Unexpected Lessons

We have reached three global sorts of lessons from building the simulation and watching it run under various conditions. One of these is renewed appreciation for the lowly error term. One is a definition of importance of key components of the system by the degree to which their outcomes surprise. And last, the simulation of our one integrated time series, *Macropartisanship*, teaches lessons about importance that are quite different from $\beta$, significance tests, and $R^2$.

*History Matters (or Random Errors Aren't).* We like to think that our theories predict outcomes. And they do. But that prediction is always with error. We tend to think of error in time-series regressions as its representation in abstract mathematics, randomness. Statistical simulation quickly cures such a misconception. There we see that the error term is a collection of all the things going on outside our theoretical system. Such things are the real backdrop of history, idiosyncratic events occurring outside the system and not explainable by it, but which nonetheless impinge upon it. What we quickly learn in simulation is that random draws will not reproduce history. If we want our predictions to be roughly in line with conditions that did occur, that is, we are in bad trouble without taking account of the error terms. The structure of relationships for our 45-year span can be reliably reproduced from random draws of error; conditions cannot be. This is most noticeable when the grand events of the period, the Civil Rights struggle, Vietnam, Watergate, and the Gulf War are occurring in the background. We know enough about these events to know something of what to expect. But the lesson also implies that events too small to come to our notice exert their effects everyday and make it impossible to re-create history without using our knowledge of it.

*Surprise.* Surprise, in the rational expectations view, is almost synonymous with causal importance. The piece of our systems model that creates most of it is election outcomes – and particularly election outcomes that alter party control. Winner-take-all election systems put a huge premium on predicting the outcome right. That turns out to be quite difficult. We assemble prediction models to forecast the vote, and we do pretty well at it by our normal evaluative standards. We come close to predicting the actual percentage split between parties in presidential elections, for example. But with depressing frequency our "close" predictions err on the wrong side of the 50–50 line that divides winners from losers. That begins to illustrate just how much surprise is inherent in the electoral system. The most obvious case is the historically close 1960 election. There, any model that improves upon a coin toss would be suspect. In statistical terms, the 1960 outcome *was* a coin toss; it is impossible to improve on 50–50 except by cheating. Many others (1968, 1976, 1988, and 1992, for example) are close enough that models with a handsome $R^2$ will call the winner wrong much of the time. After we got over feeling bad for picking the winner right only 8 or 9 times in a series of 12, we began to appreciate just how difficult the task is.

The substantive conclusion that matters is that elections inherently carry a high level of unpredictability, a function of constitutional design. That makes them decisively important turning points in our model and in the real American politics. Alesina and Rosenthal (1995) capitalize on this view for a rational expectations prediction of partisan effects on economic outcomes. This hangs on the view that the surprise associated with elections prevents rational actors from successfully anticipating the policy future, and therefore produces the large policy impacts that are normally defeated by forward-looking rational behavior. Changing election outcomes, as we have seen in one illustration, has huge consequence for our systems model, producing deviations considerably larger than the modest changes we produce by inducing increased unemployment.

*Stationarity and Integration.* None of us comes newly to time-series analysis. We have been dealing with the mathematical theory and practical issues surrounding stationary and nonstationary (e.g., integrated or "unit root") time series for decades. Emulating the two in a statistical simulation nonetheless brings a new perspective. What mathematics has always told us about integrated series comes home in the simulation. Their behavior is *very* different. Our one integrated series, *Macropartisanship*, emerges as important in a different sense from elections, for it carries little surprise. It is important because it carries all its perturbations into the future.[14]

Other parts of the model respond dynamically. They move quickly in response to some causal impetus and then that movement decays, also relatively quickly, back to a status quo approximation. Causation for these series is transient; its equilibrium expectation is zero. *Macropartisanship* responds to every perturbation by permanently altering its level. The economic recovery under FDR, for example, should still leverage Democratic partisanship and affect the outcome in elections yet to come. This kind of permanence is strikingly out of the ordinary for social theory. Its substantive message is that a unit change in such a series is vastly more important than the larger changes to be found in equilibrating time series. Partisanship is generally regarded as the key variable of American electoral research. Our view is that it may even still be underappreciated.

### THE ROAD AHEAD

This exercise in simulating the political system has proved instructive. The standard, compartmentalized understanding of American politics gets much enriched by putting the pieces together and observing their interactions. Our efforts here, however, represent a mere first step. Knowing that the components are so interdependent now suggests special care in developing comprehensive model specifications – ones that explicitly account for cross-system linkages that might safely be ignored in single-equation analysis, and it indicates renewed attention to the properties of parameter estimation in the context of a full system. This much is ordinary scientific progress that our initial efforts beg to be pursued. Perhaps more interesting would be the rigorous implementation of stochastic simulation strategies, introducing distributional properties to our more limited inferences. We would begin to see what is typical, and atypical, for the American system's political life. And more interesting yet would be an examination of how the structures of democratic politics have implications for reform. All these sorts of

14 This is a central point running throughout Carmines and Stimson (1989). Watching the eerie response of *Macropartisanship* to changes in the simulation model brought back vivid memories of parsing out racial issue effects in that now old research.

explorations, comprising a project of enormous intellectual promise, lie ahead.

The model consists of 17 separate equations of the general form

$$y_t = \beta_0 + \alpha y_{t-1} + \sum_{i=1}^{k} \beta_i x_{i,t-1} + e_t$$

All the terms of this equation may represent original measured or estimated values, denoted superscript 0 as in $y^0$, $x_i^0$, $e_t^0$, $\beta_i^0$, in which case the coefficients are best linear unbiased. The error may be actual (that is, estimated) historical errors, $e_t^0$, or (in stochastic disturbance simulation) $e_t^i$, a generated error drawn from:

$$e_t^i = N(0,\sigma)$$

where $N(0,\sigma)$ represents a draw from a normal distribution with mean 0 and standard deviation $\sigma$, the standard error of estimate for the equation, all for the $i$th iteration.

The model for *Macropartisanship* is an important exception to the general equation form. In this model, the left-hand side is the change in $y$, $\Delta y_t$, rather than $y_t$, and its specification is an error-correction model:

$$\Delta y_t = \alpha y_{t-1} + \sum_{i=1}^{k} \beta_i x_{i,t-1} + \sum_{i=1}^{k} \gamma_i \Delta x_{i,t} + e_t$$

where the right-hand side of the equation includes first difference terms of the exogenous variables and a vector of $\gamma$ coefficients. Here the $\Delta x$ terms are innovations in *Approval* and *Economic Performance*, and thus the $x$ terms are cumulated innovations. *Macropartisanship* at time $t$ is then the start-off value, $y_0$, plus the sum of all the $\Delta y_t$ terms to $t$.

Each of the parameters similarly may be the original regression results, $\beta^0$, or (in stochastic parameter simulation) they may be draws:

$$\beta^i = N(\beta^0, \sigma_\beta)$$

where $N(\beta^0, \sigma_\beta)$ is a normal draw with mean $\beta^0$ and standard deviation $\sigma_\beta$, the standard error of coefficient $\beta$.[15] Each iteration of the model constitutes a "sample" for the purpose of new draws of $\beta$.

---

15 This assumes that one can draw independently, i.e., that the expected covariance of two estimators is 0. The assumption is clearly untrue and its untruth may be consequential. The issue is of no consequence for this chapter, where all effects are calculated from the original parameter values.

# American Macro Politics: A System Model

## Models of Economic Outcomes

Estimating employment and inflation effects of party control is outside the scope of this volume. Thus, we lack both prior theory and the fully specified models that are its result. (We find ourselves in general accord with the rational expectations story of Alesina and Rosenthal (1995), in which only the surprise inherent in change of party control matters.) Thus our strategy is fully empirical. Using the historical evidence of employment and inflation changes, we estimate unrestricted distributed lag models that have coefficients for each of the 48 months of a presidential first term following change of party control of the White House. Then predicted unemployment (or inflation) is given by:

$$y_t = \beta_0 + \sum_{m=1}^{48} \beta_{p,m} + \theta_p + e_t^0$$

where the level of the indicator $y_t$ is a function of the start-off level, $\beta_0$, which party ($p$) is in the White House, what month ($m$) it is (if it is a first term), and the small expected differences by party $\theta_p$ after the first term (if it is later). For the economic outcomes models, we always employ the actual errors, $e_t^0$, because our weak model specification cannot match actual experience with random predictions. Thus predicted levels are similar to historical experience if the party of the White House is the same as for actual experience. They are not identical because the distributed lag portion of the model averages over the outcomes of all presidents of the same party. If the predicted president is not of the same party as the actual one, then the systematic portions will differ substantially from historical experience. If, for example, the model "elects" Richard Nixon and not John Kennedy in 1960, then its employment outcomes are a function of the typical (high unemployment) experience of Republicans, combined with the actual error term for the 1961–1964 period.

Figure 10.20 plots unemployment changes for each of the first 48 months of a presidential term after change of party control. The dark bars represent unemployment increases and decreases under Republican control. The light bars are comparable Democratic experience. The lines cumulate the experience over time. In general, the month-to-month changes are not reliably estimated, and few of them confidently differ from zero. The cumulations, in contrast, pick up reliably different patterns between the parties, strongly supportive of the Alesina-Rosenthal story of surprise, control, and timing.

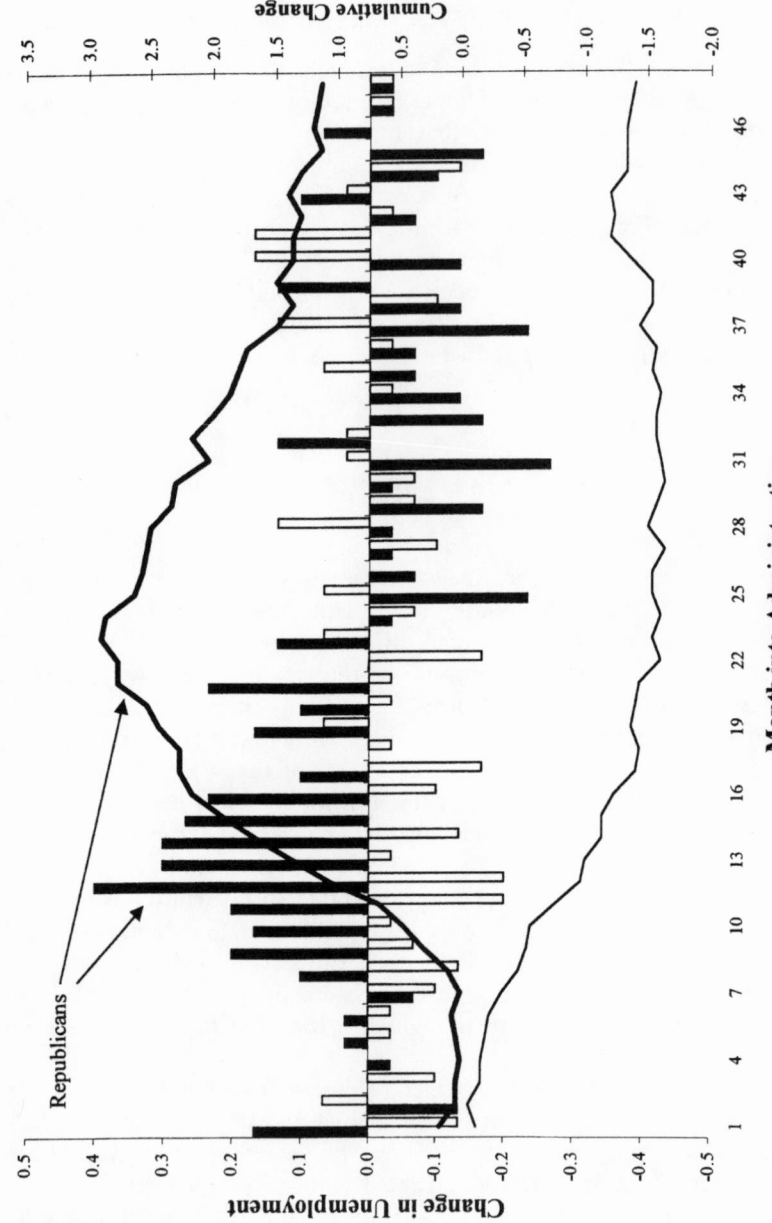

Figure 10.20. Change in Unemployment by Party: Monthly and Cumulative

424

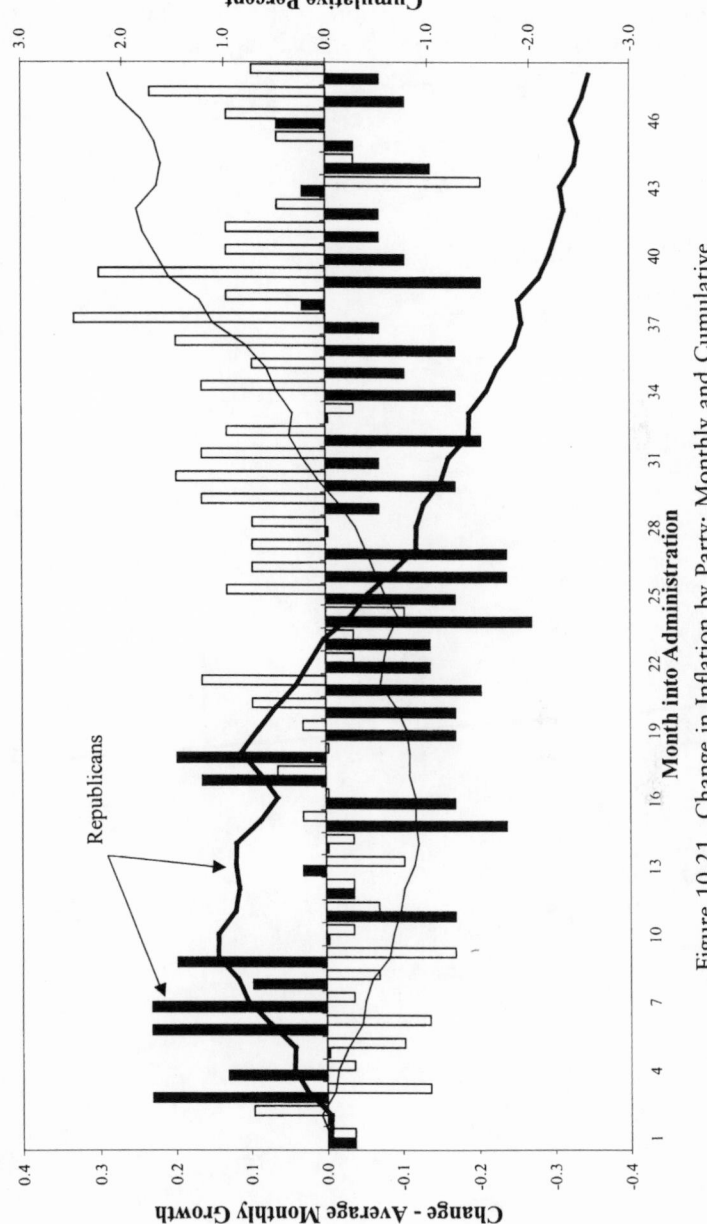

Figure 10.21. Change in Inflation by Party: Monthly and Cumulative

425

Comparable data for inflation experience are presented in Figure 10.21. Here the performance advantage favors the Republicans, who turn in consistently better cumulated inflation numbers over the term.

# 11

## The Macro Polity and Democratic Performance

For most studies of political behavior, the unit of analysis is either an individual (a citizen or politician) or a single political institution (a party or congressional committee) or a policy (a tariff or tax law) or a moment in time (an historical case study). This is the study of micro politics. Individuals and institutions and policies and moments in time also comprise the data we have used for the present book. But there is a crucial difference. Our central focus is instead on the electorate, the class of politicians, the array of political institutions, the sum of many activities and policies, and the sweep of a half-century. This makes our inquiry the study of macro politics.

### THE MACRO-POLITICAL PERSPECTIVE

Most of the patterns and relationships reported in this book become clear only upon examining macro-level data. Our unit of analysis is the American polity for a particular time segment – one month, quarter, year, or even biennium. We make no quarrel with micro-level survey research, and as individual authors have committed it ourselves many times. For the study of individual-level relationships involving political attitudes and behavior, ordinary modes of operation and clever strategy, the development of norms and small-group behavior, policy analysis, and many other things, micro-level analysis is the preferred mode of research. But to study the dynamics of political change at the national level, macro-level analysis brings special power to bear.

We understand that politics is essentially a macro phenomenon. While political life is surely experienced by individuals as individuals, what makes it specially interesting is the fact that people make their arrangements for living together through politics. And politics is practiced in a collective framework. When the nation makes a law or levies a tax or declares war, it does so as a nation in national institutions with

427

individuals acting as a collectivity. So the actions of the collectivity are worth study in their own right. By way of analogy, note that many scientific phenomena have meaning not at the micro level but only at the macro level. In physics, for example, the notion of pressure carries import as a macro phenomenon that arises from complex behavior of individual molecules. Similarly, in politics, governmental policy is a macro phenomenon that derives from the behavior of individual political actors. It is in this sense that macro behavior is the stuff of politics.[1]

To be sure, all macropolitical outcomes stem from some aggregation of micro-political behavior. We do not wish to give some special magical status to the macro outcomes or wish to divorce the macro phenomena from their constituent parts. And we need to know a good deal about how individuals and institutions act before we can make reasonable sense of the broader scale of politics. Without good micro theory, macro theory becomes sterile. But micro theory is *not* enough.[2] We want and need to understand how large-scale forces in the electorate and in the political elites move through time to govern the country.

### The Macro Public

This book has presented statistical support for a host of dynamic macropolitical causal relationships. For these relationships to make sense requires a certain level of attentiveness and rationality on the part of the American public. However, if there is anything that decades of micro-level analysis of political behavior has told us, it is that U.S. citizens are shockingly inattentive to politics and (if we allow a fuzzy definition) not very rational. How is it then that the electorate shows more attentiveness, more rationality, perhaps more political intelligence, than micro-level political behavior research would lead us to believe?

We concur with the usual empirical assessments regarding the bleak distribution of political awareness, interest, and sophistication within the American electorate. This book offers no claim that individual citizens are any more capable than the experts say to be the case. Our claim instead is that macro-level dynamics are driven by an electorate where,

---

1 In politics, as in physics, it is surely important to study molecular interactions to understand why aggregates behave the way that they do. Yet, the macro phenomena obey a qualitatively different set of scientific laws than do the micro phenomena and may usefully be studied in their own right. For more on the special character of macro as opposed to micro polities, see MacKuen (2001).

2 This reminds us of the particle physicist who proclaims that understanding the fundamental forces is all that is worthwhile in science; "All the rest is mere chemistry."

in the aggregate, the more politically capable citizens possess dominant influence. And these macro-level dynamics are statistically observable. Let us examine again the reasons why this can be the case.

A major part of the argument is the reduction of noise due to the "miracle" of aggregation (see Converse 1990). But we must be careful as to exactly what we argue here. The obvious aspect of the aggregation miracle is that when individual judgments are aggregated, error can cancel out. The usual example is Condorcet's jury theorem. Assume a set of perceptions of a common signal, each containing some random error. As defined, perceptions are not biased. As the number of participants becomes large, errors will cancel out so that the average perception will approach perfect accuracy as a reflection of the signal. We can apply this principle of aggregation not only to aggregate perceptions but to aggregate behavior, such as voting. Suppose some voters respond to policy issues while others vote unpredictably, in a way that appears random to the observer. The choices of the seemingly random voters will cancel out, while the policy voters rule the outcome.[3]

This optimistic result may be even more interesting when we understand that public judgment emanates from an interactive rather than additive process. When a jury comes to its judgment, its power stems not merely from its voting system but also, more clearly, from its deliberations. The interactions between the ignorant and the knowledgeable – in both juries and the electorate – make aggregation more exponential than additive. As thoughtful argument meets the vacuous, in daily conversation and in elite debate, the thoughtfulness gains weight with each repetition. At the end of the day, the weight of sophistication gains enormous power.[4]

---

3 Of course this line of theorizing depends on the assumption that causes of perceptions or motivations that are outside the model are in fact random. If the errors are in fact biased rather than random, the macro-level process could, while interesting, be less predictable. For instance, suppose for instance that voters come in two types. One is policy voters. The other group, instead of engaging in seemingly random behavior, systematically vote "irrationally" for candidates who offer the pleasing wizardry of smoke and mirrors. Supporters of losing candidates often see this to be the correct model. The lesson for the researcher is to control for all relevant variables. For instance, the correlation between liberal *Mood* and Democratic voting for president is virtually zero. But with other relevant variables in the model, such as party identification and candidate likes and dislikes (which are nuisances at best to a spatial modeler), controlled, *Mood* shows up handsomely as an electoral predictor.

4 For illustrative purposes, consider an interaction that has a probability of a "thoughtful" outcome of 0.51 and a "thoughtless" outcome of 0.49. Repeat that interaction 10 times and the probability of the "thoughtless" position standing firm is 0.0008.

## American Politics as a System

In addition to the empirical observations about the generally low level of political competence within the electorate, we must also deal with an established theoretical argument that says that political attention and activity is in fact "irrational" in the first place (Downs 1957). Given the busyness of daily life and the infinitesimal probability that any one individual can have any marginal impact on politics anyway, why should ordinary citizens incur the costs of staying politically informed and active? Transformed to the aggregate level, the question could be whether enough citizens are sufficiently motivated to stay sufficiently informed in order to keep the macro dynamics of politics operating.

But the better question to ask is whether political information is important enough to *some* citizens so that the overall aggregate becomes sufficiently informed. Clearly, for many policy questions there exist "issue publics" (Converse 1964, 1975) who maintain a keen interest in the matter – out of narrow self-interest or for broader ideological or philosophical reasons. On matters of equal employment for women, for example, some people pay attention because they see how policy affects their own workplace and others will see the issue in terms of a more general social stance toward gender and equality. Some issue publics may be quite small: Milk price supports and the protection of domestic sugar elicit the active interest of a relative few. Other issue publics can approach universality: an understanding of the national economy's fortunes serves the private interests of many citizens in their roles as producers, consumers, and investors.

Further, we observe that Americans possess a considerable amount of "free" information about their economic and political environment.[5] As we have pointed out, when citizens act as economic agents, they are often absorbing free information about economic conditions. Similarly, when citizens act as consumers of the mass media and when they interact socially with others, they absorb free information about politics whether they care much about politics or not. This may be a limited amount of information to be sure and unevenly distributed across the citizenry to boot. But people are capable of rationally processing the limited amounts of information they do possess. Rather than throw away their free information, people use it.

---

5 This information is "free" to the individual but it is produced by macro organizations who pursue their own private interests. The American Association of Retired Persons and the Sierra Club are eager to inform the public on matters of public policy. The mass media also, sometimes uncertainly, inform the public. And, of course, politicians and political ideologicians work to put matters forcefully to the general public. The presence of "free" information is, of course, a macro-political phenomenon.

430

## The Macro Polity and Democratic Performance

Table 11.1. *A Hypothetical Micro-Level Result*

| Probability That Individual Will Vote | Individual A | Individual B |
|---|---|---|
| Democratic | 0.53 | 0.46 |
| Republican | 0.47 | 0.54 |

Table 11.2. *A Hypothetical Macro-Level Result*

| Percentage of Electorate That Votes | Electorate A | Electorate B |
|---|---|---|
| Democratic | 53% | 46% |
| Republican | 47% | 54% |

Another reason why it is possible to observe macro-level political dynamics is that it does not take a large percentage of individuals to move in order to generate major macro-level consequences. The same political phenomenon can appear small when viewed on a micro-level landscape but large when viewed from a macro-level perspective. Consider the hypothetical micro-level data of Table 11.1. Here, we observe the voting behavior of two individuals A and B. If we view this table from the usual micro-level perspective, we see two individuals much alike in their voting behavior. Assuming the 0.07 difference in their voting behavior is not due to sampling error, the difference would probably be regarded of little substantive interest. Both individuals seem unsure about which party to support.

Instead, consider two electorates that produce a collective outcome. In Table 11.2, we see *exactly the same numerical data*, this time describing macro-political decisions of the two electorates rather than two instances of individual behavior. Now we have a winner and a loser. From the macro perspective, the smallish differences loom large.

In actuality, Electorate A and Electorate B are *not* hypothetical. Electorate A is the U.S. electorate of 1992, observed to be routinely electing into office a Democratic House of Representatives to make 40 straight years of Democratic control. Electorate B is the same U.S. electorate in 1994, which created the political earthquake of the first Republican House in 40 years. Separating the two groups is the mere 7 percentage-point difference that appears so small in the micro-level table. Elections obviously are won or lost by just a few percentage points' movement. Similarly, only a small percentage-point difference separates the distribution of party identification in the current competitive era from the

431

distribution of the same variable at the height of Democratic dominance. A small percentage-point difference can make the difference between an electorate in a liberal mood from one that is conservative. And a difference of perhaps as little as 10 percentage points can separate the politically successful president from one deemed to be a failure.

Further, understand that it is the *electorate* rather than the individual voter that commands the attention of politicians. Any given member of the House or Senate knows that winning and losing elections is paramount and that the marginal decisions of the electorate will determine political careers. Thus, what is important is not the behavior of the "typical" person but the behavior of the aggregate. In particular, what is important is *change* in the behavior of the aggregate. So politicians and political strategists attend to marginal change and to what can potentially signal future marginal change. Successful politicians do not rely on the fact that most people are committed partisans or largely uninterested in matters political. Those people provide the anchor, the dead weight, the stability in the electorate. Instead, politicians – and inevitably macro-political decisions – reflect the movement of a relative few at the margin.

Thus, three aspects of macro politics, taken together, account for the disproportionate power of sparse political intelligence. First, to the degree that people are inattentive, their perceptions and behavior tend to cancel each other out, contributing to their disappearance from the macro-level picture. Second, to the degree people hold information, they use it rather than throw it away when making political judgments. Third, it requires only a small proportion of individuals to change in response to their political environment in order to create the macro-level dynamics.[6]

### Macro Analysis Versus Micro Analysis

The pursuit of regularities of politics at the macro level requires a faith that the full attentiveness and rationality of the American electorate assert themselves at the macro level. Such a faith is rarely supported by

---

6 These arguments for macro-level analysis apply not only to time-series analysis but also to cross-sectional analysis where the units of analysis are at the macro level. An additional advantage of macro-level analysis of time series is that daunting questions of causality can be addressed. For instance, our analysis is made easier by evidence (if any is needed) that *Presidential Approval* does not affect the economy and that *Macropartisanship* does not affect *Approval*. Where causal feedback is present, as with the *Mood-Policy* connection, it is possible to analyze the two relationships in terms of lagged effects.

the literature on political behavior as a micro-level phenomenon. In fact, an argument can be made that inferences about the macro-level polity that rely on micro-level survey evidence are almost always wrong. To see this, let us consider some of our key findings and see how they compare with the easiest inference that would be available if political science were limited to its micro-level findings.

Start with the simple finding that aggregate economic perceptions trace their origins in plausible ways to the actual objective economy. While we suspect that this general argument is hardly controversial, proponents of the idea of a rationality to collective economic perceptions would be hard pressed to make their case if the sole information available was the unassailable evidence that individual citizens tend to be even more ignorant of key economic indicators than they are of public affairs (Conover and Feldman 1986; Conover et al. 1986, 1987).

Consider the argument that economic perceptions (and therefore the objective economy) affect *Presidential Approval* and presidential election outcomes. Political behavior researchers rarely challenge such claims, perhaps because survey evidence exaggerates them. Based on economic perceptions in surveys, the superficial evidence actually inflates the influence of the economy on political attitudes and voting behavior. As Kramer (1983) pointed out, cross-sectional variation in perceptions of the national economy are mere variations in perceptions of a shared constant. Especially when acting as survey respondents, people tend to communicate perceptions about the economy that are consistent with their political attitudes. The danger is that survey respondents can manufacture evidence that political attitudes are driven by economic perceptions even in instances where no such causal process exists.

The crucial variable of *Macropartisanship* provides a still different story. Studies of individual partisanship, both recent (e.g., Green and Palmquist 1990, 1994) and in the relatively distant past (e.g., Campbell et al. 1960), strongly support the notion that individual-level partisanship tends to be quite stable, with little movement. The obvious macro-level inference is that macro-level partisanship must be a virtual constant. As we have seen, this is decidedly not the case. Yet our macro-level findings of considerable macro-level movement in response to standard economic and political forces is ultimately consistent with the micro-level evidence. Why? Largely because what appears minute perhaps to the point of being unmeasurable at the individual level can take on substantive significance at the macro level. For instance, a movement of only four points in the distribution of party identification goes unnoticed in surveys. But if this shift is real and not survey error, the four-point movement can have major consequences at the macro level. For politicians, of course, a four-point swing in the normal vote is a matter of political life and death.

Next, consider *Mood*, or the electorate's relative disposition to give liberal or conservative responses to surveys. Until the corrective evidence of Stimson (1991), the tendency within the political behavior community was to see the electorate's ideological disposition as still one more constant rather than a variable. At the individual level, survey responses are known to be so prone to error that at worst they comprise mainly "doorstep opinions." But now we see that macro-level *Mood* moves and moves systematically, in response to economic conditions (unemployment vs. inflation) and to national policies. That people could move collectively in this manner can seem incredible in the light of our knowledge of the individual survey response to policy issues. For students of political behavior, the standard image of the typical voter's knowledge of recent policy is the near absence of relevant content, so ably reported by Stokes and Miller (1962) in an earlier era. We do not dispute this image or argue that voters have gotten more serious about their public affairs in the intervening decades. The reconciliation of micro-level and macro-level evidence here depends mainly on the fact that a small if imperceptible movement at the individual level can have major impact. For instance, it did not take movement by many citizens for the collective electorate to send a "go slower" signal after the apex of the Great Society legislation in the mid-1960s.

Next, consider elections. Our macro-level analysis has shown that *Macropartisanship* and *Mood* directly affect election results. Changes in electoral partisanship and ideology contribute to the outcome of presidential elections and (to a lesser extent) the national verdict of House and Senate elections. Of course, in the voluminous micro-level literature, party identification has a hallowed place as an electoral predictor. But this is the party identification of permanence and the "normal vote" (Converse 1966), not a partisanship that moves. Not only does national partisanship move, its movement holds major electoral consequences. Similarly, *Mood* has greater electoral consequences than we would surmise given the dubious level of "issue voting" by the American public. Move the electorate one percentile in its tendency to respond liberal or conservative to surveys, and one moves the Republican versus Democratic electoral tide nearly one percentage point as well.

Finally, we consider policy movement. We have presented strong evidence that the policies of national elites – both in form and substance – respond directly to small changes in public opinion. An earlier view, arising from a voting literature that stressed voters' inability to communicate policy views, held that politicians who would change policy to accord with swings in public mood would be chasing a phantom. Attributions of causality for major policy changes rarely involved public opinion. For instance, the circumstances that culminated in the Great Society liberalism of the 1960s or the conservatism of the Reagan program were rarely thought to be surges of public opinion, but rather almost the exact opposite – rare confluences of political fortune that allowed ideologically driven elites to act free of the constraints of public opinion.

In presenting these examples, we have seen several reasons why the inferences that people make about the macro polity from individual-level data are often wrong. Survey data are prone to error, both random and (worse yet) systematic, when people rationalize their reported attitudes and vote choices. As we have stressed time and time again, patterns that appear small on the micro-level landscape loom large at the macro level. The most important error of all may be the failure to recognize that systematic behavior of the aggregate is often driven by the most attentive members of the public.

The micro-level study of political behavior has dwelled at length on people's limited attention to politics and lack of political sophistication. For the study of voters or citizens as individuals rather than aggregates, it is quite appropriate to focus on the full range of human capacity in terms of political interest, political sophistication, and political knowledge. But for macro-level analysis, it is the systematic behavior that matters. And that systematic behavior rarely stems from voters at their least attentive.

A lesson can be drawn from the field of economics, where the assumption of rationality prevails among microeconomists as strongly as among the macroeconomists. The study of national economies would make little headway if economists were fixated on the seeming irrationality displayed by many individual economic actors. The study of national economies would be further thwarted if microeconomists were to scold macroeconomists for the futility of studying the effects of macro-level variables on one another because some individual consumers purchase products without regard to price or that many entrepreneurs go bankrupt. The lesson for students of the macro polity is that we should begin to theorize unabashedly as if the public will was based on at least a modicum of limited rationality.

### Macro Institutions

In addition to collapsing individual behavior into the aggregate electorate, we have also treated politicians and political coalitions as invisible parts of the main government institutions. Thus, we study the policy behavior of the House of Representatives or the U.S. government rather than any particular group of political actors. This decision is, of course, part and parcel of the *macro*-political orientation.

It does, however, lead us to concentrate on a politics that may be characteristically different from mere *micro* politics. In order to get political institutions (and particularly collections of political institutions) to act coherently requires a degree of consensus that is not necessary for smaller groupings. Thus, we expect that it will take a lot longer to get the entire government to adopt a new policy than it will take for a particular politician to sense a change in the public's preferences and to react accordingly.

Note also that it is especially difficult to get large coalitions together when issues lie along the traditional liberal-conservative ideological fault line (Quirk 1989). In such cases, the gains from cooperation on a new policy are often outweighed by the gains from political posturing.[7] This problem is especially important when we focus on *major* policy changes – ones that touch on many different political interests. And it will prove particularly poignant when we focus on the *macro*-political collections of policies that constitute the root of majoritarian politics. In fact, the *Laws* upon which we based our *Policy Mood* analyses in Chapter 9 were typically passed by large and bipartisan majorities. The sort of macro behavior that we do observe is often of a very different character than that upon which we typically focus when studying individual politicians at work.

### Macro Policy

We have kept our eye on an aggregation of different issue areas over which government makes policy. Our concepts of *Mood* and *Policy* include a wide variety of subareas that do not always have much to do with one another. In fact, one of the distinctive characteristics of American politics is its pluralistic character – with different subsystems of political elites and interested parties governing different aspects of the polity.[8] Nevertheless, it is also true that when the larger public

---

7 Of course, when one ideological faction *controls* all the institutions, this barrier to quick policy making disappears. However, note that such ideological control has proved rare in American politics.

8 Though, to be sure, the differentiation among policy areas is not complete. On the one hand, government policies typically favor producer interests and the views of the upper class. In this sense, there arise commonalities in government policies. In addition, it seems clear that in recent years the clear-cut divisions between policy domains has become a matter of evolutionary dispute – as such matters as health and environment have intruded into the producer niches.

gets invited into policy making – another characteristic trait of American politics – it comes in the guise of "majoritarian politics." And majoritarian politics is most clearly organized around the political polarities "liberalism" and "conservatism."

Thus, we find it helpful to describe the political system in terms of broader aggregates of policies. But we lose something doing so. Previous research indicates that the public can react almost immediately to changes in particular policies. More generally, Wlezien (1995) finds that the public reacts to specific budgetary changes within a year – indicating that it pays attention to the public debate rather than the longer-term consequences of budgetary change. So when we move from the specific issue area to the general policy tenor of government, we lose the ability to connect government and public directly. But this is not merely a matter of analytic fortune. In reality, the connection between public and government must run along *both* the specific and general policy lines. In fact, the majoritarian political side of the connection must be more broad-gauged and indirect than the specific policy path. To generate the idea that government has become too liberal or too conservative requires the integration of specific policies into a more general argument about political life. The party and ideological theorists must find ways to translate the specifics into the general – using a language that resonates with a modestly attentive public.[9]

Our analysis of macro policy – rather than specific policies – captures the ideological majoritarian parts of political life but misses the daily infighting of interest group politics. Much of what happens in government, well-appreciated by the K Street crowd, occurs below the radar range of ideological politics. This politics is surely well worth study and further understanding. But even the government in issue networks will be shaped by the massive movements on the national scene.

### TWO SEPARATE SYSTEMS?

The causal connections presented in this book can roughly be divided into two systems. A "competence" system involves the objective degree of economic prosperity, perceptions of that economy, *Presidential Approval*, party identification, and election outcomes. The "policy"

---

9 Sometimes we find an exception that "proves the rule." In 1994, the G.O.P. was able to portray the Clinton health-care plan as "socialized medicine" because they had at hand an old war horse that the AMA had explicitly developed in the 1940s battle over health care. Similarly, the portrayal of the plan as another hydra-headed bureaucracy played to standard themes. The Clinton political failure lay in an inability to show that this was not just politics as usual.

system involves the inflation-unemployment trade-off, *Policy Mood*, public policy, and election outcomes. So defined, the two subsystems do not come together except as they present competing sets of variables to drive election outcomes.

In the competence subsystem, we see that the objective economy drives various aggregate indicators of consumer sentiment, including both expectations and retrospections. We have observed how, among these indicators, it is mainly expectations that affect presidential approval. But approval is shaped by other factors as well, factors which we can label as "political." We have also observed how both economics and political approval affect party identification.

Election outcomes are also linked to this subsystem, as economic prosperity clearly affects the presidential vote. It would be a mistake, however, to assume that this effect represents solely the direct response of voters to their perceptions of the state of the economy. Election outcomes are also affected by the nation's distribution of party identification, indexed by *Macropartisanship*, and the electorate's affect for the candidates, indexed in part by *Presidential Approval*. We have seen that to the extent the economy prospers, people begin to like the president and shift their party identifications to the president's party. As they do so, they become more likely to vote for the presidential party. When this sequence takes place, the economy is an indirect contributor to the presidential vote outcome, without the necessity of many voters consciously taking into account the economy of the moment.

The second or "policy" system involves the electorate's ideological mood, national policy, and election outcomes. The economy is in the background of this subsystem as well. As the national mood switches liberal or conservative, policy activity by national elites responds accordingly. Major changes in national policy, reflected in our *Laws* index, take longer to actualize but do follow from national *Mood* swings. As national policy responds, the national mood that caused the policy shift recedes. Elections are the motivator for national politicians to respond to *Mood*. As *Mood* turns liberal, for instance, politicians know that they gain electorally by moving liberal.

It is interesting to view this second system from the standpoint of the typical national politician, motivated by electoral survival but with policy goals as well. Democratic politicians tend to be oriented toward liberal policies and Republican politicians toward conservative policies. Each gains rewards from achieving their policy goals. But policy gains also carry some potential cost in terms of the likelihood of reelection. Thus, the politician's equation is to find the best balance between winning on policy and winning electorally.

## The Macro Polity and Democratic Performance

Because Democrats and Republicans do pursue their own policy goals in addition to those demanded by the public, they help to generate an electoral cycle. Presidents and members of congress pursue ideological agendas. To the extent they succeed, they shift the ideological mood in the opposite direction. The result is that the electorate readjusts its decision regarding the balance of Democrats and Republicans it puts in office. In theory, it is possible for politicians to calibrate exactly just how much pursuit of an ideological agenda they must trade off against public demands. In practice, however, a precise calculation seems beyond human ken. The implication, and perhaps surprise, is that a little imprecision in these linkages produces a feedback system that is highly susceptible to cycles of policy, opinion, and electoral outcomes.

As described, the two systems do not touch each other directly. On the one hand, governments try to appear competent and in control because of the political payoff that the appearance of general competence brings. For a president and his party, perceived competence breeds approval, new party recruits, and ultimately, votes. On the other hand, governments try to provide voters with ideological satisfaction, for the reason that it also produces votes. It is in the electoral arena that the two streams are hammered together. There is no surprise that we find elections as the forge of American politics. That is where the flame and fury of electoral competition form governing coalitions and sharpen the cutting edges of public policy.

Yet, we must ask whether the two systems are connected in ways we have not yet considered. Competence is a perfect example of a "valence" issue (Stokes 1966) in the sense that competence is universally valued over incompetence. When an American president demonstrates the appearance of competence, all (or virtually all) Americans enhance their satisfaction. For instance, when George Bush transformed a potential foreign policy quagmire into the triumphant Gulf War victory of early 1991, he improved his standing as a leader with most Americans – even including opponents of military action. Similarly, when Bush appeared to blunder politically when dealing with an economic recession in late 1991 and 1992, virtually all observers, including Bush's political allies, lowered their assessment of Bush's leadership. But even as Americans changed the direction of their assessments of Bush following his military and diplomatic triumph and later his economic stumbling, their levels of support for Bush were largely fixed, with most Americans maintaining a consistent bottom-line evaluation – either approving Bush or disapproving of Bush both when he was at his high and again at his low in the polls. Policy direction, upon which people were divided, as well as competency concerns motivated evaluations of Bush.

439

Citizens divide over policy for two reasons. Most obviously, different people prefer different policies because they perceive that they have different interests. It should be no surprise when rich people favor policies that tend to favor the rich, or when the poor favor the opposite policies more favorable to their personal interests. This is the familiar struggle over dividing the pie, or the politics of distribution.

The second reason people divide over policies is that policies represent competing claims over the best means of expanding the size of the pie. When politicians and economists debate economic policies, for instance, their rhetoric rarely is pitched at the level of whose economic interests are legitimate and which not (for example, an argument that the rich are more deserving than the poor). Rather, the argument is pitched in terms of a debate over who has the best means of promoting the general welfare or (the same thing) the public interest.

From this perspective, consider the task of the ordinary citizen, trying to sort out the complexities of ideological debate. Of course, for the truly committed ideological voter, policy preferences and their associated attitudes may go forever unchanged. But consider instead more open-minded voters who combine a pragmatic bent with perhaps no more than a limited knowledge of policy outcomes and of the national well-being. Such voters might set their policy verdict to be to say yes to whatever works – for instance, if times are "good," attribute the positive showing to the policies of the "in" party and endorse them. Whatever ideology seems to work by increasing the size of the pie deserves support.

Thus, we would expect a pattern where the degree of prosperity and well-being influences ideological choices by ordinary voters, depending on who is in power and how the country is going. If times are good, and the public thinks its leaders are doing a good job, then it might become more attractive to the ideological stance of the leadership. If times are bad, the public would become more attractive to the opposite ideological position. Operationally, we should see good times under Democrats push *Mood* more liberal and good times under Republicans push *Mood* more conservative. Similarly, positive presidential approval would produce a *Mood* swing in the president's direction. And shifts in *Macropartisanship* should be accompanied by *Mood* shifts, with Republican gains producing conservatism and Democratic gains producing liberalism.

We might also expect some cross-system causality in the other direction. In particular, *Mood* could have a direct effect on *Approval* and *Macropartisanship*. For instance, when our pragmatic citizen detects an ideological excess in national policy, he or she may not only shift his or her ideological mood but also withdraw support for the president and the president's party.

## The Macro Polity and Democratic Performance

Intriguing though these hypothesized cross-system effects may be, we find little in the way of convincing statistical support for them. Consider first the effect of the economy, *Approval*, and *Macropartisanship* on *Mood*. As measured by the real or perceived economy (consumer sentiment and its components), economic performance does not correlate with annual *Mood* shifts (consistent with the president's party), either current or in the future. Annualized measures of presidential approval have no statistical relationship with *Mood* or *Mood* shifts, present or future.

Similarly, *Mood* and *Policy* appear to have no discernible effect on *Macropartisanship* or *Approval*. So far, we have generally ignored the statistical relationship between two of our most central variables, *Mood* and *Macropartisanship*. The statistical reality appears to be that the dynamics of these two variables are completely independent of each other, even though at the micro level, partisanship and ideology increasingly go together.

Figure 11.1 illustrates the *Macropartisanship-Mood* nonrelationship, where each variable is measured annually. Observing the graph, one might get the sense that until the seventies, *Mood* leads *Macropartisanship* to some extent. *Mood* became more liberal and then broke more conservative in the mid-1960s. *Macropartisanship* followed with a slight delay, moving more Democratic and then breaking more Republican in the late 1980s. But starting with the Watergate era of the 1970s, the two variables began to diverge sharply. Just as the electorate's *Mood* was becoming decidedly more conservative, Democratic Party identification received a strong second wind. Democratic president Jimmy Carter presided over a nation that was oddly Democratic even as it turned decidedly more conservative. By the mid-1980s, Democratic *Macropartisanship* finally declined to the point where it "should" have been if it followed *Mood* as it seemingly did in the 1950s and 1960s. Yet as *Mood* turned more liberal again in the 1980s and 1990s, *Macropartisanship* did not show the "predicted" Democratic increase.

Does *Approval* respond to policy or *Mood*? Neither the *Mood* index nor the *Laws* index appears statistically related to *Presidential Approval*. We can ask a similar question about the effect of specifically presidential ideology upon *Approval*. In Chapter 2, we analyzed the effect of a president's ideological posturing on *Approval*. We saw that the president's *Approval* rating does not correlate with our index of presidential liberalism (see Chapter 8 for a discussion of the index). Surely this negative finding does not mean that presidents can get away with unpopular policies without political costs. Our measure of presidential policy is crude and perhaps flawed. And the expectation that moderate policies benefit a president may be flawed. There are circumstances when a president

441

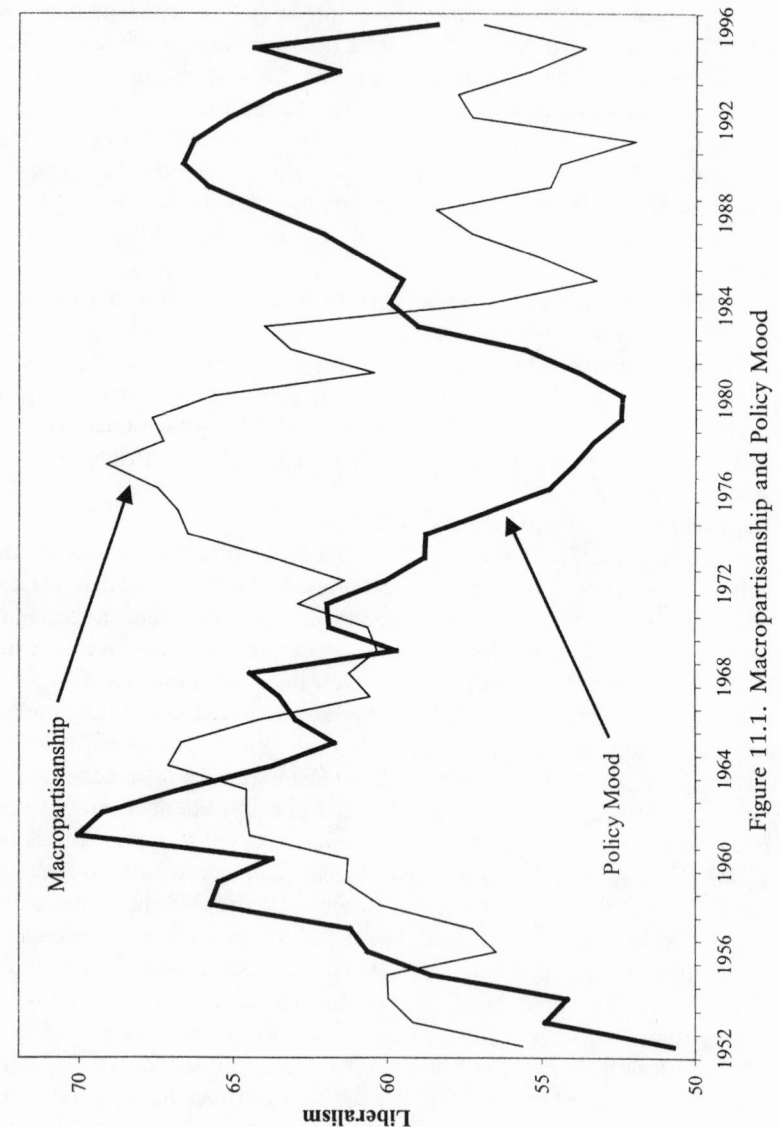

Figure 11.1. Macropartisanship and Policy Mood

would gain in *Approval* indicators by moving toward his party's ideological extreme. A very unpopular president would gain by at least shoring up his base. And moving to the center can disabuse one's core supporters. Interestingly, as Jimmy Carter conducted a relatively moderate presidency, his *Approval* suffered. Carter's *Approval* level was maintained at a higher level among independents and supporters of the other party (Republicans) than is typical for an American president. It was among Democratic identifiers that Carter's approval numbers suffered.

Another complication for observing evidence of an *Approval*-moderation connection is that if in fact moderation improves *Approval*, presidents are more likely to moderate when they are in trouble. Popular presidents may hold a more extreme agenda because they can afford the approval loss they must pay to achieve their policy gains. The two processes can cancel out. For instance, was Reagan's combination of conservatism plus evident popularity a sign that relatively extreme postures do not hurt politically or a sign that Reagan was popular enough not to need to moderate his conservative image?

When we say that we find no relationship between policy and approval, what we mean is that presidents leave no consistent trace of such a relationship. To see this, presidents would have to trade off approval for policy pursuits on a reasonably frequent basis. We have seen some instances. When Eisenhower sent troops to Little Rock in 1957, his approval among African Americans increased and his approval among southern whites plummeted. Similarly, Johnson's visible support of the Civil Rights Act of 1964 damaged his approval ratings among southerners. When Reagan broke the Air Traffic Controllers' strike in 1981, his approval rating among working-class Americans dropped predictably. And Bush's support of the 1990 compromise budget (and tax increase) hurt his rating among conservative Republicans. In each case, the *Approval* change among the relevant groups dissipated in a matter of months. And in each case, the *overall* approval ratings changed only marginally, almost invisibly. The presidents traded approval among one group for approval in the more diffuse public.

These identifiable links between policy and approval are rare, however. We should not be surprised. Presidents can only rarely be expected to take dramatic policy moves that are well known to prove politically damaging – the risks are great and the potential payoff uncertain. Such acts of "political courage" are the stuff of eulogistic biography rather than everyday politics. Statesmen, after all, are dead (or retired) politicians. Active politicians, in the heat of day-to-day battle, can be expected to risk their political capital only rarely and then only on matters of central consequence. And even then, they will do everything possible to sugarcoat the policy initiatives to minimize the political downside.

Similarly, when we find that *Macropartisanship* and *Mood* are unconnected, we may simply find that party leaderships do not consistently get
caught advocating unpopular policies. In fact, we should be surprised to
discover that parties let their images get tarnished with dramatically
unpopular policy positions. When one party or the other gains advantage by claiming an "issue," we expect that the opposition will counter
the advantage, either by reducing party distinctiveness on the issue or
(more likely) elevating alternative issue considerations. The result is that
when *Mood* swings one way or the other, party elites can be expected to
shift course so that no net advantage is systematically in place.[10]

In general, of course, this is one of the shortcomings of doing empirical research on strategic actors. We have difficulty discerning theoretical linkages that do not show themselves because the politicians[11] do not
wish to suffer the consequences.

Nevertheless, at least as far as we *can* see, the two subsystems remain
largely separate. They do merge together during election campaigns and
they do carry consequences for government. Political competence or
good fortune can yield governing coalitions that produce unwanted
policy changes. And public reaction to policy change can punish even
the most competent of governments. A more complete appreciation of
how these elements come together might give us a richer view of democratic governance. It would also yield a deeper understanding about
chance and strategic choice.

## THE POLITICAL SYSTEM AND THE ECONOMIC SYSTEM

When the interconnections between the political system and the economic system are discussed, the intersection at issue is typically the effect
of the economic system on the political realm. Typical of this pattern,
this book has discussed the impact of economic prosperity on *Presidential Approval*, *Macropartisanship*, and election outcomes. It has also
introduced a discussion of the effect of unemployment and inflation on
ideological mood. Perhaps we should also take more seriously the effects
of the political system upon the economic realm as well.

---

10 In fact, one main argument for "realignment" is when one party or the other mis-
   calculates and cedes a majoritarian issue to the opposition (Berelson et al. 1954).
   Even a major political transformation of the policy orientation of the parties,
   however, need not produce a shift in the level of *Macropartisanship* (Carmines
   and Stimson 1989).
11 In this sense, politicians are not rats.

We are not the first to express this thought. In their admirable book *Partisan Politics, Divided Government, and the Economy,* Alesina and Rosenthal assert that *"the interconnections of politics and economics is sufficiently strong that the study of capitalist economies cannot be solely the study of market forces"* (Alesina and Rosenthal 1995, p. 224, italics in original). Numerous studies appear to confirm that the party of the president has economic consequences, with Republicans focusing on the ills of inflation and Democrats on the ills of unemployment. Alesina and Rosenthal extend the discussion to the impact of electoral surprises on the economy. They argue that uncertainty about the next election outcome leads to electoral surprises, with the new president generating the policy shock given his priority of fighting inflation (if a Republican) or unemployment (if a Democrat).

For our purposes here, the interesting aspect of the Alesina-Rosenthal model is that the impact of elections on the economy is essentially passive. Elections are held and an outcome is produced by ideological tastes (including in some variants a relative distaste for inflation), economic growth, plus an exogenous shock. The economic consequences result flow from the inability to anticipate the exogenous shock. Although ideological and inflationary tastes are in the model, their effects are treated as independent of the current economy. In other words, to the extent the electorate chooses a partisan leadership based on economic *policy*, the current levels of inflation and unemployment (or growth) do not enter into the electorate's *policy* deliberations.

We speculate that electorates' policy demands respond to imbalances of the unemployment-inflation trade-off and perhaps to even more general economic considerations as well. The findings of this book provide a strong hint of a complex causal system involving the unemployment-inflation trade-off. As the relative collective worry about inflation and unemployment costs shifts back and forth, so too does the electorate's *Mood*, which in turn affects election results. In our previous discussions in Chapters 6 and 9, we treated this source of movement in *Mood* as entirely exogenous. And for purposes of coherent statistical analysis, that is the correct decision. However, consider that *Mood* affects the president's economic policy (via elections and perhaps directly as well), which feeds back to inflation and unemployment, which further alters *Mood*. Thus, with some delay, public opinion affects the course of economic action, which feeds back to public opinion.

Consider a simple model where the stylized facts are that Democratic and Republican presidents each offer their party's signature economic policy, regardless of circumstances. From the perspective of the pragmatic voters in the middle, the government should fight inflation when inflation is excessive and unemployment when it is excessive. If the electorate chooses wrong, the economy will tilt out of equilibrium. Choose Republican retrenchment when the nation faces an unemployment crisis, and it will take a long time before the natural growth rate is restored. Choose a Democratic spending binge when inflation is threatening to spiral, and the consequences will also be costly.

The policy demands represented by ideological mood are in large part demands about *economic* policy writ large. We might wish to make the heroic assumption that these actually reflect objective economic needs. Conservative *Mood* would reflect a need for government retrenchment and anti-inflationary policies. Liberal *Mood* would reflect a need for expansionary government and an emphasis on economic growth. Still, we are reminded that ideological mood is only one variable that affects the vote, so from the standpoint of the electorate's policy preferences, electoral mistakes will get made.

Is there any evidence that electoral mood provides a thermostatic device for *economic* policy? Over the post–World War II period, we have a total of six changes in presidential party that provide our observations. As measured by relative mood, in three transitions (1952, 1968, 1980), a conservative electorate placed a Republican president in the White House. In two others (1960, 1992), a liberal electorate put a Democrat in the White House. Each of these five elections represents a proper match of ideological sentiment and presidential choice. In each of these five instances, the following election was conducted in an atmosphere of exceptional economic prosperity (1956, 1964, 1972, 1984, 1996). In each instance, this new-found prosperity is generally attributed with causing the electoral landslide for the incumbent president. Could the roots of these successes be found in the electorate's collective decisions four years earlier? If we make something of this consistency, is the pattern that party change brings prosperity? Or is it that party change *consistent with national mood* brings prosperity?

For additional evidence, we note that even if *Mood* represents a prescience about economic needs, the election outcome does not always match the electorate's *Mood*. The one party transition that looks like a clear mismatch is 1976. Even though the *Mood* indicator signaled conservatism, the post-Watergate electorate chose Democrat Jimmy Carter to be president. What followed in 1980, though hardly all Carter's fault, was a presidential election held under the worst economic circumstances of any post-World War II election. In this way, the case of Carter's election and subsequent defeat provides the exception that may prove the rule. Choose the wrong party at the controls and economic distress follows. Of course, we could cite the earlier contrasting elections of 1928 and 1932 and their consequences for economic policy as well.

## DEMOCRATIC PERFORMANCE AND THE MACRO POLITY

Democratic theory comes in a strong version and a weak version. The strong version demands a politically watchful and electorally active citizenry, poised to change its leaders when they fail to provide satisfactory representation. Only when these conditions hold, would political leaders have sufficient incentive to fulfill the needs and desires of the public. The weak version holds that it is sufficient that democratic institutions survive with the occasional electoral replacement of ruling elites. The public is not capable of contributing much more to the maintenance of democracy and we should be grateful just for the public's acceptance of the legitimacy of democratic rules. The findings of micro-level political behavior have lowered our expectations of the American electorate. In this sense, the weak version of democratic theory tends to dominate our thinking regarding what is possible.

In this book, we have not challenged the usual descriptions of the American public. We do not claim to find great political wisdom where none exists. Nor should we be understood to be making Panglossian claims about the distribution of political information and power in the American polity. Rather, we point to the collective intelligence that emerges when the voices of the public are pooled into an aggregated unit. Political reactions based on the economy, for instance, are based on the collective information of those who do hold economic knowledge, not the unpredictability of uninformed actors responding in isolation. Partisanship, which rarely changes at the individual level, shows a discernible response to events when measured at the aggregate level. Even the electorate's collective ideological mood responds slowly but intelligently to the political and economic environment. In the aggregate, elections indeed are affected by the electorate's partisan disposition and its ideological mood.

Where the electorate evaluates performance and policy, we expect politicians to pay heed. And surely, we see that politicians do their very best to give the public the sorts of policy directions that they demand – immediately they generate considerable policy activity and in the longer run they change the fundamental directions of governmental policy. Elected leaders know enough to try to keep their electorate content.

We are encouraged to believe that American democracy is real. The strong version of democratic theory finds support in the past half-century. Far from the sham depicted by skeptics, politics produces a dynamic relationship between government action and citizen appraisal.

The political system, as it rewards and punishes individuals, generates the charged forces that hold politicians and public in dynamic attraction to one another. When things move out of synchrony, when political events change the political balance, the system adjusts and incorporates the changes to yield a new but stable relationship. Individual citizens, and individual politicians, and dramatic political crises, and specific policy debates come and go, but the macro polity remains fundamentally resilient.

## A MACRO-POLITICAL SCIENCE

Our macro analysis is, of course, an entry effort. We are sure that we are wrong. It is our hope that we shall spur others to take up the banner and carry on. Beyond this, the macro-level work presents puzzles that need answering. When we find that government policy generates a public response, a slow and seemingly indirect public response, we at the same time ask why so slow and why indirect. When public opinion only gradually produces a public policy response, we ask why only gradually. When matters of political competence and policy seem largely independent, we ask why do not citizens and political commentators and political entrepreneurs make the obvious connections. In our discussion, we have suggested the garden-variety explanations. But the puzzles really ask to be answered in a systematic fashion.

In particular, our pattern of results asks that we begin another form of analysis that focuses on the mechanisms that connect the micro-political world of individual citizens and politicians (that we know pretty well) and the macro-political world of economic performance, political crises, *Approval*, *Macropartisanship*, *Mood*, *Policy Activity*, and *Public Policy*. This level-bridging analysis, a sort of micro-macro linkage analysis, demands much more serious attention than we provide here. It is our hope and expectation that the patterns we have presented will intrigue others to study our governing political system.

# References

Abramowitz, Alan I. 1994. Issue Evolution Reconsidered: Racial Attitudes and Partisanship in the U.S. Electorate. *American Journal of Political Science* 38:1–25.

Abramowitz, Alan I. 2000. Bill and Al's Excellent Adventure: Forecasting the 1996 Presidential Election. In *Before the Vote: Forecasting American National Elections*, ed. James E. Campbell and James C. Garand. Thousand Oaks, CA: Sage.

Abramson, Paul R., and Charles W. Ostrom, Jr. 1991. Macropartisanship: An Empirical Reassessment. *American Political Science Review* 85:181–192.

Achen, Christopher. 1975. Mass Political Attitudes and the Survey Response. *American Political Science Review* 69:1218–1231.

Achen, Christopher. 1992. Social Psychology, Demographic Variables, and Linear Regression: Breaking the Iron Triangle in Voting Research. *Political Behavior* 14:195–211.

Achen, Christopher, and W. Phillips Shively. 1995. *Cross-Level Inference*. Chicago: University of Chicago Press.

Adamany, David. 1973. Legitimacy, Realigning Elections, and the Supreme Court. *Wisconsin Law Review* (September 1973):790–846.

Adams, Greg D. 1997. Abortion: Evidence of Issue Evolution. *American Journal of Political Science* 41:718–737.

Aldrich, John. 1995. *Why Parties? The Origin and Transformation of Party Politics in America*. Chicago: University of Chicago Press.

Aldrich, John H., and David W. Rohde. 2000a. The Republican Revolution and the House Appropriations Committee. *Journal of Politics* 62:1–33.

Aldrich, John H., and David W. Rohde. 2000b. The Consequences of Party Organization in the House: The Role of the Majority and Minority Parties in Conditional Party Government. In *Polarized Politics: Congress and the President in a Partisan Era*, eds. Jon R. Bond and Richard Fleisher. Washington, DC: CQ Press, pp. 31–72.

Alesina, Alberto, and Howard Rosenthal. 1995. *Partisan Politics, Divided Government, and the Economy*. Cambridge: Cambridge University Press.

Alesina, Alberto, John Londregan, and Howard Rosenthal. 1993. A Model of the Political Economy of the United States. *The American Political Science Review* 87:12–33.

Alt, James E. 1991. Ambiguous Intervention: The Role of Government Action in Public Evaluation of the Economy. In *Economics and Politics*, ed. Helmut

# References

Norpoth, Michael Lewis-Beck, and Jean-Dominique Lafay. Ann Arbor: University of Michigan Press.

Alt, James E., and K. Alex Chrystal. 1983. *Political Economics.* Brighton, England: Woodsheaf.

Andersen, Kristi. 1979. *The Creation of a Democratic Majority, 1928–1936.* Chicago: University of Chicago Press.

Arnold, R. Douglas, 1990. *The Logic of Congressional Action.* New Haven: Yale University Press.

Bannerjee, Anindya, Juan Dolado, John W. Galbraith, and David F. Hendry. 1993. *Co-Integration, Error Correction, and the Econometric Analysis of Non-Stationary Data.* Oxford: Oxford University Press.

Barnum, David C. 1985. The Supreme Court and Public Opinion: Judicial Decisionmaking in the Post New Deal Period. *Journal of Politics* 47:652–665.

Bartels, Larry M. 1991. Constituency Opinion and Congressional Policy Making: The Reagan Defense Buildup. *American Political Science Review* 85:457–474.

Bartels, Larry M. 1997. Specification Uncertainty and Model Averaging. *American Journal of Political Science* 41:641–674.

Baum, Lawrence. 1988. Measuring Policy Change in the U.S. Supreme Court. *American Political Science Review* 82:905–912.

Beck, Nathaniel. 1982. Parties, Administrations, and American Macroeconomic Outcomes. *The American Political Science Review* 76:83–93.

Beck, Nathaniel. 1990. Estimating Dynamic Models Using Kalman Filtering. *Political Analysis* 1:121–156.

Beck, Nathaniel. 1991. The Economy and Presidential Approval: An Information Theoretical Approach. In *Economics and Politics*, ed. Helmut Norpoth, Michael Lewis-Beck, and Jean-Dominique Lafay. Ann Arbor: University of Michigan Press.

Beck, Nathaniel. 1993. The Methodology of Cointegration. *Political Analysis* 4:237–248.

Berelson, Bernard R., Paul F. Lazarsfeld, and William N. McPhee. 1954. *Voting: A Study of Opinion Formation in a Presidential Campaign.* Chicago: University of Chicago Press.

Bishop, George F., Alfred J. Tuchfarber, and Andrew E. Smith. 1994. Question Form and Context Effects in the Measurement of Partisanship: Experimental Tests of the Artifact Hypothesis. *American Political Science Review* 88:945–954.

Bond, Jon, and Richard Fleisher. 1990. *The President in the Legislative Arena.* Chicago: University of Chicago Press.

Box-Steffensmeier, Janet M., and Renée M. Smith. 1996. The Dynamics of Aggregate Partisanship. *American Political Science Review* 90:567–580.

Box-Steffensmeier, Janet, Kathleen Knight, and Lee Sigelman. 1998. The Interplay of Macroideology and Macropartisanship: A Time Series Analysis. *Journal of Politics* 60:131–149.

Brace, Paul, and Barbara Hinckley. 1992. *Follow the Leader: Opinion Polls and the Modern Presidents.* New York: Basic Books.

Brody, Richard A. 1991. *Assessing the President: The Media, Elite Opinion, and Public Support.* Stanford, CA: Stanford University Press.

Brody, Richard, and Lee Sigelman. 1983. Presidential Popularity and Presidential Elections. An Update and an Extension. *Public Opinion Quarterly* 47:325–328.

# References

Brown, Courtney. 1991. *Ballots of Tumult: A Portrait of Volatility in American Voting*. Ann Arbor, MI: University of Michigan Press.

Budge, Ian, and Richard I. Hofferbert. 1990. Mandates and Policy Outputs: U.S. Party Platforms and Federal Expenditures. *The American Political Science Review* 84:111–131.

Budge, Ian, David Robertson, and Derek Hearl (Eds.). 1987. *Ideology, Strategy and Policy Change: Spatial Analysis of Post-war Election Programmes in 19 Democracies*. Cambridge: Cambridge University Press.

Burnham, Walter Dean. 1970. *Critical Elections and the Mainsprings of American Politics*. New York: Norton.

Caldeira, Gregory A., and James L. Gibson. 1992. The Etiology of Public Support for the Supreme Court. *American Journal of Political Science* 36:635–664.

Caldeira, Gregory A., Kevin T. McGuire, and Charles E. Smith, Jr. 1997. *Error-Correction and Decision-Making on the Merits in the Supreme Court*. Paper presented at the 1997 Annual Meetings of the Midwest Political Science Association, April 10–12.

Campbell, Angus. 1964. Issues and Voters: Past and Present. *Journal of Politics* 26:745–757.

Campbell, Angus, Philip E. Converse, Warren E. Miller, and Donald E. Stokes. 1960. *The American Voter*. New York: Wiley.

Carmines, Edward G., and James A. Stimson. 1989. *Issue Evolution: Race and the Transformation of American Politics*. Princeton, NJ: Princeton University Press.

Casper, Jonathan D. 1976. The Supreme Court and National Policy-Making. *American Political Science Review* 70:50–63.

Chappell, Henry W., Jr., and William R. Keech. 1985. A New View of Political Accountability for Economic Performance. *American Political Science Review* 79:10–27.

Clarke, H.D., and Stewart, M.C., 1994. Prospections, Retrospections, and Rationality: The "Bankers" Model of Presidential Approval Reconsidered. *American Journal of Political Science* 38:1104–1133.

Clubb, Jerome, William H. Flanagan, and Nancy H. Zingale. 1980. *Partisan Realignment: Voters, Parties, and Government in American History*. Beverly Hills, CA: Sage.

Cohen, Jeffery E. 1997. *Presidential Responsiveness and Public Policy-Making*. Ann Arbor: University of Michigan Press.

Cohen, Jeffrey E., Michael A. Krassa, and John Hamman. 1991. The Impact of Presidential Campaigning on Midterm U.S. Senate Elections. *American Political Science Review* 85:165–178.

Conover, Pamela Johnston, and Stanley Feldman. 1981. The Origins and Meaning of Liberal/Conservative Self-Identifications. *American Journal of Political Science* 25:617–645.

Conover, Pamela Johnston, and Stanley Feldman. 1986. Emotional Reactions to the Economy: I'm Mad as Hell and I'm Not Going to Take It Anymore. *American Journal of Political Science* 30:50–78.

Conover, Pamela Johnston, Stanley Feldman, and Kathleen Knight. 1986. Judging Inflation and Unemployment: The Origins of Retrospective Evaluations. *Journal of Politics* 48:565–588.

Conover, Pamela Johnston, Stanley Feldman, and Kathleen Knight. 1987. The Personal and Political Underpinnings of Economic Forecasts. *American Journal of Political Science* 31:559–583.

# References

Converse, Philip E. 1962. Information Flow and the Stability of Partisan Attitudes. *Public Opinion Quarterly* 26:578–599.

Converse, Philip E. 1964. The Nature of Belief Systems in Mass Publics. In *Ideology and Discontent*, ed. David E. Apter. New York: Free Press.

Converse, Philip E. 1966. The Concept of the Normal Vote. *Elections and the Political Order*, eds. Angus Campbell, Philip E. Converse, Warren E. Miller, and Donald Stokes. New York: Wiley.

Converse, Philip E. 1969. Of Time and Partisan Stability. *Comparative Political Studies* 2:139–171.

Converse, Philip E. 1975. Public Opinion and Voting Behavior. In *Handbook of Political Science*, Volume 4, eds. Fred Greenstein and Nelson Polsby. Reading MA: Addison Wesley, pp. 75–169.

Converse, Philip E. 1976. *The Dynamics of Party Support.* Beverly Hills, CA: Sage.

Converse, Philip E. 1990. Popular Representation and the Distribution of Information. In *Information and Democratic Processes*, eds. John A. Ferejohn and James H. Kuklinski. Urbana, IL: University of Illinois Press.

Converse, Philip E., and Gregory B. Markus. 1979. Plus ça Change. The New CPS Election Study Panel. *American Political Science Review* 73:32–49.

Cox, Gary W., and Mathew D. McCubbins. 1993. *Legislative Leviathan: Party Government in the House.* Berkeley, CA: University of California Press.

Dahl, Robert A. 1957. Decision-Making in a Democracy: The Supreme Court as a National Policy-Maker. *Journal of Public Law* 6:279–295.

Davidson, James E.H., David F. Hendry, Frank Srba, and Stephen Yeo. 1978. Econometric Modelling of the Aggregate Time-Series Relationship Between Consumers' Expenditure and Income in the United Kingdom. *The Economic Journal* 88:661–692.

DeBoef, Suzanna. 1994. Partisanship: Linking Individual and Aggregate Behavior. Doctoral dissertation, University of Iowa.

DeBoef, Suzanna. 1996. Partisanship: Identification and Evaluation. Unpublished manuscript, Pennsylvania State University.

DeBoef, Suzanna, and Jim Granato. 1997. Near-integrated Data and the Analysis of Political Relationships. *American Journal of Political Science* 41:619–640.

Delli Carpini, Michael X., and Scott Keeter. 1996. *What Americans Know About Politics and Why It Matters.* New Haven, CT: Yale University Press.

Deutsch, Karl W. 1963. *The Nerves of Government: Models of Political Communication and Control.* New York: Free Press.

Dickey, David A., and Wayne A. Fuller. 1979. Distribution of the Estimators for Autoregressive Time Series with a Unit Root. *Journal of the American Statistical Association* 74:427–431.

Downs, Anthony. 1957. *An Economic Theory of Democracy.* New York: Harper and Row.

Durr, Robert H. 1993. What Moves Policy Sentiment? *American Political Science Review* 87:158–170.

Easton, David. 1965. *A Systems Analysis of Political Life.* New York: Wiley.

Edsall, Thomas Byrne, and Mary D. 1991. *Chain Reaction: The Impact of Race, Rights, and Taxes on American Politics.* New York: Norton.

Edwards, George C., III. 1983. *The Public Presidency: The Pursuit of Popular Support.* New York: St. Martin's.

Edwards, George C., III. 1989. *At the Margins: Presidential Leadership of Congress.* New Haven, CT: Yale University Press.

# References

Edwards, George C., III, with Alec M. Gallup. 1990. *Presidential Approval: A Sourcebook*. Baltimore, MD: Johns Hopkins University Press.

Enelow, James, and Melvin Hinich. 1984. *The Spatial Theory of Voting: An Introduction*. Cambridge: Cambridge University Press.

Engle, Robert F., and Granger, C.W.J. 1987. Co-integration and Error Correction: Representation, Estimation, and Testing. *Econometrica* 55:251–276.

Engle, Robert F., and Mark W. Watson. 1981. A One Factor Multivariate Time Series Model of Metropolitan Wage Rates. *Journal of the American Statistical Association* 76:774–780.

Erbring, Lutz. 1990. Individuals Writ Large: An Epilogue on "Ecological Fallacy." *Political Analysis: 1989* 1:235–269.

Erikson, Robert S. 1976. Is There Such a Thing as a Safe Seat? *Polity* 8:623–632.

Erikson, Robert S. 1979. The SRC Panel Data and Mass Political Attitudes. *British Journal of Political Science* 9:89–114.

Erikson, Robert S. 1988. The Puzzle of Midterm Loss. *Journal of Politics* 50:1011–1029.

Erikson, Robert S., and Kent L. Tedin. 1981. The 1928–1936 Partisan Realignment: The Case for the Conversion Hypothesis. *American Political Science Review* 75:951–962.

Erikson, Robert S., and Kent L. Tedin. 1995. *American Public Opinion*. Boston: Allyn and Bacon.

Erikson, Robert S., Gerald C. Wright, and John P. McIver. 1994. *Statehouse Democracy*. New York: Cambridge University Press.

Erikson, Robert S., Michael B. MacKuen, and James A. Stimson. 1998. What Moves Macropartisanship? A Reply to Green, Palmquist, and Schickler. *American Political Science Review* 92:901–912.

Erikson, Robert S., Michael B. MacKuen, and James A. Stimson. 2000. Bankers or Peasants Revisited: Economic Expectations and Presidential Approval. *Electoral Studies* 19:295–312.

Erskine, Hazel Gaudet. 1964. Some Gauges of Conservatism. *Public Opinion Quarterly* 28:154–168.

Fair, Ray C. 1978. The Effect of Economic Events on Votes for President. *The Review of Economics and Statistics* 60:159–173.

Fair, Ray C. 1982. The Effect of Economic Events on Votes for President: 1980 Results. *The Review of Economics and Statistics* 64:322–325.

Fair, Ray C. 1993. Estimating Even Probabilities from Macroeconomic Models Using Stochastic Simulation. In *Business Cycles, Indicators, and Forecasting*, Chapter 3, eds. John H. Stock and Mark W. Watson. Chicago: University of Chicago Press.

Fair, Ray C. 1996. Econometrics and Presidential Elections. *The Journal of Economic Perspectives* 10:89–102.

Fan, David P. 1988. *Predictions of Public Opinion from the Mass Media: Computer Content Analysis and Mathematical Modeling*. New York: Greenwood Press.

Fenno, Richard F., Jr. 1978. *Home Style: House Members in Their Districts*. Boston: Little, Brown.

Fiorina, Morris P. 1977. An Outline for a Model of Party Choice. *American Journal of Political Science* 21(August):601–625.

Fiorina, Morris P. 1978. Economic Retrospective Voting in American National Elections: A Micro-Analysis. *American Journal of Political Science* 22:426–443.

# References

Fiorina, Morris P. 1981. *Retrospective Voting in American National Elections.* New Haven, CT: Yale University Press.

Fiorina, Morris P. 1989. *Congress: Keystone to the Washington Establishment,* second edition. New Haven, CT: Yale University Press.

Free, Lloyd, and Hadley Cantril. 1968. *The Political Beliefs of Americans.* New York: Simon and Schuster.

Freeman, John, Daniel Houser, Paul M. Kellstedt, and John T. Williams. 1998. Long Memoried Processes, Unit Roots, and Causal Inference in Political Science. *American Journal of Political Science* 42:1289–1327.

Fuhrer, Jeffrey C. 1988. On the Information Content of Consumer Survey Expectations. *Review of Economics and Statistics* 70:140–144.

Funston, Richard. 1975. The Supreme Court and Critical Elections. *American Political Science Review* 27:327–358.

Gates, John. 1987. Partisan Realignment, Unconstitutional State Policies, and the U.S. Supreme Court, 1837–1964. *American Journal of Political Science* 31:259–280.

Ginsberg, Benjamin. 1976. Elections and Public Policy. *American Political Science Review* 70:41–49.

Gordon, Robert J. 1994. *Macroeconomics,* sixth edition. Boston: Little, Brown.

Granger, Clive W.J., and Paul Newbold. 1974. Spurious Regressions in Econometrics. *Journal of Econometrics* 26:1045–1066.

Green, Donald Philip, and Bradley Palmquist. 1990. Of Artifacts and Partisan Stability. *American Journal of Political Science* 34:872–902.

Green, Donald Philip, and Bradley Palmquist. 1994. How Stable Is Party Identification? *Political Behavior* 16:437–466.

Green, Donald, Bradley Palmquist, and Eric Schickler. 1998. Macropartisanship: A Replication and Critique. *American Political Science Review* 92:883–899.

Grofman, Bernard, and Guillermo Owen. 1986. Condorcet Models: Avenues for Future Research. In *Information Pooling and Group Decision Making,* ed. Bernard Grofman and Guillermo Owen. Greenwich, CT: JAI.

Hall, Robert E., and John P. Taylor. 1993. *Macro Economics,* fourth edition. New York: Norton.

Haller, H.B., and Norpoth, H., 1994. Let the Good Times Roll: The Economic Expectations of American Voters. *American Journal of Political Science* 38:625–650.

Hamilton, James D. 1994. *Time Series Analysis.* Princeton, NJ: Princeton University Press.

Hastie, Reid, and Bernadette Park. 1986. The Relationship between Memory and Judgment Depends on Whether the Task Is Memory-Based or On-Line. *Psychological Review* 93:258–268.

Hendry, David F. 1995. *Dynamic Econometrics.* Oxford: Oxford University Press.

Hertzberg, Marie P., and Barry A. Beckman. 1989. Business Cycle Indicators: Revised Composite Indexes. *Business Conditions Digest* 29:97–102.

Hibbs, Douglas A., Jr. 1977. Political Parties and Macroeconomic Policy. *The American Political Science Review* 71:1467–1487.

Hibbs, Douglas A., Jr. 1987. *The American Political Economy: Macroeconomics and Electoral Politics in the United States.* Cambridge, MA: Harvard University Press.

Hibbs, Douglas A., Jr., and Christopher Dennis. 1988. Income Distribution in the United States. *American Political Science Review* 82:467–490.

## References

Hinich, Melvin J., and Michael C. Munger. 1994. *Ideology and the Theory of Political Choice*. Ann Arbor, MI: University of Michigan Press.

Hofferbert, Richard I., Ian Budge, and Michael D. McDonald. 1993. Party Platforms, Mandates, and Government Spending. *The American Political Science Review* 87:747–750.

Holbrook, Thomas M. 2000. Reading the Political Tea Leaves: A Forecasting Model of Contemporary Presidential Elections. In *Before the Vote: Forecasting American National Elections*, ed. James E. Campbell and James C. Garand. Thousand Oaks, CA: Sage.

Huckfeldt, Robert, and Carol Weitzel Kohfeld. 1989. *Race and the Decline of Class in American Politics*. Urbana: University of Illinois Press.

Hugick, Larry. 1991. Party Identification: The Disparity between Gallup's In-Person and Telephone Interview Findings. *Public Perspective* 23–24.

Hyman, Herbert. 1959. *Political Socialization*. Glencoe, IL: Free.

Iyengar, Shanto, and Donald R. Kinder. 1987. *News that Matters: Television and American Opinion*. Chicago: University of Chicago Press.

Jacobs, Lawrence R., and Robert Y. Shapiro. 2000. *Politicians Don't Pander: Political Manipulation and the Loss of Democratic Responsiveness*. Chicago: University of Chicago Press.

Jacobson, Gary C. 1991. *The Politics of Congressional Elections*, third edition. Boston: Little, Brown.

Jacobson, Gary. 1997. *The Politics of Congressional Elections*, fourth edition. New York: Longman.

Jennings, M. Kent, and Richard G. Niemi. 1968. The Transmission of Political Values from Parent to Child. *American Political Science Review* 62:169–184.

Jennings, M. Kent, and Richard G. Niemi. 1974. *The Political Character of Adolescence*. Princeton, NJ: Princeton University Press.

Katona, George. 1964. *The Mass Consumption Society*. New York: McGraw-Hill.

Katona, George. 1975. *Psychological Economics*. New York: Elsevier.

Kaufmann, Karen M., and John R. Petrocik. 1999. The Changing Politics of American Men: Understanding the Sources of the Gender Gap. *American Journal of Political Science* 43:864–887.

Keech, William R. 1995. *Economic Politics: The Costs of Democracy*. New York: Cambridge University Press.

Kellstedt, Paul, Gregory E. McAvoy, and James A. Stimson. 1995. Dynamic Analysis with Latent Constructs. *Political Analysis* 5:113–150.

Kernell, Samuel. 1978. Explaining Presidential Popularity. *American Political Science Review* 72:506–522.

Kernell, Samuel. 1993. *Going Public: New Strategies of Presidential Leadership*. Washington, DC: CQ Press.

Key, V.O. 1966. *The Responsible Electorate*. Cambridge, MA: Harvard University Press.

Kiewiet, D. Roderick. 1983. *Macroeconomics and Micropolitics*. Chicago: University of Chicago Press.

Kiewiet, D. Roderick, and Mathew McCubbins. 1991. *The Logic of Delegation: Congressional Parties and the Appropriations Process*. Chicago: University of Chicago Press.

Kinder, Donald R., and D. Roderick Kiewiet. 1979. Economic Grievances and Political Behavior: The Role of Personal Discontents and Collective Judgments in Congressional Voting. *American Journal of Political Science* 23:495–527.

# References

Kinder, Donald R., and D. Roderick Kiewiet. 1981. Sociotropic Politics: The American Case. *British Journal of Political Science* 11:129–162.

King, Gary. 1997. *A Solution to the Ecological Inference Problem: Reconstructing Individual Behavior from Aggregate Data.* Princeton, NJ: Princeton University Press.

Kingdon, John W. 1973. *Congressmen's Voting Decisions.* New York: Harper & Row.

Klein, Lawrence R., Aleksander Welfe, and Wladyslaw Welfe. 1999. *Principles of Macroeconomic Modeling.* New York: Elsevier.

Knight, Kathleen and Robert S. Erikson. 1997. Ideology in the 1990s. In *Understanding Public Opinion,* ed. Barbara Norrander and Clyde Wilcox. Washington, DC: CQ Press.

Kramer, Gerald H. 1971. Short-Term Fluctuations in U.S. Voting Behavior, 1896–1964. *The American Political Science Review* 65:131–143.

Kramer, Gerald H. 1983. The Ecological Fallacy Revisited: Aggregate versus Individual Level Findings on Economics and Elections and Sociotropic Voting. *American Political Science Review* 77:92–111.

Krause, G.A., and Granato, J., 1998. Fooling Some of the People Some of the Time? A Test of Weak Rationality with Heterogeneous Information Levels. *Public Opinion Quarterly* 62:135–151.

Lee, Rex E. 1986. Lawyering for the Government: Politics, Polemics and Principle. *Ohio State Law Journal* 47:595–601.

Lewis-Beck, Michael S. 1988. *Economics and Elections: The Major Western Democracies.* Ann Arbor: University of Michigan Press.

Lewis-Beck, Michael, and Tom Rice. 1982. Presidential Popularity and the Presidential Vote. *Public Opinion Quarterly* 46:534–537.

Lewis-Beck, Michael, and Charles Tien. 2000. The Future of Forecasting: Prospective Presidential Models. In *Before the Vote: Forecasting American National Elections,* ed. James E. Campbell and James C. Garand. Thousand Oaks, CA: Sage.

Lodge, Milton G., Kathleen M. McGraw, and Patrick Stroh. 1989. An Impression-driven Model of Candidate Evaluation. *American Political Science Review* 83:399–420.

Lodge, Milton, Marco R. Steenbergen, and Shawn Brau. 1995. The Responsive Voter: Campaign Information and the Dynamics of Candidate Evaluation. *American Political Science Review* 89:309–326.

Lord, Frederick, and Melvin R. Novick. 1968. *Statistical Theories of Mental Test Scores.* Reading, MA: Addison-Wesley.

Lupia, Arthur, and Mathew D. McCubbins. 1998. *The Democratic Dilemma: Can Citizens Learn What They Need to Know?* New York: Cambridge University Press.

Luskin, Robert C. 1987. Measuring Political Sophistication. *American Journal of Political Science* 31:856–899.

Macdonald, Stuart Elaine, George Rabinowitz, and Ola Listhaug. 1998. On Attempting to Rehabilitate the Proximity Model: Sometimes the Patient Just Can't Be Helped. *Journal of Politics* 60:653–690.

MacKuen, Michael B. 1983. Political Drama, Economic Conditions, and the Dynamics of Presidential Popularity. *American Journal of Political Science* 27:165–192.

# References

MacKuen, Michael. 2001. Political Psychology and the Micro-Macro Gap in Politics. In *Citizens and Politics: A Political Psychology Perspective*, ed. James Kuklinski. New York: Cambridge University Press.

MacKuen, Michael B., and Courtney Brown. 1987. Political Context and Attitude Change. *American Political Science Review* 81:471–490.

MacKuen, Michael B., and Calvin Mouw. 1995. *Social Class and Economic Judgments*. Paper presented at the Conference on Economics and Political Behavior. Houston, TX. April 21–23, 1995.

MacKuen, Michael B., Robert S. Erikson, and James A. Stimson. 1992. Peasants or Bankers: The American Electorate and the U.S. Economy. *American Political Science Review* 86:597–611.

MacKuen, Michael, Robert S. Erikson, and James A. Stimson. 1989. Macropartisanship. *American Political Science Review* 83:1125–1142.

Marshall, Thomas. 1989. *Public Opinion and the Supreme Court*. New York: Longman.

Matsusaka, John G., and Argia M. Sbornone. 1989. *Fear and Depression: Consumer Confidence and Economic Fluctuations*. Mimeo. University of Chicago.

Mayer, William G. 1992. *The Changing American Mind: How and Why Public Opinion Changed between 1960 and 1988*. Ann Arbor: University of Michigan Press.

Mayhew, David R. 1974. *Congress: The Electoral Connection*. New Haven, CT: Yale University Press.

Mayhew, David. 1991. *Divided We Govern: Party Control, Lawmaking, and Investigations, 1946–1990*. New Haven, CT: Yale University Press.

McDonald, Michael D., Ian Budge, and Richard Hofferbert. 1999. Party Mandate Theory and Time Series Analysis: A Theoretical and Methodological Response. *Electoral Studies* 18:587–596.

McNamara, Robert S. 1995. *In Retrospect: The Tragedy and Lessons of Vietnam*. New York: Random House.

Miller, Nicholas. 1986. Information, Electorates, and Democracy: Some Extensions and Interpretations of the Condorcet Jury Theorem. In *Information Pooling and Group Decision Making*, ed. Bernard Grofman and Guillermo Owen. Greenwich, CT: JAI.

Miller, Warren E., and Donald W. Stokes. 1963. Constituency Influence in Congress. *American Political Science Review* 57:45–46.

Miller, Warren E. 1991. Party Identification, Realignment, and Party Voting: Back to the Basics. *American Political Science Review* 85:557–568.

Mishler, William, and Reginald S. Sheehan. 1993. The Supreme Court as a Countermajoritarian Institution? The Impact of Public Opinion on Supreme Court Decisions. *American Political Science Review* 87/1:87–101.

Mouw, Calvin, and Michael MacKuen. 1992. The Strategic Agenda in Legislative Politics. *American Political Science Review* 86:87–105.

Mueller, John. 1970. Presidential Popularity from Truman to Johnson. *American Political Science Review* 65:18–34.

Mueller, John. 1973. *War, Presidents and Public Opinion*. New York: Wiley.

Murphy, Walter F. 1964. *Elements of Judicial Strategy*. Chicago: University of Chicago Press.

Neustadt, Richard E. 1964. *Presidential Power: The Politics of Leadership*. New York: Wiley.

# References

Niemi, Richard G., Richard S. Katz, and David Newman. 1980. Reconstructing Past Partisanship: The Failure of the Party Identification Recall Questions. *American Journal of Political Science* 24:633–651.

Nordhaus, William. 1975. The Political Business Cycle. *Review of Economic Studies* 42:169–190.

Norpoth, Helmut. 1996. Politics and the Prospective Voter. *Journal of Politics* 58:776–792.

Norpoth, Helmut, and Jeffrey A. Segal. 1994. Comment: Popular Influence on Supreme Court Decisions. *American Political Science Review* 88:711–716.

Ostrom, Charles W., Jr., and Dennis M. Simon. 1985. Promise and Performance. *American Political Science Review* 79:334–358.

Ostrom, Charles W., Jr., and Renée Smith. 1993. Error Correction, Attitude Persistence, and Executive Rewards and Punishments: A Behavioral Theory of Presidential Approval. *Political Analysis* 4:127–184.

Pagan, Adrian. 1999. Some Uses for Computer Simulation. *Mathematics and Computer Simulation*. June: 341–349.

Page, Benjamin I., and Robert Y. Shapiro. 1992. *The Rational Public: Fifty Years of Trends in Americans' Policy Preferences*. Chicago: University of Chicago Press.

Peffley, Mark. 1985. The Voter as Juror: Attributing Responsibility for Economic Conditions. In *Economic Conditions and Electoral Outcomes*, ed. Heinz Eulau and Michael S. Lewis-Beck. New York: Agathon Press.

Pomper, Gerald M., with Susan S. Lederman. 1980. *Elections in America: Control and Influence in Democratic Politics*, second edition. New York: Longman.

Poole, Keith T., and Howard Rosenthal. 1997. *Congress: A Political-Economic History of Roll Call Voting*. New York: Oxford University Press.

Popkin, Samuel L. 1991. *The Reasoning Voter: Communication and Persuasion in Presidential Campaigns*. Chicago: University of Chicago Press.

Popkin Samuel L., John W. Gorman, Charles Phillips, and Jeffrey A. Smith. 1976. What Have You Done for Me Lately? Toward an Investment Theory of Voting. *American Political Science Review* 70:779–805.

Quirk, Paul J. 1989. The Cooperative Resolution of Policy Conflict. *American Political Science Review* 83:905–921.

Rabinowitz, George, and Stuart Elaine Macdonald. 1989. A Directional Theory of Issue Voting. *The American Political Science Review* 83:93–121.

Riker, William H. 1962. *The Theory of Political Coalitions*. New Haven, CT: Yale University Press.

Rivers, Douglas, and Nancy L. Rose. 1985. Passing the President's Program: Public Opinion and Presidential Influence in Congress. *American Journal of Political Science* 29:183–206.

Robinson, John P., and John A. Fleishman. 1984. Ideological Trends in American Public Opinion. *Annals* 472:50–60.

Robinson, W.S. 1950. Ecological Correlations and the Behavior of Individuals. *American Sociological Review* 15:351–357.

Rogoff, Kenneth, and Anne Sibert. 1988. Elections and Macroeconomic Policy Cycles. *Review of Economic Studies* 55:1–16.

Rohde, David W. 1991. *Parties and Leaders in the Post Reform House*. Chicago, IL: University of Chicago Press.

# References

Rotunda, Ronald D. 1986. *The Politics of Language: Liberalism as Word and Symbol.* Iowa City, IA: University of Iowa Press.

Sabato, Larry J. 1988. *The Party's Just Begun: Shaping Political Parties for America's Future.* Glenview, IL: Scott, Foresman.

Salokar, Rebecca Mae. 1992. *The Solicitor General: The Politics of Law.* Philadelphia: Temple University Press.

Scammon, Richard M., and Ben J. Wattenberg. 1970. *The Real Majority.* New York: Coward-McCann.

Schattschneider, E.E. 1960. *The Semi-Sovereign People: A Realist's View of Democracy in America.* New York: Holt, Rinehart, and Winston.

Segal, Jeffrey A. 1988. Amicus Curiae Briefs by the Solicitor General during the Warren and Burger Courts: A Research Note. *Western Political Quarterly* 41:135–144.

Shapiro, Robert Y., and Bruce M. Conforto. 1980. Presidential Performance, the Economy, and the Public's Evaluation of Economic Conditions. *Journal of Politics* 42:49–67.

Shaw, G.K. 1984. *Rational Expectations: An Elementary Exposition.* New York: St. Martin's Press.

Sheffrin, S.M. 1996. *Rational Expectations,* second ed. Cambridge: Cambridge University Press.

Smith, Eric R.A.N., Richard Herrera, and Cheryl L. Herrera. 1990. The Measurement Characteristics of Congressional Roll Call Indexes. *Legislative Studies Quarterly* 15:283–295.

Stigler, George J. 1973. General Economic Conditions and National Elections. *The American Economic Review* 63:160–167.

Stimson, James A. 1976. Public Support for American Presidents: A Cyclical Model. *Public Opinion Quarterly* 40:1–21.

Stimson, James A. 1991. *Public Opinion in America: Moods, Cycles, and Swings.* Boulder, CO: Westview Press.

Stimson, James A. 1999. Public Opinion in America: Moods, Cycles, and Swings, second edition. Boulder, CO: Westview Press.

Stimson, James A. 2001. The Micro Foundations of Mood. In *Citizens and Politics: A Political Psychology Perspective,* ed. James Kuklinski. New York: Cambridge University Press.

Stimson, James A., Michael B. MacKuen, and Robert S. Erikson. 1995. Dynamic Representation. *American Political Science Review* 89: 543–565.

Stokes, Donald E. 1966. Some Dynamic Elements of Contests for the Presidency. *The American Political Science Review* 60:19–28.

Stokes, Donald E., and Warren E. Miller. 1962. Party Government and the Saliency of Congress. *Public Opinion Quarterly* 26:531–546.

Sundquist, James L. 1973. *Dynamics of the American Party System.* Washington, DC: Brookings.

Sundquist, James L. 1983. *Dynamics of the Party System: Alignment and Realignment of Political Parties in the United States,* revised edition. Washington, DC: Brookings.

Sundquist, James L. 1992. *Constitutional Reform and Effective Government,* revised edition. Washington, DC: Brookings.

Suzuki, Motoshi. 1992. Political Business Cycles in the Public Mind. *The American Political Science Review* 86:989–996.

# References

Thomas, Martin. 1985. Electoral Proximity and Senatorial Roll Call Voting. *American Journal of Political Science* 29:96–111.

Tims, Albert R., David P. Fan, and John R. Freeman. 1989. The Cultivation of Consumer Confidence: A Longitudinal Analysis of News Media Influence on Consumer Sentiment. *Advances in Consumer Research* 16:758–770.

Tufte, Edward R. 1978. *Political Control of the Economy.* Princeton, NJ: Princeton University Press.

U.S. Bureau of the Census, Current Population Reports, Series P60–184. 1993. *Money Income of Households, Families, and Persons in the United States: 1992.* Washington, DC: U.S. Government Printing Office.

Watson, Mark W., and Robert F. Engle. 1983. Alternative Algorithms for the Estimation of Dynamic Factor, MIMIC and Varying Coefficient Regression Models. *Journal of Econometrics* 23:385–400.

Wiley, David E., and James A. Wiley. 1970. The Estimation of Error in Panel Data. *American Sociological Review* 35:112–117.

Wlezien, Christopher. 1995. The Public as Thermostat: Dynamics of Preferences for Spending. *American Journal of Political Science* 39:981–1000.

Wlezien, Christopher. 1996. Dynamics of Representation: The Case of U.S. Spending on Defense. *British Journal of Political Science* 26:81–103.

Wlezien, Christopher, and Robert S. Erikson. 2000. Temporal Horizons and the Presidential Election Forecasts. In *Before the Vote: Forecasting American National Elections,* ed. James E. Campbell and James C. Garand. Thousand Oaks, CA: Sage.

Zaller, John R. 1992. *The Nature and Origins of Mass Opinion.* New York: Cambridge University Press.

Zaller, John P., and Stanley Feldman. 1988. Answering Questions vs. Revealing Preferences: A Simple Theory of the Survey Response. Paper prepared for delivery at the annual meeting of the Political Methodology Group, Los Angeles, CA.

Zaller, John, and Stanley Feldman. 1992. A Simple Theory of the Survey Response: Answering Questions and Revealing Preferences. *American Journal of Political Science* 36:579–616.

Zaller, John, with Mark Hunt. 1995. The Rise and Fall of Candidate Perot: Unmediated vs. Mediated Politics. *Political Communication* 12(1):97–123.

# Index

461

# Index

# Index

efficiency
  of expectations formation, 102–3
  in use of information, 85, 103–5
Eisenhower, Dwight, 112–13, 121, 240,
    250, 351, 395, 443
election outcomes
  campaigns and, 238n1
  candidate affect and, 240, 275
  with changed 1980 election, 411–13,
    414f, 415f
  competence system and, 438
  electoral cycle, 439
  macropartisanship and, 434
  micro-macro mismatch, 241–2
  policy preferences and, 241, 256–72
  predicting, 420
  prosperity and, 275
  reward and punishment and, 240
elections, 237–8
  deviating, 113
  forecasting, 242–3
  meaning of, 241
  models of, 20, 21f
  outcomes of. See election outcomes
  research on, 19–20
  turnover, 288, 289, 292, 306
electoral cycle
  in mood-laws dynamic, 360–8
electoral intelligence, 3
electorate. See also aggregate
  citizens vs., 428–9
  farsighted vs. myopic, 105–8
  at macro level, 5–8
  political information and, 82–3
  rationality of, 432–3
  voter vs., 1, 3
elites, 1, 3
  leadership theory, 36
  opinion, 214, 216
Engle, Robert F., 303n14
equilibrium
  dynamics and, 127–9
  of macropartisanship, 129–30, 179
  in partisanship, 127–9
equilibrium macropartisanship, 131,
    268n20, 269, 271, 272n23, 282
  predictive power of, 139–41, 146–
    7
  presidential vote and, 255
Erikson, Robert S., 2
Error Correction Mechanism, 318n23
evaluation(s)
  by citizens, 13–14, 30
  identification and, 15–16
  party disposition and, 126
  retrospective, 79–80

events. See also issues
  age and, 183n12
  identification of, 51–7
  partisan change and, 160
  party disposition and, 126
  party identification and, 116–17,
    118
  presidential approval and, 48–57, 63,
    88–9
expectations, 86, 100–2. See also
    adaptive-expectations model; business
    expectations; rational expectations;
    relative expectations
  presidential approval and, 85, 90–3,
    106–7
  voters vs. electorate, 106–7

Fair, Ray C., 242, 243n3
Fan, David P., 95
Feldman, Stanley, 83, 194, 230
Fiorina, Morris P., 79, 82, 115, 117–18,
    240
Five-Year Expectations, 96
Ford, Gerald, 51, 58n16, 110, 121
foreign policy, 196n2
  presidential approval and, 48–57
Freeman, John R., 95
funnel of causality, 238, 240

Gallup polls, 32, 110, 120–1, 136,
    138n20. See also surveys
Gallup-Thorndike Verbal Intelligence Test,
    215
gender
  macropartisanship and, 168, 171–6
General Social Survey (GSS), 194, 211,
    215. See also surveys
generations
  partisanship and, 144, 155–63
Gingrich, Newt, 29
Goldwater, Barry, 250
government(s)
  as an abstraction, 205
  attitudes toward, 195–6, 206
  citizens as consumers of, 16–17
  competence, 13
  evaluation by citizens, 13–14
  intervention by, 76, 77n1
  more vs. less, 17–18
  policy choices by, 193
  popularity of, 1
  spending, 229. See also domestic
    spending
Granger exogeneity tests, 123n8
Great Society, 349, 373, 374, 435
Green, Donald Philip, 142, 144–5
Green, Jay, 329, 330

463

# Index

# Index

465

# Index

# Index

# Index

Other books in the series (*continued*)

Made in the USA
Lexington, KY
28 January 2012